Contemporary Approaches to Migration, Identity, and Integration

Emre Cengiz
https://orcid.org/0000-0002-3854-6215
Gumushane University, Turkey

Metin Aksoy
https://orcid.org/0000-0002-3118-6739
Gumushane University, Turkey

IGI Global
Scientific Publishing
Publishing Tomorrow's Research Today

VP of Publishing Ethics & Research Integrity	Melissa Wagner
Director of Acquisitions	Mikaela Felty
Director of Book Development	Jocelynn Hessler
Production Manager	Mike Brehm
Cover Design	Jose Rosado

Published in the United States of America by
IGI Global Scientific Publishing
701 East Chocolate Avenue
Hershey, PA, 17033, USA
Tel: 717-533-8845 | Fax: 717-533-7115
Website: https://www.igi-global.com E-mail: cust@igi-global.com

Library of Congress Cataloging-in-Publication Data

Names: Cengiz, Emre editor | Aksoy, Metin editor
Title: Contemporary approaches to migration, identity, and integration / edited by: Emre Cengiz, Metin Aksoy.
Description: Hershey PA : IGI Global Scientific Publishing, [2027] | Includes bibliographical references. | Summary: "This book critically examines the issues of migration, identity and integration, which are among the most important problems of today's world, and proposes solutions. This multidisciplinary work, which encompasses many scientific disciplines, addresses the issues of migration, identity and integration from the perspectives of different scientific fields and proposes solutions"-- Provided by publisher.
Identifiers: LCCN 2026011340 (print) | LCCN 2026011341 (ebook) | ISBN 9798337385006 hardcover | ISBN 9798337385013 paperback | ISBN 9798337385020 ebook
Subjects: LCSH: South Asia--Emigration and immigration | Immigrants--South Asia | Social integration--South Asia
Classification: LCC JV8752 .C67 2027 (print) | LCC JV8752 (ebook) | DDC 304.8/54--dc23/eng/20260914
LC record available at https://lccn.loc.gov/2026011340
LC ebook record available at https://lccn.loc.gov/20260113

British Cataloguing in Publication Data
A Cataloguing in Publication record for this book is available from the British Library.

Table of Contents

Detailed Table of Contents

In everyday language, migration is most often described as the movement of people from one place to another. The definition is not wrong, but it captures little of what such movement leaves behind and what it sets in motion in the places where people settle. The number of those who move, the routes they follow, and their legal statuses undoubtedly matter. Yet the social significance of migration extends well beyond these figures. When people relocate across borders, they reshape labor markets, family relationships, cities, public services, and political debate. As migrants' expectations shift during and after the process, the settled societies that receive them find their own assumptions put to the test. Migration is therefore not an external transfer that takes place between already-completed societies. It is a historical process that transforms societies and social relations from within. It is equally misleading to present contemporary migration as a sudden, exceptional feature of globalization's most recent phase.

Migration is a complex social process, which substantially defines the personal and communal identities, altering meaning of belonging to something or another culture, and the incorporation of the social aspects. The identity and migration approaches theories talk about how the migrants negotiate the multiple or overlapping identities as a response to the new social, cultural and political circumstances. Transnationalism theory, acculturation theory, social identity theory and postcolonial approaches can provide insight into the ways migrants retain, modify or transform their identities in the process of displacement, resettlement, and social migration. Experience transfer- the sharing and the transfer of ideas, experience and cultural practices across the borders and bringing them to bear and use them in the host countries further highlight the dynamic elements in respect to the person and the societies thus bringing about personal growth as well as improvement of societies.

This chapter examines the multifaceted relationship between migration, development, and global connections in the contemporary era. Drawing on recent theoretical frameworks and empirical evidence from 2021-2025, it analyzes how international and internal migration serve as powerful drivers of economic and social development. The chapter explores key mechanisms including remittances, knowledge transfer, diaspora engagement, and transnational networks that link origin and destination communities. It investigates migration governance frameworks, integration policies, and the role of technology in facilitating global connections. The analysis reveals that migration, when properly managed, acts as a transformative force for achieving sustainable development goals.

This study defines international migration as a symbolic shift of worlds and an entry into a foreign system of recognition. The strategies developed by migrants to protect themselves from the negative labels of the host society are analyzed through Winnicott's (1960) theory of the "false self" and the proposed concept of "borrowed identities."Within the framework of Goffman's (1963) stigma theory, the "acceptable migrant" performance exhibited by the individual in order to avoid exclusion may provide short-term security, but in the long term it produces severe psychological costs such as alienation and somatization, as emphasized by Akhtar (2011) and Kirmayer (2011). Identity splits, especially observed in second generations, are addressed through the perspectives of Erikson (1968) and Sayad(1999). In conclusion, with reference to Honneth (1995) and Ataca (2005), it is argued that genuine well-being is only possible in a climate where the individual is accepted "as themselves," without wearing a mask.

This chapter examines migrant well-being through a psychosocial-ecological framework that connects migration trajectories, trauma, structural conditions, and resilience. Drawing on interdisciplinary literature, it conceptualizes migration as a multi-phase process shaped by pre-migration conditions, migration journeys, and post-migration realities. The chapter analyzes how psychosocial adjustment is influenced by language, employment, social connections, identity negotiation, and acculturation processes, while highlighting the cumulative impact of trauma, loss, and ongoing stressors. Resilience is reconceptualized as a dynamic, context-dependent process supported by family, community, cultural resources, and institutional conditions. The chapter concludes by outlining implications for research, practice, and policy, arguing that migrant well-being depends on both individual agency and inclusive social environments that enable participation, dignity, and belonging

This chapter considers international migration to be a comprehensive reorganization of social life. It critiques traditional clinical approaches that label displaced individuals as passive 'victims of trauma' and reduce responsibility for readjustment to individual coping strategies. Instead, it presents an integrative ecological framework for the post-migration period, synthesising Silove's ADAPT model, Self-Determination Theory and Honneth's theory of recognition. Accordingly, trauma is conceptualised as a profound 'social rupture' in meaning and security, while resilience is framed as an active, socially mediated process of 'reconstruction'. The chapter analyses the destructive and mediating roles of post-migration 'daily stressors'—such as status loss, legal precarity, and social exclusion—in shaping psychological well-being. Ultimately, it emphasises that the journey from trauma to resilience is influenced more by the institutional and moral conditions of recognition offered by the host society than by past adversities.

This chapter reconsiders migration, identity, and integration through the silent and tacit interactions of everyday life. While migration studies often focus on legal status, institutional participation, explicit identity claims, and visible conflicts, less attention is given to how relations between migrants and host societies are shaped through silence, caution, avoidance, observation, withdrawal, and the regulation of visibility. The chapter treats silence not as passivity or a lack of communication, but as a relational practice that produces meaning, orders relationships, and manages social distance. Drawing on approaches to everyday life, practice, tacit knowledge, and low-visibility action, silent negotiation is used not as a closed theoretical model, but as an analytical framework for understanding migrants' everyday practices of adaptation, belonging, and distance-keeping. Integration is therefore understood as a relational process shaped by fragile balances, tacit acceptances, and silent adjustments in everyday encounters.

This chapter examines immigration, fiscal contributions, and welfare state sustainability in Portugal, a country combining extreme demographic ageing with rapid migratory transformation. Drawing on administrative data and peer-reviewed literature, this chapter per the authors addresses three dimensions: migrants' fiscal contributions across the life cycle; patterns of public service use; and aggregate effects on financial sustainability. Foreign nationals contribute to social security disproportionately relative to their population share: in 2025, contributions exceeded benefits received fivefold, and public service use remained proportionally lower, consistent with the healthy immigrant effect. Without immigration, the required fiscal adjustment would quadruple. This chapter per the authors concludes that migration is an empirically documented contributor to welfare state sustainability, integration quality being the decisive factor, and that sustainability must be assessed not only by fiscal balances but by the capacity to guarantee equitable access to those who finance the system.

Migration is a profoundly gendered process shaped by unequal power relations, structural constraints, and opportunities across social, economic, and political contexts. This chapter critically examines the intersection of gender and migration by exploring how women's mobility reconstructs gender roles, transforms family and care arrangements, and reshapes agency within transnational spaces. Drawing on feminist, intersectional, and transnational perspectives, the chapter analyses both the opportunities migration offers women, such as economic participation, social empowerment, and skill development and the persistent limitations they face, including labour market precarity, gender-based violence, restrictive policies, and social exclusion. By integrating lived experiences, policy analysis, and emerging trends, the chapter highlights the central role of migrant women in sustainable human development and argues for gender-responsive migration governance that promotes equity, protection, and social inclusion.

This study approaches human rights diplomacy not merely as a domain where normative principles are articulated, but as an arena where international legitimacy is discursively constructed and redistributed among actors. The authors examine how narratives about women migrants function as a strategic tool in normative competition, arguing that four discursive frameworks (victimhood, the rescuing agent, resistance and subjectification, and crisis-threat) recur systematically in their international circulation. These frameworks let actors position themselves as humanitarian while rationalizing the hardening of border regimes through the language of protection. The authors conceptualize this as the "paradox of humanitarian justification" and, integrating it with femonationalism and intersectional hierarchies of representation, examine which migrants are made visible. They propose a research design combining critical discourse analysis with qualitative content analysis to code a multi-actor corpus across crisis periods.

This chapter examines the multidimensional phenomenon of labor migration through a systematic analysis of theoretical frameworks, circular migration conceptualization, and empirical evidence on labor market effects. The chapter traces the evolution of migration theory from Ravenstein's Foundational laws through Neoclassical Economic approaches, World-Systems Theory, Network Theory, and pluralist perspectives, demonstrating how each paradigm captures distinct dimensions of migratory decision-making. Particular attention is devoted to circular labor migration and the triple benefits it generates for sending states, receiving states, and migrants themselves. The chapter further analyzes migration's impact on labor markets. The Georgian case serves as the empirical anchor, examining how cumulative emigration of 1.3 million people since 1991, remittance flows equivalent to 9% of GDP, and recent reverse migration waves have produced ambivalent economic and demographic outcomes requiring coordinated policy responses.

The tightening of migration policy in the European Union has become a structural trend shaped by securitization and political change. This study examines the correlation between the electoral rise of far-right parties and the progressive hardening of EU migration policy through a qualitative, documentary, comparative, and normative approach based on EU legislation, institutional documents, political discourse, academic literature, reports, and journalistic materials. The findings show a growing convergence between both processes, marked by the synchronization of far-right electoral growth with tougher migration reforms, the increasing influence of these actors, and the normalization of narratives that frame migration as a threat. They also reveal a shift from a rights-based model toward one centered on control, externalization, and limits on asylum access. The study concludes that this restrictive turn is part of a broader political dynamic in which the far right plays a significant role, and it recommends stronger legal oversight and renewed protection of rights.

Climate change, one of the major challenges of our time, has brought with it the debate on climate migration. Over the last century, the number of people migrating due to climate change has been steadily increasing, and it is estimated that millions of people will be displaced by climate change in the coming years. As a result of rising air temperatures, rising sea level, increasing aridity, the depletion of water resources, the dwindling of resources essential for life, and the rise in the number of natural disasters linked to climate change, billions of people are being affected by this situation. It is also a well-known fact that the scale of conflicts and violence is beginning to change as a result of these problems. Consequently, the fact that people's living environments are becoming uninhabitable, coupled with the lack of security resulting from conflicts and acts of violence, is forcing them to migrate to more liveable places.

This chapter explores trends in Cambodian migration across different historical, sociological, and developmental contexts. It suggests that Cambodian mobility has shifted from relying on refugee and labour migration to involving more educated, skilled, and circular forms of movement. Utilising frameworks of identity, transnationalism, and integration, the chapter explores how migrants negotiate cultural belonging, preserve Khmer culture, and develop hybrid identities across host societies. It also examines how digital tools help migrants maintain emotional relationships, manage documentation, and strengthen diaspora networks. Additionally, the chapter discusses the development of host countries, emphasising how migrants contribute to their home countries through remittances, entrepreneurship, skill transfer, cultural diplomacy, and shifting narratives. Overall, it presents Cambodian migration as a continuous process of globalisation, ongoing identity negotiation, and nation-building.

This chapter addresses how migration, identity, and integration are experienced. By focusing on Gümüşhane, it contributes to an understanding of integration beyond metropolitan contexts. Themes were formed from the qualitative content analysis of semi-structured interviews conducted with 22 migrant and 22 local-community participants: identity, the local community-migrant relationship, and the acculturation process. Adopting a phenomenological approach, the study aims to reveal expectations and perceptions concerning the socio-cultural integration process, focusing on everyday encounters, social contact, cultural visibility, language use, religious commonalities, perceptions of difference, and the limits of social closeness. The findings suggest that socio-cultural integration cannot be understood solely through formal indicators. Instead, it is shaped by everyday practices, local norms, cultural expectations, and social relations. The chapter demonstrates that integration is a relational, negotiated, and context-sensitive process.

This chapter examines the national expansion of the Special Intensive Revision (SIR) process, which began in Assam, one of the North-Eastern States of India, and now functions as a de facto mechanism for citizenship scrutiny. Though presented as an electoral roll update, SIR disproportionately targets internal migrants, women, Adivasis, and residents of informal settlements, groups historically excluded from documentation systems. Drawing on legal analysis and case-based narratives, the chapter reveals how SIR redefines citizenship as a precarious, paper-dependent status. It argues for urgent procedural safeguards and a constitutional shift from suspicion to inclusion within the legal framework of India.

This chapter investigates how migration and multiculturalism reshape the foundations of India's pluralist democracy. It examines the interaction between internal and international mobility, social diversity, and political inclusion, drawing upon secondary data from the Census of India, National Sample Survey, United Nations reports, and academic studies. The chapter argues that migration places Indian pluralism "in motion," compelling institutions to reconcile constitutional ideals with demographic realities. It develops a theoretical framework combining democratic pluralism, citizenship theory, and the sociology of migration to interpret mobility as both a challenge and an opportunity for democratic renewal. The chapter concludes by proposing a shift toward a mobile and inclusive democracy that embeds portability of rights, participatory governance, and intercultural education. Migration emerges not as a threat to pluralism but as its contemporary expression, redefining belonging within a dynamic democratic framework.

Traditionally, Nepal has undergone chronic labor out-migration due to the lack of domestic labor markets, poverty, and inequalities in the regions. This paper discusses the functioning of Nepal's migrant labor networks across borders and the way in which remittances produced by such networks, results into socio-economic change on both the household and community level. It examines past and present trends of migration, recruitment procedures, labor channels, and presence of informal brokers and social networks. The paper also examines formal and informal remittance channels, online platforms and regulatory bodies that oversee remittance. At the household level, it evaluates the effects on consumption, education, health, savings, repayment of debt and social mobility. Lastly, the work also presents issues of labor exploitation, high migration costs, financial dependency and policy gap and sheds light on vulnerabilities of the remittance-based economy in Nepal.

Preface

INTRODUCTION

Migration has become one of the defining social processes of the contemporary world. Although migration is often understood primarily as the movement of people across territorial boundaries, its implications extend far beyond geographical mobility. Migration transforms identities, reshapes communities, alters labor markets, challenges political and legal institutions, and influences the ways in which belonging, citizenship, security, and social integration are understood. At the same time, migrants themselves negotiate complex processes of adaptation, identity reconstruction, recognition, and resilience as they encounter new social, cultural, economic, and political environments.

Contemporary Approaches to Migration, Identity, and Integration brings together interdisciplinary perspectives that examine these interconnected dimensions of migration. The volume approaches migration not as a single or uniform experience, but as a multidimensional process shaped by structural conditions, individual agency, historical circumstances, gender relations, environmental change, political developments, legal frameworks, and everyday social interactions. Across its contributions, the volume seeks to move beyond narrow understandings of migration as demographic movement and instead considers how mobility transforms both migrants and the societies through which they move and in which they settle.

A central concern of the volume is the question of *identity*. Migration can unsettle established forms of belonging while simultaneously creating opportunities for new identities and forms of affiliation. Migrants may negotiate between multiple cultural reference points, adapt their self-presentation to expectations in host societies, or develop hybrid and transnational identities. Such processes can involve creativity and empowerment, but they can also generate alienation, stigma, psychological distress, and tensions between individual identity and social recognition. The contributions in this volume therefore treat identity as dynamic, relational, and continually negotiated rather than as a fixed characteristic carried unchanged from one society to another.

The volume also places considerable emphasis on *integration*. Integration is examined not simply through formal indicators such as employment, legal status, education, or institutional participation, but through everyday relationships and practices. Language, cultural visibility, social contact, perceptions of difference, silence, avoidance, recognition, and the negotiation of social distance all influence whether migrants experience a meaningful sense of belonging. This perspective highlights the importance of local contexts and demonstrates that integration is a reciprocal and context-sensitive process involving both migrants and receiving communities.

Another important theme is the relationship between migration and *structural transformation*. Environmental degradation and climate change are increasingly influencing patterns of displacement and mobility. Gender shapes both the opportunities and vulnerabilities associated with migration, while labor migration affects economies, demographic structures, households, and labor markets in both sending and receiving societies. Remittances, diaspora networks, knowledge transfer, and transnational connections further demonstrate that migration creates relationships that extend across national borders and can contribute to economic and social development.

At the same time, migration takes place within increasingly complex political and institutional environments. The contributions addressing European migration policy, human rights diplomacy, citizenship scrutiny, media representations, and democratic pluralism demonstrate how migration is embedded in struggles over political legitimacy, public discourse, rights, and national belonging. Questions concerning who is recognized as a citizen, who is represented as deserving protection, whose voice is heard, and whose presence is constructed as a threat remain central to contemporary debates. The volume consequently considers migration not only as a social phenomenon but also as a field in which power, representation, and competing conceptions of rights and belonging are negotiated.

The *psychosocial dimensions of migration* constitute another significant strand of the volume. Migration may involve loss, trauma, uncertainty, status disruption, discrimination, and prolonged exposure to stress. Yet migrants should not be understood solely through the language of vulnerability or victimhood. Several contributions instead emphasize resilience, autonomy, recognition, social resources, and the institutional conditions that enable individuals and communities to reconstruct their lives. From this perspective, well-being is shaped not only by individual coping capacities but also by the social environments in which migrants attempt to establish security, dignity, participation, and belonging.

The volume also draws attention to the importance of *representation and discourse*. Media narratives, political language, humanitarian frameworks, and public perceptions can profoundly influence how migrants are understood and treated. Representations of migrants as economic contributors, victims, threats, or outsiders can shape policy responses as well as everyday interactions. Examining these representations is therefore essential to understanding the broader social conditions under which integration takes place.

Taken together, the contributions demonstrate that migration cannot be adequately understood through a single theoretical or disciplinary lens. Sociology, psychology, political science, law, economics, gender studies, migration studies, and related fields each illuminate different aspects of the phenomenon. The interdisciplinary character of this volume reflects the complexity of migration itself and encourages dialogue between approaches that are too often considered separately.

The chapters are organized to move across questions of identity, environment, gender, labor, policy, representation, everyday integration, citizenship, development, democracy, well-being, and transnational relations. While each contribution addresses a particular dimension of migration, their collective significance lies in the connections between them. Identity is influenced by political and legal structures; integration is shaped by everyday encounters; economic participation is connected to social recognition; well-being depends partly on institutional conditions; and transnational networks link individual experiences to broader processes of development and globalization.

OVERVIEW OF THE CHAPTERS

Chapter 1: Thinking Migration, Identity and Integration Together

In everyday language, migration is most often described as the movement of people from one place to another. The definition is not wrong, but it captures little of what such movement leaves behind and what it sets in motion in the places where people settle. The number of those who move, the routes they follow, and their legal statuses undoubtedly matter. Yet the social significance of migration extends well beyond these figures. When people relocate across borders, they reshape labor markets, family relationships, cities, public services, and political debate. As migrants' expectations shift during and after the process, the settled societies that receive them find their own assumptions put to the test. Migration is therefore not an external transfer that takes place between already-completed societies. It is a historical process that transforms societies and social relations from within. It is equally misleading to present contemporary migration as a sudden, exceptional feature of globalization's most recent phase.

Chapter 2: Identity and Migration:: Theoretical Perspectives and Experience Transfer

Migration is a complex social process, which substantially defines the personal and communal identities, altering meaning of belonging to something or another culture, and the incorporation of the social aspects. The identity and migration approaches theories talk about how the migrants negotiate the multiple or overlapping identities as a response to the new social, cultural and political circumstances. Transnationalism theory, acculturation theory, social identity theory and postcolonial approaches can provide insight into the ways migrants retain, modify or transform their identities in the process of displacement, resettlement, and social migration. Experience transfer- the sharing and the transfer of ideas, experience and cultural practices across the borders and bringing them to bear and use them in the host countries further highlight the dynamic elements in respect to the person and the societies thus bringing about personal growth as well as improvement of societies.

Chapter 3: Migration, Development and Global Connections

This chapter examines the multifaceted relationship between migration, development, and global connections in the contemporary era. Drawing on recent theoretical frameworks and empirical evidence from 2021-2025, it analyzes how international and internal migration serve as powerful drivers of economic and social development. The chapter explores key mechanisms including remittances, knowledge transfer, diaspora engagement, and transnational networks that link origin and destination communities. It investigates migration governance frameworks, integration policies, and the role of technology in facilitating global connections. The analysis reveals that migration, when properly managed, acts as a transformative force for achieving sustainable development goals.

Chapter 4: Borrowed Identities; The Development of the "False Self" In Migration and Its Psychological Costs: Borrowed Identities in Migration

This study defines international migration as a symbolic shift of worlds and an entry into a foreign system of recognition. The strategies developed by migrants to protect themselves from the negative labels of the host society are analyzed through Winnicott's (1960) theory of the "false self" and the proposed concept of "borrowed identities."Within the framework of Goffman's (1963) stigma theory, the "acceptable migrant" performance exhibited by the individual in order to avoid exclusion may provide short-term security, but in the long term it produces severe psychological costs such as alienation and somatization, as emphasized by Akhtar (2011) and Kirmayer (2011). Identity splits, especially observed in second generations, are addressed through the perspectives of Erikson (1968) and Sayad(1999). In conclusion, with reference to Honneth (1995) and Ataca (2005), it is argued that genuine well-being is only possible in a climate where the individual is accepted "as themselves," without wearing a mask.

Chapter 5: Psychological Adaptation and Migrant Well-being From Trauma to Resilience

This chapter examines migrant well-being through a psychosocial-ecological framework that connects migration trajectories, trauma, structural conditions, and resilience. Drawing on interdisciplinary literature, it conceptualizes migration as a multi-phase process shaped by pre-migration conditions, migration journeys, and post-migration realities. The chapter analyzes how psychosocial adjustment is influenced by language, employment, social connections, identity negotiation, and acculturation processes, while highlighting the cumulative impact of trauma, loss, and ongoing stressors. Resilience is reconceptualized as a dynamic, context-dependent process supported by family, community, cultural resources, and institutional conditions. The chapter concludes by outlining implications for research, practice, and policy, arguing that migrant well-being depends on both individual agency and inclusive social environments that enable participation, dignity, and belonging

Chapter 6: Recognition Autonomy and Resilience: Psychosocial Foundations of Migrant Well-being

This chapter considers international migration to be a comprehensive reorganization of social life. It critiques traditional clinical approaches that label displaced individuals as passive 'victims of trauma' and reduce responsibility for readjustment to individual coping strategies. Instead, it presents an integrative ecological framework for the post-migration period, synthesising Silove's ADAPT model, Self-Determination Theory and Honneth's theory of recognition. Accordingly, trauma is conceptualised as a profound 'social rupture' in meaning and security, while resilience is framed as an active, socially mediated process of 'reconstruction'. The chapter analyses the destructive and mediating roles of post-migration 'daily stressors'—such as status loss, legal precarity, and social exclusion—in shaping psychological well-being. Ultimately, it emphasises that the journey from trauma to resilience is influenced more by the institutional and moral conditions of recognition offered by the host society than by past adversities.

Chapter 7: Silent Negotiation in Migration and Integration: A Conceptual Lens on Everyday Practises of Belonging and Distance

This chapter reconsiders migration, identity, and integration through the silent and tacit interactions of everyday life. While migration studies often focus on legal status, institutional participation, explicit identity claims, and visible conflicts, less attention is given to how relations between migrants and host societies are shaped through silence, caution, avoidance, observation, withdrawal, and the regulation of visibility. The chapter treats silence not as passivity or a lack of communication, but as a relational practice that produces meaning, orders relationships, and manages social distance. Drawing on approaches to everyday life, practice, tacit knowledge, and low-visibility action, silent negotiation is used not as a closed theoretical model, but as an analytical framework for understanding migrants' everyday practices of adaptation, belonging, and distance-keeping. Integration is therefore understood as a relational process shaped by fragile balances, tacit acceptances, and silent adjustments in everyday encounters.

Chapter 8: Who Pays, Who Benefits?: Migrants, Fiscal Contributions, and Welfare State Sustainability

This chapter examines immigration, fiscal contributions, and welfare state sustainability in Portugal, a country combining extreme demographic ageing with rapid migratory transformation. Drawing on administrative data and peer-reviewed literature, this chapter per the authors addresses three dimensions: migrants' fiscal contributions across the life cycle; patterns of public service use; and aggregate effects on financial sustainability. Foreign nationals contribute to social security disproportionately relative to their population share: in 2025, contributions exceeded benefits received fivefold, and public service use remained proportionally lower, consistent with the healthy immigrant effect. Without immigration, the required fiscal adjustment would quadruple. This chapter per the authors concludes that migration is an empirically documented contributor to welfare state sustainability, integration quality being the decisive factor, and that sustainability must be assessed not only by fiscal balances but by the capacity to guarantee equitable access to those who finance the system.

Chapter 9: Gender and Migration Roles, Opportunities and Limitations

Migration is a profoundly gendered process shaped by unequal power relations, structural constraints, and opportunities across social, economic, and political contexts. This chapter critically examines the intersection of gender and migration by exploring how women's mobility reconstructs gender roles, transforms family and care arrangements, and reshapes agency within transnational spaces. Drawing on feminist, intersectional, and transnational perspectives, the chapter analyses both the opportunities migration offers women, such as economic participation, social empowerment, and skill development and the persistent limitations they face, including labour market precarity, gender-based violence, restrictive policies, and social exclusion. By integrating lived experiences, policy analysis, and emerging trends, the chapter highlights the central role of migrant women in sustainable human development and argues for gender-responsive migration governance that promotes equity, protection, and social inclusion.

Chapter 10: Gendered Human Rights Diplomacy Migrant Women's Narratives in Norm Competition

This study approaches human rights diplomacy not merely as a domain where normative principles are articulated, but as an arena where international legitimacy is discursively constructed and redistributed among actors. The authors examine how narratives about women migrants function as a strategic tool in normative competition, arguing that four discursive frameworks (victimhood, the rescuing agent, resistance and subjectification, and crisis-threat) recur systematically in their international circulation. These frameworks let actors position themselves as humanitarian while rationalizing the hardening of border regimes through the language of protection. The authors conceptualize this as the "paradox of humanitarian justification" and, integrating it with femonationalism and intersectional hierarchies of representation, examine which migrants are made visible. They propose a research design combining critical discourse analysis with qualitative content analysis to code a multi-actor corpus across crisis periods.

Chapter 11: Labor Migration and Labor Market Dynamics: Impact, Challenges, and the Circular Migration Model

This chapter examines the multidimensional phenomenon of labor migration through a systematic analysis of theoretical frameworks, circular migration conceptualization, and empirical evidence on labor market effects. The chapter traces the evolution of migration theory from Ravenstein's Foundational laws through Neoclassical Economic approaches, World-Systems Theory, Network Theory, and pluralist perspectives, demonstrating how each paradigm captures distinct dimensions of migratory decision-making. Particular attention is devoted to circular labor migration and the triple benefits it generates for sending states, receiving states, and migrants themselves. The chapter further analyzes migration's impact on labor markets. The Georgian case serves as the empirical anchor, examining how cumulative emigration of 1.3 million people since 1991, remittance flows equivalent to 9% of GDP, and recent reverse migration waves have produced ambivalent economic and demographic outcomes requiring coordinated policy responses.

Chapter 12: Mapping the Restrictive Turn in EU Migration Policy: Far Right Rise and Policy Hardening

The tightening of migration policy in the European Union has become a structural trend shaped by securitization and political change. This study examines the correlation between the electoral rise of far-right parties and the progressive hardening of EU migration policy through a qualitative, documentary, comparative, and normative approach based on EU legislation, institutional documents, political discourse, academic literature, reports, and journalistic materials. The findings show a growing convergence between both processes, marked by the synchronization of far-right electoral growth with tougher migration reforms, the increasing influence of these actors, and the normalization of narratives that frame migration as a threat. They also reveal a shift from a rights-based model toward one centered on control, externalization, and limits on asylum access. The study concludes that this restrictive turn is part of a broader political dynamic in which the far right plays a significant role, and it recommends stronger legal oversight and renewed protection of rights.

Chapter 13: Climate Migrants in the Context of Climate Change

Climate change, one of the major challenges of our time, has brought with it the debate on climate migration. Over the last century, the number of people migrating due to climate change has been steadily increasing, and it is estimated that millions of people will be displaced by climate change in the coming years. As a result of rising air temperatures, rising sea level, increasing aridity, the depletion of water resources, the dwindling of resources essential for life, and the rise in the number of natural disasters linked to climate change, billions of people are being affected by this situation. It is also a well-known fact that the scale of conflicts and violence is beginning to change as a result of these problems. Consequently, the fact that people's living environments are becoming uninhabitable, coupled with the lack of security resulting from conflicts and acts of violence, is forcing them to migrate to more liveable places.

Chapter 14: Identity, Belonging, and the Politics of Integration: Contemporary Dynamics of Cambodian Migrant Experience in a Globalised World

This chapter explores trends in Cambodian migration across different historical, sociological, and developmental contexts. It suggests that Cambodian mobility has shifted from relying on refugee and labour migration to involving more educated, skilled, and circular forms of movement. Utilising frameworks of identity, transnationalism, and integration, the chapter explores how migrants negotiate cultural belonging, preserve Khmer culture, and develop hybrid identities across host societies. It also examines how digital tools help migrants maintain emotional relationships, manage documentation, and strengthen diaspora networks. Additionally, the chapter discusses the development of host countries, emphasising how migrants contribute to their home countries through remittances, entrepreneurship, skill transfer, cultural diplomacy, and shifting narratives. Overall, it presents Cambodian migration as a continuous process of globalisation, ongoing identity negotiation, and nation-building.

Chapter 15: Migration and Integration in Everyday Local Contexts: A Qualitative Study

This chapter addresses how migration, identity, and integration are experienced. By focusing on Gümüshane, it contributes to an understanding of integration beyond metropolitan contexts. Themes were formed from the qualitative content analysis of semi-structured interviews conducted with 22 migrant and 22 local-community participants: identity, the local community-migrant relationship, and the acculturation process. Adopting a phenomenological approach, the study aims to reveal expectations and perceptions concerning the socio-cultural integration process, focusing on everyday encounters, social contact, cultural visibility, language use, religious commonalities, perceptions of difference, and the limits of social closeness. The findings suggest that socio-cultural integration cannot be understood solely through formal indicators. Instead, it is shaped by everyday practices, local norms, cultural expectations, and social relations. The chapter demonstrates that integration is a relational, negotiated, and context-sensitive process.

Chapter 16: Migration, Citizenship, and Legal Identity: The Special Intensive Revision Regime in India

This chapter examines the national expansion of the Special Intensive Revision (SIR) process, which began in Assam, one of the North-Eastern States of India, and now functions as a de facto mechanism for citizenship scrutiny. Though presented as an electoral roll update, SIR disproportionately targets internal migrants, women, Adivasis, and residents of informal settlements, groups historically excluded from documentation systems. Drawing on legal analysis and case-based narratives, the chapter reveals how SIR redefines citizenship as a precarious, paper-dependent status. It argues for urgent procedural safeguards and a constitutional shift from suspicion to inclusion within the legal framework of India.

Chapter 17: Pluralism in Motion: Migration, Multiculturalism, and the Future of Indian Democracy

This chapter investigates how migration and multiculturalism reshape the foundations of India's pluralist democracy. It examines the interaction between internal and international mobility, social diversity, and political inclusion, drawing upon secondary data from the Census of India, National Sample Survey, United Nations reports, and academic studies. The chapter argues that migration places Indian pluralism "in motion," compelling institutions to reconcile constitutional ideals with demographic realities. It develops a theoretical framework combining democratic pluralism, citizenship theory, and the sociology of migration to interpret mobility as both a challenge and an opportunity for democratic renewal. The chapter concludes by proposing a shift toward a mobile and inclusive democracy that embeds portability of rights, participatory governance, and intercultural education. Migration emerges not as a threat to pluralism but as its contemporary expression, redefining belonging within a dynamic democratic framework.

Chapter 18: Transnational Remittances and Socio-Economic Transformation: A Study of Nepalese Migrant Labor Networks

Traditionally, Nepal has undergone chronic labor out-migration due to the lack of domestic labor markets, poverty, and inequalities in the regions. This paper discusses the functioning of Nepal's migrant labor networks across borders and the way in which remittances produced by such networks, results into socio-economic change on both the household and community level. It examines past and present trends of migration, recruitment procedures, labor channels, and presence of informal brokers and social networks. The paper also examines formal and informal remittance channels, online platforms and regulatory bodies that oversee remittance. At the household level, it evaluates the effects on consumption, education, health, savings, repayment of debt and social mobility. Lastly, the work also presents issues of labor exploitation, high migration costs, financial dependency and policy gap and sheds light on vulnerabilities of the remittance-based economy in Nepal.

Chapter 19: Workplace Discrimination, Job Satisfaction, and Length of Stay among Lusophone Immigrants in Portugal: Beyond Language Proficiency

This study examines the impact of language proficiency in Portuguese on workplace discrimination and job satisfaction among immigrants in Braga, Portugal (n=161), using a questionnaire. The sample is predominantly composed of Brazilian immigrants (60.2%) and PALOP immigrants (5.6%) (Lusophone immigrants) — populations for whom Portuguese is already the official language. The study employs Mann-Whitney U tests and Spearman's rank correlation. Results indicate that language proficiency does not significantly differentiate either workplace discrimination or job satisfaction. A significant negative correlation is found between workplace discrimination and job satisfaction, and between length of stay in Portugal and perceived discrimination. One possible explanation is that discrimination among Lusophone immigrants in Braga, Portugal, is rooted in accentism, rather than linguistic barriers. Going beyond language proficiency involves examining the impact of accentism—which stems from structural, racial, and cultural stereotypes and prejudices—on job satisfaction.

CONCLUDING PERSPECTIVE

The diversity of approaches represented in this volume reflects the diversity of migration itself. Migration is simultaneously a personal experience, a social relationship, an economic process, a political issue, a legal condition, an environmental response, and a source of cultural transformation. Its consequences cannot be reduced to either opportunity or crisis; they emerge through the interaction of individual agency with institutional structures and social environments.

By bringing these perspectives together, *Contemporary Approaches to Migration, Identity, and Integration* seeks to contribute to a more nuanced understanding of mobility and its consequences. The volume invites readers to consider not only why people move, but also what happens to identities, relationships, institutions, and societies when they do. Ultimately, the chapters suggest that the future of migration studies—and of migration policy and practice—depends upon understanding mobility in connection with recognition, dignity, participation, rights, resilience, and belonging.

It is hoped that this collection will be useful to scholars, researchers, students, policymakers, practitioners, and all those interested in the complex transformations associated with contemporary migration. More importantly, it aims to encourage continued interdisciplinary dialogue about how societies can understand migration not merely as a challenge to be managed, but as a profound social process through which identities, communities, and futures are continually being negotiated.

Chapter 1
Thinking Migration, Identity, and Integration Together

Metin Aksoy
http://orcid.org/0000-0002-3118-6739
Gumushane University, Turkey

Emre Cengiz
http://orcid.org/0000-0002-3854-6215
Gumushane University, Turkey

ABSTRACT

In everyday language, migration is most often described as the movement of people from one place to another. The definition is not wrong, but it captures little of what such movement leaves behind and what it sets in motion in the places where people settle. The number of those who move, the routes they follow, and their legal statuses undoubtedly matter. Yet the social significance of migration extends well beyond these figures. When people relocate across borders, they reshape labor markets, family relationships, cities, public services, and political debate. As migrants' expectations shift during and after the process, the settled societies that receive them find their own assumptions put to the test. Migration is therefore not an external transfer that takes place between already-completed societies. It is a historical process that transforms societies and social relations from within. It is equally misleading to present contemporary migration as a sudden, exceptional feature of globalization's most recent phase.

DOI: 10.4018/979-8-3373-8500-6.ch001

INTRODUCTION

In everyday language, migration is most often described as the movement of people from one place to another. The definition is not wrong, but it captures little of what such movement leaves behind and what it sets in motion in the places where people settle. The number of those who move, the routes they follow, and their legal statuses undoubtedly matter. Yet the social significance of migration extends well beyond these figures. When people relocate across borders, they reshape labor markets, family relationships, cities, public services, and political debate. As migrants' expectations shift during and after the process, the settled societies that receive them find their own assumptions put to the test. Migration is therefore not an external transfer that takes place between already-completed societies. It is a historical process that transforms societies and social relations from within.

It is equally misleading to present contemporary migration as a sudden, exceptional feature of globalization's most recent phase. Human mobility has long been central to the making of the modern world, to the formation of states, and to economic transformation. What distinguishes the present period is less the first appearance of mobility than the growing frequency of different forms of movement, their heightened visibility, and their more intense politicization. Labor, education, family reunification, forced displacement, and the search for a particular way of life can rarely be separated by clear lines. The same person may move closer to more than one category at different stages of a single journey. For this reason the causes and consequences of migration do not run in one direction. Mobility is as much a source of new change as it is a result of social and economic change (de Haas et al., 2020). This complexity calls for caution toward the categories used to explain migration. Statistics and legal classifications lend visibility, but they also shape what research is able to see. Labels such as "migrant," "refugee," "temporary," "regular," or "irregular" should not be used interchangeably, since they point to distinct rights, obligations, and institutional relationships. Administrative classifications, however, do not always correspond to the shifting experiences of the people they name. The critique of methodological nationalism becomes relevant here (Wimmer & Glick Schiller, 2002). A perspective that treats society as coinciding naturally with national borders, that regards insiders as settled and newcomers as "other," risks placing migration in opposition to a supposedly "normal" social order from the outset. Such a starting point pushes cross-border ties, and the internal differences of receiving societies themselves, into the background.

The relationship between migration and identity demands comparable care. In common usage, identity may be imagined as a relatively fixed attribute that tells people who they are and that they carry with them when they move. Migration, however, tends to render previously taken-for-granted belongings visible and to invest them with new meaning. Positions such as language, religion, ethnicity, gender, class, and generation acquire different weight within new encounters. This shift appears not only in how migrants define themselves. The receiving society, too, repositions itself over who counts as "one of us," which differences are found acceptable, and on what conditions membership depends. Identity is therefore better treated as part of the relationships reconstituted during migration than as a ready-made cause invoked to explain it. Scholars have noted that the concept of identity carries several very different meanings at once in the social sciences (Brubaker & Cooper, 2000). It sometimes denotes an unchanging attribute, sometimes subjective self-understanding, and sometimes collective solidarity. Qualifiers such as "fluid," "multiple," or "negotiated" do not, on their own, resolve this ambiguity. In migration research the central question cannot be confined to whether a given identity exists. It must also examine the conditions under which people see themselves as close to a particular community, how they are classified by others, and what consequences those classifications produce. Seen in this way, identity ceases to be the name of fixed groups, and the context-dependent forms of identification, recognition, commonality, and division become more visible.

Belonging makes it possible to follow this relational quality of identity more clearly. To live in a country, to reside there lawfully, and to be accepted as a legitimate member of that society are not the same thing. Belonging is constituted at several levels, encompassing social positions, identifications, and emotional attachments, as well as political and ethical values (Yuval-Davis, 2006). The politics of belonging concerns which of these ties are counted as criteria of membership. Common descent, language, culture, religion, political loyalty, or economic contribution may be foregrounded in different periods. These criteria never operate neutrally; they determine who may enter the community, who must continually prove their commitment, and which differences are met with suspicion. Although the boundaries of belonging are established through formal decisions, they do not remain within the law alone. Symbolic boundaries are the conceptual distinctions used to classify people and practices (Lamont & Molnár, 2002). When such distinctions combine with the more durable inequalities that regulate access to resources and opportunities, they can harden into social boundaries. In the context of migration, characterizations such as "hardworking," "well-adjusted," "threat," "guest," or "close to our culture" are not simple descriptions. They can establish hierarchies among migrant groups, shape the conditions of everyday acceptance, and influence institutional practice. Boundaries do not always remain closed and unchanging. Contact, shared interests, political struggles, and institutional arrangements may weaken some distinctions while reinforcing others. This variability requires that migrants and local societies not be treated as two internally homogeneous blocs.

The differentiation that accompanies migration lies at the center of debates over integration. In both everyday and political language, integration is frequently used to mean the migrant's adaptation to a new society. This usage can rest on a template of an already-integrated society to which migrants are subsequently added. Once the migrant's learning of the language, employment, compliance with rules, and approximation to cultural expectations become the principal measure of the process, the institutions and inequalities of the receiving society fall outside examination. Abandoning the concept altogether by reducing it to these problematic uses, however, does not dispense with the need to name processes of settlement, participation, acceptance, and exclusion. The more productive discussion asks jointly what the concept renders visible and which assumptions it carries. Integration is better understood through migrants' participation in social life at different levels and different speeds than through any single attitude or outcome. Entering working life, settling into a home, sending a child to school, or gaining access to health services form the relatively concrete face of participation. None of these alone can serve as a sufficient indicator. Access to these domains depends largely on the institutional ground provided by rights and citizenship. Learning the language or coming to know the local culture may ease the process, while insecurity and instability can reverse it. Social ties, too, are not limited to the relationship between migrants and the local society. Familial and origin-based ties, contacts established with different groups, and the connections that provide access to institutions perform distinct functions (Ager & Strang, 2008). Integration, in short, takes shape through the simultaneous and often unequal operation of these irreducible dimensions.

Multidimensionality does not imply a process that advances in the same direction and at the same pace across every domain. A person may participate in the labor market yet remain without legal security. Access to the education system may not by itself secure social acceptance. Strong family and community ties may sustain everyday solidarity while contact with different milieus remains limited. Conversely, a perception of cultural proximity does not erase economic inequalities. Such examples make it difficult to assess integration as “successful” or “unsuccessful” along a single line. Relations among domains matter, but the assumption that they complete one another automatically is mistaken. Integration can be treated here not as a closed outcome but as the process of becoming an accepted part of society (Penninx & Garcés-Mascareñas, 2016). This process need not advance simultaneously in the legal-political, socioeconomic, and cultural-religious domains. A person may occupy an advanced position in one of these while lagging in another. Moreover, the migrant is not the sole subject of the process. The receiving society is a party to the same relationship, and the workings of organizations and institutions shape the outcome as much as individual attitudes do. It follows that acceptance cannot be explained by personal willingness or cultural disposition alone: legal arrangements, the labor market, schools, local governments, civil society organizations, and the settings of everyday interaction together determine the direction of the process.

The dimension of time is likewise decisive for understanding integration. Matters that are urgent in the initial period of settlement—shelter, income, and security—may not give way to entirely different concerns in later years. The provisional character of legal status can constrain people's long-term decisions. Although differences across generations appear in education, language use, and identification, reading them as a straight line of progress is misleading, because the receiving society's attitudes toward migrants, economic conditions, and public policies all change over time. Integration is therefore better conceived as an open-ended process in which gains can be preserved, can recede, or can be reconfigured across domains, rather than as an end point.

Taking these core critiques into account, integration is reconsidered as a process involving the interaction between individuals and institutions and encompassing both personal and social change (Spencer & Charsley, 2021). This approach does not sever integration's structural, social, cultural, civic, and identity-related domains from one another. It also attends to the spatial, temporal, and transnational dimensions of the process. Two-way interaction here is not a simple balance that measures how much the local society changes against the change expected of migrants. What is at stake is the encounter of actors endowed with unequal power and resources. The state, institutions, and majority groups do not stand on equal footing with migrants when it comes to defining the terms of membership. A relational approach must acknowledge reciprocal interaction without rendering this inequality of power invisible. The more far-reaching critiques of the concept take aim precisely at this point. The discourse of "migrant integration" imagines society as a pre-existing integrated whole and positions the migrant outside it (Schinkel, 2018). What is measured is most often not the structure of society but the presumed deficiencies of migrants. Such knowledge production can portray people of migrant origin as subjects who, generation after generation, have yet to arrive at society. Migration research has also been cautioned against reproducing the categories generated by the state's migration apparatus (Dahinden, 2016). Making "migrant-ness" the fixed explanatory center of research can subordinate other relations such as class, gender, legal position, occupation, locality, and social networks. These critiques are valuable in enabling migration and integration research to view its own concepts from the outside. It does not follow, however, that migrant status is unimportant in every case. Border regimes, citizenship law, and discriminatory practices can place people in distinct positions precisely because they are classified as migrants. The problem is not the use of the category of migrant but its transformation into an unexplained and permanent attribute. Research should show clearly when it treats the migration experience, and when it treats legal status, class position, or some other social relation, as explanatory. Integration, likewise, can be freed from serving as a normative measure that assesses only migrants and put to use instead as a question about the institutions and relations within which participation, acceptance, and inequality are produced.

The Turkish experience is especially instructive in showing that concepts do not retain the same meaning across different political and institutional settings. Research has demonstrated that the concept of integration did not reach Turkey through a linear process of academic transfer (Yükseker & Çeler, 2024). The European Union, international organizations, public institutions, civil society, and academic networks each played different roles in the concept's circulation. The English term "integration" has often been rendered in Turkey as uyum, and in the usage of international organizations at times as "social cohesion." These words cannot be regarded as mere matters of translation. Turkey's migration regime, the temporary protection status granted to Syrians, and a political discourse that does not openly acknowledge permanence have all shaped the content of the concept. The pairing of uyum with discourses of guesthood, temporariness, religious affinity, and national belonging can leave the long-term institutional consequences of settlement indeterminate. A policy concept in global circulation is thus shown to be reconstituted within its local context (Yükseker & Çeler, 2024). This observation calls for asking under what conditions integration takes on which meanings, rather than reading Turkey as a deficient instance of models developed in Western Europe. It also suggests that integration policies do not merely regulate access to services but can reproduce the boundaries of national identity and the acceptable forms of membership.

Treating migration, identity, and integration together does not mean dissolving these concepts into a single explanation. Migration studies examine the causes, forms, and social consequences of mobility. Identity brings into view the struggles over how people define themselves and others. Integration asks how participation in rights, resources, institutions, and social relations comes about. The link among them is not a linear sequence in which migration changes identities and integration marks the final stage of that change. Mobility, classification, belonging, and participation influence one another within the same process. Legal status can affect the possibility of work, working conditions can affect social relations, and those relations can affect the sense of belonging, even as the same relations produce different outcomes in different contexts. This shared frame removes the receiving society from the status of an unchanging backdrop. The participation of migrants in education, work, or cultural life is part of the inquiry, and so too are the ways institutions respond to different needs, the ways the local society draws its boundaries, and the forms of membership that public discourse deems legitimate. Such an approach does not disregard migrants' capacity to act. Nor does it place the entire burden on their choices and abilities. It seeks instead to think together the relationships between individual experiences and institutional structures, between everyday relations and national policies, and between local conditions and transnational ties.

The distance between institutional arrangements and lived experience carries particular weight here. The existence of legal rights that provide for equal access does not mean that those rights can be exercised in the same way everywhere. Application procedures, access to information, language support, the capacity of local institutions, and the practices of officials can lead people of similar status to undergo very different experiences (Buz et al., 2021). Formal objectives and everyday practice are not the same thing here. What a policy states and what institutions actually do should not be conflated (Penninx & Garcés-Mascareñas, 2016). An inclusive discourse may coexist with selective implementation, just as local institutions may develop de facto solutions where no explicit policy exists at the national level. This also removes integration from being a matter examinable at the national level alone. International organizations, central governments, local administrations, schools, employers, and civil society organizations all take part in the same process through different instruments. How authority, resources, and responsibilities are distributed among these actors is not the same in every context. Nor do institutions' aims always coincide. Tensions may arise among the security priorities of migration management, the access goals of social services, and the everyday concerns of local politics. It is therefore more illuminating to see "policy" not as the coherent result of a single will but as a combination—sometimes consistent, sometimes contradictory—of decisions and practices taken at different levels.

Differences among migrants' experiences likewise require careful interpretation of general integration indicators. People holding the same legal status may differ in age, education, income, gender, family structure, and social networks. These variables do not operate in isolation. Access to the labor market, for instance, depends on legal status but is also affected by care responsibilities, the recognition of professional qualifications, and local employment opportunities (Canlı & Buz, 2024). Knowledge of the language may reduce some institutional obstacles yet does not by itself remove discrimination or precarious working conditions. Assessing a migrant population through a single average can render invisible the obstacles some groups face while attributing the relatively favorable position of others to the group as a whole.

A similar caution is needed when speaking of the local society. The phrase "host society" can give the impression of a homogeneous majority with shared and unchanging expectations. Attitudes toward migration, however, vary according to class position, political orientation, local history, the character of contact with migrants, and economic conditions. The state's official definition of membership and the criteria of everyday acceptance may also fail to align. Even where citizenship provides an equal legal position, symbolic boundaries drawn through name, accent, appearance, or religion can persist. Conversely, people whose legal status is precarious may forge strong ties within local relationships and working life. These mismatches show that belonging is a domain wider than legal membership yet in continual interaction with the law (Lamont & Molnár, 2002; Yuval-Davis, 2006).

CONCLUSION

In the end, the principal difficulty facing scholarship on migration, identity, and integration is less the production of further concepts than making visible the limits of the concepts already in use. Grasping the place of migration within social transformation, refusing to use identity as the name of fixed groups, and declining to reduce integration to a one-sided measure of success all matter in this respect. Examining the legal, economic, social, and cultural dimensions of integration separately provides clarity. Yet a distinction drawn without asking within which power relations these dimensions take shape will remain incomplete. In the same way, belonging is not merely subjective affinity but, beyond that, a political matter that sets the conditions of acceptance.

This approach does not propose a definitive model of integration applicable to every context. It offers a more modest, but analytically more workable, point of departure. Where people come from matters, and so do the rights they hold, the institutions they encounter, how they are classified, and the kind of future they are able to build. What migration changes is not only the lives of migrants. The ways societies define themselves, the workings of institutions, and the boundaries of membership are also reshaped in the process. The explanatory power of the relationship among migration, identity, and integration should be sought precisely in its capacity to make visible this reciprocal but unequal transformation.

REFERENCES

Ager, A., & Strang, A. (2008). Understanding integration: A conceptual framework. *Journal of Refugee Studies, 21*(2), 166–191. DOI: 10.1093/jrs/fen016

Brubaker, R., & Cooper, F. (2000). Beyond "identity.". *Theory and Society, 29*(1), 1–47. DOI: 10.1023/A:1007068714468

Buz, S., Canlı, M., & Aygüler, E. (2021). *Trabzon'da yaşayan Afgan sığınmacıların profili ve gereksinimleri*. Hacettepe University Migration and Politics Research Center.

Canlı, M., & Buz, S. (2024). Trabzon'da yaşayan Afganistan uyruklu kadın göçmenlerin gündelik yaşamları. *Mavi Atlas, 12*(1), 24–39. DOI: 10.18795/gumusmaviatlas.1382617

Dahinden, J. (2016). A plea for the 'de-migranticization' of research on migration and integration. *Ethnic and Racial Studies, 39*(13), 2207–2225. DOI: 10.1080/01419870.2015.1124129

de Haas, H., Castles, S., & Miller, M. J. (2020). *The age of migration: International population movements in the modern world* (6th ed.). Red Globe Press.

Lamont, M., & Molnár, V. (2002). The study of boundaries in the social sciences. *Annual Review of Sociology, 28*(1), 167–195. DOI: 10.1146/annurev.soc.28.110601.141107

Penninx, R., & Garcés-Mascareñas, B. (2016). The concept of integration as an analytical tool and as a policy concept. In Garcés-Mascareñas, B., & Penninx, R. (Eds.), *Integration processes and policies in Europe: Contexts, levels and actors* (pp. 11–29). Springer., DOI: 10.1007/978-3-319-21674-4_2

Schinkel, W. (2018). Against 'immigrant integration': For an end to neocolonial knowledge production. *Comparative Migration Studies, 6*(1), 31. Advance online publication. DOI: 10.1186/s40878-018-0095-1 PMID: 30363772

Spencer, S., & Charsley, K. (2021). Reframing 'integration': Acknowledging and addressing five core critiques. *Comparative Migration Studies, 9*(1), 18. Advance online publication. DOI: 10.1186/s40878-021-00226-4 PMID: 32355637

Wimmer, A., & Glick Schiller, N. (2002). Methodological nationalism and beyond: Nation-state building, migration and the social sciences. *Global Networks, 2*(4), 301–334. DOI: 10.1111/1471-0374.00043

Yükseker, D., & Çeler, Z. (2024). Migrant integration in Turkey: Travels of a concept across borders and domains of knowledge production. *Migration Studies, 12*(2), mnae009. Advance online publication. DOI: 10.1093/migration/mnae009

Yuval-Davis, N. (2006). Belonging and the politics of belonging. *Patterns of Prejudice*, *40*(3), 197–214. DOI: 10.1080/00313220600769331

Chapter 2
Identity and Migration: Theoretical Perspectives and Experience Transfer

Sanjeev Kumar
http://orcid.org/0000-0002-7375-7341
Lovely Professional University, India

Pardeep Kumar
http://orcid.org/0000-0003-0308-7634
Lovely Professional University, India

ABSTRACT

Migration is a complex social process, which substantially defines the personal and communal identities, altering meaning of belonging to something or another culture, and the incorporation of the social aspects. The identity and migration approaches theories talk about how the migrants negotiate the multiple or overlapping identities as a response to the new social, cultural and political circumstances. Transnationalism theory, acculturation theory, social identity theory and postcolonial approaches can provide insight into the ways migrants retain, modify or transform their identities in the process of displacement, resettlement, and social migration. Experience transfer- the sharing and the transfer of ideas, experience and cultural practices across the borders and bringing them to bear and use them in the host countries further highlight the dynamic elements in respect to the person and the societies thus bringing about personal growth as well as improvement of societies.

DOI: 10.4018/979-8-3373-8500-6.ch002

INTRODUCTION

Migration has been one of the most significant issues in human history, shaping societies, cultures, and identities across the globe. Migration has become common in the globalized world due to economic opportunities, political wars, environmental changes, and the pursuit of better living conditions. The human race defies geographical and national borders in search of employment, education, security, and reuniting with families. These movements not only change the demographic setup of societies; they also affect the cultural, social, and psychological lives of migrants as well as host societies. One of migration's most significant aspects is its impact on identity (Kogan, 2010). Identity is not fixed or stable, but a dynamic process influenced by social experiences, culture, and individual experience. When individuals relocate to a new place, they are exposed to new environments, languages, cultures, and social practices. They therefore tend to strike a balance between their own culture and the newly modified one informed by the culture of the host society (Schuerkens, 2005). This process may shape or multiply identities, as migrants maintain ties to their home countries, adapting to the requirements of their new destinations. Migration and identity are a multidimensional relationship. Migrants tend to experience the need to belong to two or more cultural spaces. On the one hand, they have emotional, cultural, and social ties with their native country through language, traditions, family relations, and community networks.

On the other hand, they gradually become used to the lifestyles, values, and practices of the host community in an effort to integrate and live normal lives. It is a process of negotiation and adaptation that can bring both opportunities and challenges. Migration can bring emerging opportunities, resources, knowledge, and social mobility. Still, it can also result in displacement, cultural conflict, and uncertainty of identity (La Barbera, 2015). Trying to adjust to new relations in society, migrants may experience problems maintaining their cultural standards. These experiences underline the necessity to view migration as a process that not only affects people but also changes identities and social relationships.

The topic of migration and identity has become increasingly popular in the social sciences as it helps individuals and communities adapt to changing social conditions. Some theoretical perspectives that can provide insight into this process include transnationalism theory, acculturation theory, and social identity theory. Transnationalism emphasizes how migrants maintain active connections with their countries of origin in the nation in which they live. Communication technologies, remittances, and cultural interactions in the migration processes are associated with cross-border social and economic activities in which the migrants participate (Cormo , 2022). Conversely, acculturation theory focuses on the process through which migrants acculturate to the cultural patterns of the host country while still maintaining some aspects of their culture. Social identity theory focuses on how individuals identify with social groups such as ethnic, national, and cultural groups. Together, these perspectives help explain how migrants develop and recreate their identities in response to new experiences and environments. Another relevant aspect of migration is the concept of experience transfer, which can be characterized as the flow of knowledge, skills, and cultural practices across national boundaries. Migrants tend to carry with them valuable experiences from their home countries, such as work experience, educational backgrounds, and cultural practices. All these experiences may contribute to economic growth, cultural diversity, and innovation in host societies once migrants establish themselves (Brettell, 2016). In the meantime, migrants also acquire new skills and attitudes, mostly in host societies, which they can transfer to their home countries throughst-mover migration or transnational networks. This continuum of experience exchange not only enriches migrant communities but also host societies, providing opportunities to learn and develop. The study of migration as a process of identity and experience transfer aims to understand how migrants can negotiate the problems and opportunities associated with displacement and resettlement more effectively. By examining migrants' lives, the researchers can identify the social, cultural, and institutional forces that shape their ability to integrate into new societies without forgoing their cultural orientations. This knowledge will also help answer important questions related to belonging, social inclusion, and cultural diversity in multicultural societies.

These questions are significant to discuss because migration is not a purely individual experience, but also a social process that has consequences for communities, economies, a, andational policies. Awareness of the relationship between migration and identity can help policymakers, educators, and social organizations develop more accommodating and welcoming structures for migrant populations. This practice enables societies to promote social cohesion, cultural sensitivity, and respect by recognizing the differentiating nature of the migrants and their experiences (Khanlou et al., 2018). In addition, the appreciation of the value of knowledge and experience of migrants can result in the augmentation of economic growth and enrichment of their culture. In this way, interpreting migration through the prism of identity and experience transfer enables important conclusions about how society can better respond to the challenges and opportunities of an ever more globalized world (Castles, 2010).

LITERATURE REVIEW

Migration has been analyzed in different theoretical frameworks, which aim to answer the question of why people migrate and the role of migration in shaping societies and people's identities. Initial approaches to the Migration Studies discipline focused on economic aspects: migration is driven mostly by the desire to improve the livelihoods of people in sending regions by moving to countries with better employment opportunities, and this was followed by more theoretical opinions that contributed to this, adding social, political, and cultural influences that shape migration. Structural theories concentrate on the global disparity between developed and developing regions, while network theories focus on the social relations between migrants and their societies that motivate further migration (Faist, 2000). These views confirm that migration is not merely an economic process but a complex social phenomenon shaped by historical conditions, policies, and global relations. Migration also has a significant influence on the identity formation of migrant communities. Theorists within the cultural studies discipline argue that migrant identity is not fixed, but a negotiated process (Boldt, 2012). When people move to a new country or region, they have to deal with other languages, habits, and social norms that shape their self-perception and how others view them. Migrants are likely to possess a hybrid identity that incorporates both their heritage culture and that of the host society. This is especially conspicuous with respect to second-generation migrants because they grow up amid multicultural influences. Identity formation is thereby transformed into an ongoing process of balancing cultural continuity with adaptation to a new social situation.

Another significant concept in migration studies is the notion of Transnationalism, which emphasizes that migrants tend to create strong bonds with their native lands when they are away. Modern communication technologies, transport, and the global economic system allow migrants to be simultaneously active in social, cultural, and economic life across borders. For example, migrants can never stop remitting money to their loved ones, and they can also stick to their cultural festivals or participate in political discussions about their home country. Transnationalism bids farewell to the previous idea of migration, resulting in a complete break with the home. Instead, migrants are more likely to live in social spaces at the intersection of the national and transnational, creating identities that cannot be confined to a single national environment. The typical theory used to explain adaptation to a new society is Acculturation Theory, which explains how individuals adjust to a new cultural environment. This theory states that migrants can adopt different strategies for cultural change. Others assimilate into the mainstream culture by ultimately forgetting some of their original cultures.

In contrast, others maintain a strong affiliation with their cultural backgrounds and do not associate much with the host society (Lam et al., 2010). The third process is integration, in which migrants remain attached to their original cultural activities even in the host society. Marginalization can also take place whereby the migrants are detached not only from the home culture but also from the host culture. All these tendencies emphasize that migrants respond to cultural change differently and suggest that social support, discrimination, policy conditions, and individual experiences contribute to adaptation. Social Identity Theory, which explains how people define themselves as members of social groups, is also directly related to migrants' sense of belonging. In this view, people form groups of individuals with similar characteristics defined by their nationality, ethnicity, religion, or language. For migrants, belonging can be linked to the need to navigate several identities simultaneously (Museus et al., 2023). They are not only able to identify with their ethnicity, but they also desire to be acceptable by the majority population. The experiences of belonging or not belonging are important in shaping migrants' perceptions of belonging to a community. Positive interrelationships and supportive institutions can strengthen social bonds, whereas social disidentification can be strengthened by means of discrimination or social constructs (Talaat et al., 2023).

Postcolonial Studies have also been applied to the study of migration in conjunction with sociological and psychological approaches, concerning the influence of past relations of power and colonial legacies on contemporary migration patterns. Postcolonial scholars argue that without acknowledging the impacts of the colonial past, economic dependence, and the cultural distinctions developed during colonial governance, the idea of migration could not be explained. Current migration routes are mostly historical linkages between ex-colonies and their colonial masters. These relations not only dictate the direction of migration but also shape the attitudes host societies will have toward migrants (Moret, 2020). The practices of postcolonialism, therefore, focus on the relevance of race and language and the historic narratives in directing the lived experiences of the migrants and their representation in the social discourse.

CONCEPTUAL FRAMEWORK

The conceptual framework connects identity, cultural change, the transfer of experience during migration, and interaction between migrants and host societies. Migration not only means moving people across geographical locations but also altering social identities, culture, and common experiences. People carry cultural backgrounds, memories, traditions, and values when they migrate and encounter the social and cultural environment of the new society. The outcome of this process is a new identity and hybrid practices shaped by other cultures and experiences, which not only influence migrants but also the communities they enter. Identity is significant in learning about cultural change during the process of migration. Identity is not created out of stone; it is fluid and always subject to social interaction, exposure to other cultures, and experience. When migrants move into a new country or region, they are introduced to new cultural norms, new languages, and new social expectations. Such experiences can destroy their previous identity and might require them to reform or redefine it. A good example is that migrants will be able to keep their original cultural identity, such as language, religion, eating habits, and practices, and still adopt the culture of the host. This process generates cultural change, where identities become stratified or more multifaceted. Migrants do not entirely abandon their original identity, but they tend to develop a hybrid identity which comprises a legacy of the original culture and the new environment.

Cultural change also occurs through day-to-day interactions, institutions, and social networks. In attempts to retain their culture, migrants are likely to change their behaviors and cultural activities to fit into the host society. Negotiation through preservation and adaptation may lead to the development of multicultural identities. For other migrants, adherence to cultural roots is a form of belonging and continuity, especially in a new setting. At the same time, they may change their perceptions, values, and lifestyles by getting acquainted with new ideas and social structures. This change can also impact how migrants raise children in the long term, enter social life, and relate to institutions such as education and work. Migration Experience transfer entails the transfer of knowledge, skills, memories, and culture experience which the migrants have in their mother country to the host country. Migrants are not blank individuals; they carry with them their life experiences, which determine how they adapt to new environments. These experiences may include professional lifestyles, farming, entrepreneurship, social culture, or community values. As migrants integrate into the host society, they are likely to share these experiences as they work, express their culture, and interact with others. One such situation is that migrants can introduce new food, artistic trends, business ideas, or a lifestyle that may become part of the cultural diversity in the host society. The same is true with the transfer of experience. During their stay in the host country, migrants acquire new information, technology, and social practices that, over time, may be instilled in their home populations, especially when migrants have transnational relationships. Migration brings migrants' information and experiences to the families and communities of the home country, where communication, remittances, or visits occur. This exchange of knowledge and culture results in lifelong learning and change.

The interaction between the migrants and the host societies is one of the determinants of the consequences of migration. Host societies also play a major role in determining how fully migrants can assimilate and become part of social life. Factors such as government policies, public attitudes, economic opportunities, and cultural openness determine the nature of these interactions. When host societies are more inclusive and provide equal opportunities, migrants have a better chance of succeeding in their new societies and retaining their cultural identity. In that case, cultural diversity can become a source of social enrichment and innovation. However, communication between migrants and host societies can also be full of conflicts and struggles. Language, religion, s, habits, or social values might differ in some cases, which can lead to misunderstanding or bigotry. Migrants can be discriminated against and marginalized or become culturally isolated, and this may affect their ability to be part of the society. In the meantime, host societies may not be able to accommodate the cultural changes brought about by the migraine. These difficulties underscore the importance of dialogue, cultural sharing, and inclusive policies grounded in mutual understanding. Constant exposure of migrants and host societies in the long run may lead to changes in both. Migrants not only adapt to new social systems but also contribute to national development in cultural, economic, and social terms. In the meantime, host societies grow and incorporate some migrant cultures into their social arrangements. This reciprocal process demonstrates that migration is not a one-way process of accommodation but a communal transformation that reshapes identities, experiences, and communities. This theoretical framework of identity, cultural change, experience transfer, and interaction with the host society provides a holistic perspective on migration. It shows that migration is a complex social process which is correlated to adjustment, exchange, and negotiation. These processes lead to reciprocal influence between migrants and host societies, new cultures, expanded social networks, and the emergence of new identities in an increasingly connected world. The conceptual framework of Migration are shown in table 1

Table 1. Conceptual Framework of Migration

Concept	Brief Description
Identity and Cultural Transformation	Migration reshapes personal and cultural identity as migrants adapt to new cultural environments while maintaining elements of their original culture.
Experience Transfer in Migration	Migrants transfer skills, knowledge, traditions, and experiences from their home country to the host society.
Interaction between Migrants and Host Societies	Social and cultural interactions between migrants and host communities influence integration and mutual cultural exchange.

Source: Author Contributions

MIGRATION AND IDENTITY NEGOTIATION

Migration is not limited to the physical movement between one place and another. It is a complex social and cultural process that is critical to how individuals introduce and express their identities. When people travel, they are introduced to new cultural spaces, new social needs, and institutional structures that determine their sense of belonging. This typically leads to the identity negotiation process that migrants continuously experience as they balance elements of their native cultural environment with those of the host community. It can be both a positive and challenging experience, as migrants attempt to preserve their cultural heritage while acculturating into new social environments. Identity negotiation is therefore an interactive process that indicates migrants' efforts to respond to various cultural spaces and renegotiate their identity at changing social levels (Cohen & Kassan, 2018). One of the impacts of migration is the development of various and alternative identities. Human beings do not usually lose their original identities when they move to other countries or regions. Instead, they are likely to remain emotionally and culturally attached to their homeland through language, traditions, religion, and other relationships with family. At the same time, they also slowly come to share a portion of the host culture, including new social norms, values, and ways of life. The outcome of this interaction is hybrid identities, the amalgamation of aspects of both the culture of origin and the culture of a host society. Second-generation migrants and their children often experience both traditional and modern global life. Such experiences help them develop multicultural identities and interests. These hybrid identities demonstrate that identity is not fixed; it is always in flux through social experience and encounters with culture (Saar, 2018).

Alongside perspectives on cultural exchange and self-development, identity negotiation can also be defined by numerous hurdles. Social integration is one of the greatest issues migrants face. Integration is the possibility for migrants to be involved in the social, economic, and cultural life of the host society and maintain their cultural identity. Education, employment opportunities, positive social services, and non-discriminating government policies are some of the aspects that need to be combined in the integration process. When host communities welcome and support migrants in establishing a sense of belonging, their likelihood of becoming good members of society increases. However, access to legal rights, economic equality, and social services may pose barriers to integration (Liu, 2015). Another major challenge is social exclusion or discrimination. Ethnic prejudice, religious prejudice, language or cultural prejudice can be caused to migrants. Such experiences might lead to feelings of isolation, marginalization, and identity crisis. Migrants may be coerced into abandoning their cultural ways, for example, to fit mainstream culture, and may also be rejected or misunderstood by the host society. This can lead to identity tension, as migrants struggle to balance their culture with the expectations of the new world. In other cases, this struggle can be psychological and limit migrants' social mobility.

Nonetheless, several migrants become tough and resourceful enough to emerge from such issues. By creating strong community networks, joining cultural organizations, and maintaining transnational relationships with their countries of origin, migrants tend to build supportive circles where they are not restricted in expressing themselves. Other important factors that have contributed to increased understanding between migrants and host societies include education, intercultural communication, and inclusive policies (Viola, 2015). Migration can be a source of cultural enrichment and social innovation when diversity is recognized and valued. Overall, migration and identity negotiation also indicate the complex character of adapting to new social environments without depriving people of substantial components of their cultural identity. The development of multi and mixed identities, the conflict between cultural assimilation and cultural survival, and the inability to socialize describe how migration is not only a movement across borders but a renewing process that re-establishes identities and social relations. These processes can help form inclusive societies that recognize cultural diversity and contribute to the well-being of migrant populations.

TRANSFER OF EXPERIENCE, KNOWLEDGE EXCHANGE

Migration involves not only the movement of people across borders but also the exchange of knowledge, skills, and experiences between societies. Applying the notion of Migration Studies, it is noted that migrants tend to possess valuable human resources (acquired in schools, work experience, exposure to different cultures, and so on). Migrants also bring professional skills, technical knowledge, and new ideas to their host countries that contribute to the development of those societies. In the meantime, migrants tend to maintain ties with their native countries and can pass knowledge to the population of their home countries. This cross-border flow of information and expertise has been known to support development, technological growth, and cultural exchange. Migration has led to one of the most crucial outcomes: that of the transfer of skills and knowledge (Pentland et al., 2011). Skilled or professionally trained migrants tend to deploy their skills in new environments, benefiting industries such as health, education, technology, and business.

In most cases, migrants introduce new methods of working or entrepreneurial concepts that are more productive and innovative in the host country. One such situation is whereby engineering-- or medicine-trained graduates and business owners can fill skills gaps in the labor market and establish new businesses that generate employment opportunities (Argote et al., 2000). Meanwhile, returning and transnational migrants are likely to share the skills and knowledge learned abroad with their home countries or local development projects, improving professional standards. The process demonstrates how migration may be a channel for the flow of knowledge throughout the world rather than a migratory flow of labor (McNichols, 2010).

Migrant networks are also relevant to the exchange of experience and knowledge between migrants and their communities. According to sociological studies, migrant networks are social relationships that unite migrants with their relatives, friends, workmates, and the institutions of their communities in different locations. These networks provide support in career, housing, education, and legal support. Such networks help migrants share useful information about job markets, career opportunities, and integration into the host community. Newcomers manage more easily because migrant networks provide them with advice on what owhatr former migrants have gone through. Through these networks, knowledge, ideas, and resources flow between countries and communities over time. In addition, migrant networks strengthen knowledge exchange at a greater level, benefiting individuals. Professional associations, diaspora groups, and community organizations tend to be the arenas through which migrants share expertise, pursue community projects, and mentor the younger generation. Training positions, workshops, or even cultural practices can be found in such networks and help migrants remain in touch with their own cultures while also benefiting their new societies.

In most cases, diasporic communities play a key role in the transfer of technological information, business models, and educational partnerships between host and home countries (Ward et al., 2012). Such activities suggest that migrant communities are not living in isolation as a separate entity but are fully integrated into knowledge networks. The economic value of migrants is a familiar debate concerning migration and development. By contributing to the labor market, as well as through entrepreneurship and paying taxes, migrants contribute to the hostcountry's economyy. Some migrants work in sectors facing labor shortages, helping ensure the economy continues to expand and become more productive. Other companies are also established, which offer employment to migrants and natives. The needs of the migrants, in the form of remittances sent back to their families in their home countries, are also a big economic force. In the majority of cases, these funds are used to address domestic needs such as education, medical care, and residential construction, as well as some local economic expansion. Migration therefore offers cross-national economic benefits (Hope, 2016).

Migrants also make tremendous social and cultural contributions to host societies beyond economic input. Their various cultures diversify societies in terms of language, culture, food, and art. Migration tends to lead to the rise of cultural diversity and social innovations due to cultural exchange between migrants and host societies. Migrants also have access to civic affairs, local movements, and education programs, which increase social bonding. Migrant communities, in most cases, promote intercultural communication and understanding between different cultures (Grima et al., 2024). These social contributions demonstrate that migration is not just an economic process but one that enhances cultures and drives social change. Experience and knowledge which diffuse as a result of migration, in a broader sense, underline the fact that current societies are interdependent. Certainly, migrants can create connectivity between different regions of the world, and as a result, ideas, technologies, and cultural practices are exchanged. Their experiences in other social and cultural contexts allow them to develop various perceptions of their own that are useful in developing an innovation and problem-solving strategy. Migration is one of the major processes of global collaboration and development through skills transfer, migrant networks, and economic and social benefits. These dynamics help policymakers and researchers recognize the positive role of migration beyond addressing the difficulties migrants are likely to face in a new environment (Osborn et al., 2006).

STRUCTURAL AND INSTITUTIONAL FACTORS

Agencies and organizations play a critical role in the process and outcomes of migration. These variables include policies/ institutes and social structures that influence how migrants move, resettle, and become part of new societies. Social and political factors, acting on a larger scale than individual motives, are structural and institutional factors. They determine the opportunities migrants enjoy, the challenges they face, and their interactions with host communities. Among them, migration policies, social networks and support systems, and issues of discrimination, inclusion, and opportunity are particularly topical in shaping the lives of migrants. Migration policies are one of the most powerful institutional factors in shaping the lives of migrants. Governments develop policies that guide entry into the country, the terms under which migrants are allowed to stay, and the privileges they are entitled to while in the country. Such policies include visa policies, employment licenses, refugee protection, and citizenship laws. Migration policies can be either very liberal or rigid regarding the movement of people across borders (Biggart et al., 2015). To illustrate, countries with liberal immigration policies can attract skilled workers, students, and entrepreneurs by offering them opportunities and a clear path to permanent residence.

On the other hand, strict migration policies may limit the flow of migrants or create legal and administrative barriers that make it difficult for migrants to establish themselves and work diligently. Another effect of these policies is migrants' access to education, health, housing, and social services (Molosiwa & Boikhutso, 2016). These policies favor integration, making migrants more willing to participate in the host country's social and economic life. However, restrictive or ambiguous policies may create uncertain, insecure, and limited opportunities for migrants. Social networks and support systems are another influential structural determinant that can influence migration experiences. Migrants are likely to use the networks of their family members, friends, and community organizations to cope with the hardships of living in a foreign environment. These networks provide emotional and practical assistance, job opportunities, housing, education, and information on legal proceedings. Social networks connect migrants to their home countries and help them adjust to their host countries. New relatives and neighborhood agencies can help new people to adjust to new cultural standards and social expectations. In the majority of cases, migrants are inclined to migrate to regions where they already have relatives or acquaintances, which reduces the risks and uncertainties of migration. Structural and Institutional Factors Influencing Migration are shown in table 2.

Table 2. Structural and Institutional Factors Influencing Migration

Factor	Brief Description
Migration Policies	Government rules and regulations that control the entry, stay, and rights of migrants in a host country.
Social Networks and Support Systems	Family, friends, community groups, and organizations that provide emotional, social, and practical support to migrants.
Discrimination, Inclusion, and Opportunities	Social attitudes and institutional practices that affect migrants' access to jobs, education, and participation in society.

Source: Author Contributions

DISCUSSION

Migration is an evolutionary process and affects not only the flow of people within geographies but also the development and re-development of individual and group identities. Identity, migration, and experience are closely intertwined: migrants gain and reconstruct their identities depending on the setting and new social and cultural conditions. Migration exposes individuals to new cultural practices, language, values, and social expectations. Migrants also carry their experiences, traditions, and memories of their motherland, as well as the process of adjusting to the new environment. This past and present leads to a bargaining and renegotiation of identity. The migrants do not simply replace one identity with another; rather, they blend elements from other cultural settings to produce complex, dynamic identities that suggest both continuity and transformation. The interaction between identity and migration can be theorized in terms of the day-to-day lives of migrants as they move through the social, economic, and cultural environments within host societies. When migrants enter a new environment, they are subjected to new social norms, communication systems, and institutional systems. These experiences impact their self-image and others' perceptions of them. Migrants gradually acquire new skills, knowledge, and opinions through work, education, community contacts, and family life. These experiences are incorporated into the hybrid identities that create and assimilate aspects of both the host culture and the culture of origin. At the same time, migrants tend to possess strong emotional and cultural connections to their home country in terms of traditions, language, religion, and communication with their loved ones. In this way, migration can lead to a transnational identity, in which people feel they belong to two or more contexts, culturally and nationally.

Experience transfer is another aspect of the identity-migration relationship. Migrants bring with them knowledge, skills, and cultural practices that are valued in their home countries, and these can influence the society to which they relocate. Migrants can bring skills in professions, entrepreneurial ventures, and culture, as well as cultural diversity, that can enrich the social and economic life of the society in which they remain. Migration and professional activity cause migrants to share their experiences and knowledge, which can create innovation, cultural exchange, and the building of more diverse communities. At the same time, the migrants also gain new experiences in their host societies, such as education, new technologies, and new ways of working. These experiences may later be transferred to their home communities through transnational networks, remittances, or return migration. Migration hence creates a reciprocal flow of information and cultural influence that is fruitful for both sending and receiving cultures. Migration has far-reaching and diverse impacts on individuals. At the personal level, migration can provide economic, educational, and personal development. Most migrants seek better jobs, higher living standards, and access to services that may be available in their home countries. Migration also provides migrants with a chance to achieve upward social mobility and improve their family members' lives.

However, migration also involves emotional and psychological problems. Migrants can feel homesick, experience cultural shock, language barriers, and failure to adapt to new social norms. Adapting to a new environment while maintaining contact with the past can lead to uncertainty and identity conflict. Despite these problems, resilience, flexibility, and intercultural competence evolve among some migrants, helping them navigate complex social environments and build meaningful lives in their new destinations. Migration is alsohas severe implications for both the originating and receiving countries. Migrants contribute to the economies of host countries by providing labor, venturing into business, and developing innovations in different ways due to their distinct perceptions and skills. Migrants bring cultural diversity to social life, which is a blessing as new languages, traditions, cuisines, art, and cultural expression are introduced. This diversity can potentially lead to intercultural communication and social knowledge between different societies. At the same time, migration can lead to social and political debates about integration, national identity, and even the allocation of resources. These should be followed by good policies and inclusive social practices that ensure migrants can integrate without losing their cultural identities.

Country-of-origin migration might also be associated with a significant number of positive effects related to remittances, knowledge, and transnational networks. Migrants tend to invest in the families and communities they belong to, which can result in the growth of local communities and improved standards of living. Returning migrants may also introduce new skills, ideas, and worldviews that can bring both social and economic development to the mother country. This appreciation of migration brings an international exchange of experiences and resources, bringing societies together on the cross-border level. The relationship between identity and migration, and the experience as a whole, reveals the complexity and dynamism of human mobility in the modern world. Migration also reinvents identities by exposing individuals to new cultural conditions and opportunities for self-growth and development, as well as through the exchange of knowledge and experience across communities. We need to study how these influences shape one another so we can develop accommodative social policies and promote positive communication between migrant communities and their host societies. Identifying migrants' contributions and distinct identities can help societies create a conducive environment that facilitates integration, cultural diversity, and learning.

CONCLUSION AND RECOMMENDATIONS

Migration is not just about the mobility of people across boundaries; it also facilitates the transfer of knowledge, skills, and experiences across different societies. In the field of Migration Studies, scholars have identified that migrants tend to export certain valuable human capital that they earn through education, work experience, and cultural experience. The inflow of migrants into a new country brings professional experience and cultural expertise, as well as new ideas that can help societies eve. At the same time, migrants tend to preserve their connections with their home countries, and consequently transfer knowledge to their home societies. The flow of information and experience in both directions makes technological and cultural exchange across borders possible. Migration has one of the significant effects in terms of the transfer of skills and knowledge. Educated Migrants, or those who have developed professional skills, normally export their skills to new environments, where they end up operating in fields such as healthcare, education, technology, and business.

In most cases, migrants introduce new techniques, work habits, or entrepreneurial ideas that contribute to boosting productivity and innovation in the host nation. For example, qualified workers in engineering or medicine can help fill skills gaps in the labor market, and businesspeople can start new businesses that provide employment. In the meantime, returning migrants and transnational relations tend to bring the skills and expertise they have gained abroad back to their homes or to other development activities in their home countries, improving working standards. This movement demonstrates that migration may also be a source of the circulation of knowledge on the planet rather than a stream of labor. Migration networks are significant for sharing experiences and knowledge between migrants and their communities. Based on studies in the field of Sociology, migrant networks are social relationships that connect migrants and their relatives, friends, workmates, and community groups across different locations. These networks provide services to individuals in the realms of employment opportunities, housing, education, and legal services. Through these networks, migrants can share information about employment opportunities, professional opportunities, and social integration in the receiving society. These networks can also help newcomers adjust by drawing on the experiences of already-migrated members. In the long term, such networks create channels for the flow of knowledge, ideas, and resources among nations and societies. Migrant networks contribute to knowledge-sharing on a broader scale in addition to benefiting individuals. Professional associations, diaspora groups, and even community groups often exchange expertise, collaborate on projects, and mentor younger members of a community. These networks can also organize training, workshops, or cultural events, which not only allow migrants to maintain connections with their backgrounds but also serve the new societies.

In many cases, diaspora communities also play a key role in the transfer of technological knowledge, business strategies, and academic cooperation between host and home countries. Migrant communities do not remain remote in these activities because they are also involved in global knowledge networking. The economic value of migrants is generally accepted in terms of migration and development. Migrants contribute to the host country's economy through labor market participation, entrepreneurship, and tax payments. A majority of migrants work in sectors where labor supply is limited, and therefore they not only boost economic growth but also productivity. The remainder establish businesses that generate employment opportunities for migrants and local citizens. The economic importance of migration to countries of origin also includes the remittances migrants send to their families back home. These financial transfers typically support households with education, health, and housing, and they help stimulate economic development in the home country. Migration, therefore, produces global economic benefits.

In addition to their economic contributions, migrants can also contribute socially and culturally to receiving societies. They bring different cultures that make communities diverse in language, tradition, food, and art. Cultural diversity and social innovation are normally brought about by migration and the influence of local communities on cultural exchange. Migrants can also participate in civic affairs, community organizations, and educational initiatives that strengthen social cohesion. In most cases, migrant populations promote intercultural communication and improve understanding between different cultural groups. Such social contributions show that migration is not only an economic process but also a means of cultural exchange and social change. Broadly, the interdependency of modern societies is emphasized throughroughexchange of the experience and knowledge through migration. Migrants are bridges connecting the rest of the world, facilitating the sharing of ideas, technology, and cultural activities. They have been exposed to diverse social and cultural environments that help them develop distinctive personal perceptions that can be applied to innovation and problem-solving. Migration contributes to global cooperation and development through the mentthe exchange of expertise, migration networks, and economic and social impacts. This awareness of such dynamics helps policymakers and researchers value the potential that migration brings as we struggle with the problems migrants may encounter in their new surroundings.

REFERENCES

Argote, L., Ingram, P., Levine, J. M., & Moreland, R. L. (2000). Knowledge Transfer in Organizations: Learning from the Experience of Others. *Organizational Behavior and Human Decision Processes*, *82*(1), 1–8. DOI: 10.1006/obhd.2000.2883

Biggart, A., Järvinen, T., & Parreira Do Amaral, M. (2015). Institutional Frameworks and Structural Factors Relating to Educational Access Across Europe. *European Education*, *47*(1), 26–45. DOI: 10.1080/10564934.2015.1001256

Boldt, T. D. (2012). Migration biography and ethnic identity: On the discontinuity of biographical experience and how turning points affect the ethnicisation of identity. In Hackstaff, K. B., Kupferberg, F., & Négroni, C. (Eds.), *Biography and Turning Points in Europe and America* (pp. 93–124). The Policy Press., DOI: 10.2307/j.ctt9qgpjg.8

Brettell, C. B. (2016). Perspectives on Migration Theory—Anthropology. In White, M. J. (Ed.), *International Handbook of Migration and Population Distribution* (Vol. 6, pp. 41–67). Springer Netherlands., DOI: 10.1007/978-94-017-7282-2_4

Castles, S. (2010). Understanding Global Migration: A Social Transformation Perspective. *Journal of Ethnic and Migration Studies*, *36*(10), 1565–1586. DOI: 10.1080/1369183X.2010.489381

Cohen, J. A., & Kassan, A. (2018). Being in-between: A model of cultural identity negotiation for emerging adult immigrants. *Journal of Counseling Psychology*, *65*(2), 133–154. DOI: 10.1037/cou0000265 PMID: 29543472

Cormo , V. C. (2022). The Processes of Adaptation, Assimilation and Integration in the Country of Migration: A Psychosocial Perspective on Place Identity Changes. *Sustainability (Basel)*, *14*(16), 10296. DOI: 10.3390/su141610296

Faist, T. (2000). Transnationalization in international migration: Implications for the study of citizenship and culture. *Ethnic and Racial Studies*, *23*(2), 189–222. DOI: 10.1080/014198700329024

Grima, S., Chaudhary, S., Sood, K., & Kumar, S. (2024). *Business Drivers in Promoting Digital Detoxification*.

Hope, A. (2016). Creating sustainable cities through knowledge exchange: A case study of knowledge transfer partnerships. *International Journal of Sustainability in Higher Education*, *17*(6), 796–811. DOI: 10.1108/IJSHE-04-2015-0079

Khanlou, N., Bender, A., Mill, C., Vazquez, L. M., & Rojas, L. (2018). Youth Experiences of Cultural Identity and Migration: A Systems Perspective. In Pashang, S., Khanlou, N., & Clarke, J. (Eds.), *Today's Youth and Mental Health* (pp. 57–76). Springer International Publishing., DOI: 10.1007/978-3-319-64838-5_4

Kogan, I. (2010). Migration and identity: Different perspectives. *The International Journal of Psycho-Analysis*, *91*(5), 1206–1208. DOI: 10.1111/j.1745-8315.2010.00329.x PMID: 21495419

La Barbera, M. (2015). Identity and Migration: An Introduction. In La Barbera, M. (Ed.), *Identity and Migration in Europe: Multidisciplinary Perspectives* (Vol. 13, pp. 1–13). Springer International Publishing., DOI: 10.1007/978-3-319-10127-9_1

Lam, S. K., Ahearne, M., Hu, Y., & Schillewaert, N. (2010). Resistance to Brand Switching when a Radically New Brand is Introduced: A Social Identity Theory Perspective. *Journal of Marketing*, *74*(6), 128–146. DOI: 10.1509/jmkg.74.6.128

Liu, S. (2015). Searching for a sense of place: Identity negotiation of Chinese immigrants. *International Journal of Intercultural Relations*, *46*, 26–35. DOI: 10.1016/j.ijintrel.2015.03.020

McNichols, D. (2010). Optimal knowledge transfer methods: A Generation X perspective. *Journal of Knowledge Management*, *14*(1), 24–37. DOI: 10.1108/13673271011015543

Molosiwa, A., & Boikhutso, K. (2016). Low educational participation of marginalized children in Botswana's rural and remote schools: Interface between cultural, structural and institutional factors. *Africa Education Review*, *13*(2), 48–63. DOI: 10.1080/18146627.2016.1224097

Moret, J. (2020). Mobility capital: Somali migrants' trajectories of (im)mobilities and the negotiation of social inequalities across borders. *Geoforum*, *116*, 235–242. DOI: 10.1016/j.geoforum.2017.12.002

Museus, S. D., Maramba, D. C., & Teranishi, R. T. (2023). *The Misrepresented Minority: New Insights on Asian Americans and Pacific Islanders, and the Implications for Higher Education* (1st ed.). Routledge., DOI: 10.4324/9781003447931

Osborn, M., McNess, E., & Pollard, A. (2006). Identity and transfer: A new focus for home–school knowledge exchange. *Educational Review*, *58*(4), 415–433. DOI: 10.1080/00131910600971867

Pentland, D., Forsyth, K., Maciver, D., Walsh, M., Murray, R., Irvine, L., & Sikora, S. (2011). Key characteristics of knowledge transfer and exchange in healthcare: Integrative literature review. *Journal of Advanced Nursing*, *67*(7), 1408–1425. DOI: 10.1111/j.1365-2648.2011.05631.x PMID: 21466576

Saar, M. (2018). To return or not to return? The importance of identity negotiations for return migration. *Social Identities*, *24*(1), 120–133. DOI: 10.1080/13504630.2017.1310038

Schuerkens, U. (2005). Transnational Migrations and Social Transformations: A Theoretical Perspective. *Current Sociology*, *53*(4), 535–553. DOI: 10.1177/0011392105052714

Talaat, M., Elkholy, M. H., Alblawi, A., & Said, T. (2023). Artificial intelligence applications for microgrids integration and management of hybrid renewable energy sources. *Artificial Intelligence Review*, *56*(9), 10557–10611. DOI: 10.1007/s10462-023-10410-w

Viola, F. (2015). Negotiation of Identities and Negotiation of Values in Multicultural Societies. In La Barbera, M. (Ed.), *Identity and Migration in Europe: Multidisciplinary Perspectives* (Vol. 13, pp. 29–36). Springer International Publishing., DOI: 10.1007/978-3-319-10127-9_3

Ward, V., Smith, S., House, A., & Hamer, S. (2012). Exploring knowledge exchange: A useful framework for practice and policy. *Social Science & Medicine*, *74*(3), 297–304. DOI: 10.1016/j.socscimed.2011.09.021 PMID: 22014420

Chapter 3
Migration, Development, and Global Connections

Atul Kumar
http://orcid.org/0000-0003-3859-0686
Vikrant University, Gwalior, India

Gafurov Ubaydullo
Tashkent State University of Economics, Uzbekistan

Sevara Abraeva
Termez University of Economics and Service, Termez, Uzbekistan

Ismailov Bobur
Urgench State University, Urgench, Uzbekistan

Artikov Beruniy
Mamun University, Uzbekistan

Deepak Gupta
Institute of Technology and Management, Gwalior, India

Abdullayeva Marjona Asadullayevna
Bukhara State University, Uzbekistan

ABSTRACT

This chapter examines the multifaceted relationship between migration, development, and global connections in the contemporary era. Drawing on recent theoretical frameworks and empirical evidence from 2021-2025, it analyzes how international and internal migration serve as powerful drivers of economic and social development. The chapter explores key mechanisms including remittances, knowledge transfer, diaspora engagement, and transnational networks that link origin and destination communities. It investigates migration governance frameworks, integration policies, and the role of technology in facilitating global connections. The analysis reveals that migration, when properly managed, acts as a transformative force for achieving sustainable development goals.

DOI: 10.4018/979-8-3373-8500-6.ch003

1. INTRODUCTION

Migration has emerged as one of the defining features of the twenty-first century, fundamentally reshaping societies, economies, and cultures across the globe. In 2024, an estimated 281 million people live outside their country of birth, representing approximately 3.6% of the global population. This unprecedented scale of human mobility connects distant regions, creates transnational networks, and generates complex development dynamics that extend far beyond simple origin-destination relationships. The intersection of migration and development has evolved from a peripheral concern to a central policy priority for governments, international organizations, and civil society actors worldwide.

The relationship between migration and development is neither linear nor unidirectional. While classical migration theories often portrayed movement as a response to development disparities, contemporary scholarship recognizes migration itself as a catalyst for development transformation. Migrants contribute to both origin and destination countries through labor, remittances, knowledge transfer, and entrepreneurship. Simultaneously, they maintain transnational connections that create complex webs of social, economic, and cultural exchange. These dynamics challenge conventional notions of national development and highlight the importance of understanding migration within global systems of connection and interdependence (de Haas, 2021).

Recent years have witnessed significant shifts in global migration patterns, governance frameworks, and development paradigms. The COVID-19 pandemic disrupted established migration routes while simultaneously demonstrating the resilience of migrant communities and the critical importance of remittances for development. Climate change has emerged as a powerful driver of displacement and migration, raising urgent questions about environmental migration and sustainable development. Digital technologies have transformed how migrants maintain transnational connections, access financial services, and participate in development initiatives across borders (Barker et al., 2023).

This chapter provides a comprehensive analysis of the migration-development nexus through multiple analytical lenses. It synthesizes cutting-edge research published between 2021 and 2025 to examine how migration contributes to sustainable development, the mechanisms through which development impacts emerge, and the policy frameworks that shape migration-development outcomes. The chapter is structured to progressively build understanding from theoretical foundations through empirical evidence to policy implications, offering insights valuable for researchers, policymakers, and practitioners working at the intersection of migration and development.

1.1 Rationale and Significance

Understanding the migration-development nexus holds profound significance for achieving the United Nations Sustainable Development Goals (SDGs). Migration directly relates to multiple SDG targets, including poverty reduction (SDG 1), decent work (SDG 8), reduced inequalities (SDG 10), and sustainable cities (SDG 11). The Global Compact for Safe, Orderly and Regular Migration recognizes migration as a source of prosperity and sustainable development when well-managed. However, realizing migration's development potential requires evidence-based policies grounded in rigorous analysis of migration dynamics, impacts, and governance mechanisms.

The significance of this topic extends beyond academic inquiry to practical policy challenges facing nations worldwide. Origin countries seek to maximize development benefits from emigration while managing brain drain concerns. Destination countries balance economic needs with social cohesion objectives. International organizations work to facilitate cooperation on migration governance while protecting migrant rights. This chapter contributes to these efforts by synthesizing recent evidence on what works in migration-development policy and identifying promising approaches for enhancing development outcomes.

1.1.1 Contemporary Migration Trends

Contemporary migration patterns reflect complex interactions between economic opportunity, conflict, climate change, and demographic shifts. South-South migration has grown substantially, with developing countries hosting approximately 43% of international migrants. Labor migration to Gulf Cooperation Council countries dominates flows from South Asia and East Africa. Family reunification and education drive significant movements to developed economies. Irregular migration and forced displacement have increased, with global refugee numbers reaching historic highs. Understanding these trends provides essential context for analyzing migration-development linkages (Fransen & de Haas, 2022).

1.2 Chapter Objectives and Structure

This chapter pursues three primary objectives. First, it synthesizes theoretical frameworks explaining migration-development relationships, from classical push-pull models to contemporary transnational and capabilities approaches. Second, it examines empirical evidence on development impacts of migration, including remittances, human capital effects, diaspora engagement, and policy influences. Third, it analyzes governance frameworks and policy innovations that shape migration-development outcomes. The chapter proceeds through seven main sections covering theoretical foundations, development impacts, global connections, governance frameworks, integration and identity, emerging challenges, and policy implications. Each section builds on preceding analysis to construct a comprehensive understanding of migration-development dynamics.

Figure 1. Migration-Development Nexus Framework

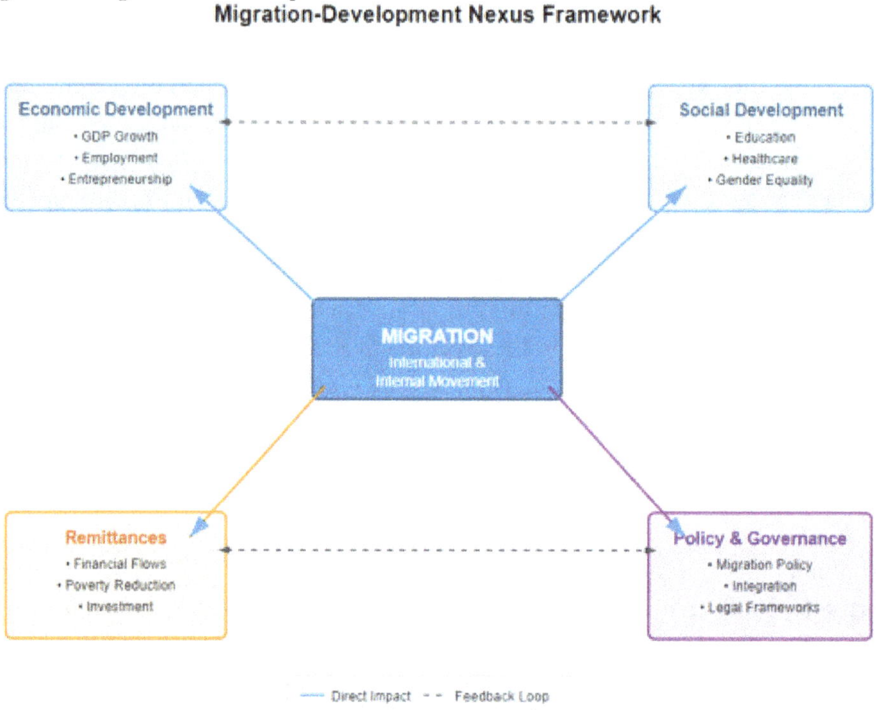

Figure 1 illustrates the interconnected relationships between migration flows and development outcomes. Direct arrows indicate primary causal pathways from migration to economic development, social development, remittances, and governance structures. Feedback loops (dashed arrows) represent how development outcomes influence future migration patterns and policy responses. The framework emphasizes the multidirectional nature of migration-development relationships rather than simple linear causation.

2. THEORETICAL FRAMEWORKS FOR UNDERSTANDING MIGRATION AND DEVELOPMENT

Theoretical understanding of migration-development relationships has evolved considerably over recent decades. Early functionalist theories viewed migration primarily as a response to wage differentials and employment opportunities, conceptualizing it as equilibrating mechanism in labor markets. These neoclassical approaches assumed migration would decrease as development reduced disparities between origin and destination regions. However, empirical evidence revealed more complex patterns, prompting development of more sophisticated theoretical frameworks that recognize migration's multifaceted relationship with development processes.

2.1 The Aspirations-Capabilities Framework

De Haas (2021) developed the aspirations-capabilities framework to address limitations in existing migration theories. This framework proposes that migration results from both aspirations to move and capabilities to realize those aspirations. Crucially, development typically increases both aspirations and capabilities, potentially expanding migration rather than reducing it. This explains the migration hump phenomenon where intermediate levels of development are associated with higher emigration. The framework integrates insights from capability approaches in development economics with migration studies, offering a more nuanced understanding of how development influences human mobility.

The aspirations dimension encompasses individuals' desires for improved living conditions, economic opportunities, education, and lifestyle preferences shaped by exposure to information about potential destinations. Capabilities include financial resources for migration costs, human capital enabling labor market integration, social capital providing networks and information, and legal status permitting movement. Development affects these dimensions differently across contexts, explaining heterogeneous migration responses to development interventions. The framework also acknowledges structural constraints including migration policies, border controls, and labor market regulations that mediate individual migration decisions.

2.1.1 Implications for Development Policy

The aspirations-capabilities framework carries significant implications for development policy. It suggests that development interventions aimed at reducing emigration may paradoxically increase migration by enhancing capabilities while raising aspirations. This underscores the importance of incorporating migration into development planning rather than treating it as failure of development. Policies should focus on maximizing development benefits from migration while protecting migrant rights, rather than attempting to prevent migration through development aid. The framework also highlights the need for destination countries to recognize their role in global development through migration policies and labor market access.

2.2 Transnationalism and Social Networks

Transnational frameworks emphasize how migrants maintain connections across borders, creating social fields that span multiple nation-states. Tedeschi et al. (2022) review current debates in transnationalism, highlighting how migrants sustain economic, political, and socio-cultural ties with origin communities while integrating into destination societies. These transnational practices include remittance sending, political participation in origin countries, circular migration, and transmission of ideas and values. Transnationalism challenges methodological nationalism in migration studies, demonstrating that migrants do not simply leave one place for another but rather occupy and create transnational social spaces.

Social network theory complements transnational perspectives by explaining how migrant networks reduce costs and risks of migration while facilitating information flows. Networks create cumulative causation effects where initial migrants establish pathways for subsequent migration through information provision, job finding assistance, and social support. These network effects help explain persistence of migration flows even when initial wage differentials narrow. Vorobeva and Jauhiainen (2023) examine how transnational practices shape identity negotiations and belonging, revealing complex processes through which migrants navigate multiple national contexts simultaneously.

2.2.1 Digital Transnationalism

Digital technologies have transformed transnational practices, enabling instant communication, real-time financial transfers, and sustained engagement with origin communities at minimal cost. Social media platforms facilitate maintenance of social ties across vast distances. Digital remittance services reduce transaction costs and increase convenience. Online platforms enable migrants to participate in origin country politics, business ventures, and social movements. This digital transnationalism intensifies connections between spatially dispersed communities while creating new forms of transnational identity and belonging (Gniniguè & Ali, 2022).

2.3 Migration Systems Theory

Migration systems theory provides a macro-level framework for understanding stable migration flows between specific origin and destination regions. These systems emerge from historical connections including colonialism, trade relationships, military presence, and cultural ties. Systems are sustained through migrant networks, transportation infrastructure, migration industries, and institutional arrangements. Trang Ha et al. (2025) analyze the globalization of international migration, examining whether migration is becoming more geographically diverse or remains concentrated in established systems. Their evidence suggests migration remains largely structured by historical systems while new corridors emerge in response to changing geopolitical and economic conditions.

3. MIGRATION AND ECONOMIC DEVELOPMENT

Economic dimensions of migration-development relationships have received extensive scholarly attention. Migration affects development through multiple channels including labor supply, remittances, human capital formation, entrepreneurship, and fiscal impacts. The net development impact depends on complex interactions between these channels, their relative magnitudes, and contextual factors shaping how migration affects economic outcomes in both origin and destination regions.

3.1 Remittances and Development Outcomes

Remittances represent the most visible and quantifiable link between migration and development. In 2024, global remittance flows to low and middle-income countries exceeded $650 billion, surpassing official development assistance by a factor of three. Remittances provide crucial income support for recipient households, enabling consumption smoothing, investment in education and health, and entrepreneurial activities. At the aggregate level, remittances can contribute to poverty reduction, improve balance of payments positions, and provide countercyclical stability during economic downturns.

Azizi (2021) examines remittance impacts on poverty and inequality in developing countries, finding that remittances significantly reduce poverty headcount ratios and extreme poverty. However, inequality effects are ambiguous, as remittances may benefit middle-income households more than the poorest who lack migration capabilities. Barkat et al. (2024) analyze how remittances contribute to sustainable development goals, revealing that financial inclusion plays a crucial mediating role.

When combined with accessible financial services, remittances generate stronger development impacts through productive investment and entrepreneurship.

3.1.1 Remittance Channels and Mechanisms

Remittances affect development through multiple channels. Direct effects include poverty reduction through increased household income. Human capital effects emerge as remittances finance education and healthcare investments. Entrepreneurship effects occur when remittances provide startup capital for small businesses. Multiplier effects arise as remittance spending stimulates local economic activity. However, potential negative effects include inflation in recipient regions, reduced labor supply through income effects, and dependency reducing recipients' work effort. Acheampong et al. (2021) analyze remittances in Sub-Saharan Africa, emphasizing interactions with financial development and institutional quality in determining development outcomes.

3.1.2 Digital Remittances and Financial Inclusion

Digital transformation of remittance services has significantly reduced transaction costs while increasing speed, convenience, and security. Mobile money platforms enable recipients without bank accounts to receive remittances directly. Blockchain-based solutions promise further cost reductions. Gniniguè and Ali (2022) examine digitalization's role in enhancing remittance impacts in ECOWAS countries, finding that digital financial infrastructure strengthens the remittance-growth relationship by facilitating productive use of funds and expanding financial inclusion among previously unbanked populations.

Figure 2. Remittances and Development Indicators (2021-2024)

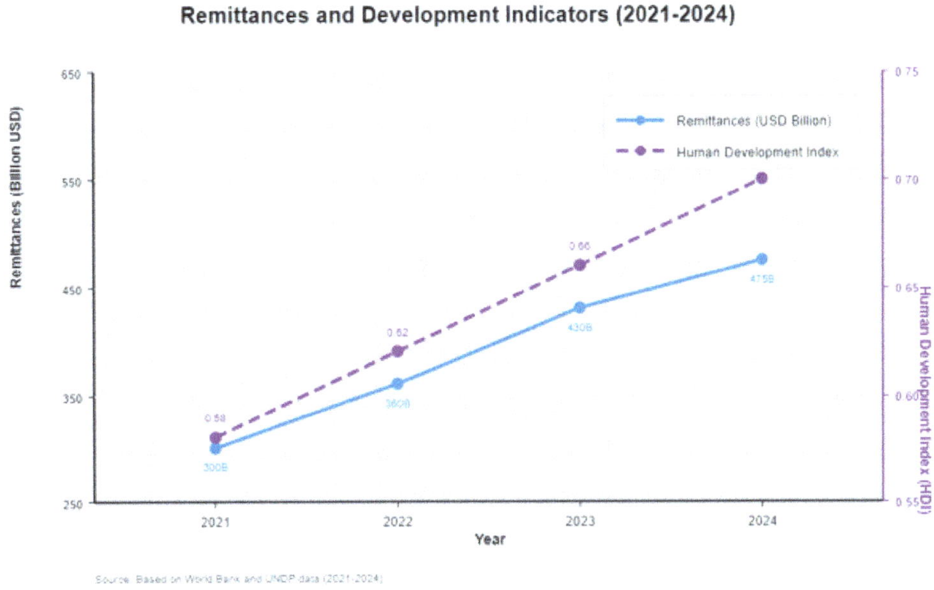

Figure 2 displays the parallel trends in global remittance flows and human development outcomes across developing countries from 2021 to 2024. The solid blue line represents aggregate remittances (left axis, billions USD), showing consistent growth from $300 billion in 2021 to $475 billion in 2024. The dashed purple line shows the composite Human Development Index (right axis) for remittance-receiving countries, demonstrating improvement from 0.58 to 0.70. The positive correlation suggests remittances contribute to broad development progress, though causality requires careful analysis controlling for confounding factors.

3.2 Labor Migration and Wage Effects

Labor migration affects economic development through impacts on labor markets in both origin and destination regions. In origin countries, emigration can increase wages for remaining workers by reducing labor supply, particularly in skill categories experiencing significant outmigration. However, it may also create labor shortages in critical sectors. McKenzie (2024) reviews evidence on whether more people should move within and from developing countries, concluding that migration restrictions prevent welfare-improving movements and that policies facilitating migration would benefit both individuals and aggregate development outcomes.

Mobarak et al. (2023) analyze returns to international migration using visa lottery data from Bangladesh, finding that successful lottery winners experience substantial income gains averaging 300% compared to unsuccessful applicants. These gains demonstrate migration's poverty-reducing potential while highlighting how migration barriers prevent welfare improvements. In destination countries, immigrant workers fill labor market gaps, particularly in sectors with aging populations or jobs unwanted by native workers. Alesina et al. (2023) examine immigration's relationship with redistribution preferences, revealing complex political economy dynamics shaping migration policy in destination countries.

3.2.1 Brain Drain and Brain Gain

Skilled migration raises distinct development concerns around brain drain—the loss of human capital when educated workers emigrate. However, contemporary research reveals more nuanced dynamics. Brain gain effects can occur when migration prospects incentivize human capital investment, with some induced investments remaining in origin countries even when individuals do not migrate. Brain circulation occurs when skilled migrants return with enhanced capabilities and connections. Diaspora effects emerge when emigrants contribute to origin country development through knowledge transfer, investment, and network provision without permanently returning.

3.3 Entrepreneurship and Innovation

Migrants demonstrate higher rates of entrepreneurship than native populations in both origin and destination countries. Returning migrants establish businesses leveraging skills, capital, and networks acquired abroad. Remittances provide startup capital for entrepreneurial ventures. Transnational entrepreneurs operate businesses spanning multiple countries, capitalizing on knowledge of multiple markets and access to diverse resources. These entrepreneurial activities stimulate economic dynamism, create employment, and facilitate technology transfer. However, structural factors including regulatory environments, access to finance, and market conditions significantly influence whether migration-related entrepreneurship translates into broad development gains.

4. MIGRATION, SOCIAL DEVELOPMENT AND WELL-BEING

Beyond economic dimensions, migration profoundly affects social development including health, education, gender relations, and social cohesion. Understanding these social impacts requires attention to household-level dynamics, community effects, and broader societal transformations associated with migration processes.

4.1 Human Development and Gender Dimensions

Nasrin et al. (2024) examine remittance effects on human and gender development in South Asian countries, revealing significant positive impacts on health outcomes, educational attainment, and gender equality indicators. Remittances enable households to invest in children's education, access quality healthcare, and improve living conditions. Importantly, migration can challenge traditional gender norms, empowering women left behind through increased autonomy and decision-making responsibility. Female migration creates opportunities for economic independence and challenges gender-restrictive cultural practices, though risks including exploitation and trafficking require policy attention.

Adger et al. (2024) analyze migration's relationship with sustainable development, emphasizing interconnections between human mobility and multiple SDG dimensions. They argue that migration should be recognized as integral to sustainable development rather than treated as separate concern. This perspective acknowledges migration's contributions to poverty reduction, health improvements, educational advancement, and gender equality while recognizing challenges including family separation, psychosocial stress, and vulnerability to exploitation that require policy responses.

4.1.1 Health and Healthcare Access

Migration affects health through multiple pathways. Remittances improve access to healthcare and nutrition in origin communities. However, migration can increase psychosocial stress, family separation impacts children's wellbeing, and migrants face health vulnerabilities during transit and in destination countries. Healthcare worker migration creates acute shortages in origin countries' health systems while destination countries benefit from immigrant health professionals. Circular migration may facilitate health knowledge transfer, with migrants adopting healthier behaviors and transmitting health information to origin communities.

4.2 Education and Skill Development

Education represents a primary channel through which migration affects intergenerational development. Remittances enable households to keep children in school longer, afford higher-quality education, and access tertiary education. Migration prospects incentivize educational investment as families recognize education's importance for migration success. Student migration creates opportunities for accessing advanced education unavailable domestically while potentially contributing to brain drain if students do not return. Lagakos et al. (2023) analyze rural-urban migration's welfare effects, finding that migration enables individuals to access better educational opportunities, though rural education improvements could reduce distress migration.

4.2.1 Knowledge Transfer and Innovation

Migrants serve as conduits for knowledge transfer between origin and destination contexts. They transmit technical skills, business practices, institutional knowledge, and social innovations. Return migration facilitates technology transfer as migrants apply knowledge gained abroad to origin country contexts. Diaspora networks enable collaboration between origin country institutions and migrant professionals abroad, facilitating research partnerships and innovation diffusion. These knowledge flows contribute to technological upgrading, productivity improvements, and institutional development in origin countries, though effectiveness depends on absorptive capacity and enabling environments.

4.3 Social Cohesion and Community Effects

Migration affects social cohesion in both origin and destination communities. In origin contexts, emigration can weaken social bonds through family separation and community fragmentation. However, transnational ties may strengthen community connections as emigrants maintain engagement with origin places. Remittances can reduce inequality within communities or increase it depending on distribution patterns. In destination contexts, immigration raises questions about social cohesion, integration, and national identity. Successful integration requires institutional support, labor market access, and welcoming attitudes among receiving populations.

5. GLOBAL CONNECTIONS AND TRANSNATIONAL NETWORKS

Contemporary migration creates dense networks of global connections that transcend national boundaries. These transnational networks facilitate flows of resources, information, and influence between spatially dispersed communities, fundamentally reshaping how we understand development in an interconnected world.

5.1 Diaspora Engagement and Development

Diaspora communities represent important development actors through remittances, investment, knowledge transfer, philanthropy, and political engagement. Kopchick et al. (2022) examine emerging diasporas and their mobilization patterns, revealing how diaspora groups organize to influence origin country politics, provide humanitarian assistance, and promote development initiatives. Governments increasingly recognize diaspora potential, implementing policies to engage emigrants and leverage their resources for development. Diaspora bonds mobilize migrant savings for infrastructure financing, while diaspora knowledge networks facilitate technology transfer and institution building.

However, diaspora engagement faces challenges including coordination difficulties, political divisions within diaspora communities, and concerns about diaspora influence on origin country affairs. Effective diaspora engagement requires institutional frameworks facilitating collaboration between diaspora groups and origin country governments while respecting political pluralism. Digital platforms increasingly enable diaspora engagement by reducing coordination costs and enabling real-time communication between diaspora members and origin communities.

5.1.1 Diaspora Investment and Entrepreneurship

Diaspora investment represents underutilized development resource. Emigrants possess capital, knowledge, and connections that could benefit origin country economic development. However, institutional constraints including property rights insecurity, regulatory burdens, and corruption limit diaspora investment. Policies reducing investment barriers, providing diaspora investment incentives, and facilitating business partnerships between diaspora members and local entrepreneurs can enhance development impacts. Transnational entrepreneurship enables diaspora members to operate businesses linking origin and destination economies, creating employment and facilitating trade.

Figure 3. Global Migration Patterns and Transnational Networks

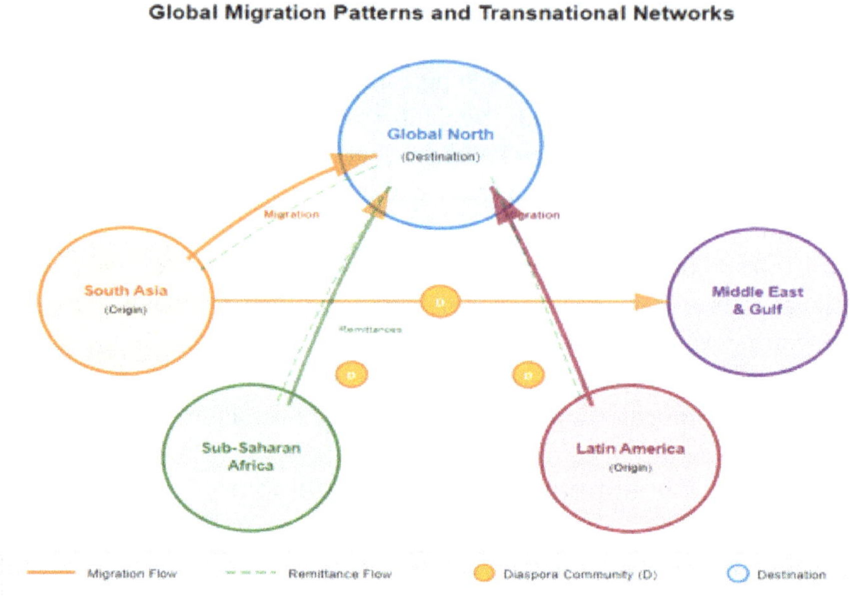

Figure 3 shows major global migration corridors and transnational network connections. Solid arrows represent primary migration flows from origin regions (South Asia, Sub-Saharan Africa, Latin America) to destination regions (Global North, Middle East & Gulf). Arrow thickness indicates relative flow volumes. Dashed lines represent remittance flows returning to origin regions. Yellow nodes marked 'D' indicate diaspora community concentrations serving as bridges between origin and destination contexts. The diagram emphasizes how migration creates complex webs of connection rather than simple unidirectional movements.

5.2 Transnational Social Fields

Ehrenfeld (2025) theorizes migration through mobile social ontologies, arguing that transnationalism creates social fields spanning multiple national contexts. These transnational spaces are characterized by sustained cross-border interactions, shared identities, and mutual influence despite geographic separation. Transnational families maintain close relationships across borders through regular communication, visits, and support exchanges. Transnational communities preserve cultural practices, celebrate shared events, and maintain social institutions linking dispersed members.

Canizales (2024) examines how transnational lives shape immigrant teen workers' aspirations and obligations, revealing complex negotiations between family expectations in origin countries and individual ambitions in destination contexts.

These transnational orientations influence educational decisions, career trajectories, and identity formation. Understanding transnationalism requires moving beyond methodological nationalism that treats nation-states as natural containers of social life, instead recognizing how contemporary migration creates social formations fundamentally organized across national boundaries.

5.2.1 Digital Technologies and Transnational Communication

Digital communication technologies have fundamentally transformed transnational practices. Video calls enable face-to-face interaction despite vast distances. Social media platforms facilitate group communication and community maintenance. Messaging apps provide real-time connection at negligible cost. These technologies enable migrants to maintain stronger ties with origin communities than was historically possible, creating what some scholars term 'digital co-presence' where migrants remain actively engaged in origin country social life despite physical absence. However, digital divides in access and literacy create unequal capacities for transnational engagement.

5.3 Transnational Political Engagement

Migrants increasingly engage politically across borders through voting in origin country elections, funding political campaigns, lobbying destination country governments on origin country issues, and participating in social movements. This transnational political engagement raises important questions about sovereignty, citizenship, and democratic participation. Some origin countries extend voting rights to emigrants, recognizing diaspora as constituency with ongoing stakes in national affairs. Destination countries increasingly consider immigrant political integration while immigrants maintain political ties to origin countries, creating complex dual political orientations.

6. MIGRATION GOVERNANCE AND POLICY FRAMEWORKS

Effective migration governance requires coordinated policy frameworks addressing migration's multifaceted dimensions while protecting migrant rights and maximizing development benefits. Contemporary governance approaches increasingly recognize migration's global dimensions, necessitating international cooperation alongside national policy reforms.

6.1 International Migration Governance

The Global Compact for Safe, Orderly and Regular Migration represents a milestone in international migration governance, establishing shared principles and commitments for managing migration cooperatively. However, implementation remains challenging as migration policy remains primarily national prerogative. Czaika et al. (2023) examine Europe's external migration policy mix, analyzing interactions between visa policies, readmission agreements, and resettlement programs. Their research reveals complex policy interactions where restrictive measures in one dimension may create pressure in others, highlighting the need for comprehensive governance approaches.

Niemann and Zaun (2023) analyze EU external migration policy and governance, exploring how the EU attempts to manage migration through partnerships with origin and transit countries. These partnerships typically link development assistance with migration control objectives, raising concerns about policy coherence and origin country ownership. Effective international governance requires balancing destination country interests in migration management with origin country development needs and fundamental migrant rights protections.

6.1.1 Regional Migration Governance

Regional governance frameworks increasingly address migration through organizations like the African Union, ASEAN, and regional economic communities. These frameworks facilitate labor mobility, harmonize migration policies, and coordinate responses to forced displacement. Regional approaches can better address migration's transnational dimensions than purely national policies while being more politically feasible than global governance. However, regional frameworks face implementation challenges including divergent national interests, capacity constraints, and concerns about sovereignty.

6.2 National Migration Policy Approaches

National migration policies encompass labor migration programs, family reunification provisions, humanitarian admission, irregular migration responses, and border management. Soto Nishimura and Czaika (2024) conduct meta-analysis of migration determinants, revealing how policy factors interact with economic, social, and demographic drivers in shaping migration flows. Effective policy requires understanding these complex interactions rather than assuming policies have simple, direct effects on migration volumes.

Destination country policies increasingly recognize skilled migration's economic benefits while remaining politically contested regarding low-skilled migration and family reunification. Points-based systems attempt to select migrants based on economic criteria, though outcomes depend significantly on how selection criteria align with labor market needs. Origin country policies increasingly focus on protecting emigrant workers' rights, facilitating remittances, and engaging diaspora for development. However, policy coherence remains challenging when objectives conflict, such as when efforts to maximize remittances conflict with goals of promoting return migration.

6.2.1 Labor Migration Programs

Labor migration programs aim to match destination country labor demand with origin country workers seeking opportunities. Temporary migration programs enable circular migration while theoretically preventing permanent settlement. However, program effectiveness depends on enforcement capacity, employer compliance, and migrant rights protections. Exploitative working conditions, wage theft, and restrictions on mobility undermine program benefits when enforcement is weak. Well-designed programs balance destination country labor needs with origin country development objectives and migrant worker rights, requiring careful attention to recruitment practices, wage provisions, and pathways to permanent residence.

6.3 Integration and Urban Governance

Zapata-Barrero (2023) examines urban migration governance through resilience lens, arguing that cities increasingly serve as critical sites of migration governance and integration. Urban contexts concentrate immigrant populations, necessitating local-level integration policies addressing housing, education, employment, and social cohesion. Cities develop innovative integration approaches while sometimes diverging from national policies, creating sanctuary cities or implementing local welcome policies. Understanding migration governance requires attention to multi-level governance dynamics where urban, regional, national, and international frameworks interact in complex ways.

Selod and Shilpi (2021) analyze rural-urban migration in developing countries, revealing how internal migration interacts with urbanization processes and development. Urban governance frameworks must accommodate rapid population growth through migration while ensuring adequate infrastructure, services, and livelihood opportunities. Successful urban integration requires coordinated approaches addressing labor markets, housing, public services, and social cohesion simultaneously rather than treating these as separate policy domains.

Table 1. Key Migration Governance Frameworks and Their Development Impacts

Governance Level	Key Frameworks	Primary Mechanisms	Development Impact
Global	Global Compact for Migration, SDG Target 10.7	Rights protection, facilitated mobility, development cooperation	Normative standards, enhanced cooperation, policy coherence
Regional	EU Free Movement, ECOWAS Protocol, African Union Framework	Labor mobility, policy harmonization, coordinated responses	Regional integration, reduced transaction costs, knowledge circulation
National	Labor migration programs, integration policies, diaspora engagement	Managed admission, rights provisions, development programs	Labor market effects, remittance flows, skill development
Local/Urban	Municipal integration strategies, urban planning, service provision	Direct service delivery, community engagement, local economic development	Social cohesion, economic integration, urban development

Note: This table synthesizes key governance frameworks operating at different scales and their primary mechanisms for affecting migration-development outcomes. Development impacts vary significantly based on implementation quality, political commitment, and complementary policies. Multi-level governance coordination is essential for maximizing positive development outcomes while protecting migrant rights.

7. INTEGRATION, IDENTITY AND BELONGING

Integration processes profoundly shape both migrant development outcomes and social cohesion in destination societies. Understanding integration requires attention to multiple dimensions including economic participation, social connections, cultural practices, and psychological identification.

7.1 Multidimensional Integration

Abdelhady and Norocel (2023) propose re-envisioning immigrant integration through multidirectional conceptual flows, arguing that integration is not unidirectional assimilation but rather mutual adaptation involving both immigrants and receiving societies. This perspective recognizes that immigrants transform destination societies while themselves being transformed, creating hybrid cultures and practices.

Integration outcomes vary across economic, social, cultural, and political dimensions, with immigrants potentially achieving high integration in some dimensions while maintaining distinct practices in others.

Laubenthal (2023) reviews integration theories, comparing assimilation, integration, and transnationalism frameworks. Classical assimilation theory predicted eventual convergence between immigrant and native populations across all dimensions. However, segmented assimilation theory recognizes divergent trajectories where second-generation immigrants may experience downward mobility into marginalized segments. Transnational perspectives challenge the assumption that integration requires weakening origin country ties, instead highlighting how transnational practices can coexist with destination country integration.

7.1.1 Economic Integration

Economic integration encompasses labor market participation, occupational mobility, earnings convergence, and entrepreneurship. Immigrants typically experience initial disadvantage due to credential recognition barriers, language limitations, and discrimination. Over time, economic integration proceeds through language acquisition, credential validation, network building, and experience accumulation. Second-generation outcomes often exceed first-generation despite persistent disparities with natives in some contexts. Policies facilitating credential recognition, language training, and anti-discrimination enforcement enhance economic integration while benefiting destination economies through fuller utilization of immigrant human capital.

7.2 Identity Formation and Belonging

Dolberg and Amit (2023) examine identity formation among 1.5 generation immigrants who migrated as children, revealing how early migration experience creates unique identity negotiations. These individuals form identities incorporating both origin and destination cultural elements while facing pressures to conform to either one or the other. Hur (2023) analyzes psychological dimensions of national belonging, arguing that migrant integration depends significantly on whether destination societies accept immigrants as legitimate national members. Exclusionary attitudes create psychological barriers to integration even when formal citizenship is achieved.

Hu and Cheung (2024) conduct meta-analysis of social identity and social integration relationships, finding that positive social identity formation facilitates integration across multiple domains. However, identity formation processes are complex, involving negotiations between imposed identities, chosen identities, and shifting identifications across contexts. Karimi and Wilkes (2024) propose a transnational amendment to assimilation theory, arguing that origin country racial status affects integration trajectories in destination contexts through transnational reference points shaping identity and status perceptions.

7.2.1 Generational Differences

Integration trajectories differ significantly across immigrant generations. First-generation immigrants maintain strong origin country connections and identities while adapting to destination contexts. Second generation individuals typically achieve higher economic and linguistic integration but may experience identity conflicts and face discrimination despite growing up in destination countries. 1.5 generation immigrants who migrate as children occupy intermediate positions, often serving as cultural brokers within families. Third and subsequent generations typically achieve full integration though may maintain ethnic identities and practices through symbolic ethnicity.

7.3 Social Integration and Networks

Social integration involves developing connections with destination society members while potentially maintaining origin country networks. Bonding social capital within ethnic communities provides support and resources but may limit broader integration. Bridging social capital connecting immigrants with natives facilitates economic opportunities and cultural adaptation. Integration policies increasingly recognize the importance of social connections, implementing initiatives promoting intergroup contact and community participation. Neighborhood composition, institutional contexts, and opportunity structures significantly influence social integration trajectories.

8. EMERGING CHALLENGES AND FUTURE DIRECTIONS

Contemporary migration-development relationships face evolving challenges requiring adaptive governance and innovative policy responses. Understanding emerging trends provides foundation for anticipating future developments and preparing appropriate responses.

8.1 Climate Change and Environmental Migration

Climate change increasingly drives migration through environmental degradation, extreme weather events, sea-level rise, and agricultural disruption. While precise predictions remain uncertain, consensus suggests substantial increases in environmentally induced migration. However, the poorest populations facing greatest climate impacts often lack resources to migrate, creating trapped populations requiring assistance. Policy responses must address both managed migration enabling climate-affected populations to move safely and adaptation investments reducing displacement necessity. International frameworks inadequately address environmental migration, creating protection gaps for affected populations.

8.1.1 Climate Migration and Development Planning

Integrating migration into climate adaptation planning represents critical development challenge. Migration can serve as adaptation strategy enabling populations to escape deteriorating environmental conditions. However, unplanned mass migration creates humanitarian crises and development setbacks. Effective approaches require anticipatory planning including investments in climate-resilient development, creation of migration pathways for affected populations, and regional cooperation on climate migration management. Development policies must acknowledge climate change's migration implications rather than treating migration as failure of adaptation efforts.

8.2 Pandemic and Crisis Impacts

The COVID-19 pandemic disrupted global migration through border closures, mobility restrictions, and economic contractions. Barker et al. (2023) analyze migration and resilience during the pandemic, finding that while migration flows temporarily declined, remittances proved remarkably resilient, demonstrating migrant commitment to supporting origin communities despite their own hardships. The pandemic highlighted migration's role in global supply chains, essential services, and economic functioning. It also revealed vulnerabilities including migrants' exposure to infection, job losses, and inadequate social protection.

Recovery from the pandemic requires policies supporting migrant workers who sustained essential services during crises. It also necessitates social protection systems including migrants regardless of legal status, recognizing their economic contributions and health interdependencies within societies. Future pandemic preparedness must incorporate migration dimensions including ensuring continued migration pathways for essential workers and protecting migrant rights during public health emergencies.

8.2.1 Post-Pandemic Migration Trends

Post-pandemic migration recovery reveals several trends including pent-up demand driving increased flows, remote work enabling new forms of mobility, and shifting destination preferences favoring countries with successful pandemic management. Labor market disruptions created temporary shortages in specific sectors while displacing workers in others. Digital transformation accelerated during the pandemic, potentially enabling greater virtual presence as alternative to physical migration. Understanding these evolving patterns requires ongoing monitoring and adaptive policy responses.

8.3 Digital Transformation and Future Mobility

Digital transformation reshapes migration-development relationships through multiple channels. Digital platforms enable remote work potentially reducing physical migration necessity. Digital financial services facilitate remittances and migrant entrepreneurship. Digital technologies enable transnational engagement at unprecedented scales. However, digital divides create new inequalities as those without digital access face mounting disadvantages. Effective policies must ensure inclusive digital access while leveraging technology's potential for enhancing migration-development benefits, while also addressing the security vulnerabilities inherent in the web-based platforms that increasingly mediate these digital interactions (Kumar et al., 2012).

Artificial intelligence and automation raise questions about future labor migration demand as technological substitution replaces certain jobs while creating new occupations requiring different skills. Development policies must anticipate these transformations, investing in education and training enabling workers to adapt to evolving labor markets. Emerging applications of artificial intelligence in education demonstrate this potential, including AI-supported instruction tailored to learners who require additional support (Dharani et al., 2022) and the reimagining of assessment and evaluation through inclusive design and digital innovation (Gupta et al., 2025). Migration policies must similarly adapt, recognizing changing skill demands and facilitating migration-development synergies in digitally transformed economies.

8.3.1 Data and Evidence Challenges

Evidence-based migration-development policy requires high-quality data on migration flows, migrant outcomes, and development impacts. However, data limitations constrain research and policy. Irregular migration escapes official statistics. Return migration and circular migration create measurement challenges. Development impact attribution faces methodological difficulties distinguishing migration effects from confounding factors. Addressing these challenges requires investment in migration data infrastructure, innovative measurement approaches leveraging technology, and rigorous evaluation designs enabling causal inference.

9. CONCLUSION AND POLICY IMPLICATIONS

This chapter has examined the complex, multifaceted relationships between migration, development, and global connections through synthesis of recent theoretical and empirical research. Several key insights emerge from this analysis. First, migration serves as powerful development force when properly managed, contributing to poverty reduction, human capital development, and sustainable development goal achievement. Second, migration-development relationships are multidirectional and context-dependent rather than uniform across settings. Third, maximizing development benefits requires coordinated policies addressing migration's economic, social, and governance dimensions simultaneously.

9.1 Key Findings

The aspirations-capabilities framework provides robust theoretical foundation for understanding migration-development relationships, explaining how development affects migration propensities and outcomes. Remittances constitute major development resource, particularly when combined with financial inclusion and supportive policy environments. Transnational networks create global connections facilitating resource flows, knowledge transfer, and innovation diffusion. Migration governance requires multi-level coordination spanning international, regional, national, and local scales. Integration represents multidimensional process requiring both immigrant adaptation and receiving society accommodation.

Emerging challenges including climate change, pandemic disruptions, and digital transformation necessitate adaptive governance frameworks. Evidence demonstrates that migration restrictions often prevent welfare-improving movements while failing to achieve purported policy objectives. Development benefits from migration depend significantly on policy choices affecting migrant rights, integration support, and diaspora engagement. Success requires moving beyond zero-sum conceptualizations recognizing mutual benefits possible through cooperative approaches.

9.1.1 Theoretical Contributions

This chapter advances theoretical understanding by synthesizing diverse frameworks into coherent analysis of migration-development relationships. It demonstrates complementarity between aspirations-capabilities approaches, transnational perspectives, and systems theories in explaining migration patterns and impacts. The analysis reveals how micro-level decisions, meso-level networks, and macro-level structures interact in shaping migration-development outcomes. It also highlights the importance of context-dependent analysis rather than seeking universal migration-development relationships applicable across all settings.

9.2 Policy Implications

Policy implications span multiple governance levels and domains. Origin countries should focus on maximizing emigration benefits through diaspora engagement, remittance facilitation, and return migration support while investing in development reducing distress migration. Destination countries should recognize migration's economic and demographic benefits, implement integration policies supporting immigrant success, and ensure migrant rights protections. International cooperation should facilitate safe, orderly migration while respecting sovereignty and ensuring development coherence.

Specific policy recommendations include: reducing remittance transaction costs below 3% as targeted by SDG 10.c; implementing portable social protection enabling coverage across borders; facilitating credential recognition and skills transferability; creating legal migration pathways reducing irregular migration; investing in integration programs including language training and labor market access; engaging diaspora through voting rights, investment facilitation, and development partnerships; mainstreaming migration into development planning; and establishing monitoring frameworks tracking migration-development outcomes.

9.2.1 Implementation Challenges

Implementing effective migration-development policies faces several challenges. Political constraints limit migration liberalization even when economically beneficial. Institutional capacity limitations hinder policy implementation in many contexts. Coordination failures across government agencies and governance levels undermine policy coherence. Resource constraints limit integration program financing. Vested interests including migration industries benefit from status quo arrangements resisting reforms. Addressing these implementation challenges requires political leadership, adequate resources, institutional development, and stakeholder engagement.

9.3 Future Research Directions

Future research should address several gaps. Long-term impacts of current migration flows require longitudinal analysis. Climate migration necessitates integrated research combining environmental science, migration studies, and development economics. Digital transformation's migration implications remain understudied. Return migration and circular migration require greater attention given their potential development benefits. Irregular migration's development dimensions need rigorous analysis despite data challenges. Regional variation in migration-development relationships merits comparative research. Policy evaluation using experimental and quasi-experimental methods can strengthen evidence base for specific interventions.

Methodological innovations including computational approaches, big data analytics, and machine learning offer promising avenues for migration research. However, these methods must be combined with traditional approaches including ethnographic research capturing lived migration experiences and qualitative analysis illuminating complex social processes. Interdisciplinary collaboration spanning economics, sociology, geography, political science, and other disciplines will enhance understanding of migration's multifaceted development relationships.

9.3.1 Emerging Research Priorities

Specific research priorities include: analyzing climate migration patterns and policy responses; evaluating pandemic impacts on migration systems; examining digital transformation's effects on migration and transnationalism; investigating migration's role in demographic transitions; analyzing South-South migration dynamics; studying migration-development relationships in conflict-affected contexts; examining gender dimensions of migration and development; and evaluating specific policy interventions' causal impacts on migration-development outcomes.

9.4 Concluding Remarks

Migration represents fundamental feature of contemporary globalization with profound implications for development. Rather than treating migration as problem requiring control or development failure requiring prevention, evidence supports conceptualizing migration as development process offering opportunities for improving human welfare when appropriately managed. This requires political will for evidence-based policymaking, institutional capacity for effective implementation, and international cooperation transcending narrow national interests.

The migration-development nexus will remain central to twenty-first century development discourse and practice. Success requires moving beyond dichotomous thinking positioning migration and development as opposing forces, instead recognizing their potential synergies. It demands policies protecting migrant rights while maximizing development benefits for origin and destination contexts. Most fundamentally, it necessitates recognizing migrants as development actors whose agency, aspirations, and contributions deserve respect and support rather than restriction and suspicion.

As global challenges including climate change, demographic shifts, and economic transformation reshape migration patterns, adaptive governance frameworks grounded in evidence and human rights principles provide the best foundation for harnessing migration's development potential. The path forward requires sustained commitment to research, policy innovation, and international cooperation, recognizing that migration-development relationships ultimately reflect fundamental questions about human opportunity, dignity, and flourishing in an interconnected world.

The evidence presented throughout this chapter demonstrates that migration, when approached through development-oriented frameworks, creates opportunities for transformative change across multiple dimensions. Economic benefits manifest through remittances, labor market contributions, entrepreneurship, and innovation. Social development advances through investments in health, education, and gender equality. Transnational connections generate knowledge flows, cultural exchange, and political engagement that enrich both origin and destination societies. These multifaceted contributions underscore migration's potential as catalyst for sustainable development.

However, realizing this potential demands fundamental shifts in how societies, governments, and international institutions conceptualize and manage human mobility. Migration governance must evolve from security-centered paradigms emphasizing border control toward development-centered approaches prioritizing human rights, economic opportunity, and social inclusion. This transformation requires acknowledging that migration results from rational decision-making by individuals and families seeking better lives, not from policy failures to be corrected through restrictions. Effective governance respects migrants' agency while creating institutional frameworks channeling migration's energy toward mutually beneficial outcomes.

The role of institutions proves critical in shaping migration-development outcomes. Strong institutions in origin countries can leverage emigration for development through diaspora bonds, knowledge networks, and return migration programs. Destination countries with inclusive institutions achieve better integration outcomes, reducing social tensions while maximizing immigrants' economic contributions. International institutions facilitate cooperation on migration management, though current frameworks remain inadequate for addressing contemporary challenges.

Institutional development at all governance levels represents essential prerequisite for positive migration-development relationships.

Looking forward, the migration-development agenda must address emerging realities reshaping human mobility. Climate change will likely become dominant migration driver, requiring proactive planning rather than reactive crisis management. Digital technologies create new possibilities for maintaining transnational connections and accessing economic opportunities, but also new risks of exclusion for those lacking digital access. Demographic divergence between aging developed economies and youthful developing regions creates complementary labor market needs that migration can address if policies facilitate rather than restrict movement. Pandemic preparedness must incorporate migration dimensions, recognizing migrants' essential roles while ensuring adequate protections.

Ultimately, migration-development relationships reflect deeper questions about global justice, human rights, and international solidarity. Current global inequalities in opportunities, resources, and life chances drive much migration, while migration barriers perpetuate these inequalities by preventing people from accessing better opportunities. Development-oriented migration policies represent not merely technical interventions but ethical commitments to expanding human capabilities and recognizing fundamental rights to mobility and opportunity. The challenge for the international community involves creating governance frameworks that respect national sovereignty while acknowledging shared responsibilities for development and human welfare transcending borders. Meeting this challenge will determine whether migration serves as force for reducing global inequalities or mechanism reinforcing them.

The path toward harnessing migration for development requires paradigm shift from viewing migrants as threats or burdens to recognizing them as agents of change and development partners. This perspective acknowledges migrants' dual contributions to both origin and destination societies while respecting their fundamental humanity and rights. Policymakers must craft frameworks enabling safe, orderly, and regular migration while protecting vulnerable populations and preventing exploitation. Researchers must continue generating evidence on what works in migration-development policy, moving beyond ideological debates toward pragmatic solutions. Civil society must advocate for migrant rights while building bridges between immigrant and native communities. Success demands collaboration across these stakeholder groups, united by commitment to migration as force for human development and global prosperity in an increasingly interconnected world.

REFERENCES

Abdelhady, D., & Norocel, O. C. (2023). Re-envisioning immigrant integration: Toward multidirectional conceptual flows. *Journal of Immigrant & Refugee Studies, 21*(2), 119–131. DOI: 10.1080/15562948.2023.2168097

Acheampong, A. O., Appiah-Otoo, I., Dzator, J., & Agyemang, K. K. (2021). Remittances, financial development and poverty reduction in Sub-Saharan Africa: Implications for post-COVID-19 macroeconomic policies. *Journal of Policy Modeling, 43*(6), 1365–1387. DOI: 10.1016/j.jpolmod.2021.09.005

Adger, W. N., Fransen, S., Safra de Campos, R., & Clark, W. C. (2024). Migration and sustainable development. *Proceedings of the National Academy of Sciences of the United States of America, 121*(3), e2206193121. Advance online publication. DOI: 10.1073/pnas.2206193121 PMID: 38190541

Alesina, A., Miano, A., & Stantcheva, S. (2023). Immigration and redistribution. *The Review of Economic Studies, 90*(1), 1–39. DOI: 10.1093/restud/rdac011

Azizi, S. (2021). The impacts of workers' remittances on poverty and inequality in developing countries. *Empirical Economics, 60*(2), 969–991. DOI: 10.1007/s00181-019-01764-8

Barkat, K., Mimouni, K., Alsamara, M., & Mrabet, Z. (2024). Achieving the sustainable development goals in developing countries: The role of remittances and the mediating effect of financial inclusion. *International Review of Economics & Finance, 95*, 103460. Advance online publication. DOI: 10.1016/j.iref.2024.103460

Barker, N., Davis, C. A., López-Peña, P., Mitchell, H., Mobarak, A. M., Naguib, K., Reimão, M. E., Shenoy, A., & Vernot, C. (2023). Migration and resilience during a global crisis. *European Economic Review, 158*, 104524. Advance online publication. DOI: 10.1016/j.euroecorev.2023.104524

Canizales, S. L. (2024). Between obligations and aspirations: Unaccompanied immigrant teen workers' transnational lives and imagined futures. *Journal of Ethnic and Migration Studies, 50*(10), 2510–2528. DOI: 10.1080/1369183X.2023.2278398

Czaika, M., Erdal, M. B., & Talleraas, C. (2023). Exploring Europe's external migration policy mix: On the interactions of visa, readmission, and resettlement policies. *Journal of Ethnic and Migration Studies, 49*(12), 3140–3161. DOI: 10.1080/1369183X.2023.2198363 de Haas, H. (2021). A theory of migration: The aspirations-capabilities framework. *Comparative Migration Studies*, *9*(1), 8. Advance online publication. DOI: 10.1186/s40878-020-00210-4 PMID: 33680858

Dharani, M., Chakravarthi, D. S., Varghese, V., Ali, B. M., & Nagendra, K. V. (2022). Influence of artificial intelligence technology on teaching slow learners. *International Journal of Early Childhood Special Education*, *14*(4), 4154–4160.

Dolberg, P., & Amit, K. (2023). On a fast-track to adulthood: Social integration and identity formation experiences of young-adults of 1.5 generation immigrants. *Journal of Ethnic and Migration Studies*, *49*(1), 252–271. DOI: 10.1080/1369183X.2022.2088484

Ehrenfeld, C. (2025). Migration theory as social theory: From transnational migration to mobile social ontologies. *European Journal of Social Theory*, *28*(3), 414–430. Advance online publication. DOI: 10.1177/13684310241274922

Fransen, S., & de Haas, H. (2022). Trends and patterns of global refugee migration. *Population and Development Review*, *48*(1), 97–128. DOI: 10.1111/padr.12456 PMID: 35874178

Gninigué, M., & Ali, E. (2022). Migrant remittances and economic growth in ECOWAS countries: Does digitalization matter? *European Journal of Development Research*, *34*(5), 2517–2542. DOI: 10.1057/s41287-021-00461-6 PMID: 34566276

Gupta, D., Siddi, S., Jadeja, K., Rao, G. S., Vijayavadivu, V., & Ahire, P. (2025). Beyond traditional testing: Reimagining assessment and evaluation through inclusive design and digital innovation. In *Innovating assessment and evaluation in higher education: Inclusive practices and technological advancements*. IGI Global. DOI: 10.4018/979-8-3373-2130-1.ch001

Hu, J., & Cheung, C. K. J. (2024). Social identity and social integration: A meta-analysis exploring the relationship between social identity and social integration. *Frontiers in Psychology*, *15*, 1361163. Advance online publication. DOI: 10.3389/fpsyg.2024.1361163 PMID: 38638525

Hur, A. (2023). Migrant integration and the psychology of national belonging. *Journal of Ethnic and Migration Studies*, *49*(13), 3245–3266. DOI: 10.1080/1369183X.2022.2132381

Karimi, A., & Wilkes, R. (2024). A transnational amendment to assimilation theory: Country of origin's racial status versus transnational Whiteness. *Ethnic and Racial Studies*, *47*(3), 459–482. DOI: 10.1080/01419870.2023.2174810

Kopchick, C., Cunningham, K. G., Jenne, E. K., & Saideman, S. (2022). Emerging diasporas: Exploring mobilization outside the homeland. *Journal of Peace Research*, *59*(2), 107–121. DOI: 10.1177/0022343320980803

Kumar, J. P., Ravi, T., & Nagendra, K. V. (2012). Analysis of security vulnerabilities for web based application. In *Proceedings of the 4th International Conference on Advances in Recent Technologies in Communication and Computing (ARTCom 2012)* (pp. 233–236). IET. DOI: 10.1049/cp.2012.2535

Lagakos, D., Mobarak, A. M., & Waugh, M. E. (2023). The welfare effects of encouraging rural–urban migration. *Econometrica*, *91*(3), 803–837. DOI: 10.3982/ECTA15962

Laubenthal, B. (2023). Introduction: Assimilation, integration or transnationalism? An overview of theories of migrant incorporation. *International Migration (Geneva, Switzerland)*, *61*(1), 84–91. DOI: 10.1111/imig.13118

McKenzie, D. (2024). Fears and tears: Should more people be moving within and from developing countries, and what stops this movement? *The World Bank Research Observer*, *39*(1), 75–96. DOI: 10.1093/wbro/lkac009

Mobarak, A. M., Sharif, I., & Shrestha, M. (2023). Returns to international migration: Evidence from a Bangladesh-Malaysia visa lottery. *American Economic Journal. Applied Economics*, *15*(4), 353–388. DOI: 10.1257/app.20220258

Nasrin, N., Haider, M. Z., & Ahsan, M. N. (2024). Well-being effect of international migration and remittance on human and gender development in South Asian countries. *PLoS One*, *19*(4), e0300597. Advance online publication. DOI: 10.1371/journal.pone.0300597 PMID: 38635690

Niemann, A., & Zaun, N. (2023). Introduction: EU external migration policy and EU migration governance. *Journal of Ethnic and Migration Studies*, *49*(12), 2965–2985. DOI: 10.1080/1369183X.2023.2193710

Selod, H., & Shilpi, F. (2021). Rural-urban migration in developing countries: Lessons from the literature. *Regional Science and Urban Economics*, *91*, 103713. Advance online publication. DOI: 10.1016/j.regsciurbeco.2021.103713

Soto Nishimura, A., & Czaika, M. (2024). Exploring migration determinants: A meta-analysis of migration drivers and estimates. *Journal of International Migration and Integration*, *25*(2), 621–643. DOI: 10.1007/s12134-023-01091-z

Tedeschi, M., Vorobeva, E., & Jauhiainen, J. S. (2022). Transnationalism: Current debates and new perspectives. *GeoJournal*, *87*(2), 603–619. DOI: 10.1007/s10708-020-10271-8

Trang Ha, J., DeWaard, J., Abel, G., Tsuchiya, K., Pinchoff, J., Levesque, C., & Price, K. (2025). The globalization of international migration? A conceptual and data-driven synthesis. *Population and Development Review*, *51*(1), 421–448. DOI: 10.1111/padr.12686 PMID: 40964514

Vorobeva, E., & Jauhiainen, J. S. (2023). Transnationalism and belonging: National identity negotiations and their outcomes. *Journal of Ethnic and Migration Studies*, *49*(13), 3389–3408. DOI: 10.1080/1369183X.2023.2184293

Zapata-Barrero, R. (2023). Urban migration governance under the resilience lens: Conceptual and empirical insights. *Ethnic and Racial Studies*, *46*(13), 2833–2862. DOI: 10.1080/01419870.2023.2166793

KEY TERMS AND DEFINITIONS

Aspirations-Capabilities Framework: A theoretical model explaining migration as resulting from both individuals' aspirations to move and their capabilities to realize those aspirations, with development typically increasing both dimensions and thereby potentially expanding rather than reducing migration.

Brain Circulation: The movement of skilled workers between countries through temporary migration, return migration, or virtual engagement, enabling knowledge transfer and skill sharing across borders without permanent brain drain.

Diaspora: Migrants and their descendants who maintain connections with their country of origin while residing in destination countries, often engaging in transnational activities including remittances, investment, political participation, and cultural preservation.

Migration-Development Nexus: The complex, bidirectional relationships between migration and development, encompassing how migration affects development outcomes in origin and destination regions and how development processes influence migration patterns and impacts.

Remittances: Financial transfers sent by migrants to family members or communities in their countries of origin, representing one of the largest financial flows to developing countries and serving as crucial development resource for poverty reduction and human capital investment.

Social Integration: The multidimensional process through which immigrants become participating members of destination societies, encompassing economic participation, social connections, cultural adaptation, and psychological identification while potentially maintaining origin country ties.

Transnationalism: The sustained cross-border connections, practices, and social fields that migrants create and maintain, enabling simultaneous engagement with both origin and destination contexts through economic, political, social, and cultural activities facilitated by modern communication and transportation technologies.

Chapter 4
Borrowed Identities:
The Development of the "False Self" in Migration and Its Psychological Costs

Sunay Güngör
http://orcid.org/0000-0001-9804-0040
Gümüşhane University, Turkey

ABSTRACT

This study defines international migration as a symbolic shift of worlds and an entry into a foreign system of recognition. The strategies developed by migrants to protect themselves from the negative labels of the host society are analyzed through Winnicott's (1960) theory of the "false self" and the proposed concept of "borrowed identities." Within the framework of Goffman's (1963) stigma theory, the "acceptable migrant" performance exhibited by the individual in order to avoid exclusion may provide short-term security, but in the long term it produces severe psychological costs such as alienation and somatization, as emphasized by Akhtar (2011) and Kirmayer (2011). Identity splits, especially observed in second generations, are addressed through the perspectives of Erikson (1968) and Sayad(1999). In conclusion, with reference to Honneth (1995) and Ataca (2005), it is argued that genuine well-being is only possible in a climate where the individual is accepted "as themselves," without wearing a mask.

DOI: 10.4018/979-8-3373-8500-6.ch004

1. THEORETICAL FRAMEWORK

1.1. The Psychic Topography of Migration and the Displacement of the Self

This process, defined by Akhtar (2011) as "third individuation," points to a radical rupture in the individual's developmental history. Unlike the processes of individuation experienced in childhood and adolescence, this third phase brought about by migration requires the individual to renegotiate not only their ties with family, but also their cultural roots. This process does not proceed under equal conditions, because the migrant is forced to speak from a position constrained by imbalances of power within society. Tatar Canbay (2012) describes this condition as the "World as a Space of Exiles." For the migrant, the world is no longer a familiar place, but a vast waiting room at the mercy of a foreign system of recognition. The struggle to survive in a new cultural geography compels the individual to adapt to the projections, expectations, and often prejudices of the host society.

At this point, the experience of migration ceases to be merely an individual process of adaptation and becomes a psychopolitical field. The host society's perception of the migrant, how it categorizes them, and within which boundaries it accepts them directly shape how the migrant constructs themselves. Therefore, identity in migration is not an internal essence, but a process that is constantly negotiated, reconstructed, and often defensively structured.

Thus, Winnicott's (1960) concept of the False Self provides a fundamental psychoanalytic tool for explaining the migrant's presentation of a "borrowed" mode of existence to the outside world, while sending the True Self into an internal exile. From a Winnicottian perspective, the "new society" functions as an oppressive environment for the individual. Rather than preserving their emotional truth and authenticity, the migrant is driven toward excessive compliance with the demands of the external world. In fact, this "borrowed identity" serves as a shield constructed to protect the true self from the destructive, humiliating, or invalidating effects of the outside world. However, the cost of this shield is quite heavy. It entails a disconnection from the individual's inner vitality, creativity, and ontological security. The mental health problems encountered by migrants and refugees are closely related not only to past traumas but also to socio-economic difficulties and cultural conflicts in the host country.

Kirmayer and colleagues (2011) emphasize that post-migration factors such as language barriers, unemployment, and social isolation constitute chronic sources of stress for migrants. In such a pressurized environment, the individual may express psychological distress not directly, but through bodily complaints (somatization) that are considered more "acceptable" socially. This situation results in a form of

Borrowed Identity in which the migrant masks their true emotional world and presents to the outside world only the identity of a "physically ill patient."

As noted by Kirmayer et al. (2011), processes of "loss and mourning" in the migrant's psychological world are in constant negotiation with the cultural expectations of the host society. In order to integrate into the new society's health and social system, the individual is forced to abandon their own cultural frameworks of meaning and to display the profile of a "compliant migrant" expected by the system. This enforced compliance feeds into what Winnicott conceptualizes as the False Self; although the individual may appear functional from the outside, they experience profound alienation and emotional emptiness in their inner world. The lack of "cultural sensitivity" emphasized in this study reinforces this false presentation, rendering the migrant's real psychological needs invisible and causing the psychological costs to accumulate exponentially.

1.2. The Concept of Borrowed Identities: A Theoretical Proposition

The concept of "borrowed identity," which is central to this section, is proposed to define forms of identity adopted by the migrant individual that do not fully correspond to their own subjective experience, but are embraced in order to ensure social acceptance, security, and existential continuity. This concept aims to go beyond terms such as "adaptation" or "assimilation," which are frequently used in the migration literature, and to make visible the psychological costs of these processes on the individual within the theoretical frameworks of figures such as Winnicott (1960) and Akhtar (2011). According to Hall (1996), cultural identity is not a fixed or essential characteristic but an ongoing process of becoming that is continuously reconstructed through historical, social, and cultural experiences. Rather than representing a stable essence, identity is negotiated within changing social contexts and shaped by interactions with different cultural environments. For migrants, identity is therefore understood as dynamic, hybrid, and continuously redefined through experiences of mobility and intercultural encounters.

Borrowed identity is situated along the line of tension between two fundamental planes:

- **True Self:** The individual's subjective existence that carries historical, cultural, and emotional continuity, maintains ties with the culture of origin, and feels "authentic" in the inner world (Winnicott, 1960).
- **Socially Approved Identity:** The performative identity displayed in order to meet the norms and expectations of the host society and, as noted by Goffman (1963), to attain an "unstigmatized" status.

1.3. Conceptual Delineations and Theoretical Boundaries

To establish the theoretical rigour of the proposed concept of "Borrowed Identity," it is essential to delineate its boundaries from interrelated psychosocial constructs in contemporary literature:

- **False Self (Winnicott) vs. Borrowed Identity:** While Winnicott's (1960) False Self is a universal psychological defense mechanisms developing in response to early caregiving environments, a Borrowed Identity is a dynamic socio-political mask specifically adopted within the asymmetrical power structures of host societies to navigate stigma and institutional discrimination.
- **Acculturation (Berry, 1997) vs. Borrowed Identity:** According to Berry (1997), acculturation involves long-term, bidirectional strategies of cultural adaptation. In contrast, a Borrowed Identity represents a performative, unidirectional coping strategy where the migrant suspends their authentic self to buy short-term social safety at a high psychological cost.
- **Identity Negotiation vs. Borrowed Identity:** Identity negotiation implies a fluid, reciprocal, and agentic interaction between the individual and society. A Borrowed Identity, however, is heavily constrained by structural violence and media-driven stereotypes, reducing the migrant's agency to an enforced compliance.
- **Hybrid Identity (Bhabha, 1994) vs. Borrowed Identity:** Bhabha's (1994) concept of hybridity highlights the creative potential of the "Third Space" where cultures merge. A Borrowed Identity, conversely, points to the pathological splitting, inner emptiness, and psychological exhaustion before a healthy synthesis can take place.

Brah (1996) argues that diaspora should not be understood merely as displacement from a homeland but as a complex social space where identities, memories, and belonging are constantly negotiated. She introduces the concept of homing desire, emphasizing that migrants seek not only to return to their place of origin but also to establish meaningful feelings of belonging in their current social environments. This perspective highlights that belonging is constructed through everyday experiences and social relationships rather than geographical location alone.

1.4. The Illusion of Temporariness and the Freezing of Time

Borrowed identity is initially experienced by the individual as a conscious survival strategy. The migrant assumes that they will use this new identity only until they become integrated into the new system; this situation parallels the "illusion of temporariness" described by Sayad (1999). The individual internally claims to have suspended their true self for a while. However, over time, this "temporary" mask begins to stick to the individual's face. The continuity of identity emphasized by Erikson (1968) is disrupted; because roles adopted "for now" begin to imitate permanent personality patterns over the years. When the individual becomes unable to distinguish which emotions belong to them and which are merely social necessities, the "borrowed" identity takes the true identity hostage.

Recent evidence further suggests that multicultural service provision can promote civic engagement and strengthen social integration among culturally diverse populations. Mansouri et al. (2024) argue that inclusive institutional practices and equitable access to public services encourage migrants to participate more actively in civic life, fostering trust, social cohesion, and a stronger sense of belonging. Their findings indicate that multicultural policies are most effective when they move beyond cultural recognition and actively facilitate participation in community and democratic processes. Consequently, successful integration should be understood as a reciprocal process involving both migrants and receiving societies (Mansouri et al., 2024).

1.5. Protective Function: Armor Against Stigma

This identity functions as a "psychosocial armor" that protects the individual from the harsh effects of the social sphere. Within the framework of Goffman's (1963/2014) stigma theory, migrant identity is often coded as "deficient" or "other." Borrowed identity opens up a space for the individual as an "acceptable foreigner" through which they can escape these negative labels.

If we relate this to Honneth's (1995) concept of "recognition," the migrant individual adopts this borrowed identity in order to be accepted as a moral and social subject. Through this armor, they are protected from discrimination and gain access to opportunities. However, this state of protection is based on an exhausting layer of performance in which the individual constantly monitors and regulates themselves (self-monitoring).

1.6. Alienating Effect and the Splitting of the Self

The most critical and costly dimension of borrowed identity is that it weakens the individual's relationship with their own inner world. According to Winnicott (1960), the false self emerges to protect the true self but eventually begins to suffocate it. While the individual is applauded in the external world as a "successful migrant," they feel a deep sense of inauthenticity in their inner world and the emptiness created by what Akhtar (2011) defines as "cultural displacement."

This process severs the individual's contact with their authentic desires and leads to the existential void frequently expressed as "I don't know who I am," along with symptoms of somatization, as often noted by Kirmayer et al. (2011). As a result, while borrowed identity is a social savior in the short term, in the long term it turns into a chronic source of alienation that threatens subjective feeling and the integrity of the self.

2. THE SOCIOPOLITICAL CONSTRUCTION OF THE FALSE SELF IN MIGRATION

2.1. Stigma, Stereotypes, and the Construction of Identity in Migration

In order to understand the process of constructing migrant identity, it is critically important to analyze the "gaze" through which the host society positions the migrant, even before the individual's own perception. At this point, stereotypes and processes of stigmatization function as decisive mechanisms that shape not only the individual's social status but also their most intimate sense of self.

2.1.1. From a Cognitive Shortcut to Structural Violence: Stereotypes

Stereotypes, in their simplest definition, are cognitive tools that individuals use to make the complex social world manageable. However, these tools, especially in the context of migration where power inequalities are pronounced, transform into a form of "structural violence" that results in the systematic negative representation of certain groups. Sayad (1999) states that the migrant is always defined through a sense of "lack" or "excess" within the host society. In this process, migrants are often associated with the following categories:

- **Security Threat:** Being linked to crime and instability.
- **Economic Burden:** The "foreigner" who harms the welfare system and consumes resources.
- **Cultural Incompatibility:** The "other" who is unmodernized, "backward," or "unassimilable."

These stereotypes do not remain confined to individual minds; they are reproduced through media, politics, and law within what Honneth (1995) emphasizes as "hierarchies of recognition." The individual encounters the wall of "prejudice" created by these stereotypes even before stepping into the public sphere.

2.1.2. Goffmanian Perspective: Stigma and Performance

Goffman's (1963) stigma theory provides a striking framework for understanding this process at the level of micro-interactions. Stigma is defined as a characteristic that damages an individual's social acceptance and reduces them from a "whole person" to a "tainted person." Migration functions in many societies as a visible (language, accent, clothing) or invisible (status, origin) stigma.

According to Goffman, a stigmatized individual must constantly engage in "impression management" in order to remain within the category of the "normal." For the migrant individual, this requires constructing every moment as if they were on a theatrical stage. This pressure of performance extends from suppressing their accent, to censoring their political views, and even to striving to be excessively polite and "invisible" in the public sphere. Akhtar (2011) argues that this constant state of vigilance drains the individual's energy and creates a burden that can be described as a "psychological watch."

2.1.3. Constant Surveillance and the Loss of Authenticity

The fear of stigmatization places the migrant in a state of "constant self-monitoring." While this weakens the individual's connection to their own needs and desires, it reinforces an existence focused on meeting external expectations. Thus, the experience of migration ceases to be a space of spontaneous living and is instead transformed into a technically optimized success story under the "surveilling gaze" of the host society.

However, the cost of this optimization is heavy. The integrity of identity emphasized by Erikson (1968) is fractured between the individual's "approved mask" and their "repressed reality." While the individual sacrifices their cultural and emotional continuity in order to protect themselves from negative external labels, they enter a spiral of deep alienation and emotional exhaustion, as indicated by Kirmayer et al. (2011). As a result, although strategies of escaping stigmatization may keep the migrant socially alive, they may psychologically condemn them to a prison of a "borrowed self."

2.2. Recognition, Power, and the Socio-Political Construction of Borrowed Identity

Borrowed identity cannot be considered solely as an individual defense mechanism or as the product of an internal conflict that develops at the micro level. This structure is produced and reinforced with almost laboratory precision under specific political climates, historical power asymmetries, and systematic mechanisms of social exclusion. From the perspective of political psychology and sociology; the "mask" that the migrant individual is forced to wear is, in fact, the concrete and often destructive reflection on the individual of state policies, hegemonic media representations, and deeply rooted social prejudices. Arias Cubas et al. (2023) emphasize that migrants' engagement with multiple cultural contexts can generate valuable intercultural capital, facilitating both social inclusion and identity development. Exposure to diverse cultural experiences enables individuals to develop intercultural competence, strengthen social networks, and foster resilience during the adaptation process. Accordingly, cultural diversity should be viewed not only as a challenge but also as a significant resource that supports successful integration and psychosocial well-being.

2.2.1. The Social Construction of Reality and the Objectified Migrant

Identity formation is directly related to the process of the "social construction of reality," as emphasized by Berger (2022). According to Berger, social reality is continuously reproduced through everyday interactions and institutional structures. In this construction process, the migrant individual transforms from a "subject" who freely defines their own identity into an "object" placed within rigid categories (burden, threat, victim) predetermined by the host society.

This process of objectification is defined by Schnapper (2005) as the "problematic relationship that modern societies establish with the other." When the migrant is turned into an "element of opposition" that defines the boundaries of national identity, they can only exist within the limits permitted by this opposition. This situation transforms the migrant's development of a false self from an individual choice into a structural necessity for survival.

2.2.2. Discursive Violence, Media, and the Burden of Proof

Media and political discourse are the most powerful instruments of power that define the boundaries of migrant identity. While analyzing the central role of the media in producing hate speech, Giritli İnceoğlu (2017) draws attention to the systematic criminalization of migrants. When the migrant is constantly represented in the public sphere as a "security threat" or an "economic parasite," this situation creates an enormous "burden of proof" on the individual.

The individual lives in a constant state of alertness in order to prove that they are the "exception" to these negative stereotypes directed at them by society. The "overly polite," "overly compliant," and "trouble-free" migrant performance exhibited in this process is actually a response to hegemonic discourse. As Çilingir (2016) states, this is a power relation; to the extent that the migrant becomes passive in this relationship, they push their real self out of the public sphere and try to exist with a borrowed identity.

2.2.3. Cognitive Shortcuts and the Narrowing Effect of Political Cognition

From a social psychological perspective, the "cognitive simplification" function of stereotypes defined by Hamilton and Sherman (1994) eliminates the uniqueness of the migrant individual. Lau (1989) emphasizes that complex realities in political cognition processes are reduced to one-dimensional representations (burden/victim).

When combined with the studies of Eagly and colleagues (1991) on the directive function of attitudes, this cognitive narrowing confines the migrant to the perception of a "homogeneous mass." When the individual realizes that society sees them as a "statistic" or a "category," they filter their authentic emotions in order to secure a safe place within that category. This filtering process feeds a permanent false self-structure that, in the Winnicottian sense, results in a "loss of vitality."

2.2.4. The "Acceptable Migrant" and the Injury of Recognition

Borrowed identity can be interpreted as a moral compromise through Honneth's (1995) theory of "recognition." The migrant adopts the mask of the "acceptable migrant" in order to compensate for the violations of rights and devaluation they experience in the domains of legal, social, and emotional recognition. The "illusion of temporariness" and "conditional acceptance" noted by Sayad (1999) make the individual feel under constant surveillance.

Excessive investment in the criteria determined by society (linguistic perfection, absolute obedience, cultural assimilation) leads the individual to perceive their own cultural origin and historical continuity as a "flaw." Ilgın and Hacıhasanoğlu (2010) state that the void created by this crisis of belonging is attempted to be filled with borrowed identities. However, this filler material is fragile; even if the individual purchases social acceptance, they experience deep alienation and ontological insecurity in their inner world.

Furthermore, sociological evidence underscores that the societal expectations imposed on foreign populations often dictate a highly scrutinized path toward validation, where individual narratives are systematically replaced by homogenized categorizations of the 'acceptable other' (Robertson, 2014). This structural surveillance directly feeds into the systemic construction of a defensive false self.

2.2.5. The Integration Paradox: The Invisibilization of Structural Violence

In their recent work, Şeker and Sirkeci (2025) draw attention to the one-sided and oppressive nature of the concept of "integration." Integration is often built on the assumption that the migrant is the side that must "change and be refined." This approach ignores the fact that the high level of integration displayed by the migrant is actually a "silent cry" or a "false self performance."

As a result, borrowed identity is a harbinger of a crisis defined by political psychology as "social trauma," which appears unproblematic on the surface but accumulates anger, grief, and disappointment deep within. A truly democratic and humane coexistence is possible in a climate where the migrant is recognized not as a "borrowed" but with their own "real" identity and can exist without being othered.

2.3. Institutional Structures and the Reinforcement of the False Self

Institutional structures such as education systems, legal frameworks, and the labor market function as tools of "normalization" that shape the identity of the migrant individual. As can be explained through Foucault's (1975) concept of "disciplinary power," these institutions impose a model of the "normative citizen," forcing the individual to conform to certain molds.

A student excluded at school because of their accent or an employee considered "unprofessional" at work due to their cultural habits demonstrates excessive compliance with these institutional expectations in order to survive. Institutional structures render the migrant's True Self invisible and reinforce the construction of the false self at a structural level by rewarding only those functional aspects that align with the system's operation.

2.4. The Process of Othering and the Psychological Reflections of Domination

Othering is not a simple state of "dislike," but, as Çilingir (2016) emphasizes, a systematic relationship of domination. When the migrant is coded as "deficient," "faulty," or "dangerous" in relation to the norms of the majority, this coding infiltrates the individual's sense of self. The process of domination keeps the individual in a constant defensive position.

Within the framework of Çilingir's analysis, othering is a form of "structural violence" sustained not only by individual prejudices but also by institutional structures and social practices. In order to avoid this violence and reduce the costs of social exclusion, the migrant rejects the "other" identity imposed upon them and adopts an "idealized mask" that will be approved by the dominant structure. However, this mask (borrowed identity) does not eliminate the relationship of domination; on the contrary, it leads the individual to internalize this pressure and to see themselves as a constantly "monitored object."

2.5. Media, Hate Speech, and Symbolic Exclusion

Media is the most powerful discursive mechanism that determines how migrant identity is reflected in the social mirror. Giritli İnceoğlu (2017) analyzes the representations in media that "criminalize" migrants and turn them into objects of hate speech, drawing attention to the destructive impact of this process on social peace.

When migrants are constantly represented in the media as a "source of problems," these collective attitudes become legitimized in individual consciences. This symbolic exclusion, as pointed out by Giritli İnceoğlu, turns the visibility of the migrant in the public sphere into a "threat." In order to avoid these violent representations in the media, to not attract attention, and to remain "invisible," the individual buries their identity even deeper. This "panopticon" effect created by the media leads the migrant to perform a "false self" as if they are constantly being watched and judged, resulting in psychological exhaustion.

2.6. The Sociological Relationship with the Other and the Boundaries of Identity

Schnapper (2005) places the concept of the "other" at the very heart of sociological thought. Within the modern nation-state structure, the migrant is coded as the "contrasting element that defines the boundaries of national unity." According to Schnapper, othering is not merely an interpersonal dissatisfaction but a socio-political construction process with historical and cultural roots.

This construction process turns the migrant experience into a state of "constant questioning." When the migrant is positioned within the cultural hierarchies of the host society, they may conceal their own cultural capital and imitate the hegemonic one in order to rise in this hierarchy or at least avoid harm. Schnapper's analysis explains why borrowed identities are not only a psychological but also a sociological necessity: for the individual marked as the “other” by society, the false self is a symbolic passport used to infiltrate the social structure.

2.7. Integrative Evaluation: A Protective and Destructive Shield

In conclusion, borrowed identities are a temporary shield that protects the individual from the symbolic and physical violence of the external world in a traumatic and uncertain process such as migration. However, over time, this shield can turn into a prison that makes it difficult for the individual to breathe.

Borrowed identities:

- **Are protective:** Because they prevent stigmatization and provide social acceptance.
- **Are destructive:** Because they hinder authentic existence and produce alienation and inner emptiness.

A genuine state of well-being is possible in a society where the individual can return what is “borrowed,” speak in their own voice, and be accepted not with their mask, but with their wounds.

3. THE PERFORMATIVE NATURE AND PSYCHOLOGICAL COSTS OF BORROWED IDENTITIES

3.1. The Performative Nature of the Self in Migration

The daily life of the migrant individual can largely be analyzed through a Goffmanian metaphor of a “stage.” On this stage, the individual is compelled to wear masks that vary according to context in order to survive and to pass through the threshold of social acceptance. This multiple role structure rests on the following three pillars:

- **“Compliant Worker” in the Workplace:** The effort to become part of the system through productivity and obedience.
- **“Unproblematic Foreigner” in the Public Sphere:** A shadow existence that does not attract attention, does not create a perception of threat, and has minimized cultural differences.
- **“Loyal Cultural Subject” in the Private Sphere:** A traditional identity that must prove loyalty to its roots within its own community.

Although this management of multiple roles may initially appear as a social skill, over time it creates not flexibility but a psychic fragmentation. Being in a constant state of performance increases cognitive load, leads to emotional exhaustion, and weakens the continuity of the self emphasized by Winnicott (1960). At this point, the "borrowed identity" ceases to be a temporary tactic and becomes the fundamental mode of organizing the individual's existence.

Drawing on Butler's (1990) notion of gender and identity as performativity, the migrant's daily existence can be understood as an exhaustive, continuous reiteration of socially approved norms. When this performative requirement is juxtaposed with Bhabha's (1994) conceptualization of hybridity and the 'Third Space,' it becomes clear that the Borrowed Identity acts as an artificial filler for the ontological gaps before a fluid, integrated hybridity can be achieved.

3.1.1. Stigmatized Identity and Strategic Self-Presentation

In the new society to which they belong, the migrant individual is often not merely a "foreigner," but a "stigmatized" figure targeted by specific social prejudices. Goffman (1963) defines stigma as a "spoiled identity" that prevents the individual's social acceptance and leads to their differentiation from those considered "normal." The migrant faces the risk that their linguistic, ethnic, or ritualistic differences will be perceived as flaws.

The "impression management" that comes into play to avoid this stigma results in the individual concealing their true self like armor and adopting a mask that will be approved by society, namely the Borrowed Identity. The tension between being "discredited" and "discreditable," as noted by Goffman, causes the migrant to live with a constant fear of being "exposed." While hiding one's accent or censoring cultural habits in the public sphere may provide temporary security, it requires immense psychological energy. In this process, the individual becomes alienated from their authentic self beneath the performance they display, constructing a deep psychological fatigue and, in the Winnicottian sense, a False Self.

3.1.2. Psychopolitical Pressure and the Identity Cost of Othering

The migration process fundamentally transforms not only the individual's physical space but also the social categories into which they are placed. Mete (2023), within the framework of Social Identity Theory, emphasizes that out-groups (the host society) tend to define groups they see as the "other" through negative stereotypes. This mechanism of othering strips the migrant of individual characteristics and reduces them to categories such as "burden" or "threat."

Under this psychopolitical pressure, the migrant is forced to suppress their unique identity in order to gain social acceptance. According to Mete's (2023) analysis, this situation creates an intense sense of identity uncertainty and worthlessness in the individual. In order to escape the negative migrant label imposed by society, the individual develops the mask of the "acceptable foreigner." However, while this defensive identity provides protection in the external world, it leads to a chronic split in the inner world and a silent suffering brought about by a "borrowed" existence.

3.1.3. Language, Discourse, and Symbolic Violence: The Invisible Governance of Identity

Language is not merely a neutral means of communication; it is also a domain in which power relations and social hierarchies are reproduced in their most refined form. For the migrant individual, language functions both as a gateway to a new world and as a constant mechanism of surveillance and judgment. Bourdieu's (1991) concept of "symbolic violence" serves as a fundamental tool for making sense of this invisible pressure to which the migrant is subjected.

The individual's accent, vocabulary, and modes of expression carrying cultural codes lose value within the "linguistic market" of the host society. When the migrant withdraws their native language from the public sphere and attempts to develop a "perfect" local accent, they are in fact enacting a practice of symbolic submission. This effort constitutes one of the most exhausting domains of the false self in the Winnicottian sense; because the individual must constantly monitor not only what they say but also the tone and emphasis of their voice (self-monitoring). This "linguistic vigilance" leads to the loss of the individual's authentic voice and, as Kirmayer et al (2011) emphasizes, causes unexpressed emotions to seek an outlet through embodiment (somatization).

3.1.4. The Psychology of Attitudes and Stereotypes: A Cognitive Prison

The studies of Eagly and colleagues (1991) on the cognitive organization of attitudes demonstrate how the social context dominates individual processes of interpretation. The established attitudes toward migrants in society function as "mental filters," causing every behavior of the migrant to be interpreted through prejudice.

As Hamilton and Sherman (1994) point out, while stereotypes simplify the complex social world, they reduce the migrant to a homogeneous, one-dimensional, and generally negative group. This cognitive prison narrows the space for the migrant to "be themselves." The individual exhibits excessive performance in order to disprove the negative expectations that society holds about them (self-fulfilling prophecy). Under this "stereotype threat," the individual calculates every step with precision in order not to make mistakes and to avoid being judged; this, in turn, causes the natural/authentic self to be replaced by a completely externally calibrated "borrowed self."

3.2. The Paradox of Adaptation and the False Self from a Winnicottian Perspective

To conceptualize the proxy identities developed in migration, the "Winnicottian" theory of the False Self provides a central theoretical ground. According to Winnicott, an individual's ability to develop a healthy self is directly related to the "good enough" environment provided by the early caregiver. This environment has the function of recognizing the child's spontaneous gestures, mirroring needs, and supporting their subjective existence.

However, when the environment fails to meet the individual's needs and instead imposes its own demands, the child develops a structure to comply with those demands in order to survive, and this structure is termed the False Self in the "Winnicottian" sense. The False Self does not completely eliminate the True Self; rather, it covers it to protect it and tries to present a socially compatible face to the outside world. When reconsidered in the context of migration, this theoretical framework suggests that the "new society" is often far from being a good enough environment for the individual. The migrant strives to exist in a social space where their needs are not recognized, their emotional reality is unseen, and their value is frequently diminished. In this context, the False Self becomes not merely an individual developmental issue but perhaps a structurally produced form of adaptation.

3.2.1. Excessive Compliance and the Withdrawal of the Self

The "Winnicottian" state of excessive compliance, also known as "compliance," is distinctly observable in migration. The migrant individual complies with the expectations of the environment at a high level in order to:

- avoid conflict
- prevent exclusion
- appear "acceptable"

However, this compliance is not a flexible adaptation but rather a submission that occurs at the expense of the self's withdrawal. In this process, spontaneous behaviors diminish, emotions are filtered, and desires are suppressed. As a result, the individual appears "functional" in the external world while becoming increasingly numb internally. In the "Winnicottian" sense, this state points to a form of existence that is "alive but unable to feel."

3.2.2. Internal Exile: The Concealment of the True Self

One of the most dramatic aspects of the False Self in migration is the exile of the True Self into an inner space. The individual suspends their own language, humor, emotional expressions, and even ways of thinking in the public sphere.

This suspension over time gives rise to questions such as:

- "What do I really feel?"
- "Who am I?"
- "Which one is me?"

These questions are not only philosophical but also frequently encountered in clinical settings. In psychotherapy, expressions by migrants such as "I don't feel real" or "It's like I'm acting" are direct reflections of the False Self structure.

3.2.3. The Hidden Cost of Successful Adaptation

In migration literature, "successful adaptation" is often considered a positive outcome. However, from a Winnicottian perspective, how this adaptation occurs is of critical importance. If adaptation:

- occurs while preserving the authentic self $\rightarrow$ healthy adaptation
- occurs through the False Self $\rightarrow$ pathological adaptation

At this point, the concept of proxy identity reveals the invisible cost behind adaptation that appears as "success." The individual may be socially successful, but this success is accompanied by inner emptiness, a sense of meaninglessness, and emotional disconnection.

3.2.4. The False Self as a Strategy of Disidentification: Escape from the Unwanted Identity

The construction of the false self in migration is not only a proactive effort arising from the desire to integrate into the new society; it is also a radical attempt to escape from the labels of "foreigner," "refugee," or "unwanted other" that cling to the individual. Daehnert (1998), by arguing that the false self functions as a "means of disidentification," draws attention to the defensive nature of this process. From this perspective, the individual presents to the external world a completely different, sterile, and artificial self in order to distance themselves from an identity they perceive as threatening, humiliating, or traumatic.

In the context of migration, as Eroğlu (2020) notes, this situation is triggered by the individual coding their own ethnic and cultural origins as a source of "shame" or a social "obstacle." In order to distance themselves from this "unwanted self," the individual adopts a flawless and polished Borrowed Identity that will be applauded by society. As emphasized in Daehnert's (1998) psychoanalytic case analyses, this disidentification builds a massive "defensive wall" that prevents the individual from confronting past losses and mourning processes. Although the migrant may present a portrait of successful integration in the external world, they sever their connection with the real parts they have rejected in their inner world. This state of "disconnection," which takes the Winnicottian (1960) perspective a step further, symbolizes the individual's escape from their own truth. As a result, although borrowed identities protect the individual from an external stigma (Goffman, 1963), they create a lasting sense of "identitylessness" and "rootlessness" in the inner world, producing a heavy ontological cost.

3.3. Developmental Disruptions and Fractures in Identity Continuity

3.3.1. Identity Development and Psychosocial Splitting: An Eriksonian Reading

To understand identity development, Erik Erikson's psychosocial development theory provides an important point of reference. According to Erikson, identity is the sense of continuity that an individual establishes between past experiences and expectations for the future. This continuity makes it possible for the individual to feel like "the same person."

The experience of migration, however, radically disrupts this continuity. The individual realizes that the identity categories they previously possessed lose their validity in the new society. This situation creates a kind of psychosocial rupture in identity development.

3.3.2. Identity vs. Role Confusion in the Context of Migration

The stage that Erikson defines as specific to adolescence, "identity achievement or role confusion," is virtually reactivated in migration. Even an adult individual faces the following questions after migration:

- "Who am I here?"
- "How should I behave?"
- "How should I appear?"

This situation shows that identity development in migration is not linear; on the contrary, it involves ruptures and reconstructions.

3.3.3. Dual Tension in the Second Generation

Second-generation immigrants grow up between two different normative systems:

- Cultural identity within the family
- Expectations of adaptation in the public sphere

This dual pressure causes the individual to develop two different representations of the self. These identities, being "one way" at home and "another way" outside, gradually become disconnected from each other. This disconnection manifests itself through emotions such as guilt ("I am betraying my family"), shame ("I am not good enough"), and lack of belonging ("I do not belong anywhere").

3.3.4. Identity Fragmentation and Loss of Continuity

The long-term effect of borrowed identities is the loss of the individual's sense of self-continuity. The healthy identity emphasized by Erikson requires a structure that can integrate different experiences. However, in migration, this integration often does not occur.

Instead, the following emerge:

- fragmented identities
- contextual selves
- inconsistent self-narratives

This situation makes it difficult for the individual to make sense of their own life story and creates an existential uncertainty.

3.3.5. Nostalgia, Mourning, and Third Individuation

Akhtar (2011) defines migration as the stage of "third individuation" in the individual's developmental process. This stage contains a deep mourning and nostalgia that comes with the loss of the familiar. The individual, striving to survive in a new geography, sends their True Self, rooted in their origins, into an internal exile in order to adapt to the projections of the host society.

From Akhtar's perspective, the excessively compliant behaviors exhibited by the migrant are in fact a defensive expression of repressed mourning and nostalgia. When the individual cannot build a bridge between the self "there" and the performance "here," they develop a functional False Self directed toward the outside. Although this structure brings social success, it also imposes the cost of an "inner sense of inauthenticity" and lack of belonging. Borrowed identities can condemn the individual to a rootless void in their psychological world.

3.3.6. A Developmental Fracture: Identity Fragmentation in Children and Adolescents

Experiences of war, forced migration, and displacement constitute not only a physical threat in the worlds of children and adolescents, but also the greatest obstacle to the construction of a healthy and integrated self. Eroğlu (2020) emphasizes that war and systematic attacks on ethnic identity fundamentally shake children's sense of self-confidence and belonging, confronting them with severe psychological trauma. These early-period traumas lead the child to develop a "defensive adaptation" toward the external world.

For an individual in adolescence, the effort to avoid being labeled as the "other" leads to the development of a rootless "borrowed identity" that conceals their own cultural and ethnic heritage and instead shows absolute adaptation to the surrounding environment. Eroğlu's (2020) research demonstrates that this process manifests in children as depression, anxiety, and a deep identity confusion. When the child suppresses their real emotions and ethnic identity in order to survive and integrate into new social support systems, they develop a False Self mechanism in the Winnicottian sense, focused on pleasing the environment. However, this image of the "successful child" contains a destructive cost that causes the adolescent to disconnect from their own inner reality. This loss of continuity in developmental processes lays the groundwork for a chronic "existential void" and alienation in adulthood.

3.4. Recognition, Existential Meaning, and Moral Injury

3.4.1. Recognition, Humiliation, and Moral Injury

Identity is not only an individual construct; it is also a process shaped by social recognition. At this point, Axel Honneth's theory of recognition offers an important perspective. According to Honneth, the individual needs recognition at three fundamental levels:

1. Emotional recognition (love)
2. Legal recognition (rights)
3. Social recognition (being valued)

The migrant individual often experiences deficiencies in all three of these areas. This deficiency is not only a deprivation; it is also an injury.

3.4.2. Psychological Consequences of Non-Recognition

The condition of non-recognition triggers in the individual feelings of worthlessness, invisibility, and humiliation. These feelings damage the relationship the individual establishes with themselves. The individual begins to evaluate their own worth through the gaze of the external world.

3.4.3. Moral Compromise as a Borrowed Identity

The migrant individual often resorts to a compromise in order to compensate for the lack of recognition:

- compromises their own values
- conforms to norms
- regulates their visibility

This compromise provides acceptance in the short term; however, in the long term, it leads the individual to become alienated from their own life story. In this sense, a borrowed identity contains not only a psychological but also a moral cost.

3.4.4. Migration, Social Reality, and the Search for Meaning

Migration is not merely a change of geographical coordinates; it is the process of the shaking of the world of meaning into which the individual is born and the radical reconstruction of social reality. Berger's (2022) theory on the "social construction of reality" and the role of religion/belief systems in this construction is indispensable for understanding the ontological dimension of migration.

When the migrant enters the host society, they encounter not only a new language or legal system, but also the invisible worlds of meaning that sustain society, which Berger calls the "sacred cosmos." In this encounter, when the migrant's own system of beliefs and values conflicts with the norms of the new structure, the "crisis of belonging" deepens. In order to gain acceptance within the new social structure, the individual may suppress their own system of meaning and display a "borrowed sacredness" or a "false cultural adaptation" in the external world. This situation leads to the formation of fractures between the individual's own truth and social reality.

3.5. Relational and Existential Diagnostics of the Borrowed Self

Although borrowed identities initially emerge as functional structures that protect the migrant individual from stigmatization and exclusion in the short term, they can produce serious psychological costs in the long term. These costs manifest not only at the individual level but also at relational, bodily, and existential levels. Therefore, borrowed identity is defined not only as a strategy of adaptation but also as a form of psychic organization with a high cost.

In this section, the psychological consequences of living with borrowed identities will be addressed along four main axes:

1. Alienation and disconnection from the self
2. Chronic emptiness and the experience of meaninglessness
3. Anxiety, depression, and burnout
4. Somatization and embodied distress

Empirical evidence from qualitative research and clinical psychiatric evaluations consistently demonstrates that individuals operating under high levels of acculturative stress show a significant propensity for somatization, converting psychological pain into chronic physical ailments (Berry, 1997; Uzun Aydın, 2024). Clinical case narratives reveal that migrants frequently report feelings of 'depersonalization' and 'existential numbness,' stating that they feel like they are merely 'acting on a stage' while their authentic self remains completely hidden from the host society.

3.5.1. Alienation from the Self: The Experience of "I Am Not Myself"

The most fundamental consequence of borrowed identities is the weakening of the individual's relationship with their own internal experience. As the individual constantly regulates themselves in order to gain acceptance in the external world, over time they have difficulty recognizing their own emotions, desires, and needs.

This situation is phenomenologically expressed through the following experiences:

- "It feels like I am acting"
- "My real self is hidden"
- "I am not myself"

These expressions indicate that the individual cannot live their own existence as an authentic experience. In "Winnicottian" terms, this situation points to a state of self that is "alive but does not feel alive."

The process of alienation progresses through the following mechanisms:

- suppression of emotions
- reduction of spontaneous behaviors
- filtering of internal experience according to external expectations

In this process, while the individual exists as a functional subject in the external world, they experience increasing numbness and disconnection in their inner world.

3.5.2. Chronic Emptiness and Existential Meaninglessness

One of the long-term effects of borrowed identities is the emergence of a chronic sense of emptiness. This emptiness is not only an emotional deficiency but also an experience of existential meaninglessness.

The individual:

- is not satisfied even when they achieve success
- does not feel a sense of belonging even when socially accepted
- cannot develop deep bonds despite forming relationships

This situation arises from the disconnection between the false self and the true self. Since the individual cannot identify with the identity they present in the external world, they cannot feel that their experiences "belong" to them.

At this point, the sense of emptiness is expressed as:

- "something is missing inside me"
- "my life does not belong to me"
- "everything is there but something is not"

Unlike classical depression, this experience carries more of a sense of ontological deficiency. In other words, the problem is not only emotional but also a rupture concerning the very foundation of the individual's existence.

3.5.3. Anxiety, Constant Self-Monitoring, and Burnout

Maintaining borrowed identities requires intense cognitive and emotional effort. The migrant individual must constantly monitor how they speak, how they appear, and how they are perceived. This situation creates a state of chronic hyper-awareness. The individual acts with the feeling that their own behaviors are constantly being observed. This leads to high levels of anxiety.

The main sources of anxiety are:

- fear of "being misunderstood"
- anxiety of "being exposed"
- concern about "appearing inadequate"

This constant state of alertness eventually turns into burnout. The individual becomes mentally exhausted, becomes emotionally depleted, and experiences loss of motivation. Burnout here is not only related to workload; it is directly related to the unsustainability of identity performance.

3.5.4. Depressive Symptoms and Inner Collapse

Living with a borrowed identity causes the individual to become disconnected from their own desires and needs. This disconnection lays the groundwork for the emergence of depressive symptoms over time.

These symptoms manifest as:

- lack of motivation
- inability to feel pleasure (anhedonia)
- inner numbness
- feelings of worthlessness

However, the important point here is that depression should be considered not only as an individual pathology but also as a socially produced condition. Because these symptoms are not independent of the structural conditions in which the individual exists.

3.5.5. The Emotional Economy of Migration: Shame, Guilt, and the Struggle for Worth

The experience of migration requires the individual to manage a vast "emotional economy" within their inner world. The fundamental units of this economy are shame, guilt, and a sense of non-belonging. From the perspective of Sara Ahmed's (2004) "cultural politics of emotion," shame functions as a social adhesive that pushes the migrant toward invisibility and to the margins of space.

The individual is caught between the guilt of "having left behind" their original society and the shame of "inadequacy" in the new one. This dual pressure leads the perception of self-worth to become entirely dependent on external validation (the mirroring of the host society). As Honneth (1995) points out, when the individual cannot satisfy their need for social recognition, they develop a form of "borrowed pride" or an "overly achievement-oriented mask" to compensate for this wound. However, this image of the "successful migrant" fails to cover the deep sense of worthlessness beneath it and creates a chronic inner emptiness.

3.5.6. Somatization: Where the Body Speaks

Migrant individuals cannot always express their psychological distress directly. Language barriers, cultural differences, and fear of stigmatization make emotional expression difficult. In this case, distress begins to be expressed through the body.

As emphasized by Laurence J. Kirmayer and his colleagues, common somatization symptoms among migrants include:

- chronic pain
- stomach problems
- headaches
- fatigue

These symptoms are not only physical ailments but also bodily expressions of unexpressed emotions. Somatization can also be considered another form of borrowed identity. Instead of expressing their psychological pain directly, the individual adopts the socially more acceptable role of being a "physically ill" person.

3.5.7. The Ontological Contradiction of Migration: Temporariness and a "Borrowed" Existence

Migration, in Sayad's (1999) striking expression, is a state of "double exclusion." The migrant is no longer fully a member of the place they left behind nor a subject of the place they have arrived in. This state of being in an "existential limbo" forces the migrant to adopt a mask of "temporariness" toward both their own society and the host society. From Sayad's perspective, the "illusion of temporariness" is a form of Borrowed Identity that conceals the reality of having been uprooted.

When the migrant is objectified in the social sphere merely as a "labor force" or a "foreign statistic," they develop a defensive False Self in order to preserve their human integrity. Sayad (1999) emphasizes that the greatest tragedy created by migration is the individual's "alienation" from themselves. Performing the "grateful, silent, and hardworking" role expected by the host society leads the individual to suppress their own memories, language, and desires. This situation results in the severing of the bond between the individual and their own truth and condemns them to a "false" existence; at this point, borrowed identities transform from a protective armor into a cage that imprisons the individual's authentic self.

4. IDENTITY IN THE DIGITAL AGE, BELONGING, AND HYBRID SELVES

4.1. Borrowed Identity in the Digital Age: Social Media and the Extension of Performance

Today, identity construction takes place not only in the physical world but also in digital environments. Social media platforms have radically transformed the way individuals present themselves. For the migrant individual, these platforms become spaces where the borrowed identity is reproduced and multiplied.

In digital environments, the migrant individual simultaneously addresses two different audiences:

- the society they left behind
- the new society in which they live

This situation requires a dual performance. The individual:

- wants to appear "successful and happy" to their former environment
- wants to appear "adapted and integrated" to the new environment

This dual pressure leads to the further idealization of digital identity. The identity displayed on social media consists of selected moments, is purified of negativity, and constantly emphasizes success and adaptation. This situation widens the gap between the individual's real experience and the identity they present. As a result, the borrowed identity becomes not only a social but also a digital mode of existence.

4.1.1. Social Media Platforms as a Digital Showcase

Social media platforms are the digital extension and "showcase" space of the Goffmanian stage performance. For the migrant individual, the digital world is a refuge where they can escape the stigmatizations (Goffman, 1963) they face in real life and construct an "idealized" reality for themselves.

The identity displayed here is often a "success story" purified of the hardships of real life, the pains of assimilation, and economic constraints. However, this digital performance further widens the gap between the individual's real self and the image they present, deepening the "loss of authenticity." While the individual nourishes their borrowed identity with the likes they collect in the digital world, the sense of inner emptiness (Akhtar, 2011) becomes chronic.

4.2. Hybrid Identities and Transnational Belonging

4.2.1. Hybrid Identities and the New Generation Migrant Experience

With globalization and digitalization, identities have taken on a more fluid and reflexive structure along the axis of what Giddens (1991) describes as "modernity and self-identity." However, this fluidity does not always create a space of freedom for the migrant individual; on the contrary, it produces a deep ontological insecurity and uncertainty. Especially for second- and third-generation migrants, identity is constructed on a hybrid plane that is neither fully "from there" nor fully "from here," defined by Homi Bhabha (1994) as the "third space."

Recent comprehensive studies in contemporary global migration frameworks emphasize that transnational belonging is no longer a static dualism but a multilayered negotiation of presence and absence across borders (Isin et al., 2024). This structural complexity further exacerbates the split between the individual's local performance and transnational reality.

4.2.2. In-Betweenness and Identity Fragmentation

This "in-betweenness" forces the individual into a constant negotiation of identity. New generation migrants are torn between the culture of origin, to which their parents expect loyalty, and the expectation of adaptation imposed by the society in which they live. The hybrid identities developed in this process sometimes offer a creative synthesis, but more often lead the individual to face both worlds with a "borrowed" self and, in the Winnicottian sense, to a "fragmentation of identity."

4.3. Belonging, In-Group Dynamics, and Social Alignment

4.3.1. Belonging and In-Group Dynamics: The Social Coordinates of Identity

Belonging is more than the individual's need to be part of a group; as Ilgın and Hacıhasanoğlu (2010) state, it is an emotional and cognitive bridge established with place and community. When migration destroys this bridge, the individual finds themselves in a "social void." Within the framework of Social Identity Theory, the migrant individual is under pressure both to maintain loyalty to their own ethnic in-group and to gain legitimacy within the host out-group.

As emphasized in the recent analyses of Şeker and Sirkeci (2025), the search for belonging is no longer unidirectional but multilayered. When the migrant is not "fully accepted" in the host society, they may cling more tightly to their own in-group; however, this situation can sometimes become a "defensive belonging" developed to protect oneself from the external world rather than an authentic bond.

4.3.2. Dual Performance of Belonging

While the individual shows excessive compliance with the norms of the in-group, they try to maintain the mask of a "compliant migrant" toward the out-group. This dual performance of belonging leads to the decentralization of the individual and to living with a sense of "borrowed belonging."

4.4. Social Cognition, Power Asymmetries, and Political Identity

4.4.1. Social Cognition and the Construction of Political Identity

Lau (1989) draws attention to the critical role of the references individuals use while categorizing the complex social world in political cognition in the construction of identity. For migrants, political identity is not merely a matter of voting or political opinion, but an effort to understand "where one stands" within the power asymmetries of the host society.

The reflection of stereotypes and prejudices in political perceptions directly determines how the migrant represents themselves in the public sphere. As Lau states, political identity is a process of "negotiation"; however, the migrant is often the weaker party in this negotiation.

4.4.2. The Political False Self and Borrowed Citizenship

Adopting the "acceptable political stance" attributed to them by society can create a kind of "political false self" in the individual. By suppressing their own political demands and struggles for rights out of fear of appearing "non-conforming," the individual develops a consciousness of "borrowed citizenship" within the limits permitted by the system.

5. CLINICAL IMPLICATIONS, INTERDISCIPLINARY SYNTHESIS, AND CONCLUSION

5.1. Visibility Strategies and Regimes in the Social Field

Migrants develop various "regimes of visibility" to cope with the processes of stigma and othering to which they are exposed. These strategies are different tactical manifestations of the borrowed identity in the social field:

- **Strategic Invisibility (Assimilation):** The individual aims to "dissolve" into the host society by smoothing out all cultural differences. This represents the most extreme point of the false self; the real self has been sent into an internal exile.
- **Selective Visibility:** The individual carefully chooses which aspect of their identity to display in which context. Goffman's (1963) impression management reaches its peak here; performing "modern-Western" roles at work and "traditional-loyal" roles at home leads to the fragmentation of the self.
- **Resistance as Performance:** In some cases, the migrant may reject the "acceptable" image imposed upon them and excessively emphasize their own cultural symbols. However, this too can sometimes function not as an authentic mode of existence but as a reactive "borrowed armor" developed against the external world.

These strategies are evidence of the migrant's effort to survive. However, each strategy distances the individual a little further from their own center, producing the cost of lifelong non-belonging and psychological exhaustion.

5.2. Clinical Implications and Psychotherapeutic Reflections

5.2.1. Borrowed Identities in the Psychotherapeutic Context

In clinical settings, the expressions most frequently voiced by migrant clients—such as "I don't know who I am" or "I am tired of wearing different masks in different worlds"—are concrete manifestations of the psychological cost of borrowed identities. In the therapeutic process, this situation appears as a loss of the individual's "sense of reality."

6. CONCLUSION: THE INVISIBLE COST OF ADAPTATION AND THE STRUGGLE FOR AUTHENTICITY

The experience of migration is often standardized in modern societies through technical and often one-sided concepts such as ''adaptation,'' ''integration,'' or ''assimilation.'' However, these concepts systematically render invisible the psychological negotiations through which adaptation occurs and the heavy costs of this process on the individual's psychic integrity.

The concept of Borrowed Identity, developed and grounded in this study, proposes rethinking the migration experience precisely through these invisible costs. Borrowed identity, while functioning as a protective shield that guards the individual against social exclusion, stigmatization, and symbolic violence, is also a mechanism of "internal exile" that, in the long term, causes the individual to move far away from their own authentic existence.

As long as a social climate is not constructed in which the individual:

Can exist without a mask,

Can establish continuity between their past and future,

Is recognized and valued not merely as a labor force but as a ''subject,''

all achieved ''adaptation'' successes will remain nothing more than an illusion. Genuine social welfare and psychological well-being are possible on a ground where the migrant can abandon performing the role of the ''acceptable other'' and speak in their own authentic voice.

Although Borrowed Identities are proof of the migrant's genius for survival, the ultimate goal is to build a world in which these borrowed elements can be returned and the individual can feel ''at home'' in reconciliation with their own truth. Migrant well-being should no longer be measured solely by economic success or language proficiency, but by the individual's capacity to exist as themselves.

REFERENCES

Akhtar, S. (2011). *The immigrant, the exile, and the experience of nostalgia*. Karnac Books.

Arias Cubas, M., Al-deen, T. J., & Mansouri, F. (2023). Transcultural capital and emergent identities among migrant youth. *Journal of Sociology (Melbourne, Vic.)*, *59*(3), 754–771. DOI: 10.1177/14407833211066969

Berger, P. L. (2022). *Kutsal şemsiye: Dinin sosyal gerçekliğinin bir kuramı* (A. Coşkun, Çev.). Rağbet Yayınları.

Berry, J. W. (1997). Immigration, acculturation, and adaptation. *Applied Psychology*, *46*(1), 5–34. DOI: 10.1111/j.1464-0597.1997.tb01087.x

Bhabha, H. K. (1994). *The location of culture*. Routledge.

Brah, A. (1996). *Cartographies of diaspora: Contesting identities*. Routledge.

Butler, J. (1990). *Gender trouble: Feminism and the subversion of identity*. Routledge.

Çilingir, S. (2016). *Tahakküm ilişkisi barındıran ötekileştirme süreçleri*. Akademik Matbuat.

Daehnert, C. (1998). The false self as a means of disidentification. *Contemporary Psychoanalysis*, *34*(2), 251–271. DOI: 10.1080/00107530.1998.10746361

Eagly, A. H., Mladinic, A., & Otto, S. (1991). Cognitive organization of attitudes: Interpretive and predictive functions. *Journal of Personality and Social Psychology*, *60*(6), 813–825. DOI: 10.1037/0022-3514.60.6.813

Erikson, E. H. (1968). *Identity: Youth and crisis*. W. W. Norton & Company.

Eroğlu, M. (2020). Etnik kimlik, savaş ve göçün çocuklara etkisi. *Sağlık Bilimlerinde İleri Araştırmalar Dergisi*, *3*(2), 121–131. DOI: 10.26650/JARHS2020-650426

Giddens, A. (1991). *Modernity and self-identity: Self and society in the late modern age*. Polity Press.

Giritli İnceoğlu, Y. (2017). *Medya ve nefret söylemi*. Ayrıntı Yayınları.

Goffman, E. (1963). *Stigma: Notes on the management of spoiled identity*. Prentice-Hall.

Hall, S. (1996). Who needs identity? In Hall, S., & du Gay, P. (Eds.), *Questions of cultural identity* (pp. 1–17). SAGE Publications.

Hamilton, D. L., & Sherman, J. W. (1994). Stereotypes. In Wyer, R. S., & Srull, T. K. (Eds.), *Handbook of social cognition*. Lawrence Erlbaum.

Honneth, A. (1995). *The struggle for recognition*. Polity Press. DOI: 10.2307/jj.18253805.13

Ilgın, C., & Hacıhasanoğlu, I. (2010). *Göç sonrası aidiyetin sorgulanması süreci*. Mimarlık Dergisi.

Isin, E. F., & Nyers, P. (Eds.). (2024). *The Routledge International Handbook of Transnational Studies*. Routledge., DOI: 10.4324/9781003690801

Kirmayer, L. J., Narasiah, L., Munoz, M., Rashid, M., Ryder, A. G., Guzder, J., Hassan, G., Rousseau, C., & Pottie, K. (2011). Common mental health problems in immigrants and refugees: General approach in primary care. *Canadian Medical Association Journal, 183*(12), 959–967. DOI: 10.1503/cmaj.090292 PMID: 20603342

Lau, R. R. (1989). Individual and collective referents in political cognition. *Political Behavior, 11*(3), 239–257. DOI: 10.1007/BF00992305

Mansouri, F., Vergani, M., & Weng, E. (2024). Parallel lives or active citizens? Examining the interplay between multicultural service provision and civic engagement in Australia. *Journal of Sociology (Melbourne, Vic.), 60*(3), 419–439. DOI: 10.1177/14407833231219033

Mete, M. (2023). Sosyal kimlik teorisi ve göçmen kimliğinin ötekileştirilmesi süreci. [Akademik İncelemeler Dergisi]. *Journal of Academic Inquiries, 18*(2), 471–490. DOI: 10.17550/akademikincelemeler.1311029

Robertson, S. (2014). Zaman ve Geçici Göç: Avustralya'daki Geçici Lisansüstü İşçiler ve Çalışma Tatili Yapanlar Örneği. *Etnik ve Göç Çalışmaları Dergisi, 40*(12), 1915–1933. DOI: 10.1080/1369183X.2013.876896

Sayad, A. (1999). *Göçmenliğin çelişkileri*. Metis Yayınları.

Schnapper, D. (2005). *Sosyoloji düşüncesinin özünde öteki ile ilişki*. İstanbul Bilgi Üniversitesi Yayınları.

Şeker, B. D., & Sirkeci, İ. (Eds.). (2025). *Güncel çalışmalarla göç ve uyum*. Transnational Press London.

Tatar Canbay, H. (2012). Sürgünler mekânı dünya. *e-Journal of New World Sciences Academy, 8*(1), 72–81.

Uzun Aydın, D. (2024). Bruno Catalano'nun heykellerinde Gestalt'ın "tamamlama" ilkesinden ve gösterge biliminden yola çıkarak "göç" olgusuna ulaşmak. *Yedi: Sanat. Tasarım ve Kültür Dergisi*, (31), 223–232. DOI: 10.54637/yedisanat.1376840

Winnicott, D. W. (1960). Ego distortion in terms of true and false self. In *The maturational processes and the facilitating environment.* Hogarth Press.

Chapter 5
Psychological Adaptation and Migrant Well-Being From Trauma to Resilience

Handan Akkaş
http://orcid.org/0000-0002-2082-0685
Ankara Medipol University, Turkey

ABSTRACT

This chapter examines migrant well-being through a psychosocial-ecological framework that connects migration trajectories, trauma, structural conditions, and resilience. Drawing on interdisciplinary literature, it conceptualizes migration as a multi-phase process shaped by pre-migration conditions, migration journeys, and post-migration realities. The chapter analyzes how psychosocial adjustment is influenced by language, employment, social connections, identity negotiation, and acculturation processes, while highlighting the cumulative impact of trauma, loss, and ongoing stressors. Resilience is reconceptualized as a dynamic, context-dependent process supported by family, community, cultural resources, and institutional conditions. The chapter concludes by outlining implications for research, practice, and policy, arguing that migrant well-being depends on both individual agency and inclusive social environments that enable participation, dignity, and belonging

1. INTRODUCTION

Migration represents one of the most significant social processes in the contemporary world. Rather than constituting a singular event or experience, migration

DOI: 10.4018/979-8-3373-8500-6.ch005

encompasses a complex field of mobility determined by labor markets, family dynamics, educational systems, conflict, persecution, environmental insecurity, global inequalities, colonial legacies, and migration controls. Foundational migration scholarship has established that international migration cannot be explained by a single cause; instead, it emerges from the interplay of economic disparities, social networks, household strategies, political contexts, historical connections, and institutional frameworks (Castles, de Haas, & Miller, 2014; Massey et al., 1993). Recent migration reports indicate that international migrants constitute a substantial proportion of the global population, with rates of forced displacement reaching unprecedented levels due to war, persecution, widespread violence, and human rights violations (IOM, 2024; UNHCR, 2024). Nevertheless, quantitative data alone cannot capture the lived realities of migration. Beneath categories such as migrant, refugee, asylum seeker, internally displaced person, unauthorized immigrant, temporary worker, or international student are lives marked by departure, waiting, separation, aspiration, uncertainty, loss, adaptation, and the pursuit of dignity.

Therefore, it is clear that there is a deeply psychological element to migration. While migration can offer the possibility of safety, employment, education, reunification, self-determination, and upward mobility, it can also expose migrants to the risks of violence, hazardous travel, uncertain legal status, social marginalization, discrimination, downward social mobility, and disruption. Moving across borders also involves entering different social environments, labor markets, cultural contexts, institutions, and social categories (Portes & Rumbaut, 2001; Castles et al., 2014). Migrants might need to renegotiate their languages, employment opportunities, social statuses, religion, gender roles, parenthood, and connections both to their countries of origin and destination. Consequently, migrants' mental well-being cannot be thought of merely as an internal psychological state; instead, it should be considered a result of interactions between individuals and the environments in which they try to reconstruct their lives (Ryan, Dooley, & Benson, 2008; Kuo, 2014).

The psychological dimension of migration encompasses multiple components, including migration trajectories, exposure to trauma, post-migration challenges, cultural meaning-making, social relationships, legal status, and institutional environments. A psychosocial-ecological perspective on migrant well-being challenges two prevalent stereotypes: the portrayal of migrants solely as vulnerable individuals defined by victimization and hardship, and the depiction of migrants as agents who invariably overcome adversity through resilience and determination. The first stereotype is reductive, while the second overlooks the extent to which resilience is contingent upon legal status, housing, employment, education, family unity, language proficiency, social recognition, and protection from discrimination (Ager & Strang, 2008; Miller & Rasmussen, 2017; Ungar, 2011). Therefore, psychological adaptation should be understood not as a linear progression from trauma to healing, but as a highly uneven process shaped by opportunities for participation, belonging, and future hope.

Four major concepts structure the discussion of migration as a social-psychological phenomenon. Psychosocial adjustment refers to the process by which migrants navigate new social, cultural, legal, economic, and emotional contexts while maintaining connections to previous environments, relationships, identities, and obligations. Well-being is conceptualized as multidimensional, encompassing safety, dignity, agency, strong social bonds, inclusion, cultural continuity, economic stability, and future prospects. Trauma is defined as lived experience, not solely as a clinical diagnosis, and includes violence, loss, dislocation, and disruptions to family, identity, social status, and future opportunities. Resilience is understood as a dynamic process in which migrants mobilize personal, familial, cultural, spiritual, communal, and institutional resources to withstand adversity and rebuild their lives (Berry, 1997; Ward, 2001; Steel et al., 2009; Masten, 2001; Lindert et al., 2023).

A solid theoretical base is necessary to understand this topic's complexity. Migration studies offer a framework for mobility, integration, transnationalism, and belonging. Psychology provides theories on coping, acculturation, adaptation, identity, distress, and resilience. Sociology and anthropology shed light on social networks, inequalities, racism, kinship, cultural suffering, and institutional exclusion. Public health and policy analysis reveal how services, legal systems, housing, education, welfare, and labor laws shape daily routines. An interdisciplinary approach is vital because migrant well-being arises from biography, social relations, culture, and institutional power (Portes & Rumbaut, 2001; Ager & Strang, 2008; Castles et al., 2014).

This chapter begins by examining migration as a multi-phase experience and subsequently addresses psychosocial adjustment, trauma, institutional barriers, resilience, support systems, positive adaptation, and practical recommendations for research, practice, and policy. The central argument is that migrants should not be viewed solely as vulnerable individuals, but also as agents whose capacity to reconstruct their lives is shaped by the circumstances they encounter.

2. MIGRATION AND PSYCHOSOCIAL ADJUSTMENT

Migration involves more than movement between territories. It reshapes everyday life, including social roles, legal status, cultural orientation, language, work, family relationships, and expectations for the future. These movements are not driven solely by individual choice, but by broader forces such as economic inequality, household strategies, social networks, political conditions, and state policies (Massey et al., 1993; Castles, de Haas, & Miller, 2014). These dynamics continue after arrival, as migrants enter labor markets, institutions, and social environments that structure possibilities for participation and belonging (Portes & Rumbaut, 2001; Penninx & Garcés-Mascareñas, 2016).

Psychosocial adjustment refers to the process through which migrants navigate these demands while sustaining identity, relationships, and cultural continuity. It includes practical engagement with institutions and less visible processes such as managing separation, renegotiating identity, and developing a sense of belonging (Ryan, Dooley, & Benson, 2008; Kuo, 2014). Adjustment is therefore relational: it depends on the interaction between migrants' resources and the conditions of reception.

2.1 Migration as a Multi-Phase Experience

Pre-Migration Conditions: Conflict, Economic Hardship, and Instability

Migration begins before departure, shaped by conditions in the origin country like economic insecurity, conflict, and family expectations. Theories show decisions are influenced by systemic inequality, labor demand, household strategies, and international relations (Massey et al., 1993; Castles et al., 2014). Even voluntary migration is often constrained by limited choices and access to safety and work.

Refugees and asylum seekers face war, persecution, detention, torture, forced recruitment, sexual violence, and threats, which have lasting psychological impacts. Their well-being also depends on post-migration factors like legal security, family reunification, social support, housing, and employment (Porter & Haslam, 2005; Li, Liddell, & Nickerson, 2016).

Labor migrants experience pre-migration pressures such as poverty, debt, unemployment, and family support responsibilities, which can cause stress if underemployed or exploited in the destination country (Kuo, 2014; Liem et al., 2021). Resources like education, health, savings, and social networks influence adjustment but depend on the context. Unrecognized qualifications, lack of documentation, or disrupted schooling increase vulnerability where support systems are weak (Ager & Strang, 2008; Ryan et al., 2008).

Migration Journey: Uncertainty, Risk, and Disruption

The journey itself may become a major phase of psychosocial disruption. Some migrants travel through regular channels with documents, employment contracts, family sponsorship, or student visas. Others move through dangerous and uncertain routes shaped by restrictive border regimes, smuggling networks, detention, exploitation, hunger, violence, or prolonged waiting in transit countries (Zetter, 2007; Gleeson et al., 2020). These experiences matter because they may disrupt trust, safety, predictability, and social continuity before settlement begins.

Uncertainty is especially significant during the journey. Migrants may not know whether they will reach safety, whether relatives are alive, whether documents will be accepted, whether they will be detained, or whether they will be permitted to remain. Such uncertainty can affect sleep, concentration, emotional regulation, and planning (Li et al., 2016; Miller & Rasmussen, 2017). For children and young people, migration journeys may interrupt schooling, friendships, language development, and everyday routines, all of which are important for developmental stability and later adaptation (Fazel, Reed, & Stein, 2015; Wong & Schweitzer, 2017).

The journey may also transform social identity. A person previously recognized as a parent, teacher, farmer, student, activist, professional, neighbor, or community member may become defined by migration categories such as refugee, asylum seeker, irregular migrant, foreign worker, or displaced person. These categories are not neutral labels. They shape rights, movement, institutional treatment, and public recognition (Zetter, 2007; Ager & Strang, 2008).

At the same time, migrants often show agency during the journey. They share information, support one another, organize safety, and form temporary communities. These actions highlight that migrants are not passive, even in highly constrained circumstances (Kuo, 2014; Lindert et al., 2023).

Post-Migration Realities: Settlement, Integration, and Identity Shifts

Arrival does not mark the end of migration. Instead, it introduces new challenges, such as finding housing, securing income, accessing healthcare, entering education, and understanding legal systems. Integration is typically understood as a multidimensional process involving employment, housing, education, health, social connections, rights, language, and safety (Ager & Strang, 2008).

Post-migration conditions can either support or undermine well-being. Access to work, education, legal security, and social recognition can facilitate adjustment. In contrast, unemployment, poor housing, discrimination, family separation, and ongoing uncertainty can create significant stress (Ryan et al., 2008; Gleeson et al., 2020). These conditions should not be seen as secondary to past trauma—they are part of the environment in which migrants attempt to rebuild their lives (Miller & Rasmussen, 2017; Li et al., 2016).

Settlement also involves changes in identity and social position. Skilled migrants may experience downward mobility if their qualifications are not recognized. Parents may become dependent on children for language support, altering family dynamics.

Young people may adapt quickly to new environments while balancing expectations from both family and society (Portes & Rumbaut, 2001; Wong & Schweitzer, 2017).

2.2 Everyday Experiences of Adjustment

Language Acquisition and Communication Barriers

Language learning plays a central role in psychosocial adjustment because it shapes access to employment, education, healthcare, legal systems, public services, and everyday social interaction. Proficiency in the dominant language can increase independence, reduce reliance on others, support access to jobs, and enable fuller participation in public life (Ager & Strang, 2008; Kuo, 2014). It also contributes to a sense of belonging, as communication is one of the primary ways migrants become visible and recognized as members of society—whether as neighbors, parents, workers, students, or citizens (Amit & Bar-Lev, 2015; Strang & Quinn, 2021).

At the same time, language barriers can create exclusion even when services are technically available. Migrants may struggle to understand medical instructions, school communications, legal documents, workplace expectations, or welfare systems. In healthcare and legal contexts, inadequate interpretation can lead to misunderstandings and reduced trust. In employment, migrants may remain in low-paid or low-skilled jobs despite having prior qualifications and experience (Kirmayer et al., 2011; Riza et al., 2020). Language difficulties can also affect self-perception, particularly when individuals who were confident and articulate in their first language feel unable to express themselves fully in a new one (Ryan et al., 2008; Kuo, 2014).

Importantly, language adaptation should not be seen as replacing one language with another. Maintaining a heritage language can support family relationships, cultural continuity, and connections across generations and borders. At the same time, learning the dominant language supports participation in institutions and broader society. The key issue is not choosing one over the other, but whether institutions recognize multilingualism as a strength rather than a limitation (Berry, 1997; Ward, 2001).

Employment, Education, and Economic Participation

Employment and education are central domains of adjustment because they provide income, structure, social contact, status, competence, and future orientation. For many migrants, work is tied to household survival, remittances, debt repayment, and aspirations for children's futures (Levitt & Glick Schiller, 2004; Liem et al., 2021). Integration frameworks identify employment as a key domain of participation, but labor-market entry alone does not guarantee inclusion if migrants are concentrated in precarious, low-paid, unsafe, or exploitative work (Ager & Strang, 2008; Castles et al., 2014).

Economic participation is shaped by structural barriers. Migrants may face non-recognition of qualifications, lack of local experience, employer discrimination, legal restrictions on work, language demands, limited childcare, or dependence on informal labor markets. Skilled migrants may experience occupational downgrading when credentials are not recognized, while asylum seekers may be prevented from working during long legal procedures (Ryan et al., 2008; Li et al., 2016). These barriers affect well-being because work is connected not only to income but also to dignity, identity, routine, competence, and social recognition (Kuo, 2014; Hajro, Stahl, Clegg, & Lazarova, 2019).

Education is equally important, particularly for children and young people. Schools can provide stability, language development, peer relationships, and pathways for future opportunities. However, migrant and refugee students may face disrupted education, unfamiliar systems, language barriers, bullying, discrimination, and limited recognition of prior learning (Fazel et al., 2015; Wong & Schweitzer, 2017). School adjustment, therefore, goes beyond academic performance—it also involves belonging, safety, identity, and relationships between families and educational institutions (Sheikh & Anderson, 2018; Keles et al., 2024).

Social Isolation Versus Inclusion

Social connection is one of the most important supports for adjustment. Migrants may rely on family, friends, co-ethnic communities, religious groups, neighbors, workplaces, schools, diaspora organizations, and digital transnational networks for practical help, emotional support, information, childcare, translation, and identity affirmation (Ryan et al., 2008; Strang & Quinn, 2021). Ager and Strang's integration framework distinguishes among social bonds within communities, social bridges across groups, and social links with institutions, showing that integration depends on multiple forms of connection rather than a single narrow measure of participation (Ager & Strang, 2008).

Social isolation may emerge from family separation, language barriers, unemployment, temporary housing, racism, gendered restrictions, long working hours, insecure legal status, or fear of authorities. Isolation matters because it can reduce access to information, weaken emotional support, and intensify feelings of invisibility or exclusion (Li et al., 2016; Gleeson et al., 2020). For asylum seekers and undocumented migrants, isolation may be intensified by dispersal policies, detention, poverty, or fear that contact with institutions could create immigration risks (Menjívar, 2006; De Genova, 2002).

Inclusion is more than just the absence of separation. A migrant might live in a diverse neighborhood and still feel left out, or have legal residence but lack real social connections. Inclusion involves recognition, participation, rights, mutual relationships, and access to institutions without humiliation (Ager & Strang, 2008; Penninx & Garcés-Mascareñas, 2016). Adjustment is therefore relational: migrants work to engage, but receiving societies must also create fair opportunities for participation.

Negotiating Identity and Belonging

Migration often requires people to renegotiate who they are in relation to place, culture, language, family, religion, race, class, gender, and citizenship. Belonging depends on both internal attachment and external recognition. A migrant may feel attached to a destination society while still being treated as foreign because of accent, name, religion, legal status, race, or cultural practice. Conversely, legal residence does not automatically produce emotional attachment or social acceptance (Amit & Bar-Lev, 2015; Strang & Quinn, 2021).

Belonging is also shaped by transnational ties. Many migrants remain connected to origin societies through remittances, digital communication, religious networks, political engagement, family obligations, and imagined or actual return. The transnational migration literature challenges the assumption that integration requires weakening ties to the origin country (Levitt & Glick Schiller, 2004; Vertovec, 2009). For many migrants, belonging is not simply here or there. It is distributed across multiple places, relationships, and obligations.

For children and young people, identity negotiation can be particularly complex. They may adapt quickly to the new society while still navigating expectations from family and heritage communities. This can create tension, but it can also lead to the development of bicultural skills, multilingualism, and flexible identities—especially when their backgrounds are recognized and valued rather than stigmatized (Portes & Rumbaut, 2001; Lee, 2020; Berry, 1997; Ward, 2001).

2.3 Acculturation and Adaptation

Acculturation Strategies: Integration, Assimilation, Separation, and Marginalization

Acculturation refers to the changes that occur when people from different cultural backgrounds come into sustained contact. In migration contexts, this can involve shifts in language, values, family life, food, religion, gender roles, social relationships, institutional participation, and identity (Berry, 1997; Ward, 2001). It is not a simple shift from one culture to another. Instead, it is a dynamic and multidimensional process shaped by broader conditions such as discrimination, policies, legal status, and expectations in the receiving society (Kuo, 2014; Kreienkamp & Bringmann, 2024).

Berry's model remains widely used because it identifies four main strategies: integration, assimilation, separation, and marginalization. Integration involves maintaining heritage culture while participating in wider society. Assimilation prioritizes dominant cultural norms over heritage culture. Separation emphasizes maintaining heritage culture while limiting wider engagement. Marginalization reflects a weak connection to both (Berry, 1997). This framework is useful because it links cultural orientation to both psychological and social adaptation, while also recognizing the role of the receiving context (Ward, 2001; Choy et al., 2021).

Although integration is often associated with better outcomes, it cannot be achieved solely by migrants. It depends on whether receiving societies allow cultural diversity, provide rights, reduce discrimination, and create real opportunities for participation. Even when migrants aim to integrate, they may face pressure to assimilate or barriers such as racism, insecure legal status, or exclusion from the labor market (Penninx & Garcés-Mascareñas, 2016; Sakamoto, 2007).

Tensions Between Cultural Continuity and Change

Migration often creates tension between preserving the past and adapting to new conditions. Cultural continuity—through language, religion, family practices, and shared memory—can support identity and well-being, especially after experiences of loss or displacement (Kuo, 2014; Silove & Klein, 2021). At the same time, adaptation requires change, including learning new systems, norms, and communication practices (Ward, 2001; Kreienkamp & Bringmann, 2024).

These tensions are often most visible within families. Parents may try to preserve cultural traditions, while children adapt more quickly through school and peer interactions. Children may also act as interpreters or cultural mediators, which can build skills but also shift family dynamics and responsibilities (Portes & Rumbaut, 2001; Wong & Schweitzer, 2017). These intergenerational tensions are not signs of failure but a common part of migration, especially when family members adapt at different speeds (Kuo, 2014; Albertini et al., 2019).

The idea of hybridity helps move beyond this tension. Rather than choosing between cultures, many migrants combine elements of both, creating flexible and layered identities. Transnational perspectives reinforce this by showing that migrants often remain connected to multiple social worlds at once (Levitt & Glick Schiller, 2004; Vertovec, 2009). Such forms of belonging can support adaptation when they are accepted rather than questioned

The Role of Host Societies in Shaping Adaptation Outcomes

Receiving societies play a major role in shaping how adaptation unfolds. Laws, institutions, labor markets, schools, housing, welfare systems, and public narratives all influence whether migrants can participate fully or remain excluded (Ager & Strang, 2008; Penninx & Garcés-Mascareñas, 2016). Adaptation is therefore not only cultural—it is also shaped by political and institutional conditions.

Even when migrants learn the language and seek work, their outcomes depend on whether their qualifications are recognized, whether discrimination occurs, whether services are accessible, and whether legal status allows long-term planning (Ryan et al., 2008; Li et al., 2016).

Public attitudes are equally important. Racism, xenophobia, and anti-immigrant narratives can undermine safety and belonging, while inclusive policies and discourse can support participation and recognition (Strang & Quinn, 2021; Cabieses et al., 2024). For this reason, integration should be understood as a shared process, involving both migrants and receiving societies.

Viewing adjustment as ongoing, relational, and shaped by social conditions helps lay the groundwork for exploring trauma and distress. Migration involves not just past experiences but also ongoing challenges related to uncertainty, loss, and unequal reception conditions.

3. TRAUMA AND PSYCHOLOGICAL DISTRESS IN MIGRATION CONTEXTS

The previous section showed that migration unfolds across multiple stages—departure, journey, arrival, settlement, and identity change. This perspective is essential for understanding trauma, because distress in migration is rarely the result of a single event. Instead, it often unfolds across phases: from violence before departure to danger during transit to uncertainty after arrival.

Research on refugees and displaced populations confirms that exposure to war, persecution, and torture is strongly linked to psychological distress. At the same time, post-migration conditions—such as legal uncertainty, poverty, social isolation, and discrimination—play a major role in shaping outcomes (Porter & Haslam, 2005; Steel et al., 2009; Li et al., 2016). Trauma should therefore be understood not only as a clinical diagnosis, but as a lived disruption of relationships, roles, and future possibilities.

3.1 Understanding Trauma as Lived Experience

Exposure to Violence, Loss, and Displacement

For many forced migrants, trauma begins in contexts of war, persecution, detention, torture, forced recruitment, or threats to loved ones. Studies show that such experiences are strongly associated with psychological distress, although outcomes vary depending on context and support systems (Steel et al., 2009; Fazel et al., 2005). These experiences are not isolated—they are shaped by broader political and historical conditions, including conflict, state violence, and unequal systems of protection (Castles et al., 2014; Zetter, 2007).

Loss is a central part of migration-related trauma. Migrants may lose family members, homes, livelihoods, social status, language environments, and familiar places. These losses can be especially difficult when they remain unresolved—for example, when relatives are missing, or mourning rituals are disrupted (Killikelly et al., 2018; Silove & Klein, 2021). In this sense, displacement is not just physical relocation, but a deeper rupture between people, places, and identities (Miller & Rasmussen, 2017).

Disruption of Social Networks and Life Trajectories

Migration often breaks the social networks that once provided stability and meaning. Family, community, work, and religious institutions offer emotional support, practical help, and a sense of belonging. When these connections are lost, migrants may lose not only relationships but also the structures that shaped everyday life (Ryan et al., 2008; Ager & Strang, 2008). Social isolation can increase distress, while strong social support is consistently linked to better outcomes (Schweitzer et al., 2006; Strang & Quinn, 2021).

Migration can also interrupt life paths. Children may lose access to education, adults may lose professional identity, and families may be separated for long periods. Since identity is built through roles—such as student, worker, or parent—these disruptions can lead to feelings of shame, helplessness, or a loss of purpose, alongside more familiar forms of distress, such as fear or sadness (Portes & Rumbaut, 2001; Wong & Schweitzer, 2017).

Cumulative and Ongoing Stressors

A psychosocial perspective highlights that trauma is often cumulative. Migrants may face hardship before, during, and after migration—ranging from violence and exploitation to poverty and legal insecurity. Research shows that post-migration stressors such as unemployment, poor housing, family separation, discrimination, and uncertain legal status are strongly linked to ongoing distress (Li et al., 2016; Gleeson et al., 2020).

Ongoing uncertainty is particularly significant. Asylum seekers may wait years for decisions, live with the threat of deportation, and remain separated from family members. These conditions can prevent recovery even after physical danger has passed. Legal status, therefore, should be seen not just as an administrative issue, but as a key factor shaping psychological well-being, affecting trust, stability, and the ability to plan for the future (Zetter, 2007; Miller & Rasmussen, 2017).

3.2 Expressions of Psychological Distress

Emotional and Behavioral Responses: Fear, Grief, Uncertainty, and Stress

Psychological distress among migrants may appear as fear, grief, sadness, anger, guilt, irritability, emotional numbness, hypervigilance, concentration difficulties, or persistent worry. These responses may be connected to traumatic exposure, but they may also be reasonable reactions to ongoing insecurity, family separation, discrimination, and loss of social position (Brunnet et al., 2020; Bryant et al., 2023). Studies of refugees resettled in high-income countries document elevated rates of post-traumatic stress, depression, and anxiety, but prevalence estimates vary because populations differ in exposure histories, legal positions, social support, host-country policies, and methods of assessment (Fazel et al., 2005; Henkelmann et al., 2020).

Fear may persist after arrival because migrants may remain concerned about relatives left behind, surveillance by political actors, asylum refusal, deportation, racism, or institutional encounters. Grief may also remain unresolved when migrants cannot return for funerals, locate missing relatives, or perform culturally meaningful mourning practices (Killikelly et al., 2018; Silove & Klein, 2021). In this sense, distress is not always a sign that the person has failed to adapt. It may be an understandable response to continuing uncertainty and to social conditions that prevent closure, safety, and recognition (Miller & Rasmussen, 2017; Gleeson et al., 2020).

Everyday Manifestations: Sleep Issues, Social Withdrawal, and Anxiety-Like Experiences

Distress is often visible in everyday life. Migrants may experience insomnia, nightmares, fatigue, appetite changes, headaches, stomach pain, concentration difficulties, avoidance, irritability, or withdrawal from social interaction. These manifestations may be associated with traumatic memories, but they may also be shaped by crowded housing, insecurity, poverty, unstable work, language barriers, or fear of authorities (Bustamante et al., 2018; Li et al., 2016). For families, distress may appear in parenting strain, intergenerational conflict, children's school difficulties, or reduced capacity to maintain routines under uncertain conditions (Hedstrom, Kovshoff, & Hadwin, 2021; Fazel, Reed, & Stein, 2015).

Social withdrawal should be interpreted carefully. It may reflect sadness, fear, mistrust, exhaustion, shame, language difficulty, experiences of racism, or lack of safe community spaces. If institutions interpret withdrawal only as personal pathology, they may overlook the exclusionary conditions that make participation difficult (Miller & Rasmussen, 2017; Strang & Quinn, 2021). A migrant who avoids services may not lack motivation; they may fear stigma, deportation, misinterpretation, or humiliation in systems that have not earned trust (WHO, 2023; Brunnet et al., 2020).

Cultural Variations in Expressing Distress

Distress is culturally mediated. Migrants may express suffering through emotional language, bodily symptoms, spiritual idioms, family concerns, moral injury, silence, or narratives of injustice. Cross-cultural work cautions against assuming that Western diagnostic categories fully capture migrants' experiences of suffering, even when those categories are useful for identifying clinical need (Kirmayer et al., 2011; Silove & Klein, 2021). Somatic expressions such as pain, fatigue, dizziness, gastrointestinal problems, and sleep disturbance may be culturally meaningful ways of communicating distress, especially where psychological labels are stigmatized or unfamiliar (Barbati et al., 2022; Brunnet et al., 2020).

Cultural meanings also shape help-seeking. Some migrants may seek support first from family, religious leaders, elders, traditional healers, peer networks, or community organizations rather than formal services. This should not be read simply as resistance to care. It may reflect culturally grounded understandings of suffering and healing, previous mistrust of state institutions, language barriers, or fear that disclosure may affect legal status or family reputation (Kirmayer et al., 2011; DeSa, Gebremeskel, Omonaiye, & Yaya, 2022). Culturally responsive support begins by asking how migrants name distress, what they believe has caused it, and what forms of care they consider legitimate (Silove & Klein, 2021; WHO, 2023).

3.3 Unequal Vulnerabilities

Refugees and Asylum Seekers

Refugees and asylum seekers often face heightened vulnerability because they are more likely to have experienced forced displacement, violence, loss, and family separation, and because their post-arrival lives may be shaped by asylum procedures, legal uncertainty, restricted work rights, and temporary accommodation (Fazel et al., 2005; Li et al., 2016). Porter and Haslam's meta-analysis showed that both pre-displacement and post-displacement conditions influence the well-being of refugees and internally displaced persons, reinforcing the argument that receiving contexts matter greatly (Porter & Haslam, 2005). Asylum seekers may be especially affected by waiting, dependency, and the threat of refusal, all of which can prolong distress after physical arrival (Gleeson et al., 2020; Zetter, 2007).

Women and Gendered Experiences of Migration

Gender shapes exposure to harm and access to protection. Women and girls may face conflict-related sexual violence, intimate partner violence, trafficking, reproductive health risks, caregiving burdens, and restricted access to work or services. At the same time, women often sustain families, transmit culture, manage care, organize community support, and navigate institutions under difficult conditions (Timshel, Montgomery, & Dalgaard, 2017; Crawford et al., 2023). Gender-diverse and LGBTQI+ migrants may face additional risks, including persecution in countries of origin, danger during transit, unsafe accommodation, discrimination in asylum systems, and exclusion from both host and co-ethnic communities (Yarwood et al., 2022; Hermaszewska et al., 2022). These patterns show that vulnerability is intersectional rather than evenly distributed across migrant populations.

Children, Youth, and Family Separation

Children and youth experience migration-related distress within developmental contexts. Violence, interrupted schooling, separation from caregivers, parental distress, poverty, and unstable housing can affect attachment, learning, emotional regulation, peer relationships, and identity formation (Fazel et al., 2015; Wong & Schweitzer, 2017). Family separation is particularly harmful because caregivers provide safety, continuity, and emotional regulation. A systematic review of children and adolescents undergoing forced separation during migration found associations with fear, sadness, insecurity, behavioral difficulties, and challenges in rebuilding trust after reunification (Oldroyd et al., 2022). For young people, belonging at school and recognition from peers and teachers can become central to recovery and adjustment (Sheikh & Anderson, 2018; Wong & Schweitzer, 2017).

The Role of Legal and Socioeconomic Precarity

Legal and socioeconomic precarity cuts across all these groups. Insecure status, poverty, unemployment, poor housing, restricted healthcare, and fear of deportation can intensify distress and reduce access to support (Li et al., 2016; Gleeson et al., 2020). Undocumented migrants may avoid healthcare, police, schools, or social services because institutions are perceived as risky or connected to enforcement (WHO, 2023). These conditions show why trauma and distress cannot be separated from the politics of reception. The next section, therefore, turns directly to the structural and social barriers that shape migrant well-being after arrival.

4. STRUCTURAL AND SOCIAL BARRIERS TO WELL-BEING

The preceding section emphasized that trauma and psychological distress in migration contexts cannot be understood only through past exposure to violence or loss. Distress is also shaped by the conditions migrants encounter after arrival. This section, therefore, turns from lived distress to the structural and social barriers that organize migrant well-being. Migration literature has repeatedly shown that incorporation into a receiving society is not simply a matter of individual motivation or cultural adaptation; it is shaped by legal status, labor-market access, housing, education, healthcare, public attitudes, discrimination, and institutional recognition (Ager & Strang, 2008; Penninx & Garcés-Mascareñas, 2016). These conditions influence whether migrants are able to participate in social life with dignity or remain suspended in uncertainty, exclusion, and dependency.

Structural barriers matter because they transform migration from a moment of movement into an ongoing condition of constraint. A migrant may have crossed a border physically but remain unable to plan a future because legal status is insecure, qualifications are not recognized, healthcare is inaccessible, or racism marks them as permanently foreign. Menjívar's concept of "liminal legality" is useful here because it shows how uncertain or temporary legal categories create lives characterized by partial inclusion, prolonged waiting, and restricted opportunity (Menjívar, 2006). Similarly, De Genova's work on migrant "illegality" and deportability demonstrates that legal precarity is not simply a neutral administrative fact; it produces vulnerability in everyday life by shaping labor, mobility, fear, and relations with institutions (De Genova, 2002).

Legal Status and Uncertainty

Legal status is one of the most consequential determinants of migrant well-being. It shapes access to employment, housing, education, healthcare, welfare support, family reunification, mobility, and long-term planning. Refugees with secure status may still face exclusion, but asylum seekers, undocumented migrants, and those with temporary or conditional status often live with heightened uncertainty (Li, Liddell, & Nickerson, 2016; Gleeson et al., 2020). Migration categories such as refugee, asylum seeker, irregular migrant, temporary worker, or undocumented person are therefore not merely descriptive labels. They structure rights, recognition, and vulnerability (Zetter, 2007).

Uncertainty has direct psychosocial consequences. Asylum seekers may wait months or years for decisions while being restricted from work, separated from family, housed in temporary accommodation, or threatened with removal. Such waiting can undermine sleep, concentration, trust, family routines, and the ability to imagine a future (Gleeson et al., 2020; Hedstrom, Kovshoff, & Hadwin, 2021). Undocumented migrants may avoid public institutions, healthcare services, police, or employers because contact with systems may be perceived as risky. In these circumstances, legal precarity becomes a social condition of fear and restricted agency, not simply a problem of documentation (De Genova, 2002; Castañeda et al., 2015).

Legal uncertainty also affects family life. Restrictions on family reunification, delays in asylum procedures, and fear of deportation may prolong separation and intensify distress for both adults and children (Oldroyd et al., 2022; Katsampa, 2024). For parents, insecure status can weaken the ability to provide stability, make educational decisions, access services, or protect children from poverty and exclusion. Legal status, therefore, operates as a structural determinant of psychosocial well-being because it shapes everyday possibilities for safety, care, and belonging (Menjívar, 2006; WHO, 2023).

Limited Access to Healthcare and Social Services

Access to healthcare and social services is another major barrier. Migrants may face restrictions due to legal eligibility requirements, lack of insurance, cost, unfamiliarity with systems, transportation difficulties, limited interpretation services, fear of authorities, and mistrust of institutions (Castañeda et al., 2015; WHO, 2023). These barriers are especially serious for refugees, asylum seekers, undocumented migrants, and those with chronic health needs, trauma histories, disabilities, pregnancy-related needs, or limited social support (Kirmayer et al., 2011; El Arab et al., 2023).

Formal entitlement does not always translate into practical access. Even where migrants are legally eligible for healthcare, they may struggle to identify services, complete forms, book appointments, explain symptoms, or understand referrals. Studies of asylum seekers and refugees show that service navigation is often shaped by "candidacy," meaning that people must learn how to present themselves as legitimate users of services within unfamiliar systems (Van der Boor & White, 2020). This process can be especially difficult when migrants do not trust providers, fear stigma, or have previous experiences of institutional violence or exclusion (Kirmayer et al., 2011; Pollard & Howard, 2021).

Social services are equally important because many sources of distress are linked to housing, income, education, childcare, legal advice, and employment support. Psychological support alone cannot resolve problems produced by destitution, unsafe accommodation, unemployment, or family separation (Miller & Rasmussen, 2017; WHO, 2023). For this reason, migrant well-being requires integrated systems in which healthcare, social care, housing, legal support, schools, and community organizations work together rather than treating distress as a separate individual problem (Riza et al., 2020; Robinson et al., 2025).

Language and Institutional Barriers

Language barriers shape nearly every domain of migrant adjustment. Limited proficiency in the dominant language can restrict access to healthcare, education, employment, housing, legal processes, welfare systems, and everyday social interaction (Ager & Strang, 2008; Kuo, 2014). In healthcare and legal contexts, inadequate interpretation can lead to miscommunication, misdiagnosis, poor treatment adherence, or inability to explain complex experiences of trauma, grief, and fear (Kirmayer et al., 2011; Brunnet et al., 2020). Language barriers may also increase dependence on children, relatives, or informal intermediaries, sometimes altering family roles and reducing privacy.

Institutional barriers go beyond language. Migrants may encounter complex bureaucracies, digital systems, eligibility rules, waiting lists, unfamiliar professional norms, and inconsistent information across agencies. These barriers can create confusion and humiliation, particularly for people who previously navigated institutions confidently in their countries of origin (Riza et al., 2020; WHO, 2023). Institutional systems often assume that users understand how to seek help, make appointments, provide documentation, and advocate for themselves. For newly arrived migrants, asylum seekers, or people with limited literacy, such assumptions can reproduce exclusion even when services are formally available (Van der Boor & White, 2020; Robinson et al., 2025).

Institutional accessibility, therefore, has psychosocial significance. Services that provide interpretation, cultural mediation, outreach, trauma-informed practice, clear information, and collaboration with trusted community organizations reduce uncertainty and support autonomy (Riza et al., 2020; Pollard & Howard, 2021). By contrast, institutions that are opaque, fragmented, or culturally unresponsive may intensify distress by making migrants feel incompetent, dependent, or unwelcome.

Discrimination, Racism, and Exclusion

Discrimination, racism, xenophobia, Islamophobia, and anti-immigrant hostility are central barriers to migrant well-being. They shape access to housing, employment, healthcare, education, policing, public space, and social recognition (Viruell-Fuentes, Miranda, & Abdulrahim, 2012; Cabieses et al., 2024). Racism is not limited to interpersonal prejudice. It also operates through institutional practices such as hiring discrimination, racial profiling, non-recognition of qualifications, exclusionary welfare policies, school segregation, and unequal treatment in healthcare (Viruell-Fuentes et al., 2012; Crawford et al., 2023).

Discrimination affects well-being both materially and symbolically. Materially, it restricts access to jobs, housing, services, and safety. Symbolically, it communicates that migrants do not fully belong, even when they have legal status or long-term residence (Ager & Strang, 2008; Strang & Quinn, 2021). Public narratives are important in this process. When migrants are represented as threats, burdens, criminals, or cultural outsiders, these narratives can legitimize exclusion and increase mistrust between migrant communities and institutions (Cabieses et al., 2024). Conversely, inclusive narratives and anti-discrimination protections can support recognition, dignity, and participation.

Exclusion is also intersectional. Migrant women may experience racism, gender discrimination, labor-market exclusion, and vulnerability to violence simultaneously. LGBTQI+ migrants may face exclusion within asylum systems, host societies, and co-ethnic communities. Disabled migrants may encounter both migration-related barriers and inaccessible services (Crawford et al., 2023; Yarwood et al., 2022; Ngondwe & Tefera, 2025). This means that structural barriers are not experienced uniformly. They are shaped by race, gender, class, religion, sexuality, disability, age, legal status, and family position.

Stigma Around Mental Health and Help-Seeking

Stigma surrounding psychological distress and help-seeking can further limit access to support. Some migrants may avoid formal services because of fear of being labeled weak, unstable, dangerous, or incapable of fulfilling family roles. Others may worry that disclosure could affect asylum claims, employment, parenting status, marriage prospects, or community reputation (Kirmayer et al., 2011; DeSa et al., 2022). Stigma may come from host societies, migrant communities, families, religious settings, or previous experiences with coercive state institutions.

Help-seeking is also shaped by cultural meanings of distress. Migrants may understand suffering through bodily symptoms, spiritual idioms, family conflict, social injustice, grief, or moral injury rather than through Western diagnostic language (Kirmayer et al., 2011; Silove & Klein, 2021). Some may seek support first from relatives, religious leaders, elders, traditional healers, or community organizations. These pathways should not be dismissed solely as barriers; they may also be culturally meaningful sources of care and trust (DeSa et al., 2022; WHO, 2023).

At the same time, stigma interacts with institutional barriers. A person who is uncertain about services, lacks interpretation, fears immigration consequences, and expects cultural misunderstanding is less likely to seek help early (Van der Boor & White, 2020; Pollard & Howard, 2021). Reducing stigma, therefore, requires more than awareness campaigns. It requires confidential, culturally responsive, linguistically accessible, community-connected services that address social conditions as well as individual distress (Riza et al., 2020; Robinson et al., 2025).

The structural barriers examined in this section demonstrate that migrant well-being cannot be explained solely by personal coping or cultural adaptation. Legal status, service access, institutional design, discrimination, and stigma shape the possibilities through which migrants recover, participate, and belong. This prepares the way for the next section's central move: resilience must be understood not as individual toughness, but as a dynamic process shaped by context, relationships, rights, and opportunities.

5. RETHINKING RESILIENCE IN MIGRATION

The structural barriers discussed in the previous section show why resilience needs to be understood differently in migration contexts. If legal status, housing, employment, healthcare, racism, language access, and social recognition all shape migrant well-being, then resilience cannot be treated as a purely individual psychological trait. Migration research shows that migrants often demonstrate strong agency, creativity, and endurance. At the same time, their opportunities for adaptation are unequally shaped by legal, economic, and social conditions (Ager & Strang, 2008; Penninx & Garcés-Mascareñas, 2016). For this reason, resilience must be understood within the wider social worlds that also shape vulnerability, including families, communities, diasporas, institutions, labor markets, welfare systems, and states (Ungar, 2011; Panter-Brick, 2014).

Resilience is useful because it moves beyond viewing migrants only as vulnerable or traumatized. However, it should not be reduced to "individual toughness," as this risks ignoring structural barriers and placing responsibility on migrants themselves. Instead, resilience is better understood as a dynamic process involving personal, social, cultural, and institutional resources that support rebuilding life under difficult conditions (Masten, 2001; Ungar, 2011). This framing supports the chapter's broader contribution to migration literature: migrant well-being is produced through the interaction of lived experience, social relationships, cultural meaning, and conditions of reception.

5.1 Resilience as a Dynamic Process

Moving Beyond "Individual Toughness"

Resilience is often used in public and policy discourse to describe people who overcome hardship through determination. While such language may appear positive, it can be misleading in migration contexts. Migrants may work, parent, study, learn languages, send remittances, support relatives, and participate in community life while simultaneously experiencing grief, exhaustion, fear, discrimination, or legal insecurity (Miller & Rasmussen, 2017; Li, Liddell, & Nickerson, 2016). Visible functioning should not be mistaken for the absence of distress. Nor should resilience be used to normalize the expectation that migrants must endure harmful conditions without adequate social protection (Panter-Brick, 2014; Theisen-Womersley, 2021).

Masten's influential concept of resilience as "ordinary magic" is useful because it shifts attention away from extraordinary heroism and toward everyday protective systems: caregiving, routines, schools, relationships, problem-solving, competence, and opportunities for participation (Masten, 2001). In migration contexts, these ordinary systems may be disrupted by displacement, family separation, legal uncertainty, or poverty. Resilience then depends not simply on the individual's inner strength, but on whether ordinary protective systems can be restored or rebuilt after movement (Fazel, Reed, & Stein, 2015; Marley & Mauki, 2019).

This approach also prevents resilience from becoming a moral demand. Migrants are often praised when they succeed despite hardship, but this praise may hide the fact that many hardships are politically produced and preventable. A person who navigates an asylum system for years, works in exploitative conditions, or raises children in insecure housing may indeed display resilience, but the deeper question is why such endurance is required in the first place (Panter-Brick, 2014; De Genova, 2002; Menjívar, 2006). Resilience should therefore be linked to justice, rights, and opportunity, not only to coping.

Ecological Perspectives: Individual–Family–Community–Society

Ecological approaches define resilience as a process distributed across multiple systems. Ungar argues that resilience depends on access to culturally meaningful resources and on the capacity of social environments to provide those resources in ways people can use (Ungar, 2011). This is especially relevant for migrants because the resources that support adaptation may include family solidarity, diaspora networks, religious communities, schools, employers, legal protections, social services, and anti-discrimination frameworks (Ager & Strang, 2008; Lindert et al., 2023).

At the individual level, resilience may involve hope, problem-solving, language learning, emotional regulation, humor, faith, persistence, and the capacity to imagine a future. At the family level, it may involve caregiving, intergenerational support, remittances, shared sacrifice, cultural transmission, and protection of children. At the community level, it may involve migrant associations, religious institutions, mutual aid, peer support, and diaspora connections. At the societal level, it depends on secure legal status, inclusive schools, fair employment, safe housing, accessible healthcare, and protection from discrimination (Ungar, 2011; Motti-Stefanidi & Masten, 2017; Lindert et al., 2023).

Migration literature on integration supports this ecological understanding. Ager and Strang's framework identifies employment, housing, education, health, social connections, rights, language, safety, and stability as interconnected domains of integration (Ager & Strang, 2008). These are also resilience-supporting conditions. Similarly, transnational migration literature shows that migrants draw on relationships and obligations across borders, not only resources in the destination society (Glick Schiller, 2004; Vertovec, 2009). Resilience may therefore be both local and transnational.

Resilience Shaped by Context and Opportunity

Resilience is shaped by opportunity. Migrants are better able to rebuild lives when they have access to legal security, language learning, education, employment, stable housing, healthcare, family reunification, and social recognition (WHO, 2023; Posselt et al., 2019). Conversely, prolonged asylum waiting, detention, deportability, poverty, racism, labor exploitation, and family separation can erode the resources through which resilience is sustained (Li et al., 2016; Gleeson et al., 2020). This means that resilience is not the opposite of vulnerability. The same person may be highly resourceful in one domain and deeply vulnerable in another.

Context also shapes what resilience looks like. In some settings, resilience may appear as educational success, employment, language acquisition, or civic participation. In others, it may appear as preserving faith, protecting children, maintaining dignity, sending remittances, sustaining cultural identity, or surviving without formal support (Kuo, 2014; Theisen-Womersley, 2021). A culturally sensitive approach, therefore, avoids imposing a single measure of successful adaptation. Instead, it asks what resources matter to migrants themselves and how receiving societies can support those resources without demanding assimilation or silence about suffering (Silove & Klein, 2021; Ungar, 2011).

5.2 Sources of Strength and Protection

Social Networks and family Ties

Social networks are among the most consistent sources of protection in migration contexts. Family members, friends, neighbors, co-ethnic communities, religious groups, schools, workplaces, and community organizations provide emotional support, practical assistance, information, translation, childcare, employment contacts, and identity affirmation (Ryan, Dooley, & Benson, 2008; Strang & Quinn, 2021). Social support has been associated with better adjustment among resettled refugees, while isolation and weak social ties are associated with poorer well-being (Schweitzer, Melville, Steel, & Lacherez, 2006; Song, Corcoran, & Zahnow, 2025).

Family ties are especially important because they provide continuity across disruption. Families may sustain migrants through shared narratives of sacrifice, obligations to children, religious commitments, remittance practices, and emotional connection across borders (Levitt & Glick Schiller, 2004; Ryan et al., 2008). Yet family can also be strained by separation, legal uncertainty, poverty, changed gender roles, parenting stress, and intergenerational language differences (Oldroyd et al., 2022; Hedstrom, Kovshoff, & Hadwin, 2021). Family support becomes most protective when social policy enables reunification, stable housing, education, work, and access to care (Miller & Rasmussen, 2017; WHO, 2023).

Community Solidarity and Diaspora Connections

Community solidarity transforms resilience from an individual process into a collective one. Migrant associations, cultural organizations, faith communities, women's groups, youth groups, advocacy networks, and informal mutual aid systems often provide support long before formal services become accessible (Villalonga-Olives et al., 2022; Posselt et al., 2019). These spaces can offer interpretation, advice, emotional support, cultural continuity, food assistance, childcare, and protection from isolation. They also allow migrants to be recognized not only as service users but as community members and contributors.

Diaspora connections further expand the geography of resilience. Transnational ties may allow migrants to maintain a sense of belonging, support relatives, participate in political or religious communities, and preserve language and memory across borders (Vertovec, 2009). Such connections can sustain hope and identity, but they may also create pressure when migrants are expected to send remittances, sponsor relatives, or demonstrate success abroad (Levitt & Glick Schiller, 2004; Liem et al., 2021). Diaspora resources are therefore ambivalent: they can protect well-being while also increasing responsibility and emotional strain.

Cultural, Spiritual, and Religious Resources

Cultural, spiritual, and religious resources are central to many migrants' resilience. Religious practice, prayer, ritual, scripture, music, food, storytelling, festivals, language, and collective memory can provide continuity, moral orientation, and meaning after disruption (Silove & Klein, 2021; Raghavan & Sandanapitchai, 2024). These resources are not only symbolic. Faith communities may also provide social networks, practical support, counseling, advocacy, and trusted spaces for help-seeking (DeSa et al., 2022; WHO, 2023).

Cultural identity can support adaptation when it is treated as a resource rather than an obstacle. Acculturation research suggests that integration—maintaining heritage culture while participating in the receiving society—can support well-being when host societies permit cultural diversity and reduce discrimination (Berry, 1997; Choy, Arunachalam, Taylor, & Lee, 2021). Cultural continuity does not mean resistance to change. Migrants may develop hybrid identities that combine heritage and destination-society practices, especially when multilingualism, religious diversity, and transnational belonging are socially recognized rather than stigmatized (Ward, 2001; Klingenberg, Luetz, & Crawford, 2021).

Education, Employment, and Stability

Education, employment, and stability are protective because they provide structure, purpose, recognition, income, social connection, and future orientation. For children and youth, schools can become sites of safety, belonging, language development, peer connection, and aspiration (Fazel et al., 2015; Wong & Schweitzer, 2017). For adults, work can restore dignity, support family obligations, reduce poverty, and create opportunities for social participation (Ager & Strang, 2008; Hajro, Stahl, Clegg, & Lazarova, 2019).

However, education and employment protect well-being only when migrants can access them under fair conditions. Non-recognition of qualifications, work restrictions, discrimination, language barriers, lack of childcare, and unstable housing can prevent migrants from using their capacities (Ryan et al., 2008; Li et al., 2016). Stability is therefore not a passive background condition; it is a foundation for adaptation. Secure status, predictable housing, family unity, school continuity, and access to healthcare reduce the chronic uncertainty that otherwise consumes emotional and practical energy (Gleeson et al., 2020; WHO, 2023).

This ecological understanding of resilience leads directly to the question of support. If resilience is sustained through relationships, culture, institutions, rights, and opportunities, then interventions cannot focus only on individual coping. The next section, therefore, examines how psychosocial well-being can be supported through everyday strategies, community-based systems, culturally responsive services, and inclusive policies.

6. SUPPORTING PSYCHOSOCIAL WELL-BEING AND RESILIENCE

The previous section argued that resilience in migration is not an individual possession but a process shaped by relationships, institutions, cultural resources, rights, and opportunities. This section extends that argument by examining how psychosocial well-being can be supported in practice. If migrant distress is produced through the interaction of pre-migration adversity, migration journeys, post-migration stressors, and unequal conditions of reception, then support cannot be limited to individual treatment or short-term crisis response (Miller & Rasmussen, 2017; Li, Liddell, & Nickerson, 2016). Support must operate across everyday life, community networks, service systems, and policy environments (IASC, 2007; WHO, 2023).

A layered approach is useful because migrants' needs differ according to legal status, migration history, age, gender, family situation, language, disability, social networks, and exposure to harm. Humanitarian and resettlement frameworks often distinguish between broad social supports for all, targeted psychosocial supports for those facing additional difficulties, and specialized care for people experiencing severe or persistent distress (IASC, 2007; Tol et al., 2011). Such an approach prevents two errors: treating all migrant suffering as a clinical disorder, and overlooking serious distress among those who require specialist support (Tribe, Sendt, & Tracy, 2019; Im, Rodriguez, & Grumbine, 2021).

6.1 Individual and Everyday Coping Strategies

Meaning-Making and Personal Narratives

Meaning-making is central to psychosocial adaptation because migration often disrupts the continuity of life stories. Migrants may need to make sense of why they left, what was lost, what remains unresolved, and how their lives can continue in a new setting. Narrative approaches to trauma and displacement suggest that recovery is not only about reducing symptoms but also about integrating painful experiences into a coherent account of self, family, history, and future (Neuner et al., 2004; Wright, Reisig, & Cullen, 2020). In migration contexts, such narratives may involve sacrifice for children, obligations to family, religious faith, political struggle, survival, return, settlement, or the search for dignity (Ryan, Dooley, & Benson, 2008; Kuo, 2014).

Meaning-making should not be treated as a purely private psychological activity. Migrants' ability to narrate themselves as agents rather than burdens is shaped by public recognition, legal status, labor-market access, family reunification, and social inclusion (Ager & Strang, 2008; Penninx & Garcés-Mascareñas, 2016). Practitioners can support meaning-making by inviting life stories beyond trauma exposure. Trauma-informed work should not pressure migrants to disclose painful memories before safety, trust, and consent are established (Im et al., 2021; Brunnet et al., 2020).

Maintaining Cultural Identity

Maintaining cultural identity can support well-being by preserving language, kinship, food, music, religious practice, rituals, moral frameworks, humor, and collective memory. Acculturation research suggests that integration—maintaining heritage-cultural ties while also participating in the receiving society—is often associated with more positive adaptation than marginalization, although outcomes depend strongly on social reception and institutional opportunity (Berry, 1997; Choy, Arunachalam, Taylor, & Lee, 2021). Cultural continuity is especially important for migrants who have experienced displacement because it can reduce the sense that migration has severed identity from place, memory, and community (Kuo, 2014; Silove & Klein, 2021).

Cultural maintenance should not be confused with resistance to adaptation. Migrants often develop hybrid or bicultural identities that combine heritage practices with new forms of participation in the destination society (Ward, 2001; Kreienkamp & Bringmann, 2024). Maintaining a heritage language can support intergenerational connection and transnational belonging, while learning the dominant language can expand access to education, work, services, and civic life (Levitt & Glick Schiller, 2004; Kuo, 2014). Supportive institutions, therefore, do not ask migrants to choose between continuity and change; they make it possible to belong without cultural erasure.

Adaptive Coping in Daily Life

Everyday coping strategies are often practical, relational, and culturally shaped. Migrants cope by learning transport systems, attending language classes, seeking work, helping children with school, cooking familiar foods, praying, exercising, contacting relatives abroad, joining community groups, or finding trusted people who can explain institutions. Research on acculturation and coping shows that migrant coping is frequently embedded in family, culture, religion, and community rather than being only an individual act of emotional regulation (Kuo, 2014; Liem et al., 2021).

However, coping should not be romanticized. Migrants may continue working, parenting, studying, translating, and supporting relatives while carrying grief, exhaustion, fear, and uncertainty (Miller & Rasmussen, 2017; Bryant et al., 2023). Visible functioning does not mean that support is unnecessary. Practical assistance with legal information, service navigation, housing, language learning, childcare, transport, and employment can reduce avoidable stress and strengthen migrants' sense of control (Riza et al., 2020; WHO, 2023).

6.2 Community-Based Support Systems

Role of Community Organizations and NGOs

Community organizations, migrant-led associations, NGOs, faith groups, and voluntary networks often provide the first accessible layer of support. They may offer interpretation, legal referrals, food assistance, housing advice, employment guidance, language classes, women's groups, youth activities, health navigation, cultural events, and advocacy (Riza et al., 2020; Shaw & Funk, 2019). These organizations are especially important for migrants who mistrust state institutions, have insecure legal status, face language barriers, or do not know how to access formal services (DeSa, Gebremeskel, Omonaiye, & Yaya, 2022; WHO, 2023).

Community-based support is effective partly because it is close to everyday life. Rather than requiring migrants to enter unfamiliar clinical or bureaucratic spaces, support may be offered in community centers, schools, places of worship, settlement agencies, neighborhood organizations, or online diaspora spaces. Reviews of community-based healthcare for migrants and refugees identify outreach, interpretation, culturally sensitive training, collaboration with community actors, and integration of health and social support as promising practices (Riza et al., 2020). Asset-based approaches are also valuable because they begin with the capacities, associations, leadership, and cultural resources already present in migrant communities rather than focusing only on deficits (Lester & Ryakhovskaya, 2023).

Peer Support and Mutual Aid

Peer support is a major source of psychosocial protection because it is grounded in shared experience and practical knowledge. Migrants frequently seek advice from others who have navigated similar asylum systems, labor markets, schools, housing systems, or language barriers. Peer support may include informal translation, childcare exchange, emotional listening, job referrals, community kitchens, women's circles, youth groups, faith-based support, or structured peer mentoring (Mahon, 2022; Gower et al., 2022). Such support can reduce isolation and increase trust because it is offered by people who understand the lived realities of migration.

Social-capital approaches show why peer support matters. Social relationships provide access to information, emotional security, practical assistance, and a sense of belonging (Villalonga-Olives et al., 2022; Song, Corcoran, & Zahnow, 2025). Peer mentoring programs for migrant and refugee women, for example, have been found to support social connection, confidence, service navigation, and settlement participation (Gower et al., 2022). Peer support should nevertheless be ethically organized. Peer workers require training, supervision, role clarity, referral pathways, and recognition of their labor, especially when they are themselves navigating trauma, legal insecurity, or precarious employment (Im et al., 2021; Mahon, 2022).

Importance of Culturally Responsive Services

Culturally responsive services recognize that distress, healing, family, spirituality, gender, authority, and help-seeking are culturally and socially mediated. Such services do not simply translate dominant models into another language. They adapt communication, assessment, intervention goals, service relationships, and referral pathways to migrants' lived realities (Kirmayer et al., 2011; Silove & Klein, 2021). Reviews of psychosocial interventions for refugees and asylum seekers emphasize that services are more likely to be acceptable when they are culturally sensitive, trauma-informed, linguistically accessible, and connected to practical settlement needs (Tribe et al., 2019; Apers et al., 2023).

Cultural responsiveness also requires attention to power. Providers should avoid treating culture as a fixed set of traits. Instead, they should ask migrants how they understand distress, whom they trust, what support they consider legitimate, and what outcomes matter to them (Kirmayer et al., 2011; WHO, 2023). This approach is particularly important for women, LGBTQI+ migrants, older adults, disabled migrants, and young people whose needs may be hidden by broad categories such as "migrant" or "refugee" (Crawford et al., 2023; Yarwood et al., 2022).

6.3 Institutional and Policy Approaches

Inclusive Integration Policies

Inclusive integration policies are psychosocial interventions because they shape the conditions through which migrants rebuild their lives. Integration should be understood as a two-way process involving both migrants and receiving societies, rather than as a unilateral demand that migrants adapt while institutions remain unchanged (Ager & Strang, 2008; Penninx & Garcés-Mascareñas, 2016). Policies that provide secure legal status, fair asylum procedures, family reunification, language education, recognition of qualifications, access to healthcare, and protection from destitution reduce chronic stress and support participation (Li et al., 2016; WHO, 2023).

When policy produces prolonged waiting, work restrictions, temporary status, detention, or family separation, it undermines adaptation even when individual support services are available (Gleeson et al., 2020; Miller & Rasmussen, 2017). Migration policy should therefore be read as part of the psychosocial environment. Legal security, rights, and recognition are not separate from well-being; they are conditions that enable recovery and participation.

Access to Education, Housing, and Employment

Education, housing, and employment provide the material foundation for psychosocial well-being. Schools can offer migrant children routine, language development, peer relationships, adult support, and future orientation when they are inclusive and responsive to migration histories (Fazel & Betancourt, 2018; Wong & Schweitzer, 2017). Housing stability allows families to establish routines, sleep safely, access local services, and build neighbourhood ties, while housing insecurity can intensify stress and social isolation (Crawford et al., 2022; WHO, 2023). Employment provides income, dignity, structure, social recognition, and opportunities for contribution, but only when migrants are protected from exploitation and when qualifications, language needs, and childcare responsibilities are addressed (Ager & Strang, 2008; Hajro, Stahl, Clegg, & Lazarova, 2019).

Anti-Discrimination Frameworks and Equitable Access to Services

Anti-discrimination frameworks are necessary because racism, xenophobia, Islamophobia, gender discrimination, and anti-LGBTQI+ exclusion damage both material opportunity and social belonging (Viruell-Fuentes, Miranda, & Abdulrahim, 2012; Cabieses et al., 2024). Effective frameworks require enforceable protections in housing, work, education, healthcare, and public services, as well as accessible reporting systems and anti-racist institutional practice (Crawford et al., 2023; WHO, 2023). Equitable access to psychosocial and social support also requires interpretation, confidentiality, affordability, community outreach, trauma-informed care, and collaboration with trusted migrant-led organizations (Riza et al., 2020; Im et al., 2021).

The logic of this section is that support must match the ecological nature of migrant resilience. Individual coping matters, but it is strengthened or weakened by community support, culturally responsive services, legal status, housing, education, employment, and protection from discrimination.

7. FROM ADVERSITY TO STRENGTH: POSITIVE ADAPTATION AND GROWTH

The shift from adversity to strength is a crucial part of the migrant journey, but it requires thoughtful reflection. Migration can involve violence, loss, separation, exclusion, and uncertainty; however, many migrants also rebuild their lives, develop new skills, support families, build communities, and engage in social, economic, cultural, and political activities. Migration literature shows that migrants are not just displaced individuals moving between countries; they are social actors who maintain transnational connections, organize resources, support households, and reshape both their home and host societies (Levitt & Glick Schiller, 2004; Castles, de Haas, & Miller, 2014). Positive adaptation, therefore, does not mean the end of suffering, but rather how migrants create continuity, agency, and opportunity under changing circumstances.

Rebuilding identity is a key part of this process. Initially, institutions may categorize migrants narrowly, using labels like refugee, asylum seeker, undocumented person, temporary worker, or newcomer. However, over time, individuals can reshape their identities as students, parents, workers, entrepreneurs, neighbors, community leaders, activists, citizens, or members of transnational families (Portes & Rumbaut, 2001; Ager & Strang, 2008). This redefinition is not only an internal process. It also relies on whether receiving societies acknowledge migrants as legitimate participants in public life. A sense of belonging grows stronger when migrants can access schools, workplaces, neighborhoods, religious communities, and civic spaces without having to abandon their heritage identities or face discrimination (Strang & Quinn, 2021; Penninx & Garcés-Mascareñas, 2016).

A sense of belonging can also be considered plural rather than singular. Transnational perspectives challenge the idea that migrants must choose between origin and destination societies. Many migrants maintain attachments across borders through remittances, digital communication, religious networks, political involvement, family obligations, and imagined or actual return (Levitt & Glick Schiller, 2004; Vertovec, 2009). These cross-border connections may help preserve identity and emotional significance, especially when migrants face marginalization in the receiving society. Simultaneously, transnational obligations can create pressure, particularly when migrants are expected to financially support relatives or to represent success abroad (Kuo, 2014; Liem et al., 2021).

Migration can also foster skills, knowledge, and agency. Migrants often develop multilingualism, intercultural competence, bureaucratic navigation skills, economic adaptability, and broader social networks. Young migrants may act as cultural brokers between family and institutions, while adults might take on new occupational, educational, or civic roles (Portes & Rumbaut, 2001; Wong & Schweitzer, 2017). These abilities should not be seen simply as coping mechanisms. They represent forms of social knowledge gained through migration, often under challenging conditions. When schools, employers, and public agencies recognize these skills, migrants' experiences can serve as assets rather than signs of deficiency (Ager & Strang, 2008; Hajro, Stahl, Clegg, & Lazarova, 2019).

Community agency is equally important. Migrants often form mutual aid networks, diaspora associations, cultural groups, women's organizations, youth groups, religious initiatives, and advocacy movements. These collective efforts offer support, maintain identity, challenge exclusion, and create new forms of belonging (Lester & Ryakhovskaya, 2023; Villalonga-Olives et al., 2022). Refugee- and migrant-led initiatives are especially vital because they challenge the notion that expertise resides only in formal institutions. They demonstrate that lived experience can generate practical knowledge about settlement, safety, care, and participation (Wood & Kallestrup, 2021; Im et al., 2023).

Positive adaptation is best seen as a relational achievement. It occurs when migrants' skills, hopes, relationships, and cultural assets meet enabling factors such as legal security, social recognition, education, employment, healthcare, stable housing, and freedom from discrimination (Ager & Strang, 2008; WHO, 2023). This perspective supports the chapter's main argument: migrant well-being is neither simply the result of personal strength nor automatically achieved by arriving in a safer place. Instead, it is created through the interaction of migrant agency with social environments that either support or restrict it.

8. RESEARCH, PRACTICE, AND POLICY

The chapter's argument has important implications for migration research, professional practice, and policy development. Conceptualizing migrant well-being as a psychosocial-ecological process requires moving beyond a narrow focus on individual symptoms, cultural adjustment, or service use. Instead, research and interventions need to consider broader structural and contextual factors, such as migration trajectories, legal status, social networks, racism, family separation, labor-market conditions, housing, education, language access, and institutional responsiveness. This view aligns with scholarship that describes integration as a multidimensional and relational process involving both migrants and receiving societies (Ager & Strang, 2008; Penninx & Garcés-Mascareñas, 2016), as well as evidence emphasizing the key role of post-migration stressors in shaping adaptation and well-being (Li, Liddell, & Nickerson, 2016; Gleeson et al., 2020).

From a research perspective, this approach highlights the importance of interdisciplinary and culturally sensitive methods. Migration involves social, psychological, political, economic, legal, and cultural factors; therefore, analyses within a single discipline may lead to incomplete explanations. While quantitative methods are crucial for detecting patterns of distress, service access, and protective factors, they should be complemented by qualitative, ethnographic, longitudinal, and participatory approaches. These approaches offer deeper insights into lived experiences, processes of meaning-making, belonging, and evolving identities over time (Kirmayer et al., 2011; Simich, Maiter, & Ochocka, 2009). Participatory research is especially valuable because it allows migrants to influence research agendas, interpret findings, and highlight priorities that might otherwise be overlooked by institutions (WHO, 2022; MacFarlane et al., 2021).

Simultaneously, research should move beyond homogenizing categories such as "migrants" or "refugees," which often obscure significant differences in legal status, race, gender, class, age, sexuality, disability, religion, education, language, and migration pathways. An intersectional lens is essential for understanding how inequalities are distributed and experienced (Crawford et al., 2023; Yarwood et al., 2022). However, this differentiation should not lead to an exclusive focus on risk. Future research should also examine flourishing, meaning-making, social contribution, community leadership, transnational belonging, and culturally specific conceptions of well-being alongside trauma and distress.

For practitioners, the main implication is that assessment should link distress with context. Those working in healthcare, education, social work, counseling, community organizations, and settlement services should ask about not only symptoms but also legal status, housing, employment, language barriers, family separation, discrimination, cultural identity, religious resources, social networks, and access to services (Kirmayer et al., 2011; Im, Rodriguez, & Grumbine, 2021). Such an approach does not require practitioners to solve all structural challenges; instead, it helps prevent misinterpreting distress as solely individual when it is often driven by uncertainty, exclusion, poverty, or institutional barriers (Miller & Rasmussen, 2017; Van der Boor & White, 2020).

Practice should be culturally responsive, trauma-informed, and strengths-based. Cultural responsiveness involves understanding migrants' views on distress, healing, family, spirituality, gender, and help-seeking (Kirmayer et al., 2011; Silove & Klein, 2021). Trauma-informed care emphasizes safety, trust, choice, collaboration, and avoiding re-traumatization for those exposed to violence, detention, persecution, or institutional betrayal (Im et al., 2021; Robinson, Musotsi, & Khan, 2025). A strengths-based approach recognizes migrants' skills, relationships, cultural knowledge, and aspirations, while avoiding narratives that hide structural inequalities (Panter-Brick, 2014; Ungar, 2011).

For policymakers, the central implication is that migration and integration policies are inherently well-being policies. Legal security, fair asylum procedures, family reunification, access to employment, education, housing, healthcare, language learning, and anti-discrimination protections all play a decisive role in shaping psychosocial adaptation (Ager & Strang, 2008; WHO, 2023). Conversely, policies that produce prolonged uncertainty—such as temporary legal status, detention, work restrictions, family separation, or fear of deportation—can exacerbate distress and hinder integration, even where formal support services exist (Menjívar, 2006; De Genova, 2002; Gleeson et al., 2020).

Policy frameworks should also promote meaningful migrant participation in service design and evaluation. Evidence suggests that such involvement enhances the relevance, trustworthiness, and responsiveness of services when participation is substantive rather than symbolic (de Freitas et al., 2014; MacFarlane et al., 2021). Migrant-led organizations, diaspora groups, peer workers, cultural mediators, and community advocates should therefore be recognized as active partners in policy implementation rather than merely intermediaries (Wood & Kallestrup, 2021; Lester & Ryakhovskaya, 2023).

Both policy and practice should be evaluated through an equity lens. The key question is not just service availability but also who can access, trust, remain excluded, and whose well-being is prioritized. Attention should focus on marginalized groups, including asylum seekers, undocumented migrants, women caregivers, children, older adults, disabled, LGBTQI+ migrants, and those with limited literacy or digital access (Crawford et al., 2023; Yarwood et al., 2022). Evaluation should go beyond service outcomes to include access, safety, dignity, participation, belonging, and institutional responsiveness. Migrant well-being is a collective, social, and political outcome shaped by the conditions under which people rebuild their lives.

9. CONCLUSION

This chapter has argued that psychological adaptation and migrant well-being must be understood as psychosocial and ecological processes. Migration is not only a movement across borders; it is a reorganization of relationships, roles, cultural meanings, legal positions, social networks, and future possibilities. For this reason, migrant well-being cannot be explained only by individual coping, trauma exposure, or cultural adjustment. It is produced through the interaction of migration trajectories, social conditions, institutional arrangements, and migrants' own forms of agency (Ryan, Dooley, & Benson, 2008; Ager & Strang, 2008; Kreienkamp & Bringmann, 2024).

The chapter has moved from migration as a multi-phase experience to trauma, structural barriers, resilience, support systems, good practices, and policy implications. This sequence has shown that trauma in migration contexts is not only a clinical category but a lived disruption of home, family, identity, social status, and future. Violence, displacement, and loss matter deeply, but post-migration conditions also shape distress and recovery. Legal uncertainty, family separation, poverty, poor housing, discrimination, restricted work rights, and limited access to services can sustain suffering long after arrival (Porter & Haslam, 2005; Li, Liddell, & Nickerson, 2016; Gleeson et al., 2020).

The chapter has also reframed resilience. Migrants may show extraordinary persistence, creativity, care, and courage, but resilience should not be reduced to individual toughness. Resilience is sustained through relationships, routines, cultural continuity, social recognition, legal rights, education, employment, housing, healthcare, and community support (Masten, 2001; Ungar, 2011; Lindert et al., 2023). This means that receiving societies do not merely observe migrant resilience; they help shape the conditions under which resilience becomes possible or is undermined.

A central contribution of the chapter is its insistence that migrants should not be represented only through vulnerability. Vulnerability is real, particularly for refugees, asylum seekers, undocumented migrants, separated children, women exposed to gendered violence, LGBTQI+ migrants, older migrants, disabled migrants, and those facing racism or poverty (Crawford et al., 2023; Yarwood, Checchi, Lau, & Zimmerman, 2022). Yet migrants are also social actors who maintain transnational ties, support families, create associations, participate in labor markets, transmit culture, build communities, and reshape both origin and destination societies (Glick Schiller, 2004; Castles, de Haas, & Miller, 2014). A balanced migration literature must therefore hold vulnerability and agency together.

Ultimately, the movement from trauma to resilience is not a simple path from suffering to recovery. It is a contested and uneven process shaped by memory, loss, hope, social connection, rights, recognition, and opportunity. Migrants rebuild lives not in isolation, but within societies that may either constrain or support their capacity to belong. The task for migration research, practice, and policy is therefore to create conditions in which migrants are recognized not only as people in need of protection, but also as agents capable of contributing to shared futures.

REFERENCES

Ager, A., & Strang, A. (2008). Understanding integration: A conceptual framework. *Journal of Refugee Studies, 21*(2), 166–191. DOI: 10.1093/jrs/fen016

Albertini, M., Mantovani, D., & Gasperoni, G. (2019). Intergenerational relations among immigrants in Europe: The role of ethnic differences, migration, and acculturation. *European Journal of Ageing, 16*, 267–277. DOI: 10.1007/s10433-017-0446-z

Amit, K., & Bar-Lev, S. (2015). Immigrants' sense of belonging to the host country: The role of life satisfaction, language proficiency, and religious motives. *Social Indicators Research, 124*(3), 947–961. DOI: 10.1007/s11205-014-0823-3

Apers, H., Van Praag, L., Nöstlinger, C., & Agyemang, C. (2023). Interventions to improve the mental health or mental well-being of migrants and ethnic minority groups in Europe: A scoping review. *Global Mental Health (Cambridge, England), 10*, e23. Advance online publication. DOI: 10.1017/gmh.2023.15 PMID: 37854435

Barbati, A., Geraci, A., Niro, F., Pezzi, L., & Sarchiapone, M. (2022). Do migration and acculturation impact somatization? A scoping review. *International Journal of Environmental Research and Public Health, 19*(23), 16011. Advance online publication. DOI: 10.3390/ijerph192316011 PMID: 36498084

Berry, J. W. (1997). Immigration, acculturation, and adaptation. *Applied Psychology, 46*(1), 5–34. DOI: 10.1111/j.1464-0597.1997.tb01087.x

Brunnet, A. E., dos Santos Lobo, N., Silveira, T., Kristensen, C. H., & Derivois, D. (2020). Migrations, trauma, and mental health: A literature update on psychological assessment. *L'Encéphale, 46*(5), 364–371. DOI: 10.1016/j.encep.2020.03.009 PMID: 32576365

Bryant, R. A., Nickerson, A., Morina, N., & Liddell, B. (2023). Posttraumatic stress disorder in refugees. *Annual Review of Clinical Psychology, 19*(1), 413–436. DOI: 10.1146/annurev-clinpsy-080921-080359 PMID: 36854285

Bustamante, L. H. U., Cerqueira, R. O., Leclerc, E., & Brietzke, E. (2018). Stress, trauma, and posttraumatic stress disorder in migrants: A comprehensive review. *The British Journal of Psychiatry, 40*(2), 220–225. DOI: 10.1590/1516-4446-2017-2290 PMID: 29069252

Cabieses, B., Belo, K., Carreño Calderón, A., Rada, I., Rojas, K., Araoz, C., & Knipper, M. (2024). The impact of stigma and discrimination-based narratives in the health of migrants in Latin America and the Caribbean: A scoping review. *Lancet Regional Health. Americas*, *40*, 100660. Advance online publication. DOI: 10.1016/j.lana.2023.100660 PMID: 39763497

Castañeda, H., Holmes, S. M., Madrigal, D. S., Young, M. E., Beyeler, N., & Quesada, J. (2015). Immigration as a social determinant of health. *Annual Review of Public Health*, *36*(1), 375–392. DOI: 10.1146/annurev-publhealth-032013-182419 PMID: 25494053

Castles, S., de Haas, H., & Miller, M. J. (2014). *The age of migration: International population movements in the modern world* (5th ed.). Palgrave Macmillan. DOI: 10.1007/978-0-230-36639-8

Choy, B., Arunachalam, K., Taylor, M., & Lee, A. (2021). Systematic review: Acculturation strategies and their impact on the mental health of migrant populations. *Public Health in Practice (Oxford, England)*, *2*, 100069. Advance online publication. DOI: 10.1016/j.puhip.2020.100069 PMID: 36101596

Crawford, G., Connor, E., McCausland, K., Reeves, K., Blackford, K., & Lobo, R. (2022). Public health interventions to address housing and mental health amongst migrants from culturally and linguistically diverse backgrounds living in high-income countries: A scoping review. *International Journal of Environmental Research and Public Health*, *19*(24), 16946. Advance online publication. DOI: 10.3390/ijerph192416946 PMID: 36554827

de Freitas, C., García-Ramírez, M., Aambø, A., Buttigieg, S. C., Dias, S., Goguikian Ratcliff, B., & de Freitas, C. (2014). Transforming health policies through migrant user involvement: Lessons learnt from three European countries. *Psychosocial Intervention*, *23*(2), 105–113. DOI: 10.1016/j.psi.2014.07.007

De Genova, N. P. (2002). Migrant "illegality" and deportability in everyday life. *Annual Review of Anthropology*, *31*(1), 419–447. DOI: 10.1146/annurev.anthro.31.040402.085432

DeSa, S., Gebremeskel, A. T., Omonaiye, O., & Yaya, S. (2022). Barriers and facilitators to access mental health services among refugee women in high-income countries: A systematic review. *Systematic Reviews*, *11*(1), 62. Advance online publication. DOI: 10.1186/s13643-022-01936-1 PMID: 35387680

Fazel, M., Reed, R. V., & Stein, A. (2015). Mental health of displaced and refugee children resettled in high-income countries: Risk and protective factors. *Lancet*, *379*(9812), 266–282. DOI: 10.1016/S0140-6736(11)60051-2 PMID: 21835459

Fazel, M., Wheeler, J., & Danesh, J. (2005). Prevalence of serious mental disorder in 7000 refugees resettled in western countries: A systematic review. *Lancet*, *365*(9467), 1309–1314. DOI: 10.1016/S0140-6736(05)61027-6 PMID: 15823380

Glick Schiller, N. (2004). *Transnational theory and study: Past, present and future*. Ayuntamiento de Madrid.

Henkelmann, J. R., de Best, S., Deckers, C., Jensen, K., Shahab, M., Elzinga, B., & Molendijk, M. (2020). Anxiety, depression and post-traumatic stress disorder in refugees resettling in high-income countries: Systematic review and meta-analysis. *BJPsych Open*, *6*(4), e68. DOI: 10.1192/bjo.2020.54 PMID: 32611475

Im, H., Rodriguez, C., & Grumbine, J. M. (2021). A multitier model of refugee mental health and psychosocial support in resettlement: Toward trauma-informed and culture-informed systems of care. *Psychological Services*, *18*(3), 345–364. DOI: 10.1037/ser0000412 PMID: 31971439

Im, H., Verbillis-Kolp, S., Atiyeh, S., Bonz, A. G., & Jani, J. S. (2023). Implementation evaluation of community-based mental health and psychosocial support intervention for refugee newcomers in the United States. *Health & Social Care in the Community*, *2023*, 6696415. Advance online publication. DOI: 10.1155/2023/6696415

Inter-Agency Standing Committee. (2007). *IASC guidelines on mental health and psychosocial support in emergency settings*. Inter-Agency Standing Committee. https://interagencystandingcommittee.org/iasc-task-force-mental-health-and-psychosocial-support-emergency-settings/iasc-guidelines-mental-health-and-psychosocial-support-emergency-settings-2007

International Organization for Migration. (2024). [IOM. https://worldmigrationreport.iom.int/]. *World Migration Report*, *2024*, •••.

Katsampa, D. (2024). *The impact of family separation on refugee men*. University of Hertfordshire. https://uhra.herts.ac.uk/handle/2299/28540

Keles, S., Devos, C., & Wang, Q. (2024). At risk or resilient? Examining the effects of having a migration background on mental and social wellbeing outcomes amongst adolescents. *Scientific Reports*, *14*, 15023. Advance online publication. DOI: 10.1038/s41598-024-65825-9

Killikelly, C., Bauer, S., & Maercker, A. (2018). The assessment of grief in refugees and post-conflict survivors: A narrative review of etic and emic research. *Frontiers in Psychology*, *9*, 1957. Advance online publication. DOI: 10.3389/fpsyg.2018.01957 PMID: 30405474

Kirmayer, L. J., Narasiah, L., Munoz, M., Rashid, M., Ryder, A. G., Guzder, J., Hassan, G., Rousseau, C., & Pottie, K. (2011). Common mental health problems in immigrants and refugees: General approach in primary care. *Canadian Medical Association Journal, 183*(12), E959–E967. DOI: 10.1503/cmaj.090292 PMID: 20603342

Klingenberg, A., Luetz, J. M., & Crawford, A. (2021). Transnationalism—Recognizing the strengths of dual belonging for both migrant and society. *Journal of International Migration and Integration, 22*(2), 453–470. DOI: 10.1007/s12134-019-00744-2

Kreienkamp, J., Bringmann, L. F., Engler, R. F., de Jonge, P., & Epstude, K. (2024). The migration experience: A conceptual framework and systematic scoping review of psychological acculturation. *Personality and Social Psychology Review, 28*(4), 402–456. DOI: 10.1177/10888683231183479 PMID: 37571846

Kuo, B. C. H. (2014). Coping, acculturation, and psychological adaptation among migrants: A theoretical and empirical review and synthesis of the literature. *Health Psychology and Behavioral Medicine, 2*(1), 16–33. DOI: 10.1080/21642850.2013.843459 PMID: 25750766

Lee, R. M. (2020). Resilience against discrimination: Ethnic-racial identity and other-group orientation as protective factors for Korean Americans. *Journal of Counseling Psychology, 67*(4), 478–490. DOI: 10.1037/cou0000417

Lester, H., Ryakhovskaya, Y., & Olorunnisola, T. S. (2023). Asset-based community development approaches to resilience among refugees and recent migrant communities in Australia: A scoping review. *International Journal of Migration, Health and Social Care, 19*(2), 77–91. DOI: 10.1108/IJMHSC-09-2022-0098

Levitt, P., & Glick Schiller, N. (2004). Conceptualizing simultaneity: A transnational social field perspective on society. *The International Migration Review, 38*(3), 1002–1039. DOI: 10.1111/j.1747-7379.2004.tb00227.x

Li, S. S. Y., Liddell, B. J., & Nickerson, A. (2016). The relationship between post-migration stress and psychological disorders in refugees and asylum seekers. *Current Psychiatry Reports, 18*(9), 82. Advance online publication. DOI: 10.1007/s11920-016-0723-0 PMID: 27436307

Liem, A., Renzaho, A. M. N., Hannam, K., Lam, A. I. F., & Hall, B. J. (2021). Acculturative stress and coping among migrant workers: A global mixed-methods systematic review. *Applied Psychology. Health and Well-Being, 13*(3), 491–517. DOI: 10.1111/aphw.12271 PMID: 33811751

Lindert, J., Samkange-Zeeb, F., Frank, L., Schouler-Ocak, M., & Barros, H. (2023). Factors contributing to resilience among first generation migrants, refugees, and asylum seekers: A systematic review. *International Journal of Public Health, 68*, 1606406. Advance online publication. DOI: 10.3389/ijph.2023.1606406 PMID: 38146483

MacFarlane, A., Ogoro, M., de Freitas, C., Niranjan, V., Severoni, S., & Waagensen, E. (2021). Migrants' involvement in health policy, service development and research in the WHO European Region: A narrative review of policy and practice. *Tropical Medicine & International Health, 26*(10), 1164–1176. DOI: 10.1111/tmi.13643 PMID: 34169612

Mahon, D. (2022). A systematic scoping review of interventions delivered by peers to support the resettlement of refugees and asylum seekers. *Mental Health and Social Inclusion, 26*(3), 206–218. DOI: 10.1108/MHSI-12-2021-0085

Marley, C., & Mauki, B. (2019). Resilience and protective factors among refugee children post-migration to high-income countries: A systematic review. *European Journal of Public Health, 29*(4), 706–713. DOI: 10.1093/eurpub/cky232 PMID: 30380016

Massey, D. S., Arango, J., Hugo, G., Kouaouci, A., Pellegrino, A., & Taylor, J. E. (1993). Theories of international migration: A review and appraisal. *Population and Development Review, 19*(3), 431–466. DOI: 10.2307/2938462

Masten, A. S. (2001). Ordinary magic: Resilience processes in development. *The American Psychologist, 56*(3), 227–238. DOI: 10.1037/0003-066X.56.3.227 PMID: 11315249

Menjívar, C. (2006). Liminal legality: Salvadoran and Guatemalan immigrants' lives in the United States. *American Journal of Sociology, 111*(4), 999–1037. DOI: 10.1086/499509

Miller, K. E., & Rasmussen, A. (2017). The mental health of civilians displaced by armed conflict: An ecological model of refugee distress. *Epidemiology and Psychiatric Sciences, 26*(2), 129–138. DOI: 10.1017/S2045796016000172 PMID: 27040595

Motti-Stefanidi, F., & Masten, A. S. (2017). A resilience perspective on immigrant youth adaptation and development. In Cabrera, N., & Leyendecker, B. (Eds.), *Handbook on positive development of minority children and youth* (pp. 19–34). Springer., DOI: 10.1007/978-3-319-43645-6_2

Neuner, F., Schauer, M., Klaschik, C., Karunakara, U., & Elbert, T. (2004). A comparison of narrative exposure therapy, supportive counseling, and psychoeducation for treating posttraumatic stress disorder in an African refugee settlement. *Journal of Consulting and Clinical Psychology, 72*(4), 579–587. DOI: 10.1037/0022-006X.72.4.579 PMID: 15301642

Ngondwe, P., & Tefera, G. M. (2025). Barriers and facilitators of access to healthcare among immigrants with disabilities: A qualitative meta-synthesis. *Health Care, 13*(3), 313. Advance online publication. DOI: 10.3390/healthcare13030313 PMID: 39942501

Oldroyd, J. C., Kabir, A., Dzakpasu, F. Q. S., Treves-Kagan, S., D'Alton, P., & O'Connor, C. (2022). The experiences of children and adolescents undergoing forced separation from their parents during migration: A systematic review. *Health & Social Care in the Community, 30*(6), e4609–e4623. DOI: 10.1111/hsc.13595 PMID: 34622499

Panter-Brick, C. (2014). Health, risk, and resilience: Interdisciplinary concepts and applications. *Annual Review of Anthropology, 43*(1), 431–448. DOI: 10.1146/annurev-anthro-102313-025944

Penninx, R., & Garcés-Mascareñas, B. (2016). The concept of integration as an analytical tool and as a policy concept. In Garcés-Mascareñas, B., & Penninx, R. (Eds.), *Integration processes and policies in Europe: Contexts, levels and actors* (pp. 11–29). Springer., DOI: 10.1007/978-3-319-21674-4_2

Pollard, T., & Howard, N. (2021). Mental healthcare for asylum-seekers and refugees residing in the United Kingdom: A scoping review of policies, barriers, and enablers. *International Journal of Mental Health Systems, 15*(1), 60. Advance online publication. DOI: 10.1186/s13033-021-00473-z PMID: 34127043

Porter, M., & Haslam, N. (2005). Predisplacement and postdisplacement factors associated with mental health of refugees and internally displaced persons: A meta-analysis. *Journal of the American Medical Association, 294*(5), 602–612. DOI: 10.1001/jama.294.5.602 PMID: 16077055

Portes, A., & Rumbaut, R. G. (2001). *Legacies: The story of the immigrant second generation.* University of California Press.

Posselt, M., Eaton, H., Ferguson, M., Keegan, D., & Procter, N. (2019). Enablers of psychological well-being for refugees and asylum seekers living in transitional countries: A systematic review. *Health & Social Care in the Community, 27*(4), 808–823. DOI: 10.1111/hsc.12680 PMID: 30417476

Raghavan, S., & Sandanapitchai, P. (2024). The relationship between cultural variables and resilience to psychological trauma: A systematic review of the literature. *Traumatology, 30*(1), 27–39. DOI: 10.1037/trm0000239 PMID: 38818343

Riza, E., Kalkman, S., Coritsidis, A., Koubardas, S., Vassiliu, S., Lazarou, D., Karnaki, P., Zota, D., Kantzanou, M., Psaltopoulou, T., & Linos, A. (2020). Community-based healthcare for migrants and refugees: A scoping literature review of best practices. *Health Care, 8*(2), 115. Advance online publication. DOI: 10.3390/healthcare8020115 PMID: 32354069

Robinson, A., Musotsi, P., Khan, Z. R. A., Nellums, L., Faiq, B., Broadhurst, K., Renolds, G., Pritchard, M., & Smith, A. (2025). Opportunities and practices supporting responsive health care for forced migrants: Lessons from transnational practice and a mixed-methods systematic review. *Health and Social Care Delivery Research, 13*(13), 1–182. DOI: 10.3310/MRWK3419 PMID: 40326302

Ryan, D., Dooley, B., & Benson, C. (2008). Theoretical perspectives on post-migration adaptation and psychological well-being among refugees: Towards a resource-based model. *Journal of Refugee Studies, 21*(1), 1–18. DOI: 10.1093/jrs/fem047

Sakamoto, I. (2007). A critical examination of immigrant acculturation: Toward an anti-oppressive social work model with immigrant adults in a pluralistic society. *British Journal of Social Work, 37*(3), 515–535. DOI: 10.1093/bjsw/bcm024

Schweitzer, R., Melville, F., Steel, Z., & Lacherez, P. (2006). Trauma, post-migration living difficulties, and social support as predictors of psychological adjustment in resettled Sudanese refugees. *The Australian and New Zealand Journal of Psychiatry, 40*(2), 179–187. DOI: 10.1080/j.1440-1614.2006.01766.x PMID: 16476137

Shaw, S. A., & Funk, M. (2019). A systematic review of social service programs serving refugees. *Research on Social Work Practice, 29*(8), 847–862. DOI: 10.1177/1049731518824405

Sheikh, M., & Anderson, J. R. (2018). Acculturation patterns and education of refugees and asylum seekers: A systematic literature review. *Learning and Individual Differences, 67*, 22–32. DOI: 10.1016/j.lindif.2018.07.003

Silove, D., & Klein, L. (2021). Culture, trauma, and traumatic stress among refugees, asylum seekers, and postconflict populations. In Friedman, M. J., Schnurr, P. P., & Keane, T. M. (Eds.), *Handbook of PTSD: Science and practice* (3rd ed.). Guilford Press.

Simich, L., Maiter, S., & Ochocka, J. (2009). From social liminality to cultural negotiation: Transformative processes in immigrant mental wellbeing. *Anthropology & Medicine*, *16*(3), 253–266. DOI: 10.1080/13648470903249296 PMID: 27269908

Song, J., Corcoran, J., & Zahnow, R. (2025). The resettlement journey: Understanding the role of social connectedness on well-being and life satisfaction among immigrants and refugees: A systematic review. *Journal of Racial and Ethnic Health Disparities*, *12*(4), 2128–2144. DOI: 10.1007/s40615-024-02036-7 PMID: 38807024

Steel, Z., Chey, T., Silove, D., Marnane, C., Bryant, R. A., & Van Ommeren, M. (2009). Association of torture and other potentially traumatic events with mental health outcomes among populations exposed to mass conflict and displacement: A systematic review and meta-analysis. *Journal of the American Medical Association*, *302*(5), 537–549. DOI: 10.1001/jama.2009.1132 PMID: 19654388

Strang, A. B., & Quinn, N. (2021). Integration or isolation? Refugees' social connections and wellbeing. *Journal of Refugee Studies*, *34*(1), 328–353. DOI: 10.1093/jrs/fez040

Theisen-Womersley, G. (2021). *Trauma and resilience among displaced populations: A sociocultural exploration*. Springer., DOI: 10.1007/978-3-030-67712-1

Timshel, I., Montgomery, E., & Dalgaard, N. T. (2017). A systematic review of risk and protective factors associated with family related violence in refugee families. *Child Abuse & Neglect*, *70*, 315–330. DOI: 10.1016/j.chiabu.2017.06.023 PMID: 28683372

Tol, W. A., Barbui, C., Galappatti, A., Silove, D., Betancourt, T. S., Souza, R., Golaz, A., & van Ommeren, M. (2011). Mental health and psychosocial support in humanitarian settings: Linking practice and research. *Lancet*, *378*(9802), 1581–1591. DOI: 10.1016/S0140-6736(11)61094-5 PMID: 22008428

Tribe, R. H., Sendt, K. V., & Tracy, D. K. (2019). A systematic review of psychosocial interventions for adult refugees and asylum seekers. *Journal of Mental Health (Abingdon, England)*, *28*(6), 662–676. DOI: 10.1080/09638237.2017.1322182 PMID: 28485636

Ungar, M. (2011). The social ecology of resilience: Addressing contextual and cultural ambiguity of a nascent construct. *The American Journal of Orthopsychiatry*, *81*(1), 1–17. DOI: 10.1111/j.1939-0025.2010.01067.x PMID: 21219271

United Nations High Commissioner for Refugees. (2024). *Global trends: Forced displacement in 2023*. UNHCR. https://www.unhcr.org/global-trends

Van der Boor, C. F., & White, R. (2020). Barriers to accessing and negotiating mental health services in asylum seeking and refugee populations: The application of the candidacy framework. *Journal of Immigrant and Minority Health*, *22*(1), 156–174. DOI: 10.1007/s10903-019-00929-y PMID: 31444614

Vertovec, S. (2009). *Transnationalism.* Routledge. DOI: 10.4324/9780203927083

Villalonga-Olives, E., Wind, T. R., Armand, A. O., Yirefu, M., Smith, R., & Aldrich, D. P. (2022). Social-capital-based mental health interventions for refugees: A systematic review. *Social Science & Medicine*, *301*, 114787. Advance online publication. DOI: 10.1016/j.socscimed.2022.114787 PMID: 35366460

Viruell-Fuentes, E. A., Miranda, P. Y., & Abdulrahim, S. (2012). More than culture: Structural racism, intersectionality theory, and immigrant health. *Social Science & Medicine*, *75*(12), 2099–2106. DOI: 10.1016/j.socscimed.2011.12.037 PMID: 22386617

Ward, C. (2001). The A, B, Cs of acculturation. In D. Matsumoto (Ed.), *The handbook of culture and psychology* (pp. 411–445). Oxford University Press.

Wong, C. W. S., & Schweitzer, R. D. (2017). Individual, premigration and postsettlement factors, and academic achievement in adolescents from refugee backgrounds: A systematic review and model. *Transcultural Psychiatry*, *54*(5–6), 756–782. DOI: 10.1177/1363461517737015 PMID: 29115909

Wood, B., & Kallestrup, P. (2021). Benefits and challenges of using a participatory approach with community-based mental health and psychosocial support interventions in displaced populations. *Transcultural Psychiatry*, *58*(2), 283–292. DOI: 10.1177/1363461520983626 PMID: 33509062

World Health Organization. (2022). *Participatory health research with migrants: A country implementation guide.* WHO. https://www.who.int/publications/i/item/9789240038196

World Health Organization. (2023). *Mental health of refugees and migrants: Risk and protective factors and access to care.* WHO. https://www.who.int/publications/i/item/9789240081840

Wright, A., Reisig, A., & Cullen, B. (2020). Efficacy and cultural adaptations of narrative exposure therapy for trauma-related outcomes in refugees/asylum-seekers: A systematic review and meta-analysis. *Journal of Behavioral and Cognitive Therapy*, *30*(4), 301–314. DOI: 10.1016/j.jbct.2020.10.003

Yarwood, V., Checchi, F., Lau, K., & Zimmerman, C. (2022). LGBTQI+ migrants: A systematic review and conceptual framework of health, safety and wellbeing during migration. *International Journal of Environmental Research and Public Health*, *19*(2), 869. Advance online publication. DOI: 10.3390/ijerph19020869 PMID: 35055698

Zetter, R. (2007). More labels, fewer refugees: Remaking the refugee label in an era of globalization. *Journal of Refugee Studies*, *20*(2), 172–192. DOI: 10.1093/jrs/fem011

Chapter 6
Recognition Autonomy and Resilience:
Psychosocial Foundations of Migrant Well-Being

Meryem Atalay
http://orcid.org/0000-0002-3879-5481
Erzincan Binali Yildirim University, Turkey

Hikmet Yazici
Trabzon University, Turkey

ABSTRACT

This chapter considers international migration to be a comprehensive reorganization of social life. It critiques traditional clinical approaches that label displaced individuals as passive 'victims of trauma' and reduce responsibility for readjustment to individual coping strategies. Instead, it presents an integrative ecological framework for the post-migration period, synthesising Silove's ADAPT model, Self-Determination Theory and Honneth's theory of recognition. Accordingly, trauma is conceptualised as a profound 'social rupture' in meaning and security, while resilience is framed as an active, socially mediated process of 'reconstruction'. The chapter analyses the destructive and mediating roles of post-migration 'daily stressors'—such as status loss, legal precarity, and social exclusion—in shaping psychological well-being. Ultimately, it emphasises that the journey from trauma to resilience is influenced more by the institutional and moral conditions of recognition offered by the host society than by past adversities.

DOI: 10.4018/979-8-3373-8500-6.ch006

1. INTRODUCTION: MIGRATION AS A PROCESS OF SOCIAL REORGANISATION

International migration is not merely physical relocation; it is a complex process that impacts an individual's existential, cultural, and relational worlds holistically, necessitating comprehensive social reorganization. Indeed, extant literature on the subject of migration consistently recognises it as a multidimensional phenomenon. While this multidimensional phenomenon can be analysed across geographical, demographic, economic, and political dimensions, this study primarily approaches it from a psychosocial perspective to analyse individuals' adaptation processes. This multifaceted and radical change poses a significant challenge to individuals' psychological boundaries, often engendering a process of 'alienation' where cultural differences and a profound sense of longing become intertwined. Forced migration, in particular, abruptly annihilates the 'average expectable environment' to which individuals are accustomed, on which their worlds of meaning are built. Consequently, this results in an enforced transition to an unfamiliar structural order, thereby rendering their prior cultural competencies and social schemas invalid.

In the existing literature on migration and mental health, the processes by which migrants adapt to this new sociocultural environment have been explained primarily through two contrasting perspectives. On the one hand, a psychiatric standpoint reduces adaptation issues solely to Post-Traumatic Stress Disorder (PTSD) stemming from pre-migration experiences; on the other hand, a sociocultural approach attempts to explain adaptation largely through superficial acculturation strategies. The fundamental critique of these two perspectives is that the clinical perspective systematically pathologises the migrant experience and, by relying on a Direct Effect Model, reduces a multidimensional social rupture into an individualised medical problem. The conventional clinical perspective portrays displaced individuals as passive and helpless "traumatised victims". By overlooking the profound social disruptions resulting from forced displacement, such as the loss of rights, de-identification, and compromised security, this perspective places the burden of adaptation solely on the individuals' internal coping mechanisms or the efficacy of medical interventions. However, it can be argued that this perspective fundamentally ignores the reality that trauma is not an isolated, temporally confined event left in the past; rather, it is an ongoing "process of social destruction" actively shaped by the structural barriers encountered in the host society.

Furthermore, the deficit-oriented and pathology-focused model is not sufficiently attentive to the active roles (agency) of individuals in the face of adverse life experiences, nor does it adequately recognise their innate capacity for resilience.

As demonstrated in Bonanno's research, conventional trauma models tend to pathologize the diverse, natural psychological responses and coping mechanisms that individuals manifest in the face of highly stressful, traumatic, or disruptive events. These models posit that in the aftermath of significant losses, individuals are obligated to engage in a protracted and arduous period of "grief work." The absence of such a process is purported to signify a pathological denial or "repressive coping." However, contemporary findings suggest that, contrary to the view that the "recovery" cycle requires prolonged clinical decline, "resilience"—a trajectory in which the individual actively maintains a stable and healthy level of functioning—is not a rare trait but rather the most common and ordinary human response. Consequently, it can be argued that the fundamental flaw of the traditional clinical model is its failure to adequately recognise human nature's capacity to survive and thrive after devastating events, completely overlooking the processes by which migrants actively engage in the "reconstruction" of a self capable of adapting to a new cultural context.

Within this theoretical framework, the primary objective of this book chapter is to shift the conceptualization of the challenges faced by migrants away from a focus on individual pathology, redefining trauma instead as a profound "social rupture" in meaning and security. In order to provide a theoretical foundation for understanding social rupture, the present study primarily focuses on Silove's Adaptation and Development After Persecution and Trauma (ADAPT) model. The ADAPT model posits that forced migration and violence do not merely affect the individual's mind (as a fear-based medical reaction) but systematically destroy five foundational pillars crucial for healthy psychosocial adaptation (Silove, 1999, 2013; Tay et al., 2015). These five pillars are as follows: safety and security; protecting physical integrity, interpersonal bonds and social networks; providing emotional support; a sense of justice against human rights violations; identity and social roles representing social status; and existential meaning offering a coherent life experience. This phenomenon may be characterised not merely as an ordinary state of being overlooked, but rather as a form of structural "social invisibility", whereby the individual is denied recognition as a moral and social being, resulting in significant damage to their self-respect. In individuals who are unable to plan for the future and who constantly experience a sense of being in "limbo," the "Safety/Security" and "Identity/Role" pillars of the ADAPT model collapse. Therefore, while this chapter conceptualises trauma as the shattering of these five fundamental pillars sustaining justice, identity, and relationships, it provides an integrative perspective that formulates adaptation (resilience) as the active "reconstruction" of these psychosocial domains and a functional, viable self-concept in a new cultural environment.

In order to achieve this objective, the chapter centres on the premise that a migrant's psychological resilience following severe trauma and losses does not depend solely on their internal strength, personal traits, or genetic makeup; in other words, psychosocial resilience does not occur in a vacuum. While the impact of pre-migration traumas and direct war experiences is irrefutable, recent studies have demonstrated that migrants' current mental health and psychological adaptation are largely shaped by the "daily stressors" to which they are exposed in the post-migration period (Dangmann et al., 2021; LeMaster et al., 2017; Miller & Rasmussen, 2010; Purgato et al., 2017).

Indeed, it can be argued that ecological factors shaped by the host society's influence – such as legal precarity, social exclusion, poverty, or loss of status – are not merely background variables; rather, they are the primary structural triggers that mediate the effects of past trauma and ultimately determine the individual's psychological breakdown or resilience.

Within this theoretical framework, the study posits that the promotion of enduring psychological well-being in migrants must encompass more than the mere absence of clinical pathology; rather, it is a process of actively reconstructing reciprocal recognition, individual agency, and social embeddedness. The psychological recovery of migrants cannot be considered a passive outcome that is achieved merely through "grief work" within the confines of a therapy room. Conversely, the concept of resilience is defined as an active, relational, and institutional process in which the shattered pillars of safety, justice, identity, and meaning (ADAPT) are simultaneously reconstructed through the migrant's dynamic interaction with the host society. This is due to the fact that the experience of migration places the continuous dilemma between the 'I' (personal identity) and the 'we' (social identity) at the very centre of social comparisons. The chapter employs a multidimensional approach to examine how individuals strive to fulfil their three basic psychological needs—autonomy, competence, and relatedness—in a new society. The study explores how exposure to social exclusion triggers protective strategies, such as clinging to ethnic identity, and how resilience is ultimately shaped along the axes of rights, love, and solidarity.

In accordance with the theoretical framework delineated above, the chapter's content is organised as follows: In the second section, the traditional Post-Traumatic Stress Disorder (PTSD) diagnostic criteria are expanded upon, with the concept of trauma being defined as a "rupture in meaning and security". Furthermore, it presents the destructive mediating role of daily stressors in the impact of trauma on migrant mental health. The third section of this study focuses on the interaction between the psychological needs of migrants and the attitudes of the host society. This interaction is explored through the mechanisms of "social exclusion and rejection-identification." In the fourth section, the passive victim narrative that is often ascribed to refugees is dismissed; instead, it is contended that resilience signifies an "active reconstruction of meaning and identity" within the framework of Honneth's Theory of Recognition. In conclusion, the focus of the study undergoes a transition from the individual to the broader ecological context in the fifth and sixth sections. The sections herein synthesise, from a holistic perspective, the premise that the trajectory from trauma to resilience is determined less by the migrant's past sufferings than by the "institutional and moral conditions" (multiculturalism, rights, and social esteem) provided by the host society. The sections conclude with relevant policy recommendations.

2. TRAUMA AS A RUPTURE IN MEANING AND SECURITY: BEYOND THE CLINICAL PTSD PARADIGM

The prevailing psychiatric approach in the domain of refugee mental health has been to focus on Post-Traumatic Stress Disorder (PTSD) to comprehend and diagnose the psychological distress experienced following forced migration. This trauma-focused approach attributes the psychological problems experienced by refugees directly to war, violence, and traumatic events. Focusing on individual symptoms and rooted in traumatic events, this clinical framework operates as a Direct Effect Model, positing that exposure to war, violence, and persecution engenders a persistent psychopathology that endures across time and geography (Purgato et al., 2017). Nevertheless, this direct effect model remains inadequate in explaining the multidimensional nature of refugee issues (Miller & Rasmussen, 2010).

In order to demonstrate the limitations of this traditional clinical approach, which fails to capture the multidimensional nature of refugee struggles, the case of a middle-aged refugee father who fled conflict in his home country to settle in a new society serves as an illuminating example. When such an individual presents to a social worker with complaints of chronic fatigue, hopelessness, and social withdrawal, the traditional clinical response is often to diagnose them with depression or PTSD, based on past war traumas, and to recommend individual therapy. However, upon closer scrutiny, it becomes apparent that the predominant issue preoccupying his mind and precipitating his decline is not the past war; rather, it is the devaluation of his labour through uninsured employment, the second-class treatment he receives at official institutions, and his exclusion from his neighbourhood through being labelled as a "foreigner." The initial encoding of trauma or depression by professionals as an individual problem is, in fact, indicative of a profound social rupture, in which the individual is systematically rendered invisible across the domains of love, rights, and solidarity. This state of exclusion, which engenders feelings of invisibility, worthlessness, and voicelessness, clearly demonstrates that trauma must be reconceptualised not merely as a medical problem fought within the individual's mind, but as the shattering of the foundations that sustain justice, identity, and relationships.

The direct effect model places significant emphasis on fear-based responses, such as intrusive memories and hyperarousal, in situations involving life-threatening experiences. However, it frequently fails to acknowledge the profound social, cultural, and existential disruptions that are characteristic of the phenomenon of forced displacement. At this juncture, an alternative conceptualisation emerges, redefining trauma not solely as an internal medical condition, but as a profound "social rupture" that shatters the very foundations sustaining safety, relationships, justice, identity, and meaning (Silove, 1999, 2013; Tay et al., 2017). This perspective entails a shift in focus from merely reducing individual symptoms to the reconstruction of the social fabric that ensures long-term functionality.

The ADAPT Model: The Five Pillars of Psychosocial Adaptation

In systematising the "social rupture" that recharacterises trauma, Silove's Adaptation and Development After Persecution and Trauma (ADAPT) model provides an integrative conceptual framework (Silove, 1999, 2013; Tay et al., 2015, 2019). The model posits that conflict and subsequent forced migration compromise five fundamental adaptive systems, each representing an interconnected psychosocial domain essential for individual adaptation.

The first pillar, Safety and Security, is designed to protect physical survival and territorial integrity. The disruption of this system has been shown to manifest in the form of ongoing threats, communal violence, and the deprivation of basic needs.

The second pillar, Bonds and Networks, encompasses the interpersonal ties, family structures, and community networks that provide emotional support and a sense of belonging. The phenomenon of forced migration has been shown to systematically disrupt these bonds through a variety of mechanisms, including familial separation, the loss of loved ones, and the erosion of trust.

The third pillar, Justice, pertains to the imperatives of securing justice against human rights violations, holding perpetrators accountable, and redressing grievances. The collapse of this pillar is evidenced by impunity for crimes, unresolved complaints, and the inability to seek legal recourse, all of which frequently engender chronic anger and social resentment in individuals.

The fourth pillar, Identity and Roles, is associated with the maintenance of social status, cultural identity, and occupational or daily functionality. Displacement has been shown to undermine this system through the abrupt loss of significant social roles, the devaluation of professional competencies, and the difficulties experienced in sustaining cultural continuity.

Finally, the Existential Meaning pillar encompasses coherent life narratives, collective purpose, and spiritual frameworks. The loss of one's homeland constitutes an existential rupture that shatters individuals' sense of continuity and future possibilities, leaving survivors to grapple with a fragmented sense of meaning and unfulfilled political or personal aspirations.

War Trauma or Daily Stress? The Ecological Framework

As outlined in the ADAPT model, the psychosocial systems that are disrupted by displacement are specified. Furthermore, contemporary ecological models reveal the specific conditions encountered in host societies that perpetuate these disruptions. The prevailing ecological models posit that the primary source of psychological distress experienced by individuals does not exclusively stem from past traumas, but is also influenced by post-migration living conditions.

In this regard, Miller and Rasmussen's (2010) ecological model, a psychosocial approach, foregrounds the material, legal, and relational conditions that shape the daily lives of refugees. This model demonstrates that "daily stressors" – comprising poverty, unemployment, housing difficulties, discrimination, social isolation, and legal precarity – partially mediate the relationship between past war exposure and current mental health outcomes. The fundamental premise of the model is that the effects of war are largely exerted through these daily stress factors.

The findings from structural equation modeling conducted across various displaced populations consistently corroborate this mediating relationship. The present findings suggest that past war trauma does not exclusively result in psychological devastation; rather, post-migration life difficulties (daily stressors) serve as a causal bridge that translates the destructive effects of war trauma into depression, anxiety, and generalised psychological distress (Dangmann et al., 2021; LeMaster et al., 2017).

The psychological harm inflicted by these daily stressors is significant due to their proximity and chronic nature, which result in perpetual activation of the individual's stress response and a profound sense of powerlessness. Conventional clinical methodologies predominantly attribute refugees' mental health challenges directly to remote past war traumas. However, Miller and Rasmussen (2010) argue that proximal daily stressors exert a far more destructive and persistent impact on refugees' mental health than the distal exposure to war.

Of particular significance is the manner in which the ADAPT and ecological models emphasise the manner in which post-migration stressors perpetuate the initial social rupture by impeding the reconstruction of the five adaptation pillars (Silove, 2013; Tay et al., 2017). For resettled refugees, the conditions that engender a chronic sense of uncertainty and "future anxiety" are inextricably linked to their legal status. The institutional barriers encountered in this context engender a state of "permanent temporariness" that erodes the capacity to plan for the future—a critical component of psychological well-being. The concurrent and ongoing adversities experienced by refugees have been shown to have several consequences. These include the sustaining of security threats, the hindrance to the re-establishment of socially meaningful roles, and the obstruction of refugees' access to supportive networks.

This compounding effect has been vividly illustrated by West Papuan refugees in Australia, who utilise the term "dua sakit" ("double sickness") to describe the entire spectrum of experiences reflecting the destructive amalgamation of past persecution and current settlement challenges (Rees et al., 2009). Consequently, the trajectory of trauma for migrants is not a discrete event relegated to the past; rather, it is an ongoing process wherein past war experiences are continuously reactivated and sustained by daily realities such as social exclusion and material deprivation within the host society (Jetten et al., 2017; Miller & Rasmussen, 2010).

To provide a concrete example of the psychological devastation wrought by the multidimensional daily stressors to which refugees are exposed within the framework of the Ecological Model, the experiences of a young mother forced to migrate with her children due to civil war are presented. For such a mother, who initially struggles to cope with the fear and losses engendered by war before migration, the truly debilitating and chronic process typically commences with the environmental conditions she encounters in the host society post-migration. The language barrier in her new environment, her spouse's unemployment, housing instability, and, most notably, the profound anxiety she harbors regarding her children's education and future, become the fundamental elements that paralyze her daily life. The subject's inability to communicate with her immediate surroundings, even at a basic level due to the aforementioned language barrier, compounded by social support being restricted to mere subsistence-level assistance, exacerbates her alienation and social isolation. The Ecological Model posits that this overarching portrait clearly demonstrates that migration is not merely a discrete war trauma relegated to the past; rather, "daily stressors"—such as unemployment, cultural adaptation difficulties, and economic pressures—constitute a multidimensional and ongoing process of social rupture that erodes the individual's psychological equilibrium just as severely as the war itself.

3. PATHWAYS OF ADAPTATION: IDENTITY AND SOCIAL EXCLUSION

In order to comprehend the psychological adaptation of migrants, it is essential to shift the focus from behavioural changes and clinical trauma models to the fundamental motivations that drive human behaviour and the social contexts that shape identity. In this regard, the psychological well-being of displaced individuals cannot be viewed as the sole achievement of the individual, but rather as an ongoing process of negotiation between the fundamental needs of the individual and the exclusionary or inclusionary dynamics of the host society.

Motivation, Status Loss, and Basic Needs: A Self-Determination Theory Perspective

Self-Determination Theory (SDT) provides a robust and empirically validated framework for conceptualising these adaptation dynamics (Ryan & Deci, 2000). This theory posits that an individual's capacity to realise their full potential, attain well-being, and facilitate psychological growth is contingent upon the fulfilment of three innate and universal psychological needs. The first of these is autonomy, which is defined as the need for behaviours to emanate from the self, accompanied by an experience of freedom and volition. This need is reflected by the desire to feel a sense of agency and have the freedom of choice. The second need is competence, which encompasses the individual's need to feel effective in pursuing goals, to believe they possess the relevant skills for success, and to have a sense of being able to demonstrate these skills. The third need is relatedness, which involves a sense of belonging and connectedness to individuals, groups, or culture, as well as the feeling of being respected and valued.

Within the domain of international migration, these three fundamental psychological needs are often impeded. Migration is not merely a geographic transition; it is also the profound disruption of the sociocultural contexts in which the individual previously fulfilled these basic needs. The aforementioned disruption becomes clearly evident upon examination of the structural barriers and limitations of post-migration environments.

Although pre-migration trauma is a significant factor in refugee mental health, contemporary ecological models emphasise that post-migration daily stressors – such as legal precarity, poverty, unemployment, and institutional marginalisation – often mediate the relationship between past adversities and current psychological distress (Miller & Rasmussen, 2010). A pervasive consequence of these ongoing stressors is the combination of profound "status loss" and highly restricted status mobility (Aycan & Berry, 1996, as cited in Berry, 1997).

In other words, when refugees arrive in a new country, they not only lose their former occupational or social positions (status loss), but they also struggle with a situation where opportunities for upward mobility and advancement in the new society are severely limited (restricted status mobility). To illustrate this point, consider a refugee who, before their displacement, was a practising lawyer in their country of origin. However, due to circumstances beyond their control, they are compelled to pursue a role as a sales clerk within the host society. This transition often results in a significant devaluation of their educational and professional qualifications, which are not formally recognised in the host nation. The failure of the environment to provide the individual with opportunities to exercise their acquired mastery and demonstrate their potential directly thwarts their psychological need for competence.

Concurrently, the legal precarity experienced by refugees, compounded by systemic barriers within institutional frameworks, systematically erodes their autonomy. This results in a perpetual state of temporality, wherein the governance of their daily lives is not derived from their own volition, but rather from external constraints and uncontrollable bureaucratic forces. This condition can be described as a "state of perpetual limbo." Insecure residency status, protracted asylum processes, and visa uncertainty have been demonstrated to deplete refugees' capacity for future planning, thereby trapping them within a state of uncertainty.

Given that forced migration is, by definition, an externally controlled and coercive life event, the framework provided by Organismic Integration Theory (OIT)—a sub-theory within Self-Determination Theory (SDT)—is critical for understanding post-migration adaptation processes. The development of this theory was driven by the necessity to comprehensively examine the various forms of extrinsic motivation and the contextual factors that either facilitate or impede the internalisation and integration of regulations for these behaviours.

It is very important to recognise that refugees and forced migrants do not voluntarily leave their countries of origin; they are compelled to do so due to external pressures, including violence, persecution, or economic collapse. Initially, this external coercion may result in a state of amotivation (a sense of unwillingness or helplessness) or external regulation (acting solely to survive or comply with the demands of the host country).

However, according to OIT, the psychological adaptation process involves an active progression from these passive, resentful, or externally controlled states towards "integrated regulation" (Ryan & Deci, 2000). The process of internalisation and integration occurs when the refugee actively transforms initially passive external cultural demands and regulations into personally endorsed values. This process enables the refugee to regain a sense of autonomy and volition in the new reality they are constructing.

A critical point to consider is that the internalisation of extrinsic motivations and new values does not occur in a vacuum; this process is fundamentally catalysed by the fulfilment of the need for "relatedness" - that is, a sense of belonging to a group or culture where individuals feel connected and respected. Consequently, the host society plays a pivotal role in this process of adaptation.

When the host society offers institutional respect, social inclusivity, and genuine belonging, it engenders "psychological safety" – the psychological state in which individuals feel secure and able to take risks in the pursuit of their personal and professional goals. This psychological safety is a prerequisite for migrants to adapt to their new environment, develop their skills, and exercise their autonomy. This condition provides the fundamental basis for the reconstruction of competence and autonomy.

Cha (2020) demonstrated that even in highly restrictive and challenging environments such as refugee camps, when students' needs for autonomy and competence are met, they exhibit significantly higher levels of "autonomous academic motivation." This finding demonstrates that institutional and environmental support play a critical role in the reconstruction of individual autonomy. In a similar vein, Kunyu et al. (2021) discovered that the daily challenges confronted by immigrant adolescents during the acculturation process have a detrimental effect on their psychological adaptation. However, when basic psychological needs (autonomy, competence, and relatedness) are met, these detrimental effects can be overcome. The research indicates that, despite external pressures, migrants can develop more autonomous motivation by internalising new values. Furthermore, Richey et al. (2022) examined institutional entrepreneurship programmes that support refugees' capacity for self-determination. The findings indicate that the presence of supportive institutional structures has the potential to liberate refugees from the constraints imposed by purely survival-oriented external regulation. Through such support, refugees can internalize and endorse their obligatory economic activities, transforming them into an integrated professional identity. When the institutions of the host society provide respect, inclusive social networks, and a genuine sense of belonging, they establish the essential interpersonal foundation that allows migrants to feel secure enough to internalise new cultural values and reconstruct their competence and autonomy.

Conversely, when the host society subjects migrants to systemic prejudice, social exclusion, ostracism, and discrimination, it engenders a toxic environment that actively thwarts the need for relatedness. This, in turn, forces individuals to adopt defensive coping strategies and precludes the integration of their new identities. In essence, the presence of an exclusionary environment, propagated by the host society, impedes the process of psychological repair, thereby engendering a defensive cycle of social exclusion among migrants.

Social Exclusion and the Rejection-Identification Mechanism

In circumstances where the discriminatory attitudes exhibited by the host society actively impede the requirement for relatedness, migrants are compelled to identify alternative mechanisms in order to preserve their psychological integrity. Pervasive perceived discrimination and social exclusion emerge as intense post-migration daily stressors, inflicting profound and direct devastation on migrants' mental health (Miller & Rasmussen, 2010). It is evident that experiences characterised by prejudice, which are rooted in exclusion and rejection by the prevailing societal norms, have the potential to compromise the fundamental psychological needs of the individual, including a sense of belonging, self-esteem, and a sense of control. Consequently, this precipitates psychological deterioration by diminishing individuals' self-esteem, sense of control, and feelings of belonging.

However, migrants should not be considered passive recipients of rejection by the host society. In response to the psychological threat posed by discrimination and exclusion, migrants may, paradoxically, strengthen their identification with their own ethnic or minority in-groups. This dynamic is comprehensively addressed in the Rejection-Identification Model (RIM) proposed by Branscombe, Schmitt, and Harvey (1999).

From a traditional standpoint, an individual subjected to exclusion or discrimination might be expected to distance themselves from this stigmatized identity or experience a psychological breakdown. However, the RIM proposes an alternative hypothesis that asserts that members of stigmatised or low-status groups who perceive rejection and discrimination from the dominant society may engage in psychological commitment and identification with their in-group as a protective coping strategy. In situations where the host society exhibits a tendency to reject or devalue individuals based solely on their group membership, these individuals often seek refuge, emotional validation, and collective meaning within their own in-group. This phenomenon can be understood as a response to external hostility. In response to the marginalisation of their group identity, members of the group exhibit a stronger adherence to that identity. In other words, rather than assimilating into or submitting to the out-group that rejects them, individuals generate psychological strength by holding more tightly to their marginalised identities. Recent empirical research supports these social identity dynamics among migrant groups. For instance, studies conducted among Arab American populations demonstrate that perceived discrimination predicts stronger ethnic identification, which in turn influences intergroup attitudes and psychological outcomes (Hakim et al., 2018; Tabbah et al., 2016). Moreover, longitudinal evidence corroborates the temporal dynamics of the model: perceived discrimination at one point in time predicts increased ethnic identification later, which subsequently predicts higher life satisfaction and support for political rights (Stronge et al., 2016). Discrimination from the host society does not necessarily indicate an absolute collapse or definitive end. Conversely, this exclusion instigates a process that engenders a more profound sense of affiliation with one's ethnic origins. This strengthening of ethnic identity is manifest through enhanced life satisfaction and political empowerment, enabling individuals to advocate for their group's rights.

The stronger adherence to one's ethnic identity, driven by the increased ethnic identification triggered by discrimination, is not merely a symbolic reaction or a cognitive labeling (e.g., stating, “I am of nationality Y”). Instead, it is a tangible resource that functions as a psychological buffer against the detrimental effects of exclusion on mental health. The strengthening of ethnic identity has been shown to have a preventative effect on psychological harm, including depression, anxiety and the erosion of self-esteem. This harm would otherwise be precipitated by the exclusion and degradation originating from the host society. The result is a safeguard for the individual's mental health.

In order to provide concrete evidence in support of the dynamic process posited by the Rejection-Identification Model (RIM), the experience of a young migrant who relocates to a host country for the purpose of education or employment, initially possessing a strong motivation to integrate with the local population, serves as an illustrative example. When an individual is subject to persistent marginalisation and exclusion from peer groups on the basis of factors such as accents, physical appearance, or cultural differences, this experience of systematic rejection can lead to the fracturing of their initial desire to adapt. In the absence of assimilation or capitulation to the exclusionary group, the individual develops a protective strategy, a phenomenon that has been predicted by the RIM. It has been demonstrated that migrants tend to congregate with others who speak their native language and share similar experiences of marginalisation. Consequently, they establish a stronger and more prominent identification with their ethnic subculture than was previously the case. This trajectory clearly corroborates the hypothesis that experiences of discrimination do not precipitate a passive psychological collapse in the migrant; conversely, they compel the individual to embrace their ethnic belonging as a psychological buffer, to construct a renewed sense of "we," and to protectively rebuild their social world.

This protective function is rooted in the Social Identity Approach (Tajfel & Turner, 1986) and is further elaborated within the framework of the "Social Cure" (Jetten, Haslam, & Haslam, 2012). The social cure paradigm is predicated on the notion that meaningful group memberships are conducive to the cultivation of critical psychological resources for individuals, comprising a sense of belonging, collective self-esteem, social support, and a shared meaning that entails collaborative endeavours towards specific, common objectives. The fundamental premise of this concept is that human beings exist not merely as isolated individuals, but as integral members of a group. It is further posited that these group memberships exert direct therapeutic effects on the individual. The possession of significant group memberships has been demonstrated to engender elevated levels of resilience and improved health outcomes in individuals. Consequently, groups are considered to possess a definitive "social cure" capacity. In response to discrimination, migrants often strengthen their ethnic identification, gaining access to collective resources that mitigate the psychological damage resulting from exclusion by the host society.

Nevertheless, alongside the healing and protective capacity of ethnic identification, it is crucial to recognise the limitations imposed by contextual realities. This is due to the Social Identity Approach positing that, within specific restrictive contexts, group identifications can act as a "social curse" (Jetten et al., 2017). This concept underscores the notion that group membership does not invariably engender a therapeutic effect; belonging to a stigmatised group can itself transform into a profound source of stress. In the absence of adequate material and symbolic resources for collective action, or if this identification results in further isolation from the host society, the maintenance of ethnic identity can, in fact, exacerbate the adverse effects of discrimination. The systematic, pervasive, and severe devaluation, exclusion, and negative stereotyping of a migrant or minority group by the host society can heighten the individual's susceptibility to prejudice.

Recent research has demonstrated that for high ethnic identification to provide psychological protection, the identity must offer the individual a meaningful sense of belonging and a feeling of "valued distinctiveness." Indeed, within a minority group that is subject to severe devaluation, an individual may experience a heightened sense of internal value within the group, yet concurrently encounter a more acute manifestation of the impact of discriminatory treatment from the broader society (Çelebi, Verkuyten, & Bagci, 2020; Molteni et al., 2024).

Consequently, in such exclusionary environments where intergroup boundaries are highly rigid, strong attachment to a severely stigmatised identity can sometimes exacerbate psychological distress, trapping individuals within a cycle of exclusion. Consequently, the adaptation processes of migrants are significantly influenced by these intricate identity dynamics, thereby underscoring the profound interconnection between migrants' resilience and the social structure of the host environment.

4. RESILIENCE AS RECONSTRUCTION BEYOND RECOVERY: THE TRAJECTORY OF RESILIENCE IN MIGRANT POPULATIONS

The psychological impacts of forced migration and displacement have long been evaluated from a pathology- and deficit-oriented perspective. However, this framing overlooks a crucial distinction regarding how human beings respond to aversive events. Bonanno (2004) proposed a definitive theoretical distinction between two primary trajectories that can emerge following trauma: recovery and resilience. The former recovery refers to a temporal pattern wherein normal psychological functioning temporarily yields to a clinical-level psychopathology, such as Post-Traumatic Stress Disorder (PTSD) or major depressive disorder, before eventually returning to the pre-trauma baseline level of functioning. This process is characterised by a "sustained disruption" across psychological, social, and occupational domains, and typically spans a prolonged period of months or years. Conversely, resilience is defined as the individual's capacity to maintain a relatively stable, healthy level of psychological and physical functioning during and immediately following exposure to highly disruptive experiences. A critical point to consider here is that resilience does not imply an absolute absence of stress or distress. Individuals exhibiting resilience may also experience "transient perturbations" in mood, sleep patterns, or concentration. The fundamental difference between resilience and the recovery process is that these disruptions are not enduring. In other words, resilient individuals do not exhibit the prolonged and clinically significant losses of functioning that define the recovery cycle.

This fundamental distinction challenges the long-standing clinical assumption—institutionalised in traditional trauma models—that all adults exposed to migration-related trauma must experience protracted distress, and that the absence of severe PTSD symptoms must be explained as pathological denial, repressed grief, or absent grief.

Indeed, the classical assumption pathologises the normal human variation in stress responses, essentially treating health as an illness. It is evident that human responses to adversity are diverse and exhibit significant variation. Many individuals possess an innate capacity to maintain their psychological equilibrium and continue with their lives (resilience) in the face of highly disruptive events. Conversely, the conventional clinical viewpoint has neglected to acknowledge "standing firm" and the absence of psychological breakdown post-trauma as a natural and healthy human response. Instead, it has presumed this trajectory to be an anomaly and an indicator of pathology (Bonanno, 2004; Wortman & Silver, 1989).

This perspective has a long history, and it has often resulted in the diagnosis of resilient individuals as psychologically avoidant or repressive. The attribution of the labels "avoidant" or "repressive" is a direct consequence of the failure to recognise resilience as a genuine psychological strength. When a migrant who has experienced severe trauma, or an individual who has suffered a profound loss, does not manifest profound psychological devastation (such as PTSD or depression), but rather continues their life stably and remains capable of experiencing positive emotions, this is indicative of resilience.

However, empirical studies contradict the notion that emotional processing and prolonged grieving are universal prerequisites for healthy adaptation; instead, they demonstrate that many individuals who do not engage in intense "grief work" still achieve positive long-term outcomes. Conventional psychoanalytical approaches posit that engaging in protracted and profound emotional processing is a universal prerequisite for healthy adaptation, mandating that every individual must actively confront their trauma to heal. Conversely, if an individual does not undergo profound psychological distress following a traumatic event and is able to resume their normal life, this is not regarded as authentic recovery. Instead, it is characterised as "denial," "avoidance," or "repression." Adopting this approach, professionals presume that individuals who do not engage in intensive grief work will inevitably experience an outburst of "delayed grief" in the future.

However, longitudinal studies have revealed that these classical expectations lack any scientific foundation. The empirical evidence indicates that there is no universal phenomenon of delayed grief, nor is there any scientific data suggesting that people presumed to have repressed their pain subsequently experience a sudden breakdown. Indeed, even in the face of highly disruptive events, the majority of individuals possess the innate capacity to maintain their lives in a healthy and functional manner (resilience) by experiencing only transient perturbations, without engaging in intensive grief work. When evaluated within this theoretical framework, it can be concluded that it is not an inevitable consequence for refugees subjected to severe trauma and displacement to enter a prolonged clinical process of excavating grief and trauma (recovery). For instance, a longitudinal study by O'Donnell et al. (2022) on refugees resettled in Australia revealed that 60.3% of the participants exhibited a "resilient" trajectory, consistently maintaining low stress levels without experiencing a clinical breakdown or an intensive "recovery" phase.

Studies conducted by Purgato et al. (2022) on refugees in Western Europe, Turkey, and Uganda corroborate this, demonstrating that among individuals following diverse psychological pathways post-trauma and migration, there is no evidence of sudden, delayed breakdowns due to repressed emotions. Conversely, the successful maintenance of persistent and consistent psychological functioning over time – that is, remaining on a resilience trajectory – has been identified as one of the most robustly observed outcomes. The conclusion drawn from these studies, which have been conducted in a variety of geographical locations, is that the capacity for resilience is not an exceptional phenomenon that is contingent solely upon a specific culture, level of prosperity, or the extensive resources provided by a host country. This finding provides scientific substantiation for the observation that, despite the variations in ecological and social conditions, refugees consistently demonstrate a psychological pattern characterised by resilience and fortitude. Contrary to popular and clinical assumptions that resilience is a rare trait unique to exceptional individuals, empirical evidence demonstrates that resilience is the most common human response to trauma and forced displacement. The extant literature has demonstrated that the majority of refugees are able to maintain their psychological functionality without succumbing to clinical deterioration. In other words, psychological robustness (resilience)—rather than breakdown—is the most frequent, natural and prevalent response among migrants facing trauma. The pervasiveness of this response underscores the imperative for a comprehensive re-evaluation of clinical practice, refugee policy, and humanitarian intervention.

Intervention frameworks must shift from a deficit-oriented and pathology-focused model to a strengths-based, resource-enhancing paradigm that recognises and fosters existing adaptive capacities. In other words, intervention approaches must be fundamentally predicated on a transition from a disease-oriented to a strengths-oriented focus. Indeed, if the majority of individuals possess an innate capacity for resilience, the present system—which views every refugee through a deficit-oriented and pathology-focused lens as a "patient" in need of psychiatric treatment—cannot possibly be functional. Consequently, rather than focusing solely on individuals' traumas or deficits, refugee policies and clinical interventions must transition to a model dedicated to enhancing strengths and resources. Such a model must recognise pre-existing coping skills, support these abilities, and provide new psychosocial resources. Recent empirical research further supports this strength-based approach across diverse contexts. Addressing these diverse needs requires culturally responsive interventions; as demonstrated by Tay et al. (2020), integrative and culturally adapted therapeutic approaches have proven empirically effective in reducing psychological distress and fostering adaptation among different ethnic refugee groups, such as the Rohingya, Chin, and Kachin communities in Malaysia.

The concept of resilience within migrant and refugee populations cannot be considered as a monolithic construct that operates uniformly across all individuals. Rather, coping pathways are to be regarded as highly diverse and multifaceted. These pathways must not be considered as mere passive survival strategies; rather, they are active, reconstructive psychological processes that enable individuals to maintain their functionality and derive meaning from adversity. In the context of resilience, the individual does not passively wait for the trauma to subside; rather, they assume an active stance, engaging in a reconstructive process to adapt to new and challenging conditions, restore meaning to their disrupted life, and sustain their functionality.

As demonstrated in the existing literature, three fundamental mechanisms have been identified as active components that facilitate individuals in maintaining their functioning and achieving psychological reconstruction following highly disruptive events. These mechanisms are: hardiness, repressive coping, and the capacity to experience positive emotions. The first of these mechanisms, hardiness, refers to the tendency of the individual to perceive encountered difficulties not as destructive threats, but as surmountable challenges; to believe they possess control over the outcomes of events; and to maintain a strong commitment that infuses their new life with meaning. The second mechanism, repressive coping, involves the tendency to minimise or avoid dwelling on negative emotional experiences. This stands in stark contrast to classical clinical orthodoxy, which mandates the continuous excavation of pain and intensive "grief work" for recovery. Despite its traditional classification as a maladaptive emotional avoidance strategy, empirical evidence demonstrates that this approach is, in fact, a highly healthy and protective coping mechanism that preserves stable functioning and facilitates a future-oriented perspective for many individuals.

In conclusion, the capacity to experience positive emotions is indicative of an individual's ability to feel gratitude, hope, and humour, even in the face of significant challenges and traumas. Despite the fact that it is frequently interpreted from a clinical standpoint as a symptom of pathological "denial", this capacity in fact serves as one of the most potent "active ingredients" that mitigates the destructive effects of negative emotions, nurtures the individual's social bonds, and facilitates psychological reconstruction following displacement.

In order to provide a concrete example of the active reconstructive processes that foster resilience, with a particular focus on cognitive flexibility and the capacity for self-enhancement, the experience of a migrant who possesses a prestigious career in their home country (for example, an award-winning artistic background or high professional status) yet is compelled to engage in unskilled or heavy manual labour in the host country due to unrecognised credentials can be used as a compelling example. From a conventional clinical standpoint, this extent of "status loss" is anticipated to engender profound existential vacuum, clinical depression, and a loss of functionality (the recovery trajectory). However, individuals on the resilience trajectory reframe this status loss through the active reconstruction of meaning rather than accepting it as a passive defeat. For instance, rather than internalising the unskilled labour as a component of their identity, such an individual might appraise it merely as a temporary instrument or a stepping stone toward future objectives (e.g. gathering artistic observations or sustaining their family). The individual's interpretation of their circumstances through such "self-enhancement," despite the presence of objective adversities, does not constitute denial or a pathological defense; on the contrary, it is a highly functional and active reconstructive strategy employed to bear the overwhelming burden of reality, stave off despair, and avert a clinical breakdown by adapting flexibly to the circumstances of a new life.

The Struggle for Recognition: Emotional Support, Rights, and Solidarity in the Migrant Experience

The concept of migrant resilience is understood as a process of "reconstruction" that is influenced by a combination of internal strengths, genetic predispositions, and personal coping skills. These factors are intertwined with the relationships and reciprocal interactions that are forged with the host society, which play a pivotal role in shaping resilience outcomes. In order to comprehend the concept of migrant resilience, it is imperative to consider it not merely as an individual psychological trait, but rather as a socially mediated process of reconstruction. In this regard, an examination of the intersubjective conditions that facilitate identity formation is essential. Axel Honneth's (1995) theory of recognition provides a robust socio-philosophical framework for this analysis. According to the theoretical framework under consideration, the development and maintenance of a healthy identity is not a process that can be realised by an isolated mind alone. The construction of a positive identity is, instead, a process that occurs through the interaction and validation of the individual by other subjects, including but not limited to other individuals, institutions, and the host society.

According to Axel Honneth's model of recognition, intersubjective recognition occurs across three fundamental dimensions required for migrants' reconstruction processes: emotional support (love), legal rights (legal recognition), and social esteem (solidarity) (Honneth, 1995). Each domain corresponds to a specific mode of the individual's relationship to the self. The formation of emotional bonds in early childhood fosters the development of fundamental self-confidence and trust in individuals, thereby laying the foundation for healthy self-esteem and self-respect. It is an irrefutable fact that rights, experienced through legal recognition and equality, are the foundational prerequisites for an individual to construct self-respect as a morally responsible agent possessing the capacity for autonomous participation in society. The legal precariousness or institutional exclusion experienced by migrants can dismantle their intersubjective status, pushing them into a state of invisibility or what has been termed "social death." Finally, solidarity or social esteem – defined as the host society valuing and appreciating the cultural distinctiveness, skills and societal contributions of migrants – fosters a sense of self-esteem within the individual.

For migrants, the process of transitioning from a state of trauma to one of resilience, and the subsequent ability to demonstrate resilience, is contingent upon the extent to which these three domains have been compromised by displacement. This, in turn, is influenced by the host society's capacity to restore them, that is to say, by providing a secure environment, legal rights, and societal value. The experience of forced migration (war, persecution, statelessness) is frequently characterised by severe disruptions across all three spheres of recognition. Displacement is known to have a detrimental effect on individuals, causing them to lose their physical security, legal status and social standing. This can result in a profound experience of disrespect and exclusion across all three domains of recognition.

In the first domain, experiences of trauma stemming from physical violence, torture, and conflict systematically erode the migrant's self-confidence and trust in the world. According to Honneth (1995), the most fundamental requirement for human beings to develop a healthy self is the protection of their bodily integrity and physical boundaries. Once this protection has been established, the individual will develop an unwavering "basic self-confidence" and trust in their own body, their needs, and the world. However, the physical violence inflicted upon refugees as a result of war, rape, or torture is widely considered to represent the most devastating violation of this fundamental sphere of recognition. Such physical abuse has been shown to inflict not only somatic pain but also to leave the individual entirely defenseless against the will of another subject. This, in turn, systematically collapses the foundational trust they harbor towards the world and themselves – their "basic self-confidence".

Within the domain of rights, the denial of legal recognition assumes a secondary form of disrespect, albeit no less detrimental. In contemporary societies, an individual's capacity to cultivate self-respect is contingent upon their legal acknowledgement as a morally responsible, fully functioning agent, endowed with equal rights within the societal framework (Honneth, 1995). However, the host society's policies, which entail the denial of permanent legal status to migrants, the complication of asylum processes, the imposition of a state of "permanent provisionality", or the restriction of access to civic participation, result in the structural exclusion of these individuals, thereby engendering a state of self-respect deprivation. This state of "legal precarity" prevents the migrant from being viewed as an equal partner within the political community and causes the individual to feel disregarded as a moral subject.

It is evident that legal rights alone are insufficient for the psychological integrity of individuals; there is a simultaneous requirement for their unique abilities, lifestyles and cultural identities to be valued by the host society. In other words, there is a need for individuals to acquire "social esteem" and "self-esteem". The third form of disrespect manifests in the domain of solidarity through the cultural denigration of migrant lifestyles.

In the event of the host society's value system denigrating or stigmatising the cultural identity, language or heritage of migrants, there is a systematic destruction of their capacity to acquire social esteem. Consequently, migrants are unable to perceive their own lifestyle and abilities as having a positive impact on the community, which results in a loss of personal self-esteem. In the most severe cases of exclusionary host society policies, this cumulative denial of recognition culminates in social invisibility or "social death." The term "social death," which is also employed in the literature to describe the disenfranchisement of slavery victims (Patterson, 1992), metaphorically illustrates that just as a physical illness threatens the body and life, social degradation and exclusion critically imperil human psychological identity and existence.

This state of social invisibility and non-recognition experienced by migrants frequently resonates with the concept of the "muted self" in the migration psychology literature. A migrant whose skills, cultural identity, and very existence are devalued by the host society (a lack of solidarity) or who is not recognised by the legal system as a legitimate individual possessing equal rights (a lack of rights) not only suffers an external injustice in the new society but also experiences profound damage to their self-worth. In the absence of the requisite social feedback and validation (mirroring) from the external world, the individual experiences a suspension of their emotions and demands, in order to maintain their functionality and avoid the pain of further rejection. This process leads to the individual's isolation within their internal world. This process of social death is accompanied by a silencing of the individual, who experiences a profound psychological alienation, resulting in a loss of their capacity for "agency". This is due to their classification as the "other" of society, a result of misrecognition, or the absence of recognition, which is termed invisibility.

However, it is important to note that migrants should not be viewed as passive recipients of disrespect. Conventional sociology posits that social conflicts are predominantly driven by financial incentives, employment opportunities, or material resources (interests). However, by illuminating the "moral grammar of social conflicts," Honneth's framework posits that the experiences of disrespect and marginalisation encountered by migrants – such as exclusion, legal precarity, or cultural denigration – are not merely material losses, but profound "moral injuries." The feelings of shame, anger and hurt experienced by migrants when subjected to such injustices serve as a moral impetus for them to demand their rights (resistance). Therefore, it is argued that migrant struggles and adaptation strategies – such as language acquisition, securing employment, or adhering to societal rules – should not be interpreted simply as mechanical and functional adjustments to a new environment; rather, they must be understood as active "struggles for recognition" that represent a much deeper psychological battle for existence. To summarise, the demands put forward by migrants for equal rights, their endeavours to maintain their culture, and their opposition to discrimination can be interpreted as a plea to the host society to acknowledge them as equals and valuable human beings.

Consequently, this recognition theory perspective posits that institutional conditions are the primary determinants of migrant resilience. The concept of individual resilience is not a standalone attribute; it cannot be achieved in isolation by relying solely on an individual's internal strength. The concept of resilience in migrants is contingent upon the host society's capacity to furnish the structural prerequisites necessary for the reconstruction of identity. For displaced individuals, the attainment of enduring psychological well-being is predicated on the facilitation of reciprocal recognition by the host environment, thereby transforming social rupture into resilient reconstruction.

5. CONTEXTUAL DETERMINANTS: THE ROLE OF THE HOST SOCIETY

An approach that seeks to comprehend the resilience and psychological adaptation of migrants exclusively through the prism of individual trauma histories or personal coping capacities represents a reductionist lens that disregards the structural and relational essence of the migratory phenomenon. In this framework, attention must be directed towards the surrounding ecological context and the institutional and moral conditions provided by the host society, rather than merely the individual's internal processes. It can be argued that an individual's capacity to reconfigure their psychological functionality within a novel sociocultural context is predominantly contingent upon the attitudes and structural policies of the host society towards migrants.

In accordance with Berry's (1997) acculturation model, the simultaneous endeavours of migrants to preserve their cultural heritage whilst concurrently engaging in the new society are regarded as the "integration" strategy, which is identified as the primary determinant of psychological well-being. However, Berry emphasises that integration is not an individual attitude that a migrant can choose unilaterally; rather, it is fundamentally predicated on an institutional process of "mutual accommodation." The mechanism of mutual accommodation necessitates that both groups acknowledge the right of the other to exist as culturally distinct communities. In this reciprocal equation, while the migrant is expected to adopt the fundamental values of the host society, the true determining factor lies in the structural steps taken by the dominant society. For integration to be fully realised, it is expected that the host society will undergo a transformation of its public institutions, including but not limited to education, healthcare and employment, with a view to meeting the needs of all coexisting groups. The successful realisation of this process is contingent upon the host society's embrace of multiculturalism, the minimisation of negative intergroup attitudes, and the institutionalisation of positive ones. When the host society fails to assume responsibility for facilitating mutual accommodation, and instead implements processes of assimilation or exclusion (marginalisation/separation), the integration strategy is unsuccessful, resulting in individuals encountering psychosocial difficulties.

Although the arduous process experienced by migrants upon contact with a new society is frequently referred to in the literature as "culture shock", this phenomenon cannot be explained merely as an issue of anxiety. The "ABC Model" (Affective, Behavioral, Cognitive) proposed by Ward, Bochner, and Furnham (2001) analyses this process within a broader structural framework. According to this model, culture shock is defined as the emotional distress experienced by migrants when acclimatising to a new environment (Affective), their deficiencies in comprehending the social structures of their new society (Behavioral), and the cognitive dissonance arising from the incongruence between their former cultural values and those of their new society (Cognitive). Consequently, the process of adaptation by migrants cannot be considered as merely the medical treatment of a symptom; rather, it is an active sociocultural learning process that requires the acquisition of social skills within a new cultural context and the holistic reconstruction of one's world of meaning.

The most critical role of the host society in the adaptation process is to officially accept migrants as "legal and equal subjects of rights" at the level of institutional recognition. In the context of Axel Honneth's (1995) Theory of Recognition, the prerequisite for an individual to respect themselves as a moral and responsible agent (self-respect) is the legal and institutional recognition of their equal rights within a society. When host societies condemn migrants to legal precarity or restrict their fundamental rights, they effectively exclude them from being equal and legitimate partners in social interaction. Indeed, the systematic denial of rights and the devaluation of migrants' cultural lifestyles propel migrants into structural invisibility, ultimately relegating them to a state of "social death" – a term also utilised in the literature to describe the condition of enslaved populations (Patterson, 1992). Consequently, the transition from trauma to resilience is contingent upon the adoption of inclusive policies and the establishment of equitable institutions by the host society, thereby ensuring the provision of legal equality and social esteem to migrants.

6. CONCLUSION

For a considerable period, the extant literature on the subjects of forced migration and displacement has been dominated by a clinical framework that focuses on pathology. Within this paradigm, migrants are depicted as passive, helpless, and "traumatised victims" of past war, violence, and persecution. The traditional Direct Effect Model conceptualises psychological distress as a consequence solely of past traumatic events, thereby placing the responsibility for adaptation on deficit-based individual clinical interventions. Nevertheless, the theoretical syntheses and empirical findings discussed in this chapter demonstrate that the primary determinant of migrants' enduring psychological well-being is not the severity of past traumas, but rather the structural, institutional and moral conditions currently provided by the host society.

As Bonanno (2004) also highlights, the most common individual response to trauma is not the "recovery" process, which is characterised by a prolonged clinical breakdown and loss of functioning. Conversely, the predominant tendency among refugees is to adopt an active approach characterised by "resilience" and "reconstruction". This entails the strategic utilisation of cognitive flexibility and individual agency to maintain functionality in the face of highly disruptive events, status losses and challenges in social life. The most significant structural impediment to this process of reconstruction, which fosters resilience among migrants, is not the memories of past wars but rather the "daily stressors" directly encountered in the host society. These stressors constitute the focal point of Miller and Rasmussen's Ecological Model. The aforementioned difficulties, which include legal precarity, poverty, discrimination, and exclusion, act in a manner that hinders the restoration of the psychosocial adaptation pillars defined in Silove's ADAPT model. These pillars were previously defined as being integral to the process of psychosocial adaptation following traumatic experiences. However, the aforementioned difficulties transform trauma into a chronic "social rupture." The restriction of refugee rights, the uncertainties experienced during the migration process, and institutional marginalisation further devastate the 'justice' and 'security' pillars that form the foundation of the ADAPT model. This, in turn, leads to a state of chronic anger, mental preoccupation, and profound moral injury among migrants. It is therefore vital that the host society provides comprehensive rights protection in essential domains, such as the legal and security spheres, thereby alleviating the impact of these daily stressors on refugees' lives if the desired enduring psychological healing is to be achieved.

It is upon this ecological and structural foundation that the most robust strategy for preserving migrants' psychosocial integrity can be adopted: integration. However, as demonstrated in John Berry's (1997) acculturation model, integration does not entail the migrant's submission to unilateral assimilation; rather, it constitutes a process of "mutual accommodation" wherein the host society institutionally supports cultural diversity.

In fact, the ABC model proposed by Ward et al. (2001) also demonstrates that individuals' capacity to overcome culture shock is directly associated with the attitudes of the host society. It is imperative to acknowledge that migrants are capable of surmounting the affective, behavioural and cognitive challenges they encounter, provided that the local population exhibits an openness to interacting with them, thereby serving as an inclusive cultural guide. Should the host society opt to evade this responsibility through the implementation of exclusionary policies, it is unlikely that migrants will succumb to a state of passive breakdown. Instead, as posited by the Rejection-Identification Model (RIM), they will cling to their ethnic identities as a psychological shield, viewing their in-group as a "social cure" mechanism against this structural exclusion. Nevertheless, this resistance strategy can be regarded as a defence mechanism rather than an ideal form of adaptation. As Honneth's (1995) theory asserts, the construction of genuine psychological integrity and self-respect in migrants is contingent upon "recognition" from the host society across three dimensions: love (emotional support), legal rights (legal recognition), and solidarity (social esteem). The rejection of this acknowledgement can result in a state of social exclusion that poses a threat to their psychological well-being.

When viewed through the lens of this integrative theoretical framework, the most critical recommendation for policymakers, institutions, and mental health professionals is to undertake a profound paradigm shift. This necessitates a fundamental transformation in both mentality and systems within current models for understanding, assessing, and intervening in refugee and migrant mental health.

Deficit-based individual clinical interventions that focus exclusively on processing past traumas and label the migrant as a "patient" inherently neglect the structural background of adaptation problems.

The effective implementation of mental health policies necessitates the adoption of "strength-based" and resource-enhancing ecological models. Before or in conjunction with the therapeutic interventions available in psychiatric clinics, these models must prioritise the mitigation of daily stressors that engender legal precarity and status loss among refugees. They must also ensure the provision of institutional rights and the promotion of a multicultural, inclusive accommodation within the host society. The establishment of an inclusive social ecology that provides structural support to migrants' pre-existing resilience has the potential to transform the post-trauma process. Rather than being viewed as a mere "recovery" phase aimed at eliminating pathology, the post-trauma process can be understood as a dynamic process of adaptation and resilience building. Conversely, the trajectory from trauma to resilience metamorphoses into an enduring existential state predicated on mutual recognition and equality.

REFERENCES

Aycan, Z., & Berry, J. W. (1996). Impact of employment-related experiences on immigrants' psychological well-being and adaptation to Canada. *Canadian Journal of Behavioural Science, 28*(3), 240–251. DOI: 10.1037/0008-400X.28.3.240

Berry, J. W. (1997). Immigration, acculturation, and adaptation. *Applied Psychology, 46*(1), 5–34. DOI: 10.1111/j.1464-0597.1997.tb01087.x

Bonanno, G. A. (2004). Loss, trauma, and human resilience: Have we underestimated the human capacity to thrive after extremely aversive events? *The American Psychologist, 59*(1), 20–28. DOI: 10.1037/0003-066X.59.1.20 PMID: 14736317

Branscombe, N. R., Schmitt, M. T., & Harvey, R. D. (1999). Perceiving pervasive discrimination among African Americans: Implications for group identification and well-being. *Journal of Personality and Social Psychology, 77*(1), 135–149. DOI: 10.1037/0022-3514.77.1.135

Çelebi, E., Verkuyten, M., & Bagci, S. C. (2020). Ethnic identification, discrimination, and mental and physical health among Syrian refugees: The moderating role of identity needs. *European Journal of Social Psychology, 51*(1), 105–119. DOI: 10.1002/ejsp.2712

Cha, J. (2020). *Refugee students' academic motivation in displacement: The case of Kakuma Refugee Camp*. Comparative and International Education Society., DOI: 10.33682/pe90-33g2

Dangmann, C., Solberg, Ø., Andersen, P. N., & Høye, S. (2021). Syrian refugee youth resettled in Norway: Mechanisms of resilience influencing health-related quality of life and mental distress. *Frontiers in Public Health, 9*, 711451. Advance online publication. DOI: 10.3389/fpubh.2021.711451 PMID: 34631646

Hakim, S., Molina, L. E., & Branscombe, N. R. (2018). How discrimination shapes social identification processes and well-being among Arab Americans. *Social Psychological & Personality Science, 9*(7), 789–798. DOI: 10.1177/1948550617742192

Jetten, J., Haslam, C., & Haslam, S. A. (Eds.). (2012). *The social cure: Identity, health and well-being*. Psychology Press. DOI: 10.4324/9780203813195

Jetten, J., Haslam, S. A., Cruwys, T., Greenaway, K. H., Haslam, C., & Steffens, N. K. (2017). Advancing the social identity approach to health and well-being: Progressing the social cure research agenda. *European Journal of Social Psychology, 47*(7), 819–835. DOI: 10.1002/ejsp.2333

Kunyu, D., Juang, L. P., Schachner, M. K., Schwarzenthal, M., Pevec, S., & Benbow, A. E. F. (2021). Acculturation hassles and adjustment of adolescents of immigrant descent: Testing mediation with a self-determination theory approach. *New Directions for Child and Adolescent Development*, *2021*(176), 99–118. DOI: 10.1002/cad.20408 PMID: 33817961

LeMaster, J. W., Broadbridge, C. L., Lumley, M. A., Arfken, E. A., Fetters, M. D., Jamil, H., & Pole, N. (2017). Acculturation and post-migration psychological symptoms among Iraqi refugees: A path analysis. *The American Journal of Orthopsychiatry*, *88*(1), 38–47. DOI: 10.1037/ort0000240 PMID: 28253013

Miller, K. E., & Rasmussen, A. (2010). War exposure, daily stressors, and mental health in conflict and post-conflict settings: Bridging the divide between trauma-focused and psychosocial frameworks. *Social Science & Medicine*, *70*(1), 7–16. DOI: 10.1016/j.socscimed.2009.09.029 PMID: 19854552

Molteni, F., Petrillo, A., & Vezzoni, C. (2024). Unpacking the integration paradox: The impact of Muslim religion, destination context, and personal characteristics on perceived discrimination. *SocArXiv*. https://doi.org/DOI: 10.31235/osf.io/6tdvc

O'Donnell, A. W., Stuart, J., & O'Donnell, K. J. (2022). Distinct trajectories of psychological distress among resettled refugees: Community acceptance predicts resilience while low ingroup social support predicts clinical distress. *Transcultural Psychiatry*, *59*(6), 737–752. DOI: 10.1177/13634615221098309 PMID: 35671154

Patterson, O. (1992). *Slavery and social death: A comparative study*. Harvard University Press.

Purgato, M., Carswell, K., Tedeschi, F., Acarturk, C., Anttila, M., Au, T., Bajbouj, M., Baumgartner, J., Biondi, M., Churchill, R., Cuijpers, P., Koesters, M., Gastaldon, C., Ilkkursun, Z., Lantta, T., Nose, M., Ostuzzi, G., Papola, D., Popa, M., & Barbui, C. (2022). Trajectories of psychosocial symptoms and wellbeing in asylum seekers and refugees exposed to traumatic events and resettled in Western Europe, Turkey, and Uganda. *European Journal of Psychotraumatology*, *13*(2), 2128270. Advance online publication. DOI: 10.1080/20008066.2022.2128270 PMID: 36237827

Purgato, M., Gastaldon, C., Papola, D., van Ommeren, M., Barbui, C., & Tol, W. A. (2017). An ecological model for refugee mental health: Implications for research. *Epidemiology and Psychiatric Sciences*, *26*(2), 139–141. DOI: 10.1017/S204579601600069X PMID: 27641739

Rees, S., Silove, D., Chey, T., Ivancic, L., Steel, Z., Creamer, M., Teesson, M., Bryant, R., McFarlane, A. C., Mills, K. L., Slade, T., Carragher, N., O'Donnell, M., & Forbes, D. (2009). Dua sakit (double sick): Trauma and the settlement experiences of West Papuan refugees living in North Queensland. *Australasian Psychiatry, 17*(6), 466–472. DOI: 10.1080/10398560902948399 PMID: 19579126

Richey, M., Ratten, V., & Suseno, Y. (2022). Building self-determination of disadvantaged groups: Insights from an entrepreneurship focused program for refugees. *International Journal of Entrepreneurial Behaviour & Research, 28*(9), 155–178. DOI: 10.1108/IJEBR-10-2021-0806

Ryan, R. M., & Deci, E. L. (2000). Self-determination theory and the facilitation of intrinsic motivation, social development, and well-being. *The American Psychologist, 55*(1), 68–78. DOI: 10.1037/0003-066X.55.1.68 PMID: 11392867

Silove, D. (1999). The psychosocial effects of torture, mass human rights violations, and refugee trauma: Toward an integrated conceptual framework. *The Journal of Nervous and Mental Disease, 187*(4), 200–207. DOI: 10.1097/00005053-199904000-00002 PMID: 10221552

Silove, D. (2013). The ADAPT model: A conceptual framework for mental health and psychosocial programming in post conflict settings. *Intervention (Amstelveen, Netherlands), 11*(3), 237–248. DOI: 10.1097/WTF.0000000000000005

Stronge, S., Sengupta, N. K., Barlow, F. K., Osborne, D., Houkamau, C. A., & Sibley, C. G. (2016). Perceived discrimination predicts increased support for political rights and life satisfaction mediated by ethnic identity: A longitudinal analysis. *Cultural Diversity & Ethnic Minority Psychology, 22*(3), 359–368. DOI: 10.1037/cdp0000074 PMID: 26460667

Tabbah, R., Chung, J. M., & Miranda, A. H. (2016). Ethnic identity and discrimination: An exploration of the rejection-identification model in Arab American adolescents. *Identity, 16*(4), 259–271. DOI: 10.1080/15283488.2016.1231609

Tajfel, H., & Turner, J. C. (1986). The social identity theory of intergroup behavior. In Worchel, S., & Austin, W. G. (Eds.), *Psychology of intergroup relations* (2nd ed., pp. 7–24). Nelson-Hall.

Tay, A. K., Mung, H. K., Miah, M. A. A., Balasundaram, S., Ventevogel, P., Badrudduza, M., Khan, S., Morgan, K., Rees, S., Mohsin, M., & Silove, D. (2020). An Integrative Adapt Therapy for common mental health symptoms and adaptive stress amongst Rohingya, Chin, and Kachin refugees living in Malaysia: A randomized controlled trial. *PLoS Medicine, 17*(3), e1003073. DOI: 10.1371/journal.pmed.1003073 PMID: 32231364

Tay, A. K., Rees, S., Chen, J., Kareth, M., & Silove, D. (2015). The Refugee-Mental Health Assessment Package (R-MHAP): Rationale, development and first-stage testing amongst West Papuan refugees. *International Journal of Mental Health Systems*, *9*(1), 29. Advance online publication. DOI: 10.1186/s13033-015-0018-6

Tay, A. K., Rees, S., Chen, J., Kareth, M., & Silove, D. (2017). The ADAPT model: Bridging the gap between psychosocial and individual responses to mass violence and refugee trauma. *Epidemiology and Psychiatric Sciences*, *26*(2), 129–141. DOI: 10.1017/S2045796016000925 PMID: 27974083

Tay, A. K., Rees, S., Chen, J., Kareth, M., & Silove, D. (2019). Defining a combined constellation of complicated bereavement and PTSD and the psychosocial correlates associated with the pattern amongst refugees from West Papua. *Psychological Medicine*, *49*(6), 993–1005. DOI: 10.1017/S0033291718002027 PMID: 30149819

Ward, C., Bochner, S., & Furnham, A. (2001). *The psychology of culture shock* (2nd ed.). Routledge.

Wortman, C. B., & Silver, R. C. (1989). The myths of coping with loss. *Journal of Consulting and Clinical Psychology*, *57*(3), 349–357. DOI: 10.1037/0022-006X.57.3.349 PMID: 2661609

KEY TERMS AND DEFINITIONS

Cognitive Flexibility: The ability of an individual to psychologically adapt to current conditions by reframing the objective difficulties and sudden status losses they encounter not as a passive defeat, but rather as a temporary instrument or a stepping stone toward future objectives.

Daily Stressors: The ongoing environmental and structural barriers—such as legal precarity, poverty, housing difficulties, unemployment, and exclusion encountered by migrants in the host society—that directly impede psychological adaptation by perpetuating the destructive effects of past war traumas.

Intersubjective Recognition: The state wherein an individual is recognised as a moral and responsible agent by other subjects and institutions within the host society across the axes of emotional support (love), legal equality (rights), and social esteem (solidarity), which is the fundamental prerequisite for developing a healthy identity and self-respect.

Mutual Accommodation: A reciprocal interaction process requiring not only that migrants adapt to the new society for successful integration to occur, but also that the host society transform its institutions, policies, and attitudes to encompass and structurally support cultural diversity.

Rejection-Identification Model: The process by which migrants who are excluded, stigmatised, or subjected to discrimination strengthen their ties and identification with their own ethnic in-groups is employed as a protective strategy to cope with the psychological devastation engendered by this rejection and to preserve their self-esteem.

Resilience: The capacity of an individual to actively maintain a healthy level of functioning and psychological equilibrium without experiencing a prolonged clinical breakdown, despite exposure to highly disruptive events, losses, and traumatic experiences.

Social Death: The condition in which migrants are deprived of legal rights, such as asylum or employment, and whose cultural lifestyles are devalued by the host society. This results in migrants being stripped of their status as equal partners in the community and propelled into civic and psychological invisibility.

Social Rupture: The destruction of the fundamental psychosocial pillars that sustain an individual's security, interpersonal bonds, sense of justice, identity, and existential meaning due to the impacts of migration and violence is a concept that is of particular interest in this study. This conceptualisation of trauma is not merely as a medical and individual pathology (PTSD) confined within the mind, but as a systemic collapse.

Chapter 7
Silent Negotiation in Migration and Integration:
A Conceptual Lens on Everyday Practises of Belonging and Distance

Metin Aksoy
http://orcid.org/0000-0002-3118-6739
Gumushane University, Turkey

ABSTRACT

This chapter reconsiders migration, identity, and integration through the silent and tacit interactions of everyday life. While migration studies often focus on legal status, institutional participation, explicit identity claims, and visible conflicts, less attention is given to how relations between migrants and host societies are shaped through silence, caution, avoidance, observation, withdrawal, and the regulation of visibility. The chapter treats silence not as passivity or a lack of communication, but as a relational practice that produces meaning, orders relationships, and manages social distance. Drawing on approaches to everyday life, practice, tacit knowledge, and low-visibility action, silent negotiation is used not as a closed theoretical model, but as an analytical framework for understanding migrants' everyday practices of adaptation, belonging, and distance-keeping. Integration is therefore understood as a relational process shaped by fragile balances, tacit acceptances, and silent adjustments in everyday encounters.

DOI: 10.4018/979-8-3373-8500-6.ch007

INTRODUCTION

Migration, identity, and integration are among the most intensively debated topics in the literatures of modern sociology, political science, and international relations. The increase in human mobility on a global scale transforms not only states' border policies, citizenship regimes, and legal arrangements, but also reshapes the everyday relations that migrants build with host societies. Migration studies have therefore long produced a comprehensive body of knowledge on adaptation policies, identity construction, cultural encounters, citizenship statuses, and forms of social acceptance and exclusion. A substantial part of this accumulated knowledge, however, prioritizes processes that are analytically more visible and more readily detectable. Explicit demands, articulated conflicts, formal citizenship processes, institutional forms of belonging, policy arrangements, and public discourses stand at the center of these studies (Castles et al., 2013). The importance of these visible domains cannot be denied. Indicators such as legal status, work permits, citizenship, education, access to health services, and political participation are indispensable for understanding migrants' social positions. Yet the relations that migrants establish with host societies cannot be explained through these formal indicators alone. The experience of living together is often shaped within the ordinary encounters of everyday life, beyond institutions, laws, and explicit discourses. A continuous process of mutual adjustment operates between migrants and members of the host society in neighborly relations, at the workplace, at school, on the street, in the marketplace, on public transport, in contacts with official institutions, and across the various planes of the public sphere. This process does not always emerge in the form of open dialogue, visible demands, or direct conflict. On the contrary, it frequently proceeds through silence, caution, avoidance, observation, withdrawal, the regulation of visibility, and indirect forms of interaction. Understanding migration and integration processes therefore requires focusing not only on explicitly articulated demands and visible institutional processes, but also on the more tacit and silent domains of interaction in everyday life.

The point of departure for this study is precisely these low-visibility domains of interaction. In migration studies, the question of which silent and tacit practices manage living together, belonging, distance, and adaptation in everyday life often remains a secondary concern. Yet silence cannot be regarded merely as the absence of speech in social interaction. Silence is a social practice that produces meaning, orders relationships, renders power relations visible or invisible, and allows actors to position themselves (Jaworski, 1992; Zerubavel, 2006). In the context of migration, silence must therefore be treated not as deficiency, passivity, or communicative failure, but as one of the constitutive elements of everyday social order. This chapter discusses how the processes of migration, identity, and integration are frequently shaped in everyday life through silences, avoidances, tacit acceptances, and implicit adjustments.

Aksoy and Cengiz (2025) approach migration not merely as a spatial displacement but as a complex sociocultural process in which identity and belonging are called into question anew. For these authors, the migrant is positioned within a dynamic field of interaction between their own cultural heritage and the cultural codes of the host society. In this process, integration is a reciprocal and dynamic rather than one-directional process that encompasses the migrant's participation in social, economic, cultural, and political life. This approach reinforces the need to evaluate integration not solely through institutional participation or legal status, but through the practices of belonging, distance, and relationship management established in everyday life.

Here silence is understood not merely as a state of not speaking, but as a relational practice that serves to manage boundaries, expectations, risks, and forms of belonging in social relations. The processes through which migrants become part of a new social context do not always proceed through open, rational, and mutually defined dialogues. Particularly in contexts marked by unequal power relations, normative uncertainty, legal precarity, and the riskiness of open speech, individuals manage social boundaries and mutual expectations through more tacit means (Goffman, 1969; Pugh, 2018). At this point, the phrase silent negotiation is used in this chapter not as a closed and completed theoretical model, but as an analytical framework that serves to make visible the tacit dimensions of everyday interactions. This framework aims to understand how individuals and groups manage their identities, belongings, and social distances through avoidance, postponement, caution in speech, the regulation of visibility, and indirect forms of interaction rather than through open conflict or direct confrontation. From this vantage point, integration must be conceived not merely as a process of participation in the state or official institutions, but as a relational process shaped through the tacit compromises, fragile balances, and continually readjusted social distances established in everyday life.

The aim of this chapter is to reveal the analytical value of silent and tacit interactions by rereading the existing theoretical and empirical accumulation in the migration and integration literature. Rather than claiming to construct a new and closed theory, the chapter develops an interpretive perspective that connects existing studies to one another. Throughout the study, themes such as psychological adaptation, legal identity, infrastructure-based integration, gendered vulnerabilities, and media representations are reassessed along the axis of everyday interactions and silent adjustments. What these themes share is that the mutual expectations between migrants and the host society are frequently shaped without being explicitly articulated, within the small, ordinary, and repeated practices of everyday life. Within this framework, the chapter argues that migration and integration studies must take seriously, in analytical terms, not only what is visible but also what is left unsaid, what is postponed, what is implied, and what is silently arranged.

BACKGROUND

Migration studies were long shaped around state-centered and macro-level analyses. Border regimes, migration policies, citizenship systems, asylum procedures, labor markets, and international migration flows constituted the principal research fields of this literature. This approach made important contributions to understanding migrants' structural positions, legal statuses, and relations with the state. Nevertheless, macro-level analyses often fail to render sufficiently visible the uncertainties migrants face in everyday life, their small-scale interactions, and their tacit forms of relationship. A similar limitation can be observed in the integration literature. Integration is most often addressed through measurable indicators such as language learning, participation in the education system, inclusion in the labor market, housing acquisition, citizenship applications, and access to social services (Ager & Strang, 2008). The importance of these indicators cannot be denied. Yet confining integration to these domains alone can push into the background the more nuanced processes of how migrants are accepted in everyday life, under what conditions they are excluded, in which situations they withdraw, and in which domains they limit their visibility.

A migrant's legally possessing certain rights does not mean that they can exercise those rights safely and comfortably in everyday life. Likewise, language learning or labor-force participation cannot be regarded as sufficient indicators that social acceptance has been completed. Identity studies, for their part, most often concentrate on representation, discourse, recognition, and identity claims. This literature provides an important theoretical ground for understanding how identities are expressed, how they become politicized, and within which forms of representation they are constructed. Yet identity does not always emerge as an explicitly articulated demand or a visible declaration of belonging. Migrants often render certain aspects of their identities visible while keeping others in the background. Language, accent, dress, religious practices, dietary habits, forms of public conduct, and social relationship networks are important parts of these adjustments of visibility. Identity must therefore be evaluated not only as an expressed form of belonging, but also as a relational position that is at times concealed, postponed, silently preserved, or rearranged according to context.

At this point the analytical importance of everyday life becomes evident. Everyday life is not a domain in which migrants act merely as a consequence of their structural positions. It is also a ground on which they interpret these positions, test boundaries, calculate risks, and reconstruct their own spaces of movement through small practices. Understanding migration and integration processes therefore requires more than focusing on state policies, official institutions, or explicit discourses. Practices such as remaining silent, withdrawing, postponing speech, becoming invisible, avoiding attention, and behaving cautiously in particular situations must also be included in the analysis. This approach distances itself from interpretations that position migrants as passive actors. Silence is treated here not as passive acquiescence, but as a pragmatic form of relationship management that actors develop within existing power relations. Particularly in contexts where legal status is uncertain, economic precarity is intense, and the risk of social exclusion is high, speaking openly, demanding rights, or being visible may not always be a safe option. In such situations, silence becomes part of the individual's strategy of self-protection, sustaining social relations, and reducing risks. Silence thus acquires meaning not merely as the absence of communication, but as a relational practice that serves to manage uncertainties, adjust social distances, and render fragile relations sustainable within everyday life.

MAIN FOCUS OF THE CHAPTER

Silence, Practice, and Everyday Life: A Theoretical Framework

Treating silence as a social practice is closely related to micro-sociological approaches, theories of practice, and the sociology of everyday life. Traditional approaches to communication often place speech, expression, and open action at the center. From a sociological standpoint, however, silence cannot be evaluated merely as the absence of speech. Silence is a form of action that acquires meaning according to context, is interpreted relationally, and plays a role in the production of social order (Jaworski, 1992; Zerubavel, 2006). In some situations it may signify consent, in others objection, and in still others fear, caution, or distance. The meaning of silence therefore emerges within the power relations, normative expectations, and interactional context that surround it. The work of Goffman (1959, 1969) on the presentation of self and strategic interaction in everyday life offers a strong theoretical ground for this discussion. According to Goffman, individuals regulate social relations not only through what they say, but also through what they conceal, which impressions they manage, and which information they withhold. For migrants, this stage management frequently involves a continuous assessment of the contexts in which differences will be rendered visible, the contexts in which they will be withdrawn, and the situations in which remaining silent will be more appropriate. In this respect, the migrant experience is not only a process of becoming part of a new society, but also a process of rearranging the self and identity before different audiences. Theories of practice likewise offer an important theoretical contribution to understanding silence and tacit interactions. These approaches emphasize that social order is produced not only through explicit norms and institutional rules, but also through repeated everyday practices, habits, bodily dispositions, and tacit knowledge (Bourdieu, 1990; Schatzki et al., 2001). Within this framework, migrants' adaptation to a new society is not confined to attending language courses, learning legal procedures, or establishing relations with official institutions. Adaptation also involves learning tacit rules such as when to speak, how to address others, which conduct is deemed appropriate, how to move within a given space, and to what extent particular differences will be rendered visible. This tacit learning process frequently takes place through silent observation, imitation, trial and error, and experience. A glance, a silence, a distant reply, a bureaucratic redirection, coldness in a neighborly relation, or an excluding implication at the workplace may carry important information for the migrant about what is acceptable and what is risky.

The approach to tacit knowledge developed by Polanyi (2009) offers a complementary theoretical ground for understanding migrants' everyday practices of adaptation and relationship management. According to Polanyi, individuals often know more than they can explicitly articulate. This knowledge is acquired within experience, intuition, bodily habit, observation, and practice rather than through formal rules or explicit instruction. Migrants' learning of when to speak in a new social context, which conduct will be deemed appropriate, which identity markers to render visible, or in which situations to withdraw also occurs largely through such tacit-knowledge processes. Silent negotiation is therefore related not only to communicative reticence, but also to a practical way of knowing that is acquired within everyday life and often operates without being put into words.

The approach of de Certeau (1984) to the practices of everyday life likewise makes an important contribution to this discussion. De Certeau argues that ordinary actors do not always develop open forms of resistance against powerful structures, but frequently create everyday and tactical spaces of movement. These tactics may carry no visible political claim, yet they can provide individuals with the possibility of opening up space for themselves within the existing order. For migrants, this may take the form of avoiding certain places, using public space at particular hours, keeping some relations limited, not rendering certain differences visible, or creating alternative domains of belonging within their own safe social networks. The concepts of infrapolitics and hidden resistance advanced by Scott (1990) point to a similar issue. In contexts where power relations are asymmetrical, open resistance is often neither possible nor safe. Powerless actors therefore develop more tacit, indirect, and low-visibility practices in everyday life. For migrants, silence in this sense is not merely acquiescence; in some situations it functions as a form of self-protection, avoidance of open conflict, and the creation of an alternative space of movement. Interpreting silence simply as passivity therefore leads to a deficient reading of migrants' everyday strategies and of the forms of relationship management they develop within limited possibilities. Silence is not a void lying outside social order, but one of the domains in which this order is produced, sustained, and readjusted.

Tacit Interactions, Power Relations, and Normative Uncertainty

Understanding migrants' everyday interactions requires evaluating power relations and normative uncertainties together. In terms of legal status, economic resources, language competence, cultural capital, and level of social acceptance, migrants are frequently in a more precarious position than members of the host society. This precarity can limit their capacities to communicate openly, demand rights, or object. Being visible can generate new risks for the individual, particularly in situations such as temporary protection, asylum-seeking, irregular migration, or uncertain residence status (De Genova, 2002; Menjívar, 2006). At this point a direct relationship emerges between legal uncertainty and everyday interaction. Where legal status is precarious, the individual may be compelled to behave more cautiously not only before state institutions, but also before employers, landlords, neighbors, school administrations, health personnel, and local bureaucracy. There is not always a direct transition between holding a right and being able to exercise that right safely in everyday life. Even when applying for a service to which they are legally entitled, a migrant may factor in the possibility of stigmatization, exclusion, mistreatment, or bureaucratic trouble. This calculation frequently becomes visible in the form of silence, withdrawal, or a turn toward informal networks.

Normative uncertainty is another important factor that deepens this process. Migrants cannot always know in advance, in the social context they have newly entered, which conduct is acceptable and which will provoke a reaction. Which topics may be spoken of, which demands will be deemed appropriate, which identity markers will be welcomed, or in which situations visibility will carry risk is often learned through everyday experience. The uncertainty reduction approach of Berger and Calabrese (1975) emphasizes that in the initial stages of social relations, actors develop various strategies to understand the expectations of the other party. In the context of migration, this uncertainty acquires a more structural and more enduring character, because the migrant is confronted not only with individual persons but also with different institutions, social groups, and normative orders. The approach of Luhmann (1995) to uncertainty and expectation structures in social systems is likewise functional for this discussion. Social order is founded on actors being able to predict, to a certain degree, one another's mutual expectations. For migrants, however, these expectations are frequently neither clear nor predictable. Migrants therefore frequently turn toward forms of conduct that reduce risk. In this context, silence functions not merely as avoidance of communication, but as an everyday security strategy developed in the face of uncertain expectations.

The understanding of power advanced by Foucault (1980) also allows silence to be understood not as an individual preference alone, but as a position produced within power relations. Power operates not only through repression, but through norms, discourses, institutions, and everyday practices. Even when they are not directly prohibited, migrants are frequently constrained by particular normative expectations. Expectations such as not causing trouble, appearing compliant, not being overly demanding, and reducing visible differences are felt in everyday relations even when they are not explicitly articulated. In the face of these expectations, remaining silent becomes, in some situations, the price of sustaining social acceptance. Silent negotiation can therefore be evaluated as an everyday form of relationship management that emerges at the intersection of unequal power relations and normative uncertainties. The balance between silence and visibility is not established in the same way in every context; a migrant group's legal status, class position, language skills, gender, religious belonging, visible differences, and the social structure of the city in which they settle shape this balance in different ways.

Everyday Practices of Belonging and Distance

In migration studies, belonging is frequently addressed together with the processes of identity, citizenship, settlement, and social acceptance. Belonging, however, is not limited to the individual's feeling of belonging to a place or community. It is also related to processes of being accepted, recognized, and regarded as legitimate by others. As Yuval-Davis (2006) emphasizes, belonging is a multilayered phenomenon interwoven with emotional, political, and social boundaries. For migrants, belonging does not mean merely living in a new social context. It is also shaped together with everyday questions such as to what extent one will be visible, which differences will be preserved, which norms will be complied with, and which distances will be maintained. In everyday life, belonging and distance are frequently established through silent practices. A migrant's avoidance of speaking their mother tongue in public space, their attempt to conceal their accent, their adjustment of dress to the surrounding environment, their keeping away from certain places, or their more cautious conduct in some social relations all demonstrate the everyday balance between belonging and distance. These practices are not always the result of open pressure. At times they arise from the individual's previous experiences, observations, and sensed social expectations. In every case, however, these practices serve to silently regulate the migrant's position in the social domain.

The study by Papatzani (2021) of migrants' settlement practices in the urban space of Athens is important for showing how migrants act tactically in everyday life in the face of racist practices and excluding encounters. Migrants may code certain streets, institutions, or public spaces as safer or riskier. This coding is not always explicitly articulated; instead, it manifests itself in choices of route, in neighborhood preferences, and in strategies of public visibility. The city thus ceases to be merely a physical space for migrants and turns into a social map that is continually read and negotiated in silence. The everyday practices of belonging emerge not only in public space, but also in domestic and community domains. Within the home, migrants can preserve their own belonging through food, language, religious rituals, family relations, and cultural habits. The study by Sandu (2013) of transnational home-making practices reveals migrants' efforts to create safe, familiar, and meaningful spaces of their own in the new country. In this respect, the home is not merely a place of shelter; it is also a domain in which cultural continuity and emotional security are established against the uncertainties of the outside world. The study by Plöger and Kubiak (2019) of high-skilled migrants likewise shows that belonging is not an issue confined to disadvantaged migrant groups. While positioning themselves as internationals, high-skilled migrants manage the distance between themselves and the local society through different practices. This shows that the management of belonging and distance cannot be explained solely through legal precarity or economic deprivation. Class position, educational level, professional identity, and spatial settlement are also among the important determinants of this process. Migrants are neither fully assimilated nor fully excluded actors; they develop strategies of visibility, adaptation, distance, and protection at different levels in different contexts.

The Everyday and Relational Dimension of Integration

The concept of integration continues to be one of the most contested concepts in migration studies. Traditional approaches most often define integration through migrants' learning of the host society's language, participation in the labor market, inclusion in the education system, fulfillment of legal obligations, and compliance with social norms. This approach is important in that it allows integration to be evaluated through measurable indicators. At the same time, it carries the risk of construing integration as a one-directional, normative process of adaptation frequently expected of migrants. The perspective of everyday practices proposed in this chapter makes it possible to think of integration as a more relational, dynamic, and context-sensitive process. From this vantage point, integration does not mean merely migrants' adaptation to the institutions of the host society. It is also a reciprocal process in which members of the host society rearrange their ways of living together with migrants, their expectations, and their social boundaries. This mutual arrangement does not always take place under equal conditions. Migrants are frequently confronted with a greater burden of adapting, withdrawing, and behaving more cautiously. Even so, integration must be evaluated as a two-directional and relational process in which mutual expectations, boundaries, and distances are reestablished within everyday interactions.

The integration framework of Ager and Strang (2008) emphasizes the importance not only of structural domains such as employment, housing, education, and health, but also of dimensions such as social bonds, social bridges, language, cultural knowledge, safety, and rights. This framework offers a valuable contribution to understanding the multidimensional nature of integration. Yet the silent and tacit dimensions of everyday interactions require further deepening within such models, because a migrant's finding work, enrolling at a school, or accessing health services does not eliminate the questions of how they are received in these domains, which tacit expectations they encounter, and in which situations they feel compelled to remain silent. A migrant child's remaining silent at school, a mother's hesitation to speak at a parent-teacher meeting, an employee's not objecting when treated unjustly at the workplace, a family's keeping a distant relationship with neighbors, or a young person's avoidance of speaking their mother tongue in public space all point to the frequently invisible dimensions of integration. These practices cannot be read, on their own, as the success or failure of integration; they should rather be evaluated as everyday signs that show how migrants interpret the normative, institutional, and social context in which they find themselves. This perspective treats integration not as a point of arrival, but as a continuous process of relationship management that is reproduced within everyday life, negotiated, and reacquires meaning in different contexts. In this process, silence can at times become the medium of adaptation, at times of protection, at times of distance-keeping, and at times of invisible resistance.

Psychological Adaptation, Coping, and Silent Burdens

The processes through which migrants become part of a new society must be addressed not only in their legal, economic, and institutional dimensions, but also in their psychological effects. Displacement, linguistic loss, cultural unfamiliarity, loss of status, separation from family, the expectation of an uncertain future, and experiences of exclusion can produce deep effects on migrants' inner worlds. The work of Berry (1997) on acculturation and adaptation shows that migrants develop different strategies in their relations with the new society and that these strategies are decisive for psychological adaptation. Explaining psychological adaptation solely through individual coping capacity is nevertheless insufficient. Migrants' psychological experiences are also shaped by the social conditions in which they find themselves, by power relations, by forms of acceptance and exclusion, and by the quality of everyday interactions. In this context, silence can be evaluated as one of the important but frequently invisible dimensions of psychological adaptation. Migrants' practices of remaining silent, withdrawing, or avoiding conflict may be interpreted from the outside as indicators of adaptation, calmness, or the absence of problems. Yet this appearance leads, in some situations, to the invisibilization of psychological burdens. When a migrant subjected to discrimination, exclusion, or injustice does not react openly, this silence does not always mean acquiescence. On the contrary, it may be related to the suppression of inner stress, anxiety, anger, resentment, or a sense of helplessness.

Migrants may also, in some situations, prefer silence in order to preserve their own psychological integrity. Entering open conflict, constantly voicing a negative experience, or reacting to every excluding behavior can be both exhausting and risky for the individual. In such cases, silence can function in the short term as a psychological defense and self-protection strategy. In the long term, however, these silent burdens can deepen feelings of loneliness, alienation, mistrust, and social distance. Silence therefore functions, on the one hand, as a protective practice that enables the individual to sustain everyday life, while on the other hand producing invisible psychological costs. From the outside, a migrant may appear adapted, calm, or untroubled, yet behind this appearance there may lie a continuous risk assessment, emotional control, and relationship management. This constant inner accounting regarding when to speak, what to voice, in which situation to withdraw, and which experience not to share is one of the invisible psychological labors of migrancy. Attention must therefore be paid not only to explicitly articulated traumas, visible conflicts, or voiced grievances, but also to the emotional burdens carried in silence and to everyday coping strategies.

Legal Identity, Infrastructure-Based Integration, and Everyday Access

Legal identity forms the basis of the relationship that migrants establish with the state, with institutions, and with rights regimes. Categories such as citizenship, residence permit, work permit, temporary protection status, international protection application, or irregular status determine individuals' rights, obligations, and spaces of movement. Legal status, however, does not automatically secure integration in everyday life. The determining effect of legal status on everyday life becomes even more visible in the case of persons displaced by climate change. Cengiz et al. (2025) emphasize that the refugee definition of the 1951 Geneva Convention provides an internationally binding framework, but that persons forcibly displaced due to climate change are not explicitly included within this definition. According to the authors, processes such as drought, natural disasters, sea-level rise, and the depletion of water and food resources linked to climate change place millions of people at risk of displacement; yet the non-recognition of these persons as refugees creates a significant gap in legal protection. This shows that legal status is not merely a technical matter of classification, but also an element that directly shapes migrants' everyday experiences of security, access to services, visibility, and vulnerability.

Rights recognized on paper can become limited in practice due to bureaucratic obstacles, lack of information, language problems, discriminatory attitudes, or social stigmatization. A direct and untroubled relationship therefore cannot always be established between legal recognition and de facto access. At this point, infrastructure-based domains of integration acquire importance. Education, health, housing, transport, social assistance, municipal services, and local support mechanisms are fundamental domains that directly affect migrants' everyday lives. Yet access to these domains is not merely a matter of legal eligibility. How migrants are received in their relations with institutions, in which language they can communicate, which documents they must submit, how they interpret bureaucratic processes, and what kinds of risks they feel when applying are all decisive. When applying for a social assistance to which they are legally entitled, a migrant may experience the anxiety of being stigmatized as a burdensome foreigner. When enrolling their child at school, a family may fear being misunderstood due to insufficient language skills. When applying to a health institution, a patient may worry about having their status questioned, being mistreated, or encountering an excluding attitude. In such situations, silence cannot be evaluated merely as ignorance, indifference, or unfamiliarity with institutional processes; it is related rather to the precarity, uncertainty, and perception of risk produced by institutional encounters.

In this context, informal networks play an important role. When official channels are uncertain, complex, or difficult to access, migrants can seek information and support through kinship, fellow-townsman ties, religious communities, migrant associations, acquaintances, and relations of trust. These networks frequently function as domains of silent knowledge transfer. Information such as how to approach which institution, which official is helpful, which documents are required, which application might be risky, or by which route a given service can be reached circulates through the sharing of everyday experiences rather than through official guides. This shows that integration is not shaped solely through state institutions and official service mechanisms; it is also established through the silent knowledge networks, experience-based guidance, and informal relations of solidarity that migrants develop among themselves. Legal identity and infrastructure-based integration must therefore be analyzed not only through formal rights and indicators of institutional access, but also through how these rights are used in everyday life, in which situations they are postponed, and by which silent strategies they are supported.

Gendered Vulnerabilities and Silent Labor

The migration experience differs according to variables such as gender, age, position within the family, and sexual identity. Women, men, children, the elderly, and individuals of different sexual identities do not experience the migration process in the same way. The gender dimension of migration and integration processes must therefore be addressed not merely as an additional heading of analysis, but as a fundamental element that directly shapes the organization of everyday life. Migrant women frequently encounter multilayered disadvantages arising from being both a migrant and a woman (Hondagneu-Sotelo, 2003). Limited access to language-learning opportunities, the obstacles faced in labor-market participation, domestic care obligations, intra-family power relations, and safety concerns in public space differentiate women's integration experiences from those of men and other migrant groups. In this context, women's silence frequently carries a more intense, more multilayered, and harder-to-detect character. Migrant women may be less visible in public space, yet this invisibility does not mean that they are ineffective in integration processes. On the contrary, many domains such as sustaining the domestic order, children's adaptation to school, the follow-up of health services, the building of neighborly relations, the continuation of cultural transmission, and the bearing of emotional labor are carried out through women's frequently invisible labor.

Field studies conducted in the Turkish context likewise show that the everyday life experiences of migrant women differ along gendered lines. The study by Buz et al. (2021) on the profile and needs of Afghan asylum-seekers living in Trabzon reveals that Afghan asylum-seekers face multilayered difficulties in the domains of housing, employment, education, health, social assistance, and social cohesion, and that they largely sustain their everyday lives within these constraints. Within this general ground of vulnerability, the qualitative study conducted by Canlı and Buz (2024) with women migrants of Afghan nationality living in Trabzon shows that being a woman in the migration process markedly differentiates the difficulties encountered. The study finds that Afghan women experience specific vulnerabilities in their pre-migration, migration, and post-migration experiences with respect to patriarchal assumptions, mobility restrictions, the risk of violence, access to social rights, and relations established with the local society. At the same time, the study shows how gender assumptions and practices are reconstructed after migration, and how women of Afghan nationality establish differences with local women in terms of social rights and freedoms while establishing similarities in terms of religious elements, which relates directly to the practices of silent belonging, distance, and everyday adaptation discussed in this chapter.

This silent labor performs a decisive function in enabling migrant households and communities to survive in everyday life. Migrant women preserve cultural continuity within the home while at the same time managing their children's processes of adaptation to the new society. They are confronted, on the one hand, with the expectation of sustaining traditional norms within the family, and on the other hand, with the host society's expectations regarding education, language, conduct, and public visibility. This dual pressure requires women to strike a continuous balance in everyday life. This balance is frequently not discussed openly, but rather carried out silently within food practices, language use, child-rearing patterns, neighborly relations, forms of appearance in public space, and intra-family decision processes. Gendered silence should not be read merely as women's withdrawal or exclusion from public space. In some situations, women can influence intra-family decisions through silent, indirect, and low-visibility means, be decisive in their children's educational processes, build support networks through neighborly relations, and rearrange the boundaries of cultural transmission. Women's silence must therefore be evaluated not only through vulnerability and subordination, but also through everyday agency, relationship management, and the capacity to produce tacit influence.

Media Representations, Stereotypes, and Silencing

The media is one of the most influential public domains that shape how migrants are perceived by the host society. Within news language, visual representations, political discourses, and social media debates, migrants are frequently represented as a threat, a burden, a victim, a criminal, or an element of crisis. These representations not only shape public perception, but also affect how migrants are received in everyday life, which attitudes they confront, and within which social expectations they are positioned. The study by Olier and Spadavecchia (2022) of the visual representation of migrants in different countries shows that media images can produce stereotypes, disproportions, and power asymmetries. Media representations shape not only the host society's view of migrants, but also migrants' own strategies of visibility. Migrants who are continually associated with negative images may tend to attract less attention in everyday life, behave more cautiously in public space, limit their identity markers, or keep away from certain debates. In this respect, the intense and frequently noisy discourse produced by the media can lead migrants to withdraw their own voices further.

A paradoxical relationship thus emerges between media visibility and everyday silence. Migrants are continually rendered visible in public discourse, yet are frequently deprived of the opportunity to speak on their own behalf and to represent their own experiences. This paradox shows that the silent-negotiation perspective can also contribute to media studies. Migrants are not merely represented objects, but actors who develop everyday strategies in the face of these representations. Some migrants may try to appear more compliant in order to keep away from negative stereotypes. Some may deliberately keep away from media debates. Some may produce alternative narratives within their own community networks. Others may prefer silence because they regard public visibility as risky. These strategies show that media representations are effective not only at the discursive level, but also within the everyday practices of building relationships, being visible, withdrawing, and self-protection. It is therefore insufficient to examine media representations solely through how migrants are depicted; how these representations affect migrants' everyday behaviors, choices of visibility, searches for belonging, and strategies of silence must also be analyzed.

SOLUTIONS AND RECOMMENDATIONS

The silent-negotiation perspective carries several implications for policy and practice in the fields of migration and integration. First, integration policies should not be assessed solely through measurable structural indicators such as employment, language acquisition, or legal status. Because a migrant's formal access to schools, the labor market, health services, or social assistance mechanisms does not eliminate the questions of how they are received in these domains, which tacit expectations they confront, and in which situations they feel compelled to remain silent, institutions should attend to the quality of everyday encounters as much as to the existence of formal rights. Reducing the stigmatization, discriminatory attitudes, and perceptions of risk produced within institutional encounters is at least as important for effective integration as the expansion of formal entitlements.

Second, the silent labor carried out by migrant women within the home and the community should be rendered visible and supported rather than overlooked. Policies that recognize women's roles in cultural transmission, children's schooling, and the building of neighborly support networks, and that expand their access to language-learning and labor-market opportunities, would strengthen integration processes that currently depend heavily on invisible labor. Third, informal networks of trust and experience-based knowledge transfer among migrants should be acknowledged as complementary to official service mechanisms. Local institutions and civil-society organizations could work with these networks rather than around them, using them as channels for accurate information about rights, procedures, and services.

Fourth, media actors and public communicators bear a responsibility to move beyond representations that frame migrants as threats, burdens, or crisis elements, since such representations can silence migrants and push them toward reduced visibility. Providing migrants with opportunities to speak on their own behalf and to represent their own experiences would help address the paradox between media visibility and everyday silence. Taken together, these recommendations point toward integration policies that take seriously not only what is visible and measurable, but also the tacit, relational, and everyday dimensions of living together.

FUTURE RESEARCH DIRECTIONS

The analytical perspective developed in this chapter offers a productive ground for future empirical research. The conditions under which different migrant groups' strategies of silence, avoidance, adaptation, and distance-keeping change stand out as an important field of investigation. How variables such as legal status, class position, gender, religion, language, ethnic belonging, and spatial settlement shape these strategies should be examined in greater detail through comparative and context-sensitive research designs. In addition, the meanings that members of the host society ascribe to migrants' silence should be included in the analysis, because silence can function, in some situations, as adaptation, in others as protection, in others as distance, and in others as a form of resistance.

This approach also has important methodological implications. Silence is not a datum that is easy to measure directly. The researcher must attend not only to what is said, but also to what is left unsaid, to hesitations, to avoidances, to gaps in the narrative, to recurring silences, and to the patterns of everyday practices. Qualitative research, ethnographic observation, in-depth interviews, narrative analysis, and contextual interpretation offer important possibilities for grasping the social meaning of silence. The fundamental point to be observed, however, is not to fill silence with the researcher's own assumptions. Silence acquires analytical value only when it is interpreted together with context, power relations, experience, and patterns of practice; otherwise, it ceases to be a social practice that must be explained and turns into a carrier of the meanings the researcher ascribes to it. Future research attentive to these considerations could substantially enrich the understanding of the everyday, relational, and tacit dimensions of migration and integration.

CONCLUSION

This chapter has sought to show that, in the context of migration, meaning, belonging, and exclusion are shaped not only through explicitly articulated discourses, but also through meanings left unsaid, avoidances, and silences. The relations that migrants establish with the host society do not always proceed through open demands, visible conflicts, or formal processes of adaptation. These relations are frequently established within the ordinary encounters of everyday life, through silent observations, cautious behaviors, avoidances, distance adjustments, and tacit compromises. Silence should therefore not be evaluated as passivity or as a lack of communication. Silence is a relational practice that acquires meaning within power relations, normative uncertainties, legal precarities, social expectations, and searches for belonging. When migrants remain silent, they do not merely avoid speaking; they frequently calculate risks, read social boundaries, test domains of acceptance, adjust the visibility of their identities, and try to open up, however limited, a space of movement for themselves. Silence should therefore be regarded as one of the constitutive social practices that the sociology of migration must address with greater care.

Within this framework, the concept of silent negotiation has been treated not as a completed and closed theoretical model, but as an analytical sensibility that makes it possible to rethink migration and integration processes at the level of everyday interactions. This approach aims to go beyond forms of explanation that evaluate integration solely through legal status, institutional participation, or indicators of cultural adaptation. Instead, it focuses on the fragile balances, tacit expectations, implicit acceptances, and frequently unarticulated practices of mutual adaptation established within everyday life between migrants and members of the host society. From this vantage point, integration can be grasped not only through formal institutions, legal arrangements, and visible mechanisms of participation, but also through the meanings, boundaries, and forms of relationship silently produced within everyday encounters.

The silent-negotiation approach distances itself from forms of explanation that position migrants as passive actors or as actors merely expected to adapt. Migrants frequently act within limited resources, precarious statuses, and uncertain social expectations, yet this does not mean that they are entirely passive within everyday life. On the contrary, they continually assess, in different contexts, when to speak, which demands to voice, in which situations to withdraw, which differences to render visible, and in which relations to keep distance. This assessment process does not always emerge in the form of open negotiation; it frequently operates within silent, indirect, cautious, and context-sensitive practices. In the context of migration, social adaptation and conflict do not occur solely at the level of visible discourses, open demands, and institutional processes. Behind these processes there frequently operates a silent, tacit, and interactional social fabric that goes unnoticed. Integration cannot therefore be evaluated as a formal process shaped solely through laws, institutions, and policies. It is also reproduced daily in glances on the street, in the distances established in neighborly relations, in silences at the workplace, in cultural continuities within the home, and in adjustments of visibility in public space. One of the fundamental tasks of the sociology of migration is therefore to take seriously, in analytical terms, not only what is explicitly said, but also the meanings left unsaid, the tacit acceptances, and the silent arrangements of everyday life.

REFERENCES

Ager, A., & Strang, A. (2008). Understanding integration: A conceptual framework. *Journal of Refugee Studies, 21*(2), 166–191. DOI: 10.1093/jrs/fen016

Aksoy, M., & Cengiz, E. (2025). Göç, kimlik arayışı ve entegrasyon tartışmaları. In Aksoy, M., & Cengiz, E. (Eds.), *Göç, kimlik ve entegrasyon: Disiplinlerarası yaklaşımlar* (pp. 1–16).

Berger, C. R., & Calabrese, R. J. (1975). Some explorations in initial interaction and beyond: Toward a developmental theory of interpersonal communication. *Human Communication Research, 1*(2), 99–112. DOI: 10.1111/j.1468-2958.1975.tb00258.x

Berry, J. W. (1997). Immigration, acculturation, and adaptation. *Applied Psychology, 46*(1), 5–34. DOI: 10.1111/j.1464-0597.1997.tb01087.x

Bourdieu, P. (1990). *The logic of practice.* Stanford University Press. DOI: 10.1515/9781503621749

Buz, S., Canlı, M., & Aygüler, E. (2021). *Trabzon'da yaşayan Afgan sığınmacıların profili ve gereksinimleri.* Hacettepe University Migration and Politics Research Center.

Canlı, M., & Buz, S. (2024). Trabzon'da yaşayan Afganistan uyruklu kadın göçmenlerin gündelik yaşamları. *Mavi Atlas, 12*(1), 24–39. DOI: 10.18795/gumusmaviatlas.1382617

Castles, S., de Haas, H., & Miller, M. J. (2013). *The age of migration: International population movements in the modern world* (5th ed.). Palgrave Macmillan.

Cengiz, E., Uğur, Ö., & Aksoy, M. (2025). Mültecilerin hukuki durumuna ilişkin sözleşme kapsamında iklim mültecileri. *ISARC International Science and Art Research Center*, 547–553.

De Certeau, M. (1984). *The practice of everyday life.* University of California Press.

De Genova, N. P. (2002). Migrant "illegality" and deportability in everyday life. *Annual Review of Anthropology, 31*(1), 419–447. DOI: 10.1146/annurev.anthro.31.040402.085432

Foucault, M. (1980). *Power/knowledge: Selected interviews and other writings, 1972–1977.* Pantheon Books.

Goffman, E. (1959). *The presentation of self in everyday life.* Doubleday.

Goffman, E. (1969). *Strategic interaction.* University of Pennsylvania Press.

Hondagneu-Sotelo, P. (2003). *Gender and U.S. immigration: Contemporary trends.* University of California Press. DOI: 10.1525/9780520929869

Jaworski, A. (1992). *The power of silence: Social and pragmatic perspectives.* Sage Publications.

Luhmann, N. (1995). *Social systems.* Stanford University Press.

Menjívar, C. (2006). Liminal legality: Salvadoran and Guatemalan immigrants' lives in the United States. *American Journal of Sociology, 111*(4), 999–1037. DOI: 10.1086/499509

Olier, J. S., & Spadavecchia, C. (2022). Stereotypes, disproportions, and power asymmetries in the visual portrayal of migrants in ten countries: An interdisciplinary AI-based approach. *Humanities & Social Sciences Communications, 9*(1), 133. DOI: 10.1057/s41599-022-01430-y

Papatzani, E. (2021). Encountering everyday racist practices: Sociospatial negotiations of immigrant settlement in Athens, Greece. *International Journal of Urban and Regional Research, 45*(2), 254–271. DOI: 10.1111/1468-2427.12984

Plöger, J., & Kubiak, S. (2019). Becoming "the internationals": How place shapes the sense of belonging and group formation of high-skilled migrants. *Journal of International Migration and Integration, 20*(2), 493–511. DOI: 10.1007/s12134-018-0608-7

Polanyi, M. (2009). *The tacit dimension.* University of Chicago Press. (Original work published 1966)

Pugh, J. D. (2018). Negotiating identity and belonging through the invisibility bargain: Colombian forced migrants in Ecuador. *The International Migration Review, 52*(4), 978–1010. DOI: 10.1177/0197918318781845

Sandu, A. (2013). Transnational homemaking practices: Identity, belonging and informal learning. *Journal of Contemporary European Studies, 21*(4), 539–556. DOI: 10.1080/14782804.2013.865379

Schatzki, T. R., Knorr-Cetina, K., & von Savigny, E. (Eds.). (2001). *The practice turn in contemporary theory.* Routledge.

Scott, J. C. (1990). *Domination and the arts of resistance: Hidden transcripts.* Yale University Press.

Yuval-Davis, N. (2006). Belonging and the politics of belonging. *Patterns of Prejudice, 40*(3), 197–214. DOI: 10.1080/00313220600769331

Zerubavel, E. (2006). *The elephant in the room: Silence and denial in everyday life*. Oxford University Press.

ADDITIONAL READING

Lamont, M., & Molnár, V. (2002). The study of boundaries in the social sciences. *Annual Review of Sociology, 28*(1), 167–195. DOI: 10.1146/annurev.soc.28.110601.141107

Lynch, M. (1999). Silence in context: Ethnomethodology and social theory. *Human Studies, 22*(2-4), 211–233. DOI: 10.1023/A:1005440501638

Nonaka, I., & Takeuchi, H. (1995). *The knowledge-creating company: How Japanese companies create the dynamics of innovation*. Oxford University Press. DOI: 10.1093/oso/9780195092691.001.0001

KEY TERMS AND DEFINITIONS

Belonging: A multilayered process involving not only an individual's subjective sense of attachment to a place or community but also recognition, acceptance, and legitimation by others.

Everyday Life: The domain of ordinary, repeated encounters and practices in which social order, belonging, and distance are continually produced and readjusted beyond formal institutions and explicit discourses.

Integration: A reciprocal, dynamic, and relational process of mutual adjustment between migrants and the host society that extends beyond measurable structural indicators to the tacit arrangements of everyday interaction.

Normative Uncertainty: A condition in which migrants cannot reliably predict which behaviors, demands, or identity markers will be deemed acceptable in a new social context, prompting risk-reducing and cautious conduct.

Regulation of Visibility: The context-sensitive practice through which migrants decide when and to what extent to render aspects of their identity, difference, or presence perceptible in public and institutional spaces.

Silence: A relational social practice that, rather than signifying mere absence of speech, produces meaning, orders relationships, and manages uncertainty and risk within specific contexts of power and expectation.

Silent Labor: The frequently invisible, largely gendered work—cultural transmission, care, relationship-building, and emotional management—through which migrant households and communities sustain everyday life.

Silent Negotiation: An analytical framework describing the tacit, indirect, and low-visibility ways in which migrants and host-society members manage identity, belonging, and social distance without resorting to open dialogue or direct confrontation.

Tacit Knowledge: Practical, experiential knowledge acquired through observation, habit, and repetition that individuals possess but cannot fully articulate, and that guides migrants' everyday judgments about appropriate conduct.

Chapter 8
Who Pays, Who Benefits?
Migrants, Fiscal Contributions, and Welfare State Sustainability

Paula Sousa
http://orcid.org/0000-0003-4876-490X
Universidade de Tras os Montes e Alto Douro, Portugal

José Luis Almeida
http://orcid.org/0000-0003-1824-9587
Universidade de Trás os Montes e Alto Douro, Portugal

Daniela Monteiro
http://orcid.org/0000-0002-3968-1531
Universidade Aberta, Portugal

ABSTRACT

This chapter examines immigration, fiscal contributions, and welfare state sustainability in Portugal, a country combining extreme demographic ageing with rapid migratory transformation. Drawing on administrative data and peer-reviewed literature, this chapter per the authors addresses three dimensions: migrants' fiscal contributions across the life cycle; patterns of public service use; and aggregate effects on financial sustainability. Foreign nationals contribute to social security disproportionately relative to their population share: in 2025, contributions exceeded benefits received fivefold, and public service use remained proportionally lower, consistent with the healthy immigrant effect. Without immigration, the required fiscal adjustment would quadruple. This chapter per the authors concludes that migration is an empirically documented contributor to welfare state sustainability, integration

DOI: 10.4018/979-8-3373-8500-6.ch008

quality being the decisive factor, and that sustainability must be assessed not only by fiscal balances but by the capacity to guarantee equitable access to those who finance the system.

1. INTRODUCTION

Contemporary debate on migration and the financial sustainability of the welfare state is laden with political tensions, incomplete readings, and deeply polarised narratives. The central question of who pays and who benefits, whilst apparently simple, opens onto a complex web of relationships between fiscal contributions, public service use, demographic dynamics, labour markets, and social perceptions. Over recent decades, public debate has oscillated between extremes: on one side, discourses portraying migrants as a permanent burden on already-pressured public systems; on the other, interpretations presenting them as an almost magical solution to the challenges of population ageing. Both, with equal determination, ignore the multifaceted reality that academic research and administrative data have been steadily revealing.

A useful analogy for understanding this debate is that of the "intertemporal fiscal balance": much like a financial investment, migratory flows generate returns that only become fully and clearly visible when evaluated over a sufficiently long time horizon. The tendency to assess migrants' contribution in the short term is methodologically equivalent to judging a pension fund by its weekly return: imprecise, misleading, and potentially counterproductive. This temporal trap is systematically flagged in the literature (Dustmann & Frattini, 2014; Christl et al., 2022; Bernardino et al., 2025) and constitutes one of the epistemological foundations of this chapter.

It is precisely this dual simplism that this chapter seeks to overcome, proposing an approach that articulates three essential dimensions: (1) how migrants contribute fiscally across the life cycle; (2) how they use social services and benefits; and (3) the real effects of that balance or imbalance on the sustainability and legitimacy of the welfare state. In addition, the analysis incorporates a fourth dimension, of an institutional and political nature: how governmental configurations and public perceptions mediate the translation of migrants' economic contribution into effective public policy (Qi, 2025).

This analysis takes Portugal as its case study, not merely for empirical reasons but because of its particular relevance as a demographic and institutional laboratory. Portugal combines extreme ageing with rapid migratory transformation, a hybrid social protection model, and a political context in which demagogic discourses on migration have gained considerable visibility (Carvalho & Duarte, 2020). These conditions make the country a privileged setting for understanding how, when, and why migration may contribute to reinforcing, or indeed challenging, fiscal and social sustainability.

From a methodological standpoint, the chapter draws on a diverse range of sources: national administrative data (GEP/MTSSS, AIMA, ISS), academic literature published in journals indexed in Web of Science and Scopus, European simulation models (EUROMOD, EUROPOP2023), and comparative panel studies. This methodological triangulation enables the conclusions to be grounded in both empirical and theoretical robustness. The choice of a plurality of sources also responds to an ethical imperative: on a subject as politically charged as this one, the solidity of the evidence is the first line of defence against ideological distortion.

2. PUBLIC PERCEPTIONS, POLITICAL DISCOURSE, AND (MIS)ALIGNMENT WITH EVIDENCE

There is a peculiar consistency in the way European societies perceive immigration: they are systematically wrong. People tend to overestimate the number of migrants, believe without evidence that migrants draw more benefits than nationals, and associate migration with criminality in ways that the data simply do not support. Populist political discourses exploit this misalignment through techniques such as statistical exaggeration, the construction of an external enemy, and the artificial causal association between migration and pre-existing structural problems (Carvalho & Duarte, 2020).

The Portuguese case is particularly instructive in this regard. Boeri (2009), analysing Eurobarometer data for the EU-15, documents that in Portugal the proportion of citizens who agreed with the statement that "minority groups exploit the social protection system" rose from 22.2% in 1994 to 49.5% in 2000, the largest absolute increase recorded across the entire EU-15 during that period. What makes this finding particularly striking is that it occurred precisely when the same research confirmed the absence of residual welfare dependency among migrants in Portugal. The gap between perception and evidence in Portugal is, therefore, empirically documented and is by no means a recent phenomenon.

This misalignment does not exist in a vacuum, nor is it politically neutral. Qi (2025) provides the theoretical framework for understanding why this misalignment translates into different policies depending on the type of government. In single-party majority governments, anti-immigration public sentiment is more readily converted into restrictive policy: without internal veto players, the governing party is fully exposed to the electoral cost of policies perceived as favourable to migrants. In coalition or minority governments, by contrast, public pressure is mediated by multiple actors with divergent preferences, which attenuates the influence of majority hostility on social spending decisions.

Portugal has frequently been identified as a favourable case in the domain of integration policies. According to the Migrant Integration Policy Index (MIPEX) 2025, Portugal ranks among the leading countries in migrant integration, achieving a score of 83/100 (Table 1). This positive assessment stands in marked contrast to the intensification of restrictive discourses in public political debate, illustrating with particular clarity the gap between the formal institutional framework and the effective political dynamic.

Table 1. Portugal's Scores in the Migrant Integration Policy Index (MIPEX) 2025

Domain	Score	Assessment
Labour market mobility	94	Favourable
Family reunification	93	Favourable
Education	74	Slightly favourable
Health	71	Intermediate
Political participation	80	Favourable
Permanent residence	71	Slightly favourable
Access to nationality	86	Favourable
Anti-discrimination	100	Favourable (maximum)

Note. Own elaboration based on MIPEX (2025). Available at https://www.mipex.eu/portugal

The recent legislative cycle on migration — culminating in Law No. 61/2025 and the Constitutional Court's partial annulment of stricter family reunification provisions on grounds of the fundamental right to family life — illustrates the tension between restrictive political discourse and the constitutional limits that frame legislative sovereignty in migration matters.

This gap between perception and evidence is not a marginal phenomenon: it structures public debate, shapes policy, and undermines the institutional standing of professionals who work with migrant populations. Empirical rigour is no longer merely a methodological option; it becomes an ethical and political imperative. It is precisely to address this challenge that the sections that follow mobilise systematic evidence around three central questions: how migrants contribute fiscally to the Portuguese welfare state; how they use public services across the life cycle; and what the real effects of that balance are on the sustainability of the social protection system in a context of accelerated demographic ageing. The data that follow are the empirical response to the problem this chapter has just framed (Dustmann & Frattini, 2014; Bernardino et al., 2025; Oliveira, 2023).

3. PORTUGAL AS A CASE STUDY: METHODOLOGICAL JUSTIFICATION

The choice of Portugal as the central empirical axis is not arbitrary. The country combines a singular set of characteristics that make it a case study of exceptional comparative relevance for research on migration and the welfare state. First and foremost, it is a late-building democracy: the 1974 transition inaugurated a universal welfare state at a time when most European partners had already consolidated their systems over several decades. Moreover, Portugal has compressed into a very short period two transitions that elsewhere in Europe unfolded over more than a century: the shift from an emigration to an immigration country, and the shift from a young to an ageing population structure. Finally, since 2022 the country has been navigating a period of strong ideological fragmentation around migration, making it a particularly vivid laboratory for observing how empirical evidence and political discourse so rarely converge.

3.1. Extreme Demographic Ageing

Portugal is today one of the most rapidly ageing countries in Europe. The ageing index, understood as the number of elderly people per 100 young people, exceeded 159 in 2021 and is projected to surpass 300 by 2050. This profound inversion of the age pyramid directly affects the financing of pension systems, specialist health services, and long-term care structures. The pay-as-you-go (PAYG) system, which depends on the ratio between the active population and the elderly, therefore faces enormous structural pressures. In 2021 there were approximately 3.3 people of working age for every older person; by 2050 there will be only 1.5. Without intervention, this ratio seriously jeopardises the financial balance of the welfare state, bringing to the fore a question that is no longer merely academic: whether and how migratory flows can partially compensate for demographic deterioration.

In this system, labour migration functions as a supplementary engine: it adds contributors without, in the short and medium term, generating a proportional increase in beneficiaries, directly improving the system's balance (Bongaarts, 2004; Han, 2013; Bernardino et al., 2025).

From the perspective of pension political economy, the architecture of any PAYG system can be formalised in a simple equation that makes explicit its structural vulnerability nodes: the contribution rate required to balance the system (c) is the product of the beneficiary-to-contributor ratio (B/C), known as the system dependency ratio, and the average pension-to-average wage ratio (P/W), the benefit ratio, minus external fiscal transfers (S) that the state may inject into the system (Hinrichs, 2021). Immigration acts directly on the denominator C, increasing the number of contributors without generating, in the short and medium term, a proportional increase in beneficiaries B, which is why immigration is structurally beneficial to PAYG pension systems.

3.2. Recent Transformation of Migratory Flows

For most of the twentieth century, Portugal was primarily a country of emigrants. Over the past three decades, however, it has become a significant destination for immigration, growing from approximately 100,000 foreign residents in 1990 to over 1,543,697 in December 2024 (AIMA, 2025). But this growth is not merely quantitative; it is also qualitative. Migrants account for only 7% of the total population, yet represent approximately 15% of the active population between the ages of 25 and 40, precisely the age group that contributes most fiscally and makes the least use of high-cost health services.

Currently, Brazilian nationals remain the largest foreign resident community (31.4%), whilst Indian nationals have moved into second position (98,616 residents) (AIMA, 2025). This diversification of origins is directly reflected in the diversification of contributory profiles and service use patterns (Table 2).

Table 2. Foreign Residents by Continent and Nationality in Portugal (2024)

Continent	No. by continent	Nationality	No.	Rank
South America	528 401	Brazil	484 596	1st
Africa	315 609	Angola	92 348	3rd
Asia	311 955	India	98 616	2nd
European Union	194 094	Italy	40 021	12th
Europe (other)	164 165	Ukraine	79 232	4th
North and Central America	27 999	—	—	—

Note. Own elaboration based on data from the Report on Migration and Asylum 2024 (AIMA, 2025).

3.3. The Hybrid Architecture of the Portuguese Welfare State

The welfare state in Portugal has followed a singular historical trajectory within the European context, marked by a late construction heavily shaped by the authoritarian political path of the twentieth century and by the democratic rupture of 1974. Unlike the democracies of Northern and Central Europe, where social protection systems were consolidated in the post-World War II period, Portugal only assembled the political, institutional, and normative conditions for the development of a universally based welfare state under democratic rule. The literature indicates that responses to the "social question" rested on a corporatist-inspired model, strongly dependent on formal employment and with limited coverage, falling well short of a universal system of social rights (Amaro, 2018; Amaro & Guerra, 2024; Carolo & Pereirinha, 2010).

The Portuguese welfare state combines elements of three models: a contributory system of Bismarckian origin, universal services of Beveridgean inspiration (the NHS, education), and means-tested targeted support. This hybrid architecture generates contradictory dynamics: it incentivises formal employment whilst penalising fragmented careers; it guarantees universal access to services whilst feeding perceptions of concentrated costs. Migrants navigate this mosaic asymmetrically, sometimes encountering the worst of each model: they contribute as Bismarckian workers whilst accessing services as second-tier citizens (Branco, 2017; Calado et al., 2019). In Esping-Andersen's (1990) typology, Portugal is typically classified as a "Mediterranean" or "Southern European" regime, sharing with Spain, Italy, and Greece a combination of strong family dependency, low coverage of universal services, and high stratification of contributory benefits, characteristics that produce specific patterns of access and exclusion for the migrant population.

In Bismarckian systems like Portugal's, this structural logic is especially pronounced: the link between current contributions and current benefits is immediate, so every additional contributor in the workforce directly reinforces the system's short-term balance (Hinrichs, 2021; Han, 2013).

3.3.1. Social Security

The Portuguese social security system constitutes the most directly relevant pillar for the analysis of migrants' fiscal contributions, operating as it does within a predominantly contributory logic in which access to monetary benefits depends on the registration of formal contributory careers (Carolo & Pereirinha, 2010; Amaro, 2018). The Social Security Framework Law (Law No. 4/2007 of 16 January) enshrines the principle of universality, recognising the right to social security for all who legally reside or work in national territory, regardless of nationality. In practice, access to contributory benefits is conditional upon the fulfilment of qualifying periods, which structurally disadvantages workers with fragmented employment histories (Eiras et al., 2024; Oliveira & Caleiras, 2025).

Analysis of GEP/MTSSS data allows this asymmetry to be quantified. In 2022, foreign nationals accounted for 13.5% of total social security contributions whilst representing only 7.5% of the resident population. The ratio of contributions to benefits received was systematically more favourable to the system than that observed for the national population, reinforcing the view that migrants function, in aggregate terms, as net contributors (Oliveira, 2023). This surplus, which Dustmann and Frattini (2014) term the immigrant fiscal dividend, represents the net fiscal gain from immigration when contributions and transfers across the life cycle are both taken into account.

The asymmetry between contributions and benefit use is particularly pronounced in the old-age pension sub-system, which constitutes the largest item of expenditure in Portuguese social security. Data from the European Community Household Panel (ECHP) show that, in Portugal, the average age of non-EU migrants is 43.6 years, compared with 49.9 years for nationals, and that the pension participation rate among migrants is only 18.2%, compared with 24.6% for Portuguese citizens (Han, 2013). This 6.4 percentage-point difference, structurally favourable to the system, reflects the fact that migrants actively contribute to the financing of current pensions without yet having consolidated entitlements to their own retirement pensions, a feature inherent to the PAYG logic and systematically documented across 14 European countries (Han, 2013).

The Portuguese legal framework formally enshrines equal rights of access to social security for migrants in regular status, including the portability of rights under bilateral social security agreements concluded with relevant countries of origin, such as Brazil, Cape Verde, Mozambique, and Ukraine. Yet the distance between formal entitlement and rights actually exercised remains a central challenge for social work practitioners. This tension is compounded by the structural tendency of European parametric reforms to tighten the principle of equivalence between career contributions and pension levels, which disproportionately penalises workers with non-linear careers, including the majority of economic migrants in Portugal (Hinrichs, 2021; Casquilho-Martins et al., 2025).

3.3.2. Employment

In the domain of the labour market, Portugal formally guarantees equal access to employment for migrants with legal residence, applying the Labour Code to them under the same conditions as national workers. Despite this formal framework, the immigrant population is, in general terms, strongly associated with precarious employment conditions, characterised by contractual instability, low earnings, and greater exposure to social risks (Eiras et al., 2024; Arruda, 2023). These conditions limit the effective exercise of formally recognised rights and constrain subsequent access to social protection. From the perspective of social work, this gap between written law and lived experience is one of the most urgent and, paradoxically, least visible domains of intervention, which the literature refers to as the problem of "invisible administrative justice" (Casquilho-Martins et al., 2025; Dominelli, 2010).

Labour market segmentation is one of the most documented mechanisms for the reproduction of inequality among migrant populations. Data from the INE Labour

Force Survey reveal that foreign workers are overrepresented in low-skilled and highly precarious sectors, notably hospitality, tourism, construction, and intensive agriculture, sectors simultaneously characterised by high contractual turnover and seasonal cycles that impede the accumulation of continuous qualifying periods (Eiras et al., 2024). The phenomenon of deskilling through migration, already noted from a fiscal returns perspective, is equally a labour market phenomenon: more than one third of migrants in Portugal work in roles below their formal qualification level, which represents, simultaneously, a productivity loss for the economy, a reduction in contributory potential for the pension system, and a violation of equality of opportunity (Observatório das Migrações, 2026).

Despite formal anti-discrimination provisions in Portuguese labour law, discrimination in access to employment and career progression remains structurally documented across several migrant communities, particularly those from sub-Saharan Africa and South Asia (Arruda, 2023). Social workers are well placed to bridge this gap, directing migrants towards legal and employment support structures, a dimension that Dominelli (2010) integrates into anti-oppressive practice in transnational contexts.

3.3.3. Education

In the field of education, Portugal guarantees free access to public schooling for all children and young people resident in the country, regardless of nationality, enshrining a universalist framework. Yet inequalities persist, associated with linguistic and cultural barriers that constrain the full educational integration of children and young people from migrant families (Ramos & Ramos, 2025; Pinho & Ançã, 2023). Sacramento et al. (2023) demonstrate that cultural diversity in Portuguese schools has increased significantly over the past decade, posing multiple challenges to the education system, most notably the need to strengthen the teaching of Portuguese as a foreign language.

The presence of pupils of migrant origin in Portuguese schools has grown rapidly over the past decade, reaching approximately 12% of all pupils in primary and secondary education by 2024, with a particular concentration in the metropolitan areas of Lisbon and Porto. This reality poses considerable challenges to the education system that have not been fully matched by a proportional expansion of support resources. The teaching of Portuguese as a Foreign Language (PLNM), whilst formally mandated in legislation since 2008, has been implemented unevenly across schools and school clusters, with significant gaps in teacher-specific training and in the availability of bilingual psychosocial support (Pinho & Ançã, 2023; Sacramento et al., 2023). These gaps have a direct impact on the academic trajectories of pupils of migrant origin, with rates of grade retention and early school leaving that are systematically higher than those for the national population.

Rodrigues et al. (2022) demonstrate that the local community can partially compensate for school shortcomings by building the affective bonds critical for educational persistence. The Escolhas Programme, created in 2001, funds social inclusion projects in more vulnerable territories with documented positive impacts on schooling rates, albeit with difficulties in sustaining results beyond funding cycles.

For social work, the school is far more than an intervention setting: it is the place where tensions between culture of origin and host culture manifest earliest and most acutely, as when a six-year-old child who cannot understand what the teacher is saying. The perspectives of anti-oppressive practice (Dominelli, 2010) and culturally competent care (Challinor, 2012) converge in the demand that practitioners working in multicultural educational contexts develop the capacity for critical reading of the power dynamics that structure relations between institutions, families, and migrant pupils. This capacity is not merely a technical competence: it is an ethical imperative that connects directly to the guarantee of the right to education as a precondition for all subsequent social rights.

3.3.4. Health

The universalist principle of the Portuguese NHS recognises the right to health protection regardless of origin, and migrants with a residence permit generally enjoy full access. However, Challinor (2012) shows that "equal treatment for all" applied uncritically can produce subtle exclusions when cultural difference is reinterpreted as an individual deficit — what the literature terms "institutional cultural blindness" (Casquilho-Martins et al., 2025).

In practice, access to the National Health Service (NHS) for migrants in regular status is formally guaranteed by Law No. 27/2002 of 8 November. However, migrants in irregular status operate within a more restricted framework that includes emergency care and some primary health services, but frequently excludes the full range of scheduled care (Casquilho-Martins et al., 2025). The existence of language barriers, unfamiliarity with the health system, fear of administrative exposure, and the concentration of migrant populations in geographic areas with lower primary care density combine to produce a pattern of underuse of preventive care and relative overrepresentation in emergency services, the last-resort access circuit (Kennedy et al., 2015).

Beyond access, the cultural diversity of migrant populations poses adaptation challenges to the NHS. Health practices, illness perceptions, and relationships with medical authority vary considerably between communities, requiring active cultural competence (Challinor, 2012). The dominant biomedical model's tendency to treat these differences as patient deficits rather than legitimate cultural rationalities erodes institutional trust and drives withdrawal from primary health services.

Perhaps the most silent domain of this vulnerability is that of mental health. The migratory process frequently entails relational ruptures, migratory grief, exposure to discrimination and housing precarity, all of which are social determinants of mental health risk. Compounding this vulnerability is the scarcity of culturally adapted specialist responses within the NHS and the stigma attached to seeking psychological help in several communities of origin. Social work, by virtue of its interface position between health systems and communities, occupies a strategic place in the early identification of psychosocial distress and in referral to appropriate responses (Casquilho-Martins et al., 2025; Dominelli, 2010).

3.3.5. Housing

Housing is constitutionally recognised in Portugal regardless of nationality. Housing policy has been predominantly residual, and recent legislative packages — the New Generation of Housing Policies (2018), the Housing Framework Law (2019), and Mais Habitação (2023) — represent attempts to reverse that orientation (Pereira, 2024).

The overrepresentation of migrants in situations of housing inadequacy is one of the most robust indicators of social inequality in Portugal. Data from the Observatory on Migration (2026) indicate that foreign families exhibit rates of housing overcrowding substantially higher than those of Portuguese families, with a particular incidence in the metropolitan areas of Lisbon and Porto. This concentration is not solely a function of lower incomes: it also results from discrimination in access to the private rental market, documented in situational testing studies that reveal systematic refusals on ethnic or national-origin grounds (Tosi, 2012). The structural housing crisis affecting Portugal in recent years has significantly compounded this situation, as pressure on the rental market has reduced availability and raised prices in the segments where lower-income migrants had concentrated their options.

Social housing policies in Portugal, historically characterised by a residualist orientation and insufficient coverage, have only recently begun to explicitly incorporate the immigration variable. The 1.º Direito programme, created in 2019, and the Porta de Entrada programme, aimed at recognised refugees, constitute the main mechanisms of access to publicly supported housing for foreign nationals in severe housing need. Nevertheless, their effective coverage remains limited relative to the scale of need, and the administrative access requirements constitute, in practice, specific barriers for recently arrived migrants, who frequently have not yet accumulated the required periods of residency (Pereira, 2024; Jorge, 2024).

Housing is the material condition without which all other rights are difficult to realise: it affects labour integration, schooling, health access, and civic participation. Tosi (2012) underlines that precarious housing constitutes a form of social invisibilisation that deprives individuals of the possibility of exercising their rights — an exclusion social work has a responsibility to interrupt through integrated intervention with municipal structures and welfare organisations.

3.4. The Rise of Populist Discourses and Distorted Perceptions

Since 2020, Portuguese political debate on migration has been increasingly shaped by populist rhetoric that exaggerates figures, associates migration with criminality, and attributes to migrants responsibility for structural problems that preceded their arrival, such as the housing crisis or the underfunding of the health system (Carvalho & Duarte, 2020). These narratives distort public perceptions, generate social fear, legitimise counterproductive policies, and weaken social cohesion. The landmark study by Citrin and Sides (2008) demonstrates that in virtually every European country the population systematically overestimates by two to three times the actual proportion of immigrants, a cognitive bias with direct and measurable political consequences for support for integration policies. Experimental research by Alesina et al. (2023) confirms that correcting this bias with factual information significantly increases support for redistributive policies that include migrants.

4. MIGRATION AND FISCAL CONTRIBUTIONS

4.1. Labour Market Insertion and Contributory Formalisation

At the beginning of the twenty-first century, the foreign resident population in Portugal stood at under 230,000 individuals, representing approximately 2.2% of the total population (INE, 2001). Two and a half decades later, that figure has surpassed 1.5 million people (AIMA, 2025). This demographic shift has left a clear mark on the pension system: in 2000, contributions from foreign workers to Social Security were residual within the overall contributory revenue picture; by 2025, they exceeded 4.162 billion euros, representing approximately 15% of all contributions for a population that accounts for only 7.5% of benefit recipients (GEP/MTSSS, 2026; Oliveira, 2023).

Between 2017 and 2022, the total number of foreign nationals in formal employment and contributing to social security more than trebled, rising from 166,000 to 534,000 (European Commission, 2025). By 2023, with migrants injecting 2.7 billion euros into the Social Security system, against 15.8 billion disbursed in total benefits, the contribution of the foreign population already represented approximately 17% of the system's financing. The ratio of contributions to benefits received, which stood at approximately 3.5:1 in 2015 and reached around 5:1 in 2025, reflects the young age structure of the migrant population: a population that contributes intensively during its active phase and has not yet, for the most part, reached the ages of greatest use of old-age and invalidity benefits (Table 3).

Table 3. Social Security Contributions and Benefits Received by the Foreign Population in Portugal

Indicator	2015	2020	2025
Social Security contributions	491.5 M€	1,823 M€	4,162.3 M€
Benefits received	137.2 M€	498 M€	827.1 M€
Contribution/benefit ratio	~3.5:1	~3.7:1	~5:1
% foreign pop. in total pop.	~4%	~5.5%	~7,5%

Note. Own elaboration based on GEP/MTSSS (2026) and Oliveira (2023).

There is, however, a fundamental distinction that aggregate figures tend to obscure: the formalisation of an employment contract is not equivalent to full integration into the social protection system. The existence of fixed-term contracts, seasonal work, and precarious arrangements, patterns overrepresented in the migrant population, generates contributory discontinuities that may prevent the fulfilment of qualifying periods required for benefit access (Eiras et al., 2024; Oliveira & Caleiras, 2025). A migrant worker may thus accumulate substantial contributions over many years without ever consolidating full entitlements to the corresponding benefits, which amplifies the system's net positive contributory balance, but at an equity cost that cannot be disregarded from the social work perspective (Casquilho-Martins et al., 2025; Dominelli, 2010).

4.2. Fiscal Capture Mechanisms

The mechanisms that convert contributory potential into effective revenue include the reduction of legal and fiscal bureaucracy, administrative simplification, withholding at source, and the combating of informality. Effective labour market integration policies and the recognition of qualifications substantially increase the fiscal capacity of migrants, particularly in the medium and long term (Cook, 2018; Oliveira, 2023). Comparative research by Fiorio et al. (2024), applying the EUROMOD model to 14 EU countries, demonstrates that migrants are net contributors to public finances across the European average, contributing approximately 1,500 euros per capita annually above natives, a difference amplified where labour integration policies are more robust.

Viewed from the perspective of social work, fiscal capture is neither automatic nor merely administrative: it is also an act of capacity-building and institutional mediation. Migrant workers who are unaware of their labour rights, or who face linguistic barriers in accessing employment services, are frequently excluded from formal circuits, generating not only a loss of social security revenue but also a deepening of social vulnerabilities. The case for "active integration" as an investment with measurable pension returns (Cook, 2018) finds here its most concrete expression.

4.3. Diversity of Profiles and Fiscal Impact

Fiscal impact differs significantly between migrant groups: young migrants generate positive net contributions over many years; highly qualified migrants contribute above average; migrants in precarious situations produce lower formal contributions but frequently above their level of service use. Portugal's migratory diversity thus constitutes an analytical advantage for studying multiple fiscal equilibria. It is important to underline that the pension sustainability argument in favour of immigration does not depend exclusively on migrants' qualifications: as Bernardino et al. (2025) demonstrate, immigration improves fiscal balances even when migrants have low qualifications, provided their lifetime contributions exceed those of newborn natives.

This finding has far-reaching policy implications: the public debate that conditions the validity of migrants' contribution on academic qualifications has no robust empirical foundation. Skills-selective immigration may have merits in other domains, for example in responding to specific labour market needs, but it does not constitute a necessary criterion for ensuring the positive fiscal contribution of migratory flows. What ultimately determines the magnitude of that contribution is the quality of integration policies that transform potential into realisation.

5. USE OF PUBLIC SERVICES ACROSS THE LIFE CYCLE

5.1. Health

When one examines the pattern of health service use by the migrant population in Portugal, an asymmetry emerges that tends to surprise those approaching the question with different assumptions: migrants use less, not more. Migrants tend to use fewer specialist and high-cost health services than nationals, which is largely explained by their age structure: this is a predominantly young and working-age population, a life-cycle stage in which demand for differentiated hospital care is statistically lower (Casquilho-Martins et al., 2025).

This pattern is well established in the international literature under the name of the healthy immigrant effect. The concept describes the tendency of recently arrived migrants to exhibit health indicators superior to those of the native population at equivalent ages, an advantage research has consistently documented across multiple national contexts (Kennedy et al., 2015). The most widely accepted explanatory hypothesis rests on self-selection: those who migrate are, on average, the healthiest and most resilient members of their communities of origin. This effect tends to fade progressively with years of residence, as living and working conditions take their toll on migrant workers' health, a phenomenon described in the literature as the "weathering effect" (Geronimus et al., 2006).

From a fiscal perspective, below-average use of high-cost health services represents a net benefit to the system. This fiscal advantage is, however, temporary across the life cycle horizon: as the migrant population ages, its usage patterns will progressively converge with those of the national population (Kennedy et al., 2015). This dynamic implies that the net fiscal benefit of immigration in health is a decreasing function of length of stay, which reinforces the importance of continued migratory flows, rather than merely accumulated stocks, for sustaining fiscal balance.

5.2. Education

Education occupies a singular position in this picture: it is the domain in which migrant families make greatest use of public services and, simultaneously, the one in which that use generates the most substantial intergenerational fiscal returns. Migrant families make intensive use of the Portuguese education system, particularly for school-age children, a pattern reflecting both the young demographic structure of this population and the high value placed on education as a vehicle for social mobility (Sacramento et al., 2023; Ramos & Ramos, 2025).

The literature on second-generation immigrants demonstrates that educational investment produces fiscal and economic returns that substantially outweigh the initial costs. Children of immigrants educated in Portugal tend to access more qualified labour market positions, earn higher incomes, and contribute more intensively to social security throughout their careers (Rodrigues et al., 2022). This phenomenon of upward intergenerational social mobility constitutes one of the most robust arguments in favour of public investment in the educational integration of migrants' children. From a social cost-benefit perspective, each euro invested in the educational integration of migrant children is estimated to generate deferred fiscal returns substantially higher than the initial outlay, although the precise measurement of these returns varies across methodologies and national contexts (Fiorio et al., 2024).

Yet it would be naive not to add a caveat: this entire intergenerational value chain only works if school integration is genuinely effective. A system that formally includes but materially marginalises through insufficient support resources for Portuguese as a foreign language, the stereotyping of academic expectations, or ignorance of the cultural dynamics of migrant families, squanders the intergenerational potential that, in pension terms, justifies the investment itself. The Escolhas Programme and the Learning and Inclusion Support Measures (MSAI) are examples of policies that seek to address these gaps, with results that research has been documenting in an increasingly systematic manner (Rodrigues et al., 2022; Sacramento et al., 2023).

5.3. Social Protection

The empirical evidence available for Portugal is consistent with patterns documented elsewhere in Europe: migrants draw, in per capita terms, fewer social benefits than national citizens with comparable socioeconomic characteristics (Oliveira, 2023). This finding is not, however, entirely attributable to lower objective need; it results in part from institutional, administrative, and informational barriers that limit effective access to formally recognised entitlements. Boeri (2009), in a landmark study on non-EU migrants' access to social transfers, confirms that once individual characteristics are controlled for, the so-called residual dependency, defined as the probability that a migrant receives more than a national with the same characteristics, disappears in virtually all countries analysed, including Portugal.

This conclusion is reinforced by Römer (2023), in a large-scale study analysing data from 21 OECD countries between 1980 and 2010. Using dynamic panel models with error correction, the author demonstrates that there is a negative and statistically robust association between net migration and social expenditure in the short term, given that migrants add more to GDP than they draw in benefits, and that in the medium and long term there is no evidence that migration increases social expenditure. Römer (2023) concludes that there is little empirical foundation for the thesis that migration has an overburden or erosion effect on the welfare state.

The pattern of under-access to social benefits by migrants, combined with their relatively high contributory level, generates a systematically positive balance for the system. Yet this pattern also contains an ethical dimension: a social protection system that migrant workers finance but access at a disproportionately low rate constitutes, in practice, a transfer of resources from an already vulnerable population to society as a whole. This tension between fiscal efficiency and social justice is one of the structural dilemmas of the relationship between immigration and the welfare state, with social work being one of the few institutional spaces where that tension is simultaneously acknowledged and actively addressed (Oliveira & Caleiras, 2025; Eiras et al., 2024; Dominelli, 2010).

6. THE SUSTAINABILITY OF THE WELFARE STATE IN A CONTEXT OF ACCELERATED DEMOGRAPHIC AGEING

6.1. Structural Pressures

The Portuguese welfare state is not in sudden crisis: it is under growing structural pressure, driven by a confluence of forces that any demographic projection makes increasingly difficult to ignore. Demographic projections from INE (2023) indicate that the proportion of the population aged 65 or over will rise from the current approximately 23% to over 35% by 2050, in the central scenario. Eurostat projects an increase in pension expenditure of approximately 3 to 4 percentage points of GDP by 2070 in the Portuguese case, one of the most pronounced increases in the European Union (EUROPOP2023).

Hinrichs (2021), in a comprehensive review of EU pension reforms over the past three decades, identifies the main adjustment instruments available to governments: reduction of the benefit ratio (through indexation to inflation rather than wage growth, reduction of accrual rates, incorporation of demographic factors); extension of working life (raising the statutory retirement age, closing early retirement routes); and the construction of multi-pillar systems. Portugal has, since the 2008 crisis and under pressure from the European Commission and the IMF, followed a path that simultaneously combines several of these instruments. By reducing the benefit ratio, these reforms increase the risk of old-age poverty, particularly for workers with fragmented contributory careers, a situation that disproportionately encompasses migrants with histories of precarious employment. The scale of this structural pressure is illustrated by the working-age population projections and old-age dependency ratios presented in Figures 1 and 2.

Figure 1. Projections of the working-age population (15–64 years) by migratory scenario, Portugal 2015–2060.

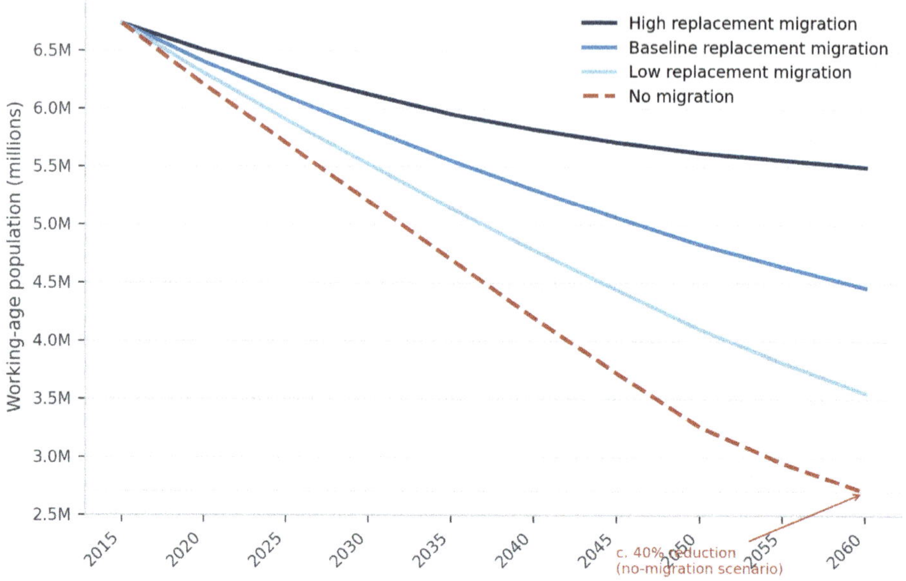

Note. Source: Own elaboration based on Alves et al. (2019), Tables 5 and 7. The no-migration scenario projects a reduction of approximately 40% in the active population between 2015 and 2060.

Figure 2. Old-age dependency ratio (pop. 65+/pop. 15–64) by migratory scenario, Portugal 2015–2060.

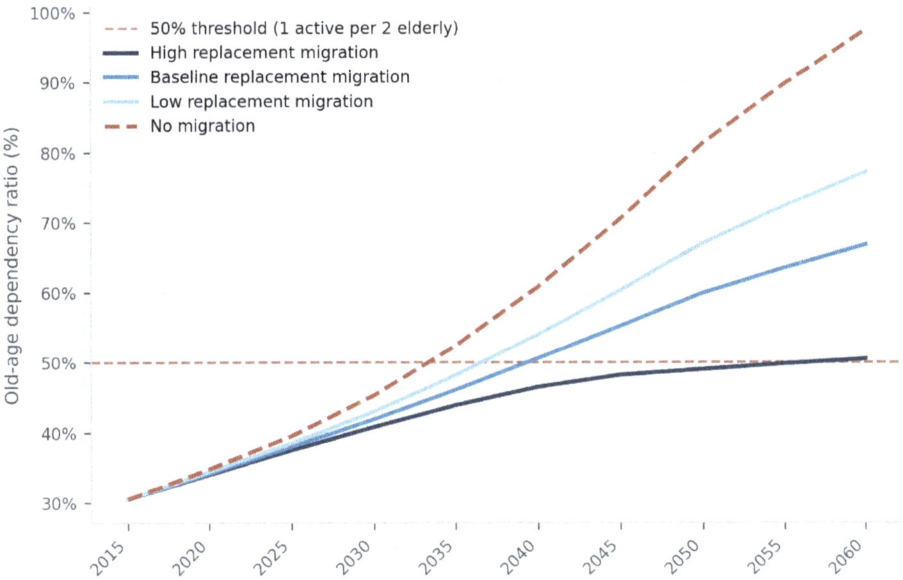

Note. Source: Own elaboration based on Alves et al. (2019), Tables 5 and 7. The dashed red line marks the 50% threshold, corresponding to one person of working age for every two older persons.

6.2. The Potential Contribution of Migration

The study by Bernardino, Franco, and Teles Morais (2025), the most recent to focus directly on the Portuguese case, puts concrete numbers on a dependency that qualitative projections had indicated but not measured. Using a demographic model combined with original estimates of migrants' fiscal contributions in Eurozone economies, the authors demonstrate that eliminating immigration increases the fiscal burden of ageing by 16%, whilst doubling inflows reduces it by only 9%, an asymmetry whose fiscal implications are asymmetric: restricting immigration carries substantially higher public finance costs than does equivalent expansion.

For Portugal specifically, the authors estimate that, in a scenario of maintaining current migratory flows (0.5% of the population per year), the fiscal adjustment required to ensure the sustainability of public finances in the face of ageing would amount to 2.9 percentage points of GDP; in a zero-immigration scenario, that effort rises to 10.8 percentage points, and the total fiscal burden would need to reach 43% of GDP (Bernardino et al., 2025). In individual terms, the average net contribution of a 30-year-old national taxpayer would need to increase by 631 euros per year in the baseline scenario; without immigration, that figure rises to 1,700 euros annually. This difference constitutes the most rigorous monetary estimate available for the Portuguese case of immigration's pension-system value under conditions of accelerated demographic ageing.

In a retrospective analysis spanning 14 European countries between 1981 and 2009, Han (2013) reaches a conclusion with direct bearing on the Portuguese case: labour migration actively restrained the reduction of pension benefit levels, cuts in public pension expenditure, and the expansion of private pension funds. This effect is substantially larger in countries with Bismarckian pension systems, such as Portugal, which depend on current contributions to finance current benefits, unlike countries with Beveridgean systems. Bongaarts (2004) adds an equally relevant long-run perspective: an increase in the annual net migration rate of 1 per 1,000 inhabitants reduces the ratio of public pension expenditure to GDP in 2050 by approximately 5%, a sensitivity comparable to an increase in fertility of 0.1 births per woman.

The convergence between Römer (2023) and Han (2013) — two independent studies with different samples and methodologies arriving at the same finding — is a degree of agreement unusual in a field characterised by contested results: migration sustains rather than erodes the generosity of public pension systems.

The magnitude of this contribution depends, however, on more than demographic and economic variables. Qi (2025), in a panel analysis of 28 advanced countries between 1980 and 2019, demonstrates that the effect of immigration on social expenditure is ambiguous when analysed unconditionally, becoming systematically positive only under certain institutional configurations. In coalition and minority governments, where multiple veto players hinder the adoption of restrictive policies and where electoral accountability is diffused across coalition partners, the effect of immigration on social expenditure is significantly larger than in single-party majority governments. The financial consequences of different migratory scenarios for the old-age pension sub-system are set out in Figures 3 and 4.

Figure 3. Financial balance of the old-age pension sub-system with and without replacement migration, 2015–2060.

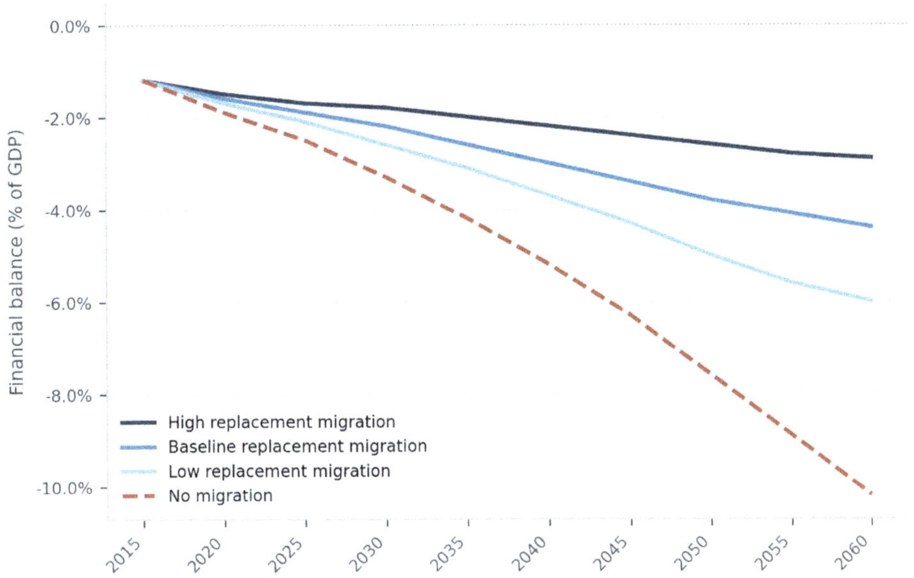

Note. Source: Own elaboration based on Alves et al. (2019), Table 8 (Case I). Solid lines = scenarios with replacement migration; dashed lines = scenarios without migration. Values expressed as a percentage of GDP.

Figure 4. Differential in the financial balance between scenarios with and without replacement migration (percentage points of GDP), 2020–2060.

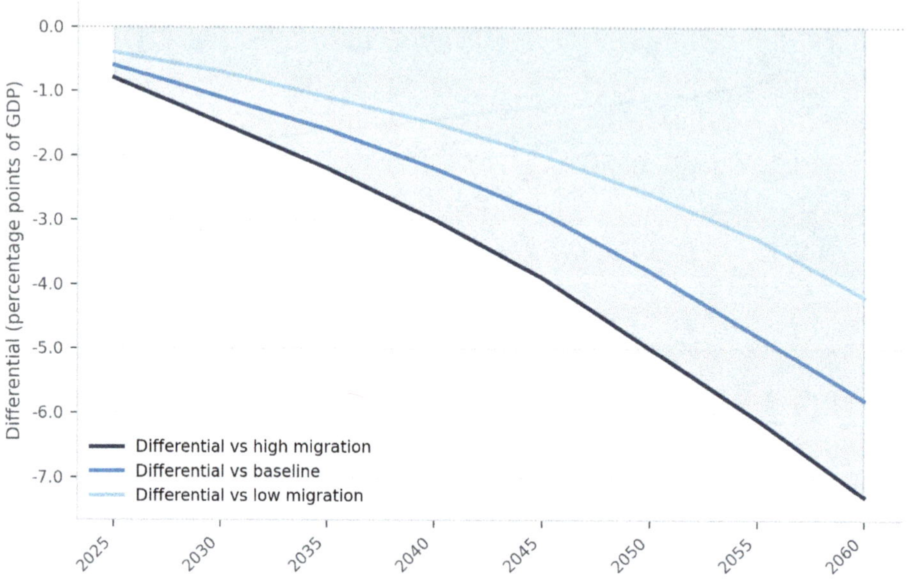

Note. Source: Own elaboration based on Alves et al. (2019), Table 8 (Case I). Negative values indicate deterioration of the balance in the absence of replacement migration relative to the equivalent scenario with migration.

6.3. Fiscal Return Scenarios

The returns on integration investment play out across three distinct time horizons, each with its own logic.

In the short-term horizon (2025–2035), pension returns are dominated by the immediate effect of contributions from migrants already present in the formal labour market. Improving formalisation rates through the regularisation of irregular situations, the recognition of qualifications, and the combating of undeclared work constitutes the primary lever for pension revenue in this period. Franco et al. (2020) demonstrated that different migratory assumptions produce significant divergences in pension balances even within a 10 to 15-year horizon, with higher-formalisation scenarios generating substantial gains relative to stagnation or migratory contraction scenarios.

In the medium-term horizon (2035–2050), qualification recognition becomes the critical lever: with over 35% of migrants in Portugal overqualified for the roles they perform (Observatório das Migrações, 2026), deskilling through migration represents a structural contributory waste of hundreds of millions of euros annually.

Santos and Domínguez-Fabián (2012) quantified the migratory flows required for pension solvency in this horizon — an exercise empirically validated by current GEP/MTSSS data.

In the long-term horizon (2050 and beyond), the pension impact of the second generation assumes analytical primacy. Fiorio et al. (2024) demonstrate that, in the EU, migrants contribute more than natives to public finances, partly because they are younger and have a lower probability of receiving accumulated pensions. Public investment in the educational integration of the second generation, through programmes such as Escolhas, the teaching of Portuguese as a foreign language, and psychosocial support in schools, can be analysed not merely as social expenditure, but as an investment with high-magnitude deferred pension returns (Rodrigues et al., 2022; Sacramento et al., 2023).

7. BEYOND THE MYTHS: TENSIONS, OPPORTUNITIES, AND DILEMMAS

It would be too easy, and intellectually dishonest, to conclude that the data presented resolve the problem. They do not. What they do reveal is a set of structural tensions that will not be resolved by good intentions alone. The first tension is that between formal contribution and effective access: a system in which migrant workers contribute in proportion above their demographic representation, but access benefits in proportion below their objective need, is not merely fiscally efficient; it is also unjust from the standpoint of social justice. This tension is structurally embedded in the Bismarckian architecture of the Portuguese system and requires deliberate intervention to be corrected.

The second tension exists between contributory potential and professional deskilling. With more than 35% of migrants in Portugal overqualified for the roles they perform, there is a structural waste of human capital that translates directly into lost pension revenue. The recognition of foreign qualifications, one of the most persistent bottlenecks in the Portuguese integration system, is not merely a matter of individual equity: it is also a question of economic efficiency and pension sustainability (Alves et al., 2019; Observatório das Migrações, 2026).

The third tension is temporal in nature: the fiscal benefits of immigration are structurally deferred in time, whilst integration costs are immediate. This temporal asymmetry favours discourses that emphasise visible costs and minimise invisible benefits, generating a distorted perception of the fiscal balance that fuels populist narratives. Addressing this tension requires public communication instruments capable of translating long time horizons into accessible language, a task in which social work can play a crucial role as mediator and critical voice capacity-builder (Dominelli, 2010; Casquilho-Martins et al., 2025).

There are also real opportunities. The youth of the migrant population is a first-order demographic resource; the diversity of origins and competencies carries innovation potential; and Portugal's historical ties to Brazil, Lusophone Africa, and Asia create unique conditions for a skilled migration hub. These assets only materialise through integration policies that translate potential into realisation.

The dilemmas, in turn, are ethical and political in nature. The central dilemma is that between the instrumentalisation of migration as a fiscal resource and the recognition of the intrinsic dignity of migrants as rights-bearing subjects. An approach that justifies openness to migrants exclusively through their contributions to public finances is not only ethically problematic but also empirically fragile: the data demonstrate that migrants contribute because they work, not because they work in order to contribute. The normative framework must recognise this principle without surrendering it to a purely utilitarian narrative that, in moments of economic crisis, can easily reverse into hostility. Social work, as a profession committed to social justice and human dignity, bears a particular responsibility for guarding this boundary (Dominelli, 2010; Casquilho-Martins et al., 2025).

8. CONCLUSIONS

Seven conclusions follow from this analysis. Some are empirical summaries; others are, in effect, claims about what the evidence requires of us as researchers, practitioners, and citizens.

First, migration contributes positively to fiscal revenues: GEP/MTSSS (2026) data demonstrate that foreign nationals contributed, in 2025, five times more to social security than they received in benefits. This 5:1 ratio is not a temporary anomaly: it reflects the age structure of the migrant population and the logic of the PAYG system, being structurally sustained for as long as migratory flows continue and integration policies ensure the formalisation of employment. That said, this ratio is not merely an indicator of fiscal efficiency: it is also a mirror of a structural asymmetry that demands both political and ethical response.

Second, use of public services is proportional to or lower than that of the national population, particularly in specialist health care. This pattern, consistent with the healthy immigrant effect (Kennedy et al., 2015), has a temporary component resulting from the youth of current migratory flows and tends to diminish as this population progressively ages.

Third, migration can partially mitigate the effects of demographic ageing by slowing the deterioration of the active-to-inactive ratio. The evidence from Bernardino et al. (2025) is particularly clear: without immigration, the fiscal effort required to ensure the sustainability of public finances in Portugal would quadruple, from 2.9 to 10.8 percentage points of GDP. Migration is, in these terms, one of the indispensable components of any credible pension sustainability strategy, albeit not the only one.

Fourth, one should not shy away from an uncomfortable fact: the data this chapter presents have existed for decades, yet the gap between public perceptions and empirical evidence regarding migrants has not narrowed. The Portuguese case documented by Boeri (2009) is instructive: in 2000, half the Portuguese population believed that migrants were exploiting the social protection system, at a moment when scientific evidence demonstrated the contrary. That gap has not narrowed; if anything, it has deepened.

Fifth, the contribution of immigration to the welfare state is not an automatic demographic given: it is the product of deliberate policy choices. The recognition of qualifications, tackling labour informality, promoting educational inclusion for the second generation, and ensuring effective access to social protection are the pillars of any integration agenda capable of delivering demonstrable pension returns.

A sixth conclusion emerges from the comparative institutional analysis: the pension contribution of immigration does not materialise automatically. As Qi (2025) demonstrates, it is the type of government, and the institutional architecture that distributes power and responsibility among multiple actors, that determines the extent to which migrants' fiscal contributions are translated into effective social protection policies. In coalition and minority governments, immigration tends to generate more social expenditure than in majority governments, because internal veto mechanisms and the diffusion of electoral accountability attenuate the conversion of anti-immigration sentiment into restrictive policy. This institutional dimension is therefore a public policy variable on a par with the demographic or the economic.

A seventh conclusion, normative in nature, constitutes the central ethical argument of this chapter. The sustainability of the welfare state must not be assessed solely by the positive balance of the pension system. A 5:1 ratio between contributions and benefits received can be read simultaneously as an indicator of fiscal robustness and as an alarm signal about the equity of the system: if those who contribute most access proportionally less of what they finance, the welfare state is functioning as a mechanism for transferring resources from a structurally vulnerable population to society as a whole, without guaranteeing the reciprocity that legitimises the social contract. The concept of the immigrant fiscal dividend, as used by Dustmann and Frattini (2014), describes a real and measurable fiscal surplus. Its existence, however, only constitutes a full contribution to the welfare state when that dividend is reinvested in guaranteeing equitable access to benefits for those who generated it. The criterion for evaluating the welfare state in a migratory context must therefore be twofold: not only "how much do migrants contribute?", but also "how much of what they contribute is guaranteed to them?". The distance between these two questions is the measure of the system's ethical debt to migrant workers. Social work bears the singular responsibility of making this debt visible and translating it into demands for political intervention. The conclusions drawn from the Portuguese case are relevant to the many European countries facing the same triple challenge: rapid ageing, pressure on public systems, and the rise of populist discourses that instrumentalise migration without acknowledging the ethical debt the system owes to those who sustain it.

AI DISCLOSURE STATEMENT

The author(s) used Perplexity and Microsoft Copilot to assist with outlining and structuring the chapter (e.g., organising headings and the sequence of topics). The author(s) also used DeepL for translation support to improve the readability of text originally written by the author(s). These tools were not used to generate original scholarly content (e.g., arguments, analysis, results, or conclusions), nor to create, generate, or modify figures/images. All AI-assisted outputs were critically reviewed, verified, and edited by the author(s), who take full responsibility for the final manuscript.

COMPETING INTERESTS

The author(s) declare no competing interests.

REFERENCES

AIMA. I.P. (2025). Relatório de migrações e asilo 2024. Agência para a Integração, Migrações e Asilo. https://aima.gov.pt/media/pages/documents/fec4d6a712-1760603125/relatorio-migracoes-e-asilo-2024.pdf

Alesina, A., Ferroni, M., & Stantcheva, S. (2023). Perceptions of racial gaps, their causes, and ways to reduce them. *AEA Papers and Proceedings. American Economic Association, 113*, 1–6. DOI: 10.1257/pandp.20231009

Alves, J., Esteves, R., & Pinheiro, M. (2019). Migração e o saldo financeiro do sistema público de pensões em Portugal. *Notas Económicas*, (49), 5–22.

Amaro, A. R. (2018). The late construction of Portugal welfare state: The failure of the social corporatist state (1933–1974). *Memoria y Civilización, 21*. Advance online publication. DOI: 10.15581/001.21.005

Amaro, A. R., & Guerra, J. (2024). Capitalismo, democracia e Welfare State em Portugal. *Textos & Contextos (Porto Alegre), 23*(1), e46874. DOI: 10.15448/1677-9509.2024.1.46874

Arruda, M. de S. (2023). Pro-immigrant digital platforms in Portugal: An overview. *E-Journal of International and Comparative Labour Studies, 12*(1), 1–17.

Bernardino, T., Franco, F., & Teles Morais, L. (2025). The costs of building walls: Immigration and the fiscal burden of ageing in Europe [Working Paper]. Nova SBE / IIES – Stockholm University. https://ssrn.com/abstract=4932922

Boeri, T. (2009). Migration policy and the welfare state. In *Reinventing the Welfare State* (pp. 1–22). Netspar / Tilburg University.

Bongaarts, J. (2004). Population ageing and the rising cost of public pensions. *Population and Development Review, 30*(1), 1–23. DOI: 10.1111/j.1728-4457.2004.00001.x

Branco, R. (2017). Entre Bismarck e Beveridge: Sociedade civil e Estado-Providência em Portugal (1960–2011). Análise Social, (224), 534–558. DOI: 10.31447/AS00032573.2017224.02

Calado, A., Capucha, L., & Estêvão, P. (2019). Welfare State development in Portugal: From “Stage Zero” to the post-crisis “leftist” compromise against austerity. *Comparative Sociology, 18*(5–6), 658–686. DOI: 10.1163/15691330-12341515

Carolo, D. F., & Pereirinha, J. A. (2010). The development of the Welfare State in Portugal: Trends in social expenditure between 1938 and 2003. Revista de Historia Económica / Journal of Iberian and Latin American Economic History, 28(3), 469–501. DOI: 10.1017/S0212610910000133

Carvalho, J., & Duarte, M. C. (2020). The politicization of immigration in Portugal between 1995 and 2014: A European exception? *Journal of Common Market Studies*, *58*(6), 1469–1487. DOI: 10.1111/jcms.13048

Casquilho-Martins, I., Ferreira, S., & Alves, D. R. (2025). Addressing migrant access to healthcare in Portugal: Promoting rights in a landscape of socio-political polarization. Trabajo Social Global–Global Social Work, 15(Extra), 214–242. DOI: 10.30827/tsg-gsw.33392

Challinor, E. (2012). Medical citizenship, culture and power in perinatal and pediatric immigrant care. *Saúde e Sociedade*, *21*(1), 76–88. DOI: 10.1590/S0104-12902012000100009

Christl, M., Bélanger, A., Conte, A., Mazza, J., & Narazani, E. (2022). Projecting the fiscal impact of immigration in the European Union. *Fiscal Studies*, *43*(4), 365–385. DOI: 10.1111/1475-5890.12314

Citrin, J., & Sides, J. (2008). Immigration and the imagined community in Europe and the United States. *Political Studies*, *56*(1), 33–56. DOI: 10.1111/j.1467-9248.2007.00716.x

Cook, M. L. (2018). Portugal's immigration and integration policies: A case apart? *Journal of International Migration and Integration*, *19*(3), 771–789. DOI: 10.1007/s12134-018-0569-x

de Oliveira, C. R. (2023). *Indicadores de integração de imigrantes: Relatório estatístico anual 2023 (Imigração em Números, 8)*. Observatório das Migrações, Alto Comissariado para as Migrações.

Dominelli, L. (2010). *Social work in a globalizing world*. Polity Press.

Dustmann, C., & Frattini, T. (2014). The fiscal effects of immigration to the UK. *Economic Journal (London)*, *124*(580), F593–F643. DOI: 10.1111/ecoj.12181

Eiras, A. A., Toledo, A. F., Monteiro da Silva, D. J. M., & Ferreira, M. E. F. (2024). Questão social em Portugal: Indicadores e desafios para o Serviço Social. *Eleuthera*, *27*(1), 127–143. DOI: 10.17151/eleu.2025.27.1.8

Esping-Andersen, G. (1990). *The three worlds of welfare capitalism*. Polity Press.

Fiorio, C. V., Frattini, T., Riganti, A., & Christl, M. (2024). Migration and public finances in the EU. *International Tax and Public Finance, 31*(3), 635–684. DOI: 10.1007/s10797-023-09787-9

Franco, F., Rodrigues, P. G., & Pereira, T. (2020). Cenários de imigração e sustentabilidade das finanças públicas portuguesas: Pensões e contribuições como itens-chave. *Portuguese Economic Journal, 19*(3), 195–220.

Gabinete de Estratégia e Planeamento do Ministério do Trabalho, Solidariedade e Segurança Social. (2026). Síntese de informação estatística da Segurança Social: Janeiro de 2026. https://www.gep.mtsss.gov.pt/documents/10182/37639/siess202601.pdf

Geronimus, A. T., Hicken, M., Keene, D., & Bound, J. (2006). "Weathering" and age patterns of allostatic load scores among Blacks and Whites in the United States. *American Journal of Public Health, 96*(5), 826–833. DOI: 10.2105/AJPH.2004.060749 PMID: 16380565

Han, K. J. (2013). Saving public pensions: Labor migration effects on pension systems in European countries. *The Social Science Journal, 50*(2), 152–161. DOI: 10.1016/j.soscij.2012.12.001

Hinrichs, K. (2021). Recent pension reforms in Europe: More challenges, new directions. An overview. *Social Policy and Administration, 55*(3), 409–422. DOI: 10.1111/spol.12712

Instituto Nacional de Estatística. (2023). *Projeções de população residente em Portugal 2022–2080*. INE.

Kennedy, S., McDonald, J. T., & Biddle, N. (2015). The healthy immigrant effect and immigrant selection: Evidence from four countries. *Social Science & Medicine, 130*, 217–222. DOI: 10.1016/j.socscimed.2015.02.023

Observatório das Migrações. (2025). *As políticas de nacionalidade numa perspetiva comparada (Versão 1)*. AIMA.

Observatório das Migrações. (2026). *Relatório anual de monitorização da integração de imigrantes*. AIMA/Observatório das Migrações.

Oliveira, M. C., & Caleiras, J. (2025). So far and yet so close: Labour market activation and social policy in Portugal and Chile. *Journal of Comparative Policy Analysis, •••*, 1–20. DOI: 10.1080/13876988.2025.2596831

Padilla, B., & Ortiz, A. (2012). Fluxos migratórios em Portugal: Do boom migratório à desaceleração no contexto de crise. Balancos e desafios. *Revista Interdisciplinar da Mobilidade Humana, 20*(39), 159–184. DOI: 10.1590/S1980-85852012000200009

Pereira, S. M. (2024). Portuguese reactions to the housing crisis: Is it possible to move from the residualisation to post-neoliberalisation of housing policies? *Critical Housing Analysis, 11*(2), 204–215. DOI: 10.13060/23362839.2024.11.2.578

Pinho, J., & Ançã, M. H. (2023). Aprender português língua de acolhimento, em contexto não formal: Imigrantes e refugiados em Portugal. *Revista Lusófona de Educação, 58*(58), 31–49. DOI: 10.24140/issn.1645-7250.rle58.02

Pires, R. P., Vidigal, I., Pereira, C., Azevedo, J., & Veiga, C. M. (2025). *Emigração portuguesa 2024: Relatório estatístico. Observatório da Emigração e Rede Migra.* CIES-Iscte.

Qi, H. (2025). Immigration, government type, and social welfare spending. *Policy Studies Journal: the Journal of the Policy Studies Organization, 53*(2), 349–364. DOI: 10.1111/psj.70015

Ramos, M. D. C. P., & Ramos, N. (2025). Olhares e perspetivas sobre educação e imigração em Portugal: Do ensino básico ao ensino superior. *Estudos Avançados, 39*(115), e39115315. DOI: 10.1590/s0103-4014.202539115.018

Rodrigues, R., Amorim, J. P., & Neves, T. (2022). "The holiness of minute particulars": Can the community compensate for the schools' shortfalls in affection? *Pastoral Care in Education, 40*(1), 41–60. DOI: 10.1080/02643944.2020.1855672

Römer, F. (2023). How immigration affects the welfare state in the short and long run: Differences between social spending and policy generosity. *European Policy Analysis, 9*(1), 69–90. DOI: 10.1002/epa2.1140

Sacramento, O., Challinor, E., & Silva, P. G. (2023). The challenges of education in contexts of increasing migratory diversity: (Mis)adjustments, adaptative practices and creativity in Portuguese schools. REMHU: Revista Interdisciplinar da Mobilidade Humana, 31(69), 73–89. https://doi.org/DOI: 10.1590/1980-85852503880006906

Santos, J. A., & Domínguez-Fabián, I. (2012). Imigração como solução para o sistema previdencial português: Quantificação dos fluxos necessários para a solvência. Em Reforming Pension Systems (Cap. 8). FMI. https://www.elibrary.imf.org/downloadpdf/display/book/9781484353844/ch08.pdf

Tosi, A. (2012). Homeless people. In *International encyclopedia of housing and home* (pp. 74–79). Elsevier., DOI: 10.1016/B978-0-08-047163-1.00331-3

KEY TERMS AND DEFINITIONS

Demographic Ageing Index: A demographic indicator calculated as the ratio between the population aged 65 or over and the population aged under 15, multiplied by 100. It expresses the relative weight of the elderly in relation to the young within a given population and is one of the main indicators used to measure the pace of population ageing.

Deskilling Through Migration: A structural phenomenon in which migrant workers perform functions below their formal qualification level in the host country, due to non-recognition of foreign qualifications, language barriers, or discrimination in the labour market. This phenomenon generates a simultaneous loss of individual human capital, productive efficiency for the economy, and contributory potential for the social security system.

Healthy Immigrant Effect: The empirically documented tendency for recently arrived migrants to present superior health indicators relative to the native population of equivalent age, attributed primarily to self-selection mechanisms in migration: those who migrate tend to be healthier and more resilient than those who remain in the country of origin. This advantage tends to diminish with length of residence.

Immigrant Fiscal Dividend: The net fiscal surplus generated by immigration when both tax and social security contributions and transfers received across the life cycle are accounted for. The concept reflects the tendency of migrants, particularly those of working age, to contribute more to public finances than they draw in benefits, at least during the initial decades of residence.

Intergenerational Fiscal Return: The fiscal revenue generated in subsequent generations as a result of public investment in the education and integration of the children of migrants. This concept encompasses the multiplying effect of educational investment: the improved labour market integration and higher earnings of the second generation translate into increased social security contributions across their working lives, generating deferred returns to the pension system.

Pay-As-You-Go (PAYG) System: A pension financing model in which current contributions paid by the active working population are used directly to fund the benefits of current retirees, without prior accumulation of capital. The financial sustainability of this model depends structurally on the ratio between active contributors and benefit recipients.

Residual Welfare Dependency: The statistical probability that a migrant individual receives a higher volume of social transfers than a national individual with identical socioeconomic characteristics. When individual characteristics are controlled for, the empirical literature systematically demonstrates that this residual probability tends to zero or is absent, contradicting the assumption that migrants are disproportionate users of social protection systems.

Welfare Chauvinism: A political and ideological orientation that advocates the restriction of access to welfare state benefits to citizens of the host country, excluding migrants or conditioning their access more severely. It represents a selective version of the welfare state in which social rights are linked to national origin rather than residence or contribution, and has been associated with the growth of populist parties in Europe.

Chapter 9
Gender and Migration Roles:
Opportunities and Limitations

Zahid Ahmad Thoker
http://orcid.org/0009-0002-6897-5835
Lovely Professional University, India

Lovleen Marwaha
http://orcid.org/0000-0002-5175-2590
Lovely Professional University, India

ABSTRACT

Migration is a profoundly gendered process shaped by unequal power relations, structural constraints, and opportunities across social, economic, and political contexts. This chapter critically examines the intersection of gender and migration by exploring how women's mobility reconstructs gender roles, transforms family and care arrangements, and reshapes agency within transnational spaces. Drawing on feminist, intersectional, and transnational perspectives, the chapter analyses both the opportunities migration offers women, such as economic participation, social empowerment, and skill development and the persistent limitations they face, including labour market precarity, gender-based violence, restrictive policies, and social exclusion. By integrating lived experiences, policy analysis, and emerging trends, the chapter highlights the central role of migrant women in sustainable human development and argues for gender-responsive migration governance that promotes equity, protection, and social inclusion.

DOI: 10.4018/979-8-3373-8500-6.ch009

1. INTRODUCTION

Migration is a social process that has been in existence since humans have been present, and this has changed society, economy, culture, and even political systems over time and space. Although the initial migration literature has tended to be tightly male-centric in its studies about labour mobility and economic factors, modern-day literature has come to acknowledge migration as highly gendered and as a determinant of social change (Kofman and Raghuram, 2015). The increased acknowledgment of the independent roles women played in the transnational movements over the past decades has been a challenge to the previous thinking of the migrant women as being primarily dependents or followers of their male counterparts. As the paradigm shift where women migrate in large numbers in most parts of the world is commonly referred to as the feminisation of migration, it should be noted that a large percentage of migrants across the globe are female and migrate either to work, study, build families, or seek refuge (Piper, 2008).

Gendered migration is important because it helps to highlight how notions of power, chances, and susceptibilities are unequally distributed among migration systems. Gender is intertwined with class, ethnicity, legal status, age, and nationality to influence migration, in what conditions, and with what result. The migration patterns of women are often determined by labour requirements across the global feminised regions like household work, care labour, and services (Bastia, 2023). It is these dynamics that subject migrant women to different types of vulnerability, such as precarious work, restricted access to social services, and high chances of exploitation and gender-based violence. Migration, on the other hand, may provide avenues to economic self-sufficiency, social mobility, and increased agency, especially when women work, are educated, or mobilize communities overseas.

Gendered migration is therefore critical in understanding migration to enhance scholarly and policy development. The gender-blind models of migration do not correspond to the actual needs and contributions of women migrants, which leads to the failure to cover the areas of protection, integration, and social inclusion (Teodorescu, 2024). This chapter provides an addition to the general discussion about social justice, human rights, and sustainable development by foregrounding gender as one of the key analytic categories to outline that migration processes reproduce and reinforce the existing gender hierarchies at the local, national, and global scales.

Conceptualising Gender within Migration Studies

Gender is theorised as a relation-specific system of roles, roles, and norms that are socially constructed to define the experiences of individual people and institutional setups in the context of migration studies (Christou, 2022). According to feminist and gender sociologists, the process of migration is a gendered and gendering one: it not only reproduces the current gender relations but can also transform them by occupying labour markets, family roles, and transnational networks with gender relations. Based on gender affects migration aspirations, migration modes, resource accessibility, and settlement or returning outcomes (Kofman and Raghuram, 2015).

The conceptualisation of gender within migration studies has been substantially shaped by the pioneering contributions of feminist migration scholars who challenged the male-centred assumptions of traditional migration theories. Among the earliest contributions, Mirjana Morokvasic (1984) argued that women should be recognised as independent migrants rather than merely accompanying spouses, thereby drawing attention to the invisibility of women in migration research. Building on this foundation, Pierrette Hondagneu-Sotelo (1994) demonstrated that migration is fundamentally a gendered process that reshapes family relations, labour participation, and household dynamics. Subsequently, Patricia R. Pessar and Sarah J. Mahler (2003) introduced the influential concept of the "gendered geographies of power," illustrating how gender interacts with social location, institutional structures, and transnational processes to influence migration experiences. More recently, Eleonore Kofman and Parvati Raghuram (2015) expanded these perspectives by examining skilled migration, care work, social reproduction, and migration governance through feminist and intersectional lenses. Collectively, these studies transformed gender from a peripheral demographic variable into a central analytical framework for understanding migration processes, inequalities, and social change.

One of the theoretical innovations that has been made in gendered migration studies is the use of intersectionality, which emphasizes the fact that gender cuts across a broad range of power systems, like race and class and legal status, and age. Black feminist thinking gave rise to intersectionality to articulate the effects of intersecting systems of oppression in defining complex social positions (White, 2025). The intersectional approach to migration studies can aid in seeing, among other things, how an undocumented migrant woman of colour can have accumulated disadvantages that are not inherent to the experience of a female skilled professional migrant or a male migrant in the same socio-economic status.

The other important theoretical aspect is the dimension of transnationalism, which highlights that migration does not cut off the relationship with the country of origin but is frequently redefining social relationships across borders by remittance, care, practices of culture, and family duties. As guardians, laborers, and negotiators of the expectations across societies, women often maintain transnational families and bargain various obligations (Piper, 2008). Gender conceptualisation of migration, therefore, needs to consider both structural limitations and the daily practices of migrant women who have agency within the intersectional social worlds.

Rationale, Scope, and Objectives of the Chapter

This chapter is based on the argument that the analysis and policy gaps about gendered migration are persistent. Despite a significant growth in the academic acknowledgement of the contributions of women to the process of migration, the bulk of analysis persists in marginalising the issue of gender or reducing it to the status of a demographic factor rather than an organising principle of migration. This limitation is attempted to be overcome in this chapter by making gender central to the study of migration, as well as by critically analysing the impact of migration on the re-formation of gender relations within families, labour markets, communities, and institutional structures in both sending and receiving societies.

The chapter is purposefully interdisciplinary and global and is based on the knowledge of sociology, gender studies, anthropology, economics, and development studies. The chapter takes a middle ground and a critical view of migration and acknowledges that migration could create viable opportunities for women, such as greater autonomy, economic gains, skill development, and social network access. Meanwhile, it does not ignore the structural constraints that still limit the agency of women, including gendered division of labour, discrimination, legal/policy constraints, and social marginalization. This interaction between the two dimensions helps the chapter to evade the simplistic descriptions of women as either being empowered or victimized; rather, it shows a complex view of migration experience among the women.

It is through this analysis of the concepts of migration that the chapter seeks to conceptualise migration as a social process that is inherently gendered based on power relations and structural inequalities. It aims to examine how migration can provide women with opportunities and constraints, especially regarding labour market engagement, social integration, and autonomy, as well as make its own contribution to policy and general academic discussions. The chapter seeks to enhance the insight into the gendered aspects of migration and to inform future research, policy formulation, and advocacy on gender justice in modern migration systems by formulating the gaps in the current migration governance frameworks and suggesting some gender-responsive solutions.

Study Aim and Problem Statement

Although women are now recognised as active agents in international migration, there is still a lack of understanding of the impact of migration processes on women's social, economic, and political lives, and how gendered power relations shape these processes in various migration contexts. Gender-neutral migration policies and theories have often used a lens that fails to capture the overlapping experiences of migrant women across class, ethnicity, legal status, age, and cultural norms. As a result, the experiences, contributions, and vulnerabilities of female migrants are often poorly captured in the governance and policy process of migration. In this context, the main objectives of this chapter are to critically analyze migration as a gendered social process by examining the reconstruction of gender relations, the opportunities and limitations experienced by female migrants, and the role of policy, technology, and governance in determining migration outcomes. This chapter aims to offer a holistic and integrated view of gendered migration, drawing on interdisciplinary literature and current theories of migration, and highlighting critical research gaps and policy priorities to support the development of more inclusive, equitable, and gender responsive migration systems.

2. THEORETICAL FOUNDATIONS OF GENDER AND MIGRATION

Feminist Migration Theories

Feminist migration theories were developed in response to the earlier migration models, which were more androcentric and economically reductionist. Classical migration theories tended to idealise the migrants as rational male laborers reacting to wage differentials, and thus made the women invisible or passive dependents in the family reunification initiatives. Feminist scholars challenged these assumptions by foregrounding women's agency and highlighting how migration is embedded within gendered social relations, labour markets, and power structures (Kofman, 1999). In this sense, migration is not purely an economic choice but a socially placed phenomenon that is informed by patriarchal conventions and caregiving roles and the gendered expectation of work and movement.

The focus on social reproduction and care labour is one of the major contributions of the feminist migration theory. Feminist researchers have illustrated that migration flows around the world are perpetuated by transnational migration of reproductive labour, especially in the form of domestic work, elder care, and childcare, which are undertaken by the migrant women (Piper, 2003). These types of labour have become undervalued, informal, and not covered by labour protections, which strengthens gendered inequalities in global economic systems. The feminist migration theory, therefore, broadens the scope of analytical interest outside the production and households, families, and emotional labour to become a crucial place of migration governance and inequalities.

Further, the feminist approaches disapprove of the binary representations of migrant women as victims or self-sufficient actors. They instead focus on relational agency and the fact that women move through limited structural environments and negotiate opportunities and risks actively. This theoretical prism allows a more sophisticated interpretation of the way migration can, at the same time, reproduce the gender hierarchies and create the space of resistance, role renegotiation, and social change (Kofman et al., 2000).

Intersectionality and Transnational Feminist Perspectives

Intersectionality has also taken root as a guiding model in gendered migration research, and it can be a potent instrument in the study of the interactions between various systems of power in order to understand the implications of migration. Intersectionality was first formulated to describe the addition of the cumulative impact of race and gender, but since then it has also been used extensively to analyse the interactions of gender with class, ethnicity, race, religion, age, and legal status in migration studies (Crenshaw, 1989). This method, in the context of migration, will demonstrate why migrant women are not a homogeneous group and why their experiences are quite different in relation to social places and geopolitical settings.

An intersectional lens has the benefit of enabling scholars to internalize the differentiated vulnerability and privilege that inform the migration patterns of women. As an example, undocumented migrant women can be at a disadvantage because of legal precarity, and highly skilled women migrants can be disadvantaged because of deskilling and racialised gender discrimination in the professional labour markets. Intersectionality, therefore, changes the analytical focus, which is on individual identities, to the intricate formations of power that define mobility and immobility (Kofman and Raghuram, 2015).

Transnational feminist views also contribute to enriching gendered migration theory with the focus on the cross-border character of social relations and inequalities. These views are critical of Western-centric paradigms and emphasize the role of global political economy, colonial past and uneven developments in influencing the migration of women in the Global South to the Global North. Transnational feminism is able to place migrant women in the network of global care chains, remittance economies, and transnational households and is able to see how gender relations are renegotiated across spatial and cultural boundaries (Pessar & Mahler, 2003). Collectively, intersectional and transnational feminism approaches offer a holistic approach to explaining migration as a multi-scalar process full of power.

Gendered Power Relations in Mobility and Immobility

Gendered power relations become very decisive in defining who can migrate, under what circumstances, and with what level of autonomy. Mobility as such is a resource with gendered variables, informed by cultural practices, family bargaining, state policies, and economic restrictions. In a wide range of situations, the migration choices that women make are mediated by social norms that govern respectability and honour, taking into account their duties as caregivers, and family constraints, which may limit free mobility or force women into particular migration patterns (Kofman, 2014).

Simultaneously, immobility, or the lack of or the restriction to movement, is also becoming a part of migration analysis. Gendered immobility can be caused by restrictive immigration policies, undocumented status, financial reliance, or caregiving responsibilities, which disfavorably affect women. According to feminist scholars, the state of immobility should not be perceived as the inability to move but as a state that is actively created under the influence of gendered power relations and institutional restrictions (Schewel, 2020).

The process of migration can also reorganize families and communities to create new power dynamics. The involvement of women in paid employment in foreign countries can put an end to the rigid gender hierarchies, as they will change the decision-making power and financial reliance. Nevertheless, such developments are usually disproportional and reversible, especially when women are still focused on low-status or informal jobs. Gendered power relations in mobility and immobility can therefore be analysed in the manner of the two to provide a more comprehensive insight into the way in which the outcomes of migration are influenced by the structural inequalities as opposed to individual choice.

Structural and Institutional Determinants of Gendered Migration

Institutional and structural forces are very critical in developing patterns and experiences of gendered migration. Labour market segmentation, immigration policies, welfare regimes, and social protection systems are not gender neutral; they tend to reproduce the existing inequalities by giving a preference to some types of mobility and discriminating against others. The labour markets that are urbanized on gender lines, such as gender-based division of labour in the low-paid care and service sectors, generate the demand for migrant women and restrict the mobility and accessibility of labour rights (Piper, 2008).

The gendered outcomes are also further organised by immigration and asylum policies, in which the legal categories may not be able to recognise the experiences of women who are persecuted, experience violence, or are burdened with care duties. Feminist researchers have noted that restrictive migration regimes tend to increase the vulnerability of women by subjecting them to irregular status, reliance on employers or partners, as well as denying them access to social services. These institutional factors highlight the significance of the gender-responsive consideration of migration governance.

On the macro level, the interaction of global inequalities, the neoliberal restructuring of the economy, and demographic transitions leads to the creation of gender-differentiated migration flows. The feminisation of migration is associated with structural adjustment policies, environmental degradation, and deficiencies of care in ageing societies, which restrict the protection of migrant women at the same time. It is necessary to understand these structural and institutional determinants, therefore, to create fair migration structures that cannot view women as migrants, but as workers, caregivers, and rights-bearing people.

3. GLOBAL TRENDS IN FEMALE MIGRATION

Historical Trajectories of Women's Migration

The involvement of women in migration is not a recent event, but most of the history of migration was under-theorised and under-documented. The initial wave of migration linked with the colonial expansion, the industrialisation, and the national building of the nation states incorporated both large numbers of women as settlers, agricultural or household workers. Nonetheless, hegemonic trends in migration discourse in the nineteenth and early twentieth centuries were mostly the view of migrants as breadwinners, with women being theorised as dependants who migrated to reunite with their families (Morokvasic, 1984). This invisibility of history was a portrayal of gender bias across the social science research community, and not the lack of women in migration flows.

Since the middle of the twentieth century, economic restructuring at the global level, decolonisation, and the growth of service economies have played a part in slowly directing the migration patterns of women. Women were moving out on their own to work, to get an education, and to get social mobility, especially in areas that were related to care, textiles, nursing, and hospitality. Feminist researchers commenced to record these patterns and dispel theories that focused on male migration and emphasised the agency of women and the structural factors that defined women's mobility (Donato et al., 2006). As historical analysis would show, the so-called Feminisation of migration is not the recent development of women migrants but a change in perceptions of women migrants, in terms of measurement and conceptualisation in migration studies.

Contemporary Patterns: Labour, Forced, and Voluntary Female Migration

In the modern world, migration mechanisms, there are almost equal numbers of women among the international migrant population, and the distribution differs widely by region and type of migration. The most noticeable form of female mobility is still the migration of labour, especially in the feminised sectors of the economy that include domestic work, caregiving, health services, agriculture, and export-oriented manufacturing. Such forms of labour markets are typically informal, poorly paid, and with fewer legal protections, which places migrant women in structurally precarious employment relations (Kofman and Raghuram, 2015).

Coupled with the labour migration, forced migration has also become a very important aspect of the movement of women. The armed conflict, political persecution, climate-related displacement, and humanitarian crisis have increased in cases of women who need asylum or refugee status. Women refugees are also vulnerable to gender-related dangers such as sexual violence, trafficking, and obstacles to accessing asylum procedures, which fail to acknowledge gender-based persecution (Daly et al., 2016). Meanwhile, voluntary migration in education, marriage, and family formation remains the determinant of the transnational movements of women, which are frequently intermarriage with labour and legal vulnerability.

These categories of migration defy strict lines between voluntary and forced migration. Migration decisions by women often come out as choices that are very limited due to economic need, social pressure, and structural imbalances, and not necessarily entirely out of choice. The need to develop analytical frameworks that embrace complexity, agency, and constraint at the same time is therefore emphasised by the contemporary trends of female migration.

Push–Pull Dynamics in Gendered Mobility

Migration flows have been traditionally explained with references to push-pull frameworks, whereas gender-sensitive approaches show that the processes differ in terms of women and men. Gender factors that cause push are the lack of access to education and employment, gender violence, lower social norms, and inequality of inheritance or property rights in countries of origin. Migration is a way of going out of the patriarchal restrictions, attaining livelihood, or satisfying family demands for many women with remittance (Bastia, 2023).

The pull factors, on the other hand, are influenced by the global demand for labour, demographic ageing in receiving nations, and institutional structures that direct women into particular sectors. The need for care workers in high-income countries has been central in consolidating the migration of low-income countries to fill the workforce in a developing global care chain that relocates reproductive labour to other countries. These pull factors cannot be said to be gender neutral because they are entrenched in social constructs of femininity, care, and emotional labour that place women as an apparently inherent fit to specific types of labour.

Notably, migration policies, recruitment practices, and social networks mediate gendered push-pulls. There is a tendency to lock women away in terms of mobility and bargaining power in temporary labour schemes, sponsorship systems, and employer-tied visas, which make women more dependent and vulnerable. To even conceive of gendered mobility, though, one must go beyond the simplistic economic account of gendered mobility to a structural analysis of power, institutions, and gender norms.

Regional Variations and Global South–North Dynamics

There are significant differences in the female migration patterns across territories, depending on economic development, demographic changes, cultural beliefs, and migration management systems. Women's migration is highly related to poverty alleviation measures and family sustainability in most of the Global South areas, and remittances are significant in the local economies. Migration to the Global North, on the contrary, is also defined by the labour deficit in care and service industries, immigration policies, and racialised labour structures (De Haas., al., 2019).

The change in migration flows with a South-North direction points to the existence of gross global inequalities that organise women's mobility. Despite their high level of skills or education, women in the Global South are often given low-status, precarious jobs in the destination countries. The main characteristics of these migration paths include deskilling, the lack of qualification appreciation, and discrimination. Meanwhile, South-South migration is a significant yet less noticeable element of global female migration as it is often informal, less safeguarded, and regionalised in nature to labour markets (Bakewell, 2009). The regional differences also indicate the difference in gender regime and social norms. Although in certain situations the migration can be associated with opportunities to renegotiate the gender roles, in other cases, it can support the old expectations, especially when the mobility of women is presented as temporary or conditional. A global trend analysis of female migration necessitates a focus on both the macro-level inequalities and region-specific processes that determine the experience of mobility and settlement of women. Table 1 provides a comparative overview of the major dimensions of female migration and highlights the evolving nature of women's mobility across different historical and contemporary contexts.

Table 1. Global Trends and Patterns in Female Migration

Dimension	Key Characteristics	Gender-Specific Implications
Historical Migration	Women migrated largely through family reunification and colonial labour systems.	Women's agency is historically under-recognised
Labour Migration	Concentration in care, domestic work, health, textiles, and services	Economic participation with high precarity
Forced Migration	Rising number of women refugees and asylum seekers	Heightened risk of gender-based violence
Voluntary Migration	Education, marriage, and professional mobility	Expanding autonomy but unequal recognition
South–South Migration	Regional and informal mobility	Limited protection and policy visibility
South–North Migration	Movement toward high-income countries	Deskilling and racialised labour segmentation

4. RECONSTRUCTION OF GENDER RELATIONS IN MIGRATION PROCESSES

Migration as a Catalyst for Transforming Gender Roles

Migration often serves as an agent of change in altering the established gender roles by changing access to income, mobility, and power to make decisions. In instances where women immigrate as individuals or become the main income earners, families actively renegotiate the previously gendered division of labour within the household. The feminist migration scholars support that migration has the power to threaten the patriarchal norms by increasing the economic and social presence of women, especially where the employment of women in paid jobs was previously a privilege of their gender (Hondagneu-Sotelo, 1994). Such changes are usually most evident in cases where migrant women participate in wage labour, learn new skills, or have an experience of other gender regimes in the destination societies.

The transformative potential of migration, however, is neither homogenous nor a given thing. Class position, legal status, cultural expectations, and labour market segmentation mediate gender role change. In most instances, migrant women endure a form of two-fold load, as they are not only in paid employment but also have to bear the burden of unpaid domestic and care work (Kofman & Raghuram, 2015). Migration can therefore both undermine and strengthen gender hierarchies. Although the financial contribution of women can enhance their bargaining power in the households, ingrained social norms might attenuate the level at which the gains can be converted to gender equality in the long term. Notably, gender role change is a negotiable process that is dynamic as opposed to a migration effect. These might be interim changes, contentious changes, or changes that are reversed on returning or reuniting with family. Migration as a source of gender change should be analysed in terms of structural opportunities and existing limitations that define the lives of women in various migration conditions, therefore. It is also demonstrated in Fig.1 below that there are gender role dynamics, power/agency negotiation, family/care work changes, and transnational householding.

Figure 1. Overview of migration as a catalyst for transforming women's gender roles

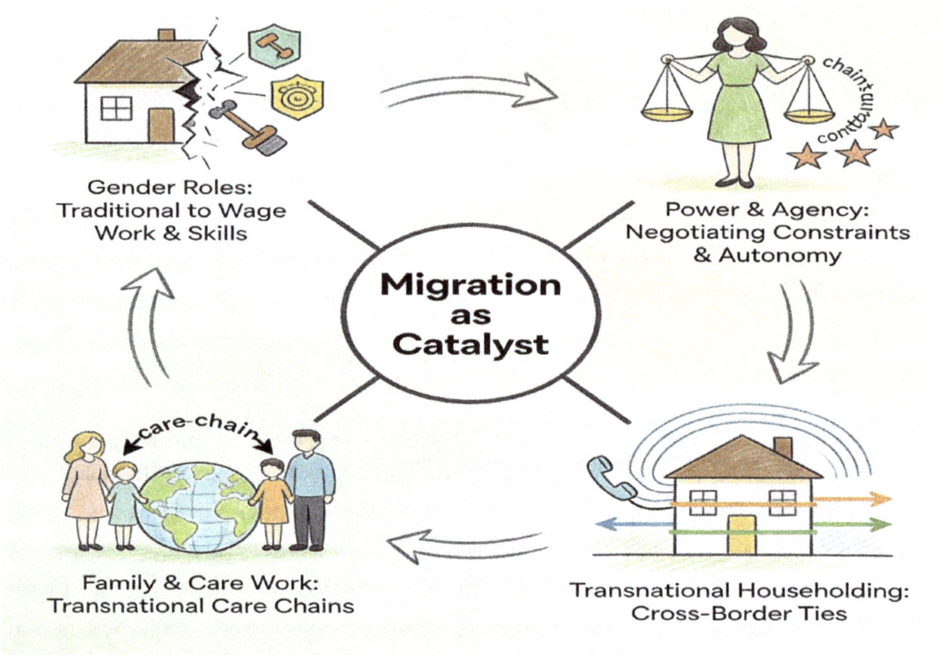

Negotiation of Power, Agency, and Autonomy

The key to the issue of gender reconstructions during migration is power relations. Feminist scholarship underlines that agency is exercised not individually but is negotiated in the context of power asymmetrical structures with the influence of legal systems, labour markets, and social norms (Pessar & Mahler, 2003). Migration can increase the autonomy of women by enhancing their income, mobility, and life decisions, especially in situations where women migrate alone or where they also take an active role in the transnational decision-making.

Simultaneously, the agency of women is frequently limited by the policy of immigration, which restricts the freedom of movement and makes women dependent on employers or husbands. The temporary labour migration schemes, as well as the sponsorship systems, can also strengthen the power asymmetry by limiting job mobility and access to social protections (Anderson, 2010). Such institutional setups determine the terms in which women overcome autonomy, and in most cases, these women must contend between survival tactics and structural vulnerability.

Agency in migration, however, should be viewed as relational and contextual. Women exert power in daily activities as they may do in the management of remittances, transnational relations, or even confronting exploitation, even in limited situations. Upon acknowledging these agencies, the simplicity of the agency-defined dichotomy between powerless victims and fully empowered actors is avoided, and the gendered negotiations of migration along migration trajectories are viewed through the lens of complexity.

Changes in Family Structures, Care Work, and Reproductive Roles

Migration has a drastic change in family structures, and it redistributes care to the opposite side of the border. Where women migrate, traditional caregiving can be reorganised, and this has resulted in the development of transnational families where care is outsourced to other members of the extended family or paid workers in the homeland (Parreñas, 2005). These structures provoke traditional conceptions of maternity and femininity, and at the same time, reinforce the couple as a result, women are expected to be responsible for caring and childbirth, despite geographical separation.

The internationalisation of care labour has been theorised in terms of the idea of global care chains, according to which reproductive labour is being relocated between poorer and richer areas because of the migration of women (Yeates, 2009). Although involvement in care labour may offer an income and a mobility opportunity, it also recreates global gendered inequalities by undermining care work and subjecting migrant women to exploitation and emotional trauma.

Alterations in the family and reproductive roles are frequently coupled with moral evaluation and social conflicts, especially in the native communities, where the migration of women can be seen as an abandonment of the traditional gender roles. These processes remind us that the gender reconstruction process via migration is integrated into more general cultural and affective economies, which define the women's identity and their social standing.

Transnational Householding and Gendered Responsibilities

Transnational householding has been a characteristic aspect of modern-day migration, especially of women migrants. Remittances, communication technologies, and emotional labour are some of the ways that are used to maintain transnational households by connecting the members of the family across borders. In most cases, women take centre stage in upholding these relationships, financial matters, nurturing arrangements, and social duties at various locations.

Gendered roles in transnational families often become more and more acute, instead of being reduced. Migrant women could be expected to be financially contributing, and at the same time, they are required to meet the moral demands of caring and family unity. This two-fold duty may cause emotional stress and solidify the gendered attitudes, despite the economic independence of women (Morokvašić, 2014). Meanwhile, transnational practices have the potential to provide the opportunity of renegotiating power and redefining the role of kinship, especially when the women are the main decision makers.

The gender perspective of transnational householding can be understood as the restructuring of social reproduction on the global level as a result of migration. It demonstrates the necessity to examine migration not just through the prism of individual movers but to think about the long chains of duty and support that facilitate transnational lives. This analysis was essential in formulating policies that will acknowledge the latent labour and social costs of migrant women.

5. OPPORTUNITIES FOR FEMALE MIGRANTS

Economic Empowerment and Labour Market Access

Migration can create significant opportunities for women's economic empowerment by facilitating access to paid employment, income generation, and financial autonomy. For many women, particularly those from contexts characterised by limited labour market participation or wage inequality, migration represents a pathway to economic inclusion and improved household bargaining power. Feminist economists have shown that women's access to income through migration can enhance decision-making authority within families, increase investment in children's education and health, and contribute to poverty reduction in countries of origin through remittances (Kabeer, 2012).

Labour market access for migrant women is, however, highly segmented and gendered. While many women find employment in care, service, agriculture, and manufacturing sectors, these roles often provide entry points into formal or semi-formal labour markets that were previously inaccessible. In some cases, migration enables women to accumulate work experience, develop transferable skills, and gain exposure to alternative labour regimes that value women's paid work more highly than in origin contexts (Kofman & Raghuram, 2015). Despite structural constraints, participation in paid labour can strengthen women's sense of autonomy and economic self-worth.

Economic empowerment through migration should therefore be understood as a relational and context-dependent process. While labour market inclusion does not automatically translate into equality, it can expand women's capacity to negotiate resources, mobility, and life choices. Recognising these opportunities is essential for moving beyond deficit-oriented narratives and acknowledging migrant women as economic actors within global labour systems.

Educational, Social, and Political Opportunities

Migration also opens avenues for educational advancement and social mobility for women, particularly through access to formal education, vocational training, and professional development opportunities. Female migrants who pursue education abroad may benefit from improved credentials, language acquisition, and cultural capital that enhance long-term career prospects. Even among labour migrants, exposure to new social environments can foster informal learning and skill acquisition that contribute to personal development.

Beyond education, migration can create opportunities for social and political participation. Migrant women often engage in community organisations, advocacy groups, and civil society initiatives that promote rights awareness and collective action. Such engagement can strengthen social capital and foster leadership skills, particularly among women who were previously excluded from public participation (Izaguirre et al., 2025). In some contexts, migrant women become active political actors through trade unions, migrant associations, or transnational advocacy networks.

These forms of participation challenge assumptions that migrant women are politically passive or socially isolated. While structural barriers remain, migration can provide spaces for women to articulate interests, claim rights, and participate in public life. Educational and social opportunities thus play a crucial role in shaping women's integration trajectories and long-term empowerment outcomes.

Access to Networks, Support Systems, and Diaspora Resources

Social networks and diaspora communities are critical resources that shape women's migration experiences and opportunities. Networks facilitate access to employment, housing, information, and emotional support, often reducing the risks associated with migration. Research has demonstrated that migrant women actively mobilise kinship ties, community organisations, and informal support systems to navigate labour markets and settlement processes (Ryan et al., 2009).

Diaspora resources can also provide platforms for collective empowerment. Women's associations within diaspora communities often address gender-specific needs such as childcare, legal assistance, health services, and protection from violence. These organisations can function as spaces of solidarity and resistance, enabling women to share knowledge and advocate for improved conditions both locally and transnationally (Anthias, 2008).

Importantly, access to networks is not evenly distributed. Legal status, class, ethnicity, and language proficiency shape women's ability to benefit from diaspora resources. Nevertheless, social networks remain a key mechanism through which migrant women exercise agency, mitigate vulnerability, and expand opportunities. Recognising the role of networks highlights the importance of relational dimensions of empowerment within migration processes.

Empowerment through Entrepreneurship and Skills Development

Entrepreneurship has emerged as a significant avenue for empowerment among migrant women, particularly in contexts where access to formal employment is restricted. Migrant women entrepreneurs often establish small businesses in sectors such as retail, food services, care, and cultural production, drawing on transnational knowledge, ethnic markets, and community networks (Fairlie & Lofstrom, 2015). Entrepreneurship can provide flexibility, income stability, and a sense of control over working conditions, especially for women balancing paid work and caregiving responsibilities.

Skills development is closely linked to entrepreneurial and economic opportunities. Migration may enable women to acquire new technical, linguistic, and managerial skills through work experience, training programs, or informal learning. These skills can enhance employability, support business creation, and facilitate upward mobility over time. However, access to skills development opportunities is often constrained by legal status, cost, and time availability, reinforcing inequalities among migrant women.

Despite these challenges, entrepreneurship and skills acquisition represent important pathways through which migrant women transform constraints into opportunities. Supporting these processes through inclusive policies, access to finance, and targeted training can contribute to more equitable migration outcomes and harness the economic potential of migrant women for both origin and destination societies.

6. LIMITATIONS AND BARRIERS IN THE MIGRATION JOURNEY

Pre-Migration, Transit, and Post-Migration Barriers

Migration is a process that is characterised by a spectrum of obstacles that are manifested before migration, in the process of migration, and in the context of the destination. Gendered disparities like inaccessible education, finances, information, and movements usually limit the migration preference of women in their pre-migration phases. The patriarchal family systems, high social constraints, and the lack of equal property or inheritance rights further reduce the potential of women to migrate on their own or to enjoy safe and legal migration routes.

Migration often puts migrant women at a greater risk, especially in cases where migration is done via irregular pathways. Women might be exposed to physical insecurity, smuggling, extortion, and sexual violence when crossing borders and when travelling across extensive distances. Such dangers are worsened by the confining immigration policies that push migrants on illegal and unsafe paths (Daly et al., 2016). Gender(s) vulnerabilities in transit are not about personal vulnerabilities to transit, but rather failures of migration governance and protection systems.

The post-migration barriers continue to exist in the destination societies, where women can experience precarious jobs, social isolation, language barriers, and access to health care and social services. Women's ability to integrate and exercise rights is determined by legal status, acknowledgement of qualifications, and cultural expectations. Combined, these pre-, during-, and post-migration barriers indicate that the experience of women's migration is organised based on the intersecting nature of inequality throughout the migration process.

Gender-Based Violence, Exploitation, and Vulnerability

One of the most pragmatic and widespread restrictions on migrant women is gender-based violence (GBV). Violence can be perpetrated at different points of migration and can have many different forms, such as domestic violence, sexual violence, trafficking, workplace violence, and violence in the state system through detention or asylum seekers. Feminist studies point out that migration may further promote the current gender disparities, and women are exposed to increased risks through legal precarity, economic reliance, and social isolation (Castañeda et al., 2015).

Low regulation and weak supervision characterise many labour areas in which migrant women play a crucial role in the labour force, like domestic work and care labour. The fact that live-in arrangements, employer-related visas, and being excluded by labour laws may provide situations where exploitation and abuse are a possibility (Anderson, 2010). The context of forced migration also intensifies vulnerability since refugee and asylum-seeking women might suffer violence in the displacement process, in the camps, or due to a lack of proper protection systems in the countries of destination.

Notably, the susceptibility to violence cannot be perceived as an intrinsic issue of migrant women but rather a structurally created problem of inequality of power relations and failure of institutions. It is important to note that a systemic approach needs to be taken to deal with GBV in migration through gender-sensitive asylum processes, labour protection, and access to justice, and not solely by individual coping mechanisms.

Legal, Policy, and Institutional Constraints

Political and legal frameworks are determining factors in the migration experiences and opportunities of women. Immigration regimes tend to pay more focus to the economic productivity or family dependency models that do not acknowledge the multiple migration motivations and vulnerabilities of women. Policies that require residence permits based on employers or spouses may limit the independence of women and create more chances of victimisation and abuse (Kofman, 2014).

Gender biases in asylum systems are also widespread as they often fail to consider the types of persecution that disproportionately impact women, including domestic violence, forced marriage, or reproductive control. Despite the achievements in acknowledging gender-based asylum claims, the practice is still disproportionate in different nationalities (Freedman, 2015). Inaccessible social protection, child-care, health services, and legal assistance are also considered a type of institutional constraints that disproportionately impact migrant women who have to take care of their children and work are disproportionately impacted.

These institutional and legal obstacles highlight the weaknesses of the gender-neutral migration policies. In the absence of gendered responsive frameworks, migration governmental frameworks will replicate inequality and marginality. The solution to these limitations is policy reforms based on the centralisation of women's rights, the understanding that there are varied migration routes, and access to protection and social services should not be limited to those with legal status.

Social Exclusion, Discrimination, and Stereotyping

Social exclusion and discrimination are some of the endemic factors towards the full participation of migrant women in destination societies. Gender cuts across race, ethnicity, religion, and migration status to form stratified forms of marginalisation. Migrant women often face stereotypes based on racialisation and gender that depict women as submissive, unskilled, or culturally incompatible, which influences the attitude of people and institutions (Essed et al., 2002).

Discrimination is evident in various areas that include employment, housing, education, and healthcare. Deskilling and occupational segregation curb the upward mobility of women, despite having qualifications and work experience. Isolation and a sense of breakdown of psychological well-being are other outcomes of cultural stereotyping that inhibit social interaction and belonging.

Nevertheless, migrant women are stronger in their struggle against exclusion by organising their communities, expressing their culture, and engaging in daily resistance activities. Nonetheless, structural discrimination is one of the limitations that cannot be tackled with the help of individual adaptation alone. Overcoming social exclusion requires society and institutions to actively challenge stereotypes, promote inclusion, and recognize migrant women as full participants rather than a marginalized group. Table 2 summarises the major gender-specific barriers encountered by women across different stages of the migration cycle, highlighting how structural, legal, and social challenges evolve from pre-migration to post-migration contexts and influence women's migration experiences.

Table 2. Gender-Specific Barriers across the Migration Cycle

Migration Stage	Major Barriers	Gendered Outcomes
Pre-Migration	Limited education, financial dependency, restrictive norms	Reduced mobility and choice
Transit	Irregular routes, trafficking, violence	Physical and psychological vulnerability
Destination	Precarious work, legal dependency, discrimination	Social exclusion and exploitation
Legal Status	Employer/spouse-tied visas	Restricted autonomy
Social Integration	Stereotyping, racism, and language barriers	Marginalisation and isolation

7. LIVED EXPERIENCES OF FEMALE MIGRANTS

Narratives of Agency, Resistance, and Adaptation

Lived experiences of female migrants show complicated stories of agency, resistance, and adaptability that disrupt monistic responses of migrant women as mere victims of structural forces. Feminist migration studies highlight the idea that women are involved in the interpretative, negotiating, and responding to migration restrictions by daily practices that affirm independence and strength (Pessar & Mahler, 2003). Agency is not perceived as free will in this context but as the ability to act in anything of significance in structurally constrained circumstances.

Migrant women practise agency by using a variety of ways, such as selective compliance with labour requirements, negotiation of domestic roles, upholding transnational relationships, and collective organising in migrant communities. The resistance can be non-violent and hidden within everyday life, like the redefinition of motherhood in what it means to be distant, to mess with exploitive employers, or to take charge of remittances and family decision-making (Parreñas, 2005). Such practices show the ways through which women will fit migration experiences to personal aspirations in dealing with unequal power relations.

Adaptation stories also bring out the fact that women can learn, change, and redefine themselves in new social situations. The main aspects of this process are language acquisition, cultural negotiation, and identity reconstruction. Adaptation allows the migrant women to form a new hybrid identity, which is a continuity and transformation at the same time, giving them the ability to survive and, in certain instances, prosper in the transnational space.

Emotional, Psychological, and Social Adjustment

Migration involves many emotional and psychological difficulties that define the lived experiences of women in terms of their effects. The process of being separated due to family members, the role of a caregiver in a different location, being uncertain about legal status, and facing discrimination may lead to emotional distress, loneliness, and anxiety (Ryan et al., 2009). To numerous migrant women, emotional labour may be a very elusive yet very crucial aspect of the migration experience, which involves trying to maintain family relationships, dealing with expectations, and dealing with loss and displacement.

Social support, employment conditions, legal security, and cultural acceptance are some of the factors that affect psychological adjustment. Research has shown that migrant women who have access to support groups and secure jobs are more psychologically strong and resilient (Bhugra, 2004). Social isolation and extended precarity, on the other hand, can increase the vulnerabilities of mental health, especially in women who have been exposed to trauma or exploitation.

The processes of social adjustment also consist of the process of negotiating belonging and identity in the destination societies. Migrant women are frequently involved in an exclusionary world in attempting to forge social relationships in terms of community organisations, religious institutions, and informal networks. The process of emotional and psychological adjustment, thus, should not be viewed as an individual process only, but a socially mediated one that is conditioned by structural inclusion or exclusion.

Intersectionality: Class, Ethnicity, Religion, Age, and Legal Status

Intersectionality offers a critical approach to the diversity in lived experiences by migrant women. Gender overlaps with class, ethnicity, religion, age, and legal status to create differentiated migration moves and results (Anthias, 2012). These overlapping identities define access to resources, their exposure to risk, and integration opportunities in the destination societies.

The migration motive is affected by position in classes, and post-migration possibilities are defined by the phenomenon of deskilling of women of high skills and devaluation of their credentials, as well as by precarious labour and low protection of low-income migrants. Ethnicity and religion also define the experiences of discrimination and belonging, especially in a situation where there is racism and cultural exclusion. Legal status is also one of the most determining factors in how access to employment, welfare, healthcare, and mobility are organised.

The age factor is also very crucial since younger migrant women can easily adjust to the new cultural environment, and older women can feel more isolated and dependent. An intersectional lens helps to understand that the lived experience of women cannot be generalised, but instead, it is produced by stratified systems of power at work together. Scholars and policymakers must recognize this complex situation in their analyses and designs.

Case Studies from Different Regions

The empirical case studies represent the areas of the globe, and they are examples of how gendered migration experiences are being influenced by particular social, economic, and political boundaries. The migration of women to domestic and care employment in the Middle East and East Asia has exposed the income opportunities and increased vulnerability to exploitation by the restrictive sponsorship systems (Piper, 2008). Migration of women into North America from Latin America shows the flagship of transnational maternity and survival tactics founded on remittance (Hondagneu-Sotelo and Avila, 1997).

The migration of the African women in and out of the continent, as well as into Europe, shows how the South–South migration and the informal mobility are increasingly important with little institutional protection and social status (Adepoju, 2008). Another factor that defines the migration of women in South Asia is gender norms, labour recruitment policies, and regulatory frameworks that both facilitate and limit women's mobility.

The case studies of these regions serve as a reminder that the experiences of women are contextual and cannot be detached and isolated from the larger structural circumstances. The comparative analysis shows similar patterns as well as regional dynamics, and supports the necessity of context-sensitive and gender-responsive migration frameworks.

8. POLICY FRAMEWORKS AND GOVERNANCE MECHANISMS

The role of gender in international migration governance has become more pronounced, as global policy frameworks have come to appreciate the unique experience of migration, vulnerability of women, and their contribution to international migration. One of the ways international organisations have contributed to the development of gender sensitive migration discourse is by recasting migration as a human rights problem instead of analysing it through the prism of economic or security to understand its nature. Gender has been progressively being integrated into global standards on labour migration, refugee protection, and human trafficking, and this change of direction towards more inclusive forms of governance. These frameworks are an indication that there is increased understanding that migration processes impact women and men in different ways, and gender-blind policies usually do not resolve structural inequalities experienced by migrant women.

This development implies that processes of gender integration are still unequal and rather superficial in the international migration governance. Gender is commonly approached as a cross-cutting issue, unknown as a primary organising principle, and thus, no adequate operationalisation has been developed at the national and local level. International frameworks tend to be based on wide normative commitments with fewer enforcement mechanisms, accountability frameworks, or monitoring systems, which lowers their practical effects on the lived experiences of migrant women (Freedman, 2015). A significant gap persists between global gender ideals and the realities faced by migrant women. They navigate oppressive migration policies, insecure labor markets, and marginalizing institutional practices. In the absence of long-term political will, gender-disaggregated data and regular assessment mechanisms, gender policies will always be symbolic and not transformative.

Gender-responsive migration policies at the national level should be focused on meeting the specific needs of women and discussing equality in the access to rights, services, and opportunities. These policies can be labour rights of migrant women, acknowledgement of gender-based asylum seekers, access to medical services and social amenities, and protection from exploitation and assault. There are indications that those countries whose policy frameworks are gender-sensitive tend to have better results in other spheres, including labour market integration and anti-abuse protection (Kofman, 2014). Nevertheless, many migration policies of nations are gender blind or implicit in a manner that perpetuates inequality. The Family reunification policies can limit the autonomy of women by linking the legal status to the spouses, and labour migration programmes often direct women into the low-wage, insecure jobs with insufficient labour protection. Those discrepancies between the migration policy and the labour and welfare policy also result in the institutional gaps that disfavour migrant women to a disproportionate degree.

Non-governmental organisations, civil society organisations, and community-based organisations are very important in the policy-to-practice gaps. These actors frequently offer key services, which include legal services, housing, health services, language education, and psychosocial services, especially in situations where state protection is minimal or absent in some way (Izaguirre et al., 2025). In addition to providing services, civil society organisations have been used as advocacy, empowerment, and political mobilisation tools to allow women migrants to engage in policy discussions and rights campaigns. NGOs provide support but impose structural constraints, as their limited resources cannot replace state responsibilities. Sustainability in migration governance thus necessitates institutional cooperation among civil actors in society and the governments.

There are major disparities between the policy intent and implementation that still cripple the gender-responsive migration governance. The absence of quality gender-disaggregated information, decentralised governance, repressive political systems, and the increasing anti-immigrant sentiments hinder quality policy implementation (Castañeda et al., 2015). To fill these gaps, it is necessary to go beyond the symbolic inclusion of gender to transformative governance strategies that put the issue of accountability, intersectional justice, and the active involvement of migrant women in the process of decision-making on the agenda.

9. TECHNOLOGY, MEDIA, AND REPRESENTATION OF MIGRANT WOMEN

Digital technologies have grown more prominent in the processes that have been influencing the experiences of migrant women and developing new avenues of empowerment, communication, and protection in the context of migration. Smartphones, social media, and online financial service providers allow migrant women to maintain transnational family connections, find essential information about migration, labour laws and regulations, and more easily regulate remittances. It has also been demonstrated that digital connectivity minimises the effects of social isolation and improves the ability of women to navigate multifaceted migration systems, especially the pre-migration planning, transit, and post-settlement stages (Alencar, 2018). Internet technologies are essential lifelines to several migrant women, particularly to those who experience linguistic, geographic, or institutional obstacles in practice and are thereby disadvantaged when making decisions, in terms of emotional health as well as social inclusion.

In addition to communication and connectivity, digital technologies are becoming forms of protection and advocacy of rights. There is availability of information on the law, emergency support services, and reporting abuse, exploitation, and labour violations through online platforms. With migrant women who are denied physical mobility or access to formal institutions, digital spaces may act as supplementary spaces for seeking help and claiming rights. Nevertheless, the availability of such technologies is still uneven and heavily influenced by the structural imbalance of literacy, language knowledge, cost, digital literacy, and legal position (Leurs and Smets, 2018). In addition, digitalisation presents new threats such as surveillance, exploiting data, spreading misinformation, and online harassment despite the valuable opportunities. The absence of gender-responsive digital governance structures means that emerging technological innovations will continue to create the inequalities that migrant women face instead of empowering them and improving their security. Figure 2 depicts that the digital experience is mediated by digital technologies of empowerment and protection, media representations, narrative, and feminist digital activism to shape the agency, visibility, and rights claims in the migration context.

Figure 2. Conceptual overview of migrant women's digital experiences

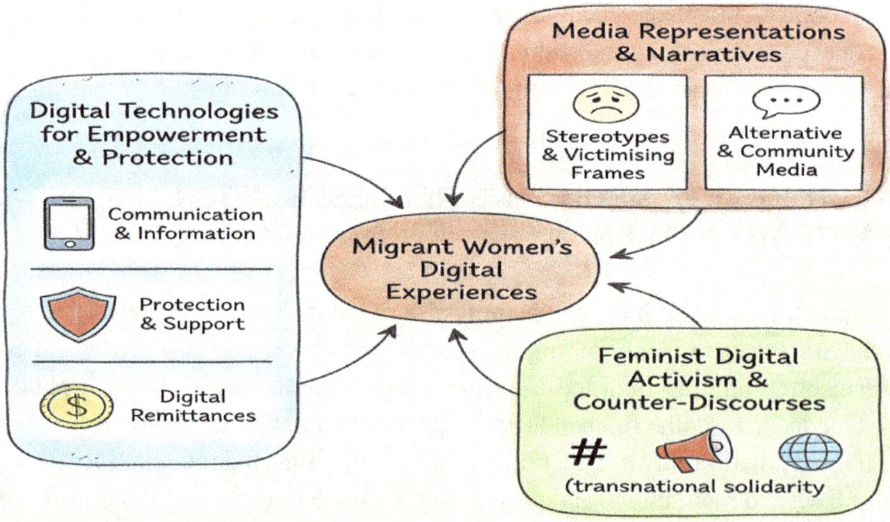

The power of media representations is that they can create the collective opinion of the migration of women and alter the discourse of policy. Migrant women are often perceived through the prism of a fixed and rather simple lens in mainstream media: either they become victims of trafficking, or they are passive, reliant people, or people who strain the welfare systems. These images distort the agency of women, their labour input, and involvement in society, as well as support racialised and gendered inequalities (Chouliaraki and Zaborowski, 2017). Male and female migration discourses tend to dramatise victimhood, especially where refugee and asylum-seeking women are involved. It is crucial, though, not to focus solely on violence and distress, as a sole emphasis on suffering may lead to the depoliticisation of structural factors that contribute to inequality and justify the paternalistic policies (Kofman and Raghuram, 2022).

Feminist digital activism has come up in reaction to these hegemonic representations to act as a counter-reference to the dominant representations. By spreading information about themselves on the internet, social media movements, and online storytelling efforts, migrant women and their supporters attack misinformation, challenge stereotypes, and demand rights and recognition. Digital activism makes transnational connections possible, as it unites women internationally and magnifies local struggles in the global networks (Milan & Treré, 2019). However, the problems with feminist digital activism are not absent, too, because online platforms may create the same atmosphere of exclusion, harassment, and surveillance that racialised and undocumented women struggle to overcome. Despite such constraints, counter-discourses produced by the digital platform are crucial in transforming the narratives, making them more visible, and promoting more gender-just and inclusive migration agendas.

10. FUTURE DIRECTIONS AND RESEARCH GAPS

The literature related to gender and migration has undergone substantial development during the past few decades, and the recent global trends continue to mold the focus and methodology of the literature. The increasing focus of the recent global trends includes and encompasses the increasing acknowledgment related to the aspect of climate change and environmentally mediated migration. Such change primarily affects the lives of women and, therefore, the lack of focus related to the concerns and aspects of gender and the subsequent implications related to climate change and migration remains inadequately examined (Hunter et al., 2015). The critical focus related to the intersectionality of the environment and the social and political roles, expectations, and influences related to gender and migration initiatives remains an essential and primary aspect related to the methodology and focus of the literature.

Another significant emerging theme has to do with the digital transformations of experiences and governance related to migration. Digital technologies are increasingly influencing recruitment methods, border control systems, labor surveillance in host countries, and communication networks for migrants. Although digital technologies may improve connectivity, access to information, or empowerment, there are also gender-related hazards associated with access to privacy, surveillance, exclusion generated by algorithms, and differentiated access to digital capabilities. A key theme in feminist literature regards the importance of a critical approach to digital infrastructures, which are identified for their potential in reproducing power relations, inequality, and mobility (Leurs & Smets, 2018).

Future governance of migration must go beyond tokenistic expressions of commitment to gender equality and implement gender-responsive and intersectional approaches. Current governance structures often neglect the various migration experiences, caregiving roles, and vulnerabilities of women. Gender-responsive governance entails incorporating gender analysis into every step of the policymaking process and every migration experience, from recruitment and management of borders to integration, protection, and return (Kofman, 2014). Policymakers must ensure the effective and systematic collection and use of gender-disaggregated data for evidence-based policymaking. In the absence of this, the undertapped contributions and challenges of migrant women remain unrepresented, and policymaker actions may end up perpetuating inequality (Piper, 2003). Another important factor is enhancing the role of migrant women within policymaking, identifying them not just as recipients of protection but rather rights-holders.

Despite the important progress, there are still important research gaps in the field of gender and migration. A first important gap refers to the long-term consequences of migrations on the relationship between the two sexes. In other words, even if the short-term consequences of migrations on the labor market are relatively well known, much less has been studied on how the norms, aspirations, and inequalities related to the two sexes are transformed by the migrations themselves (Donato et al. 2006). There are also important research gaps related to the phenomenon of South-South migrations, which represent the main component of the global mobility of females. There is a need for important research related to the particular migration systems in the context of Africa, Asia, and Latin America, to propose non-Global-North-centered theories (Bakewell, 2009). Methodologically, there must be more emphasis on mixed-method approaches, participation, and feminist methodological approaches, taking into consideration the non-conventional, emotional aspects of the migrations.

To pursue sustainable and equitable gendered mobility, it is important to reconceptualize migration not just as the movement of workers, but as a type of social process that is also situated within broader global systems of inequality, care, and development. Sustainable migration policies should address the economic and social role of migrant women while also acknowledging the "hidden costs" associated with caregiving and exposure to risks, as stated by Yeates in 2009. There is a crucial need to synchronize migration governance alongside broader development goals that target decent work, gender equality, and social justice.

11. CONCLUSION

This chapter has explored how migration can be seen as a 'gender project,' in which women's experiences of migration are subject to intersecting frameworks of power, inequality, and opportunity. By moving through feminist, intersecting, and transnational theory, this chapter has illustrated how gender roles are remade, power relations are reframed, and family roles are redesigned in borderlands by migrant flows. Although there are ways in which women may achieve empowerment, inclusion, and agency in/host countries through their experiences of migration, this is in many ways mediated by labor segmentation, legal frameworks, violence against women, and exclusion in the host country. In other words, Women actively shape their migration experiences rather than simply being acted upon. They navigate intersecting frameworks of power and inequality in everyday ways.

Integrating gender, migration, and sustainable human development, the chapter made it clear that migrant women have played a crucial role in maintaining household and economic sustainability, as well as transnational social reproduction. Contributions made by migrant women through their paid as well as unpaid labour, remittances, caregiving, and community participation have been fundamental to development outcomes in both countries of origin and countries of destination. However, the sustainability of such contributions is dependent upon addressing the underlying hidden costs of social and emotional reproduction that migrant women endure. Development policies that neglect gender issues have the potential to perpetuate the problem of exploitation and threats to sustainable social cohesion. Thus, gender-equitable migration governance is important to ensure that migration is also incorporated within the broader framework of equity, dignity, and sustainable development. Taking cognizance of the abovementioned aspects, the chapter proposes that gender-equitable migration policies need to receive equal emphasis to enhance migration paths and access to rights and protection, and associated social services. There is an important need for development to ensure that civil society organisations receive equal emphasis for their amplification and protection. For research, future studies should receive important emphasis at the intersectionality levels to ensure that longitudinal studies and research from the global south receive important emphasis to enhance gender migration dynamics.

REFERENCES

Adepoju, A. (2008). *Migration in Sub-Saharan Africa*. Nordiska Afrikainstitutet.

Alencar, A. (2018). Refugee integration and social media: A local and experiential perspective. *Information Communication and Society*, *21*(11), 1588–1603. DOI: 10.1080/1369118X.2017.1340500

Anderson, B. (2010). Migration, immigration controls, and the fashioning of precarious workers. *Work, Employment and Society*, *24*(2), 300–317. DOI: 10.1177/0950017010362141

Anthias, F. (2008). Thinking through the lens of translocational positionality: an intersectionality frame for understanding identity and belonging. *Translocations: Migration and social change, 4*(1), 5-20.

Anthias, F. (2012). Transnational mobilities, migration research, and intersectionality. *Nordic Journal of Migration Research*, *2*(2), 102–110. DOI: 10.2478/v10202-011-0032-y

Bakewell, O., de Haas, H., Castles, S., Vezzoli, S., & Jónsson, G. (2009). South-South migration and human development: reflection on African experiences.

Bastia, T., Datta, K., Hujo, K., Piper, N., & Walsham, M. (2023). Reflections on intersectionality: A journey through the worlds of migration research, policy, and advocacy. *Gender, Place and Culture*, *30*(3), 460–483. DOI: 10.1080/0966369X.2022.2126826

Bhugra, D. (2004). Migration and mental health. *Acta Psychiatrica Scandinavica*, *109*(4), 243–258. DOI: 10.1046/j.0001-690X.2003.00246.x PMID: 15008797

Castañeda, H., Holmes, S. M., Madrigal, D. S., Young, M. E. D., Beyeler, N., & Quesada, J. (2015). Immigration as a social determinant of health. *Annual Review of Public Health*, *36*(1), 375–392. DOI: 10.1146/annurev-publhealth-032013-182419 PMID: 25494053

Chouliaraki, L., & Zaborowski, R. (2017). Voice and community in the 2015 refugee crisis: A content analysis of news coverage in eight European countries. *The International Communication Gazette*, *79*(6-7), 613–635. DOI: 10.1177/1748048517727173

Christou, A., & Kofman, E. (2022). Gendered migrations and conceptual approaches: Theorising and researching mobilities. In *Gender and migration: IMISCOE short reader* (pp. 13–31). Springer International Publishing. DOI: 10.1007/978-3-030-91971-9_2

Crenshaw, K. W. (1989). Demarginalizing the intersection of race and sex: A black feminist critique of antidiscrimination doctrine (pp. 139–168). In the *University of Chicago legal forum* (Vol. 1).

Daly, F., Spicer, N., & Willan, S. (2016). Sexual rights but not the right to health? Lesbian and bisexual women in South Africa's National Strategic Plans on HIV and STIs. *Reproductive Health Matters, 24*(47), 185–194. DOI: 10.1016/j.rhm.2016.04.005 PMID: 27578352

De Haas, H., Castles, S., & Miller, M. J. (2019). *The age of migration: International population movements in the modern world.* Bloomsbury Publishing.

Donato, K. M., Gabaccia, D., Holdaway, J., Manalansan, I. V. M.IV, & Pessar, P. R. (2006). A glass half full? Gender in migration studies. *The International Migration Review, 40*(1), 3–26. DOI: 10.1111/j.1747-7379.2006.00001.x

Essed, P., & Goldberg, D. T. (2002). Cloning cultures: The social injustices of sameness. *Ethnic and Racial Studies, 25*(6), 1066–1082. DOI: 10.1080/0141987022000009430

Fairlie, R. W., & Lofstrom, M. (2015). Immigration and entrepreneurship. In *Handbook of the economics of international migration* (Vol. 1, pp. 877–911). North-Holland.

Freedman, J. (2015). *Gendering the international asylum and refugee debate.* springer.

Hondagneu-Sotelo, P. (1994). *Gendered transitions: Mexican experiences of immigration.* Univ of California Press.

Hondagneu-Sotelo, P., & Avila, E. (1997). "I'm here, but I'm there": The meanings of Latina transnational motherhood. *Gender & Society, 11*(5), 548–571. DOI: 10.1177/089124397011005003

Hunter, L. M., Luna, J. K., & Norton, R. M. (2015). Environmental dimensions of migration. *Annual Review of Sociology, 41*(1), 377–397. DOI: 10.1146/annurev-soc-073014-112223 PMID: 29861536

Izaguirre, L., Bastia, T., Walsham, M., & Cortés, P. P. (2025). Neglected intersections: A view from the South. *Comparative Migration Studies, 13*(1), 45. DOI: 10.1186/s40878-025-00456-w

Kabeer, N. (2012). Women's economic empowerment and inclusive growth: Labour markets and enterprise development. *International Development Research Centre, 44*(10), 1–70.

Kofman, E. (1999). Female "birds of passage" a decade later. *The International Migration Review, 33*(2), 269–299. DOI: 10.1177/019791839903300201 PMID: 12319733

Kofman, E. (2014). Towards a gendered evaluation of (highly) skilled immigration policies in Europe. *International Migration (Geneva, Switzerland)*, *52*(3), 116–128. DOI: 10.1111/imig.12121

Kofman, E., & Raghuram, P. (2015). Gendered migrations and global social reproduction: Vol. 122. *No. 7*. Palgrave Macmillan.

Leurs, K., & Smets, K. (2018). Five questions for digital migration studies: Learning from digital connectivity and forced migration in (to) Europe. *Social Media + Society*, *4*(1), 2056305118764425. DOI: 10.1177/2056305118764425

Milan, S., & Treré, E. (2019). Big data from the south(s). *Television & New Media*, *20*(4), 319–335. DOI: 10.1177/1527476419837739

Parreñas, R. S. (2005). *Children of Global Migration: Transnational Families and Gendered Woes Stanford*. Stanford Univ. DOI: 10.1515/9781503624627

Pessar, P. R., & Mahler, S. J. (2003). Transnational migration: Bringing gender in. *The International Migration Review*, *37*(3), 812–846. DOI: 10.1111/j.1747-7379.2003.tb00159.x

Piper, N. (2003). Bridging gender, migration, and governance: Theoretical possibilities in the Asian context. *Asian and Pacific Migration Journal*, *12*(1-2), 21–48. DOI: 10.1177/011719680301200102

Piper, N. (2008). Feminisation of migration and the social dimensions of development: The Asian case. *Third World Quarterly*, *29*(7), 1287–1303. DOI: 10.1080/01436590802386427

Ryan, L., Sales, R., Tilki, M., & Siara, B. (2009). Family strategies and transnational migration: Recent Polish migrants in London. *Journal of Ethnic and Migration Studies*, *35*(1), 61–77. DOI: 10.1080/13691830802489176

Schewel, K. (2020). Understanding immobility: Moving beyond the mobility bias in migration studies. *The International Migration Review*, *54*(2), 328–355. DOI: 10.1177/0197918319831952

Teodorescu, L. (2024). Women on the move: Understanding the female face of migration to develop targeted policies. *European View*, *23*(1), 55–63. DOI: 10.1177/17816858241246662

White, J., Cordova-Gomez, A., Mejía, R., & Clayton, J. A. (2025). Intersectionality and interseccionalidad—The best of both worlds. *Lancet Regional Health. Americas*, *41*, 41. DOI: 10.1016/j.lana.2024.100974 PMID: 40321657

Yeates, N. (2009). Globalizing care economies and migrant workers: Explorations in global care chains.

Chapter 10
Gendered Human Rights Diplomacy:
Migrant Women's Narratives in Norm Competition

Oğuzhan Bal
http://orcid.org/0009-0005-1830-3565
Karadeniz Technical University, Turkey

ABSTRACT

This study approaches human rights diplomacy not merely as a domain where normative principles are articulated, but as an arena where international legitimacy is discursively constructed and redistributed among actors. The authors examine how narratives about women migrants function as a strategic tool in normative competition, arguing that four discursive frameworks (victimhood, the rescuing agent, resistance and subjectification, and crisis-threat) recur systematically in their international circulation. These frameworks let actors position themselves as humanitarian while rationalizing the hardening of border regimes through the language of protection. The authors conceptualize this as the "paradox of humanitarian justification" and, integrating it with femonationalism and intersectional hierarchies of representation, examine which migrants are made visible. They propose a research design combining critical discourse analysis with qualitative content analysis to code a multi-actor corpus across crisis periods.

INTRODUCTION

In the first quarter of the twenty-first century, migration has become one of the areas where the most intense normative and political tensions in international

DOI: 10.4018/979-8-3373-8500-6.ch010

politics are played out. The Syrian civil war, deaths in the Mediterranean, Central American caravans, evacuations from Afghanistan, and mass asylum requests from Ukraine have reframed foreign policy agendas through the language of human rights. In these reframing processes, the experiences of women migrants have emerged as a privileged narrative resource that mobilizes public sensitivity and enables states to justify their positions on moral grounds. Representations of asylum-seeking mothers, children lost at the border, women fleeing sexual violence, and survivors of rape along migration routes have become central elements of humanitarian aid campaigns and public diplomacy (Chouliaraki, 2013; Johnson, 2011). However, the intensification of these representations has signaled not merely an expansion of sensitivity but also a new international legitimacy economy in which narratives are strategically circulated.

Traditional literature has largely treated human rights diplomacy as a set of tools states use to disseminate normative standards and expand legal binding force (Donnelly, 2013; Forsythe, 2017; Risse et al., 1999, 2013). Critical literature, however, has demonstrated that human rights discourse serves not only to disseminate norms but also to produce legitimacy (Anghie, 2005; Douzinas, 2007; Fassin, 2012; Mutua, 2001). The language of human rights has become a tool for answering questions about who is civilized, who is responsible, and who is an acceptable international partner. The role of stories about migrant women has been of particular importance in mobilizing this resource. By bringing together themes of high emotional intensity—such as trauma, vulnerability, motherhood, and self-sacrifice—these narratives have produced a narrative capital conducive to legitimizing foreign policy decisions at the level of moral intuition (Ahmed, 2004). This high emotional intensity has highlighted the question of which elements are selected in the construction of the narrative and which are systematically excluded. While experiences related to border violence, exploitation of undocumented labor, legal uncertainty, and daily bureaucratic humiliation are often pushed to the margins of the narrative economy, segments that enhance the visibility of the rescuer have circulated more easily (Hyndman, 2010; Johnson, 2011).

The theoretical framework of this study draws from four bodies of literature. The first is the Feminist International Relations approach, which began with Cynthia Enloe (2014) and expanded through the works of Tickner (1992, 2001), True (2012), and Sjoberg (2013). The second body of literature is the norm contestation framework developed by Wiener (2018), Acharya (2004), and Sandholtz (2008). The third is the strategic narratives approach developed by Miskimmon et al. (2013). The fourth cluster is the intersectionality and femonationalism literature shaped by the works of Crenshaw (1989, 1991), Yuval-Davis (2006), and Farris (2017). At the intersection of these four bodies of literature, the central argument of the chapter is formulated as follows: the stories of women migrants, in the forms in which they are circulated internationally, are part of a technology of legitimacy that functions as an instrument of normative competition. On the one hand, these stories have the potential to make violations visible; on the other hand, through selective representations, they have served to frame actors' own policies as humanitarian and rights-based, and to soften border control practices through the language of protection. This simultaneity points to the mechanism conceptualized in this study as the "paradox of humanitarian justification."

The study seeks to answer the following research questions: Through which discursive frames do foreign policy actors circulate the stories of women migrants? Through which mechanisms do these frames shape the production of international legitimacy and normative competition? Under what conditions do these representational practices generate a line of rights advocacy, and under what conditions do they contribute to the normalization of border regimes' language of protection? Which women migrants' stories are made visible, and how does this selectivity reproduce racial, class, and geographical hierarchies? To what extent can counter-narratives erode this technology of legitimacy? To address these questions, a research design combining critical discourse analysis (Fairclough, 2003; Hansen, 2006) with qualitative content analysis (Krippendorff, 2018; Mayring, 2014) is adopted. A multimodal corpus comprising government statements, reports from international organizations, public diplomacy materials, mainstream media representations, and counter-narratives from civil society sources examines three crisis periods (the 2015–2016 European refugee crisis, the 2018–2019 Central American caravans, and the 2021–2022 Afghanistan–Ukraine shift).

The remainder of the chapter is structured as follows. The background section presents the conceptual framework, discussing the reinterpretation of human rights diplomacy as a technology of legitimacy, the perspective of normative competition, the strategic narratives approach, the contributions of the Feminist International Relations approach, and the intervention of intersectional-feminist critique. The subsequent sections analyze the four frameworks, address the paradox of humanitarian justification and the pattern of selective humanitarianism using the example of Ukraine, and assess the capacity and limitations of counter-narratives. The chapter then presents the research design, discusses the theoretical implications of the analysis, identifies future research directions, and offers concluding remarks.

BACKGROUND

Human Rights Diplomacy: From Normative Claim to Legitimacy Technology

In the classical literature, the concept of human rights diplomacy has been used to define the entirety of diplomatic activities undertaken by states and international organizations to disseminate human rights norms and strengthen legal frameworks (Donnelly, 2013; Forsythe, 2017). Risse, Ropp, and Sikkink's (1999, 2013) spiral model presented an institutionalized form of this approach, linking human rights diplomacy to a positive transformation dynamic by depicting a learning process in which norms are internalized through supranational networks. Critical literature, however, has pointed out that this framework does not sufficiently account for the nature of the discourse in question, which is intertwined with power relations. Costas Douzinas (2007) argued that the claim of the universality of human rights is underpinned by specific civilizational assumptions, while Makau Mutua (2001) demonstrated that the human rights discourse cannot escape an Orientalist logic within the representational matrix he termed the "savior-victim-savage" triad. Antony Anghie (2005) analyzed that the foundational elements of international law are based on the assumption of a civilizational divide, while Didier Fassin (2012) revealed that the rise of "humanitarian reason" has transformed aid practices into a biopolitical sphere of governance.

This critical line of inquiry makes it possible to reframe human rights diplomacy as a technology of legitimacy. Here, legitimacy is understood not as a quality that can be acquired and preserved once and for all, but as a claim that is constantly constructed and tested (Hurd, 2007; Reus-Smit, 2007). Actors mobilize various resources in the discursive arena—legal references, moral examples, visual evidence—to legitimize themselves and their actions, and this mobilization proceeds hand in hand with objections to rivals' claims to legitimacy. The language of human rights has been one of the most powerful tools of this mobilization. While using this language to frame their own positions as humanitarian and rights-based, actors have also employed it to label their rivals as violators, insensitive, or uncivilized. The production of legitimacy operates at three interconnected levels. The first level is identity discourse, which concerns how an actor positions itself as part of a particular normative community. The second level is the justification of action, which encompasses the normative foundation upon which specific policies are grounded. The third level is the marking of the other, which involves identifying which actor or practice is deemed outside the norm. Stories of women migrants serve as a functional resource at all three of these levels.

Norm Competition, Contestation, and the Contested Nature of Legitimacy

Classical constructivist literature has explained the processes of norm acceptance through a relatively linear logic. Finnemore and Sikkink's (1998) norm life-cycle model posits that norms pass through stages of emergence, cascade, and internalization. However, this model does not sufficiently address the fact that norms remain contentious even after they are accepted, and that their meanings are constantly renegotiated in practice. The norm contestation approach developed by Antje Wiener (2018) fills this gap by demonstrating that norms are inherently open to debate and that their meanings are shaped through the interpretations of practitioners and institutional practices. Acharya's (2004) thesis on norm localization reveals that norms are reinterpreted in recipient contexts using local cultural resources, while Sandholtz (2008) shows that norm change proceeds through dynamics of conflict, negotiation, and reformulation.

This literature enables an analysis of human rights diplomacy through the lens of normative competition. Even when actors invoke norms presumed to be universally accepted, they produce competing interpretations. This competition often manifests not as a rejection of norms, but as norms being pulled in different directions. For example, the protection norm has been mobilized both to safeguard the rights of refugees and to tighten border regimes (Andrijasevic, 2007; Sharma, 2005). This study proposes the following contribution to the perspective of normative competition: competition operates not only through the content of norms but also through regimes of evidence. Actors highlight specific types of evidence to support their interpretations; legal references, statistics, images, testimonies, and stories constitute this repertoire of evidence. Stories of female migrants function as a type of evidence with high emotional intensity and easy public access within this regime of evidence, thereby imparting a narrative character to the competition of norms.

Strategic Narratives and the Narrative Dimension of Foreign Policy

The strategic narratives approach conceptualizes foreign policy not merely as a process of negotiation among decision-makers, but also as a practice of meaning-making directed at publics. Miskimmon, O'Loughlin, and Roselle (2013) proposed a three-level distinction while developing this approach: system narratives, identity narratives, and issue narratives. Consistency among these three levels enhances the narrative's persuasive power. In the field of foreign policy, narratives do not merely serve as communicative tools; they also function as cognitive maps, instruments of emotional mobilization, and devices for rationalizing action. By positioning themselves as the heroes of the story and their rivals as enemies or obstacles, actors make complex policy domains morally comprehensible. Lawrence Freedman's (2006) analysis of cognitive superiority in conflict environments and Sara Ahmed's (2004) work on the political economy of affect reveal the emotional foundation of narratives.

Stories of women migrants constitute one of the areas where strategic narratives are most concentrated in terms of this affective mobilization. Figures such as the vulnerable mother, the child who dies at the border, and the young woman fleeing violence generate empathy at the individual level while also compelling the adoption of moral stances at the collective level. This study proposes an expansion of the strategic narratives approach by incorporating the critical sensibilities of Feminist International Relations. The persuasive power of narratives is not merely a matter of technical design; it is also tied to gender representations, racial coding, and class visibility. Questions such as which woman is made visible as a victim, which woman is deemed worthy of rescue, and which woman is ignored directly determine the strategic impact of the narrative.

Feminist International Relations and Gendered Representation

The Feminist International Relations approach reveals that the discipline's central concepts are built upon gendered assumptions. Cynthia Enloe's (2014) question "Where are the women?" examines how the invisibility of women's experiences enables international politics, while Tickner (1992, 2001) demonstrates that reducing the concept of security to military threats renders everyday forms of violence invisible. True (2012) analyzes gendered forms of violence within the global political economy, while Sjoberg (2013) and Sjoberg and Gentry (2007) elucidate the operational logic of women's representations in war and security discourses. The implications of this literature for migration studies are of particular significance. Hyndman (2000, 2010) examines the geographical and gendered dimensions of refugee management, Johnson (2011) analyzes the tensions between vulnerability and agency in representations of refugee women, Squire (2009) examines the role of representations of refugee women in the politicization of migration discourse, and Mountz (2010) documents the gendered patterns of bureaucratic violence in the asylum process through fieldwork.

These studies converge on a common finding. Women migrants are predominantly positioned between two extremes in the international economy of representation. At one extreme lies the figure of the vulnerable, passive victim in need of protection; at the other, the figure of the resilient, adaptable success story. Although both figures generate visibility, the constitutive logic of representation often produces an effect that limits the subject's political agency, depoliticizes their experience, and dissolves structural inequalities into individual dramas. This structure is intertwined with an issue that postcolonial feminist criticism has long highlighted. Spivak's (1988) analysis, which critiques the logic of white men rescuing brown women from brown men, demonstrates how rescue discourses rationalize imperial intervention; Abu-Lughod (2002, 2013) reveals that calls for protection often shift political intervention choices onto a moral plane; and Mohanty (1988, 2003) criticizes the homogenizing violence of representations of the standardized "Third World woman." These critiques provide a reference framework that should be consulted when analyzing the international circulation of stories about women migrants.

Intersectionality, Femonationalism, and Selective Humanitarianism

The category of women migrants is not homogeneous; the hierarchies established within this category directly shape the economy of legitimacy. Kimberlé Crenshaw's (1989, 1991) concept of intersectionality demonstrates that race and gender are not separate axes but structurally intertwined axes that operate simultaneously. The framework Patricia Hill Collins (2000) termed the "matrix of domination" shows that the axes of gender, race, class, and nationality operate as intertwined planes of power, while Yuval-Davis (2006, 2011), through her situated intersectionality approach, emphasizes that the very question of which social categories come to the fore in which contexts is itself a political issue.

An intersectional reading necessitates questioning which subjects are made visible and which are ignored in the circulation of stories about migrant women. The experiences of women who are non-white, Muslim, working in the informal labor market, or living in legal limbo are often reduced to narratives of cultural violence (as evidence of the barbarism of their communities of origin) or framed as security threats. Groups such as trans migrants, queer individuals, women with disabilities, elderly care workers, and young girls who have run away from home, however, remain almost entirely on the margins of the economy of representation. This hierarchy of visibility reflects an implicit decision regarding which subjects deserve moral attention and obscures the racialized and classed grounds of international legitimacy struggles.

At this point, Sara R. Farris's (2017) conceptualization of "femonationalism" offers the theoretical framework closest to the central argument of this study. Farris documents a discursive regime in the European context in which nationalist-populist parties, center-right governments, and even some liberal feminists use the rhetoric of protecting women's rights as a political weapon against Muslim and migrant men. While this regime positions women's rights as a sign of progress and native identity, it constructs migrant men as a threat to these values. Femonationalist discourse positions female migrants either as victims in need of rescue (from their own men) or as a showcase for integration success, while categorically rendering migrant men as suspect subjects. The international diplomatic reflections of femonationalism are not limited to domestic political discourse. The EU's border regime discourse, U.S. policies toward the Middle East, and the intervention priorities of international funds often rely on frameworks that extend this logic to the international scale. Abu-Lughod's (2013) analysis of the "rescue of Muslim women" discourse, Mahmood's (2005) studies on secular-religious representations of women, and Grewal's (2005) critique of global feminism's imperial articulations bring to light different facets of this international dimension.

This framework enables the analysis of the pattern of selective humanitarianism observed in recent years. Europe's development of an admission regime at an unprecedented pace following the 2022 Ukraine crisis, its activation of the Temporary Protection Directive for the first time in history, and the launch of comprehensive support programs for Ukrainian women concretely demonstrate for which women admission capacity can be mobilized. At the same time, the persistence of border violence, pushback practices, and detention conditions faced by Syrian, Afghan, and Sub-Saharan African women reveals that the distribution of moral attention is structured along racial and geographical lines. This disparity is as much a result of political choices as it is a consequence of the moral economy produced by feminist discourse on an international scale. Pallister-Wilkins' (2015, 2022) conceptualization of the "humanitarian border" provides analytical tools to show which subjects the protection discourse is open to and which it excludes; this selectivity forms the empirical basis for the paradox of humanitarian justification.

THE DISCURSIVE ARCHITECTURE OF WOMEN MIGRANT NARRATIVES: FOUR FRAMEWORKS

Identifying recurring discursive patterns in the international circulation of women migrants' stories is a necessary step to make visible their function within the technology of legitimacy. The authors propose that four fundamental frames recur systematically: victimhood, the rescuer, resistance and subjectification, and crisis-threat. These frames may be derived deductively from the literature and reformulated through inductive refinement in corpus analysis to develop sub-codes. While the frames can be analytically distinguished, in practice they often intertwine to produce complex narrative compositions.

Victimization Framework

The victimization framework expresses the narrative pattern in which the violence, trauma, and losses experienced by the female migrant are central. Within this framework, the female subject is predominantly portrayed as passive, in need of protection, and in a position where she cannot survive without external intervention. The experience of violence forms the emotional core of the narrative, while a language of urgency and calls for intervention frame the narrative. This framework serves as a highly effective tool for mobilizing public sensitivity, constituting one of the most frequently invoked discursive sources in human rights campaigns and asylum advocacy. The political power of this framework stems from its ability to rapidly mobilize moral intuition.

Critical feminist literature has long debated the structural limitations of this framework. The first issue is the erasure of agency. The centralization of victimhood can render the female subject's capacity to shape her own life and her forms of resistance invisible. The second issue is the tendency toward culturalization (Volpp, 2001). Violence is often attributed to the cultural characteristics of the society to which the woman belongs, pushing structural, economic, and political causes into the background. The third issue is depoliticization (Brown, 1995). Narratives focused on individual suffering render the legacy of colonialism, global inequalities, and the structural violence of border regimes invisible. The diplomatic use of victimhood often walks a fine line between advocacy and political instrumentalization. The boundaries of deservingness are drawn by implicit standards regarding the purity of victimhood (Ticktin, 2017). Victimhood is not a category distributed equally among all subjects; rather, it functions as a capital of deservingness distributed hierarchically. Within the competition of norms, actors can highlight the victimhood of women living under their rivals' policies to label their rivals as norm violators, while simultaneously presenting the stories of women under their own protection to position their own policies as morally superior.

The Rescuer-Agent Framework

The rescuer-agent framework forms a twin structure with the victimhood framework. The victim's suffering gains meaning only through a rescuer's intervention; consequently, the narrative highlights the rescuer-agent's visibility, thereby attributing moral authority to them (Mutua, 2001; Spivak, 1988). Within this framework, states, international organizations, and civil society organizations are positioned as agents who rescue, protect, and shelter migrant women. While the agency of the helper is made visible, the agency of the recipient is pushed into the background.

The visual economy of the framework comes to the fore in a distinct manner. Figures such as the soldier transporting women at the border, the volunteer offering a blanket to a female refugee, and the rescue team extracting children from destroyed homes become iconic components of public diplomacy materials. The aesthetics of the imagery serve to compositionally ground the claim of moral superiority. Chouliaraki's (2006, 2013) studies on the representation of the suffering other analyze the moral structure of the viewer-witness position; the viewer often experiences moral satisfaction by placing themselves in the position of the helping agent. Analyses by authors such as Sontag (2003) and Sliwinski (2011) on the political circulation of images of suffering reveal the historical continuity of this visual regime. One of the structural issues with this framework is that it establishes the helper's intent, capacity, and moral superiority on unquestionable ground. The conditions, limits, and unintended consequences of aid become invisible; aid is presented not as a political choice but as a natural moral act. From the perspective of normative competition, this framework serves as a direct instrument for the construction of identity. While a state positions itself as the protector of humanitarian values, it morally excludes actors it does not intervene with.

The Framework of Resistance and Subjectification

The framework of resistance and subjectification emerges as a response to the passivity created by the victimhood and rescuer-agent frameworks, and it articulates a narrative pattern that represents the migrant woman as a resilient, re-emerged subject. Within this framework, the female subject takes an active central position in the narrative, emerging as a figure who has overcome her circumstances, rebuilt her life, and contributes to the new society. The discourse of resistance initially serves as a response to the problem of the erasure of agency in feminist criticism (Mahmood, 2005).

However, the resistance framework is not immune to its own structural issues. The dominant form of this framework in its international circulation is often intertwined with neoliberal success narratives (Rose, 1999). Being resilient is equated with capacities for adaptation, such as standing on one's own two feet in the market, sustaining oneself through small-scale entrepreneurial activities, and adapting to the new society. This articulation transforms the discourse of resistance from a tool of structural critique into a case study of market subjectivity. The process Táíwò (2022) terms "elite capture" explains the dynamic by which concepts belonging to marginalized subjectivities are absorbed by the hegemonic discourse. The emergence of the model migrant figure within the framework of resistance draws attention.

Representing a subjectivity that conforms to the values of the host society, adheres to rules, is economically productive, and politically reasonable, this figure functions as a source of discipline that redraws the distinction between the deserving and the undeserving. This discursive economy prevents the establishment of migrant rights on a universal foundation, instead tying rights to a merit-based conditionality.

The Crisis-Threat Framework and Securitization

The crisis-threat framework articulates a discursive pattern that removes narratives of women migrants from the humanitarian sphere and incorporates them into the realm of security and control. To understand the operation of this framework, it is illuminating to draw on the securitization theory developed by the Copenhagen School. Buzan, Wæver, and de Wilde (1998) demonstrate that when an issue is removed from the ordinary political sphere and framed as an existential threat, it is subjected to a discursive order that legitimizes extraordinary measures. Hansen (2000, 2006) incorporates a feminist perspective into this framework, revealing that securitization processes reproduce gendered hierarchies and systematically silence the voices of certain subjects. Huysmans (2006) analyzes the securitization of migration in Europe, while Bigo (2002) examines the normalization of border control through practices he terms the "management of unease."

Within the crisis-threat framework, women migrants are either placed into threat categories themselves (fake asylum-seekers, welfare fraud) or the harms they have suffered (human trafficking, prostitution, forced marriage) are used as justifications for border control. The first form represents a relatively explicit anti-migration discourse. The second form, however, operates with a more subtle logic and constitutes the core of the humanitarian justification paradox. The rise of the human trafficking discourse is one of the most visible examples of this framework. The call to combat traffickers exploiting female migrants initially appears to carry a content of rights advocacy; however, in practice, it often serves to justify policies that criminalize irregular migration and restrict the mobility of asylum seekers. Andrijasevic (2007) demonstrates that in the EU's anti-trafficking campaigns, the female body is represented as a "beautiful dead body," and that this representation is embedded in a moral economy that legitimizes border control; Sharma (2005), meanwhile, argues that the anti-trafficking discourse has become the discursive infrastructure of a global apartheid regime. Pallister-Wilkins' (2015, 2022) analyses of the EU border regime and Frontex document this logic's humanitarian face at the institutional level.

Reading the crisis-threat framework through the lens of Feminist International Relations reveals the paradoxical nature of the protection discourse. Iris Marion Young's (2003) analysis of masculine protection logic exposes the capacity of the agent providing protection to legitimize its own domination within the framework of protection. This logic persists in the practice of states exercising border control in the international arena in the name of protecting female migrants; the protective actor derives the right to restrict the freedom of movement of the population it protects from its own position of patronage. Thus, the crisis-threat framework reveals the most sophisticated form of the humanitarian justification paradox.

THE HUMANITARIAN JUSTIFICATION PARADOX AND SELECTIVE HUMANITARIANISM

The simultaneous operation of the four frameworks discussed above produces a mechanism conceptualized in this study as the humanitarian justification paradox. The core formulation of this paradox is as follows: rather than eroding the legitimacy of control policies, humanitarian discourse serves to repackage control within a more acceptable rhetoric (Fassin, 2012; Ticktin, 2011). Protection and exclusion coexist without contradiction within the same narrative universe, and even reinforce one another.

The operation of this paradox can be observed in various concrete practices in the field of foreign policy. The first is the practice of externalization. The agreements the EU has made with transit countries such as Turkey, Libya, and Tunisia establish a framework that shifts refugee reception processes outside EU borders; these agreements are justified with the rhetoric of preventing migrants from undertaking dangerous journeys and curbing human trafficking (De Genova, 2017; Pallister-Wilkins, 2022). The second is the softening of detention practices through the language of protection (Mountz, 2010). The administrative detention of asylum seekers is often framed as being carried out for their own safety. The third is the renaming of return practices as "protective return." Voluntary return programs are presented as a protective version of return processes, though the voluntary nature of these programs often emerges under conditions of structural coercion. The fourth is the conditional nature of funding practices. Funds from international organizations and donor states are often tied to conditions aimed at strengthening recipient countries' border management capacities. These linkages ensure that protection and control transform into institutionally intertwined practices.

The operation of this paradox at the level of the moral economy is also significant. The process conceptualized by Fassin (2012) as the rise of "humanitarian reason" reveals that the visibility of suffering has become the fundamental basis for legitimizing aid practices in contemporary international governance. Within this framework, aid shifts from being a rights-based obligation to taking the form of a moral gift, and the constitutive logic of the gift relationship requires the recipient to remain in a position of indebtedness to the giver. Ticktin's (2017) conceptualization of the "innocent victim" reveals the implicit logic of selection regarding which sufferings are deemed worthy of moral consideration. Stories of female migrants occupy a prominent place within the regime of evidence of the gift relationship, providing a continuous flow of testimony that constantly renews the moral superiority of the aid-giving actor.

Selective Humanitarianism and Racialized Hierarchies: The Ukraine Example

Perhaps the most concrete manifestation of this paradox emerged in the selective admission regime observed during the 2022 Ukraine crisis. Within weeks of the start of Russia's invasion, the EU activated the Temporary Protection Directive (2001/55/EC) for the first time in its history, establishing a comprehensive reception framework that provided Ukrainians with unconditional residence permits, the right to work, access to healthcare, and educational guarantees. During the same period, refugees from Syria, Afghanistan, Yemen, Sudan, and Sub-Saharan Africa continued to face pushback practices at the borders of Bulgaria, Greece, Poland, and Italy, were held for indefinite periods in detention centers, and were subjected to accelerated return procedures.

The discursive dimension of this distinction holds particular significance. The way European leaders and the media represented Ukrainian women offered a different narrative framework compared to those long used for Syrian and Afghan women. Ukrainian women were often positioned directly within a category of racial, geographical, and religious affinity—as "our European sisters" or as part of European civilization. The same logic of categorization often positioned Syrian and Afghan women within a framework of cultural distance, in terms of integration challenges, and even within the context of security concerns. This discursive asymmetry provides a concrete example of how Farris's (2017) framework of femonationalism operates on an international scale. Pallister-Wilkins' (2015, 2022) conceptualization of the "humanitarian border" analytically reveals how the same border regime can present different faces to different racialized subjects. While the humanitarian face remains open to white European refugees, the securitized face of the same border remains directed toward refugees from Sub-Saharan Africa and the Middle East. This duality is not an inconsistency but a constitutive feature.

This selectivity provides crucial evidence for the central argument of this study. The selective visibility of women migrants' stories in international discourse is not merely a narrative preference but emerges as a discursive reflection of the racialized operation of institutional reception capacities, funding flows, and legal frameworks. The answer to the question of which woman is deemed worthy of protection is shaped not merely by the level of evidence of victimization, but by the victim's proximity to the categories of whiteness, Christianity, European-ness, and modernity. This structure demonstrates why the analytical intervention of critical race studies (Goldberg, 2002) is necessary in understanding the operation of human rights diplomacy as a technology of legitimacy. The paradox of humanitarian justification reveals that the language of human rights can serve as both a source of criticism and a linguistic architecture that absorbs criticism.

COUNTER-NARRATIVES AND THE DIRECTION OF NORM COMPETITION

The functioning of human rights diplomacy as a technology of legitimacy is not limited to state-centered and rescuer-centered representations. The self-narratives of women migrants, content produced by diaspora networks, and counter-narratives from civil society possess the capacity to intervene in official diplomatic representations and shift the direction of normative competition (Squire, 2009). These counter-narratives can expose structural inequalities by undermining the central figures of rescuer-centered representations, and by bringing experiences such as border violence, discrimination, and legal uncertainty to the international agenda, they erode official claims to legitimacy. Social media platforms, podcast ecosystems, and alternative media formats enable a circulation of narratives that is partially independent of traditional media's gatekeeping role. Bayat's (2010) concept of "non-movements" makes visible the forms of political intervention produced by marginalized subjects in the porous spaces of daily life, thereby enabling a theoretical reading of the political agency of women migrants.

Interventions by civil society and international organizations operate at both the local and supranational levels. Reports by human rights organizations, refugee support associations, monitoring studies by academic institutions, and legal support networks document and present to the public practices concealed within official discourse. Most of these reports rely on a narrative language that interprets the experiences of women migrants within structural conditions, makes their agency visible, and avoids a rescuer framework. Diaspora activism also functions as a political subject intervening in the discursive arena of normative competition. Activists who have fled oppressive conditions in their countries of origin can develop critical interventions targeting the migration policies of host countries and create a two-way accountability pressure on the international stage.

The circulation capacity of counter-narratives is severely constrained by structural limitations. The first limitation is the inequality of platform access. While official actors' public diplomacy budgets and international media connections enable them to rapidly disseminate their frames to broad publics, counter-narratives circulate on smaller platforms with more limited resources. The second limitation is the language barrier. Content produced in the languages of source countries often has to undergo translation and adaptation processes. The third limitation is the algorithmic policy of digital platforms. The process that Couldry and Mejias (2019) term "data colonialism" demonstrates that digital platforms' visibility distribution mechanisms are tied to the accumulation of corporate capital. The fourth limitation is the filtering effect of hegemonic media agendas. Counter-narratives are often framed as exceptional cases or thematically ignored in mainstream media. These inequalities show that norm competition operates not only through the content of norms but also through the conditions under which claims about norms circulate.

Certain concrete patterns where counter-narratives have proven effective show that the direction of normative competition can indeed shift. In Europe, images of migrants drowning in the Mediterranean and the testimonies of survivors managed to bring criticism of the EU's border regime to the forefront of the public agenda for a time, while in the United States, rising public backlash against the family separation policy led to the reversal of certain administrative measures. These examples show that counter-narratives possess the capacity to erode the legitimacy claims of official discourse under certain conditions. However, the success of these examples often depends on a temporary public outcry and requires a more sustained pressure infrastructure to translate into long-term institutional transformation.

METHODOLOGY AND RESEARCH DESIGN

The research design proposed in this study is based on a mixed-methods approach combining critical discourse analysis with qualitative content analysis. Critical discourse analysis, drawing on the theoretical framework developed by Fairclough (2003), van Dijk (1993), and Hansen (2006), enables an examination of how language is intertwined with power relations and which discursive strategies serve the production of legitimacy. Qualitative content analysis, drawing on the frameworks of Krippendorff (2018) and Mayring (2014), enables the recording of the frequency of frames and patterns of articulation through systematic coding.

Corpus Design and Sampling

The corpus is designed as a multimodal and multi-actor structure. The first group of actors consists of state institutions, including statements by foreign ministries, parliamentary speeches, press releases, and official social media accounts. Examples from EU member states (particularly Germany, France, Italy, Greece, and Poland), the United States, Turkey, neighboring states of Syria, and Latin American countries are included in the corpus. The second group of actors consists of international organizations, including reports and campaigns by organizations such as UNHCR, IOM, UN Women, ILO, and UNICEF. The third group of actors consists of mainstream media, with examples selected from international and local outlets such as the BBC, Reuters, Al Jazeera, Le Monde, The New York Times, Anadolu Agency, and Süddeutsche Zeitung subjected to thematic coding. The fourth group of actors consists of civil society organizations. The fifth group of actors comprises diaspora and migrant-focused platforms. The corpus selection is based on a chronological framework. Three crisis periods are taken as the focus: the 2015–2016 European refugee crisis, the 2018–2019 Central American caravans period, and the 2021–2022 Afghanistan–Ukraine shift. Samples are selected from the pre-crisis (three months), during-crisis (three months), and post-crisis (six months) sub-periods for each phase.

Coding Scheme and Reliability

The coding scheme is constructed around four core frameworks. These frameworks are initially derived deductively from the literature, and sub-codes are subsequently developed through inductive refinements based on a pilot sample. Sub-codes within the victimization framework include an emphasis on sexual violence, the drama of motherhood, and narratives of cultural violence. Sub-codes within the rescuer-agent framework include images of rescue operations and the visibility of international organizations. Sub-codes within the resistance framework include narratives of entrepreneurship, educational success, and stories of adaptation, while sub-codes within the crisis-threat framework include discourse on human trafficking, an emphasis on border security, and discussions on reception capacity. Additionally, sub-codes related to racial, geographic, and religious categories are developed for intersectionality analysis. The coding process is conducted independently by two coders; inter-coder reliability is calculated using the Krippendorff alpha coefficient, and an acceptable threshold of $\alpha \geq .80$ is established (Krippendorff, 2018). For subcategories with lower values, coder training is repeated to achieve reliability above the threshold. A qualitative data analysis software environment is used for coding, and a multimodal analysis framework is applied in the coding of visual materials (Kress & van Leeuwen, 2006).

Triangulation and Reflexive Stance

A four-level triangulation strategy is applied to enhance the reliability and validity of the analysis. The first level is source triangulation, which involves comparing data obtained from different groups of actors. The second level is methodological triangulation, which involves the combined use of discourse analysis and content analysis. The third level is theoretical triangulation, which is based on the simultaneous use of the literature on Feminist International Relations, norm contestation, strategic narratives, and intersectionality. The fourth level is coder triangulation. Methodological limitations are explicitly acknowledged. The corpus selection is necessarily selective; the loss of linguistic subtleties introduced by translation is a concern; and the dimension of reception remains outside the scope of the study. Building on Haraway's (1988) concept of situated knowledge and Harding's (1995) proposal of strong objectivity, the authors adopt a reflexive stance that incorporates the researcher's situatedness into the analysis as a methodological necessity, justifying analytical decisions and explicitly stating the partial nature of the results.

SOLUTIONS AND RECOMMENDATIONS

The theoretical framework and methodological design of this study make four contributions to the literature. The first pertains to the literature on normative competition. Existing studies on normative contestation (Acharya, 2004; Sandholtz, 2008; Wiener, 2018) have largely focused on the contested interpretations of norms in legal and political texts. This study expands this literature by analyzing gendered narrative regimes of evidence, demonstrating that norms compete not only in an argumentative sphere but also within a narrative and affective one. Stories of women migrants function as a type of evidence in the struggle over what content norms should embody, and this type of evidence possesses a mobilization capacity distinct from other types of evidence.

The second contribution relates to the literature on strategic narratives. Existing studies (Miskimmon et al., 2013) have largely treated strategic narratives as a tool for states to communicate their positions on the international stage. This study demonstrates that the persuasive power of narratives is not independent of gender hierarchies, racial coding, and class visibility by linking strategic narratives with gendered and racialized representations. The success of strategic narratives depends on which subjects can be made visible under which conditions, and these conditions of visibility result from a structural economy of representation.

The third contribution pertains to the Feminist International Relations approach's focus on migration and human rights studies. Existing feminist literature (Hyndman, 2010; Johnson, 2011; Squire, 2009) has critically analyzed the problematic structures of representations of women migrants. This study emphasizes that representation is not merely an ethical issue but a political practice that shapes foreign policy outcomes by incorporating the conceptualization of "technologies of legitimacy" into this critical analysis. Gendered representations are not merely a discursive epiphenomenon; they are part of a material and discursive complex that shapes institutional policy preferences, funding flows, and border regimes.

The fourth contribution relates to the literature on intersectionality and femonationalism. Farris's (2017) femonationalism framework, developed at the national level, is applied to the international diplomatic arena in this study to test the concept's explanatory capacity. The study demonstrates that femonationalist logic operates not only within domestic political discourse but also in the discourses of international organizations, the justification of border regimes, and the diplomatic repertoire of explanations. This step lays the groundwork for a research agenda that extends Farris's theoretical intervention into the field of International Relations and could be conceptualized as international femonationalism.

The practical implications of these contributions are noteworthy. The humanitarian justification paradox serves as a call for strategic vigilance among actors engaged in rights advocacy. The effectiveness of victimhood-based campaigns in generating short-term public mobilization must be evaluated alongside the question of which institutional outcomes these campaigns legitimize in the long term. Rights advocates may therefore benefit from foregrounding the structural conditions and the agency of women migrants rather than relying on rescue-centered imagery that can be absorbed into border-control rhetoric.

FUTURE RESEARCH DIRECTIONS

Several limitations of this study open avenues for future research. The corpus design is geographically concentrated at the intersection of Europe, North America, and the Middle East, and its validity in other migration corridors needs to be tested. Because the articulation of discourse and institutions is analyzed without directly testing the causality regarding institutional policy outcomes, future studies should deepen this analysis through a detailed examination of the causal mechanisms of this articulation. The exclusion of a separate qualitative field study on the self-narratives of female migrants opens the door to a future research agenda supported by direct ethnographic data.

Future research agendas can be summarized under the following headings: adapting the theoretical framework to other representational economies (climate migrants, ethnic minorities, LGBT+ subjects); the empirical investigation of the dimension of reception; the systematic examination of the transformative impact of digital platforms on the representational economy; the analysis of the political power of women migrants' own narratives within transnational solidarity networks; and the testing of the conceptualization of international femonationalism in different regional contexts. The Turkish case, in particular, offers fertile ground for analyzing how a host state with a large migrant population constructs its own gendered representation regime, which the present framework identifies but does not yet examine in depth.

CONCLUSION

By reinterpreting human rights diplomacy as a technology of legitimacy and treating the international circulation of women migrants' stories as a central component of this technology, this study proposes an analytical framework that conceptualizes the political nature of narrative at the intersection of migration, human rights, and foreign policy. The central argument is that stories of women migrants are not merely objects of ethical sensitivity but functional components of international legitimacy struggles. Organized around four key frameworks, these stories enable actors to position themselves as humanitarian and rights-based, to label their rivals as violators, and to justify inclusion-exclusion policies through the language of protection.

The conceptualization of the "humanitarian justification paradox" developed in this study reveals a mechanism through which protection and exclusion can coexist without contradiction within the same narrative universe. The operation of this mechanism takes concrete forms in externalization agreements, protective detention practices, voluntary return programs, funding conditionalities, and, particularly following the 2022 Ukraine crisis, in patterns of selective humanitarianism. The extension of femonationalist logic to the international scale provides a theoretical analysis of contexts where the discourse on women's rights is instrumentalized to legitimize anti-migration policies. The discussion regarding the capacity of counter-narratives, meanwhile, emphasizes that normative competition operates not only through the content of norms but also through the conditions under which claims regarding norms circulate.

In conclusion, human rights diplomacy has become as much a political field as an ethical one, and gendered narratives function as a central constitutive element of this political field. The international circulation of migrant women's experiences serves, on the one hand, as a crucial tool in the struggle against invisibility, while on the other hand, it remains part of a representational economy that reproduces power relations. Awareness of this dual effect makes it possible to conceptualize human rights discourse more sophisticatedly at the theoretical level and to structure human rights advocacy practices more critically and strategically at the practical level.

REFERENCES

Abu-Lughod, L. (2002). Do Muslim women really need saving? Anthropological reflections on cultural relativism and its others. *American Anthropologist, 104*(3), 783–790. DOI: 10.1525/aa.2002.104.3.783

Abu-Lughod, L. (2013). *Do Muslim women need saving?* Harvard University Press. DOI: 10.4159/9780674726338

Acharya, A. (2004). How ideas spread: Whose norms matter? Norm localization and institutional change in Asian regionalism. *International Organization, 58*(2), 239–275. DOI: 10.1017/S0020818304582024

Ahmed, S. (2004). *The cultural politics of emotion*. Edinburgh University Press.

Andrijasevic, R. (2007). Beautiful dead bodies: Gender, migration and representation in anti-trafficking campaigns. *Feminist Review, 86*(1), 24–44. DOI: 10.1057/palgrave.fr.9400355

Anghie, A. (2005). *Imperialism, sovereignty, and the making of international law*. Cambridge University Press. DOI: 10.1017/CBO9780511614262

Bayat, A. (2010). *Life as politics: How ordinary people change the Middle East*. Stanford University Press. DOI: 10.5117/9789053569115

Bigo, D. (2002). Security and immigration: Toward a critique of the governmentality of unease. *Alternatives, 27*(1_suppl, Suppl.), 63–92. DOI: 10.1177/03043754020270S105

Brown, W. (1995). *States of injury: Power and freedom in late modernity*. Princeton University Press. DOI: 10.1515/9780691201399

Buzan, B., Wæver, O., & de Wilde, J. (1998). *Security: A new framework for analysis*. Lynne Rienner.

Chouliaraki, L. (2006). The spectatorship of suffering. *Sage (Atlanta, Ga.).*

Chouliaraki, L. (2013). The ironic spectator: Solidarity in the age of post-humanitarianism. *Polity*.

Collins, P. H. (2000). *Black feminist thought: Knowledge, consciousness, and the politics of empowerment* (2nd ed.). Routledge.

Couldry, N., & Mejias, U. A. (2019). *The costs of connection: How data is colonizing human life and appropriating it for capitalism*. Stanford University Press.

Crenshaw, K. (1989). Demarginalizing the intersection of race and sex: A Black feminist critique of antidiscrimination doctrine, feminist theory, and antiracist politics. *University of Chicago Legal Forum, 1989*(1), 139–167.

Crenshaw, K. (1991). Mapping the margins: Intersectionality, identity politics, and violence against women of color. *Stanford Law Review, 43*(6), 1241–1299. DOI: 10.2307/1229039

De Genova, N. (Ed.). (2017). *The borders of "Europe": Autonomy of migration, tactics of bordering*. Duke University Press. DOI: 10.1215/9780822372660

Donnelly, J. (2013). *Universal human rights in theory and practice* (3rd ed.). Cornell University Press. DOI: 10.7591/9780801467493

Douzinas, C. (2007). *Human rights and empire: The political philosophy of cosmopolitanism*. Routledge. DOI: 10.4324/9780203945117

Enloe, C. (2014). *Bananas, beaches and bases: Making feminist sense of international politics* (2nd ed.). University of California Press. (Original work published 1989) DOI: 10.1525/9780520957282

Fairclough, N. (2003). *Analysing discourse: Textual analysis for social research*. Routledge. DOI: 10.4324/9780203697078

Farris, S. R. (2017). *In the name of women's rights: The rise of femonationalism*. Duke University Press. DOI: 10.1215/9780822372929

Fassin, D. (2012). *Humanitarian reason: A moral history of the present*. University of California Press.

Finnemore, M., & Sikkink, K. (1998). International norm dynamics and political change. *International Organization, 52*(4), 887–917. DOI: 10.1162/002081898550789

Forsythe, D. P. (2017). *Human rights in international relations* (4th ed.). Cambridge University Press. DOI: 10.1017/9781316874929

Freedman, L. (2006). *The transformation of strategic affairs* (Adelphi Paper 379). Routledge.

Goldberg, D. T. (2002). *The racial state*. Blackwell.

Grewal, I. (2005). *Transnational America: Feminisms, diasporas, neoliberalisms*. Duke University Press. DOI: 10.1215/9780822386544

Hansen, L. (2000). The Little Mermaid's silent security dilemma and the absence of gender in the Copenhagen School. *Millennium, 29*(2), 285–306. DOI: 10.1177/03058298000290020501

Hansen, L. (2006). *Security as practice: Discourse analysis and the Bosnian war*. Routledge.

Haraway, D. (1988). Situated knowledges: The science question in feminism and the privilege of partial perspective. *Feminist Studies*, *14*(3), 575–599. DOI: 10.2307/3178066

Harding, S. (1995). "Strong objectivity": A response to the new objectivity question. *Synthese*, *104*(3), 331–349. DOI: 10.1007/BF01064504

Hurd, I. (2007). *After anarchy: Legitimacy and power in the United Nations Security Council*. Princeton University Press.

Huysmans, J. (2006). *The politics of insecurity: Fear, migration, and asylum in the EU*. Routledge. DOI: 10.4324/9780203008690

Hyndman, J. (2000). *Managing displacement: Refugees and the politics of humanitarianism*. University of Minnesota Press.

Hyndman, J. (2010). Introduction: The feminist politics of refugee migration. *Gender, Place and Culture*, *17*(4), 453–459. DOI: 10.1080/0966369X.2010.485835

Johnson, H. L. (2011). Click to donate: Visual images, constructing victims, and imagining the female refugee. *Third World Quarterly*, *32*(6), 1015–1037. DOI: 10.1080/01436597.2011.586235

Kress, G., & van Leeuwen, T. (2006). *Reading images: The grammar of visual design* (2nd ed.). Routledge. DOI: 10.4324/9780203619728

Krippendorff, K. (2018). *Content analysis: An introduction to its methodology* (4th ed.). Sage.

Mahmood, S. (2005). *Politics of piety: The Islamic revival and the feminist subject*. Princeton University Press.

Mayring, P. (2014). *Qualitative content analysis: Theoretical foundation, basic procedures and software solution*. Klagenfurt. https://nbn-resolving.org/urn:nbn:de:0168-ssoar-395173

Miskimmon, A., O'Loughlin, B., & Roselle, L. (2013). *Strategic narratives: Communication power and the new world order*. Routledge.

Mohanty, C. T. (1988). Under Western eyes: Feminist scholarship and colonial discourses. *Feminist Review*, *30*(1), 61–88. DOI: 10.1057/fr.1988.42

Mohanty, C. T. (2003). *Feminism without borders: Decolonizing theory, practicing solidarity*. Duke University Press. DOI: 10.1215/9780822384649

Mountz, A. (2010). *Seeking asylum: Human smuggling and bureaucracy at the border*. University of Minnesota Press.

Mutua, M. (2001). Savages, victims, and saviors: The metaphor of human rights. *Harvard International Law Journal, 42*(1), 201–245.

Pallister-Wilkins, P. (2015). The humanitarian politics of European border policing: Frontex and border police in Evros. *International Political Sociology, 9*(1), 53–69. DOI: 10.1111/ips.12076

Pallister-Wilkins, P. (2022). *Humanitarian borders: Unequal mobility and saving lives*. Verso.

Reus-Smit, C. (2007). International crises of legitimacy. *International Politics, 44*(2–3), 157–174. DOI: 10.1057/palgrave.ip.8800182

Risse, T., Ropp, S. C., & Sikkink, K. (Eds.). (1999). *The power of human rights: International norms and domestic change*. Cambridge University Press. DOI: 10.1017/CBO9780511598777

Risse, T., Ropp, S. C., & Sikkink, K. (Eds.). (2013). *The persistent power of human rights: From commitment to compliance*. Cambridge University Press. DOI: 10.1017/CBO9781139237161

Rose, N. (1999). *Powers of freedom: Reframing political thought*. Cambridge University Press. DOI: 10.1017/CBO9780511488856

Sandholtz, W. (2008). Dynamics of international norm change: Rules against wartime plunder. *European Journal of International Relations, 14*(1), 101–131. DOI: 10.1177/1354066107087766

Sharma, N. (2005). Anti-trafficking rhetoric and the making of a global apartheid. *NWSA Journal, 17*(3), 88–111. DOI: 10.2979/NWS.2005.17.3.88

Sjoberg, L. (2013). *Gendering global conflict: Toward a feminist theory of war*. Columbia University Press.

Sjoberg, L., & Gentry, C. E. (2007). *Mothers, monsters, whores: Women's violence in global politics*. Zed Books.

Sliwinski, S. (2011). *Human rights in camera*. University of Chicago Press. DOI: 10.7208/chicago/9780226762784.001.0001

Sontag, S. (2003). *Regarding the pain of others*. Farrar, Straus and Giroux. DOI: 10.3917/dio.201.0127

Spivak, G. C. (1988). Can the subaltern speak? In C. Nelson & L. Grossberg (Eds.), *Marxism and the interpretation of culture* (pp. 271–313). University of Illinois Press.

Squire, V. (2009). *The exclusionary politics of asylum*. Palgrave Macmillan. DOI: 10.1057/9780230233614

Táíwò, O. O. (2022). *Elite capture: How the powerful took over identity politics (and everything else)*. Haymarket Books. DOI: 10.2307/j.ctv2g591sq

Tickner, J. A. (1992). *Gender in international relations: Feminist perspectives on achieving global security*. Columbia University Press.

Tickner, J. A. (2001). *Gendering world politics: Issues and approaches in the post-Cold War era*. Columbia University Press.

Ticktin, M. (2011). *Casualties of care: Immigration and the politics of humanitarianism in France*. University of California Press. DOI: 10.1525/9780520950535

Ticktin, M. (2017). A world without innocence. *American Ethnologist, 44*(4), 577–590. DOI: 10.1111/amet.12558

True, J. (2012). *The political economy of violence against women*. Oxford University Press. DOI: 10.1093/acprof:oso/9780199755929.001.0001

van Dijk, T. A. (1993). Principles of critical discourse analysis. *Discourse & Society, 4*(2), 249–283. DOI: 10.1177/0957926593004002006

Volpp, L. (2001). Feminism versus multiculturalism. *Columbia Law Review, 101*(5), 1181–1218. DOI: 10.2307/1123774

Wiener, A. (2018). *Contestation and constitution of norms in global international relations*. Cambridge University Press. DOI: 10.1017/9781316718599

Young, I. M. (2003). The logic of masculinist protection: Reflections on the current security state. *Signs (Chicago, Ill.), 29*(1), 1–25. DOI: 10.1086/375708

Yuval-Davis, N. (2006). Intersectionality and feminist politics. *European Journal of Women's Studies, 13*(3), 193–209. DOI: 10.1177/1350506806065752

Yuval-Davis, N. (2011). The politics of belonging: Intersectional contestations. *Sage (Atlanta, Ga.)*.

ADDITIONAL READING

Bhabha, J. (2014). *Child migration and human rights in a global age*. Princeton University Press.

Boswell, C., & Geddes, A. (2011). *Migration and mobility in the European Union*. Palgrave Macmillan. DOI: 10.1007/978-1-137-28548-5

Fiddian-Qasmiyeh, E. (2014). *The ideal refugees: Gender, Islam, and the Sahrawi politics of survival*. Syracuse University Press.

Freedman, J. (2015). *Gendering the international asylum and refugee debate* (2nd ed.). Palgrave Macmillan. DOI: 10.1057/9781137456236

Malkki, L. H. (1996). Speechless emissaries: Refugees, humanitarianism, and dehistoricization. *Cultural Anthropology*, *11*(3), 377–404. DOI: 10.1525/can.1996.11.3.02a00050

Nyers, P. (2006). *Rethinking refugees: Beyond states of emergency*. Routledge.

Olivius, E. (2016). Refugee men as perpetrators, allies or troublemakers? Emerging discourses on men and masculinities in humanitarian aid. *Women's Studies International Forum*, *56*, 56–65. DOI: 10.1016/j.wsif.2015.12.004

Ticktin, M. (2011). The gendered human of humanitarianism: Medicalising and politicising sexual violence. *Gender & History*, *23*(2), 250–265. DOI: 10.1111/j.1468-0424.2011.01637.x

Turner, L. (2021). The politics of labelling refugee men as "vulnerable.". *Social Politics*, *28*(1), 1–23. DOI: 10.1093/sp/jxz033

Wöhl, S., & Wigger, A. (2021). Gendering the European Union's migration and asylum regime. *Journal of Common Market Studies*, *59*(S1), 130–146.

KEY TERMS AND DEFINITIONS

Counter-Narrative: An account, often produced by migrants themselves, diaspora networks, or civil society, that challenges official, rescuer-centered representations and brings concealed experiences of border violence, discrimination, and legal precarity onto the international agenda.

Femonationalism: A discursive regime in which the rhetoric of protecting women's rights is mobilized as a political weapon against migrant and Muslim men, positioning female migrants as victims to be rescued or as showcases of integration while rendering migrant men suspect.

Humanitarian Justification Paradox: A mechanism through which humanitarian discourse, rather than eroding the legitimacy of control policies, repackages border control and exclusion within a more acceptable rhetoric of protection, allowing protection and exclusion to coexist without contradiction.

Intersectionality: An analytical framework holding that race, gender, class, and nationality operate not as separate axes but as structurally intertwined planes of power that shape which migrant subjects become visible within the economy of legitimacy.

Norm Competition: A process in which actors invoking ostensibly shared norms produce rival interpretations, pulling norms in different directions; this competition operates through both the content of norms and the regimes of evidence used to support interpretations.

Selective Humanitarianism: A pattern in which reception capacity, funding, and legal protection are mobilized for some migrant populations while withheld from others, distributing moral attention along racial, geographical, and religious lines.

Strategic Narratives: Purposive accounts deployed by foreign policy actors to shape the perceptions of domestic and international publics, functioning as cognitive maps and instruments of emotional mobilization that rationalize policy action.

Technology of Legitimacy: A conception of human rights diplomacy as a practical apparatus through which international legitimacy is continuously constructed, tested, and redistributed among actors, rather than a fixed normative attribute.

Chapter 11
Labor Migration and Labor Market Dynamics:
Impact, Challenges, and the Circular Migration Model

Khatuna Kharkhelauri
http://orcid.org/0000-0002-1390-5816
Georgian Technical University, Georgia

Tamari Kajaia
http://orcid.org/0009-0008-5842-4603
Georgian Technical University, Georgia

ABSTRACT

This chapter examines the multidimensional phenomenon of labor migration through a systematic analysis of theoretical frameworks, circular migration conceptualization, and empirical evidence on labor market effects. The chapter traces the evolution of migration theory from Ravenstein's Foundational laws through Neoclassical Economic approaches, World-Systems Theory, Network Theory, and pluralist perspectives, demonstrating how each paradigm captures distinct dimensions of migratory decision-making. Particular attention is devoted to circular labor migration and the triple benefits it generates for sending states, receiving states, and migrants themselves. The chapter further analyzes migration's impact on labor markets. The Georgian case serves as the empirical anchor, examining how cumulative emigration of 1.3 million people since 1991, remittance flows equivalent to 9% of GDP, and recent reverse migration waves have produced ambivalent economic and demographic outcomes requiring coordinated policy responses.

DOI: 10.4018/979-8-3373-8500-6.ch011

INTRODUCTION

Labor migration constitutes one of the most critical socio-economic processes in the modern global economy and society. In the context of globalization, economic inequality, technological advancement, and the transformation of labor markets, labor migration has acquired an increasingly large-scale, dynamic, and multifaceted character. Both sending and receiving countries undergo significant demographic, economic, and social changes as a result of migratory processes, lending particular urgency to the scientific analysis of this phenomenon.

The theoretical understanding of migration is historically rooted in various paradigmatic approaches that explain the causes and consequences of migratory behavior in different ways. Theories developed across different eras interpret the drivers, mechanisms, and outcomes of migration diversely. Early migration theory emerged from Ravenstein's laws of migration (Ravenstein, 1885) and was later systematized through Lee's Push-Pull model (Lee, 1966), subsequent Neoclassical Economic Theory (Sjaastad, 1962; Harris & Todaro, 1970) and the Dual Labor Market Theory (Ranis & Fei, 1961) view the migrant as a rational "Homo Economicus," making decisions based on a calculation of costs and benefits.

However, in the era of modern globalization, explaining migration solely through economic factors is insufficient. This chapter critically analyzes the shortcomings of classical theories, which fail to explain the so-called "immobility paradox" or the continuation of migration after economic incentives have been exhausted. To address these gaps, this work proposes a synthesis of the latest paradigms: the New Economics of Labor Migration (NELM) (Stark & Bloom, 1985), social capital, transnationalism (Castles & Miller, 2003), and migratory systems (Massey et al., 1993). Due to this diversity, the analysis of labor migration requires a complex and critical approach.

Since the second half of the 20th century, the classical paradigm of a one-time, permanent move from one country to another has increasingly failed to reflect the reality of international labor migration. In the 21st century, fluid mobility in the field of employment is considered the norm rather than the exception, bringing phenomena such as return, repeat, and circular migration to the forefront. In recent decades, particularly in the European Union, the decline of the working-age population, industrial automation, and the structural transformation of the labor market have created an urgent political need for managed, circular migration systems. In this context, the correct conceptualization of circular migration is not only a matter of theoretical interest but a practical necessity for effective policy formation. This phenomenon significantly alters the classical perception of migration and creates new opportunities for both individuals and states.

The impact of migration on the labor market represents a central direction of research. In receiving countries, immigration often plays a complementary role, filling labor shortages and increasing economic activity. Conversely, in countries of origin, emigration causes both challenges (reduction of labor resources, "brain drain") and opportunities (remittances, return of knowledge, growth of entrepreneurship). Particularly significant is the transition from the concept of "brain drain" to "brain circulation," which emphasizes the dynamic and reciprocal nature of migration.

Emigration from Georgia represents one of the most significant socio-economic challenges on the country's path to development. Following the collapse of the Soviet Union in 1991, economic chaos, civil conflicts, and poverty served as the primary catalysts for mass emigration. According to IMF (2024) data, the cumulative number of emigrants from Georgia between 1994 and 2024 reached 1.3 million, accounting for 30 percent of the population. This figure gains particular gravity considering that the total population of the country stands at 3.7 million.

Labor migration, by its nature, is an ambivalent phenomenon. On one hand, it weakens the local labor market, reduces the stock of human capital, and accelerates the process of population aging. On the other hand, emigrants send significant financial resources to the country, while returning migrants bring new competencies and experience.

This chapter seeks to demonstrate the multidimensional nature of the labor migration process and to provide an integrated analysis of its interconnected dimensions, structured around four analytical objectives: (1) a historical and theoretical overview of migration dynamics; (2) a critical evaluation of circular migration as a policy instrument; (3) an analysis of migration's impact on labor market dynamics; and (4) an assessment of its macroeconomic effects, with particular reference to the case of Georgia.

Research Methodology

This chapter adopts a qualitative, desk-based research design and employs a narrative synthesis approach to analyze the existing academic and policy-oriented literature on labor migration and circular migration. The study does not involve the collection of primary data or the development of original statistical models. Instead, it is based on a critical review, comparison, and synthesis of existing theoretical, empirical, and policy-related studies in order to develop an integrated analytical understanding of the relationship between labor migration and labor market dynamics.

The sources used in this study are grouped into three main categories. The first category comprises classical and foundational theoretical works on migration (Ravenstein, 1885; Lee, 1966; Harris & Todaro, 1970; Stark & Bloom, 1985; Massey et al., 1993), which provide the conceptual foundation for the analysis. The second category includes peer-reviewed academic articles and studies published between 2000 and 2025, focusing on labor migration (de Haas, 2008), circular migration (Adeusi et al., 2025), return migration (Adda, Dustmann, & Görlach, 2022), labor market outcomes, and human capital mobility (Constant, Nottmeyer, & Zimmermann, 2012; Constant, 2020). The third category consists of reports and statistical data published by international organizations, including the International Monetary Fund (IMF), the Organisation for Economic Co-operation and Development (OECD), the World Bank, the International Organization for Migration (IOM), the United Nations (UN), and the European Training Foundation (ETF).

The analytical framework of the chapter follows a funnel-shaped approach, progressing from the general to the specific. The discussion begins with an examination of the major theories of migration, then moves to the conceptual and policy dimensions of circular migration, followed by an analysis of migration's effects on labor markets, and finally narrows its focus to the case of Georgia.

Several limitations should be acknowledged. First, the study relies exclusively on secondary sources. Second, internationally comparable data on circular migration remain limited, which constrains the scope of empirical analysis. Nevertheless, the methodology provides a reliable and rigorous basis for examining the relationship between labor migration, labor market dynamics, and economic development, enabling a comprehensive assessment of migration's socioeconomic implications.

1. THEORETICAL FOUNDATIONS OF LABOR MIGRATION

Neoclassical Premises: Ravenstein's "Laws" and the Conceptualization of the "Push-Pull" Model.

The epistemological foundation of modern migration theories was laid at the end of the 19th century. The scientific study of migration is associated with the name of the German-British cartographer and statistician, Ernst Georg Ravenstein. Between 1885 and 1889, based on British census data, he formulated the "Laws of Migration", which are still considered the classical foundation of migration studies (Ravenstein, 1885). Ravenstein's approach was a classic example of empirical positivism, aimed at identifying the behavioral patterns of migratory flows.

The postulates formulated by Ravenstein remain relevant today; specifically:

1. The Distance Factor: The majority of migrants travel short distances, while long-distance migration is primarily directed toward major industrial and commercial centers (The principle of Distance Decay).

2. Gradualism: Migration occurs in stages (Step-by-step migration) - from village to town, from town to small city, and ultimately to the metropolis.
3. Technological Determinism: The development of technology, communications, and transport increases the volume of migration in direct proportion.
4. Dominance of the Economic Factor: Despite other factors, the primary driving force of migration is economic gain.

In the second half of the 20th century, these laws were systematized by sociologist Everett Lee, who gave the final form to the so-called "Push-Pull" model in his seminal 1966 work, "A Theory of Migration" (Lee, 1966). According to Lee, the migratory decision is the result of the interaction between four factors:

1. Factors associated with the area of origin (Push factors — unemployment, low income, political repression);
2. Factors associated with the area of destination (Pull factors — high wages, security, better social environment);
3. Intervening obstacles (e.g., distance, physical borders, visa regulations);
4. Personal factors (age, education, attitude toward risk).

Although the "Push-Pull" model is still used today as a basic heuristic framework, it is frequently criticized in modern academic discourse for ignoring historical context and for its overly mechanical perception of the process. The model fails to view humans as complex social beings with emotions, fears, and family obligations. Furthermore, it treats migration as an individual act and fails to account for structural forces (such as global inequality or the structural interdependence between center and periphery) that often determine a migrant's "choice" independently of their own will.

Despite the fact that migration issues receive relatively little attention in mainstream economic theory, economic explanations of migration have occupied a dominant position in academic discourse (Haas, 2008).

Neoclassical Economic Theory: The Neoclassical Equilibrium Perspective.

This theory was the most influential in migration research during the 20th century. The core idea of this theory is the existence of a geographical imbalance: factors of production (labor and capital) are unevenly distributed throughout the world, and migration is a natural mechanism that brings the economic system into equilibrium. Proponents of this theory view migration as the efficient redistribution of labor resources by market forces (supply and demand). The theory is divided into two main levels: macro (country level) and micro (individual level).

At the macro level, migration is viewed as the redistribution of labor from poor (developing) regions or countries—where there is a surplus of labor but a scarcity of capital (money/technology) and low wages—to wealthy (developed) regions or countries where capital is abundant, but labor is scarce and wages are high. This process continues until wages equalize (equilibrium). As a result of migration, labor becomes less scarce in receiving territories and scarcer in sending regions, while capital (investments) flows in the opposite direction (toward cheap labor). This process should lead to factor price equalization (Heckscher–Ohlin model) (Jones, 2008).

At the micro level, neoclassical economic theory is based on the principle of "Rational Choice". On an individual level, this perspective relies on the concept of "Homo Economicus" (Economic Man). According to this concept, migrants are rational actors who make the decision to migrate based on a cost-benefit analysis.

Neoclassical theory views rural-to-urban migration as an organic part of the development process. Surplus rural labor moves toward the urban industrial economy (Lewis, 1954). The Fei-Ranis model of economic growth is known in development and welfare economics as the "Dualism Model" and can be considered a more complex vision of Lewis's "Dual Sector Model". The model examines a country characterized by two sectors: (1) the traditional sector (agriculture), characterized by surplus labor and low productivity, and (2) the modern sector (industry), characterized by capital accumulation and high technology (Lewis, 1954), (Ranis & Fei, 1961). The model outlines three phases of development: (1) the initial phase (LMP = 0), when surplus labor migrates from agriculture to the industrial sector at low wages ("subsistence level") without harming agricultural output; and (2) the subsequent phase (LMP > 0), where the outflow of labor continues, but the rural population decreases. At this stage, the departure of a worker reduces agricultural production. Food shortages lead to rising prices, and (3) this marks the turning point phase. Agriculture itself transforms into a business. The workers remaining in the rural areas receive wages equal to the real value of their labor. Industry and agriculture now compete with each other for labor; wages rise in both sectors, and the economy becomes developed. The industrial sector is forced to increase wages so that workers can afford expensive food, which, in turn, slows industrial growth.

Later, neoclassical economic theory evolved to incorporate migration into the human capital framework, where migration is viewed as an investment. An individual invests money and effort (by moving abroad) to achieve higher returns in the future. Larry Sjaastad (Sjaastad, 1962) argues that the individual is a rational actor who calculates expected income and subtracts the monetary costs (transportation, costs of searching for housing and employment), opportunity costs (lost income during the job search period, temporary unemployment), and psychological costs (leaving behind family, environment, and social ties). If the benefits outweigh the costs, the individual chooses to emigrate. The benefits of migration are manifested in higher wages, better employment opportunities, increased productivity, and sometimes consumption benefits (e.g., improved living conditions).

This approach evolved into the so-called Harris-Todaro model, according to which labor migration from rural to urban areas—and on a broader scale—is determined not by actual wage differentials, but by expected income differentials. Migration continues as long as the expected income in the city (wages multiplied by the probability of employment) exceeds the actual rural income (Harris & Todaro, 1970). The model attempts to explain why the movement of rural populations to cities continues in developing countries despite rising urban unemployment.

Although these models were originally developed for internal migration, they can also be adapted for the analysis of international migration. George Borjas (Borjas, 1989) proposed the idea of an international migration market, while Todaro and Maruszko developed a model of illegal international migration that incorporates the risks of apprehension and deportation (Todaro & Maruszko, 1987). According to this model, the probability of apprehension/deportation multiplied by the costs of fines/deportation is also subtracted from the expected income. As long as this difference remains higher than the wages available in the home country, migrants will continue to take the risk.

While these approaches are particularly strong in terms of economic logic, they pay insufficient attention to market imperfections, neglect institutional factors (such as borders and visas), and focus primarily on the individual rather than the family or the structural environment. Instead of the promised "equilibrium", in reality, migration often further widens the gap between poor and wealthy countries (Haas, 2008). Nevertheless, they remain classic and fundamental works in the economic analysis of migration.

Historical-Structuralist Determinism

This is a broad theoretical framework that emerged in the analysis of migration and development during the 1960s–1980s.

Immanuel Wallerstein's World-Systems Theory (Wallerstein, 1974) argued that the global economy is divided into the core, semi-periphery, and periphery. Migration is a result of the capitalist world-system, and the periphery is structurally dependent on the core. Within this framework, migration is perceived as a product of the global capitalist structure, while individual choice is considered secondary.

The central thesis of Andre Gunder Frank's Dependency Theory (Frank, 1966) is that development and underdevelopment are interconnected, and the core "developed" through the exploitation of the periphery. Migration is viewed here as a result of structural inequality and a component of capitalist expansion.

Samir Amin's concept of the structural subordination of the periphery (Amin, 1974) views migration as a mechanism for global capital accumulation and the outflow of labor from the periphery to the core.

In the field of migration studies, the historical-structuralist (structure-oriented) view explicitly treats migration as a result of the needs of capitalist production and a product of the structural demand of the labor market, while virtually ignoring individual choice (Castles & Kosack, 1973). This approach was criticized by pluralist theories for overemphasizing structural constraints and neglecting the agency[1] of individuals and families.

Social Capital: Migration Networks and Systems

Although economic factors are often considered one of the primary drivers of migration, and individuals tend to gravitate toward locations with better living conditions, this single factor alone cannot explain certain forms of migration.

Network theory examines migration through the lens of social capital. Its central argument is that the continuation and expansion of migration are driven not only by economic factors but also by interpersonal ties-such as kinship, friendship, and shared community origins.

The central concept of this theory is "chain migration", where pioneer migrants act as "outposts" at the destination, providing subsequent arrivals with information, housing, and employment opportunities. This process reduces the costs and risks associated with migration, making it accessible to a broader range of people-consequently, migration becomes less selective.

According to Douglas Massey, once network ties reach a critical threshold, migration becomes self-sustaining and continues even after the original causes have disappeared. "Cumulative Causation" is one of Massey's most significant concepts. Its essence lies in the fact that migration itself generates further migration. Furthermore, transnational identity explains the phenomenon of remittances, which neoclassical theory fails to account for (Massey et al., 1993).

However, the theory also has its weaknesses. It fails to explain what eventually causes the weakening of these networks. Furthermore, migrants do not always act as "outposts" - they can also become "gatekeepers" when they refuse to assist new arrivals. Networks can also be exclusionary in nature, meaning that for those outside of kinship groups, migration remains unattainable.

Migration Systems Theory expands the logic of network theory and places migration within a much broader systemic context. According to its authors, a migration system is a group of places linked by reciprocal flows of people, goods, capital, and information (Mabogunje, 1970).

A fundamental principle of the theory is that migration entirely transforms the socio-economic environment in both the origin and destination areas, thereby determining the character of future migration. This reciprocal, dynamic feedback loop is the primary distinction from network theory, which focuses mainly on interpersonal ties.

The theory also explains the geographical structuring of migration: migration flows are clustered, and specific territories are linked to specific destinations—for example, North Africa to the European Union, or Mexico to the USA. Neoclassical economic factors fail to explain this clustering pattern (Massey et al., 1993).

Particularly significant is the concept of "social remittances" (Levitt, 1998): the ideas, behaviors, and values that flow back to the donor community shape people's aspirations and subsequent migration decisions. Thus, the theory posits that the impact of migration should be assessed not only on the migrants themselves but on the sending society as a whole, including non-migrants.

The concept of migration networks and systems differs from its predecessors, particularly neoclassical theories, in several aspects. The neoclassical model fails to explain remittances, as there is no motive for transfers within an individualistic logic; in contrast, network theory finds a natural explanation for remittances in transnational ties and a sense of social belonging. Furthermore, while neoclassical theory views migration as a temporary phenomenon that ceases once wages equalize, network theory demonstrates that networks prolong migration even after the original economic causes have disappeared.

Pluralist Perspectives on the Interaction Between Labor Migration and National Development Levels

The understanding of the nexus between migration and development has undergone significant transformation over time, particularly after the 1980s with the emergence of the so-called pluralist approach. This paradigm arose as a reaction to the one-sidedness of both neoclassical and historical-structuralist theories, aiming to integrate structural and agency-based factors (Giddens, 1984).

At the core of the pluralist view lies the assumption that the interaction between migration and development is neither unambiguous nor linear. On the contrary, it represents a multifaceted and heterogeneous process driven by both macro-level structural conditions (political, economic, and institutional environments) and micro-level decisions and strategies. In this context, particular emphasis is placed on "agency" - the capacity of individuals and households to act within existing constraints and, to some extent, transform their environment.

A significant contribution to the development of the pluralist approach was made by the New Economics of Labor Migration (NELM) (Stark & Bloom, 1985),which views migration not as an individual decision but as a household-level choice (Massey et al., 1993). According to this theory, migration serves as a strategic tool aimed not only at income maximization but also at risk diversification and minimization (Statk & Levhari, 1982). Thus, migration functions as a form of "insurance mechanism", especially in conditions where financial and insurance markets in developing countries are imperfect.

In parallel with NELM, the "livelihood" approach emerged, emphasizing that households employ various strategies to maintain and improve their well-being (Carney, 1998); (Ellis, 2000). Within this framework, migration is viewed as a vital component of a broader livelihood strategy that encompasses both agricultural and non-agricultural activities. In this context, migration is perceived not merely as a response to a crisis, but as a pre-planned and rational decision aimed at stabilizing income and expanding investment opportunities.

Another vital dimension of the pluralist view is the concept of transnationalism, which focuses on the multi-local social, economic, and cultural ties of migrants (Castles & Miller, 2003). (Faist, 1998). The transnational perspective rejects the traditional dichotomy between 'origin' and "destination" countries and asserts that migrants can be simultaneously engaged in both spaces. Thus, the integration of migrants into the host country does not preclude their active participation in the development of their country of origin.

Contemporary studies indicate that transnational ties, such as remittances, investments, and social networks, play a significant role in the development of local economies. Furthermore, the pluralist approach emphasizes that the impact of migration is not uniform and is context-dependent, necessitating a complex and interdisciplinary analysis (Kharkhelauri & Kajaia, 2026).

Ultimately, the pluralist view provides a more balanced and realistic framework for analyzing the nexus between migration and development, as it integrates both structural constraints and the active role of individuals and households. This approach is particularly significant in the context of developing countries, where migration often constitutes a vital element of development strategy.

2. CIRCULAR LABOR MIGRATION: DEFINITION AND CONCEPTUALIZATION

In the second half of the 20th century, the classical paradigm of a one-time, permanent move from one country to another increasingly failed to reflect the reality of international labor migration. In the 21st century, fluid human mobility in the field of employment is considered the norm rather than the exception, as the phenomena of return, repeat, and circular migration come to the forefront (Constant, 2020). Among OECD countries in Europe, the average outflow rate of migrants who arrived between 2010 and 2014 was approximately 50% after five years of residence. In the USA, this figure is around 15%, while in Canada, it stands at 21%. It should be noted that these figures include both voluntary and forced (deportation) returns. Assisted Voluntary Return and Reintegration (AVRR) programs account for only a small fraction of total returns (at most 5%) (OECD, 2024). Approximately 26-31% of migration flows in any given period represent returns to the country of origin (Azose & Raftery, 2018).

In recent decades, particularly in the European Union, the decline of the working-age population, industry automation, and the structural transformation of the labor market have created an urgent political need for the formation of managed, circular migration systems (Privarova, 2024). In this context, the proper conceptualization of circular migration is not merely a matter of theoretical interest but a practical necessity for the formulation of effective policy.

Core Conceptual Approaches to Definition

The issue of defining circular migration is primarily linked to its conceptual ambiguity. There is no universally accepted definition for circular, repeat, or return migration. This is due to the fact that migrant behavior is dynamic, context-dependent, and frequently changes throughout the migration process (Constant, 2020). In academic literature, it is often defined as the repeated, systematic movement of migrants between their countries of origin and destination, primarily for the purpose of (Constant, Nottmeyer, & Zimmermann, 2012).

However, international organizations such as the IOM, the European Commission, and the World Bank often view circular migration as a policy instrument. Their approach is more normative, emphasizing migration management, the regulation of labor flows, and the promotion of development. Consequently, a distinction arises between the theoretical (academic) approach, which focuses on behavioral, economic, and social dynamics, and the political approach, which regards circular migration as a management mechanism.

The issue intensifies when moving from the conceptual level (what is circularity?) to the operational level (how do we measure it?). At the conceptual level, circular migration encompasses a broad spectrum: seasonal, professional, and transnational movements. At the operational level, however, it is often restricted to specific programs, such as temporary work visas and bilateral agreements.

The Task Force (UNECE, 2016) highlighted that for operational purposes, strict criteria are required:

(1) Frequency: A minimum of two cycles (departure and return).
(2) Duration: The temporary nature of the stay (e.g., up to 12 months).
(3) Legality: Possession of a valid residence permit (right of residence).

Thus, while circularity is flexible at the conceptual level, it is often narrowed at the operational level to encompass only regulated labor migration. Such a discrepancy leads to methodological difficulties, particularly in data collection and empirical research, as countries often lack systematic information regarding the multiple movements of migrants.

"The Win-Win-Win Concept"

In the academic and political discourse on circular migration, the "win-win-win" model is widely prevalent, implying benefits for three key actors:

(1) Destination (Host) Countries:
- Filling labor market shortages;
- Flexible workforce;
- Stimulating economic growth.

(2) Countries of Origin:
- Remittances, which reached $656 billion in 2023;
- Return of skilled human capital (brain gain);
- Reduction of unemployment.

(3) Migrants:
- Higher income;
- Accumulation of skills and experience;
- Improvement of living standards;
- Maintaining family ties.

The theoretical evolution of the concept was followed by empirical support. Studies show that circularity is not merely a theoretical construct. Constant and Zimmermann (2012) establish that more than 60% of the so-called "guest workers" in the German labor market were repeat or circular migrants—individuals who used Germany as a base for systematic movement between their homeland and the host country.

In the study of Turkish migrants in Germany, a direct correlation was identified between return intentions and the accumulation of human capital. The authors argue that migrants invest in their skills based on where they intend to utilize them. Migrants who plan to circulate or return soon spend less time acquiring skills specific to the host country (such as perfect language proficiency or local legal nuances). Instead, they focus on skills that will be beneficial upon their return home. Research shows that work experience gained in the host country is "capital" whose value increases upon return, as the migrant is regarded in their homeland as a professional with international experience (Constant, 2020), (Adda, Dustmann, & Görlach, 2022).

Research identifies the key determinants of the return decision.

(1) Consumption Preference: For many migrants, living and consuming in their home country provides higher utility than doing so abroad, despite the higher wages available there.
(2) Price Differential (Purchasing Power): Migrants often accumulate capital in the host country to later utilize these funds in their home country, where the cost of living is lower and the purchasing power of their savings is significantly higher.
(3) Optimal Length of Stay: Each migrant has their own "optimal point", where an additional euro earned in the host country no longer outweighs the cost of being away from their home country.

The 2024 Rabat Process document confirms that circular migration programs between Africa and Europe (e.g., Talent Partnerships) are already yielding empirical results in terms of skills recognition and transferability (Rabat Process, 2024). However, it must be noted that success depends on "innovative policy interventions", such as the portability of social protection and flexible visa renewal systems (Adeusi, et al., 2025).

While research confirms the triple-win potential of circular migration for skilled migrants, this model is also subject to criticism. In practice, issues such as irregular overstaying, labor exploitation, social integration difficulties, and the negative effects of "split families" frequently arise. Within the context of the global labor market, its practical implementation faces numerous legal and administrative constraints. Without proper management, circular migration can easily become permanent. All these policy instruments encounter a practical paradox: interventions by host countries are often counter-productive (Constant, 2020). In various European countries, monetary incentives for voluntary return (pay-to-go) or the tightening of entry requirements ultimately serve as incentives for permanent settlement. Migrants prefer to bring their families rather than incur the costs and risks of re-entry each time. The most crucial policy principle in the conceptualization of circular migration is offering a guarantee of repeated legal return. Thus, the "win-win-win" remains more of a normative ideal than a universally achievable reality.

Thus, in modern discourse, migration is no longer viewed as a zero-sum game, but rather as a dynamic process that can be mutually and multilaterally beneficial.

3. THE IMPACT OF MIGRATION ON THE LABOR MARKET

Migration represents one of the primary driving forces of the global economy, influencing labor market structures, economic growth, and social dynamics. In recent years, particularly in the post-pandemic period, migratory processes have intensified significantly, as evidenced by the latest reports from the World Bank and the International Organization for Migration (2023–2024).

Migration encompasses both emigration and immigration, and its impact varies between host and origin countries. Consequently, its analysis requires a complex, multifaceted approach.

Labor Market and Workforce Shortages in Host Countries

In host countries, immigration represents a crucial mechanism for labor market stabilization. According to OECD (2024) data, the labor markets of many developed nations are already dependent on immigrants, particularly in the following sectors:

- Healthcare
- Information Technology (IT)
- Construction
- Agriculture

These sectors are characterized by both labor shortages and low levels of local workforce participation, which renders immigrants a critical economic resource.

Immigrants fill workforce shortages, reduce vacancy durations, and boost economic activity.

Table 1. Migration (Immigration) and Employment in OECD Countries (2019–2023)

Year	Immigration-mln	Employment-rate %
2019	5.1	69.8
2020	3.7	67.5
2021	4.8	68.9
2022	5.9	70.5
2023	6.5	71.6

Source: (OECD, 2024)

The data reveals that an increase in immigration does not reduce employment. On the contrary, between 2021 and 2023, both indicators increased simultaneously. This indicates that immigrants:

- Do not substitute for the local workforce
- Address structural market deficits

This trend confirms the theory of complementarity and indicates the labor market's capacity for adaptation. Immigration enhances labor market flexibility and reduces structural unemployment, particularly in regions experiencing demographic aging.

According to the latest projections from the International Monetary Fund (International Monetary Fund, 2024), immigration has a significant multiplier effect, which is reflected in a 1-2% increase in GDP over the long term.

Recent research (OECD, 2024); (IMF, 2024) demonstrates that:

- Immigration increases productivity
- It has a positive impact on wages in the long term
- It fosters innovation

According to the International Monetary Fund, immigration increases GDP by 1–2% over the long term.

Table 2. The Impact of Immigration on Key Economic Indicators

Parameter	Degree of Impact	Mechanism and Outcome
Productivity	**Growth**	Immigrants bring new skills that complement the competencies of the local workforce.
Wages	**Positive (Long-term)**	Increased productivity leads to economic expansion, which is reflected in wage growth.
Innovation	**High**	Migrants generate more patents and scientific papers (the so-called "High-skilled flow").
GDP	**+1% - 2%**	Labor force growth and efficient allocation increase the overall volume of the economy.
Fiscal Base	**Expansion**	Tax revenues (Income Tax, VAT) increase, and the demographic pressure on the budget is reduced.

Source: (International Monetary Fund, 2024)
(International Monetary Fund, 2024)

Furthermore, immigration contributes o the expansion of the fiscal base, as it increases both tax revenues and domestic consumption.

Countries of Origin (Emigration)

Emigration generates significant economic benefits in the form of remittances.

Table 3. Global Remittance Dynamics and Their Economic Significance (2015–2024)

Year	Remittances-bln
2015	440
2017	520
2019	548
2021	630
2023	656
2024	700

Source: (World Bank, 2024)

The data reveals a steady growth in remittances, which in turn reduces poverty, increases consumption, and promotes the development of small businesses. Nevertheless, this is accompanied by negative consequences. Specifically, the economy may become dependent, and incentives for domestic production may diminish.

From Brain Drain to Brain Circulation

Traditionally, migration has been viewed within the context of 'brain drain" - as a loss of human capital for developing countries. According to OECD (2022) data, the number of migrants with higher education has increased by 70% over the last decade. The flow of skilled migrants grew two and a half times faster than that of unskilled migrants (Privarova, 2024).

Table 4. Growth Trend of Highly Skilled Migration (Brain Drain) (2010–2024)

Year	High-skill-%
2010	28
2015	32
2020	35
2022	37
2024	39

Source: (United Nations Department of Economic and Social Affairs, 2024)
(OECD, 2024)

The trend is upward, which, from the perspective of the traditional "brain drain" approach, signifies:

- Developing countries lose human capital
- The potential for innovation decreases

However, the development of the circular migration concept has shifted this narrative. Circular migration creates opportunities for "brain circulation", where knowledge and skills return to the country of origin. Migrants act as conduits for technology and innovation, while transnational networks strengthen investment and trade. Recent empirical studies show that returning migrants significantly increase the likelihood of entrepreneurship, accumulate capital, and disseminate knowledge and practices that stimulate local economic development (Adeusi, et al., 2025). This is explained by two factors:

(1) Risk tolerance: The decision to migrate itself already indicates an individual's readiness for risk, which is an essential trait for entrepreneurship.
(2) Psychological capital: The experience of adapting to a foreign environment increases self-efficacy and problem-solving skills.

According to data from Adda, Dustmann & Görlach (2021) and EPRS (2025), the funds saved by migrants often become start-up capital upon their return home. In many developing countries, the local population lacks access to bank credits; returning migrants overcome this barrier using their own savings. They not only finance their own businesses but also become "angel investors" for other local projects.

The dissemination of knowledge and practices (Social Remittances) is the most crucial aspect of "Brain Circulation". According to Rabat Process (2024) and Přívarová (2024) documents, returnees bring back:

(1) Technological know-how: Modern standards of production or services acquired in developed countries.
(2) Institutional practices: Business ethics, management styles, and quality control mechanisms that increase competition in the local market.
(3) Market knowledge: They understand the demands of foreign markets, which helps local production to become export-oriented.

The IJSRA (2025) study shows that enterprises established by migrants are more inclined toward innovation and create jobs not only for themselves but for the community as well. This creates a "multiplier effect" in the local economy.

4. THE GEORGIAN CASE STUDY

Emigration from Georgia represents one of the most significant socioeconomic challenges on the country's path to development. Following the dissolution of the Soviet Union in 1991, economic chaos, civil conflicts and widespread poverty became the primary catalysts for mass emigration. According to data published by the International Monetary Fund (International Monetary Fund, 2025), the cumulative number of individuals who emigrated from Georgia between 1994 and 2024 reached 1.3 million, representing 30% of the total population. This figure takes on particular gravity when considered against the backdrop that the total population of the country is 3.7 million.

Migration is, by its very nature, an inherently ambivalent phenomenon. On the one hand, it weakens the local labor market, depletes the stock of human capital, and accelerates the aging of the population. On the other hand, emigrants remit substantial financial resources to the country, while returning migrants bring new competencies and professional experience. This paper aims to present a comprehensive analysis of these interrelated processes, structured around four analytical objectives: (1) a historical overview of migration dynamics; (2) an evaluation of circular migration policy; (3) an analysis of labor market effects; and (4) an assessment of macroeconomic impacts.

Migration Dynamics: Historical Context and Trends

External migration from Georgia can be divided into three principal phases. The first phase (1991-2003) encompasses the period of post-Soviet economic collapse, during which the most intensive emigration was recorded. Russia constituted the primary destination during this period. The total number of Georgians who emigrated to Russia between 1997 and 2023 exceeded 240,000, representing 7% of the country's population (Giguashvili, Khorguashvili, & Makasarashvili, 2023).

The second phase (2004-2017) is characterized by a geographic reorientation of the emigration flow. The principal destination countries during this period were Germany, Italy, Greece, Spain, and France. The IMF (2025) further highlights that approximately 60% of these flows were directed toward Western Europe, primarily for employment purposes.

The third phase (2017-present) opens with the visa liberalization agreement with the European Union in 2017. This agreement will significantly ease pathways for legal migration. Subsequently, according to data from the Organisation for Economic Co-operation and Development (OECD, 2022), the flow of Georgian emigrants to the European Union member states increased from 3,500 individuals in 1995 to 33,000 by 2022.

Socio-Demographic Profile of Emigrants

According to data published by the United Nations Department of Economic and Social Affairs (United Nations, 2020) among the 861,077 individuals who emigrated from Georgia in 2020, the gender composition was nearly balanced: 50.2% female and 49.8% male. The European Training Foundation (European Training Foundation, 2021) highlights that in certain destination countries, particularly Italy and Greece, a pronounced gender imbalance of emigration is evident, with a substantial proportion of Georgian women emigrants employed in domestic care and elderly support services. In terms of age structure, the highest share of emigrants belongs to the 20-64 age group — 58.4% according to 2020 data — while the 65+ age group constitutes 20.2%, indicating a comparatively older age composition among emigrants.

With respect to geographic distribution, ETF (2021) confirms that 80.2% of Georgian emigrants reside in Europe, 14.8% in Asia (predominantly Russia), and 4.9% in North America. Among the top 10 destination countries, Russia leads (449,973 individuals), followed by Greece (85,065), Ukraine (65,475), Azerbaijan (48,815), and the United States (39,422). The IMF (2025) clarifies that following 2022, the number of Georgians residing in Russia declined sharply as a result of the Russia-Ukraine war. Immigration patterns are also dynamic: ETF (2021) reports that as of 2020, the primary countries of origin for foreign immigrants residing in Georgia were Russia (37,267), Armenia (12,789), and Ukraine (12,203).

Concerning educational attainment, ETF (2021) and IMF (2025) arrive at the convergent conclusions: Georgian emigrants, similarly to emigrants from comparable countries, exhibit above-average levels of educational attainment relative to the domestic population (ETF and Business Consulting Group Research (Georgia), 2013) (OECD, 2017). In 2020/2021, among Georgian emigrants residing in OECD countries, 31% held tertiary education, 30% had low educational attainment, and 39% had intermediate qualifications. By contrast, within Georgia's domestic labor market during the same period, 40% held tertiary qualifications, while only 4.5% had low educational attainment. ETF (2021) particularly emphasizes that the comparatively small proportion of emigrants who departed for educational and research purposes constitutes a meaningful loss of intellectual capital for the country. Taking them into consideration is particularly important, however, the principal destination countries for Georgian students are Germany (1,955), Ukraine (1,851), Armenia (1,045), Turkey (758), and the United States (579) (ETF, 2021; UNESCO, 2019).

Eurostat data on first residence permits (2010-2023) reveal significant variation in emigrant profiles by destination country. The IMF (2025) elaborates: Poland primarily admitted men aged 30-44 for short-term employment purposes; Greece admitted women aged 45-64 on long-term humanitarian visas; and Germany admitted young people aged 0-29, primarily for educational purposes. The Center for Global Development (Center for Global Development, 2021) confirms that labor migration flows toward lower-skilled occupations — welders, construction workers, and freight drivers — are also intensive, particularly toward Poland. During the

IOM pilot program (Georgia-Poland-Estonia) conducted between 2015 and 2017, 1,200 potential candidates were assessed, of whom 409 registered and 19 workers were actually placed in employment. This demonstrates that the boundaries of formal circular programs remain sharply distinct from the broader informal migration flows (Center for Global Development, 2021). Accounting for this differentiation is essential for sound policy design.

The conceptualization of the **"Immobility Paradox"** is particularly salient in the Georgian context, as classical "Push-Pull" models fail to explain why the most economically deprived segments of the population often remain immobile. In the case of Georgia, this phenomenon underscores that migration is contingent not merely upon the desire to leave, but upon access to specific resources: a lack of **social capital**, information asymmetry, and the high initial financial costs of departure create a "trapped" effect, effectively stripping the most vulnerable groups of the opportunity for international mobility.

Georgia's State Policy on Circular Migration and Key Challenges

Georgia's state policy on circular migration has developed incrementally. According to Giguashvili et al. (2023), the Law on Labor Migration, adopted in 2015, provided the foundational framework for a system of bilateral agreements. On January 1, 2020, the State Employment Promotion Agency (SEPA) was established to facilitate employment both within the domestic market and abroad through bilateral agreements. Furthermore, the Migration Strategy of Georgia 2021-2030 sets four principal priorities: the promotion of legal migration; the reintegration of returning migrants; the engagement of the Georgian diaspora in national development; and the expansion of circular migration schemes.

By the end of 2023, Georgia had concluded four bilateral circular migration agreements: with France (2013), Bulgaria (2019), Germany (2020), and Israel (2020). Stulb and Dzhvarsheishvili (2023) emphasize that Germany, applying the concept of Global Skill Partnerships, trains Georgian migrants in their home country before subsequently providing them with employment in the sectors facing the greatest labor shortages in Europe — namely agriculture and logistics. The IMF (2025) also references the South Korean experience as a model: the country offers relocation grants, job placement services, tax incentives, and start-up subsidies to returning specialists.

Within the framework of the IOM's Assisted Voluntary Return and Reintegration (AVRR) program between 2016 and 2020, 11,000 migrants returned to Georgia — primarily from Europe — and 3,400 individuals received reintegration assistance The

IMF (2025) notes that these programs require expansion and that regular evaluation of their effectiveness is desirable.

Influence on the Labor Market

The most immediate impact of emigration on the labor market is manifested in the quantitative reduction of the workforce. According to IMF (2025) data, between 2014 and 2023, Georgia's working-age population (aged 15-64) declined by 5%, primarily as a result of external migration. This trend translates into practical difficulties for businesses: according to the EU Business Climate Survey (2024), two-thirds of the surveyed business entities reported avoiding new projects and opening new branches due to labor shortages. This indicator suggests that emigration has effectively become a structural barrier to economic growth.

The outflow of young professionals is of particular concern. Stulb and Dzhvarsheishvili (2023) report that in 2022, the 15-29 age cohort had declined by 10% over the preceding five years. The primary motivations cited by young specialists for emigration are unemployment (at 47.4% among the 15-19 age group and 37.3% among the 20-24 age group), lack of adequate career prospects and the increasing accessibility of global labor markets. Research by Stulb and Dzhvarsheishvili (2023) also found that 76% of Georgian students and recent graduates report feeling insufficiently prepared for the international labor market, principally due to deficiencies in foreign language proficiency and practical skills.

One of the key paradoxes characterizing the Georgian labour market is that, despite a significant demand for workers with vocational and middle-level technical qualifications, emigration rates among this group remain high. Empirical evidence suggests that the shortage of skilled labour is a major constraint for businesses, with 66% of firms identifying high emigration as a primary cause of labour shortages and 65% pointing to weaknesses in the vocational education system (Kharkhelauri & Kajaia, 2025). At the same time, the main drivers of emigration are strongly linked to economic incentives, including higher wages, better working conditions, and broader career development opportunities abroad (EBA Georgia, 2024). As a result, a structural imbalance emerges: although domestic demand for medium-skilled labour is considerable, a substantial share of this workforce exits the country, further exacerbating skill shortages and reducing the efficiency of the local labour market. This pattern indicates that, in the Georgian context, migration is driven not only by unemployment but also by wage differentials and the search for improved employment conditions, reinforcing the central role of economic disparities within the classical "push–pull" framework.

Despite concerns about brain drain, the IMF (2025) indicates that this phenomenon remains relatively moderate in Georgia. The impact of Georgian emigration on human capital is less severe than in the neighboring countries, given that emigrants are on average less educated than the population that remains in the country. Analysis by OECD (2022) confirms that the share of highly educated individuals among Georgian emigrants residing in OECD countries declined from 38% in 2015/2016 to 31% in 2020/2021, while the proportion of highly educated individuals in the domestic labor market remained at 40%.

However, the European Union Agency for Asylum (EUAA, 2022) report highlights that, according to expert assessments, emigration among qualified specialists — particularly in the fields of law, media, and the digital economy — has increased in recent years due to political factors associated with the contraction of civic space within the country. This trend warrants close monitoring.

The IMF (2025) emphasizes that from 2012 to the present, an average of two-thirds of those who emigrated have returned to Georgia. This proportion represents a significant source of human capital renewal for the country. A particularly distinctive situation emerged in 2022-2023: following the outbreak of the Russia-Ukraine war, more than 150,000 individuals arrived in Georgia annually, consisting primarily of Russian citizens and ethnic Georgians who had been residing in Russia or Ukraine (IMF, 2025; German Economic Team, 2023). This flow differed substantially in scale from the usual patterns of return migration. The IMF (2025) confirms a direct link between this wave and subsequent economic growth: Georgia recorded growth of 10.9% in 2022 and 10.5% in 2021. The connection is straightforward — a significant portion of the new arrivals, particularly IT specialists and entrepreneurs, established new companies and spent in the services sector, directly increasing revenues for Georgian employers, suppliers, and the state budget.

Effects on the Economy

The most tangible positive effect of emigration is manifested in the form of remittances. According to IMF (2025) data, net remittances received by Georgia in 2024 amounted to USD 3 billion, equivalent to 9% of the country's gross domestic product (GDP) — more than double the USD 1.2 billion recorded in 2012. According to data from the National Bank of Georgia (2024), the largest sending countries are the United States (USD 560 million), Italy (USD 550 million), and Russia (USD 500 million). Total inflows from European Union member states (Italy, Germany, Greece, Spain, France, and Poland) exceeded USD 1.3 billion in 2024, reflecting significant growth following the visa liberalization of 2017.

Data from the World Bank (2024) and the National Bank of Georgia (2024) confirm that gross remittance inflows surpassed USD 4 billion in 2022, reaching USD 4.1 billion in 2023 and USD 4.3 billion in 2024. Giguashvili et al. (2023) further note that while remittances serve as a significant instrument for poverty reduction, they have thus far proven unable to transform into the more structurally productive investments required for sustained economic development.

IMF (2025) research at the micro level reveals that 6-7% of households receive remittances; in 2023, the average monthly transfer amounted to GEL 895 (approximately USD 330). The income of remittance-receiving households is on average 25-30% higher than that of households that do not receive such transfers. Educational expenditure in these households is 60% higher — a positive effect on human capital formation. However, remittance-receiving households are 20% less likely to seek employment, which reduces labor market participation rates. EUAA (2022) also confirms that emigrants have consistently maintained strong ties with their homeland, and remittances constitute one of the most tangible expressions of these bonds.

Applying standard macroeconomic estimation methodology, the IMF (2025) calculates that the 5% decline in the workforce recorded between 2014 and 2023 generated an annual negative effect on the economy of approximately 2%. In parallel, the influx of war-displaced individuals (exceeding 150,000) in 2022-2023 reinvigorated economic growth: Georgia achieved GDP growth of 10.9% in 2022 and 10.5% in 2021 (Giguashvili et al., 2023).

Migration balance statistics published by the National Statistics Office of Georgia (2024) confirm that Georgia's net migration balance turned positive in 2022 (+54,000) and remained positive in 2023 (+43,000). This flow produced ambivalent economic effects: on one hand, consumption increased, the services sector expanded, and business activity intensified; on the other, rental prices in Tbilisi rose by 101% within a single year in 2022, inflation exceeded 13%, and pressure on urban infrastructure increased markedly (EUAA, 2022).

The problem of demographic imbalance constitutes a long-term economic challenge. According to the IMF (2025), the old-age dependency ratio (the ratio of the population aged 65 and above to those aged 15-64) has increased over the past decade and is the highest among countries of the Caucasus and Central Asia (CCA) region. This trend exerts growing pressure on social protection and pension systems. The Ministry of Finance characterizes this effect as manageable; however, the long-term fiscal risk is objectively present.

Empirical evidence from IMF (2024) supports the argument that remittances in Georgia are predominantly utilized for immediate consumption rather than productive investment. This creates a cycle of external dependency, where households fail to establish self-sustaining income sources. Furthermore, the transition from individual labor migration to family reunification abroad fundamentally alters the migratory cycle. As migrants integrate and bring their family members to destination countries, the initial intent of return diminishes, leading to long-term demographic depletion for Georgia.

While circular migration theory posits that the transfer of accumulated knowledge and skills is a primary benefit for the country of origin, its validity in the Georgian context, specifically regarding the care sector, remains highly questionable. Research by (Women Engage for a Common Future [WECF] - Georgia, 2023) and ETF (2021) indicates a significant trend of 'deskilling' among Georgian migrant women. When highly educated professionals are employed in low-skilled caregiving roles abroad, they experience a loss of professional human capital. Furthermore, the absence of formal recognition for informal care skills in the Georgian labor market renders the 'knowledge transfer' argument largely symbolic, as returned migrants often find themselves back in precarious economic conditions without a viable path to professional reintegration.

In conclusion, in the case of careworkers, the 'positive effect' of circular migration for the country of origin is almost entirely reduced to financial remittances rather than the transfer of skills.

CONCLUSIONS AND POLICY RECOMMENDATIONS

Conclusion

The present paper has addressed three interrelated areas of inquiry: the theoretical foundations of labour migration, the conceptualisation of circular migration and the challenges of its practical implementation, and finally, the specific case of Georgia, where these broader tendencies have manifested with particular intensity. Drawing together these three dimensions makes it possible to formulate two categories of conclusion: analytical — concerning what has been revealed about the nature of migration — and political — concerning the challenges that now face states and international institutions.

The theoretical analysis demonstrates that the academic study of migration has undergone a gradual yet profound epistemological evolution from the late nineteenth century to the present day. From Ravenstein's empirical laws and Lee's Push-Pull model, through the neoclassical conception of Homo Economicus, to the historical-structuralist critique and the pluralist synthesis - this trajectory reflects the continuous refinement of our understanding. Particularly significant is the shift that took place in the late twentieth century: attention moved away from the individual migrant's rational calculation and towards household strategy, the logic of social networks, and the interplay of structural and agentive forces. This means that migration can no longer be studied as a one-dimensional economic optimisation problem - it is always simultaneously a social, cultural, and political phenomenon.

The study of circular migration's conceptualisation reveals a fundamental problem: what is treated in theoretical discourse as a fluid, flexible phenomenon — systematic movement between countries of origin and destination — is frequently narrowed at the operational level to the boundaries of specific legal schemes. The UNECE (2016) criteria -frequency, duration, and legality-constitute an instrument of systematic measurement, yet they do not exhaust the full empirical breadth of circularity. Failure to account for this conceptual gap may lead us to methodological error: who counts as a circular migrant depends on researchers' operational choices, which in turn complicates the comparability of findings.

Notwithstanding this conceptual complexity, the paper confirms that the win-win-win potential of circular migration- benefits for receiving countries, countries of origin, and migrants themselves - is neither impossible nor guaranteed. The studies of Constant and Zimmermann (2011) on Germany's guest workers and the analysis by Adda, Dustmann and Goerlach (2022) of human capital accumulation confirm that circularity creates a distinctive investment logic: migrants acquire competencies that will prove valuable upon return to their country of origin. Remittances - amounting to 656 billion dollars globally in 2023 - represent a significant lever for poverty reduction and human capital investment. At the same time, the shift from "brain drain" to "brain circulation" is gaining growing empirical support, even if this transformation is not automatic and requires the systematic support of institutional conditions.

The findings of this research indicate that labor migration in Georgia has entered a critical phase characterized as a "migration trap". Although theoretical models of circular migration emphasize "brain circulation" and the productive transfer of skills, the Georgian reality paints a starkly different picture.

First and foremost, a profound trend of "brain waste" (deskilling) has emerged: highly qualified Georgian migrants, particularly those within the caregiving sector, undergo significant professional degradation. This process of de-qualification renders their professional reintegration into the domestic labor market nearly impossible upon return. Furthermore, financial remittances-which constitute approximately 13–15% of the national GDP-are predominantly funneled into immediate consumption and debt servicing. The critically low level of productive investment suggests that migrant households fail to establish self-sustaining income sources, thereby fostering a perpetual state of external dependency on foreign inflows.

The most alarming trend identified is the structural transformation of migration from a temporary labor activity into permanent emigration. The process of family reunification in host countries fundamentally dissolves the motivation for return, resulting in an irreversible loss for Georgia—not only in terms of its immediate labor force but also its long-term demographic and human capital potential.

Policy Recommendations

In response to these systemic challenges, the Government of Georgia and relevant stakeholders should implement the following strategic interventions:

1. Recognition of Non-formal Education and Skills (VNFIL):

It is essential to establish institutional mechanisms for the validation and certification of experience acquired abroad (e.g., in the caregiving or service sectors). This would empower returnees to secure formal employment within Georgia's healthcare and social service industries, effectively converting informal experience into recognized professional assets.

2. Incentivizing the Productive Investment of Remittances:

The state should design targeted investment programs for the diaspora (e.g., "Agro-Diaspora" initiatives or tax incentives for Small and Medium Enterprises). The objective is to facilitate the transition of remittances from consumption to capital accumulation, enabling households to generate sustainable internal revenue long after the migrant's return.

3. Redesigning the "Return Strategy":

National policy must pivot from merely legalizing outflows (circular schemes) toward robust reintegration packages. This includes educational adaptation programs for the children of returning migrants to ensure that family reunification occurs within Georgia rather than abroad, thereby mitigating demographic depletion.

4. Skills Forecasting and Vocational Education (VET) Modernization:

There must be a rigorous synchronization between labor market demands and the educational system (Skills Alignment). By strengthening Vocational Education and Training, Georgia can reduce youth unemployment and ensure that young graduates do not perceive emigration as their only viable survival strategy.

The overall conclusion may be distilled into three concentrated messages. First: labour migration is a structurally ambivalent phenomenon- it is simultaneously an opportunity and a challenge, a lever of economic benefit and a risk of human capital depletion. This ambivalence itself rules out any one-dimensional narrative. Second: the win-win-win potential of circular migration is real, but it is not guaranteed - it is the product of political will, institutional maturity, and mutual commitment. The portability of social protection, guaranteed rights of re-entry, and mutual recognition of qualifications are critical instruments without which circularity frequently transforms into permanent emigration. Third: Georgia - with its scale of emigration, the significance of its remittances, the irregular flows generated by nearby geopolitical upheaval, and the evolving adaptation of its state institutions - represents a laboratory of analytical and political interest where theory and practice of migration find particularly close proximity.

In conclusion, this paper confirms that in the twenty-first century, labour migration can no longer be understood through economic logic alone, regulated solely by legal norms, or evaluated exclusively through the prism of national interest. It demands integrated, multidisciplinary analysis - and a state policy that respects this complexity.

REFERENCES

Adda, J., Dustmann, C., & Görlach, J.-S. (2022). The dynamics of return migration, human capital accumulation, and wage assimilation. *The Review of Economic Studies*, *89*(6), 2841–2871. DOI: 10.1093/restud/rdac003

Adeusi, O. O., Ajeboriogbon, T., Adjadeh, J.-P., Obiono, S. M., Adebayo, Y. O., & Adebayo, Y. O. (2025). Circular migration models with innovative policy interventions to balance economic growth, workforce needs and migrant welfare between host and origin countries. *International Journal of Science and Research Archive*, *14*(1), 1735–1742. DOI: 10.30574/ijsra.2025.14.1.0298

Amin, S. (1974). *Accumulation on a world scale*. Monthly Review Press. https://dokumen.pub/accumulation-on-a-world-scale-a-critique-of-the-theory-of-underdevelopment-2-volumes-1-2-0853452725-9780853452720.html

Azose, J. J., & Raftery, A. E. (2018). Estimation of emigration, return migration, and transit migration between all pairs of countries. *Proceedings of the National Academy of Sciences of the United States of America*, *116*(1), 116–122. DOI: 10.1073/pnas.1722334116 PMID: 30584106

Borjas, G. J. (1989). Economic theory and international migration. *The International Migration Review*, *23*(3), 457–485. DOI: 10.1177/019791838902300304 PMID: 12282789

Carney, D. (1998). *Sustainable rural livelihoods: What contribution can we make?* Department for International Development.

Castles, S., & Kosack, G. (1973). *Immigrant workers and class structure in Western Europe*. Oxford University Press / The Institute of Race Relations.

Castles, S., & Miller, M. J. (2003). *The age of migration*. Palgrave Macmillan.

Center for Global Development. (2021). *Migration pathways: Temporary labor migration of Georgian workers to Poland and Estonia*. https://gsp.cgdev.org

Constant, A. F. (2020). *Time-space dynamics of return and circular migration: Theories and evidence* (GLO Discussion Paper Series No. 446). Global Labor Organization. https://hdl.handle.net/10419/210984

Constant, A. F., Nottmeyer, O., & Zimmermann, K. F. (2012). *The economics of circular migration* (IZA Discussion Paper No. 6940). Institute for the Study of Labor. https://docs.iza.org/dp6940.pdf

Ellis, F. (2000). *Rural livelihoods and diversity in developing countries: Evidence and policy implications.* Oxford University Press ETF and Business Consulting Group Research (Georgia). (2013). *MIGRATION AND SKILLS IN GEORGIA.* European Training Foundation and Business Consulting Group .

European Training Foundation. (2021). Skills and migration country fiche: Georgia. https://www.etf.europa.eu/sites/default/files/2021-11/etf_skills_and_migration_country_fiche_georgia_2021_en_0.pdf

European Union Agency for Asylum (EUAA). (2022). Georgia as a country of origin: Migration drivers report. Ridgeway Information & Stop The Traffik. https://www.euaa.europa.eu/sites/default/files/publications/2022-08/2022_08_MDR_Georgia_Origin_EN.pdf

Faist, T. (1998). *International migration and transnational social spaces: Their evolution, significance and future prospects.* Institut für Interkulturelle und Internationale Studien.

Frank, A. G. (1966). The Development of Underdevelopment. *Monthly Review (New York, N.Y.), 18*(4), 17–31. https://www.bresserpereira.org.br/terceiros/cursos/2010/1970.The_Development_of_Underdevelopment.pdf. DOI: 10.14452/MR-018-04-1966-08_3

Georgia, E. B. A. (2024). *EU business climate report: Georgia 2024.* European Business Association Georgia. https://eu4georgia.eu/wp-content/uploads/EU-Business-Climate-Report_2024-1.pdf

Giddens, A. (1984). The Constitution of Society - Outline of the Theory of Structuration. *University of California Press.* http://www.communicationcache.com/uploads/1/0/8/8/10887248/the_constitution_of_society.pdf

Giguashvili, G., Khorguashvili, T., & Makasarashvili, T. (2023). Mechanisms for managing circular labor migration in Georgia. *Proceedings of the 7th International Scientific and Practical Conference: Current Issues and Prospects for the Development of Scientific Research,* 151, pp. 77-88. Orléans. DOI: 10.51582/interconf.19-20.04.2023.007

Haas, H. d. (2008, 02). *Migration and development A theoretical perspective.* Retrieved from International Migration Institute: https://www.migrationinstitute.org/publications/wp-09-08

Harris, J. R., & Todaro, M. P. (1970). Migration, Unemployment and Development: A Two-Sector Analysis. *The American Economic Review,* •••, 126–142. https://www.jstor.org/stable/1807860

International Monetary Fund. (2024, April). *World Economic Outlook: Steady but slow: Resilience amid divergence.* International Monetary Fund. https://www.imf.org/en/Publications/WEO/Issues/2024/04/16/world-economic-outlook-april-2024

International Monetary Fund. (2024, April). *World Economic Outlook—Steady but Slow: Resilience amid Divergence.* Washington,DC. https://www.imf.org/-/media/files/publications/weo/2024/april/english/text.pdf

International Monetary Fund. (2025). *Impact of Emigration On the Georgian Labor Market.* IMF Selected Issues Paper., DOI: 10.5089/9798229021029.002

Jones, R. W. (2008). *Heckscher–Ohlin Trade Theory.* The New Palgrave Dictionary of Economics., DOI: 10.1057/978-1-349-95121-5_1116-2

Kharkhelauri, K., & Kajaia, T. (2025). Adaptation of Vocational Education to Labor Market Requirements. *Works of Georgian Technical University*, 77-83. DOI: 10.36073/1512-0996-2025-1-77-83

Kharkhelauri, K., & Kajaia, T. (2026). Theoretical aspects of labour migration (A comparative analysis of classical and contemporary approaches). *Georgian Academy of Business Sciences. Moambe*, (58), 9–18. DOI: 10.52340/gbsab.2026.58.01

Lee, E. S. (1966). A Theory of Migration. *Demography*, *3*(1), 47–57. http://links.jstor.org/sici?sici=0070-3370%281966%293%3A1%3C47%3AATOM%3E2.0.CO%3B2-B. DOI: 10.2307/2060063

Levitt, P. (1998). Social Remittances: Migration Driven Local-Level Forms of Cultural Diffusion. *The International Migration Review*, *32*(4), 926–948. DOI: 10.1177/019791839803200404 PMID: 12294302

Lewis, W. A. (1954). Economic Development with Unlimited Supplies of Labour. *Manchester School*, *22*(2), 139–191. DOI: 10.1111/j.1467-9957.1954.tb00021.x

Mabogunje, A. L. (1970). Systems Approach to a Theory of Rural-Urban Migration. *Geographical Analysis*, *2*(1), 1–18. DOI: 10.1111/j.1538-4632.1970.tb00140.x

Massey, D. S., Arango, J., Hugo, G., Kouaouci, A., Pellegrino, A., & Taylor, J. E. (1993). Theories of International Migration: A Review and Appraisal. *Population and Development Review*, *19*(3), 431–466. DOI: 10.2307/2938462

OECD. (2017). *Interrelations between public policies, migration and development in Georgia.* Organisation for Economic Co-operation and Development, & CRRC-Georgia. . OECD Publishing. . DOI: 10.1787/9789264272217-en

OECD. (2022). *A Review of Georgian Emigrants, Talent Abroad.* OECD Publishing., DOI: 10.1787/00df3f32-

OECD. (2024). *International Migration Outlook 2024.* Paris. DOI: 10.1787/50b0353e-en

OECD. (2024). *Migration Data Reports.* https://www.oecd.org/en/topics/migration.html

OECD. (2024). *Return, Reintegration and Re-migration.* Paris: OECD Publishing. https://www.oecd.org/content/dam/oecd/en/publications/reports/2024/01/return-reintegration-and-re-migration_0e5de901/625fb5e6-en.pdf

Privarova, M. (2024). CIRCULAR MIGRATION OF HIGHLY SKILLED LABOR IN EU COUNTRIES AND ITS IMPACT ON MIGRATION POLICIES. *Economy & Business*, 89-96.

Rabat Process. (2024). *Circular migration: a cycle of opportunities and skills.* Euro-African Dialogue on Migration and Development, Morocco. https://www.rabat-process.org/en/activities/technical-meetings/circular-migration

Ranis, G., & Fei, J. C. (1961). A Theory of Economic Development. *The American Economic Review*, •••, 533–565. http://www.jstor.org/stable/1812785

Ravenstein, E. G. (1885). The Laws of Migration. *Journal of the Statistical Society of London*, *48*(2), 167–235. https://www.jstor.org/stable/2979181. DOI: 10.2307/2979181

Sjaastad, L. A. (1962). The Costs and Returns of Human Migration. In U.-N. B. Research, *Investment in Human Beings* (pp. 80 - 93). The Journal of Political Economy. DOI: 10.1086/258726

Stark, O., & Bloom, D. E. (1985). *The New Economics of Labor Migration.* The American Economic Review. https://www.jstor.org/stable/1805591

Stark, O., & Levhari, D. (1982). On migration and risk in LDCs. *Economic Development and Cultural Change,* https://www.journals.uchicago.edu/doi/10.1086/451312

Todaro, M. P., & Maruszko, L. (1987). Illegal Migration and US Immigration Reform: A Conceptual Framework. *Population and Development Review*, *13*(1), 101–114. DOI: 10.2307/1972122

UNECE. (2016). Defining and measuring circular migration. UNECE Task Force on Measuring Circular Migration. *United Nations Economic Commission for Europe.* https://unece.org/fileadmin/DAM/stats/publications/2016/ECECESSTAT20165_E.pdf

United Nations. (2020). *International migrant stock 2020* (POP/DB/MIG/Stock/Rev.2020). United Nations Department of Economic and Social Affairs.

United Nations Department of Economic and Social Affairs. (2024). *International migration report 2024.* https://www.un.org/development/desa/pd/news/international-migration-report-2024

Wallerstein, I. (1974). *The Modern World-System.* Academic Press. http://pombo.free.fr/wallersteini.pdf

Women Engage for a Common Future [WECF] - Georgia. (2023). *Socioeconomic stability for Georgian labor migrant women: Study of return and reintegration.* WECF. https://www.undp.org/georgia/publications/georgian-migrant-women-study

World Bank. (2024). *Migration and development brief 40.* KNOMAD / World Bank. https://www.knomad.org/publication/migration-and-development-brief-40

ENDNOTE

1 In the context of migration, the term "agency" implies that migration is not merely a "forced outcome" of economic inequality; rather, individuals and families actively formulate their own strategies, assessing risks, opportunities, and prospects.

Chapter 12
Mapping the Restrictive Turn in EU Migration Policy:
Far Right Rise and Policy Hardening

Fernando Casado Gutierrez
http://orcid.org/0000-0003-0818-3924
Universidad Técnica de Manabí, Ecuador

Rebeca Sanchez
Universidad Rey Juan Carlos, Spain

ABSTRACT

The tightening of migration policy in the European Union has become a structural trend shaped by securitization and political change. This study examines the correlation between the electoral rise of far-right parties and the progressive hardening of EU migration policy through a qualitative, documentary, comparative, and normative approach based on EU legislation, institutional documents, political discourse, academic literature, reports, and journalistic materials. The findings show a growing convergence between both processes, marked by the synchronization of far-right electoral growth with tougher migration reforms, the increasing influence of these actors, and the normalization of narratives that frame migration as a threat. They also reveal a shift from a rights-based model toward one centered on control, externalization, and limits on asylum access. The study concludes that this restrictive turn is part of a broader political dynamic in which the far right plays a significant role, and it recommends stronger legal oversight and renewed protection of rights.

DOI: 10.4018/979-8-3373-8500-6.ch012

INTRODUCTION

In recent decades, international migration has emerged as one of the central axes of global political debate, particularly in contexts characterized by humanitarian crises, armed conflicts, economic transformations, and growing global inequalities. Within this scenario, human mobility has intensified and acquired an increasingly significant political dimension, positioning itself at the center of debates on sovereignty, security, identity, and human rights, thereby contributing to its progressive politicization (Pereira Peñalver, 2023). Migration governance has thus become a field of tension between protection-oriented approaches and control-oriented models, reflecting broader disputes over the role of the state, border management, and the definition of political belonging in contemporary societies.

In Europe, this phenomenon has gained particular relevance, not only due to its impact on public policy but also because of its capacity to reshape the political system and dominant discursive frameworks. The European Union, historically conceived as a project grounded in values of openness, rights, and cooperation, currently faces internal tensions arising from the management of migration flows, leading to a gradual shift toward more restrictive approaches (Pérez, 2020; Nissen, 2022). This process has been further intensified by the so-called "refugee crisis" of 2015, which not only exposed the limitations of the Common European Asylum System but also contributed to the consolidation of migration as a security issue (Porras Ramírez, 2025). In this context, migration policy has become a privileged arena of political contestation, where state interests, electoral pressures, and transformations in public opinion intersect.

At the same time, the electoral rise of far-right parties has significantly reshaped the European political landscape, contributing to a shift in the center of political debate toward more restrictive positions on migration (Bello, 2024). These parties have not only increased their institutional representation but have also influenced the political agenda through the dissemination of discourses that construct migration as a threat to security, identity, and social cohesion. In this regard, the relationship between the rise of the far right and the tightening of migration policies cannot be understood merely as a temporal coincidence, but rather as the result of a complex interaction between political, normative, and discursive dynamics.

This article examines this relationship by proposing a "mapping of the restrictive turn" that integrates these dimensions. The main objective is to analyze the correlation between the rise of the far right and the hardening of migration policies in the European Union, guided by the following research questions: To what extent has the growth of the far right influenced the transformation of the European migration framework? What political and discursive mechanisms explain this convergence? And how is it reflected in the recent normative architecture? These questions enable the phenomenon to be examined from an analytical perspective that goes beyond the description of specific policies, focusing instead on identifying structural patterns and interaction dynamics between actors and institutions (Lang, 2024).

To address these questions, a qualitative approach of a documentary, comparative, and normative nature is employed, based on the systematic review of primary sources—such as European legislation, institutional documents, and political discourse—and secondary sources, including academic literature, reports, and journalistic materials. The analysis is supported by the construction of analytical matrices that facilitate the identification of temporal, normative, and discursive patterns. This approach is particularly suitable for examining complex phenomena in which political, legal, and symbolic dimensions converge, allowing for the reconstruction of processes of change through the articulation of multiple levels of analysis (Pereira Peñalver, 2023).

This research is justified by the need to understand the implications of the restrictive turn in terms of fundamental rights and European governance, in a context marked by the increasing politicization of migration. In particular, it is essential to assess the extent to which recent normative transformations are compatible with the foundational principles of the European Union and its international commitments to human rights protection. The scope of the study covers the period from 2000 to 2026, with particular attention to key milestones such as the 2015 refugee crisis, the 2024 New Pact on Migration and Asylum, and the 2026 Return Regulation. However, the study is subject to limitations inherent to its qualitative design, particularly regarding the inability to establish direct causal relationships and the absence of empirical analysis on the impact of these policies on migrants, thereby opening avenues for future research that may complement this analysis through quantitative approaches and case studies.

The Restrictive Turn in European Migration Policy

The adoption of migration policies grounded in a predominantly securitarian perspective has decisively shaped the recent normative development of the European Union. This approach, widely conceptualized in the literature as Fortress Europe, refers to the progressive reinforcement of border controls, the externalization of migration management, and the subordination of international protection for migrants and asylum seekers to state security imperatives (Pérez, 2020; Nissen, 2022). Far from constituting a temporary response, this paradigm has become a structural axis of EU migration policy.

This restrictive turn has intensified throughout the twenty-first century in parallel with the electoral growth and institutional consolidation of far-right parties across most Member States. As various scholars have noted, the influence of these actors extends beyond their direct participation in government, operating also through indirect mechanisms that push mainstream parties to adopt more restrictive positions in order to avoid electoral losses. As a result, measures that at the end of the twentieth century were considered socially, politically, and legally unacceptable have increasingly become part of the ordinary repertoire of migration policy (Lang, 2024).

Within this framework, European migration policies have undergone a gradual shift from a rights-based approach toward a logic of risk management, in which migration is increasingly associated with threats to security, public order, and social cohesion (Pereira Peñalver, 2023). This process of securitization involves not only changes in policy design but also transformations in the interpretative frameworks that shape public perceptions of migration. Migration is no longer primarily conceived as a humanitarian issue but rather as a security problem, thereby legitimizing the adoption of restrictive and exceptional measures.

The consolidation of this approach has been closely linked to the growing influence of anti-immigration political discourses, which have gained prominence in the center of public debate. These narratives, often characterized by xenophobic and exclusionary elements, simplify complex phenomena and channel social discontent toward migrant populations. In contexts marked by crises of neoliberalism, rising inequality, and increasing precarization, such discourses play a key role by providing accessible explanations and scapegoats for deeper structural transformations.

In this regard, Robinson (2019) warns of the emergence of contemporary authoritarian projects that, while not mechanically reproducing the features of twentieth-century fascism, share with it the instrumentalization of fear, the securitization of "the other," and the mobilization of xenophobia as a central political resource. Unlike historical fascisms, these new expressions operate within a context of globalization and weakened labor and left-wing movements, facilitating the electoral normalization of exclusionary discourses and their translation into restrictive public policies, particularly in areas such as migration and asylum (Castro Romero, 2024).

Instruments and Consolidation of Migration Policy Restriction

The restrictive turn has materialized in a complex normative architecture that combines both internal and external instruments. At the internal level, the European Union has promoted reforms aimed at accelerating asylum procedures and strengthening border controls. Among these, accelerated border procedures—introduced within the framework of the Migration Pact—stand out, as they allow for the examination of applications for international protection under conditions that may limit effective access to legal safeguards.

At the same time, the external dimension of migration policy has been consolidated. Through both formal and informal agreements with third countries, the European

Union has sought to contain migration flows before they reach European territory. These agreements include return and readmission mechanisms, cooperation in border control, conditional visa facilitation, and financial assistance. Taken together, these measures reinforce the externalization of migration control and consolidate the logic of Fortress Europe (Lang, 2024).

The so-called "refugee crisis" that began in 2015 constituted a turning point in this process. The arrival of large numbers of people from countries affected by prolonged armed conflicts, such as Syria, Afghanistan, and Iraq, exposed the limitations of the Common European Asylum System and the lack of effective solidarity mechanisms among Member States. At the same time, this episode contributed to the consolidation of migration as a security issue to be prevented, contained, or managed, reinforcing threat-based narratives with significant penetration in public opinion (Porras Ramírez, 2025).

From 2015 onwards, there was a marked intensification of border control policies and a greater willingness among Member States to resort to exceptional measures. These included the temporary reintroduction of internal border controls within the Schengen Area, the strengthening of the European Border and Coast Guard Agency (Frontex), and the expansion of agreements with third countries aimed at curbing migration flows before they reach EU territory. Although initially justified as temporary responses to a crisis situation, these measures have tended to become institutionalized, leading to the normalization of exceptional practices in migration governance.

This process has significantly transformed the European asylum regime, shifting the balance from protection toward control. Migration management is increasingly framed as a matter of security, reinforcing the centrality of instruments aimed at deterrence and containment.

The Rise of the Far Right and Its Influence on Migration Policy

Alongside normative developments, the twenty-first century has witnessed a significant rise and expansion of far-right parties in Europe. This process has entailed a gradual de-marginalization of these formations, which have moved from peripheral positions to become relevant actors with the capacity to influence both the public and legislative agenda. The consolidation of an anti-immigration narrative has been one of the central elements of this phenomenon (Bello, 2024).

Whereas at the peak of the refugee crisis only Poland and Hungary had far-right governments, by 2019, ten Member States were governed either directly, in coalition, or with parliamentary support from xenophobic populist parties, all of which were represented within European Union institutions (González Páramo, 2019). In many other countries, these political forces consolidated themselves as the main opposition parties, exerting constant pressure on traditional governments to adopt more restrictive positions on migration.

Currently, with few exceptions, virtually all Member States have at least one far-right party with parliamentary representation, underscoring the structural nature of this phenomenon. The 2024 European Parliament elections confirmed this trend, with the consolidation of the Patriots for Europe group as the third political force, reinforcing earlier warnings regarding the impact of the rise of the far right on migration policies and on the European Union's commitment to human rights (Bidaguren, 2019).

The impact of the far right on migration policy is not limited to its institutional presence. Even when not in government, its capacity for influence remains significant. Traditional parties, in an effort to contain its electoral advance, tend to adopt more restrictive positions, thereby contributing to a shift in the political center. This dynamic generates a progressive convergence between far-right proposals and the policies implemented by governments across the ideological spectrum.

Convergences, Legal Tensions, and the New Pact on Migration and Asylum

The correlation between the rise of the far right and the tightening of migration policies materializes through the convergence of political discourses and normative frameworks. Anti-immigration narratives resonate within the policies adopted by the European Union, creating a feedback loop that consolidates the restrictive turn.

In this context, in May 2024, the European Union reached agreement on the New Pact on Migration and Asylum after years of negotiations among Member States. This new normative framework introduces reforms aimed at strengthening external border control, reconfiguring responsibility-sharing mechanisms, and deepening cooperation with third countries in matters of return. As De Zwaan (2025) notes, the Pact incorporates innovations in external border control arrangements, the principle of "flexible solidarity" for determining the Member State responsible for examining applications for international protection, and new approaches to cooperation with third countries regarding the return of migrants.

However, the New Pact on Migration and Asylum, composed of nine regulations and one directive, has been subject to substantial criticism from international organizations, civil society actors, and human rights experts. Recent reports warn that several of its provisions may conflict with international human rights and asylum law, particularly regarding effective access to protection procedures, the extensive use of border detention, and the risk of violations of the principle of non-refoulement (Oxfam Intermón, 2025).

These criticisms highlight the tensions between the European Union's international legal obligations and the restrictive orientation of its new migration architecture. In this sense, the Pact reflects not only the institutionalization of the restrictive turn but also the limits and contradictions of a model that seeks to reconcile migration control with the protection of fundamental rights.

The "mapping of the restrictive turn" thus reveals a complex and bidirectional relationship between the electoral rise of the far right and the hardening of migration policies. Both processes reinforce one another, shaping a structural dynamic that redefines contemporary European migration policy and poses significant challenges for the future of the European project in terms of human rights and political cohesion.

METHODOLOGY

The present study aims to analyze the correlation between the electoral rise of far-right parties and the hardening of migration policies in the European Union, based on their normative, discursive, and institutional manifestations. In line with this objective, a qualitative approach of a documentary, comparative, and normative nature is adopted, suitable for examining complex processes in which political dynamics, legislative production, and discursive transformations converge.

The qualitative approach enables not only the identification of the coexistence of these phenomena but also the understanding of the mechanisms of interaction and feedback that connect them. In this regard, the analysis is oriented toward interpreting how the electoral growth of the far right—evidenced by the sustained increase in its representation in the European Parliament from 2004 to 2024 (Camas & Ferrándiz, 2024; Sangiao, 2024)—relates to the progressive adoption of more restrictive migration policies, particularly following the turning point represented by the 2015 refugee crisis (Del Valle, 2020).

The methodological design is documentary in nature, based on the systematic collection and analysis of both primary and secondary sources. Primary sources include European legislation on migration and asylum—particularly the 2024 New Pact on Migration and Asylum and the Return Regulation—as well as electoral programs, manifestos, and official discourses of European far-right parties since 2015. This corpus is complemented by institutional documents of the European Union and reports from specialized bodies.

Secondary sources include academic literature, reports by non-governmental organizations, and analyses from research centers, as well as high-quality journalistic coverage documenting both the electoral evolution of the far right and the development of the European migration policy framework (Europa Press, 2023; Carrascón & Vilches, 2024; Sahuquillo, 2026). Additionally, studies addressing xenophobia as a central discursive axis are incorporated (Hernández-Carr, 2011; González-Páramo, 2019; Rodríguez, 2020; Sanahuja & López, 2024; Pérez Gallo, 2026), along with relevant cases such as Brexit (EFE, 2016; Marea Granate, 2017; González de la Calleja, 2016).

Data collection techniques are centered on systematic document review and the construction of an analytical corpus organized around two main dimensions: the rise of the far right and the hardening of migration policies.

Data processing is carried out through the development of systematization instruments derived from document analysis, which allow for the structured organization of the empirical corpus in accordance with the research objectives. Specifically, this process takes the form of three analytical tables that synthesize the main dimensions of the phenomenon under study.

First, a temporal and descriptive table is developed to reconstruct the evolution of the far right's electoral rise in the European Parliament, classifying information according to chronological milestones (2000–2024), levels of representation, and key political events. This table enables the identification of longitudinal trends and situates the growth of these political forces within the European institutional context.

Second, a table oriented toward normative and sequential analysis is constructed, systematizing the main milestones in the tightening of European Union migration policy. It organizes key events—such as the 2015 refugee crisis, the 2016 Brexit referendum, the adoption of the 2024 New Pact on Migration and Asylum, and the 2026 Return Regulation—alongside the measures associated with each of them (Oxfam Intermón, 2025). This table allows for the observation of the cumulative evolution of the normative framework and its progressive orientation toward migration control.

Third, an analytical-synthetic table is developed, linking the main theoretical categories of the study—xenophobia, securitization, externalization, de-marginalization, and discursive normalization—with the empirical evidence identified and its manifestation in public policy. This table enables the systematic connection between discursive, political, and institutional levels, facilitating the identification of convergences between the rise of the far right and the hardening of migration policies.

In addition, the analysis incorporates a comparative dimension across national cases—Hungary, Italy, France, and Germany—which, although not presented in tabular form in the results section, informs the interpretation of differentiated trajectories of the far right and their relationship with migration policies in specific contexts.

The analysis is conducted through a dual comparative and normative strategy. At the comparative level, transformations are examined across two dimensions. First, at the temporal level, contrasting the period prior to the 2015 crisis with the subsequent cycle culminating in the 2024 New Pact on Migration and Asylum. Second, at the spatial level, analyzing how the relationship between the far right and migration policy restriction manifests across Member States with distinct trajectories.

At the normative level, the study critically evaluates the compatibility of the main innovations in the European migration framework with international human rights standards. This analysis focuses on elements such as the expansion of the "safe third country" concept, the externalization of migration control, detention measures, and the risk of violating the principle of non-refoulement (Domínguez, 2024; RTVE.es, 2026; Banchón, 2026).

Finally, the analysis is structured around key analytical categories, including securitization of migration, externalization of border control, xenophobia as a discursive axis, normalization of the far right, and tensions with human rights. These categories enable the construction of a "mapping of the restrictive turn" that identifies the interrelations between the rise of the far right and the transformation of the European migration framework.

RESULTS

The Rise of the Far Right in Europe

The analysis of the systematized documentary corpus reveals a substantial transformation in the position of the far right within the European political system since the beginning of the twenty-first century. Based on the organization of information into temporal and documentary matrices, a transition can be observed from a context of political isolation to one of progressive normalization and institutional influence. This shift not only entails an increase in electoral representation but also a reconfiguration of the boundaries of what is considered politically acceptable, expanding the sphere of legitimacy of previously marginal discourses and policy proposals.

In 2000, the participation of the Austrian Freedom Party (FPÖ) in government—after securing more than 26% of the vote and forming a coalition with the People's Party (ÖVP)—triggered sanctions from the European Union, reflecting a political consensus aimed at containing the far right (Europa Press, 2023). However, the systematization of electoral data reveals a sustained evolution in the opposite direction. Whereas Members of the European Parliament from Eurosceptic and far-right groups accounted for only 8.7% of the chamber in 2004, this figure increased in successive elections: 2009 (11.8%), 2014 (15.7%), and 2019 (18%) (Camas & Ferrándiz, 2024). This trajectory reflects a steady and continuous growth of the far right within the European Parliament, demonstrating its consolidation within the European political system and its growing capacity to reshape the balance of power within the institution.

Beyond its quantitative dimension, this trend also reflects a qualitative transformation: the far right has shifted from being a reactive actor to a proactive one, capable of shaping the legislative agenda and influencing the direction of political debate at the European level. This development indicates an increasing permeability of the political system to its positions, even in contexts where it does not directly hold executive power.

Table 1. Evolution of the Electoral Rise of the Far Right in the European Union

Year	Representation (%)	Key Event
2000	—	EU sanctions on Austria following FPÖ participation in government
2004	8.7	Marginal presence of Eurosceptic forces
2009	11.8	Sustained increase
2014	15.7	Electoral consolidation
2019	18	Significant growth
2024	22–28	Consolidation as a relevant political bloc

Note. Author's own elaboration based on European Parliament data and secondary sources (Europa Press, 2023; Camas & Ferrándiz, 2024; Carrascón & Vilches, 2024; Sangiao, 2024).

This process intensified following the 2024 European Parliament elections. The far right continued to expand and is now represented across several of the eight political groups in the European Parliament. More conservative estimates place far-right forces as the second-largest political bloc, with 159 seats (22% of the total), primarily within the European Conservatives and Reformists (ECR) and Identity and Democracy (ID) groups (Carrascón & Vilches, 2024).

However, subsequent analyses conducted after the formal constitution of parliamentary groups suggest an even higher level of representation. Led by the German party Alternative for Germany (AfD), and joined by smaller formations such as Spain's Se Acabó la Fiesta (SALF), a third far-right group—Europe of Sovereign Nations—was established, reaching 25 Members of the European Parliament. If these three far-right groups were to unite, they would form the second-largest bloc in the Parliament with 187 seats, just one seat behind the European People's Party. When adding 11 non-attached far-right members and 7 additional members within the EPP, the total rises to 205 seats, representing more than 28% of the European Parliament (Sangiao, 2024).

This level of representation not only confirms the electoral consolidation of the far right but also introduces a key analytical dimension: its growing capacity to influence legislative processes through coalition-building, negotiation, and strategic positioning. Even without holding a majority, its parliamentary weight enables it to shape alliances, influence agendas, and exert pressure on mainstream political actors, thereby contributing to a reconfiguration of institutional dynamics.

It is therefore not surprising that far-right parties emerged as the most voted political forces in several key EU countries—such as France, Italy, Austria, and Belgium—in the most recent European elections. Nevertheless, their trajectory is not without setbacks. In Hungary, the April 2026 elections resulted in the defeat of Viktor Orbán, a central figure within the far-right bloc, whose long tenure had been marked by the obstruction of key EU decisions requiring unanimity. His departure opens the possibility for institutional reforms, such as the removal of unanimity in foreign policy decision-making, as proposed by the European Commission amid concerns over potential future far-right electoral victories (Sahuquillo, 2026).

This development introduces an important nuance: while the rise of the far right appears structural, it is neither linear nor irreversible. Rather, it remains subject to dynamics of political fatigue, internal competition, and broader transformations within party systems.

Currently, three distinct far-right parliamentary groups coexist and, to some extent, compete with one another. While all share Eurosceptic positions, ultranationalist orientations, and xenophobic discourses, they differ in the degree of radicalism of their proposals (Castro & Sánchez, 2024). Some factions advocate for deep reforms within the European Union, whereas others promote more disruptive and confrontational positions. In particular, groups such as Patriots for Europe and Europe of Sovereign Nations embody the most radical stances, including controversial links to external actors such as Russia, which have generated political tensions and institutional concerns (Voytyuk & Müller, 2026).

This internal fragmentation suggests that the European far right does not constitute a homogeneous bloc but rather a heterogeneous political field in which strategies of integration and rupture coexist. However, this diversity does not preclude convergence around key policy areas, particularly migration.

The growth of far-right parties in Europe has thus become a structural trend since the second decade of the twenty-first century. Xenophobia, as a central unifying feature, has been widely documented in the literature (Hernández-Carr, 2011; González-Páramo, 2019; Rodríguez, 2020; Sanahuja & López, 2024; Pérez Gallo, 2026). Anti-immigration discourses, systematically repeated across contexts, function as mechanisms of ideological cohesion and electoral mobilization.

From an analytical perspective, these discourses serve not only an identity function but also a strategic one, enabling the simplification of complex socio-economic problems and the redirection of social discontent toward specific groups, thereby enhancing their political effectiveness in contexts of uncertainty.

In the context of European domestic politics, xenophobia also played a central role in the Brexit campaign. Pro-Brexit actors, including Boris Johnson and Nigel Farage, framed their messaging around border control and the perceived threat of immigration (EFE, 2016; Marea Granate, 2017). These narratives resonated with widespread public perceptions regarding excessive immigration levels, mobilizing specific socio-economic segments of the electorate (González, 2016).

The Brexit case illustrates how the interaction between political discourse and public perception can translate into far-reaching political outcomes, highlighting the performative role of anti-immigration narratives in reshaping the European political landscape.

The systematized evidence demonstrates that the rise of the far right in Europe is not a temporary phenomenon but a sustained process combining electoral growth, institutional reconfiguration, and discursive consolidation. This process establishes the structural conditions necessary to understand its influence on the hardening of migration policies, providing a robust empirical foundation for analyzing the correlation between both phenomena.

The Hardening of European Migration Policy

The analysis of the documentary corpus reveals a progressive and cumulative process of tightening European migration policy, the intensification of which is closely linked to the 2015 refugee crisis. Through the systematization of information in a temporal matrix, this episode emerges as a critical turning point that reshaped both the normative framework and the political perception of migration within the European Union. Beyond its immediate humanitarian dimension, the crisis functioned as a catalyst for the redefinition of migration governance, shifting the balance between protection and control in favor of the latter and accelerating pre-existing securitization trends.

The 2015 crisis left a profound mark on the European project, exposing the limitations of the Common European Asylum System and the lack of effective solidarity mechanisms among Member States. As Del Valle (2020) argues, this moment represented not only a "terrifying human tragedy" but also a significant deterioration in Europe's image as a moral power and civilizational reference. From that point onward, migration governance increasingly shifted toward a logic centered on control, containment, and deterrence. This shift reflects a broader transformation in the political framing of migration, in which humanitarian obligations become subordinated to considerations of state sovereignty and internal security, thereby altering the normative foundations of European asylum policy.

This transformation materialized in a series of normative reforms culminating in May 2024 with the adoption of the New Pact on Migration and Asylum. As shown in Table 2, the development of this framework does not result from a single policy measure but from a sequence of political and legislative milestones that reflect a progressive intensification of the restrictive approach. The temporal sequencing of these measures suggests a path-dependent dynamic, in which earlier responses to crisis conditions generate institutional precedents that facilitate the adoption of increasingly restrictive policies over time..

Table 2. Key Milestones in the Hardening of European Migration Policy

Year	Instrument / Event	Main Measure
2015	Refugee crisis	Turning point in migration policy
2016	Brexit	Political instrumentalization of anti-immigration discourse
2024	New Pact on Migration and Asylum	Comprehensive reform of the asylum system
2024	Adoption of the Pact	Accelerated procedures and reinforced border control
2026	Return Regulation	Expansion of the "safe third country" concept and facilitation of deportations

Note. Author's own elaboration based on academic, legal, and documentary sources (Del Valle, 2020; Calvo, 2024), as well as the New Pact on Migration and Asylum and the European Union Return Regulation.

The 2024 Migration and Asylum Pact is structured as an integrated system composed of ten legislative instruments, including the Regulation on Asylum and Migration Management, the Border Screening Regulation, the Asylum Procedures Regulation, the Border Return Procedure Regulation, the Eurodac Regulation, the Reception Conditions Directive, and the Crisis and Force Majeure Regulation, among others. This normative framework aims to provide a faster and more uniform response to migration arrivals, combining mechanisms of responsibility and solidarity among Member States. However, the emphasis on procedural acceleration and border management reveals an underlying prioritization of efficiency and control over the strengthening of protection guarantees, reinforcing the structural shift toward a securitized governance model.

The documentary analysis suggests that the adoption of the Pact was influenced by short-term political considerations, particularly the need to reach agreements ahead of the 2024 European Parliament elections and in anticipation of the electoral growth of far-right parties (Calvo, 2024). This temporal alignment between electoral cycles and normative reform indicates that migration policy is not only shaped by structural pressures but also by strategic political calculations, in which regulatory outcomes are conditioned by the need to respond to shifting electoral landscapes. This context helps explain both the speed of its approval and the restrictive orientation of several of its provisions.

Following the 2024 elections, the European political landscape underwent significant changes, including the consolidation of parliamentary alliances between traditional conservative parties and far-right formations. This dynamic is particularly evident in the approval of the Return Regulation, which was supported by a majority of 389 votes due to the convergence between the European People's Party (EPP) and the European Conservatives and Reformists (ECR), Patriots for Europe (PfE), and Europe of Sovereign Nations (ESN). Such alliances illustrate the erosion of the so-called "cordon sanitaire" and signal a normalization of cooperation between mainstream and far-right actors, with direct implications for policy outcomes.

The Return Regulation introduces substantial modifications to the concept of a "safe third country," allowing its application even in the absence of a direct connection between the asylum seeker and the destination country. Specifically, it establishes that Member States may consider as "safe" any country through which the applicant has transited, under the assumption that effective protection could have been sought there. This reinterpretation represents a significant doctrinal shift, as it expands the scope of admissibility restrictions and redefines the criteria for responsibility in international protection, potentially undermining the individualized assessment of asylum claims.

Moreover, the regulation allows for the adoption of measures aimed at preventing the risk of absconding, including restrictions on freedom of movement or the detention of applicants during the processing of their claims. These provisions have been interpreted as a form of criminalization of migration, insofar as irregular mobility is treated as a threat to be contained through coercive mechanisms. From a governance perspective, this reflects the increasing reliance on preventive and punitive tools, which blur the boundary between administrative regulation and security enforcement.

The regulatory framework also introduces limitations on the right to remain during appeal procedures, establishing that applicants will not automatically have the right to stay within the territory of a Member State while their appeal is being processed. This provision raises profound legal concerns, as it weakens procedural safeguards and increases the likelihood of premature returns, potentially in violation of international protection standards. In particular, it poses risks in relation to the principle of non-refoulement, a cornerstone of international protection law.

In parallel, the regulation strengthens the external dimension of European migration policy through the possibility of establishing "return hubs" in third countries—that is, processing and return centers located outside EU territory. This approach draws inspiration from policies such as Italy's establishment of detention centers in Albania, where migrants rescued in the Mediterranean are transferred, detained, and subsequently expelled (Domínguez, 2024). The expansion of such mechanisms reflects a broader strategy of externalization, aimed at relocating migration management beyond EU borders in order to reduce legal accountability and political costs within Member States.

The response from civil society has been largely critical. More than 200 non-governmental organizations have warned that these measures may violate fundamental rights, weaken legal safeguards, and exacerbate conditions of irregularity. At the political level, Member of the European Parliament Mélissa Camara described the adoption of the regulation as “a vote of shame and a betrayal of the fundamental values of the European Union” (RTVE.es, 2026). Similarly, parliamentary groups from the Greens, social democrats, liberals, and the left—totaling 206 votes against—criticized both the content of the regulation and the alliance between the EPP and far-right parties (Banchón, 2026).

These reactions highlight the existence of a normative cleavage within the European political system, between actors advocating for a rights-based approach and those prioritizing control-oriented strategies. This tension underscores the contested nature of migration governance and reflects broader ideological divisions within the European Union.

The systematized evidence demonstrates that the tightening of European migration policy does not stem from a single isolated reform but rather from a cumulative process combining normative changes, political transformations, and discursive reconfigurations. Taken together, these elements reveal a structural shift in the European migration regime, in which control, deterrence, and externalization increasingly define the core logic of policy design. This process is characterized by the growing centrality of mechanisms of control, externalization, and restriction of access to asylum, thereby shaping a migration governance architecture that is progressively oriented toward containment rather than protection.

Convergence Between the Rise of the Far Right and the Hardening of Migration Policies

The integrated analysis of the documentary corpus reveals a process of progressive convergence between the electoral rise of the far right and the tightening of migration policies in the European Union. This convergence should not be interpreted as a direct or unidirectional causal relationship, but rather as a complex process of interaction in which political, normative, and discursive dimensions mutually reinforce one another. In this sense, the relationship operates through mechanisms of co-evolution, where changes in one domain—such as electoral dynamics—reshape the conditions of possibility in others, including policy design and public discourse.

From a temporal perspective, as demonstrated in the previous sections, both processes exhibit parallel trajectories. The sustained growth of the far right since the beginning of the twenty-first century—particularly from the 2010s onward—coincides with the intensification of reforms oriented toward migration control, especially following the 2015 refugee crisis. The adoption of the New Pact on Migration and Asylum in 2024 and the Return Regulation in 2026 can be situated within this same cycle of transformation. This simultaneity suggests the presence of a broader structural shift in European governance, in which migration becomes a central axis through which political competition, institutional reform, and identity-based narratives are articulated.

However, it is at the political-institutional level that this convergence becomes most visible. The gradual erosion of the so-called "cordon sanitaire" has enabled the incorporation of far-right parties into decision-making dynamics at the European level. As noted, the approval of the Return Regulation was supported by a coalition involving the European People's Party (EPP) and far-right groups such as the European Conservatives and Reformists (ECR), Patriots for Europe (PfE), and Europe of Sovereign Nations (ESN), reflecting a reconfiguration of parliamentary alliances (Banchón, 2026). This development is particularly significant, as it signals not only a shift in power balances but also a transformation in the normative boundaries of political legitimacy, whereby positions once considered marginal are increasingly integrated into mainstream policymaking processes.

Within this context, the discursive dimension plays a crucial role as a mechanism linking both processes. As previously discussed, xenophobia constitutes a central unifying element of far-right discourse (Hernández-Carr, 2011; González-Páramo, 2019; Rodríguez, 2020; Sanahuja & López, 2024; Pérez Gallo, 2026), and its gradual normalization within public debate contributes to legitimizing the adoption of more restrictive policies. The construction of migration as a threat—whether economic, cultural, or security-related—facilitates the social acceptance of measures focused on containment, control, and externalization. From an analytical standpoint, this framing process operates as a form of cognitive and political simplification, enabling complex structural issues to be translated into accessible narratives that justify restrictive policy responses.

The Brexit case provides a paradigmatic example of this dynamic. The instrumentalization of anti-immigration discourse during the 2016 referendum campaign not only contributed to the victory of the "Leave" option but also demonstrated the capacity of such narratives to shape large-scale political decisions (EFE, 2016; Marea Granate, 2017; González, 2016). Importantly, these discourses did not remain confined to the national level but circulated across the European political space, influencing broader debates and contributing to the reconfiguration of both political alignments and policy orientations at the EU level.

Table 3. Convergences Between Political Discourse and Migration Policy in the European Union

Dimension	Empirical Evidence	Manifestation in Public Policy
Xenophobia	Anti-immigration discourse in far-right parties and Brexit campaign	Restriction of access to asylum (reinforced context after 2016)
Securitization	Construction of migration as a security threat	Border procedures and detention measures (intensified since 2015)
Externalization	Third-country centers (e.g., Albania) and external agreements	Delegation of migration control outside the EU (visible implementations in the 2020s; Italy–Albania case cited in 2024)
De-marginalization	Alliances between mainstream and far-right parties	Approval of restrictive legislation such as the Return Regulation (2026)
Discursive normalization	Repetition of anti-immigration narratives in public debate	Political legitimation of restrictive migration policies (consolidated after 2015 and reinforced in 2024)

Note. Author's own elaboration based on documentary corpus analysis and specialized literature (Hernández-Carr, 2011; González-Páramo, 2019; Rodríguez, 2020; Sanahuja & López, 2024; Pérez Gallo, 2026), as well as journalistic sources (EFE, 2016; Marea Granate, 2017; González, 2016; Banchón, 2026). The analytical categories reflect the articulation between political discourse and public policy in the European context.

As illustrated, the convergence between these processes is articulated through a set of interrelated mechanisms. First, xenophobia and securitization operate as interpretative frameworks that redefine migration as a security issue, displacing its humanitarian dimension. This transformation is not merely rhetorical but has concrete implications for policy design, as it reorients institutional priorities toward risk management and border enforcement. Second, the externalization of migration control reflects a structural shift in how the European Union manages its borders, transferring responsibilities to third countries. This strategy can be understood as a form of governance displacement, aimed at minimizing legal accountability and redistributing the political costs associated with migration management.

Third, the de-marginalization of the far right enables the incorporation of its policy agendas into formal decision-making processes, while discursive normalization contributes to their broader social acceptance. Together, these mechanisms generate a feedback loop in which political influence, policy change, and discursive shifts reinforce one another, consolidating the restrictive turn as a dominant paradigm.

Finally, the findings suggest that the hardening of migration policies should be understood as a political dynamic that extends beyond a purely technical response to the management of migration flows, in which the rise of the far right plays a significant role. Both processes develop in an interdependent manner, shaping a "cartography of the restrictive turn" in which normative, political, and discursive transformations are deeply intertwined and mutually reinforcing. This interdependence highlights the structural nature of the phenomenon and underscores the need to analyze migration policy not in isolation, but as part of broader transformations within the European political order.

CONCLUSIONS

The findings of this study indicate that the so-called "restrictive turn" in European Union migration policy is neither an isolated nor a conjunctural phenomenon, but rather the outcome of a structural transformation in which political, normative, and discursive dynamics converge. Based on the systematic analysis of the documentary corpus, it has been possible to reconstruct a consistent relationship between the electoral rise of the far right and the progressive tightening of the European migration framework, demonstrating the existence of a multicausal and cumulative convergence between these processes.

One of the main findings lies in the identification of a significant temporal synchronicity between the growth of the far right and the intensification of migration reforms. Since the beginning of the twenty-first century—and particularly from the 2010s onward—a sustained expansion of these political forces can be observed, accompanied by a parallel process of normative transformation oriented toward migration control. The 2015 refugee crisis emerges as a critical turning point that accelerates both dynamics, while the adoption of the New Pact on Migration and Asylum in 2024 and the Return Regulation in 2026 represent key moments of institutional consolidation of this trend. This temporal alignment suggests that migration policy developments are closely embedded within broader political cycles, rather than being driven solely by functional or administrative considerations.

Beyond this temporal coincidence, the analysis identifies a second key finding: the emergence of a political-institutional convergence expressed through the progressive de-marginalization of the far right and its increasing capacity to influence decision-making processes. The erosion of the so-called "cordon sanitaire" and the formation of parliamentary alliances between mainstream parties and far-right actors reflect a qualitative shift in the European political system. This transformation expands the operational space of far-right parties and reshapes the normative boundaries of political legitimacy, allowing previously excluded positions to enter the sphere of policy formulation. As a result, restrictive proposals have become increasingly integrated into the legislative framework.

A third central finding operates at the discursive level. The research demonstrates that the normalization of narratives framing migration as a threat constitutes a key mechanism linking these processes. Xenophobia and securitization function as interpretative frameworks that mobilize electoral support and legitimize policies focused on containment, externalization, and restriction of access to asylum. In this regard, anti-immigration discourse should be understood not merely as a reflection of political contexts, but as an active driver in the reconfiguration of migration governance. Its performative capacity lies in shaping public perception and, consequently, expanding the political feasibility of restrictive measures.

The integration of these dimensions supports the argument that the tightening of migration policies in the European Union cannot be understood exclusively as a technical response to the management of migration flows. Rather, the findings show that this process is embedded in a broader political dynamic in which the rise of the far right plays a significant role, both directly—through institutional participation—and indirectly, by shifting the center of political debate and normalizing specific discursive frameworks. This dual mechanism of influence highlights the importance of considering both formal and informal channels of political power in the analysis of policy change.

Another relevant finding concerns the transformation of the normative architecture of European migration policy, characterized by the increasing centrality of mechanisms of control and externalization. Instruments such as the New Pact on Migration and Asylum and the Return Regulation reflect a reconfiguration of the balance between protection and control, in which the latter assumes a dominant role. This shift entails profound implications for migration management and for the foundational principles of the European Union and its commitment to human rights, raising questions about the long-term sustainability of its normative framework.

Furthermore, the findings indicate that this transformation is not confined to the European context but forms part of a broader global trend toward the securitization of migration. In this sense, the European Union should not be understood as an exception, but rather as a particularly illustrative case in which wider tensions between state control, domestic political dynamics, and international human rights obligations are expressed with notable intensity. This positioning situates the European case within a comparative framework, opening avenues for cross-regional analysis.

From a methodological perspective, the use of analytical matrices proved essential for identifying these dynamics of convergence, enabling the organization of empirical material and the visualization of relationships that go beyond the fragmented analysis of individual events or policies. This approach facilitated the construction of a "mapping of the restrictive turn," providing a descriptive account and an interpretative framework capable of capturing the structural logic underpinning policy transformations.

While the study presents limitations inherent to its qualitative and documentary approach—particularly regarding the inability to establish direct causal relationships or measure concrete impacts—these limitations also point to opportunities for further research. Future studies could advance the quantitative measurement of the relationship between electoral variables and normative changes, as well as examine the concrete effects of these policies on migrants and asylum seekers. In addition, exploring the mechanisms of production, circulation, and contestation of anti-immigration discourses remains a key area for further investigation.

In terms of implications, the findings highlight the need to reconsider the balance between control and protection in European migration policy, as well as to pay closer attention to the role of political discourse in shaping public policy. Beyond specific legislative reforms, the analysis suggests that any meaningful transformation will require a critical reassessment of the interpretative frameworks that structure the debate on migration, as these ultimately define the scope and direction of policy responses.

REFERENCES

Alberdi Bidaguren, J. (2019). The rise of the far right in the 2019 European Parliament elections and its consequences for migration policies. In EuroBasque (Ed.), *Citizen reflections on the EU ahead of the 2019 European Parliament elections* (pp. 73–77). EuroBasque. https://dialnet.unirioja.es/servlet/articulo?codigo=8953032

Banchón, M. (2026, March 26). European return regulation: The crime of being a migrant. *DW.* https://www.dw.com/es/reglamento-europeo-del-retorno-el-crimen-de-ser-migrante/a-76541786

Bello, C. L. C. (2024). The de-marginalization of the far right and the anti-immigration narrative. *Revista Diarios del Terruño*, (17), 149–153.

Camas, P., & Ferrández, J. (2024, June 7). The rise of the far right in Europe, in data. *eldiario.es*. https://www.eldiario.es/internacional/auge-extrema-derecha-europa-datos_129_11395177.html

Carrascón, I., & Vilches, S. (2024, June 10). The far right wins in France, Italy, Austria, and Belgium, securing 159 seats, 22% of the European Parliament. *Newtral*. https://www.newtral.es/ultraderecha-parlamento-europeo/20240610/

Castro, I., & Sánchez, R. (2024, May 25). The two factions of the far right compete for hegemony in Europe. *eldiario.es*. https://www.eldiario.es/internacional/facciones-extrema-derecha-compiten-hegemonia-europa_1_11390194.html

Castro Romero, G. A. (2024). *Venezuelan migration and the production of irregularity: The case of Venezuelan migrants in transit through Mexico (2018–2023)* (Master's thesis, Universidad Nacional Autónoma de México). UNAM Institutional Repository. https://ru.dgb.unam.mx/server/api/core/bitstreams/613e9720-c6a9-4aff-8150-9af1679ea500/content

De Zwaan, J. W. (2025). The evolution of the immigration and asylum policy of the European Union: From the internal market to the New Pact. *European Review of Public Law*, *37*(1), 335. https://openurl.ebsco.com/

Del Valle Gálvez, A. (2020). The rescue of people in the Mediterranean: On the unfeasibility of the European external border model in the Mediterranean. *Revista Española de Derecho Internacional*, (72), 187–196.

Domínguez, I. (2024, October 17). An Italian bubble in Albania where migrants become invisible. *El País*. https://elpais.com/internacional/2024-10-17/

EFE. (2016, June 29). Brexit fuels resurgence of xenophobia in the United Kingdom. *La Vanguardia*. https://www.lavanguardia.com/

Europa Press. (2023, June 18). The evolution of the far right in European governments. *Onda Cero*. https://www.ondacero.es/

González de la Calleja, P. (2026, June 19). Xenophobia leads the campaign for the UK's exit from the EU. *Público.es*. https://www.publico.es/

González Páramo, A. (2019). The rise of the far right in Europe and xenophobic discourses. *Anuario CEIPAZ*, (12), 27–42. https://dialnet.unirioja.es/

Hernández-Carr, A. (2011). The populist radical right in Europe: Discourse, electorate, and explanations. *REIS*, (136), 141–160.

Lang, I. G. (2024). The re-emergence of "Fortress Europe.". *European Foreign Affairs Review*, *29*(4).

Marea Granate Londres. (2017, January 24). Brexit and the normalization of xenophobia. *eldiario.es*. https://www.eldiario.es/

Nissen, A. (2022). *Europeanisation of the contemporary far right: Generation Identity and Fortress Europe* (1st ed.). Routledge., DOI: 10.4324/9781003226604

Oxfam Intermón. (2025, February). *Impact of the European Pact on Migration and Asylum: A human rights-based interpretative framework* [Working paper]. https://www.oxfamintermon.org/

Pereira Peñalver, C. A. (2023). Securitization and migration in the European Union. *Diario La Ley*, (10297).

Pérez, A. (2020, October 30). Fortress Europe: An authoritarian-populist construct? (ARI 122/2020). *Real Instituto Elcano*. https://media.realinstitutoelcano.org/

Pérez Gallo, H. (2026). Youth, far right, and meaning construction: A critical approach to Vox narratives. *Papers* (in press), e3416, 1–28. https://zaguan.unizar.es/

Porras Ramírez, J. M. (2025). Integrated migration and border management as a strategic priority of the European Union: When "à la carte solidarity" serves security. *Revista de las Cortes Generales*, (119), 199–228. DOI: 10.33426/rcg/2025/119/1862

Rodríguez, G. (2020). The crisis of the European Union and the rise of the far right. *RIPS*, *19*(1), 93–108.

RTVE.es. (2026, March 26). The European Parliament approves regulation allowing migrant centers abroad. *RTVE.es*. https://www.rtve.es/

Sahuquillo, M. (2026, April 14). Von der Leyen proposes ending unanimity in EU decision-making in response to blockages such as Hungary. *El País*. https://elpais.com/

Sanahuja, J., & López, C. (2024). Variations in the geopolitics of the neo-patriotic far right and contestation of the international order, (11), 17–36. https://docta.ucm.es/

Sangiao, S. (2024, July 14). Three parliamentary groups and 200 far-right MEPs: The new European Parliament. *Público.es*. https://www.publico.es/

Voytyuk, A., & Müller, A. (2026, March 31). Audio leaks show Hungary sharing information with Russia and Orbán's alignment within the EU. *La Sexta*. https://www.lasexta.com/

Chapter 13
Climate Migrants in the Context of Climate Change

Emre Cengiz
http://orcid.org/0000-0002-3854-6215
Gümüşhane University, Turkey

ABSTRACT

Climate change, one of the major challenges of our time, has brought with it the debate on climate migration. Over the last century, the number of people migrating due to climate change has been steadily increasing, and it is estimated that millions of people will be displaced by climate change in the coming years. As a result of rising air temperatures, rising sea level, increasing aridity, the depletion of water resources, the dwindling of resources essential for life, and the rise in the number of natural disasters linked to climate change, billions of people are being affected by this situation. It is also a well-known fact that the scale of conflicts and violence is beginning to change as a result of these problems. Consequently, the fact that people's living environments are becoming uninhabitable, coupled with the lack of security resulting from conflicts and acts of violence, is forcing them to migrate to more liveable places.

INTRODUCTION

Looking at the history of humankind as a whole, migration appears to be a phenomenon that has continued since the very first day humans set foot on Earth. At times, natural phenomena and disasters have forced people to migrate, whilst at other times, economic hardship and the desire for a better standard of living have

DOI: 10.4018/979-8-3373-8500-6.ch013

been the main reasons for migration. Furthermore, incidents of violence and wars have driven people to seek safer places to live.

The 20th century stands out as a significant period in migration studies, as it encompasses a wide range of causes and examples of migration. The two world wars, economic crises, pandemics, acts of terrorism and the large number of countries undergoing their initial industrialisation are regarded as the principal causes of migration. By the 1950s, we can see that a new cause of migration was gradually making itself felt across the world. "Environmental issues" had begun to come to the fore and were starting to affect people. Mass deaths caused by greenhouse gases and problems arising from deteriorating air quality began to dominate the agenda. These environmental problems led to the emergence of an environmental consciousness. The economic policies implemented caused increasing pressure on the environment and natural resources, and alongside the view that environmental problems should be seen as a consequence of economic development, there was also discussion of the need to overlook these issues. It has also been argued that the environmental problems experienced are limited solely to the area where pollution occurs. However, it is also known that environmental policies implemented in response to such problems generally focus on attempting to remedy the pollution that has already occurred (Cengiz et al. 2025a). From the 1960s onwards, we began to observe that these views gradually started to change as environmental problems and the number of people affected by them began to increase. The notion that environmental problems were confined solely to the location where they occurred was replaced by the realisation that they were "transboundary" issues. Consequently, rather than attempting to remedy environmental pollution after it had occurred, the concept of "prediction and prevention" began to take on greater importance in the formulation of environmental policies (Cengiz et al. 2025b).

Since the 1970s, the United Nations and civil society organisations have been drawing attention to the problems that have arisen and seeking solutions. The 1970s are significant as the period when the first steps towards global awareness of environmental issues began to be taken. Furthermore, it was during this period that human consumption of natural resources began to exceed the Earth's capacity to regenerate them within a single year. In 1973, this capacity was seen to have been exceeded, and 26 November was designated as Earth Overshoot Day. As shown in Figure 1, Earth Overshoot Day has been occurring earlier in the year since 1973.

Figure 1. Earth Overshoot Days (1972–2024)

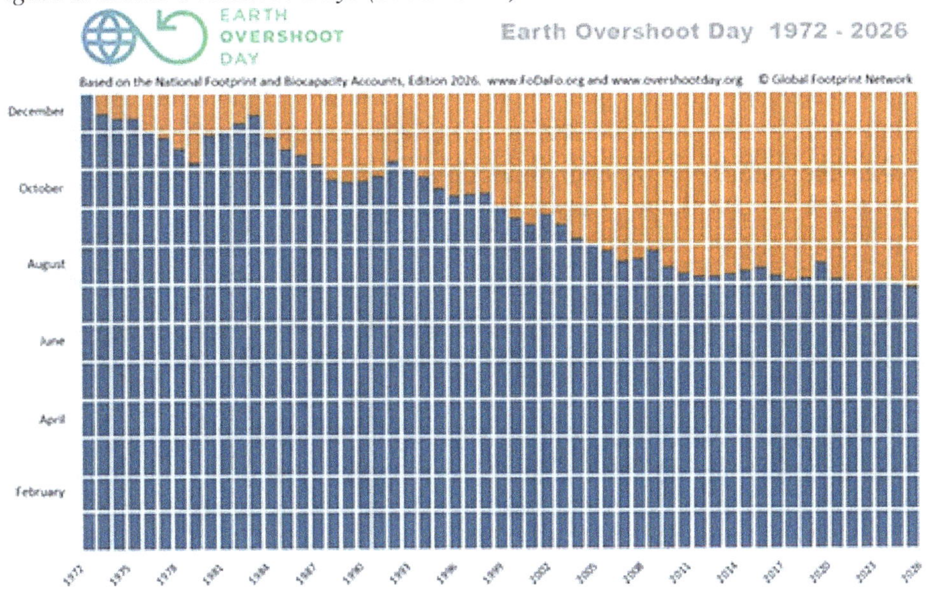

Source: Past Earth Overshoot Days, https://overshoot.footprintnetwork.org/newsroom/past-earth-overshoot-days/

Looking at Figure 1, we can see that Earth Overshoot Day which began in November 1973 has in recent years moved forward to July, meaning that the rate at which the world's natural resources are consumed in a single year has accelerated even further. It is also a well-known fact that, as things stand today, we would need 1.8 Earths to sustain our consumption of natural resources.

The rapid increase in environmental problems, accompanied by global warming and climate change, as well as the excessive consumption of natural resources, is causing the ecological balance to be disrupted and has become one of the most significant causes of migration in today's world. This situation, which we might briefly describe as the climate crisis, does not merely affect people living in the areas where these problems occur; it has a negative impact on all of humanity. Alongside the challenges faced by migrants, social, sociological, economic and security issues are among the most pressing problems facing humanity today. This study examines the phenomenon of climate-induced migration whilst seeking to develop proposed solutions for the future.

CLIMATE CHANGE, MIGRATION AND DISPLACEMENT

It is well known that, from the second half of the 20th century to the present day, climate change has been the subject of debate worldwide, with efforts being made to find solutions. Both international organisations and the academic community are conducting research into climate change the most pressing issue of our time and are striving to raise global public awareness.

It is important to note that research into climate change began in the 19th century. In 1856, Eunice Foote published a two-page article entitled "Circumstances Affecting the Heat of the Sun's Rays" in the American Journal of Art and Science, in which she sought to explain the relationship between carbon dioxide and atmospheric warming.

"The highest effect of the sun's rays I have found to be in carbonic acid gas. One of the receivers was filled with it, the other with common air, and the result was as follows: The receiver containing the gas became itself much heated—very sensibly more so than the other—and on being removed, it was many times as long in cooling. An atmosphere of that gas would give to our earth a high temperature; and if, as some suppose, at one period of its history the air had mixed with it a larger proportion than at present, an increased temperature from its own action as well as from increased weight must have necessarily resulted. On comparing the sun's heat in different gases, I found it to be in hydrogen gas, 104°; in common air, 106°; in oxygen gas, 108°; and in carbonic acid gas, 125°." (p.383)

Eunice Foote's study indicates that the rise in carbon dioxide levels traps solar heat within the atmosphere and causes temperatures to rise.

We see that the first climate modelling was carried out in the article entitled "On the Influence of Carbonic Acid in the Air upon the Temperature of the Ground", written by Svante Arrhenius in 1896. Arrhenius (1896) states that an increase in the amount of carbon dioxide in the atmosphere would lead to a rise in air temperature.

"One may now ask, How much must the carbonic acid vary according to our figures, in order that the temperature should attain the same values as in the Tertiary and Ice ages respectively? A simple calculation shows that the temperature in the arctic regions would rise about 8° to 9°C., if the carbonic acid increased to 2.5 or 3 times its present value. In order to get the temperature of the ice age between the 40th and 50th parallels, the carbonic acid in the air should sink to 0.62--0.55 of its present value (lowering of temperature 4°- 5°C.). The demands of the geologists, that at the genial epochs the climate should be more uniform than now, accords very well with our theory. The geographical annual and diurnal ranges of temperature would be partly smoothed away, if the quantity of carbonic acid was augmented." (p. 268)

In his article entitled "The Artificial Production of Carbon Dioxide and Its Influence on Temperature", published in 1938, Guy Stewart Callendar stated that 150 billion tonnes of carbon dioxide had been released into the atmosphere between the Industrial Revolution and 1938, and that the global temperature had risen by 0.005 degrees Celsius per year (Callendar, 1938).

"By fuel combustion man has added about 150,000 million tons of carbon dioxide to the air during the past half century. The author estimates from the best available data that approximately three quarters of this has remained in the atmosphere. The radiation absorption coefficients of carbon dioxide and water vapour are used to show the effect of carbon dioxide on " sky radiation." From this the increase in mean temperature, due to the artificial production of carbon dioxide, is estimated to be at the rate of 0.003OC. per year at the present time. The temperature observations at zoo meteorological stations are used to show that world temperatures have actually increased at an average rate of o.oo5°C. per year during the past half century." (p. 223)

In an article published in 1958 by Charles D. Keeling, entitled "The concentration and isotopic abundances of atmospheric carbon dioxide in rural areas", it was demonstrated that the concentration of carbon dioxide in the atmosphere was steadily increasing, and the effects of fossil fuel use were explained. (Keeling, 1958).

"Carbon dioxide in the atmosphere has been studied for more than a hundred years. Nineteenth century measurements showed its concentration to vary, especially over continental areas. Causes for variation were not always understood, but the activity of plants explained the diurnal periodicity often observed for rural air, and the burning of fuel accounted for the high values of urban air reported." (p. 322)

From the 19th century to the 1960s, numerous studies investigated the effects of fossil fuels on climate change, and articles were published on the subject. A few of the studies considered significant have been mentioned. As noted in the introduction, it is also known that efforts to raise public awareness have been underway worldwide since the 1960s.

Migration is a phenomenon as old as human history itself. We can observe climate-induced migration from the past to the present day. An example of such climate change can be seen in the collapse of the Maya Empire between 660 and 1000 AD. Looking at the more recent past, the dust storms that occurred in America in the 1930s and the drought in the Sahel between the 1970s and 1980s forced people living in those areas to migrate (Sherbinin).

Discussions regarding the impact of climate change on migration actually date back to the 1960s. When Wolpert (1966) examined migration patterns, he argued that environmental changes should also be taken into account.

The concept of migration refers to the permanent or semi-permanent relocation of people from their places of residence. Migration may take place within a country or to another country. Migrants may relocate either involuntarily or voluntarily. Another important concept that must be explained alongside that of migration is the concept of displacement. We can observe the concept of displacement throughout the period from the earliest humans to the present day. Even before people adopted a settled way of life, they were subject to displacement. People who subsisted on hunting and lived as nomads were forced to leave their homes whether due to threats from other people or as a result of natural disasters or natural phenomena and migrated to other settlements or regions (Cengiz, 2019). Displacement refers to people being forced to leave their homes as a result of economic and physical changes in the areas where they live. Economic and physical changes encompass development projects, environmental issues, natural disasters, war and acts of terrorism, as well as the changes and transformations occurring in residential areas (McDowell and Morrell, 2010).

In a report prepared by El-Hinnawi (1985) for the United Nations Environment Programme (UNEP), the concept of "environmental refugees" was examined in detail. The report explains the concepts of refugees and environmental refugees. It also addresses the natural disasters, soil degradation, environmental accidents and wars that cause people to be displaced.

The report defines the concept of "environmental refugees" as follows:

"Environmental refugees are defined as those people who have been forced to leave their traditional habitat, temporarily or permanently, because of a marked environmental disruption (natural and/or triggered by people) that jeopardized their existence and/or seriously affected the quality of their life. By "environmental disruption" in this definition is meant any physical, chemical and/or biological changes in the ecosystem. (or the resource base) that render it, temporarily or permanently, unsuitable to support human life. According to this definition, people displaced for political reasons or by civil strife and migrants seeking better jobs purely on economic grounds are not considered environmental refugees." (p. 4)

By 1990, a report by the Intergovernmental Panel on Climate Change (IPCC) had stated that the greatest impact of climate change would be on human migration (IPCC, 1990; IOM 2008). Research conducted from 1990 to the present day has indicated that the number of migrants is set to rise rapidly. Looking at projections for 2050, it is estimated that 200 million people may be forced to migrate due to climate change (IOM, 2008). This trend is rising even further in the latest research.

The concept of climate change-induced displacement, which began to be discussed extensively in the 2000s, is generally addressed and explained within the broader context of displacement caused by environmental issues; however, researchers wishing to highlight the significance of the issue have begun to examine it under a separate heading (Warner, 2012).

Climate change is leading to an increase in the number of natural disasters, drought, deforestation, a decline in water resources and rising sea levels. Consequently, it is hindering people's ability to carry on with their daily lives and, as a result, is forcing them to migrate.

LEGAL AND POLITICAL CHALLENGES FACED BY CLIMATE MIGRANTS

There are issues relating to climate migrants that need to be resolved today. Shortcomings must be addressed, both in terms of determining which rights should be granted from a legal perspective and in terms of building consensus amongst all countries worldwide during policy-making processes.

The most significant of the issues encountered begins with seeking an answer to the question of which term to use: "migrant" or "refugee". Should the term "climate migrant" be used, or should it be "climate refugee"? We see that the term "climate migrant" is the one generally accepted and in use. We can see that, whilst climate migrants do not possess "refugee" rights, the UN has stated in its resolutions that those displaced by climate change should not be returned, as there is a risk of a violation of their right to life.

Although the terms "migrant", "refugee", "asylum-seeker" and "displaced person" may appear similar, there are differences between them in terms of legal rights.

Migrant: This term refers to people who choose to migrate not because of a threat to their lives or persecution, but for reasons such as improving their lives, accessing a good education or family reunification. There are no obstacles preventing them from returning to their home countries, and there are no barriers to their return. Furthermore, they can return to their home country whenever they wish without encountering any problems. Migrants are subject to the national laws of the country to which they have migrated (UNHCR, 2016).

Internally Displaced Person: These are people who have been forced to leave their homes due to conflict, violence, persecution and natural disasters, but who have not crossed their country's borders (UNHCR).

Asylum-seeker: People who have been forced to leave their homes due to war, persecution and human rights violations. They are individuals seeking international protection. Their applications for refugee status or subsidiary protection may not yet have been processed, or they may not yet have applied for such protection but intend to do so (UNHCR).

Refugee: People who are forced to flee to neighbouring countries because their safety, freedom and lives are at risk in their home country due to death threats, internal strife, armed conflict and persecution (UNHCR, 2016).

Article 1 of the 1951 Convention Relating to the Status of Refugees provides a definition of a refugee;

> "(1) Has been considered a refugee under the Arrangements of 12 May 1926 and 30 June 1928 or under the Conventions of 28 October 1933 and 10 Feb-

ruary 1938, the Protocol of 14 September 1939 or the Constitution of the International Refugee Organization;

Decisions of non-eligibility taken by the International Refugee Organization during the period of its activities shall not prevent the status of refugee being accorded to persons who fulfil the conditions of paragraph 2 of this section;

(2) As a result of events occurring before 1 January 1951 and owing to well-founded fear of being persecuted for reasons of race, religion, nationality, membership of a particular social group or political opinion, is outside the country of his nationality and is unable or, owing to such fear, is unwilling to avail himself of the protection of that country; or who, not having a nationality and being outside the country of his former habitual residence as a result of such events, is unable or, owing to such fear, is unwilling to return to it.

In the case of a person who has more than one nationality, the term "the country of his nationality" shall mean each of the countries of which he is a national, and a person shall not be deemed to be lacking the protection of the country of his nationality if, without any valid reason based on wellfounded fear, he has not availed himself of the protection of one of the countries of which he is a national" (UNHCR, 1951).

With the 1967 Protocol Relating to the Status of Refugees, the issue of limiting refugee status to a specific time period a matter frequently debated in the Geneva Convention was resolved, and the phrase "events occurring prior to 1 January 1951" in Article 1 of the Geneva Convention was removed.

Climate migrants are not classified as refugees and do not enjoy the rights afforded to refugees. Whilst it is often assumed that climate migrants do not face significant issues such as conflict, violence and persecution which are necessary for refugee status this is not entirely the case. It is important to recognise that, as the effects of climate change intensify, there is a likelihood of increased conflict, violence and internal unrest in their living environments. A Security Council Report published in the United Kingdom in 2007 actually highlights the problems that may arise alongside climate change. Under the heading "Energy, Security and Climate", the report emphasises the need to promote sustainable development in the face of climate change. Increased dependence on fossil fuels could accelerate climate change and heighten the risk of conflict. Climate change will give rise to border disputes, migration, and shortages of energy resources, water, arable land and other resources, which will in turn lead to increased social tensions and humanitarian crises (Security Council Report 2007).

The UNFCCC states that climate change indirectly contributes to an increase in conflicts, in line with the issue highlighted. It notes in particular that the most vulnerable groups are becoming even more vulnerable, emphasising that there is no group today more vulnerable than those forced to flee their countries due to conflict and who are feeling the effects of adverse climatic conditions. Finally, it states that the likelihood of those displaced by both conflict and climate change and environmental degradation returning to their homes is very low (UNFCCC). In light of this information, an action plan must be drawn up without delay to address the situation of those displaced by climate change.

The World Bank published the Groundswell Reports in 2018 and 2021. Both reports emphasised that millions of people would be forced to migrate internally as a result of the climate crisis. The report published in 2018 states that 143 million people in Sub-Saharan Africa, South Asia and Latin America will be forced to migrate internally by 2050. (Groundswell, 2018) Furthermore, this situation is illustrated in the report by the figure below.

Figure 2. Internal migration that could occur by 2050 according to three scenarios

Source: Groundswell PREPARING FOR INTERNAL CLIMATE MIGRATION, 2018, World Bank p. xx

A closer look at the figure reveals the difference in migration rates between the "Pessimistic scenario" and the "Climate-adapted scenario". When measures are taken to adapt to climate change, migration rates are reduced by almost half.

In 2021, the World Bank (2021) published its second "Groundswell Report". The report states that 216 million people across six regions could be affected by migration by 2050 (Figure 3).

Figure 3. Groundswell's migration projections for 2050

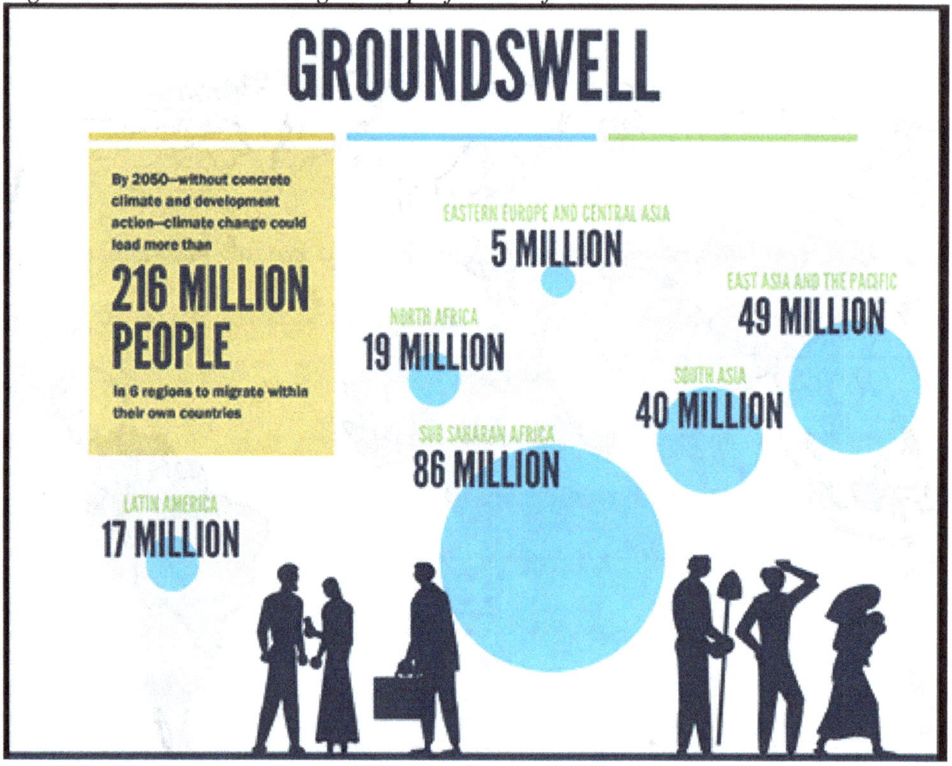

Source: *Groundswell ACTING ON INTERNAL CLIMATE MIGRATION, 2021, World Bank, p. xv*

Various studies have been carried out on the climate crisis, one of the greatest challenges of our time. The findings of a study conducted in 2020 are particularly striking. It revealed that, unless a solution to the climate crisis is found, within 50 years 3 billion people will be trying to live in areas considered to be extremely hot. Los Angeles and Paris are among these places. The study also showed that the communities most affected by the climate crisis are the most vulnerable ones, who bear the burden of the crisis despite not being responsible for greenhouse gas emissions or polluting the environment (CBD).

The Institute for Economics and Peace, an international think tank, paints an even bleaker picture. It states that by 2050, 1.2 billion people could be displaced due to rising temperatures and natural disasters (IEP).

In the coming years, virtually every region of the world will be adversely affected by the impacts of climate change. Hundreds of millions of people will either be displaced or face difficulties in sustaining their livelihoods. The most important issue in this regard will be to rethink the concept of "refugees".

As the concept of a "climate migrant" does not provide legal protection, the adoption of the concept of a "climate refugee" is important from the perspective of legal protection. In this regard in 2023, the UN Special Rapporteur on Human Rights and Climate Change Ian Fry, called for the drafting of a protocol to the 1951 Convention for those displaced by climate change (Hattem). In 2020, the UN Human Rights Committee stated that the climate crisis constitutes a valid ground for preventing deportation.

The Falepili Agreement, signed between Australia and Tuvalu in 2023, is significant for climate migrants. The agreement involves granting visas to 280 Tuvaluan citizens due to the climate crisis (Hattem). In fact, the idea of a climate visa was first raised in 2017. New Zealand established a climate refugee visa programme for residents of the island nations of Kiribati and Fiji. However, six months later, the government abandoned the programme (Surman).

It should also be borne in mind that climate change may increase the likelihood of civil wars and acts of violence. In such circumstances, it is considered that the criteria for refugee status set out in the 1951 Refugee Convention may apply to persons displaced as a result of civil wars and acts of violence (UNHCR – Law and policy for protection and climate action).

However, in order to fully resolve the conceptual confusion, the term "climate refugee" must be firmly established in the literature in place of "climate migrant". Theriot (2025) identifies six criteria for being classified as a climate refugee. She emphasises that those who satisfy these criteria should be recognised as climate refugees;

- Forced migration,
- Temporary or permanent relocation,
- Crossing national borders,
- Being linked to climate change,
- Sudden or gradual environmental degradation,
- Human influence on environmental degradation is a necessary condition.

It is worth considering that recognising those who meet the above-mentioned criteria as "climate refugees" would resolve the confusion and ensure that those forced to relocate as a result of climate change enjoy full legal protection.

CONCLUSION

There is a need to establish a new definition for people forced to migrate due to climate change. In other words, rather than the internationally recognised term "climate migrant", the term "climate refugee" which has been used in recent years to highlight the importance of the issue should become the generally accepted term. This should not be viewed merely as an effort at conceptualisation. This is because, once the term "climate refugee" becomes the generally accepted term, people displaced by climate change will acquire legal rights and be afforded full protection.

Whilst it is recognised that visa requirements exist between countries due to climate change, it is also evident that these visa requirements do not provide full protection. As climate-related issues are a global concern, resolving them is a shared responsibility of the entire world.

The criteria for being recognised as a "climate refugee" must be defined, and these criteria must be accepted by international consensus. The idea of adding a supplementary protocol to the 1951 Refugee Convention is important. The proposed additional protocol should be designed in such a way that it removes the issue of "climate refugees" from a situation where the majority of countries might express reservations, and instead establishes a framework whereby countries fulfil their responsibilities in accordance with their levels of economic development.

REFERENCES

Arrhenius, S. (1896). On the influence of carbonic acid in the air upon the temperature of the ground. *The London, Edinburgh and Dublin Philosophical Magazine and Journal of Science, 41*(251), 237–276. DOI: 10.1080/14786449608620846

Callendar, G. S. (1938). The artificial production of carbon dioxide and its influence on temperature. *Quarterly Journal of the Royal Meteorological Society, 64*(275), 223–240. DOI: 10.1002/qj.49706427503

Cengiz, E. (2019). *Mega etkinlikler ve yerinden edilme – Olimpiyat oyunları etkisi.* On İki Levha Yayıncılık.

Cengiz, E., Aksoy, M., & Uğur, Ö. (2025b). *İklim krizi bağlamında yerinden edilmeleri yeniden düşünmek. In 5. Uluslararası Gaziantep Bilimsel Araştırmalar Kongresi.* İKSAD Publishing House.

Cengiz, E., Uğur, Ö., & Aksoy, M. (2025a). *Mültecilerin hukuki durumuna ilişkin sözleşme kapsamında iklim mültecileri. In 5. Uluslararası Gaziantep Bilimsel Araştırmalar Kongresi.* İKSAD Publishing House.

De Sherbinin, A. (n.d.). Climate impacts as drivers of migration. Migration Policy Institute. https://www.migrationpolicy.org/journal/feature/climate-impacts-drivers-migration

El-Hinnawi, E. (1985). *Environmental refugees.* United Nations Environment Programme.

Foote, E. (1856). Circumstances affecting the heat of sun's rays. *The American Journal of Science and Arts, 22*(66), 382–383.

Global Footprint Network. (n.d.). Past Earth Overshoot Days. https://overshoot.footprintnetwork.org/newsroom/past-earth-overshoot-days/

Groundswell. (2018). Groundswell: Preparing for internal climate migration. World Bank.

Groundswell. (2021). Groundswell 2.0: Acting on internal climate migration. World Bank.

Intergovernmental Panel on Climate Change. (1990). *Climate change: The IPCC scientific assessment.* Cambridge University Press.

International Organization for Migration. (2008). *World migration 2008: Managing labour mobility in the evolving global economy*. International Organization for Migration.

Keeling, C. D. (1958). The concentration and isotopic abundances of atmospheric carbon dioxide in rural areas. *Geochimica et Cosmochimica Acta, 13*(4), 322–334. DOI: 10.1016/0016-7037(58)90033-4

McDowell, C., & Morrell, G. (2010). *Displacement beyond conflict: An overview of forced migration in the developing world.* Berghahn Books. DOI: 10.3167/9781845457723

Sussman, C. M. (2023). A global migration framework under water: How can the international community protect climate refugees? *Chicago Journal of International Law*, *2*(1), 41–68.

United Nations Framework Convention on Climate Change. (n.d.). Conflict and climate. https://unfccc.int/news/conflict-and-climate

United Nations High Commissioner for Refugees. (1951). The 1951 Refugee Convention and 1967 Protocol relating to the status of refugees.

United Nations High Commissioner for Refugees. (2016). UNHCR viewpoint: "Refugee" or "migrant"—Which is right? https://www.unhcr.org/news/stories/unhcr-viewpoint-refugee-or-migrant-which-right

United Nations High Commissioner for Refugees. (n.d.). Law and policy for protection and climate action. https://www.unhcr.org/us/law-and-policy-protection-and-climate-action

United Nations High Commissioner for Refugees. (n.d.). Who is an "asylum-seeker"? https://www.unhcr.org/about-unhcr/who-we-protect/asylum-seekers

United Nations Security Council. (2007). Energy, security and climate.

Warner, K. (2012). Human migration and displacement in the context of adaptation to climate change: The Cancun Adaptation Framework and potential for future action. *Environment and Planning. C, Government & Policy*, *30*(6), 1061–1077. DOI: 10.1068/c1209j

Wolpert, J. (1966). Migration as an adjustment to environmental stress. *The Journal of Social Issues*, *22*(4), 92–102. DOI: 10.1111/j.1540-4560.1966.tb00552.x

Chapter 14
Identity, Belonging, and the Politics of Integration:
Contemporary Dynamics of Cambodian Migrant Experience in a Globalised World

Sovanna Huot
http://orcid.org/0009-0006-8335-442X
Department of Political Science, University of Delhi, New Delhi, India

Kimyut Phin
http://orcid.org/0009-0009-5667-7313
Department of English, University of Heng Samrin Thbongkhmum, Tboung Khmum, Cambodia

ABSTRACT

This chapter explores trends in Cambodian migration across different historical, sociological, and developmental contexts. It suggests that Cambodian mobility has shifted from relying on refugee and labour migration to involving more educated, skilled, and circular forms of movement. Utilising frameworks of identity, transnationalism, and integration, the chapter explores how migrants negotiate cultural belonging, preserve Khmer culture, and develop hybrid identities across host societies. It also examines how digital tools help migrants maintain emotional relationships, manage documentation, and strengthen diaspora networks. Additionally, the chapter discusses the development of host countries, emphasising how migrants contribute to their home countries through remittances, entrepreneurship, skill transfer, cultural diplomacy, and shifting narratives. Overall, it presents Cambodian migration as a continuous process of globalisation, ongoing identity negotiation, and nation-building.

DOI: 10.4018/979-8-3373-8500-6.ch014

I. INTRODUCTION

Cambodia has experienced the most rapid transformations in Southeast Asia over the past two decades. The nation has transitioned from a landscape characterized by civil conflicts, authoritarian governance, and limited global connectivity to a state of enhanced integration within regional and international mobility, labor, and cultural exchange systems. Hughes (2009) argues that the post-war development of Cambodia has been affected by both liberalization and reconstruction, while Ear (2013) argues that Cambodia's rapid growth came with macroeconomic stabilization and the country's integration into ASEAN in 1999. Specifically, Cambodia's integration into ASEAN has influenced the nation's socio-economic frameworks and the perceptions of Cambodian citizens regarding opportunities, mobility, and their sense of belonging and identity in the global context.

Economic growth has been a transformative force for Cambodia, highlighting the changes the country is currently undergoing. GDP growth has been around 7% for most of the 2010s, and has encouraged diversification of industries such as textiles, construction, and tourism (ADB, 2024; Chhair & Ung, 2016; Clark, 2020). In the same manner, Khamjalas (2024) states that the tourism sector, the growth of economic zones, and foreign direct investment have created labor demand and led to rural-to-urban cross-border migration. Education has also changed rapidly. Peou (2021) and Kheang (2024) point out that post-conflict reconstruction led to rapid growth in secondary and tertiary education enrolment, and Sen (2019) shows that scholarship programs, private universities, and international exchanges created a generation of Cambodians focused on the global economy. The growth of human capital has also contributed immensely to migration, as people with education and training are now seeking employment opportunities beyond their borders (Fielding, 2015). Cambodia is a member of ASEAN, a significant contributor to regional mobility. The creation of the AEC (ASEAN Economic Community) has encouraged the movement of people, especially professionals, within Southeast Asia, though the movement is not equal (Rigg, 2016). On the other hand, Co et al. (2025) argue that improved transport, economic corridors, and visa agreements have increased cross-border movement between Cambodia, Thailand, Laos, and Vietnam, marking a shift from necessary movement to seeking opportunities. Cambodia is now moving beyond being a refugee transit point to participating in regional labor markets, transnational education, and global trade networks.

Bordering on a new era of global integration, Cambodia's challenges with post-conflict recovery have deep implications for its sense of identity. For example, Derks (2010) and Yeoh and Ramdas (2014) propose that it draws on a psychological mechanism that restructures how Cambodians envision themselves. In the digital age, virtual and physical migration happen simultaneously, making Cambodia unique.

Historically, Cambodia was mainly a source of migrants with lower education. Now, there's an outflow of highly educated citizens with higher expectations, marking a new era. The rise in educational and occupational migration from Cambodia is significant. Legally, both the volume and purpose of out-migration have increased, especially for work. Hugo (2014) notes this in a review of bilateral agreements between Australia and Asia that have launched formalized recruitment processes in exchange for the labor of Cambodian citizens. In the same way, Sophal (2009) notes this increase at the upper end of the migration employment system, where there is less wage labor and more professional and technical apprenticeships, as well as seasonal contracted labor. The phenomenon has fundamentally changed the conceptual framework for migration from Cambodia; educated migrants are more than laboring survivors. Furthermore, educational migration has been center stage. According to the Map of Fong and Shibuya (2020), literate migrants are gaining mobility scholarships, especially to China, South Korea, Australia, and Europe. In this regard, migrants have become part of even the global middle-class educational aspirations of Waters (2016).

The steadily expanding Cambodian diaspora communities are changing. Lee (2010) and Chan (2015) argue that the community's expansion is in the United States, France, Australia, and Canada, and describes a generational process of establishing community associations, Buddhist temples, and student organizations, thereby continuing Khmer culture. Lucas (2001) describes the Cambodian diaspora community in newer host countries, Japan, South Korea, and Singapore, where the Cambodian community is in the early stages and marks the digital community, the young migrant labor force, and the circulation of temporary work contracts. Hall (1994) notes that identity is never a fixed construct but is always a work in progress, the result of difference, displacement, and articulation. Similarly, instead of defining migrants in a singular form, Vertovec and Wessendorf (2010) describe migrants as having multi-local identities that comprise their place of origin, their place of settlement, and their transnational connections. Cambodian migrants face a unique negotiation in which they must navigate a complex blend of Khmer culture and global influences. As migrants, it is possible to adjust to the host country's desires and expectations while simultaneously holding onto symbolic ties to the homeland through food, language, ritual practices, and emotional attachments (Frohlick, 2013).

This is intensified with globalization. Through the mediation of migration, technology, and imagination, Appadurai (1996) posits that global cultural flows deepen the complexity of cultural crossings, ultimately forming new scopes of belonging. As Cambodian migrants, they remain actively involved in cultural flows through Facebook, TikTok, and Telegram, as well as in diaspora media that help retain cultural memory even amid dislocation. There has been growing recognition of the role of hybrid identity spaces created by Khmer migrants through the use of digital platforms in both global diasporic and local spaces (Lim, 2023). Therefore, it can be assumed that identity negotiation is not a singular process, but has a broad scope. Along with the reproduction and preservation of Khmer culture, the migrants' identity as Cambodians encompasses a reinterpretation of what it means to be Cambodian. Rashid (2025) states that transnational identity is a combination of both pride and ambivalence: pride in having a continuum of culture and ambivalent undercurrents formed by displacement, especially through experiences of discrimination, language barriers, and class inequities. This chapter has five primary objectives, each guided by the transformations mentioned earlier:

1. Identify the socio-cultural impacts of each of the host societies and how these impacts affect the self-perception of Cambodian migrants and the host society analysis.
2. Identify and analyze the Cambodian diaspora community in host societies, focusing on the analysis of the community in the diaspora, the community's host society, and religious and cultural activities.
3. Identify and analyze the host society's legal, socio-political, and economic structures and how these structures affect socio-political and economic integration.
4. Identify the socio-economic contributions of migrant workers and the socio-economic contributions of migrant workers.
5. Analyze the migration of the Global South with particular reference to the migration of South-East Asia.

This study is significant for several interconnected reasons. Firstly, it examines a gap in migration scholarship. Brickell (2020) notes that Cambodian migration studies focus on vulnerability and exploitation, whereas contributors to agency, education, innovation, and cultural diplomacy are ignored. This study focuses on identity formation and developmental contributions, reframing Cambodian migrants as active architects of global belonging. Secondly, the chapter offers a theoretical contribution.

2. HISTORICAL AND CONTEMPORARY CAMBODIAN MIGRATION PATTERNS

2.1 Historical Waves of Migration

The most emotionally charged and well-documented phase of Cambodian migration occurred in the late 1970s and early 1980s. During this time period, the Cambodian civil war, forced collectivization, and genocidal violence led to the

Khmer Rouge regime and the overwhelming displacement of close to two million Cambodians (Chandler, 1979). Chandler (1993) suggests that the Pol Pot era caused one of the most extreme social disruptions in modern Southeast Asia, affecting the most basic and essential elements of Khmer identity. Hence, this social rupture shaped the pattern of movement, as survival was the most important reason for displacement.

Cambodians fled to Thailand, and camps like Khao-I-Dang and Site Two processed them. Heder (1979) and Heder and Ledgerwood (2016) state that these camps were not only humanitarian spaces; they were also political spaces where new community identities were formed and changed in response to Cold War geopolitics and international humanitarianism. Mabbett and Chandler (1995) also argue that these were spaces where the displaced people constructed and altered Khmer culture and where ritual practices and the dominant culture got engaged, aided, and governed. Then, large-scale resettlement to third countries, such as the US, Australia, Canada, and France, began. Ong (2003) shows that for most of the refugees who resettled to the Global North, there was immense cultural dislocation, alienation, and the complexities of language and race, resulting in trauma and relocation narratives. For the US, which became home to more than 150,000 Cambodians, Schlund-Vials (2012) states that Cambodian-American identity is the outcome of intergenerational negotiation between the identities of first-generation survivors and those of transnationally educated, culturally hybrid millennials who were social, political, and cultural activists.

As a result of the UN-led reconstruction following the 1991 Paris Peace Agreements, Cambodia gradually transitioned from a humanitarian crisis to a developmental recovery state. With the return of stability in the region, labor migration became a phenomenon of mobility. Derks (2008) states that escalating impoverishment, unequal development in rural areas, and the absence of employment opportunities in Cambodia led young Cambodians to migrate to countries such as Thailand, Malaysia, and South Korea in search of employment. Unlike refugee migrations, this type of migration was primarily economic and often undocumented (Bonjour, 2014). The first Cambodian workers to migrate laboriously went to the bordering provinces of Thailand. Due to insufficient documentation, many Cambodian migrants who crossed borders informally to work in construction, fisheries, agriculture, domestic work, and other sectors were absorbed by Chairattana and Khanawiwat (2019). Such movements bring to mind what Kelly (2013) refers to as circulatory migration, in which migrants engage in temporary return migration to avoid permanent settlement in Thailand.

In the early 2000s, Malaysia and Taiwan became new destinations for migrant workers in factories and domestic work. Ford et al. (2012) believe this was the genesis of the labor brokerage system, where the first formal recruitment agencies emerged to contract, train, and collect migration fees. Although such systems provided formal job prospects, they also created new forms of exploitation, including debt bondage, confiscation of identity documents, violations of labor rights, and the like. The Cambodian labor migration during this period was, as Platt et al. (2017) have argued, the most modern and unique of its kind, but also exemplified the most exploitation and social exclusion.

2.2 Modern Migration Dynamics

Informal migration systems become semi-formal when a country partially develops legal mechanisms to regulate migration. This is the case for Cambodia after it acceded to ASEAN in 1999 and after it participated in the ASEAN Economic Community in 2015. Piper (2017) argues that ASEAN regionalism reframes labor not as a national surplus but as a regional resource, and crafting agreements for the temporary movement of labor allows regional states to keep host-country control. In that regard, Thailand developed formalized recruitment systems for Cambodian migrant workers in the agriculture, manufacturing, fisheries, and domestic care sectors. Sophal (2009) argues that migration from Cambodia to Thailand has become one of the most important labor corridors in Southeast Asia, influenced by bilateral agreements, nationality verification mechanisms, and regional migration governance frameworks. Although there are still irregular documentation and workplace vulnerabilities, Oishi (2017) argues that the employment conditions have improved due to the introduction of wage regulations, the inclusion of social security, and the establishment of cross-border social protection. In Vietnam and Laos, migration is on a smaller scale but is culturally embedded. Rigg (2016) identifies the persistence of everyday transnationalism as a result of historical kinship relations, borderland economies, and shared livelihoods around the Mekong.

Yeoh et al. (2018) suggest that Asian migration systems are shifting towards differentiated mobility, in which the acquisition of higher education enables the attainment of professional and/or permanent residency, with the possibility of returning home. South Korea and Japan are also popular. According to Park (2024), many Cambodians are attracted to technical internships, factory work, and agricultural contracts. In contrast, Australia and Europe are common destinations for Cambodian postgraduate students. In their study, Walker (2012) and Fong and Shibuya (2020) assert that the Australia Awards, Erasmus, and Chinese government scholarships have significantly increased the number of Cambodians studying postgraduate programs overseas. Educational migration also creates a form of cultural capital mobility (Tan & Chen, 2025; Waters, 2016). Students learn to navigate the global economy and develop social skills and networks, alongside their academic qualifications and a multidimensional identity. Many can secure highly skilled employment, which, in turn, contributes to what Saxenian (2006) termed brain circulation in Cambodia, where talent and knowledge move internationally while also providing economic and innovative contributions to the home country.

Return migration is increasingly pivotal in Cambodian migration. In the past, most migrants relocated overseas and stayed there permanently. Currently, migrants return home, bringing new wealth, knowledge, and international connections (Aletheiani, 2025). According to Naudé et al. (2017), returnees foster activity in entrepreneurship and the public sector, as well as in development, culture, and the creative economy. Returned labor migrants work in agribusiness, real estate, and retail; engineers in infrastructure and digital sectors; academics in teaching, research, and consultancy at think tanks. However, the return journey has challenges. Long (2013) notes that returnees struggle with a range of identity conflicts stemming from overseas expectations and local communities' social standards. Zapata-Barrero and Rezaei (2020) state that returnees can be used as a means of cultural communication and that they have a new view of work, a new attitude towards technology, and a new concept of citizenship.

2.3 Cambodia's Development and Global Image

Cambodia's development has changed migration patterns, self-perceptions, and perceptions of Cambodian migrants. For years, narratives on Cambodia have depicted genocides, poverty, and humanitarian crises. Edwards (2007) states that Cambodia has been constructed through Western media as a suffering nation. This media representation has created stereotypes of Cambodian refugees. Recently, however, economic growth, urban development, and cultural resurgence have shifted Cambodia's global image positively. Cambodia has been rebranded as an emerging nation thanks to the growth of its Angkor tourism, garment exports, ASEAN diplomacy, and the construction of skyscrapers in Phnom Penh. Strangio (2014) states that Cambodia has entered an era of developmental ambition, shifting from a humanitarian discourse to a regional market focus.

Perceptions of host countries have shifted. Despite stereotypes, Cambodians are now seen as skilled migrants in Japan, students in Australia, entrepreneurs in Paris, and digital migrants in Seoul. According to Ford (2024), recognition of labor contributions in Southeast Asia, driven by ASEAN integration, has created a sense of pride among mobile workers. Cambodian migrants navigate belonging through a history of displacement and an embodiment of achievement. The Cambodian migration experience has been shaped by trauma and survival, then later by economic necessity, and now increasingly by education, skills, and global interconnectedness (Tong, 2011). Each stage produces different forms of belonging, community building, and identity construction. Therefore, to understand Cambodian migrant identity today, it must be examined in the context of the complex history of mobility. This is where refugees became diasporas, laborers became regional workers, students became global citizens, and return migrants became transformative agents (Berry, 1997). Contemporary Cambodian migration is the latest trend in a long history of resilience, adaptability, and aspiration, as outlined in Table 1.

Table 1. Historical and Contemporary Cambodian Migration Patterns

Component	Summary
Historical Waves	Refugee migration (1970s–80s), post-Khmer Rouge displacement to the U.S., France, Canada, Australia.
Labor Migration (1990s–2000s)	Economic push factors to informal movement to Thailand, Malaysia, and South Korea, work-driven survival mobility.
Modern Migration Dynamics	Increasing skilled labour and student migration to Asia, Europe, and Australia.
Return Migration	Growing trend of returnees bringing capital, skills, and networks to brain circulation.
Key Significance	Cambodia's mobility evolved from trauma, livelihood and global opportunity.

3. CONSTRUCTING AN IDENTITY AS A CAMBODIAN MIGRANT

Identity construction among Cambodian migrants is still ongoing and remains complex. For Cambodians living outside Cambodia, their identity is influenced by memories of their homeland, the expectations of host societies, and the pressures of economic survival and the opportunities of global belonging. A well-established view is that identity emerges, develops, and is constructed through differing and transformative processes (Hall, 1994). This view suggests that identity is produced rather than merely a possession. For example, in relation to migrant identities, the term multi-local describes identities that are formed, constructed, and contextualized in both the origin and the destination (Vertovec & Wessendorf, 2010).

Cambodian migrants have to balance their lived Khmer experiences and values with those of their host society and learn to negotiate what each society values most. Schiller et al. (1995) claim that migrants are not simply culture-less actors but transmigrants who develop distinct identities across locations. In that sense, the Cambodians must manage and negotiate the expectations that come with *sampeah* respect, the ethics of Buddhism, the responsibility to one's family, and the hierarchical structure of society. Most Khmer migrants do what Derks (2010) and Yeoh and Ramdas (2014) call identity work involves migrants maintaining Khmer cultural practices while adopting new behaviors for integration, such as punctuality, workplace responsibility, and technology use in South Korea or Japan, alongside celebrating Khmer traditions and speaking Khmer at home.

While many details contribute to cultural continuity, the day-to-day aspects of this process are especially compelling. Edwards (2007) identifies one of the primary features of belonging to a culture, or community, as the ability to use a particular language. Because language is central to cultural belonging, Cambodian diasporic families often advocate for children to use Khmer to preserve intergenerational cohesion. However, the success of language retention efforts depends on the community context. For example, in her analysis of the Khmer diasporic community in Long Beach, California, Kang and Park (2018) found that the community's religious, educational, and media resources promote Khmer language retention. In contrast, dispersed European Cambodian refugee communities are losing it. Language loss is separate from cultural identity but may lead to forming new communities beyond mother-tongue fluency. Religion also influences social structuring through Cambodian Buddhism. As Ebihara et al. (1994) noted, Khmer language schools and dance groups are part of cultural activities by Buddhist temples in host countries. During festivals like Pchum Ben, Kathina, and Khmer New Year, Cambodian migrants reenact homeland rituals, exercising memory and pride. Temples also foster intergenerational relations and reduce transgenerational conflict by providing a collective space that eases relations between Khmer conservatism and global youth culture. In the words of Nguyen (2024), the diasporic communities also use food as a vehicle for expressing their identity. The scents of amok, kuy teav, and somlor machu are examples of an autobiography of a collective community.

Identity for first-generation migrants includes memory, survival, and obligation, while second-generation Cambodian youth focus on negotiation, aspiration, and future imagination. Born, raised, educated, and socialized in the host country, their identity centers on choices rather than losses. According to Zhou and Bankston (1998), the second generation's identity results from selective acculturation, in which the youth of a particular society adopt the norms of the host society while retaining their ethnic culture through family and community structures. There are second-generation Cambodians in the U.S., France, and Australia, and their identity development varies widely. Some embrace their Khmer culture, while others feel no connection, and many experience a pendulum effect, swinging between inclusion and exclusion. According to Schlund-Vials (2012), from the point of view of youth identity, the powerful influence of intergenerational trauma, memory of wars, and the narrative of refugees is particularly notable in the emerging communities that are the result of resettlement.

Cambodian youth in East Asia are in a unique position to construct their own identities. They can do so without many resources or institutional support because most of their parents are temporary contract workers (Ledgerwood, 1996). Many Southeast Asian children bear the weight of difficult and emotionally taxing identity negotiation as they deal with a combination of cultural isolation, communication barriers, and the impact of their racial difference, as Kwon (2022) illustrates the case of Southeast Asian migrants in East Asia. While the process can be difficult, Cambodian youth in the East Asia region express their identity formation in positive ways. In creative ways, such as the active reformation of Khmer culture in their dance and rap groups, online language lessons, and youth associations, and the creation of contemporary culture online, Khmer culture is being actively reformed to the present. Such a view of identity aligns with Hall (2003), who argues that identity in the diaspora is the result of active cultural creation and is not simply bequeathed to an individual or a community.

In today's world, a person's identity is tied not only to a specific geographical location but also to a virtual one. For Cambodians who migrated, their virtual identity also involves using social networking and messaging platforms like Telegram and TikTok. Lim (2023) notes that a digital diaspora fosters 'networked belonging' by enabling migrants to situate themselves within multiple cultures. Cambodian migrants also participate in various activities, such as live temple ceremony streams, Khmer drama, online political debates, and digital remittances. Such activities support and reinforce their cultures and help sustain emotional sentiments. Supporting each other online is also possible. For instance, Bylander (2015) notes that migrant communities on Facebook have used their networks to share information on employment opportunities, visas, housing, recruitment agencies, workers' rights, and more. This is also what Madianou and Miller (2013) termed as ambient co-presence, the sense of a social compact created without the actual presence of people.

Support networks are evident among Malaysian domestic workers, Japanese students, and diaspora Khmer youth, who express their cultural identity through Khmer meme pages to foster Khmer culture. Symbolic attachment is particularly strong as the physical return is the exception rather than the norm. Nations are, as Anderson (2008) puts it, imagined communities and are maintained through memory and storytelling. Cambodian migrants practice symbolic nationhood through the display of flags, classical dance, apsara imagery, icons of the Buddha, and participation in diaspora festivals. In exile, migrants curate and reinterpret their heritage to foster a sense of attachment and emotional investment. For most migrants, the homeland is more than a geographical space; it is a moral reference point. While transnational identities are often described as fragmented, Rashid (2025) argues that they are emotionally anchored in the homeland through nostalgia, family obligations, and ritual duties. Remittances embody moral duty and citizenship, extending beyond economic needs. Return visits for Pchum Ben or ancestral rituals are more than cultural acts; they represent kinship and spiritual ties. Even second-generation young people, who might feel disconnected, show attachment through heritage journeys, Khmer tattoos, and digital cultural expressions.

Transnational attachment and belonging are marked by ambiguity. Migrants often feel longing and loss and may feel suspended in an in-between space. Parreñas (2005) suggests that migrants inhabit a space of transnational melancholia in which emotional bonds are strong despite the absence of physical presence. While migratory tensions may be painful, they can also be productive. Such tensions create a fertile ground for hybrid creativity, such as in diaspora poetry, fusion cuisine, transnational activism, and bilingual theatre. Thus, Cambodian identity in the diaspora is not simply preserved; it is transformed, as depicted in Table 2.

Table 2. Identity Construction Among Cambodian Migrants

Component	Summary
Cultural Identity	A hybrid belonging between Khmer tradition and global culture
Heritage Maintenance	Language, religion, food, and festivals sustain cultural continuity
Youth Identity	Second-generation forms bicultural identity, negotiates belonging in host-country society
Agency and Expression	Youth assert pride through cultural production, education, and online creativity
Transnational Belonging	Digital communication sustains emotional connection to homeland and heritage

4. HOST SOCIETY INTEGRATION POLITICS

For Cambodian migrants, integration becomes a highly political process, with differential impacts shaped by the host society's migration labor regime, citizenship acquisition, cultural recognition, racialization, diasporic community, and transnational identity. While many Cambodians move in search of opportunity, their experiences abroad depend on how host countries define belonging and worthiness for permanent inclusion. According to de Haas et al. (2019), integration is relational and moves beyond assimilation into a dominant mainstream to capture the flow of migrant agency in relation to the structural determinants within the host society. For Cambodian migrants, such agency differs across regions, from labor-induced mobility in the ASEAN region to the more liberal, open, and multicultural frameworks of the Western world to the more regulated, temporally confined zones of East Asia.

Integration differs in each country. Host societies sponsor distinct models of migrant inclusion: multicultural, assimilation, segmented, or temporary labor. Each constructs a different Cambodian migrant identity. Within ASEAN, migration frameworks tend to be labor rather than citizenship-focused. Piper (2017) argues that ASEAN mobility prioritizes economic profit over social integration, producing a paradox in which migrants are accepted as workers but not as people. In Thailand, Cambodia's most important destination, migrant workers have only legal routes for temporary jobs via MoUs, while permanent settlement is nearly impossible. Chairattana and Khanawiwat (2019) argue that the regularisation of programs strengthens labor protection, but seldom grants migrants any political or civic rights. Here, integration is rather pragmatic.

Migrants are not social outsiders; they integrate into society by learning the dominant workplace language and culture (Bonjour & Chauvin, 2018). In Malaysia and Singapore, Cambodian domestic workers are valorized economically as described by Parreñas (2005) as "servant citizenship", but socially, men are not recognized. Often migrants are included in the house, but socially excluded outside. Therefore, inclusion is integration of private spheres, not in public ones. Japan and South Korea are highly selective in regulating labor migration. Both countries, according to Park (2024), rely extensively on Southeast Asian workers through trainee and EPS programs, treating them as temporary labor rather than potential citizens. Integration is predicated on discipline, supervision, and labor productivity. Migrants must do the work, learn the language of the employer, comply with workplace hierarchies, and, in most cases, are excluded from permanent residence. Oishi (2017) argues that social integration in East Asia is "conditional." Economic participation is the only route to social inclusion.

Migrants retain a certain level of agency despite limitations. In the Cambodian diaspora, communities in Osaka, Ibaraki, and Busan organize temple festivals, create student networks, and form Facebook support groups. These activities help build a community within an immigration system that promotes temporary stays and discourages long-term integration. Oh et al. (2025) note that the promotion of a diasporic identity blooms outside the realm of legality. Social flourishing of diasporic identity is largely evident within the legal constraints of the Asia-Pacific region. In the European and North American contexts, Lee's (2010) observations apply to the social flourishing of diasporic identity within the legal and social frameworks of a fully inclusive citizenship. Kymlicka (2011) notes that citizenship is vested within a nation. Multiculturalism recognizes minority rights and cultural diversity. Ong (2003) describes the Cambodian refugee family contexts as a confluence of extreme poverty, trauma of displacement, and welfare citizenship, which shaped a form of early integration that was entirely reliant on the state and its systems. This was not a form of integration that empowered families. Schlund-Vials (2012) describes the degree to which Cambodian second-generation migrants are racialized as Asian or ethnic minority to the exclusion of their national origin. This process is a source of alienation from the nation-state. Within varying geopolitical contexts, Cambodian migrants experience integration through distinct regimes:

- Dominant Model and Implications by Region

- Labor-based temporary mobility in the ASEAN region offers limited rights and prioritizes mobility over settlement.
- East Asia offers controlled inclusion and conditional rights. In this region, work integration is prioritized over citizenship.
- In Europe and North America, multiculturalism offers citizenship with rights, but retains racialized belonging.

The political economies of migration shape international mobility. When migrants are viewed as workers, their rights are limited, while as settlers, their belonging is mediated through race and identity. Their legal standing, such as Cambodians in Thailand or Malaysia, shows how they participate in society, often depending on renewal, employer sponsorship, or legal mandates. Bylander (2015) says that when legal clarity is in short supply, migrants manage a conditional existence, where the fear of being arrested or deported is ever-present. As a result of such insecurity, the sense of identity and belonging is often constructed outside the borders of the host nation and is instead anchored in a transnational framework. Under South Korea's Employment Permit System (EPS), migrant workers experience employer-controlled job access and job-market control through employer extensions. As Kim (2021) states, such schemes focus on extracting economic resources rather than recognizing migrant workers as social entities. Temporary social adjustments rarely restore citizenship. The EU follows a similar pattern: France uses family reunification and naturalization for citizenship, but integration involves moralized criteria like language and civic tests, reflecting standards of homogeneous societies. Legality is control, with Cambodian migrants facing varied legal routes depending on location.

- United States, France, Canada, and Australia: citizenship is attainable and opens participation in the political sphere with the same rights as naturally born citizens. Cambodians' access to citizenship drove the change of Cambodian-American communities from a refugee enclave to an active diaspora community (Chan, 2015).
- Japan & South Korea: citizenship is unattainable, and where residency is difficult and long-term integration (if ever) remains an unattainable aspiration. Oishi (2017) describes East Asia's perspective as 'guest labor citizenship' whereby migrant workers are useful, but are not welcome as integrated members of society.
- Thailand, Malaysia, Singapore: Integration is labor market dependent; pathways to citizenship are nearly non-existent. Migrants are temporary circulators, not settlers.

Citizenship access expresses global mobility hierarchies: Western states offer settlement with integration, while Asian market economies offer employment without incorporation. Integration is not simply a legal concept; it is lived and manifested in temples, markets, classrooms, workplaces, and online spaces. Cambodian migrants leverage parallel structures of community-building alongside state frameworks to create a sense of belonging. Within the diaspora, Buddhist temples are the most significant social anchors. Ebihara et al. (1994) and Ebihara (2018) state that temples are miniature cultural states that regulate morality, sponsor community festivals, mediate family disputes, and teach Khmer civics.

Community associations also facilitate social inclusion. Frohlick (2013) states that Khmer cultural associations in the United States and Canada offer legal aid, job placement services, mental health assistance, and tutoring. Cambodian student unions in France and the UK blend heritage and French civic engagement, exemplifying what Werbner (2002) terms diasporic citizenship. In South Korea and Japan, the Cambodian worker collectives formed more recently and disseminate information regarding contracts, rights, unions, and remittances. These create counter-integration structures (Oh et al., 2025), in which solidarity is built laterally through migrant networks rather than inclusively through state participation. Community life offers alternative forms of belonging, even when formal integration is limited. Socially embedded, legally temporary migrants create what Oh et al. (2025) call parallel public structures of integration. They establish markets for prahok, dance troupes for apsara dances, football clubs, and Khmer-language Bible or Dharma groups. Perceptions of migrants contribute significantly to their integration. The early portrayals of Cambodia, genocide, poverty, and corruption, shaped the perception of Cambodians abroad. Edwards (2007) comments on Western media portray Cambodia as trauma-focused, neglecting other Khmer identities and reducing it to suffering. Refugees are viewed with pity, not respect.

The country's developmental achievements are beginning to change this perception. Urban development, the rising middle class, tech innovation, and Phnom Penh's cultural visibility show that the narrative of being a backward nation is false. Strangio (2014) argues that Cambodia now shows ambition and competitiveness within ASEAN. This is a significant change in migrants' identity. Once migrants see their nation improving rather than stagnating, they begin to hold themselves in higher esteem. Young migrants from Cambodia have begun to express their identity with more confidence, sporting Khmer scarf patterns on their clothing, hip-hop with tro and roneat, and promoting Khmer cuisine. The perception of host societies has changed with the success of these migrants. Cambodians are now seen as hard workers in Japanese factories, top-performing students in Australia, successful entrepreneurs in Paris with their bai sach chrouk restaurants, and digital workers in Seoul speaking fluent Korean. Abubakar and Islam (2025) note that achievers from the diaspora are seen as cultural diplomats as they increase respect and soft power. Migrants represent countries, not governments. Fighting stereotypes is political, not only for the sake of feeling good. It positions Cambodians as professionals, pioneers, and cultural creators.

Integration politics influence how Cambodian migrants live, work, and see their futures abroad. In ASEAN, they lack citizenship; in East Asia, they work under conditional tolerance; in Western countries, they face limited rights and racialization. Diaspora communities challenge legal limits by building belonging through temples, associations, and digital networks. As the nation-state develops, stereotypes weaken; successful migrants reshape their environment and define their identity beyond survival. Thus, integration is a disruptive process seeking recognition, dignity, and control over narratives, as shown in Table 3.

Table 3. Politics of Integration in Host Societies

Component	Summary
ASEAN Integration	Temporary labour mobility; rights limited and citizenship rare
East Asia Model	Controlled inclusion — labour valued, belonging conditional
Western Multicultural Contexts	Accessible pathways to residency/citizenship, yet racialised social integration
Community Institutions	Temples, associations, and diaspora networks enable social inclusion beyond state structures.
Shifting Narratives	Cambodia's development improves global perception and migrant confidence

5. DIGITAL DIASPORA AND TRANSNATIONAL NETWORKS

Migration from Cambodia has become a far more involved process than in the past. Digital technologies have transformed the process from a unilateral removal of the individual from their home country to a transnational experience. Earlier generations would stay in touch with their home country through letters and remittances, with occasional visits from migrants. Today's migrants engage in a continuous transnational digital space that incorporates their migrant identities with other elements of their transnational experience. Appadurai (1996) postulates that electronic media reinvigorates communities' imaginations worldwide and reshapes technoscapes.

New migration-related cultural practices among Cambodians include using digital infrastructure, such as social media platforms like Facebook, TikTok, YouTube, and Telegram. These sites provide Cambodians with spaces for elaborate storytelling, memory construction, and heritage preservation; Miller and Slater (2020) talk about such places as virtual homes. Through social media, migrants have found a sense of cultural belonging in their new home. For transnational Cambodians, Facebook has become the most important social networking site. Lim (2023) claims that Cambodian Facebook networks are not only social but also political; they discuss social and political issues related to national development, stream devotional and cultural celebrations in temples, and share cultural material. South Korean and Thai migrants, as well as parents and Monks, from Khmer New Year live-stream celebrations while they preach and conduct devotional or cultural services.

YouTube playlists serve culturally-preserving functions within the diaspora by offering cooking tutorials, historical documentaries, storytelling podcasts, and Cambodian-language teaching videos. Memory and identity are intertwined, and as Nguyen (2024) explains, food and narratives are vehicles for identity; migrants remember by documenting themselves preparing samlor korko, sewing hol kben, or chanting Buddhist prayers. Telegram groups, by contrast, allow for information sharing about jobs, migration risks, visas, and emergency fundraisers. The unity of the digital diaspora is born out of cultural pride and practical reasons. The online storytelling of the diaspora serves to create collective memory. Videos such as Life in Korea as a Khmer Worker or Growing Up Cambodian-American are examples of migrants documenting their experiences and creating what Hall (2003) terms identity narratives. These are the stories of a people, for a people, and by a people, unlike the dominant identity narrative of the colonizers. These stories defy historical silence; they give migrants space to articulate their joy, struggles, ambitions, and transformations.

Digital networks also act as scaffolding for migrant survival, workforce mobility, and skill acquisition. For students in precarious economies, information is a lifeline; for workers, networks are gateways to opportunity. Bylander (2015) argues that contemporary Cambodian migration is sustained, in addition to remittances, by the circulation of information about contracts, wages, border crossings, and recruitment agencies. On Facebook and Telegram, Cambodian migrants have established job-hunting groups that advertise factory jobs in Thailand, seasonal farming positions in Japan, domestic work in Malaysia, and Internships in South Korea. Platt et al. (2017) state that these networks defy broker hierarchies by fostering peer-to-peer knowledge transfer. Migrants share information on workers' rights, union contacts, and how to avoid exploitation. Digital networks, therefore, perform a regulatory function where formal regulations do not exist. Some groups offer support through fundraising efforts during crises. In cases of illness, deportation, or workplace accidents, diaspora networks act quickly. Horst (2006) labels it as transnational moral obligation, the moral imperative to assist each other within a borderless context. For international students, digital networks enable collaboration on academic work, provide mental support, and guide them through the educational journey. The Cambodian Student Associations in Korea, Japan, Australia, and France also run Facebook groups that provide information on scholarships, updates on visa regulations, accommodation, and academic culture. Waters (2016) asserts that these networks are the basis for acquiring cultural capital, enabling youth to utilize a transnational educational experience in pursuit of global employment.

Online educational platforms and resources allow youth to learn skills not part of a degree, such as programming, languages (including Japanese and Korean), IELTS tutoring, and entrepreneurship, through videos from peers and webinars hosted by the diaspora. This phenomenon represents what Saxenian (2006) describes as brain circulation, the skills of a diaspora that return to the transnational networks of their origin, in this case, Cambodia. When formal social integration is missing, informal and digital networks offer support, belonging, and security. Digital diaspora networks connect migrants across borders, making the Internet a social structure for movement and care. Transnational migration separates families physically but keeps them emotionally connected. Parreñas (2005) writes about this phenomenon in migrant families as transnational intimacy and describes it as sustained by telephone calls, video calls, remittances, and ritual communication. Cambodian families are strong examples of what Transnational intimacy looks like in practice. Remote live video dinners, daily voice messages, and shared photos of kids are ways that Cambodian families mitigate the emotional and spatial distance of migration. "Ambient co-presence" is the phenomenon used by Madianou and Miller (2013) to describe the text of a mother's digital presence in Malaysia helping her child in Phnom Penh via Messenger, and a father in Korea live-streaming Buddhist prayers for parents to join. Digital co-presence lessens separation but adds emotional and financial duties. Some parents view cultural transmission as a barrier, sharing traditional dances and proverbs. YouTube tutorials serve as digital temples in the Khmer community, helping preserve culture online. For instance, a child in France can learn Pchum Ben on TikTok, and a youth in Japan can access Khmer slang through memes. While digital retention is common, signs of digital assimilation emerge, especially when cultural exposure makes youth feel distant, with cultures inherited asymmetrically. Despite language barriers, emotional bonds often remain. (Rashid, 2025).

Instead of signaling loss, this shows transformation: identity becomes hybrid, digitally sustained, and self-interpreted. Many Cambodian children are left with their grandparents as their parents are migrant workers. Such instances are referred to as global care chains by Hochschild (1983), where cross-border emotion work is performed. Video calls symbolize parental presence, remittances show love, and stories transmit cultural identity without co-residency. The Cambodian digital diaspora shows migration involves digital connections, reshaping economies and identities, offering new ways to connect with home. Migrants shape their identities via social media, build economies, access education, and develop skills. Digital networks keep families culturally and emotionally linked. The transnational self involves communication, memory, and creativity. As Table 4 shows, technology enhances a country's origin, not replaces it.

Table 4. Digital Diaspora and Transnational Networks

Component	Summary
Identity Online	Facebook, TikTok, and YouTube are used as platforms for cultural storytelling.
Cultural Continuity	Digital sharing preserves tradition, language, and ritual memory.
Digital Support Networks	Online job-sharing, student groups, and skill-sharing communities enhance migrant mobility.
Transnational Family	Emotional intimacy is maintained via video calls, messaging, and livestream rituals.
Heritage for Youth	Children learn culture digitally — a hybrid identity carried across generations.

6. THE ROLE OF CAMBODIAN MIGRANTS IN THE COUNTRY'S DEVELOPMENT

The contribution of Cambodian migrants to the development of their home country is complex, as they help build the country economically, socially, intellectually, culturally, and diplomatically. Earlier studies of Cambodian migration focused on migrants' vulnerabilities and exploitation, whereas more recent studies highlight migrants' ability to influence, innovate, and engage on a transnational scale. Levitt (1998) describes migrants as social remitters because they not only send money but also new social ideas, values, and practices, as well as new skills. In Cambodia, social remittances stimulate the local economy, change how citizens perceive their government, and demand new professional and managerial behaviors. Thus, migrants are not on the periphery of development; instead, they are key architects of their country's development.

A significant part of the Cambodian migrants' contributions comes from remittances. Samreth and Aiba (2026) say remittances have helped provide household livelihood security, especially in rural areas where jobs are scarce. Families use remitted income to build houses, purchase land, pay for education, invest in farming, and pay for health care. Samreth and Aiba (2026) indicated that remittances help poor rural families and boost consumer spending. This then helps circulate money through the economy, into building construction, and into the purchase of motorbikes, phones, and food. In rural areas of Cambodia, remittances help build roads and rural homes in provinces such as Banteay Meanchey, Kampong Cham, Prey Veng, and Siem Reap. Sophal (2009) claims that money used to build rural homes helps raise the standard of living in rural areas and provides jobs for builders, carpenters, and suppliers. Migration also becomes an individual development strategy; however, it also helps drive the rural economy. The economic impact is primarily not physical. Bylander (2015) argues that remittance dependence increases the family's educational expectations, delays marriage, and increases female empowerment. Income from jobs in Bangkok or Busan also increases the family's aspirations for life.

Many returnee Cambodian migrants are also returning to Cambodia to set up businesses. Naudé et al. (2017) say that returnee migrants often use the money and skills acquired from working in another country to set up businesses. This helps create jobs in that area and is positive because it fosters more businesses, strengthens the economy, and helps people manage their businesses. Returned migrants commonly establish:

- Global-style mini-marts, cafes, and restaurants
- Korean and Japanese-style bakeries and beauty salons
- Farms that utilize innovative seed technologies and/or new irrigation techniques
- Information technology businesses that connect Phnom Penh to the global digital marketplace

According to Zapata-Barrero and Rezaei (2020), such entrepreneurs warrant the title of innovation brokers as they introduce and apply norms of efficiency, customer service, and workplace punctuality that they learned while living abroad. Although small, the changes are critical to the Cambodian economy's evolution.

Educational migrants bring intellectual resources and help modernize the Cambodian state. Fong and Shibuya (2020) explain that new pedagogical methodologies, research, and professional ethics introduced by Australian, Japanese, French, and Korean graduates transformed Cambodian higher education and the civil service. These returnees influence the dominant ideas on governance, urban development, climate change, and digital technologies. Foreign-trained nurses and doctors elevate the standard of techniques and practices in surgery, public health, maternal health, and epidemiology. According to Chan (2015) and Clark (2020), the increasing compliance of hospitals in Phnom Penh and Siem Reap with global standards of care is due to the presence of Western-trained personnel. Moreover, there is the same trend in civil engineering and hydraulic works. Instead of permanently returning to Cambodia, some professionals participate in 'brain circulation', working in other countries while remaining engaged with Cambodia. Saxenian (2006) sees these types of networks as the most beneficial for diaspora development, as they help create collaborations in research, business, and technology transfer across multiple countries. For example, in South Korea, some Cambodian computer science graduates are working with startups in Cambodia, while in Australia, some Khmer PhD researchers are working with researchers at the same University. This type of digital collaboration, in itself, speeds up the whole process, as demonstrated by (Levitt & Waters, 2002). Digital networks create a continuous flow of diaspora intellectual capital.

Cambodian diasporas preserve their home country's culture abroad while also supporting its globalization. Ebihara et al. (1994) and Ebihara (2018) note that, from a cultural diplomacy perspective, Cambodian diaspora temples in Long Beach, Montreal, and Paris host New Year celebrations, Pchum Ben festivities, and Royal Ballet shows. Khmer culture introduces the host culture community through food, dance, costume, and spirituality. In the diaspora, artists reinterpret tradition by merging apsara dance with hip-hop, making silk-patterned streetwear, and videotaping shadow plays and publishing them on YouTube. This is cultural reinvention, Lim (2023) argues, helping boost youth involvement and global relevance. This reflects a cultural paradigm shift; instead of the assumed fragile history of the culture, the migrant community chooses and demonstrates an actively living culture. An increase in Cambodians living abroad, especially in the USA, demonstrates an increase in soft power (Nye, 2017) attributed to the Cambodian diaspora. Cambodian American chefs win Michelin stars, documentarians screen their work at European festivals, and artists exhibit their mixed-media works with Khmer motifs in prestigious galleries.

Recognition of these Cambodians abroad shifts perceptions of Cambodia in the international cultural sphere. In support of their own cultures, diaspora community organizations in the USA have campaigned diplomatically on behalf of the Cambodians and their preserved heritage. Lee (2010) and Chan (2015) showed that US legislative lobbying post-political crackdown in Cambodia and illustrated that the Cambodian diaspora is acting as moral agents in the governance of the diaspora. Migration narratives within Cambodia have historically focused on exploitation, trafficking, and trauma. Edwards (2007) points out that these narratives position migrants as passive sufferers. Current patterns of migration, however, create a different scenario. Young, mobile Cambodians are motivated by education, entrepreneurship, and global networking, with labour survival a by-product. Strangio (2014) suggests that, with Cambodia's rapidly growing economy, migrants no longer need to negotiate their identity apologetically, as shown in Table 5.

Table 5. Cambodian migrants contribute to national development through multiple channels

Contribution Domain	Impact Summary
Economic	Remittances reduce poverty, stimulate rural development, and fund new businesses.
Knowledge & Skills	Brain circulation strengthens industry, education, health, and innovation.
Cultural Diplomacy	Diaspora events and media elevate Cambodia's global image.
Narrative Transformation	Migrants redefine identity—from trauma to achievement.

7. CONCLUSION AND RECOMMENDATIONS

Cambodian migration has evolved from a history of displacement and survival to a contemporary landscape of opportunity, global participation, and hybrid identities. This chapter illustrates the diverse impacts of Cambodian migrants, including their contributions to the economy via remittances and investments, as well as their roles in shaping national development through intellectual, cultural, and diplomatic efforts. Migrants' identities are reshaped by the interaction of cultural persistence, digital connectivity, and host society policies. Migration now encompasses more than just physical movement; it is a complex process.

The research outlines three key migration phases: the refugee exodus of the 1970s and 1980s, the rise of informal labor migration in the 1990s and 2000s, and today's migration of skilled, educated, and circular migrants. Each phase involved a redefinition of identity and belonging. Refugee communities fostered diasporic memories rooted in trauma and rebuilding, labor migrants supported families through remittances, and modern migrants forge global futures through educational and professional pursuits. These histories intertwine in identity construction. Cambodian migrants, maintaining their cultural practices like language, religion, cuisine, and rituals, adapt and create hybrid lifestyles within a global society. In a digitized world, feelings of belonging and emotional bonds are strengthened, and physical distance no longer prevents cultural learning and practice.

Integration experiences vary considerably. In ASEAN and East Asia, migrants primarily engage as economic participants and workers. Conversely, in Western nations, economic involvement is linked with worker citizenship and cross-border activities, though racialized social acceptance remains a challenge. Despite structural obstacles, Cambodian migrants pursue various forms of social integration. Beyond sending remittances, they also foster development in both host and home countries through entrepreneurship, sharing knowledge, cultural exchange, and changing narratives. Migration should be viewed as a development opportunity rather than a vulnerability.

Migration trends in Cambodia are shifting towards temporary and circular patterns instead of permanent relocation. As the country advances economically and educationally, Cambodian migrants are increasingly pursuing transnational careers rather than settling abroad permanently. The evolution of digital tools will facilitate the exchange of ideas across borders, with returning academics leading innovation at their universities. The diaspora is expected to contribute to technological advances and developments in agriculture and culture. Emerging migration trends include digital outsourcing, medical training, climate research, and the creative economy. Greater international visibility will showcase Cambodia's cultural talents and boost its soft power. While work migration offers opportunities, it also presents challenges that require policies addressing rights, inclusion, and reintegration beyond economic concerns.

For Cambodian migrants, identity remains an ongoing process, reinforced through speech, memory, celebration, and struggle. The sense of belonging is negotiated in various settings—from dining tables and mosques to TikTok, factories, and classrooms. Integration is a gradual lived experience characterized by adaptation, recognition, and pride. Cambodian migrant identities are multifaceted, blending traditional cultural elements like sampeah with influences from K-pop and hip-hop, reflecting a hybrid, transnational, and bilingual youth culture. For Cambodians, especially young people, migration is more about expanding and reshaping identity rather than dissolving it.

Understanding migration from Cambodia reveals potential. Moving past simple narratives of loss, the Cambodian international community exemplifies humanity's resilience, creativity, and ambition. Cambodian migration has reshaped economies and societies—whether rural areas dependent on remittances, urban digital startups, student exchanges, circulatory 'brain' networks, or refugees who now represent Cambodia worldwide. Yet, appropriate support is crucial. Responsibilities are layered: the state, host countries, and the diaspora. When Cambodia recognizes its migrants as development contributors, treats host nations as equal partners, and sees the diaspora as a network of solidarity, Cambodian migration can serve as a significant force for local and global progress.

Cambodia can boost migrant protections by improving pre-departure training on language, contracts, rights, and access to social services and complaint channels abroad. Reintegration, including returnee grants, vocational training, business support, and skill recognition, should be sustainable and future-oriented. Promoting brain circulation via research with the diaspora, innovation, remote teaching, and research networks is also key. Host countries can better support migrants by creating integration policies that simplify access to permanent residency, offer flexible work permits, and ensure full legal rights and protections regardless of immigration status.

Providing language assistance, intercultural training, and employer and educator competency development can help reduce discrimination and social exclusion. To improve collaboration, Cambodia and host countries should invest in diaspora networks, including student groups, religious communities, and digital platforms that strengthen professional and cultural ties. Government and community partnerships, such as diaspora advisory councils and alumni networks, can connect overseas expertise with national development goals. Cambodian migration is a permanent reality, and with effective policies, cross-border cooperation, and a growing migratory flow, the diaspora will play a crucial role in Cambodia's future.

REFERENCES

Abubakar, Y. W., & Islam, M. N. (2025). Diaspora civil society: The nexus of civil society, soft power and foreign policy. *Journal of Applied And Theoretical Social Sciences*, *7*(4), 362–378. DOI: 10.37241/jatss.2025.135

ADB. (2024). *Cambodia's economic diversification: A country diagnostic study*. Asian Development Bank. https://www.adb.org/sites/default/files/publication/1009916/cambodia-economic-diversification.pdf

Aletheiani, D. R. (2025). Southeast Asian diaspora communities and consciousness. *Diaspora, Indigenous, and Minority Education*, *19*(3), 216–226. DOI: 10.1080/15595692.2025.2516009

Anderson, B. (2008). Imagined communities: Reflections on the origin and spread of nationalism. In Seidman, S., & Alexander, J. C. (Eds.), *The new social theory reader* (pp. 282–288). Routledge., DOI: 10.4324/9781003060963-46

Appadurai, A. (1996). *Modernity at large: Cultural dimensions of globalization*. University of Minnesota Press.

Berry, J. W. (1997). Immigration, acculturation, and adaptation. *Applied Psychology*, *46*(1), 5–34. DOI: 10.1111/j.1464-0597.1997.tb01087.x

Bonjour, S. (2014). The transfer of pre-departure integration requirements for family migrants among member states of the European Union. *Comparative Migration Studies*, *2*(2), 203–226. DOI: 10.5117/CMS2014.2.BONJ

Bonjour, S., & Chauvin, S. (2018). Social class, migration policy and migrant strategies: An introduction. *International Migration (Geneva, Switzerland)*, *56*(4), 5–18. DOI: 10.1111/imig.12469

Brickell, K. (2020). *Home SOS: Gender, violence, and survival in crisis ordinary Cambodia*. John Wiley & Sons. DOI: 10.1002/9781118898338

Bylander, M. (2015). Depending on the sky: Environmental distress, migration, and coping in rural Cambodia. *International Migration (Geneva, Switzerland)*, *53*(5), 135–147. DOI: 10.1111/imig.12087

Chairattana, S., & Khanawiwat, T. (2019). *The Report on the route of migration from Myanmar and Cambodia to Thailand*. Plan International Organisation. https://www.dol.gov/sites/dolgov/files/ILAB/Report_on_Migration_from_Myanmar_and_Cambodia_to_Thailand.pdf

Chan, S. (2015). Cambodians in the United States: Refugees, immigrants, American ethnic minority. In Dailey, J. (Ed.), *Oxford research encyclopedia of American history*. Academic., DOI: 10.1093/acrefore/9780199329175.013.317

Chandler, D. P. (1979). The tragedy of Cambodian history. *Pacific Affairs*, *52*(3), 410–419. DOI: 10.2307/2757655

Chandler, D. P. (1993). *The tragedy of Cambodian history: Politics, war, & the revolution since 1945*. Yale University Press.

Chhair, S., & Ung, L. (2016). Cambodia's path to industrial development: Policies, lessons, and opportunities. In Newman, C., Page, J., Rand, J., Shimeles, A., Söderbom, M., & Tarp, F. (Eds.), *Manufacturing Transformation: Comparative studies of industrial development in Africa and emerging Asia* (pp. 213–234). Oxford University Press., DOI: 10.1093/acprof:oso/9780198776987.003.0011

Clark, H. A. (2020). *Beyond borders, beyond banking: The ACLEDA bank story, 2005-2019*. Springer. Co, N. D., Ba, L. V., Thi, T. T., & Binh, N. T. (2025). Cooperation in border areas among some Southeast Asian mainland countries: A case study of the Cambodia-Laos-Vietnam development triangle. *Cogent Arts & Humanities*, *12*(1), 1–14. DOI: 10.1080/23311983.2025.2463203

de Haas, H., Castles, S., & Miller, M. J. (2019). *The age of migration: International population movements in the modern world*. Bloomsbury Publishing.

Derks, A. (2008). *Khmer women on the move: Exploring work and life in urban Cambodia*. University of Hawaii Press. DOI: 10.21313/hawaii/9780824831288.001.0001

Derks, A. (2010). Migrant labour and the politics of immobilisation: Cambodian fishermen in Thailand. *Asian Journal of Social Science*, *38*(6), 915–932. DOI: 10.1163/156853110X530804

Ear, S. (2013). *Aid dependence in Cambodia: How foreign assistance undermines democracy*. Columbia University Press.

Ebihara, M., Mortland, C. A., & Ledgerwood, J. (1994). *Cambodian culture since 1975: Homeland and exile*. Cornell University Press. DOI: 10.7591/9781501723858

Ebihara, M. M. (2018). *Svay: a Khmer village in Cambodia*. Cornell University Press. DOI: 10.7591/9781501714801

Edwards, P. (2007). *Cambodge: The cultivation of a nation, 1860-1945*. University of Hawaii Press.

Fielding, T. (2015). *Asian migrations: Social and geographical mobilities in Southeast, East, and Northeast Asia*. Routledge. DOI: 10.4324/9781315863566

Fong, E., & Shibuya, K. (2020). Migration patterns in East and Southeast Asia: Causes and consequences. *Annual Review of Sociology*, *46*(1), 511–531. DOI: 10.1146/annurev-soc-121919-054644

Ford, M. (2024). *The politics of cross-border mobility in Southeast Asia*. Cambridge University Press. DOI: 10.1017/9781108673914

Ford, M., Lyons, L., & Van Schendel, W. (2012). Labour migration and human trafficking: An introduction. In M. Ford, L. Lyons, & W. van Schendel (Eds.), *Labour migration and human trafficking in Southeast Asia* (pp. 1–22). Routledge. https://doi.org/DOI: 10.4324/9780203121535-1

Frohlick, S. (2013). *Sexuality, women, and tourism: Cross-border desires through contemporary travel*. Routledge.

Hall, J. M. (2003). Analyzing women's roles through graphic representation of narratives. *Western Journal of Nursing Research*, *25*(5), 492–507. DOI: 10.1177/0193945903252422 PMID: 12955967

Hall, S. (1994). Cultural identity and diaspora. In Williams, P., & Chrisman, L. (Eds.), *Colonial discourse and post-colonial theory* (pp. 392–403). Routledge., DOI: 10.4324/9781315656496

Heder, S. (1979). Kampuchea's armed struggle the origins of an independent revolution. *Bulletin of Concerned Asian Scholars*, *11*(1), 2–23. DOI: 10.1080/14672715.1979.10424028

Heder, S., & Ledgerwood, J. (2016). *Propaganda, politics and violence in Cambodia: Democratic transition under United Nations Peace-keeping*. Routledge. DOI: 10.4324/9781315285894

Hochschild, A. R. (1983). *The managed heart: Commercialization of human feeling*. University of California Press.

Horst, C. (2006). *Transnational nomads: How Somalis cope with refugee life in the Dadaab camps of Kenya*. Berghahn Books. DOI: 10.3167/9781845451295

Hughes, C. (2009). *Dependent communities: Aid and politics in Cambodia and East Timor*. Southeast Asia Program Publications. DOI: 10.7591/9781501719295

Hugo, G. (2014). The role of international migration in Australia's research workforce. *Asian and Pacific Migration Journal*, *23*(1), 27–54. DOI: 10.1177/011719681402300102

Kang, M. Y., & Park, B. (2018). Sustainable corporate social media marketing based on message structural features: Firm size plays a significant role as a moderator. *Sustainability (Basel), 10*(4), 1–14. DOI: 10.3390/su10041167

Kelly, P. F. (2013). *Migration, agrarian transition, and rural change in Southeast Asia*. Routledge. DOI: 10.4324/9781315877884

Khamjalas, K. (2024). Nexuses between food, energy, and water consumption on urban-rural income gap in South-Eastern Asian countries using difference in difference in modelling technique. *International Journal of Economics and Financial Issues, 14*(2), 186–195. DOI: 10.32479/ijefi.15923

Kheang, T. (2024). Leading educational reconstruction in post-conflict Cambodia: Perspectives of primary school leaders. *Educational Management Administration & Leadership, 52*(1), 189–207. DOI: 10.1177/17411432211058942

Kim, K. (2021). Framing immigrant rights in politics: Comparative evidence from Japan and South Korea. *Pacific Focus, 36*(2), 287–315. DOI: 10.1111/pafo.12187

Kwon, H. (2022). Inclusion work: Children of immigrants claiming membership in everyday life. *American Journal of Sociology, 127*(6), 1818–1859. DOI: 10.1086/720277

Kymlicka, W. (2011). Multicultural citizenship within multination states. *Ethnicities, 11*(3), 281–302. DOI: 10.1177/1468796811407813

Ledgerwood, J. L. (1996). Politics and gender: Negotiating conceptions of the ideal woman in present day Cambodia. *Asia Pacific Viewpoint, 37*(2), 139–152. DOI: 10.1111/apv.372003

Lee, J. H. X. (2010). *Cambodian American experiences: Histories, communities, cultures and identities*. Kendall Hunt Publishing.

Levitt, P. (1998). Social remittances: Migration driven local-level forms of cultural diffusion. *The International Migration Review, 32*(4), 926–948. DOI: 10.1177/019791839803200404 PMID: 12294302

Levitt, P., & Waters, M. C. (2002). *The changing face of home: the transnational lives of the second generation*. Russell Sage Foundation.

Lim, M. (2023). From activist media to algorithmic politics: The Internet, social media, and civil society in Southeast Asia. In Hansson, E., & Weiss, M. L. (Eds.), *Routledge handbook of civil and uncivil society in Southeast Asia* (pp. 25–44). Routledge., DOI: 10.4324/9780367422080-3

Long, K. (2013). *The point of no return: Refugees, rights, and repatriation*. Oxford University Press. DOI: 10.1093/acprof:oso/9780199673315.001.0001

Lucas, R. E. (2001). *Diaspora and development: Highly skilled migrants from East Asia*. Boston University: Institute for Economic Development. https://www.bu.edu/econ/files/2012/11/dp120.pdf

Mabbett, I. W., & Chandler, D. P. (1995). *The Khmers*. Blackwell.

Madianou, M., & Miller, D. (2013). *Migration and new media: Transnational families and polymedia*. Routledge. DOI: 10.4324/9780203154236

Miller, D., & Slater, D. (2020). *The Internet: An ethnographic approach*. Routledge. DOI: 10.4324/9781003087007

Naudé, W., Siegel, M., & Marchand, K. (2017). Migration, entrepreneurship and development: Critical questions. *IZA Journal of Migration*, *6*(1), 1–16. DOI: 10.1186/s40176-016-0077-8

Nguyen, C. H. (2024). The sense-making of home among Vietnamese returning graduates. *Journal of International Students*, *14*(1), 210–228. DOI: 10.32674/jis.v14i3.5777

Nye, J. (2017). Soft power: The origins and political progress of a concept. *Palgrave Communications*, *3*(1), 1–3. DOI: 10.1057/palcomms.2017.8

Oh, I., Seol, D.-H., & Choi, M. (2025). Managing Diasporic Returns: Contrasting Approaches to Peoplehood and Returnee Integration in Japan and Korea. In Sahoo, A. K. (Ed.), *Routledge Handbook of Asian Diaspora and Nationalism* (pp. 317–333). Routledge., DOI: 10.4324/9781003487432-25

Oishi, N. (2017). Gender and migration policies in Asia. In Tittensor, D., & Mansouri, F. (Eds.), *The politics of women and migration in the global south* (pp. 27–48). Springer., DOI: 10.1057/978-1-137-58799-2_3

Ong, A. (2003). *Buddha is hiding: Refugees, citizenship, the new America*. University of California Press.

Park, W. (2024). *State governance and less-skilled migrant workers in South Korea*. University of Kentucky.

Parreñas, R. (2005). Long distance intimacy: Class, gender and intergenerational relations between mothers and children in Filipino transnational families. *Global Networks*, *5*(4), 317–336. DOI: 10.1111/j.1471-0374.2005.00122.x

Peou, S. (2021). *Cambodia: Change and continuity in contemporary politics.* Routledge.

Piper, N. (2017). Migrant domestic workers as' agents' of development in Asia: Collective organising at the intersection of temporality and transnationality. *European Journal of East Asian Studies, 16*(2), 220–247. DOI: 10.1163/15700615-01602003

Platt, M., Baey, G., Yeoh, B. S., Khoo, C. Y., & Lam, T. (2017). Debt, precarity and gender: Male and female temporary labour migrants in Singapore. *Journal of Ethnic and Migration Studies, 43*(1), 119–136. DOI: 10.1080/1369183X.2016.1218756

Rashid, A. (2025). Trauma, memory, and identity of women in the Cambodia diaspora. In Ashton, J. C. (Ed.), *The Routledge handbook of heritage and gender* (pp. 212–223). Routledge., DOI: 10.4324/9781003258193-19

Rigg, J. (2016). *On more than rural: Textures of Thailand's Agrarian transformation.* University of Hawaii Press.

Samreth, S., & Aiba, D. (2026). *Microfinance in Cambodia: Development, role, and prospects.* Routledge. DOI: 10.4324/9781003647935

Saxenian, A. (2006). *The new argonauts: Regional advantage in a global economy.* Harvard University Press.

Schiller, N. G., Basch, L., & Blanc, C. S. (1995). From immigrant to transmigrant: Theorizing transnational migration. *Anthropological Quarterly, 68*(1), 48–63. DOI: 10.2307/3317464

Schlund-Vials, C. J. (2012). *War, genocide, and justice: Cambodian American memory work.* University of Minnesota Press. DOI: 10.5749/minnesota/9780816670963.001.0001

Sen, V. (2019). Hybrid governmentality: Higher education policymaking in post-conflict Cambodia. *Studies in Higher Education, 44*(3), 513–525. DOI: 10.1080/03075079.2017.1379985

Sophal, C. (2009). *Review of labour migration management, policies and legal framework in Cambodia.* ILO.

Strangio, S. (2014). *Hun Sen's Cambodia.* Yale University Press.

Tan, S., & Chen, W. (2025). Transnational politics of Cambodian American ethnic organizations. *Journal of Southeast Asian American Education & Advancement, 20*(1), 1–28. https://www.jstor.org/stable/48854958. DOI: 10.7771/2153-8999.1335

Tong, K. (2011). Migration, remittances and poverty reduction: Evidence from Cambodia. *CDRI Cambodia Development Review, 15*(4), 7–12. https://cdri.org.kh/storage/pdf/cdr11-4e-2_1617846166.pdf

Vertovec, S., & Wessendorf, S. (2010). Assessing the backlash against multiculturalism in Europe. In Vertovec, S., & Wessendorf, S. (Eds.), *The multiculturalism backlash European discourses, policies and practices* (pp. 1–31). Routledge., DOI: 10.4324/9780203867549

Walker, K. (2012). Cambodia's postgraduate students: Emerging patterns and trends. *ASEAN Journal of Teaching and Learning in Higher Education*, *4*(1), 1–13.

Waters, J. L. (2016). Education unbound? Enlivening debates with a mobilities perspective on learning. *Progress in Human Geography*, *41*(3), 279–298. DOI: 10.1177/0309132516637908

Werbner, P. (2002). *Imagined diasporas among Manchester Muslims: The public performance of Pakistani transnational identity politics*. James Currey.

Yeoh, B. S., Huang, S., & Lam, T. (2018). Transnational family dynamics in Asia. In Triandafyllidou, A. (Ed.), *Handbook of migration and globalisation* (pp. 413–430). Edward Elgar Publishing. DOI: 10.4337/9781785367519.00034

Yeoh, B. S., & Ramdas, K. (2014). Gender, migration, mobility and transnationalism. *Gender, Place and Culture*, *21*(10), 1197–1213. DOI: 10.1080/0966369X.2014.969686

Zapata-Barrero, R., & Rezaei, S. (2020). Diaspora governance and transnational entrepreneurship: The rise of an emerging social global pattern in migration studies. *Journal of Ethnic and Migration Studies*, *46*(10), 1959–1973. DOI: 10.1080/1369183X.2018.1559990

Zhou, M., & Bankston, C. (1998). *Growing up American: How Vietnamese children adapt to life in the United States*. Russell Sage Foundation.

Chapter 15
Migration and Integration in Everyday Local Contexts:
A Qualitative Study

Muhlise Canli
http://orcid.org/0000-0001-6051-4677
Gümüşhane University, Turkey

Neslihan Koc
http://orcid.org/0009-0000-5119-2290
Gumushane University, Turkey

ABSTRACT

This chapter addresses how migration, identity, and integration are experienced. By focusing on Gümüşhane, it contributes to an understanding of integration beyond metropolitan contexts. Themes were formed from the qualitative content analysis of semi-structured interviews conducted with 22 migrant and 22 local-community participants: identity, the local community-migrant relationship, and the acculturation process. Adopting a phenomenological approach, the study aims to reveal expectations and perceptions concerning the socio-cultural integration process, focusing on everyday encounters, social contact, cultural visibility, language use, religious commonalities, perceptions of difference, and the limits of social closeness. The findings suggest that socio-cultural integration cannot be understood solely through formal indicators. Instead, it is shaped by everyday practices, local norms, cultural expectations, and social relations. The chapter demonstrates that integration is a relational, negotiated, and context-sensitive process.

DOI: 10.4018/979-8-3373-8500-6.ch015

INTRODUCTION

Throughout different periods of history and across various regions of the world, internal and international migrations driven by wars, civil conflicts, and economic, political, and social causes have left deep marks on societies. Castles and Miller described the age in which we live as the "Age of Migration" (Castles & Miller, 1998). The phrase is significant for characterizing a present in which national and international human mobility is ever more pronounced. Turkey, situated at the meeting point of Asia, Europe, and Africa, has long been a country of transit, destination, and origin for such movement, and the everyday encounter between migrants and the settled population has become an increasingly visible feature of its cities.

Once migration is underway and basic needs have been met, the process of integration begins for migrants. Research on integration has come to emphasize that this is not a one-way process but a set of multiple processes unfolding across different domains (Aksoy, 2025). Integration is a multidimensional and multi-actor process through which individuals take part in social, cultural, political, and economic life, develop relations across groups, and form shared belongings. In line with the principle of reciprocity, it unfolds as a responsibility of both migrants and members of the local community.

One notable feature of this way of thinking is its tendency to treat integration as a reciprocal and relational process. The ways in which local communities receive migrants, their practices of creating social distance, and their attitudes toward cultural difference matter as much as migrants' own efforts to adapt. Such an approach holds the potential to move beyond conventional views that place the entire burden of integration on migrants. For this reason, by focusing on the forms of mutual relationship between migrants and local communities rather than on migrants' conduct alone, this chapter offers a valuable perspective on the everyday texture of socio-cultural integration in a small-scale city.

BACKGROUND

The concept of socio-cultural integration encompasses a multidimensional process. For this reason, before socio-cultural integration itself is defined, it is important to define the related concepts of integration, identity, culture, and acculturation. In this study, the concept of socio-cultural integration is defined only after these related concepts have been set out.

Integration

Although the concept of integration is used very frequently in the migration literature, there is no clear consensus on its definition. Historically, the classical assimilation theories that pioneered integration research defined settlement and integration as a more or less linear process in which migrants were expected to change almost entirely in order to merge with the mainstream culture and society. Warner and Srole (1945), who introduced the concept at the end of the Second World War, for example, assumed that all groups in U.S. society would evolve toward the American way of life. Even as they treated this as a linear process, these authors noted that its pace could vary with factors such as cultural distance (the Anglo-conformity gap) and racial categorization, and therefore depended largely on the characteristics of migrant groups. Safi (2011) groups the principal criticisms of this one-sided view into three categories. The first concerns the problematic nature of the notion of a "mainstream," since it implies the existence of a more or less homogeneous and cohesive social environment. The second stresses the importance of structural inequalities—such as discrimination in housing and labor markets—that can slow or even block migrants' integration. The third points to the plurality of integration processes, which depend on collective actors (such as the state and its policies, public opinion, ethnic communities, and civil society) and on contextual factors (such as economic conditions) (Garcés-Mascareñas & Penninx, 2016).

Empirical and theoretical insights from a rich body of research have led to growing recognition of the complexity of integration. Moving away from linear understandings of migrant assimilation, contemporary conceptualizations have become more nuanced and multidimensional. Analyses increasingly treat integration as a process, which brings a better grasp of temporal dimensions and of the significance of processes at the local level. It is now widely accepted that integration is "two-way" and involves both migrants and society at every level. Integration has been examined as multiple processes occurring in different domains rather than as a single process. There is, however, no consensus on theoretical and methodological concepts, and different theoretical developments exist across disciplines and geographies. Alba and Foner, for instance, treat integration as a societal goal shared by many, defining it in terms of processes that—through participation in major institutions such as the education and political systems and the labor and housing markets—enhance the opportunities of migrants and their descendants to access a society's valued resources and to gain social acceptance. On this view, full integration implies equal life chances with members of the native majority and recognition as a legitimate part of the national community. Olwig and Paerregaard, by contrast, argue in a normative register that integration is not "a neutral concept denoting the coming together of different population groups" but rather "part of the vocabulary of the nation-state."

For Favell, likewise, integration is defined in connection with the nation-building project (Spencer & Charsley, 2021). Whereas earlier definitions were dominated by the idea that a one-way process (such as the assimilation of a migrant or migrant group) ought to operate, the inadequacy of this framing became apparent as social conditions changed and transformed. Underlying the differences in definition is a shared recognition that integration is a two-way process, bound up with the positions both sides take, and the tolerances they display, when migrants and members of the local community meet within a shared space.

Penninx and Garcés-Mascareñas (2016) offer a basic definition of integration as the process by which it is determined whether people can become an accepted part of society. In this context they identify three analytically distinct dimensions of integration: the legal-political, the socio-economic, and the cultural-religious.

The *legal-political dimension* refers to residence and political rights and statuses. It concerns whether, or to what extent, migrants are accepted as full members of the political community.

The *socio-economic dimension* concerns the social and economic position of residents, independent of their national citizenship. Within this dimension, migrants' positions, their access to domains of vital importance for anyone residing in a given place, and their participation in those domains can be examined and analyzed.

The *cultural-religious dimension* concerns the perceptions and practices of migrants and of the receiving society, as well as their mutual responses to difference and diversity. If newcomers see themselves as different and are perceived by the receiving society as culturally or religiously different, expectations arise about gaining a recognized place in the new society in these respects. The receiving society, in turn, may or may not accept cultural and religious diversity.

These three dimensions of integration operate in relation to one another. The legal-political dimension can shape, and be shaped by, the socio-economic and cultural-religious dimensions.

Identity

For individuals caught up in the migration process, the boundaries of the identities they hold can shift. For those who migrate, a situation of reconciliation or conflict arises between the identity or identities they held in their country of origin and the identity or identities they hold, or are expected to hold, in the destination country (Aksoy & Cengiz, 2025). This renders the perception of identity complex and full of uncertainty for migrants. For some, identity serves as a means of preserving the values of the country of origin; for others, it becomes a vehicle of change in adapting to the new society. Because socio-cultural integration is multidimensional and complex, clarifying the phenomenon of identity is therefore important.

According to Bilgin (1996), identity is, first, an evaluative mechanism through which we adjust the various options the social system offers us to what we wish to do. Second, because the norms and values imposed on us are open to interpretation and, through social change, cease to be absolute and become relative—thereby easing the move toward new norms and values—identity is a system of improvisation that provides us with a space of freedom and initiative in relation to existing rules. Third, in the search between the role allotted to the individual and freedom, identity is a system of negotiation that gives concrete form to the articulation between our desires and reality—between what we want and what is wanted from us (Balcı, 2022). Within this frame, identity is a phenomenon through which the individual, in the struggle to be and remain oneself, develops strategies of survival amid changing and transforming conditions of social life. Identity is sometimes a reflection of a person's life practices, sometimes something acquired through the social groups to which one belongs, and sometimes an argument used by oneself and by those outside one's group to define the individual. It also serves as a means through which similarities and differences between migrants and members of the local community are constructed. In this study, the identities held by migrants are seen to bear on social and cultural acceptance. A Muslim identity supports the construction of shared belonging and rapprochement between migrants and the local community. Yet differences in religious practice and in the groups' ways of life lead both migrants and local residents to create social distance. "Turkishness," as an identity through which local residents set themselves apart from the "other," constructs a differentiating identity that is decisive in relations with migrants. In defining migrants' identities, local residents disregard ethnic, religious, social, and class differences and produce a homogeneous identity ascription.

Culture and Acculturation

Although culture is widely used in both academic and everyday language, it is a concept that is difficult to define and on which social scientists have not reached consensus. Culture is at once the product of a society and its builder. It is the whole range of behavioral systems a society uses to sustain its life and to solve its problems (Bahar, 2005). Within this frame, culture resides in the mind as the sum of the thoughts and values of the individuals who belong to a society. Migrant groups' motivations to preserve, sustain, or change the cultural values they hold are decisive for their integration with the local community.

The encounter between migrants and members of the local community—in other words, the beginning of a relationship between two different cultures within a shared space—gives rise to the process of acculturation. Acculturation may be expressed as "cultural enrichment, cultural adaptation, and cultural interaction" (Zafer, 2016). It is "the process that arises from continuous and direct contact between groups of individuals from different cultures, resulting in changes in the original cultural patterns of both groups or of one of them; acculturation takes place at both the cultural and the psychological level" (Berry, 2005). Migration is one of the causes that give rise to acculturation. Individuals who carry culture into contact generally hold initial ideas—habitus, in other terms—about what they are trying to do or what the culture they are in contact with is trying to do to them. These ideas shape the choices of members of both groups within the field of acculturation. In the specific case of Gümüşhane, the encounter of two different cultures (local community and migrant) heightens the visibility of cultural differences. Differences such as cleanliness and items of cultural dress in everyday life show that the reciprocity presumed in the integration process does not, in fact, operate. As an indicator of intercultural interaction, the forms of contact between the two groups in the city remain at the level of greeting and do not deepen.

Socio-Cultural Integration

"The phenomenon of migration denotes a multidimensional process of transformation in which individuals carry with them not only a change of physical space but also their cultural identities, values, and life practices" (Yılmaz & Önay Doğan, 2025). The interaction of those who arrive through migration with the settled society, and the accompanying process of social change, is defined as integration (Penninx & Garcés-Mascareñas, 2016). Integration is a multifaceted concept. The first distinction between psychological and socio-cultural integration was drawn by Ward (1996). Psychological integration largely concerns an individual's psychological and physical well-being, whereas socio-cultural adaptation refers to how well an individual undergoing acculturation is able to manage everyday life in the new cultural context (Berry, 2005). "Socio-cultural integration encompasses dimensions such as a sense of community formed around shared values and norms, active participation in public life, cultural continuity, the fair sharing of resources, and mutual responsibility" (Yılmaz, 2025). "The factors affecting socio-cultural integration include individual variables such as a person's level of education, age, gender, physical characteristics, regional differences, prior migration experiences, language proficiency, legal status, and traumatic events experienced before and after migration, as well as various social dynamics such as the host society's stance, media discourses, the political atmosphere, the level of social acceptance, and exclusion or discrimination" (Yılmaz & Önay Doğan, 2025). Socio-cultural integration thus encompasses various changes and transformations for both migrants and the local community. Its development in societies rests on mutual acceptance, respect, and realistic expectations. "In multicultural societies with dense migrant populations, socio-cultural adaptation is of vital importance, particularly for forestalling forms of maladaptation such as exclusion, assimilation, and marginality" (Yılmaz, 2025).

Given the redefinition of integration from a one-way to a two-way process, and given its several dimensions, this study assesses migrant–local community relations in terms of socio-cultural integration. The integration that takes place in legal and economic terms differs from the integration that occurs in everyday life. In everyday integration, factors such as cultural adaptation between the local community and migrants, social acceptance, identity negotiations, forms of contact, migrants' participation in social life, and similarities and differences with the local community become decisive for socio-cultural integration. For understanding and accounting for local community–migrant relations in a small-scale city, socio-cultural integration is a workable lens. Although the literature offers various definitions of socio-cultural integration, it is valuable to analyze it through Bourdieu's concepts.

Pierre Bourdieu's Sociological Approach

The ground of Bourdieu's sociological approach lies in overcoming the opposition between objectivity and subjectivity. With this approach Bourdieu contributed to the development of classical sociology. He held that sociology should be interrogative in character: for Bourdieu, sociology ought to be a science that lifts the veil over realities and makes trouble. He expressed this critical and interrogative approach through the concepts he developed. Drawing on the circumstances of his own life, Bourdieu defined the concepts of habitus, social capital, and field (Ritzer, 2011; Palabıyık, 2011).

The Concept of Habitus

The concept of habitus, which lies at the center of Bourdieu's sociological theory, had been used before him by many thinkers in different works. Durkheim employed it in his lectures on "The Evolution of Pedagogy in France," Marcel Mauss in his essay "Techniques of the Body," and Max Weber in *Economy and Society*. None of these thinkers, however, assigned habitus the decisive role in their theory that Bourdieu did (Palabıyık, 2011).

In his work, Bourdieu focused on the "mode of coming into being" of practices—that is, on their origins. Unlike Foucault, he concentrated less on what practices produce than on what produces practices, and this focus led him to the concept of habitus (de Certeau, 1984). Habitus consists of the "mental or cognitive structures" through which people deal with the social world. People are endowed with a set of internalized schemas that mediate their perception, understanding, appreciation, and evaluation of the social world. Through these schemas they both produce their practices and perceive and evaluate them. Dialectically, habitus is "the product of the internalization of the structures" of the social world (Ritzer, 2011). For Bourdieu, rather than an individually reductive and deterministic notion, habitus is a structuring mechanism and a principle for generating strategies suited to circumstances, enabling social actors to cope with the changing practices of life. In this sense it is a concept that allows individuals to escape the impasses in which necessity places them. Habitus is not an unchanging fate but a set of dispositions that transform and take shape according to the new situations individuals encounter (Bourdieu & Wacquant, 1992).

"Habituses reflect objective divisions within the class structure, such as age groups, genders, and social classes. A habitus is acquired as a result of long occupancy of a position within the social world. Habitus therefore varies with the nature of one's position in the world: not everyone has the same habitus. Yet those who occupy the same position within the social world tend to have similar habituses" (Ritzer, 2011). Bourdieu's emphasis on change is important for both migrants and members of the local community. Habitus refers to the sets of knowledge present in individuals' minds. In this respect, both migrants and local residents generate strategies within the new situations and social conditions they encounter by drawing on acquired stores of knowledge and past experience.

Many commentators (such as Aristotle and Mauss) have understood habitus in connection with the notion of habit. For Bourdieu, however, habitus is the continuous embodiment of acquired habits and their shaping by culture (Kaplan & Yardımcıoğlu, 2020).

The Concept of Capital

The origins of the concept of capital may be traced to the sociology of Karl Marx. By capital Marx meant not only monetary wealth but everything that makes the bourgeois bourgeois, placing the assets, equipment, machinery, and similar resources that contribute to the bourgeoisie within the concept. In other words, Marx built the concept of capital entirely on economic grounds (Palabıyık, 2011; Wallace & Wolf, 2012). Through his own work on capital, Bourdieu gave a social and cultural dimension to the concept Marx had founded on the economy, and it is this that makes his notion of capital distinctive.

The social world is accumulated history, and if this history is not to be reduced to a discontinuous series of instantaneous, mechanical equilibria among interchangeable actors treated as particles, it is impossible to account for the structure and functioning of the social world without considering capital in all its forms (Bourdieu,

1986). Following the process of accumulation present in Marx's account of capital, Bourdieu argued that capital is not merely economic accumulation but a social and cultural one as well. Within this frame he defined capital in three interrelated forms: economic, cultural, and social.

"Economic capital refers to the money or material assets individuals possess. In this form of capital we encounter the situation Marx sought to express—namely, the capital possessed and the utilitarian condition it brings with it" (Palabıyık, 2011). Cultural capital can exist in three forms: in the embodied state (as long-lasting dispositions of the mind and body), in the objectified state (as cultural goods such as pictures, books, dictionaries, instruments, and machines), and in the institutionalized state (such as educational qualifications) (Bourdieu, 1986). Cultural capital helps explain how educative education is, and under certain conditions it can be converted into economic capital (Erel, 2010).

Social capital is the sum of the actual or potential resources that accrue from possessing a durable, more or less institutionalized network of relationships based on mutual acquaintance and recognition; in other words, it is membership in a group that provides support to each of its members (Bourdieu, 1986). Bourdieu shapes the concept of social capital through its reciprocal relations with habitus, capital, and field. Social capital is a form of capital that provides useful support when needed and that arises from individuals' social relations; it is characterized as capital because it furnishes resources for group members (Kaplan & Yardımcıoğlu, 2020; de Haas, 2010). The volume of social capital an individual possesses depends on the size of the network of connections that individual can effectively mobilize and on the volume of capital (economic, cultural, or symbolic) possessed in his or her own right by each person to whom the individual is connected. This means that, although social capital is relatively irreducible to the economic and cultural capital possessed by a given individual or even by all those to whom that individual is connected, it is never wholly independent of it (Bourdieu, 1986).

Social capital is important in the construction of everyday relations between migrants and members of the local community. For migrants, the social capital they hold serves in some cases as a resource for meeting basic and human needs—finding housing or work, for example—and in others as a means of securing the connections that ease the need for socialization and the maintenance of culture and cultural values. The connections social capital provides allow migrants to sustain relations with their countries of origin and to socialize within their own group. On the other hand, when a migrant meets everyday social needs within his or her own group, this can create a zone of resistance to building relations with the local community, which may impede socio-cultural integration. For the local community, the social capital held with respect to migrants often affects relations with them. Local residents' claims that "Afghans are not like Syrians," for instance, are in many cases indicative of a hierarchical outlook formed through social capital. In this sense, the social capital held by both the local community and migrants can be said to determine the quality and scope of the relations built in everyday life and, with it, to affect the socio-cultural integration process.

The Concept of Field

Bourdieu defines the concept of field not structurally but relationally. A field is bound up with objective positions and with the positions of the individuals who occupy them (Ritzer, 2011). Just as there are different forms of capital, Bourdieu notes, so too are there different fields that these forms of capital bring into being. He holds that the concept of field encompasses multidimensional positions and that social life cannot be reduced to the direct relations and interactions established between individuals. The network of structural and objective relations present in a field shapes the form and content of the visible relations and interactions among individuals (Palabıyık, 2011). To put Bourdieu's concept of field another way, it is an arena in which capital is expressed—a space in which the various forms of capital (economic, cultural, social) are used and mobilized. Actors' positions within a field depend on the volume of capital they possess, and depending on the quantitative and qualitative properties of that capital, they can make themselves felt in the appropriate fields (Kaplan & Yardımcıoğlu, 2020; Ritzer, 2011). "At the basis of Bourdieu's theory of the field is the idea that the social world is the site of a process of 'gradual differentiation.' First, a field imposes its own determinations on whatever is positioned within it—this, in Bourdieu's terms, is the 'field of power.' Second, a field is an arena of struggle in which the actors within it seek to preserve or change their current position, where a hierarchical war is at stake; Bourdieu calls this the 'field of struggle.' Alongside this, a field appears as something that emerges, develops, changes, and disappears over time. This is its third property, namely its 'degree of autonomy'" (Palabıyık, 2011). The encounters between migrants and members of the local community in everyday life, and their use in those encounters of the stores of knowledge (habitus) present in their minds, express precisely what Bourdieu terms a field. The social capital and habituses that members of both communities possess largely determine the social relations they will build within a field. The power struggle that unfolds in Bourdieu's field through the encounter of local community and migrant proceeds through each side's selective use of habitus and social capital. This struggle takes place not through open conflict but invisibly and implicitly, through selected symbolic mechanisms. It is carried out through hidden, deeply operating strategies bound up with processes of recognition, legitimacy, and the acquisition of symbolic capital, rather than through actors relating to and openly confronting one another. According to Bourdieu (1977), symbolic capital is such that, even when—as in gift exchange—it carries an expectation of future return, the parties do not present it openly as a relationship of credit and debt. It involves a process of social recognition that makes an economic and social exchange appear valuable in terms of values such as respect and generosity, rather than a relationship built on explicit expectations. In the field, local residents and migrants use the social, economic, and cultural capital they possess to build social relations on the one hand and to establish recognition and legitimacy on the other. In this sense, the symbolic capital the parties hold bears on relations of power. The power struggle is sustained not only through the social, cultural, and economic capital possessed but also through symbolic capital such as recognition and legitimacy. Who will be recognized in the field, and who will be deemed legitimate, is determined through symbolic struggles.

Berry's Acculturation Model

The focus of Berry's acculturation model is how individuals who have developed within a particular cultural context adapt to the new contexts that arise as a result of migration (Berry, 1997).

As a result of migration, many societies become culturally plural—that is, people from different cultural backgrounds begin to live together in a diverse society. In most cases this produces cultural groups that are unequal (numerically, economically, or politically). These differences of power have given rise to popular terms in the social sciences such as "mainstream," "minority," and "ethnic group."

While acknowledging the unequal effects and changes present in the acculturation process, Berry's model uses the term "cultural group" to refer to all groups, and, where such a difference exists and is relevant to the discussion, the terms "dominant" and "non-dominant" to express their relative power.

According to Berry, all plural societies—and the cultural groups within them, whether in dominant or non-dominant positions, together with the individuals in those groups—must confront the question of *how* to acculturate. Strategies with respect to two central issues are generally developed by groups and individuals during their daily interactions with one another: *cultural maintenance* (the extent to which cultural identity and characteristics are deemed important and effort is made to preserve them) and *contact and participation* (the extent to which they should become involved with other cultural groups or remain primarily among themselves). When these two issues are considered together, the concepts of integration, assimilation, separation, and marginalization emerge.

Integration

According to Berry (2006), integration is generally the most successful of the acculturation strategies. The integration option operates where the migrating individual is interested both in maintaining his or her own heritage culture and in engaging in daily interaction with members of the new society (Berry, 2005). The process of integrating can be "freely" chosen and successfully pursued by non-dominant groups only when the dominant society's attitude toward cultural diversity is open and inclusive. Integration therefore requires mutual accommodation, which includes both groups' acceptance of the right of all groups to live as culturally different peoples (Berry, 1997). In relations between the local community and migrants, the fact that everyday contact remains at the level of greeting, that everyday restrictions exist on migrants' living out their cultural values in public spaces, and that social distance is maintained by members of both groups indicates that integration in the city is limited.

Assimilation

The assimilation strategy operates when migrating individuals, on beginning to live in a new society, do not wish to preserve the cultural identities, values, norms, and attitudes they adopted in the past and instead seek daily interaction with the new society (Berry, 1997). Assimilation is the process of relinquishing one's cultural heritage and being absorbed into the dominant society, and it too results from contact between cultural groups (Berry, 2005). Local residents can be said to be largely in a state of cultural-assimilation expectation, wanting migrants to come to resemble them in language and conduct. The abandonment or complete alteration of migrants' cultural identities affects the socio-cultural experience adversely.

Separation

Separation occurs when individuals or groups entering a new society wish, on the one hand, to sustain their own cultural values, norms, and attitudes while, on the other, avoiding interaction with the new society. Here individuals keep away from relations with other cultural groups and turn toward their own cultural heritage. Migrants experiencing this undergo psychological, emotional, and cognitive confusion of meaning. Those eager to maintain their own cultural values may encounter problems when meeting other cultures, particularly when they resist taking on the cultural values of the society they have newly entered (Berry, 1997; Tokmak, 2022). Migrants' living out their own cultural values at home, sustaining relations with people in the country of origin, having limited relations with local residents, and the absence of friendship between migrants and local residents are indicators of separation. This separation is less a one-sided choice than a situation on which both sides largely agree.

Marginalization

Marginalization occurs when migrant individuals or groups have little interest in maintaining their cultural heritage (often for reasons of enforced cultural loss) or little interest in relating to members of the new society (often for reasons of exclusion or discrimination). In marginalization, the migrant feels like a minority and belongs neither to the culture of origin nor to the new society. In this situation the migrant fails to adapt and enters a cycle of conflict (Berry, 2001).

Berry's acculturation model is used here not as a rigid typology for classifying migrants' relations with the local community but as an analytical frame that helps in understanding cultural continuity and the forms of everyday contact.

RESEARCH METHODOLOGY

Research Design

Qualitative research is a naturalistic and interpretive approach concerned with understanding the meanings that participants attach to phenomena (actions, decisions, beliefs, values, and so on) in their social worlds (Snape & Spencer, 2003). Through qualitative research it is possible to understand the structure of everyday life—the perceptions and experiences of research subjects and how social structures, discourses, and relations are formed (Mason, 2002).

This study set out to explore adult male and female migrants' perceptions of migrant status, their experiences of the migration process, their everyday lives, the relationships they hold, and their thoughts about the future, and a qualitative method was used. The qualitative method was chosen because it suits the aim of the research, allows a relationship to be established with subjects on an equal footing, and gives weight to subjects' freely expressing their own circumstances. According to Creswell (2018), there are five qualitative research approaches: case study, narrative research, ethnographic research, grounded theory, and phenomenological research. This study used the phenomenological approach.

The phenomenological approach holds that individuals' experiences and perceptions of a phenomenon are influential as they construct their social worlds, and it therefore maintains that understanding social reality is possible by discovering the meanings individuals attach to it (Spencer, Pryce, & Walsh, 2014; Kümbetoğlu, 2012). For understanding and accounting for the systems of meaning of both migrants and local residents within everyday life, the phenomenological approach proves functional for this study. Given the migrants in the study group, it is expected that, although participants underwent a similar process of experience, their personal assessments of that similar process will not be identical but will differ.

Data Collection Instrument

Because a qualitative method was used and a phenomenological approach adopted, a semi-structured interview guide was employed. The main aim in choosing this method was to obtain in-depth information from participants and to analyze their perceptions of migrant status, their experiences of the migration process, their everyday lives, the relationships they hold, and their thoughts about the future.

So that focus would not be lost during the interviews and the study's aim would not be departed from, all interviews were conducted with the interview guide at hand. A structured interview guide can lead participants to express their thoughts within fixed limits (Tutty, Rothery, & Grinnell, 1996); to prevent this, a balance was sought through a semi-structured interview form. Semi-structured guides create a safe environment for interviewer and participant alike while reducing the loss of data and time (Creswell, 2020). For these reasons a semi-structured interview guide was functional in the study.

After an extended period of reading in the field, the semi-structured interview guide was developed. It was prepared comprehensively so as to bring out in detail adult male and female migrants' perceptions of migrant status, their experiences of the migration process, their everyday lives, the relationships they hold, and their thoughts about the future. The questions were ordered appropriately from the general to the specific, and care was taken that they were phrased in a manner that would not discomfort participants, that they were structured so participants could express themselves freely, and that they were neither value-laden nor leading. The interviews were conducted with migrants who spoke Turkish.

Participants

The study was conducted with adult female and adult male migrants residing in Gümüşhane and with local community members consisting of adult women and men. Gümüşhane was chosen because it offers more spaces in which migrants and local residents come into contact than do other provinces of the Black Sea region.

Within the scope of this study, in-depth interviews were conducted with 44 people: 22 adult migrants and 22 members of the local community. Because qualitative research focuses on relatively small, purposively selected samples—and sometimes on a single case—purposive sampling is widely used (Patton, 2014; Kümbetoğlu, 2012). Purposive sampling offers the opportunity to explore and understand the topic in detail and to reach subjects within the studied group who have high data-generating potential and can express themselves (Neuman, 2014). The purposive sampling technique was used in this study.

The purposive sampling technique made it possible to reach participants with different characteristics. Migrants with differing attributes—in terms of gender, age, marital status, level of education, year of arrival in Gümüşhane, and occupation—were included.

The researcher assigned descriptive codes to interviewees so that qualitative data analysis could be carried out easily. These descriptive codes also make it easier for readers to follow the participants.

Information on the migrants and the local community members is provided in the tables below.

Table 1. Data on the Migrant Participants

Code	Country of Origin	Gender	Age	Marital Status	Occupation (Gümüşhane)	Years Resident (Gümüşhane)	Turkish Proficiency
G1	Ukraine	Female	32	Married	Delicatessen assistant	9 years	Good
G2	Tunisia	Male	25	Single	Barista	8 months	Good
G3	Afghanistan	Male	20	Single	Pide restaurant worker	4 years	Intermediate
G4	Syria	Male	42	Married	Baker	9 years	Good
G5	Afghanistan	Male	20	Single	Shepherd	6 years	Intermediate
G6	Afghanistan (Turkmen)	Male	29	Single	Fruit-pulp (pestil-köme) factory worker	9 years	Good
G7	Afghanistan (Turkmen)	Male	47	Married	Former shepherd (not working)	8 years	Good
G8	Cameroon	Female	33	Single	Master's student	5 years	Good
G9	Syria (Turkmen)	Female	40	Married	Homemaker	8 years	Good
G10	Iran (Afghan origin)	Female	20	Single	Hairdresser	14 years	Good
G11	Syria (Turkmen)	Female	31	Married	Homemaker	13 years	Good
G12	Syria (Turkmen)	Female	37	Widowed	Homemaker	9 years	Good
G13	Syria (Turkmen)	Male	30	Married	Marble craftsman	11 years	Good
G14	Syria (Turkmen)	Female	26	Married	Homemaker	3 years	Intermediate
G15	Syria (Turkmen)	Female	33	Married	Homemaker	9 years	Intermediate
G16	Syria (Turkmen)	Male	34	Married	Glazier	10 years	Good
G17	Syria	Female	35	Married	Master's student	4 years	Intermediate
G18	Azerbaijan	Male	19	Single	Student / Sales representative	2 years	Good
G19	Afghan (Uzbek)	Male	21	Single	Labourer	6 years	Good

continued on following page

Table 1. Continued

Code	Country of Origin	Gender	Age	Marital Status	Occupation (Gümüşhane)	Years Resident (Gümüşhane)	Turkish Proficiency
G20	Afghan (Uzbek)	Male	28	Married	Greengrocer worker	10 years	Good
G21	Syria (Turkmen)	Male	32	Married	Construction worker	8 years	Good
G22	Syria	Male	35	Married	Construction foreman	10 years	Good

Table 2. Data on the Local Community Participants

Code	Gender	Age	Marital Status	Occupation
Y1	Male	32	Married	School administrator (counsellor)
Y2	Female	45	Married	Beautician
Y3	Female	36	Married	Banker
Y4	Female	46	Married	Sociologist
Y5	Female	55	Married	Cook
Y6	Female	31	Married	Paramedic
Y7	Male	50	Married	Businessperson
Y8	Female	39	Married	Handicrafts instructor
Y9	Female	29	Single	Driving instructor
Y10	Male	69	Married	Tailor
Y11	Male	40	Married	Baker
Y12	Male	36	Married	Optician
Y13	Male	60	Married	Upholsterer
Y14	Male	42	Married	Fruit-pulp (pestil-köme) worker
Y15	Female	30	Single	Qur'an course instructor
Y16	Female	38	Single	Architect
Y17	Male	63	Married	Religious official
Y18	Male	38	Married	Shoe-shop owner
Y19	Female	58	Married	Curtain retailer
Y20	Female	48	Married	Entrepreneur
Y21	Male	34	Married	Non-commissioned officer
Y22	Female	41	Married	Support staff

Interviews

To bring out the experiences of the subjects, this study used in-depth interviewing, one of the most widely used techniques in qualitative research. In-depth interviews allow the subjects' experiences, perceptions, and meaning systems to be examined in detail and in their own words.

Within the scope of this study, interviews were conducted with adult women and men residing in different neighborhoods of Gümüşhane. Meetings were arranged at times and places convenient for the participants, and the interviews proceeded on the basis of the semi-structured guide.

All interviews were audio-recorded and all participants signed a consent form. The recordings were later transcribed in full for analysis.

In order to obtain fuller information about participants' lives, economic situations, and social positions, the interviews were conducted in a manner that allowed follow-up questions and elaboration where relevant.

Data Analysis

Unlike quantitative research, which relies on questionnaires, standardized tests, and experimental designs for data collection, this study analyzed the interview data through qualitative content analysis. In qualitative content analysis, the data are read repeatedly, meaningful units are coded, and the codes are gathered under categories and themes. In line with the statements of the migrant and local participants, three main themes were identified as functional for understanding socio-cultural integration: identity, the construction of living together, and the cultural adaptation strategy.

Limitations and Strengths of the Study

Within the scope of this study, considerable effort and time were required to reach both migrant and local community participants; establishing trust and arranging interviews in a small-scale setting was demanding. A further limitation is that the interviews were conducted only with migrants who spoke Turkish, which leaves outside the study the experiences of those who do not.

A strength of the study is that, in keeping with the principle of maximum variation within the purposive sampling technique, it reached participants of differing origins, ages, genders, occupations, and lengths of residence in Gümüşhane. Presenting the experiences of migrants and local residents together in the analysis is a further strength, as it makes the relational and two-way character of socio-cultural integration visible.

Ethical Considerations

The ethical suitability of the research, carried out within the scope of a master's thesis, was assessed and approved by the relevant ethics committee before fieldwork began.

Throughout the process, care was taken to observe the rules regarded as the ethical principles to be followed.

Participants were informed that participation in the study was entirely voluntary and that they could withdraw at any stage.

Participants were assured that the principle of confidentiality would be observed unconditionally, that recording would take place only where permission was granted, and that their identities would be protected through the use of codes.

The principle of not harming participants was observed in the interviews. In keeping with this principle, care was taken to avoid questions that might disturb participants, and the interviews were ended whenever a participant wished.

MAIN FOCUS OF THE CHAPTER

Through qualitative content analysis of the semi-structured, in-depth interviews conducted in Gümüşhane with 22 migrant and 22 local community participants, themes were developed. The experiences and perceptions of the participants are presented together in the analysis. In line with the statements of the migrant and local participants, three main themes were identified as functional for understanding the socio-cultural integration taking place in the case of Gümüşhane: identity, the local community–migrant relationship, and the process of cultural adaptation.

Identity

In the process of socio-cultural integration, the identity or identities through which individuals define themselves are significant, because identity—bound up with the answer to the question "who am I?"—constitutes the process through which similarities and differences with other individuals are constructed. In this respect identity bears directly on socio-cultural integration. When the statements of migrant and local individuals are analyzed, it can be said that local residents define migrants by nationality as "Syrian, Afghan, African," that discourses of "Muslim" and "Muslimness" constitute a shared identity perception, and that discourses of "Turk" and "Turkishness" constitute a differentiating one.

Identity ascriptions refer to the differences between the other and the self. Despite the existence of different identity ascriptions, the migrants living in Gümüşhane are defined by their countries of origin, with their ethnic, religious, social, and class differences disregarded. Used as homogeneous ascriptions, the identity labels "Syrian, Afghan, African" show that the local resident forms a general judgment about the migrant's identity and that the national identities migrants hold are evaluated differently.

"Afghans are loyal to their work, clean, good people." (Y7)

"The Afghans I know are very well-mannered." (Y15)

"Afghans, in my view, are very well-adjusted and very easygoing." (Y8)

Looking at local residents' statements, migrants with an "Afghan" identity are seen to be described as hardworking, respectful, and well-adjusted. In the classification of migrants by national identity, the same participants do not make comparably positive statements about "Syrian" migrants.

"In general I don't like Syrians; they're dirty." (Y7)

"I don't want Syrians at all; they don't appeal to me and I don't like them." (Y15)

The negativity in local residents' descriptions of "Syrian" migrants is noticed by the migrant, as in the statement, "Some people don't look kindly on me because I'm Syrian" (G13). This shows that the hierarchy local residents construct through national identity is also perceived on the migrant's side.

For local residents, among the migrants they define by national identity, another group is defined as "African."

"African people seem dirty to me; I wouldn't want them to go to the same school as us." (Y15)

"In Gümüşhane they don't like Africans." (Y20)

In local residents' descriptions of "African" migrants, negative attributions and a marked social distance come to the fore. When local residents' statements are examined, migrants are placed in a hierarchical ordering through their national identities: an "Afghan" identity is met relatively positively, a "Syrian" identity more negatively, and an "African" identity with the sharpest distance.

While a hierarchical classification is constructed between migrants through the perception of national identity, a shared Muslim identity comes to the fore as a facilitator. Local residents describe closeness with migrants through religious commonality.

"Because our religion is the same, their way of life largely resembles ours." (Y14)

"They're Muslims too, conservative like us; their customs and traditions suit ours." (Y4)

In terms of socio-cultural integration, religious elements are seen to operate similarly for migrants as well, easing their adaptation.

"I'm a Muslim, and the fact that the people here are Muslim too made my adaptation here easier." (G17)

"The similarity of our cultures was an ease for me; being a Muslim in particular helped me get used to this place." (G9)

In line with the participants' statements, the religious similarity that proceeds through a Muslim identity operates as a facilitator of socio-cultural integration for both groups. Alongside this shared identity, however, "Turkishness," which the local resident defines as an identity that sets the self apart from the "other," functions as a differentiating identity.

"Whatever nation they come from, they can never be like a Turk." (Y17)

"Our view of them is so different, as if we were a race superior to them, looking down on them." (Y3)

In line with the participants' statements, "Turkishness" is decisive in relations with migrants and is held to be superior to migrant identity. It thereby forms the ground for regarding the migrant as "other," and, in the view of local residents, becomes a reason why migrants cannot fully attain social acceptance.

The Construction of Living Together

"Migration is not only a spatial mobility but also a process in which individuals' cultural identities, values, and everyday practices are reshaped" (Aksoy & Cengiz, 2025). When the statements of migrants and local residents are examined, the everyday construction of socio-cultural integration is seen to proceed through both facilitating similarities and complicating differences.

In line with the participants' statements, socio-cultural integration is eased through religious similarity (being Muslim). A shared Muslim identity supports rapprochement and a sense of common belonging between the two groups.

"They're Muslims too, conservative like us; their customs and traditions suit ours." (Y4)

"Because our religion is the same, their way of life largely resembles ours." (Y14)

With migration, however, the encounter of two different cultures heightens the visibility of differences. Alongside the facilitating role of religious commonality, differences in everyday life—around cleanliness and cultural dress, for example—become grounds on which distance is built.

"They're more disorderly than us; for instance, we don't throw rubbish on the ground, but they do. It's not part of our culture." (Y3)

"Where we come from it's quite normal to drop rubbish on the ground, but here it's frowned upon. I learned that later." (G6)

"I've never come across a clean Syrian." (Y3)

"They're dirty; they have different habits. Their clothes are dirty, they're not clean people." (Y15)

"I'd like to wear clothes belonging to our own culture, but when I do, they tell me to go back to my own country." (G13)

That the ground of difference between the local community and migrants is built around cleanliness and cultural visibility in everyday life shows that the reciprocity presumed in the integration process does not operate. The differences that become visible are attributed by local residents to the migrants and treated as markers of an unbridgeable distance.

Socio-cultural adaptation can be gauged by the level of contact (Berry, 1997). In this frame, the forms of contact between local residents and migrants matter for socio-cultural integration.

When the participants' statements are examined, the relations local residents build with migrants are seen to remain, for the most part, at the level of greeting.

"We have a relationship only at the level of greeting." (Y5)

"I've seen them, but I know only one person, and even with him my contact is limited to greeting." (Y9)

"In ordinary life I don't know any migrants, but in the work setting I sometimes come across them." (Y11)

In line with local residents' statements, the local community keeps its distance at the point of building relations with migrants, and contact does not deepen beyond greeting.

In line with the participants' statements, another form of contact between local residents and migrants in Gümüşhane takes the shape of a customer relationship.

"I have no one I meet on friendly terms, but there are people I see around and know as customers." (Y18)

"There are migrants I know, but they're not people I chat with or am friends with; I know them as customers." (Y2)

"Many come and go to the bakery, but I've never once had a proper conversation; I've had no such chance." (Y11)

In line with local residents' statements, the customer-relationship form of contact remains bounded by commercial exchange and does not turn into a social bond.

In line with the participants' statements, a further form of contact is the work relationship. Local residents come into contact with migrants as employers.

"Our relationship was generally limited to the employer–employee dimension, but I'm pleased with them." (Y7)

"One of them is an Afghan and I give him work. There are fabrics here; I take orders for trousers, and he does them." (Y10)

The statement of the participant coded G3, "They like the way I work and that I'm reliable. When I apply for a job, people who know me say I do my work well and even act as references for me," and that of the participant coded G6, "They constantly speak highly of how well I do my work," show that the work relationship is seen by the migrant as a form of recognition and legitimacy.

That the contact established between local residents and migrants on economic grounds does not continue as a social bond creates a negative in the experience of socio-cultural integration. Where contact that begins as an economic relationship turns into a social one, it allows two different cultures to come to know each other and can constitute the experience of socio-cultural integration.

The Cultural Adaptation Strategy

For individuals who have migrated from various countries of origin to another country for various reasons, the conditions of life in the new country matter. As migrants of different cultures begin to live alongside individuals who sometimes share and sometimes hold different cultural and social codes, the encounter of two different cultures is set in motion. This process operates, for both migrants and local residents, largely through adaptation strategies and patterns of expectation formed in everyday encounters. "In all plural societies, cultural groups—and the individuals within them—who are in both dominant and non-dominant positions must confront the question of how to acculturate. Acculturation strategies are generally developed by groups and individuals during their daily interactions" (Berry, 1997). Within this frame, the statements of migrants and local residents were analyzed in terms of Berry's acculturation-strategy model. The analysis yielded the categories of assimilation expectation, conditional multiculturalism, the impossibility of full adaptation, and cultural threat.

When the participants' statements are examined, local residents can be said to be largely in a state of cultural-assimilation expectation toward migrants. This expectation is bound up with migrants coming to resemble them in language and conduct.

"As long as they don't learn my language, in my eyes they're mute; it means nothing, it says nothing to me." (Y6)

"Since they came here, it's really they who should learn this language and communicate with us." (Y15)

"People out there don't understand their language, so there's no point in them speaking it; let them speak Turkish." (Y22)

For local residents, speaking Turkish is the clearest expression of adaptation. This expectation of adaptation operates in the form of assimilation. "Turkishness," defined as a differentiating identity, sustains itself as an assimilation expectation in the migrants' adaptation process. For local residents, migrants' knowing and widely using Turkish establishes Turkish culture as the hegemonic determinant. Migrants who do not or cannot speak Turkish are characterized by local residents as maladjusted and are excluded. That expectations regarding knowledge and use of the language limit migrants' opportunities to build and develop social relations with the local community is also evident in migrant participants' statements: "When I speak my own language I meet with a reaction—they say you're foreigners, why are you here, if you've come here you have to speak the language of this place" (G11).

"Sometimes when I speak Arabic people judge me—why are you speaking this language, this is Turkey, some react." (G13)

Migrants' completely relinquishing or altering the cultural attributes they hold affects the experience of socio-cultural integration adversely, because in socio-cultural integration it is important that groups preserve and sustain their own identities to a certain degree.

"Wherever you go, you'll adapt to that place. If they keep up their own cultures, they'll stand out more, catch the eye more." (Y5)

"They should be able to fit their culture to ours... they should be integrated into our culture." (Y1)

These statements show that assimilation also operates, for local residents, through behavioral expectations. That this expectation is perceived by migrants, and that behavioral change follows, is expressed by the participant coded G13: "Where we come from, swinging prayer beads is quite normal... but I didn't know it was misread in Turkey... After that day I never did it again."

"The process of integrating can be successfully pursued by non-dominant groups only when the dominant society's attitude toward cultural diversity is positive and inclusive. The integration strategy can be implemented only in societies that are explicitly multicultural" (Berry, 1997). Multiculturalism denotes a structure that holds two or more cultures within it and works to preserve cultural values. Looking at the integration process within the study, and in line with local residents' statements, a conditional multiculturalism is evident in Gümüşhane, because conditional multiculturalism ties the recognition of cultural differences to the fulfillment of certain obligations. Under conditional multiculturalism, migrants' social acceptance is made contingent on particular conditions. Local residents' statements—

"Let them keep their holidays and their culture alive in their own homes, but it makes no sense for them to display their culture outside." (Y7)

"There's no harm in their keeping it up within the family, at home, but in public spaces I'd want them to conform to our culture." (Y19)

"They can sustain their own culture within the family, but they can't do so once they step outside." (Y21)

"If they have practices that clash, let them do them at home, but not out in society." (Y8)

"Let them practice their own cultural traditions at home, but when they go out, let them adapt to here." (Y12)

—show an expectation that migrants' culture may be free in their own private spaces but restricted in public. That this is also perceived and even accepted by the non-dominant group appears in migrants' statements: "Outside I behave in ways suited to your culture, but at home I behave according to my own" (G3); "At home I keep my own culture alive through my dress and our food, but outside I do none of it" (G9). This rare accord can be read as the de facto contract of living together. The cultural difference with the dominant group is confined by the non-dominant group to the private sphere, and public conformity is achieved. Both the dominant and the non-dominant group accept this tacit rule. Yet it does not take place among equals. The rule about how one is to be in public—about how cultural visibility is to be managed—is set by local residents, and the migrant complies. Conditional multiculturalism is an asymmetrical peace, because the recognition of migrants' cultural values and differences, and their social acceptance, are determined through the inequality of power present in the field. Migrants' displaying and sustaining their differences and taking part in social life are settled not through equal negotiation but by the power of local residents. The principle of reciprocity present in socio-cultural integration therefore does not, in this sense, obtain. In the specific case of Gümüşhane, the local community–migrant relationship is built around conditional multiculturalism, and the asymmetrical outlook it involves is plainly visible in these statements.

Turkish identity and Turkish culture—on which local residents strongly agree among themselves and which they see as the ground of their difference from the migrant—are influential in the integration process.

"We'll never be able to fully embrace them, that's certain. They'll remain a Syrian, an Afghan; we won't be able to say they're one of us." (Y1)

"Just as I wouldn't become like a German when I go to Germany, they can't become like a Turk here; they adapt, but they can't become one." (Y2)

"A person carries the traits of the soil they were raised in. Whatever nation they come from, they can never be like a Turk." (Y17)

"They can't become like someone from Gümüşhane; one doesn't become of Gümüşhane, one is born of Gümüşhane." (Y12)

In line with these statements, the structural impossibility of integration rests, it can be said, on the dominant cultural group's regarding its own cultural values as superior. For the local community, national culture matters and becomes the reason migrants' social acceptance is not fully realized. That this is accepted by migrants appears in the statement of the participant coded G5: "In my view it's not possible; I think people would judge them."

Despite local residents' emphatic statements about the determining and superior character of Turkish culture, they perceive migrants' presence in the city as a cultural threat.

"Their growing numbers change our culture... society is being spoiled, its character is being lost." (Y8)

"In my view it causes a deformation... of course there's damage." (Y16)

"Let them not spoil our cultural, homogeneous structure." (Y12)

"They've spoiled our whole order, our moral structure." (Y3)

These statements show the inward-looking anxiety of cultural threat. The statement of the participant coded G12—"I don't want to forget my traditions; I want my children to grow up with Turkish culture, but I also want them to know our own traditions"—shows that the migrant has no such intent to "spoil" as local residents claim, but rather seeks a balance between preserving his or her own culture and adapting. Alongside anxieties that the migrant will spoil Turkish culture, local residents also express anxieties that the place, the city, will be overrun by migrants.

"If not today then tomorrow they'll overrun this place... once their numbers rise, there'll be trouble." (Y18)

"One day these people will be the kings of the country; then they'll make us work and not pay us... if it goes on like this, they'll throw us out." (Y20)

"In Esenyurt I witnessed such a scene, as if we were in Damascus. Arabic signs everywhere; you're in the middle of Istanbul, but it's as if you're in Damascus at the same time." (Y12)

"At one point migrants had overrun the islands in Istanbul; there were no Turks at all, the character of the place had changed." (Y16)

These statements are indicative of the spatial and demographic extreme of the threat perception toward migrants. Formed through a nativist discourse, this perception arises less from individuals' own experience than from what they know of other cities, from what they have heard in the media, and from a fear of numbers. The statements of the participant coded G4, "I'll go back to my country," and the participant coded G16, "I'm thinking of returning to my country," show that migrants speak in a language of temporariness and return and have no such aim of "overrunning."

CONCLUSION

This study has set out the experience of socio-cultural integration in its various dimensions along the axis of local contexts. The relations built between local residents and migrants in everyday life have been examined in terms of socio-cultural integration.

For socio-cultural integration to succeed, the recognition of migrants' identities and sub-identities is important. Yet migrants were found to be defined, according to their countries of origin, within a homogeneous structure under a national-identity heading, as "Syrian, Afghan, African." These identity ascriptions by local residents were found to reflect a hierarchical approach to migrant groups and prejudicial conduct, at various levels, through national identity.

Local residents and migrants were found to agree on a "Muslim" identity, which is used as a means of integration in socio-cultural terms. While the shared Muslim identity takes on a facilitating function in socio-cultural integration, differences in religious practice between local residents and migrants were found to construct distinctions and to lead migrants to experience exclusion. Within this frame, alongside its positive, shared effect in socio-cultural integration, the Muslim identity was found to give rise to separation through differences of religious practice.

The "Turkishness" identity held by local residents was found to be decisive in the relations built, to be regarded as superior to migrant identity, and, for that reason, to underpin an agreement that the migrant cannot succeed in socio-cultural integration. Appearing as a differentiating identity for both local residents and migrants, Turkishness was found to form the ground for viewing the migrant as "other."

In the socio-cultural integration process, similarities serve a facilitating function while differences create complicating ones. The social relations between local residents and migrants were found to be built on the similarity of being Muslim, which has a positive effect on socio-cultural integration for both groups. The differences that begin to stand out as two cultures live side by side were found to be constructed by local residents around factors such as migrants' cleanliness and ethnic dress.

The level of contact matters in socio-cultural integration. The forms of contact between local residents and migrants were found to take place at a superficial level—greeting, customer relationships, work relationships. That these economically grounded forms of relationship gain no social dimension shows that socio-cultural integration is not realized. The absence of friendship between local residents and migrants is a specific finding indicating that socio-cultural integration remains very limited. Interaction and mutual acquaintance between two cultures are important in socio-cultural integration, and friendship is the plainest expression of such a relationship. The absence of friendship in the findings is, despite the small scale of the city, an indicator of the limits of the socio-cultural integration process.

In the cultural adaptation process that begins with the everyday encounter of local residents and migrants, local residents were found to hold intense expectations that migrants conform to the local culture. Turkish—through which the differentiating Turkish identity gains visibility in everyday life—was seen by local residents as the clearest expression of adaptation and was evaluated both as an expression of adaptation and as a means of cultural assimilation. Migrants who do not speak Turkish were found to fail in building social relations, while for migrants, knowing Turkish was evaluated as functional for easing everyday life and gaining acceptance from the local community.

Local residents were found to adopt a conditional multiculturalism in their relations with migrants, whereby cultural differences between the local community and migrants are confined to the private sphere and public conformity is produced. This was found to be the de facto contract of living together between settled residents and migrants: settled residents decide how, and to what degree, cultural visibility will appear in public space, and the migrant complies with this rule.

Local residents who emphasize that the local culture ought to be the hegemonic determinant were found to perceive migrants' presence in the city as a cultural threat. Against this, migrants' statements were found to show an effort to strike a balance between preserving their own culture and adapting.

In conclusion, in a small-scale local context such as Gümüşhane, socio-cultural integration can be said to be eased by religious commonality but to operate as a fragmented process, strained by perceptions of national identity, everyday norms, and limited contact.

REFERENCES

Aksoy, M. (2025). Göç dinamikleri: Tarihsel evrim, kültürel dönüşüm ve küreselleşme çağında yeni yönelimler. In Aksoy, M., & Cengiz, E. (Eds.), *Göç, kimlik ve entegrasyon* (pp. 17–38). Nobel Akademik Yayıncılık.

Aksoy, M., & Cengiz, E. (2025). Göç, kimlik arayışı ve entegrasyon tartışmaları. In Aksoy, M., & Cengiz, E. (Eds.), *Göç, kimlik ve entegrasyon* (pp. 1–16). Nobel Akademik Yayıncılık.

Bahar, H. İ. (2005). *Sosyoloji*. USAK Yayınları.

Balcı, M. E. (2022). Zorunlu göç: Kimlik, aidiyet ve uyum çerçevesinde bir değerlendirme. *Tezkire, 81*, 110–116.

Berry, J. W. (1997). Immigration, acculturation, and adaptation. *Applied Psychology, 46*(1), 5–34. DOI: 10.1111/j.1464-0597.1997.tb01087.x

Berry, J. W. (2001). A psychology of immigration. *The Journal of Social Issues, 57*(3), 615–631. DOI: 10.1111/0022-4537.00231

Berry, J. W. (2005). Acculturation: Living successfully in two cultures. *International Journal of Intercultural Relations, 29*(6), 697–712. DOI: 10.1016/j.ijintrel.2005.07.013

Berry, J. W. (2006). Stress perspectives on acculturation. In Sam, D. L., & Berry, J. W. (Eds.), *The Cambridge handbook of acculturation psychology* (pp. 43–57). Cambridge University Press. DOI: 10.1017/CBO9780511489891.007

Bourdieu, P. (1977). *Outline of a theory of practice*. Cambridge University Press. DOI: 10.1017/CBO9780511812507

Bourdieu, P. (1986). The forms of capital. In Richardson, J. G. (Ed.), *Handbook of theory and research for the sociology of education* (pp. 241–258). Greenwood Press.

Bourdieu, P., & Wacquant, L. J. D. (1992). *An invitation to reflexive sociology*. Polity Press.

Castles, S., & Miller, M. J. (1998). *The age of migration: International population movements in the modern world*. Macmillan Press. DOI: 10.1007/978-1-349-26846-7

Creswell, J. W., & Poth, C. N. (2018). *Nitel araştırma yöntemleri: Beş yaklaşıma göre nitel araştırma ve araştırma deseni* (Bütün, M., & Demir, S. B., Trans.). Siyasal Kitabevi.

de Certeau, M. (1984). *The practice of everyday life*. University of California Press.

de Haas, H. (2010). The internal dynamics of migration processes: A theoretical inquiry. *Journal of Ethnic and Migration Studies, 36*(10), 1587–1617. DOI: 10.1080/1369183X.2010.489361

Erel, U. (2010). Migrating cultural capital: Bourdieu in migration studies. *Sociology, 44*(4), 642–660. DOI: 10.1177/0038038510369363

Garcés-Mascareñas, B., & Penninx, R. (Eds.). (2016). *Integration processes and policies in Europe: Contexts, levels and actors*. Springer Open., DOI: 10.1007/978-3-319-21674-4

Kaplan, M., & Yardımcıoğlu, M. (2020). Alan, habitus ve sermaye kavramlarıyla Pierre Bourdieu. *Toplumbilim Dergisi, 1*, 23–37.

Kümbetoğlu, B. (2012). *Sosyolojide ve antropolojide niteliksel yöntem ve araştırma* (3rd ed.). Bağlam Yayınları.

Mason, J. (2002). *Qualitative research* (2nd ed.). SAGE Publications.

Neuman, W. L. (2014). *Toplumsal araştırma yöntemleri: Nicel ve nitel yaklaşımlar* (5th ed.). Yayın Odası.

Palabıyık, A. (2011). Pierre Bourdieu sosyolojisinde habitus, sermaye ve alan üzerine. *Liberal Düşünce, 15*(61–62), 121–141.

Patton, M. Q. (2014). *Nitel araştırma ve değerlendirme yöntemleri* (Bütün, M., & Demir, S. B., Trans.). Pegem Akademi.

Penninx, R., & Garcés-Mascareñas, B. (Eds.). (2016). *Integration processes and policies in Europe: Contexts, levels and actors*. Springer Open.

Ritzer, G. (2011). *Modern sosyoloji kuramları*. De Ki Basım Yayım.

Snape, D., & Spencer, L. (2003). The foundations of qualitative research. In J. Ritchie & J. Lewis (Eds.), *Qualitative research practice: A guide for social science students and researchers* (pp. 1–23). Sage Publications.

Spencer, R., Pryce, J. M., & Walsh, J. (2014). Philosophical approaches to qualitative research. In Leavy, P. (Ed.), *The Oxford handbook of qualitative research* (pp. 81–98). Oxford University Press.

Spencer, S., & Charsley, K. (2021). Reframing 'integration': Acknowledging and addressing five core critiques. *Comparative Migration Studies, 9*(1), 18. Advance online publication. DOI: 10.1186/s40878-021-00226-4

Tokmak, M. C. (2022). Kültürleşme sürecinin kitle iletişim araçlarında temsili: Spanglish modeli. *4. Boyut Medya ve Kültürel Çalışmalar Dergisi, 21*(21), 1–22. DOI: 10.26650/4boyut.2022.1204077

Tutty, L. M., Rothery, M. A., & Grinnell, R. M. (1996). *Qualitative research for social workers: Phases, steps, and tasks*. Allyn & Bacon.

Wallace, R. A., & Wolf, A. (2012). *Çağdaş sosyoloji kuramları* (Elburuz, L., & Ayas, R., Trans.). Punto Yayınları.

Yılmaz, H. (2025). Göç ve dijital medyanın kesişiminde sosyo-kültürel uyum: YouTube üzerine nitel bir inceleme. *Ortadoğu ve Göç, 15*(2), 258–305. DOI: 10.31834/ortadoguvegoc.1784575

Yılmaz, H., & Önay Doğan, B. (2025). Sosyokültürel uyumun iletişim perspektifinden analizi: İstanbul ve Gaziantep'teki Suriyeli üniversite öğrencileri üzerine bir inceleme. *Gaziantep Üniversitesi Sosyal Bilimler Dergisi, 24*(3), 1186–1208.

Zafer, A. B. (2016). Göç çalışmaları için bir anahtar olarak kültürleşme kavramı. *Uludağ Üniversitesi Fen-Edebiyat Fakültesi Sosyal Bilimler Dergisi, 17*(30), 75–92.

KEY TERMS AND DEFINITIONS

Acculturation: The change in the original cultural patterns of one or both groups that results from continuous, direct contact between people of different cultures, occurring at both the cultural and the psychological level.

Conditional Multiculturalism: An arrangement in which cultural difference is recognized only on condition that it remain confined to the private sphere while public conformity to the dominant culture is required, producing an asymmetrical accommodation set by the dominant group.

Field: In Bourdieu's sociology, a relational arena of objective positions in which actors deploy their economic, cultural, and social capital and struggle, often through symbolic means, over recognition and legitimacy.

Habitus: In Bourdieu's sociology, the set of durable, internalized dispositions through which individuals perceive, evaluate, and act in the social world, acquired through long occupancy of a social position and reshaped by new situations.

Phenomenological Approach: A qualitative approach that seeks to understand social reality by exploring the meanings individuals attach to their experiences of a phenomenon within everyday life.

Purposive Sampling: A qualitative sampling technique in which participants are selected deliberately for their capacity to provide rich, relevant information about the phenomenon under study rather than for statistical representativeness.

Socio-Cultural Integration: The process through which migrants and members of a receiving society come to know one another and take part in shared social life via cultural adaptation, social acceptance, identity negotiation, and everyday contact, understood as relational and two-way rather than as a one-sided outcome measured only against migrants.

Symbolic Boundary: A conceptual distinction used to classify people and practices that, when combined with durable inequalities of access to resources, can harden into a social boundary between groups.

Chapter 16
Migration, Citizenship, and Legal Identity:
The Special Intensive Revision Regime in India

Naresh Prajapati
http://orcid.org/0000-0002-0752-3651
School of Law, Bennett University, Greater Noida, India

Anwesha Ghosh
http://orcid.org/0000-0003-4167-2121
Kirit P. Mehta School of Law, Shri Vile Parle Kelvani Mandal's Narsee Monjee Institute of Management Studies (Deemed to be University), Mumbai, India

ABSTRACT

This chapter examines the national expansion of the Special Intensive Revision (SIR) process, which began in Assam, one of the North-Eastern States of India, and now functions as a de facto mechanism for citizenship scrutiny. Though presented as an electoral roll update, SIR disproportionately targets internal migrants, women, Adivasis, and residents of informal settlements, groups historically excluded from documentation systems. Drawing on legal analysis and case-based narratives, the chapter reveals how SIR redefines citizenship as a precarious, paper-dependent status. It argues for urgent procedural safeguards and a constitutional shift from suspicion to inclusion within the legal framework of India.

DOI: 10.4018/979-8-3373-8500-6.ch016

INTRODUCTION

The debate over the question of citizenship, which has already been dealt with in the Constitution of India, has, over the past few years, shifted to the periphery of national debate and transformed the relationship between the individual and the state (Jayal, 2013; Austin, 1966). Though citizenship has never been a light matter in the legal and political sense of any country, its definition and application have started to drift towards more administrative and technical approaches (Scott, 1998; Torpey, 2000). The Special Intensive Revision (SIR) process is one such mechanism, formally situated within electoral roll revision but increasingly relevant to wider debates on legal identity, documentation, and civic inclusion (Chakravarty, 2019). What began in the specific context of Assam has generated concerns about whether electoral verification practices may, in some contexts, take on the character of citizenship scrutiny. While presented as a normal precaution to keep the electoral lists accurate, the reality of how the SIR process works is more on the side of intrusion and coercion (Human Rights Watch, 2019; The Guardian, 2025; Economic Times, 2025). This is especially important for a volume concerned with migration and integration, because documentary exclusion can affect not only formal voting rights but also broader questions of social belonging, civic participation, and recognition within the political community.

This chapter deals with document-based identity becoming entrenched in the law and administration of India (Torpey, 2000; Hull, 2012). In a nation where the documentation is not even and is traditionally based on caste, class, gender, migration status, and geography, the transformation into the paper-based citizenry establishes new exclusionary patterns (Deshingkar & Akter, 2009; Kabeer, 2005; Norwegian Centre for Human Rights, 2021). Legal identity, which was previously assumed to be stable due to birth, residence, or long-term community membership, is becoming more and more conditional (Hari & Nagpal, 2022). The inability to provide documents, the existence of discrepancies, or the absence of fixed addresses can now put people into the doubtful voter category or, worse still, the category of potential non-citizens. Through the SIR mechanism, the state does not merely authenticate identity; it also shapes the conditions under which identity, membership, and belonging are recognized.

The importance of the SIR regime is based on the fact that it is a hybrid system of governing, in which the electoral system is linked to the migration management system and definitions of legal statuses. Ordinary electoral revision is designed to update voter lists by adding, deleting, or correcting entries. The NRC process, by contrast, concerns the verification of citizenship status, particularly in Assam. D-voter classification refers to the marking of certain voters as "doubtful" where their citizenship is questioned. SIR occupies a more ambiguous position because, although it is framed as an electoral exercise, its documentary requirements and consequences may overlap with citizenship verification. The SIR was first conceived in the special post-Partition and post-Assam Accord situation of Assam and was intended to identify and disqualify so-called ineligible voters, the ones suspected to be undocumented immigrants. But the copying of such a model outside Assam happens in an empty space of the law; there is neither an Act nor a parliamentary discussion that sanctions such a shift. However, However, when SIR-style verification practices are discussed or used beyond Assam, they raise difficult legal questions, especially where the statutory basis, procedural safeguards, and relationship with citizenship law remain unclear. This brings up some serious constitutional issues. What are the legal norms of this process? What are the rights of people who are wrongfully discriminated against? Who is the one who is required to prove identity, and according to what criterion? And what safeguards, such as there exist, are there for the flagged or the excluded?

This chapter explores how SIR has been changed to mean and enforce citizenship in modern India. In its essence, the chapter aims to find the answers to three questions, which are interrelated: the first one, how is the SIR process, as an administrative mechanism, redefining the boundaries of legal citizenship in India? Second, what are the communities most impacted by this process and what historical, social or economic factors predispose them to it? Third, what are the implications of the SIR regime in general on the participation of democracies, equal treatment under the law, social integration, civic inclusion, and belonging?

To answer such questions, the current chapter takes on a qualitative, interdisciplinary approach, which is based purely on secondary data. The methodology implies a critical and comprehensive analysis of the legal framework followed in India, such as the Citizenship Act (1955), the Foreigners Act (1946), the electoral legislation, as well as the procedural guidelines issued by the Election Commission of India. Moreover, the work deals with major Indian judicial rulings, including Sarbananda Sonowal v. Union of India and Abdul Kuddus v. Union of India. The interpretation of citizenship, burden of proof, and procedural fairness has been developed by the Union of India, which has influenced the interpretation of those provisions. The conceptual framework is provided by the academic literature of law and political science, sociology, migration studies, and journalistic research. The analysis is based on the lived realities of the reports provided by the civil society organisations and journalistic inquiries. The chapter is not based on fieldwork or primary interviews; rather, it uses the triangulation of different sources of published knowledge in the construction of a legally acceptable and socially based argument.

The chapter contributes to existing scholarships by bringing together debates that are often examined separately: citizenship verification, electoral administration, migration governance, and social integration. Existing studies have examined the

NRC, statelessness, migration, and documentary citizenship in India, but less attention has been paid to how electoral revision practices may become sites where legal identity, political participation, and belonging are contested. This chapter addresses that gap by treating SIR not merely as a technical administrative exercise, but as a process with implications for democratic inclusion and integration.

The chapter takes the form of seven sections. After this introduction, the second part offers a historical and legal background of how migration, the Partition and the Assam Accord helped create the exclusionary citizenship practices in India. It then presents the development of Indian citizenship law and the way electoral law had developed to include identity-checking processes. In the third part, the authors change the focus to the mechanics of the SIR process and how a voter list revision exercise is an informal test of citizenship in India, which operates by administrative discretion and opaque criteria. The fourth part explores the most vulnerable to exclusion, such as internal migrants, women, *Adivasis* and the urban poor, and the combination of social marginality and document scrutiny leads to systematic disenfranchisement. The fifth part critically analyses the SIR regime from an Indian constitutional law perspective and pays attention to the concepts of due process, equality and the right of recognition. It analyses the judicial interventions and determines the legal grey areas on which such a process could thrive without proper checks and balances. It is the sixth section that draws comparative lessons of other international contexts with references to the examples of the United States, Myanmar and the Gulf states, as well as the involvement with the theories of critical modes of state power and bureaucratic governance in order to place the Indian experience within the larger theoretical context. Lastly, the conclusion section summarises the main findings and gives policy suggestions. It advocates a change in the state practice towards surveillance to care, suspicion to inclusion and a narrow view of citizenship as documentation is replaced by a broader view of belonging as a constitutional right.

Placing the SIR process under intense examination, this chapter not only attempts to record the exclusionary consequences of the process, but is also an attempt to engage in a discussion on the nature of a citizenship regime that is assumed in India. Even the silence of the administration with which millions of people are being shoved into the fog is indefensible in a democracy where equality and dignity are guaranteed by the Constitution of India. The present chapter poses the following questions in the prism of SIR: who is allowed to be considered a citizen, and who makes decisions?

HISTORICAL AND LEGAL BACKGROUND

When India got its independence in 1947, the issue of citizenship was not only the status of the law but also a moral and political question closely connected with the Partition and mass migration, as well as with the new identity of the Indian Republic. The first foundation of citizenship was established by the Constitution of India, which came into force on 26 January 1950 in Articles 5 to 11. These were given to resolve who would become a citizen of India when the Constitution came into force, especially those migrants who had previously come and those who had come to India as a result of the Partition. This was because the framers intentionally left more specific guidance about future citizenship to the parliament, which was a result of the unsettled conditions in the demographics and politics of that era.

In 1955, the parliament passed the Citizenship Act, which has been the fundamental law governing citizenship by birth, descent, registration, naturalisation and incorporation of territory. Although the original Act appeared to be a fairly open method, its amendments, particularly those that followed in 1986, 2003 and 2019, were characterised by the obvious transition towards more restrictive and security-focused citizenship policies. In the 1986 amendment, a parental qualification to birth-based citizenship was added, which marked the beginning of a trend in which states were becoming increasingly concerned with undocumented migration. The amendment of 2003, more importantly, gave the structure of the National Register of Citizens (NRC) and the state was permitted to make a National Population Register (NPR), which formed the foundation of creating document-based citizenship checks. The most recent amendment, the Citizenship (Amendment) Act (CAA) 2019, left the general principles of a secular constitution and started the process of politicising citizenship by making religion a factor in certain naturalisation procedures.

A key historical event that emerged as a defining factor in the citizenship discourse was the Assam Movement (1979-1985) that took place as a result of the mass mobilisation against the alleged illegal immigration of people of Bangladesh. The movement culminated in the Assam Accord being signed in August 1985 between the Government of India and the leaders of the All-Assam Students' Union (AASU). The Accord gave a cut-off date of 24 March 1971, the date by which any foreigners had to be detected and expelled, in effect from 24 March 1971 onwards, defining citizens and non-citizens in terms of documentary presence in India before that date. This has become section 6A of the Citizenship Act and has generated a special citizenship category in Assam. Following the Assam Accord, several exceptional legal and administrative practices developed in Assam, including Foreigners Tribunals, the NRC process, and the marking of certain persons as Doubtful Voters, or D-voters, on the electoral roll. These mechanisms should be distinguished from one another. The NRC concerns citizenship verification; D-voter classification refers to the marking of voters whose citizenship is placed under doubt; and electoral roll revision is formally concerned with the accuracy of voter lists. SIR occupies an ambiguous position because it is framed as an electoral revision exercise but may, in practice, overlap with citizenship scrutiny where documentary proof and suspicion-based verification are involved. These classes of administration subjected the burden of proof to individuals to show that they were citizens, which was commonly done using documents that many could not afford because of poverty, displacement, or illiteracy. Whilst these mechanisms were reasonable as reactions to local demographic anxiety, they institutionalised mistrust and process obstacles in such a way that would subsequently shape national policies.

Migration- internal and cross-border has been a characteristic of Indian demographic and economic life. But in some political and geographical circumstances, it happened that the migrants have come to be regarded not as an economic resource or a displaced people, but as a source of a threat to cultural identity, national integrity, or security. In the northeastern states of India, in particular, migration has been associated with anxieties of demographic change, displacement of land rights and eradication of culture. This framing has played a central part in the formation of legal regimes that are characterised by the blurring of the distinction between migrants and so-called infiltrators. With time, the demarcation between citizens and non-citizens has been progressively mediated by the capacity to generate a set of documents of a certain nature, which is usually done in circumstances of arbitrary inspection.

The exclusion of migratory populations due to law and bureaucracy is a manifestation of the transformation of the state's attitude to citizenship. Instead of seeing citizenship as a status that has a presumption of validity, particularly in the case of persons born in the country or long-time residents, the focus has shifted to a check-up regime. Not only cross-border migrants but also internal migrants are touched upon by this trend, because of mobility, the lack of a permanent address, or non-uniform documents, they are the subject of suspicion. The women are especially vulnerable, especially those who marry and change names or those who do not have property documents (Kabeer, 2005; Chowdhury, 2004). For such groups, documentary citizenship is not only a legal issue but also an issue of social integration, because exclusion from documentation can affect access to voting, welfare, mobility, and recognition within the community.

Along the same lines as the changes in citizenship law, the transformation of the electoral law and voter registration processes in India has also started. The rules developed under the Representation of the People Act, 1950, contain the preparation and revision of electoral rolls. To make these rolls accurate, the Election Commission of India is granted the authority to carry out regular revisions of the same, which include special and intensive revisions. Electoral integrity requires such revision processes. However, where intensive revision is combined with documentary scrutiny and suspicion-based identification, it may move beyond ordinary electoral administration and acquire the character of identity verification.

The SIR process involving a door-to-door validation and document inspection is not clearly spelt out in the statute, but it is carried out according to administrative circulars. This process was used in Assam in conjunction with the so-called D-voter marking and allusions to Foreigners Tribunals. SIR should not be treated as identical to the NRC or D-voter classification. Rather, it should be understood as an electoral roll revision mechanism that may produce citizenship-related consequences when it is linked to documentary burdens, doubtful voter identification, or exclusion from the electoral roll. Similarly, claims about the spread of SIR-style practices outside Assam must be made cautiously. Available reports suggest that similar verification practices have been discussed or used in some other contexts, but their legal basis, scope, and connection to citizenship law require closer official documentation and institutional verification. This uncertainty itself raises concerns about transparency, discretion, and access to legal remedies.

In this way, the SIR is a perfect example of the interplay between the electoral regulation, law of citizenship and administrative discretion, where a certain group of people who were already marginalized. The historical and legal background therefore suggests that citizenship in India is increasingly shaped not only by formal legal entitlement, but also by the practical ability to prove identity through documents. This has direct implications for integration, because those unable to satisfy documentary requirements may remain legally present but civically insecure, socially excluded, and politically vulnerable.

HOW SIR WORKS: MORE THAN JUST A VOTER CHECK

The Special Intensive Revision (SIR) process, in its official version, being a voter roll update system. However, where it involves intensive documentary scrutiny, field verification, and possible exclusion from electoral rolls, it may operate in practice as a form of identity verification (Hull, 2012). Not only has the increased scrutiny of SIR made it stand out from ordinary electoral maintenance, but it is also the ability to change the relationship between individuals and the state fundamentally. As it is now, the procedure includes door-to-door validation by local enumerators, the collection of documents, fieldwork, and the designation of a person as a Questionable Voter, which has drastic implications on the legal identity of an individual and their rights to vote. It is important to distinguish this from the NRC and D-voter processes: NRC is a citizenship verification exercise, D-voter classification refers to voters whose citizenship is marked as doubtful, while SIR is formally an electoral revision process that may acquire citizenship-related consequences when linked to documentary suspicion and exclusion. SIR is not reflected in primary legislation; however, it takes the form of executive directions given by electoral authorities, with different levels of transparency and procedural protection. The absence of a standardised framework allows discretionary power to be exercised by the lower-level authorities, in that an administrative exercise might carry out the role of legal adjudication and frequently without judicial review (Economic Times, 2025).

On its operational level, SIR starts with a field visit of officials, usually, Booth Level Officers (BLOs), whose responsibility is to ascertain the entries in the electoral roll. These officers also demand physical presence and documentary evidence of people whose citizenship is questioned or who have a record of inconsistency in their records in places that have been designated as subject to intensive scrutiny. The focus lies in the delivery of legacy documents like land records, birth certificates, school leaving certificates, or evidence of living over a few decades (Human Rights Watch, 2019). The need to find such historical documentation is especially hard to meet in situations of displacement, informal settlement, or intergenerational illiteracy. Where documentary evidence is treated as the main basis of recognition, persons with weak documentary histories may face exclusion even when they have long-standing social and residential ties to a community.

Even though it is structured as an impersonal administrative undertaking, the procedure is subjective to several people. Citizens, and in particular socio-economically disadvantaged members of the community, are not usually notified before their citizenship status is put in question. In most cases, even when the names of individuals who are suspected have been noted as such, they are not even advised and only find out about the exclusion when they are refused access to any public services, or when they come to vote. The absence of transparency in the procedure and notification to the population further contributes to the inequality of power between state actors and regular residents. Although constitutional principles should support fair treatment and procedural safeguards, SIR-style verification may shift the practical burden onto individuals to prove their eligibility and belonging, rather than requiring the state to justify exclusion through clear and accountable procedures.

This fact is because the burden of proving SIR lies almost solely on the individual, irrespective of the structural impediments that he/she faces in seeking to get the documents (Scott, 1998). The effect of this demand is not a neutral effect. All these are disproportionately experienced by women, as there are gendered patterns of documentation. Most women do not have property documents or school certificates, and their names are easily changed upon marriage; hence, documentary consistency becomes a challenge. In the same way, the Scheduled Tribes and other communities living in the forests of India are frequently unable to generate land records because of custom or collective ownership of the land not recognised by the state (Xaxa,

2008). Internal migrants do not avoid their own problems, as they might not have continuous residency documentation or voter IDs, depending on their current residence. These difficulties show why SIR is not only a technical electoral issue but also an issue of integration: documentary gaps can affect civic participation, access to welfare, and recognition within the political community.

Discretion is a key factor in the dynamics of the SIR process (Foucault, 1991). The subjective judgments of the local officials are not legally prepared, and therefore cannot be questioned by the court of law in the courts of law regarding the sufficiency and integrity of the documents provided. In most instances, the enumerators are guided by local information, rumours, or random judgments when deciding on the legitimacy of an individual to be a citizen. Lack of formality or standardised evidentiary levels sets up the room for prejudice, inaccuracy, and exploitation. Besides, the so-called doubtful are not supplied with the specifications and a chance to be heard before disenfranchising. This sabotages fundamental constitutional principles of natural justice, such as *audi alteram partem*, the right to a fair hearing. It is not just a list of qualified voters but a more intricate, more perversive redefinition of citizenship itself that comes out of this process. The SIR is not a process that takes place in the sphere of open legal investigation; the structure of its creation is such that it is impossible to establish limits between governance and surveillance. Citizenship, which has always been granted by law and which is guaranteed by the constitution of India, was becoming conditional in nature-it depended upon the records available, upon the opinion of local authorities, and upon adherence to a constantly changing bureaucratic norm by individuals (Jayal, 2013). These fears are only intensified by the silent spread of SIR to other states of India other than Assam. Though it has not been endorsed by a policy or even a legislative amendment to give it national implementation, electoral authorities in several states have started to copy the model. This copying is done within a regulatory vacuum where there is neither a legislative discussion nor judicial questioning or consultation with the populace. The outcome of this is an increasing normalisation of suspicion-based checking in which specific groups of people are regularly placed into a disproportionate check because of an administrative imperative. As a matter of fact, SIR institutionalises the regime of selective vigilance, which is directed towards individuals whose identities are not compatible with conventional accounts of belonging.

The broader consequences are not on the electoral participation. When an individual is branded as a suspicious voter, the label accompanies them on their new journey in various spheres, this is since the label affects their welfare program, state jobs and various other services that would need them to demonstrate they are citizens. The exclusion is both social and legal. When documentation is being employed as a gatekeeping tool and is more powerful in a society, failure to fashion an identity on paper is equated with a lack of identity itself. This has direct implications for civic inclusion and belonging, because individuals may remain physically present in a community while being administratively uncertain or politically insecure.

The SIR compromises the entire assumption that the status of citizenship is settled and secure by turning a voter list revision procedure into an informal procedure of legal verification. It changes the landscape of rights to compliance, recognition to suspicion and legal certainty to administrative discretion. Although made to look like a harmless practice in electoral hygiene, the real effect of it is much more drastic, altering the outlines of inclusion in such a way that those who are already peripheral to the legal order are disproportionately impacted. The process does not simply record who is non-belonging, but it actually creates the categories of non-belonging, those who are not, without due process, without clarity or without a remedy.

WHO IS AFFECTED AND HOW?

The impacts of the SIR process are not equally distributed. Although it is formally used as a uniform administrative exercise, its effect is disproportionately felt by those communities that are already marginalized vis-a-vis a state recognition (Deshingkar & Akter, 2009). The kind of structure and the needs involved in the process, especially the reliance on documentary evidence and residence-checking, increase the weaknesses of certain social categories. Migrants, women, *Adivasis*, *Dalits* and people living in informal settlements prove to be the main target group not in terms of a legal deficiency of their status, but rather in terms of historical and structural circumstances that have rendered their access to documentation fractured, sporadic, or non-existent. Internal migrants, particularly those involved in circular or seasonal labour, may not have documentation of residence continuity (Hari & Nagpal, 2022; Norwegian Centre for Human Rights, 2021; Castles et al., 2014; Deshingkar & Akter, 2009). Most of them fail to renew their voter ID or ration card with every movement (Deshingkar & Akter, 2009), and also reside in common or temporary setups, which do not meet the bureaucratic requirements of demonstrating residency. There is a more deeply rooted suspicion against cross-border migrants, and more so of the Bangladesh-origin cross-border migrants who settled in the border areas of the Indian states of Assam and West Bengal decades ago (Banerjee, 2020; Chatterji, 2007). Their mere existence is not a socio-economic reality but a national identity threat. The stories of migration and political language often mix such that migration is confused with illegality and simplified charges of infiltration of complex histories of migration, displacement and settlement. This framework is incorporated into the SIR process, whereby specific names, accents, or places of origin are used as a point of further examination.

The exclusion of women is especially prone to SIR because of the gendered patterns of documentation in India (Kabeer, 2005; Chowdhury, 2004). In many cases, Patriarchal standards lead to a situation whereby women possess fewer documents in their names. In the case of married women, the name, address, and place of residence change will cause discrepancies in documents. A woman who was born in one village, married in another and lives in a third village because of migration or displacement may not have any uninterrupted line of identity to meet the bureaucratic requirements as required during SIR. In most instances reported in Assam, women who had previously voted in several other past elections were all at once identified as D-voters since they could not connect the legacy documents of their fathers to their marriage identity. What follows is a denial of civic prominence based not on any established illegality but on formal vacuums the system is unsuited to receive.

In the case of *Adivasis* and *Dalits*, the situation is further complicated by the fact that they have been excluded by a long history of exclusion from formal land and educational systems. Most of the *Adivasi* villages have been found in remote forested regions with land titles that are not recognised in the conventional revenue records and held collectively, in most cases. Here, lack of individual documents does not amount to non-citizenship but to the inability of states to incorporate the communities into their official record-keeping systems. Secluded or informal areas are also a problem faced by the *Dalits* who live in those areas. The fact that they are historically marginalised from bureaucratic processes implies that they are disproportionately represented by those people who are not able to provide the necessary paperwork when they are subjected to verification drives. Furthermore, their social position usually restricts their access to legal counsel or procedural expertise that is required to challenge exclusion. Informal settlements or slums are also vulnerable to the people dwelling there. These locals often reside in an unowned piece of land, most of which is a product of forced migration, urban settlement, or poverty. Their speeches are not registered, their names might not be present in the city books, and their everyday life is beyond official state recognition. In SIR, the residents would either not be enumerated or the residents would be indicated as not eligible due to failure to provide long-term residence evidence. In Delhi, the SIR-style checking of the electorate has been seen to dishonour thousands of the urban poor in the electoral lists, most of whom had lived in the same locality for years, but had no documents to satisfy the requirements of the electoral office.

Migration is constructed through a narrative framing of politics (Samaddar, 2016; Banerjee, 2020 ; Roy et al., 2021), which is an important factor in the legitimisation of such exclusions (Samaddar, 2016). Migration is not regarded as a structural characteristic of the economic life in India (Castles et al., 2014; Banerjee,

2020).; instead, it is usually disruptive. In Assam, years of political mobilisation against so-called illegal Bangladeshi immigrants have established an environment where migration is the equivalent of illegitimacy. This suspicion is not just of the cross-border migrants; it is also of internal migrants in the Indian states of Bihar, West Bengal, and Uttar Pradesh who are considered to be foreign to the northeast states. These stories have infiltrated administrative logics, in which mobility is a sign of unreliability. Settlement and issuing a trail of documents turns out to be a requirement of recognition, and movement is equated with fraudulence or avoidance.

This logic is applied in practice as shown in case studies in Assam (Human Rights Watch, 2019; Chakravarty, 2019; Times of India, 2025). In a single case, which received a lot of publicity in Barpeta district, a woman who had cast her vote in all elections since 1996 was called a suspicious voter in 2015 (Human Rights Watch, 2019). Although she presented her documents, such as her electoral photo identity card, school certificate, and marriage registration, the case was taken to a Foreigners Tribunal on the grounds of the non-matching of the name of her father in the records (Amnesty International, 2019). She was eventually recognised as an Indian citizen, but it took her a lengthy legal struggle that cost the family a lot of time and money (Human Rights Watch, 2019; NRC Assam Reports, 2019). In a different instance, a worker in a tea garden in Dibrugarh was not counted in the NRC as he did not even have land records, yet he had been working in the same plantation for more than thirty years (Chakravarty, 2019; Human Rights Watch, 2019). His work history was not considered a strong enough argument for citizenship (Jayal, 2013). These instances show the reality of an actual experience of a process favouring paper over presence, and form over substance (Torpey, 2000; Scott, 1998).

Exclusionary effects are being manifested outside the Indian state of Assam as well (The Guardian, 2025). Local activists in Hyderabad and Mumbai have registered instances of Odisha and Jharkhand migrant workers being dropped off voter lists during voter verification campaigns in the two cities. Even in such situations, police have mentioned the absence of evidence of local address, even though the residents have been staying and working in those places for several years. The vote denial, although legally reversible, is an indicator of a wider loss of belonging, in which the presence and participation are no longer regarded by the state as adequate evidence of belonging. These reported instances should be treated as emerging concerns rather than conclusive evidence of a uniform national pattern, and they require stronger official or institutional documentation.

RIGHTS, LAW, AND THE CONSTITUTION OF INDIA

The Indian Constitution, both in letter and spirit, undertakes the state to safeguard the dignity, equality and basic freedoms of all individuals. The legal regime of citizenship and civic inclusion is based on core constitutional guarantees (Seervai, 1996; Baxi, 1982), including equality before the law (Article 14), nondiscrimination based on religion, race, caste, sex, or place of birth (Article 15), and the right to life and personal liberty (Article 21). These principles cannot be understood as idealistic ideals but practical rights that require the state should act fairly, transparently and accountably. The cornerstone of these safeguards is what is called due process, and this is the right to hear before any decision is made that can impact negatively on the legal status of an individual. However, in the context of the operational environment of the Special Intensive Revision (SIR) process, these constitutional guarantees are not only blurred but, in most cases, they are also not made available (Pandey, 2025).

SIR, despite being presented as a procedural means of updating electoral rolls, is effectively a de facto citizenship scrutiny tool. Being characterised by the use of the informal procedures, the discretionary power and the lack of outlined legal security, it is the direct violation of natural justice (Baxi, 1982). In case of Marked Doubtful Voters, there is no obligation that the grounds upon which they have been marked may be told to them, or that they should be given a pre-decisional hearing. Such procedural secrecy is a violation of the *audi alteram partem* rule, which has been restated on multiple occasions by the Supreme Court as being a critical part of a fair decision in Articles 14 and 21. The refusal to give notice, reasons and the right to appeal the decision provides a scenario where people are deprived of their rights without even knowing the motive behind the action or what can be done to effectively appeal against the decision.

Jurisprudence in the Supreme Court has long been the position that a decision by an administrative agency that involves fundamental rights should meet the requirements of reasonableness and non-arbitrariness. In Maneka Gandhi v. Union of India (1978), the Court broadened the scope of Article 21 to add procedural fairness to the right to life and personal liberty. Nevertheless, SIR is in effect working around these constitutional requirements. Being unofficial on the classification as a process that influences citizenship, it does not encounter the rigour of the process and the legal redress that would otherwise be provided in such circumstances. This legal confusion is intentional so that the identity verification can be performed even without considering the legal implications of its practice. In Assam, judicial involvement with processes related to the same, specifically those involving citizenship and voter identity, one can gain an idea of the tensions underlying administrative practice as challenged by constitutional law. In the case of Sarbananda Sonowal v. Union of India (2005), the Supreme Court declared the Illegal Migrants (Determination by Tribunals) Act,

1983, illegal, saying that it made it too hard to detect and deport illegal migrants and that it endangered national security. Although the decision supported the interest of the state in controlling citizenship, it also provided the citizenship law a punitive tone, raising the suspicion above the rights-based protection. The court conceded a point by the state that the illegal immigration between Bangladesh and Assam was changing the demographic profile of the state and thus warranted extraordinary administrative actions (Lynch & South, 2018). In Abdul Kuddus v. Union of India (2019), the Supreme Court looked at the issue of whether the decisions made by Foreigners Tribunals were open to appeal by the writ jurisdiction of High Courts. The Court believed that the Tribunals had a quasi-judicial role and could thus have their decisions reviewed by the Court under Article 226. It also noted, though, that these decisions did not involve strict adherence to the code of civil procedure or the Evidence Act. This decision validated the jurisdictional power of Foreigners Tribunals with the legal flexibility of the process at the same time. The resultant effect has been a system in which the quasi-judicial authorities have the power to render a person stateless without having to follow any formal evidentiary procedures, and the burden of action is placed on the individual themselves with little or no access to legal counsel or the right to know the procedural process. The exclusion cases have been identified to contain procedural flaws by other High Courts. The Gauhati High Court has been successful in several instances in striking down Tribunal orders which had been made ex parte or without justifiable reasons. However, all these corrective actions are after the fact, when they have denied people their voting rights, stigmatised them socially, or even imprisoned them. The remedial process is not only lengthy but also not easily accessible by the uninformed, unrepresented and poor in the country. Equal protection by the constitution, therefore, is conditional upon the ability to manoeuvre through a legal system that is still obscure and exclusionary.

The issue with the structure is that there is no statutory framework that could determine the legal nature, scope, and procedural safeguards of SIR. It acts under internal directions, circulars, and orders made by electoral authorities, none of which is subject to parliamentary discussion and debate. Since SIR is not a mechanism prescribed by law as a device to check citizenship, its application is not subject to the protection that would otherwise be mandatory under Indian administrative law. It does not contain a distinct notice requirement, no statutory requirement of capturing reasons of exclusion, and no entitlement to an appeal or redress. This grey zone of the law allows non-accountability in the denial of recognition by the state.

The presence of the non-justiciable nature of SIR-related exclusions only adds to the issue. Those suspected of being dubious voters can be taken to Foreigners Tribunals, but the process of making such a referral is not transparency-based. In numerous instances, the names are not put on the electoral roll, and without any Tribunal procedure, an official record of the reasons why the exclusion took place is not kept. The invisibility that ensues from the exclusion, neither quite legal nor distinctly administrative, deprives individuals who are the subject of it of the benefits of procedural rights in either sphere. This brings about a two-regime system wherein there are citizens with the protection of the law under the law and those who are governed by an administrative system that does not follow the law. Effectively, SIR will present an informal disenfranchisement architecture. It changes the burden of establishing what the law should assume on citizens and leaves the challenge to them, instead of individuals. Such inversion is not a mere procedural anomaly but a structural betrayal of the constitutional pledge of equality and dignity.

GLOBAL AND CONCEPTUAL REFLECTIONS

Although the SIR regime of India has a specific context in terms of its law and history, it is not completely isolated. This tendency of bureaucratic instruments of inquiry, limitation or disenfranchisement is a general tendency of the world, whereby administrations become instruments of inclusion and exclusion (Borders Within, 2024). The purpose of comparison here is not to equate India with other contexts, but to show how documentation-based governance can affect citizenship, participation, and belonging in different political settings. In the transnational character of what might otherwise be perceived as a localised policy, legal identity becomes increasingly entangled with state-administered documentation, producing a wider shift from citizenship-as-right to citizenship-as-proof.

The politics of voter identification is a contentious process in the United States (U.S.) whereby the right to be able to democratically participate is selectively controlled. As the legal system of the U.S. does not explicitly disfranchise any citizens on documentary grounds, the existence of the state level laws that require government-issued photo identifications disproportionately affects African American, Latino, low-income, and elderly voters, the groups that are less likely to have the necessary forms of ID (Hasen, 2012; Levitt, 2007). The ruling of the U.S. Supreme Court in Crawford v. Indiana Marion County Election Board 2008, affirmed the voter ID law in the state, citing the interest of the state to reduce voter fraud. Nevertheless, empirical research has constantly demonstrated that the real cases of voter fraud are statistically insignificant, but the effects of disenfranchisement are real and far-reaching. The comparison with SIR is limited but relevant: both cases show how electoral integrity measures can produce unequal access to democratic participation when documentary requirements are not accompanied by adequate safeguards.

Bureaucratic marginalization has become more devastating and harsher in Myanmar. Disenfranchisement of the Rohingya Muslim minority through the systematisation of the 1982 Citizenship Law is rooted in the strict national system of registration that, in effect, makes the Rohingya Muslims stateless. The Rohingya, although they have often lived many generations, are not considered a national race, and the exclusion of this group is supported with the help of the documentation regimes that do not recognise their historical existence. Identification documents have been issued and revoked selectively, and whole people have been locked out of the electoral lists, deprived of education and sent back to the refugee camps and the borders. National registries in Myanmar can help us understand the way in which the state can use documentation as a tool to suppress rights and deny recognition itself (Cheesman, 2017). This example should be treated with caution because Myanmar's political history, ethnic classification system, and scale of rights deprivation differ significantly from the Indian context. Its relevance lies not in direct equivalence with SIR, but in showing how documentation regimes can become tools of exclusion when state recognition is made conditional on contested categories of identity.

Equally, the historical memory of the Liberation War of 1971 still has an effect on citizenship discourses in Bangladesh. Organisations perceived as collaborators or whose roots can be traced to the Urdu-speaking Bihari community have been put in a long legal limbo. They were refused citizenship papers decades ago, and now, thousands of them are stateless or marginalised. In spite of slow judicial interventions that have given them their rights, there is bureaucratic obstruction and stigma. In India, and similar documentations are the place where disputed histories and political identities are determined, but not through the courts, but through clerks and local officials. This example shows how historical conflict can shape documentary citizenship, especially where identity papers become the practical basis for recognition, mobility, and civic participation.

Statelessness in the Gulf Cooperation Council (GCC) countries, especially in Kuwait and the United Arab Emirates, linked to restrictive citizenship regimes, migration governance, and the exclusion of some long-term residents from recognised citizenship routes (Longva, 1997). The Kuwaiti Bidoon, such as the example of the Bidoon, are long-term inhabitants of the state who obtain no citizenship because they do not have a historical right of recognition by the state. Though most of them occupy positions in the state institutions, such as the army, they are deprived of the full status of civic participation due to their undocumented status. The status of the Bidoon, as well as those outside of SIR in India, demonstrates how the non-recognition of documentation can produce civic insecurity among long-term residents. In this regard, statelessness is not only an absence of status but may also be produced by policy and administrative classification.

Knowledge of these global parallels makes one ponder further on the theoretical view. The concept of biopolitics introduced by Michel Foucault can be useful to understand the functioning of such regimes as SIR. Foucault contends that contemporary states are not just exercising their sovereignty by way of law and prohibition; instead, they control life itself by monitoring population, watching, and categorising. Such bureaucratic apparatuses as the SIR can be seen as technologies of power that the state monitors, classifies, and punishes bodies not through the explicit enforcement of repression but through the apparently neutral mechanisms. The verifications that occur at the door to door, the requirement of the legacy papers and labeling people as doubtful is not in the form of coercion. Nevertheless, they establish an order of legitimacy, according to which only some of the lives are considered administratively visible and thus legal.

The strain on state rationality developed by Foucault is particularly relevant to the interpretation of the rationalisation of SIR as a simple practice of accuracy in registering records, with concrete effects of exclusion. The process may seem objective and methodical, yet it performs a specific role of making some population groups suspicious. In this respect, SIR can be regarded as a kind of surveillance that conceals its disciplinary nature behind the administrative procedure. This means that the individual is not the presumed citizen until the state makes it so; citizenship is contingent, in other words and administered by bureaucratic reason and not constitutional right.

Another interpretation is provided by the concept of the bare life developed by Giorgio Agamben and the state of exception. Agamben postulates that sovereign power is becoming more and more active with the exclusion of certain people from the political community and yet subjecting them to the force of law. These people are denied their rights, but still, they stay in the sphere of state manipulation alive, but deprived of the rights that should be guaranteed to them by law. Applied cautiously, this idea helps illuminate the condition of people who remain residents, workers, taxpayers, or community members, yet face uncertainty in voting rights or legal recognition because of documentary deficiencies. The Indian situation is therefore not identical, but it shows a comparable problem of administrative uncertainty, where those marginalised in SIR or termed under D-voters may occupy an insecure civic position. They still remain in the territory, pay taxes, are under policing and regulation, but they are still not allowed to take part in the democratic process. Their subjectivity in the law is held in suspension, but not by a court decree, but by a governmental action.

The state of exception according to Agamben is not of an extraordinary legal action, but it is the normalisation of a state where legal rights are selectively denied to those they choose to withdraw them. The SIR process is in this same zone. It is not empowered by the law, but it carries out the state roles that have very serious implications. It is an exercise that takes place beyond the rule of law and has a profound impact on those that are counted by the rule of law.

Foucault and Agamben both contribute to understanding how the law order perpetuates exclusion not by blatantly being illegal, but by the same tools that are utilized to maintain the order. The SIR, which resembles the Myanese registry systems or the American voter ID legislation, makes rights a conditional offer, intermediated by document, discretion, and discipline.

CONCLUSION AND SUGGESTIONS

As it has been indicated above, the SIR process, which, on the face of it, is largely of an administrative nature, has started to represent a potent tool that remakes the meaning and accessibility of citizenship in India (Jayal, 2013). Even with the document verification, electoral roll verification and discretionary categorisation, SIR has eroded the fundamental distinction between citizen and non citizen, shifting what previously formed a legal status to a status that has to be continuously demonstrated (Hari & Nagpal, 2022; The Guardian, 2025; Torpey, 2000). This has not been in the transparent frameworks of statutory law, and neither has it been an issue of long-term debate. Rather, it has emerged as executive orders, veiled field processes, and an informal logic of suspicion, especially towards people and groups that are already excluded by the system.

The process is disproportionate towards the people who are at the periphery of the bureaucratic vision of the Indian state (Deshingkar & Akter, 2009; Norwegian Centre for Human Rights, 2021). All internal migrants whose addresses have not been documented continuously, women whose identities were formed through marriage and migration, *Adivasi* and *Dalit* people historically left out of record-keeping, and the residents of informal settlements without a legal title to their land, all end up at the mercy of the SIR uneasily. The fact that they are not able to provide legacy documents is not a product of some fraudulent motive but rather indicative of the heavily institutionalised social and administrative injustices. However, the structural disadvantage is misinterpreted in the SIR framework as failure by individuals to that effect, as they are categorised as either Doubtful Voters or they are not on the electoral list without any meaningful way of appealing.

This has led to a scenario where, instead of insisting on democratic participation being a guarantee of constitutional membership, it is mediated through a bureaucratic trial of credibility. The very right to vote, which has been considered the foundation of democratic citizenship, is now conditional, and cannot be fulfilled by many people. Instead of serving as an inclusionary and verification device, SIR is a filtration and exclusion device. A presumption of illegitimacy has been substituted with the assumption of legitimacy, especially for those already in (Baxi, 1982).

The structural issues brought up by the SIR process are not going to be amended through an incremental administrative correction. It requires a re-evaluation of the state policy towards the concept of identity and citizenship, the one that reinstates constitutional guarantees and renegotiates the principle of dignity in the construction and execution of electoral and citizenship policies. The introduction of clear legal protections against people labelled as "Doubtful Voters" will be the first and most immediate course of action. No person should be omitted from the electoral roll or sent to a Foreigners Tribunal without being notified in advance, in writing the reason and having his say. These minimum procedural safeguards should not remain at the mercy of administrative discretion, but should be enshrined.

In addition to that, SIR process oversight should be independent. Currently, Booth Level Officers and other local electoral officials make decisions without a lot of scrutiny, and the results are arbitrary and, in most cases, prejudiced. It would be of use to have independent monitoring bodies, those that consist of legal professionals, representatives of civil society, and other human rights institutions, so that decisions could be reviewed and also adjusted according to the provisions of the constitution. The power of appeal should also be enhanced. Those who have been refused a place on voter lists must be offered free legal assistance and a time-limited process to appeal such decisions, particularly where SIR is once more applied in states not provided by statute.

The transparency should be instilled throughout the process. The current criteria of identifying suspicious voters, the form of documents acceptable, and the logic of applying a single exclusion are not clear and are similar to those of other regions. It is imperative to publish a set of clear and uniform instructions and translate them into the local languages, to avoid taking arbitrary measures and to guarantee the awareness of the population. Electoral officers should not only be responsible for the correctness of the rolls but also the constitutional validity of the process by which they have been verified.

Primarily, there is a need to change the state orientation, which is between suspicion and inclusion. Citizenship should never be a privilege that has to be acquired through compliance with the bureaucracy, but it is a right of the law and a right accepted by lived belonging. Their role as a state is to guard and not to police its citizens. In a digital era, in which identification schemes, like Aadhaar, voter ID and ration cards, are more and more networked, this duty is of particular concern: failures in one area can lead to a wave of rights revocation. The increase in surveillance capabilities should be accompanied by an increase in the legal frameworks and procedural safeguards.

India is trying to be a digital democracy and is thus forced to deal with the contradictions of the citizenship regime where documentation is prioritised over presence, compliance over recognition and control over care. The systems should not be created in such a way that they exclude those who do not fit in the thin end of the bureaucratic eligibility, but rather to integrate them into the law. The state has to acknowledge that it has administrative failures of its own, including holes in record keeping, inconsistencies in application and the absence of access to legal assistance, which should not be used to prosecute individuals. A rights-based system should not expect the most vulnerable groups to maintain perfect records; rather, it should provide accessible procedures, correction mechanisms, and institutional support.

Even the SIR process, as it is designed and deployed at the moment, is a form of departure from the constitutional vision of a democratic, inclusive, and egalitarian society. Otherwise, it can easily create a parallel government of exclusion, unresponsive, administrative, and silent, a government that is contrary to the very promises of the republic. It is not merely the process itself that needs reforming; it is the principles that it should be governed by that must be reclaimed. Citizenship should not be pauperised, whereby rights will depend on perfect archives. Rather, it should be the embodiment of the constitutional promise to acknowledge the individual before the state, not the pieces of paper in his or her file (Scott, 1998).

REFERENCES

Amnesty International. (2019). *Designed to exclude: How India's courts are failing foreigners*. Amnesty International Ltd.

Assam, N. R. C. (2019). *National Register of Citizens: Final draft report*. Government of Assam.

Austin, G. (1966). *The Indian Constitution: Cornerstone of a nation*. Oxford University Press.

Banerjee, P. (2020). Citizenship, identity, and migration in West Bengal: Contestations and challenges. *Economic and Political Weekly, 55*(6).

Baxi, U. (1982). *The crisis of the Indian legal system*. Vikas Publishing.

Castles, S., de Haas, H., & Miller, M. J. (2014). *The age of migration: International population movements in the modern world* (5th ed.). Guilford Press. DOI: 10.1007/978-0-230-36639-8

Chakravarty, S. (2019). NRC and the politics of citizenship in Assam. *Economic and Political Weekly, 54*(31).

Chatterji, J. (2007). *The spoils of partition: Bengal and India, 1947–1967*. Cambridge University Press. DOI: 10.1017/CBO9780511497384

Chowdhury, P. (2004). *Gender and citizenship in India*. Oxford University Press.

Deshingkar, P., & Akter, S. (2009). *Migration and human development in India*. United Nations Development Programme.

Economic Times. (2025). Caught between NRC logjam and elections: Citizenship rules stall Assam's SIR. The Economic Times.

Foucault, M. (1978). The history of sexuality: Volume 1: An introduction. Pantheon Books.

Foucault, M. (1991). Governmentality. In Burchell, G., Gordon, C., & Miller, P. (Eds.), *The Foucault effect: Studies in governmentality* (pp. 87–104). University of Chicago Press.

Hari, A., & Nagpal, R. (2022). The National Register of Citizens (NRC) in India and the potential for statelessness in situ: A cautionary tale from Assam. Journal of Immigration, Asylum and Nationality Law, 36(2).

Hasen, R. L. (2012). *The voting wars: From Florida 2000 to the next election meltdown*. Yale University Press.

Hull, M. S. (2012). *Government of paper: The materiality of bureaucracy in urban Pakistan*. University of California Press.

Human Rights Watch. (2019). *"We are like on a death list": India's NRC citizenship verification process*. Human Rights Watch.

Jayal, N. G. (2013). *Citizenship and its discontents: An Indian history*. Harvard University Press.

Kabeer, N. (2005). Gender equality and women's empowerment: A critical analysis of the third millennium development goal. *Gender and Development*, *13*(1), 13–24. DOI: 10.1080/13552070512331332273

Levitt, J. (2007). *The truth about voter fraud*. Brennan Center for Justice.

Longva, A. N. (1997). *Walls built on sand: Migration, exclusion, and society in Kuwait*. Westview Press.

Lynch, C., & South, A. (2018). Myanmar's contested citizenship. *Journal of Contemporary Asia*, *48*(4), 617–634.

Norwegian Centre for Human Rights. (2021). *Citizenship registration in India: Case of NRC*. University of Oslo.

Pandey, T. (2025). Constitutional validity and ethical perspective of the Citizenship Amendment Act. *International Journal of Creative Research Thoughts*, *13*(4).

Roy, S., Mukherjee, M., Sinha, P., Das, S., & Mukherjee, A. (2021). Exploring protest dynamics against NRC–CAA in India. arXiv preprint arXiv:2102.10531.

Samaddar, R. (2016). *The postcolonial age of migration: Dimensions of contemporary global migration*. Routledge.

Scott, J. C. (1998). *Seeing like a state: How certain schemes to improve the human condition have failed*. Yale University Press.

Seervai, H. M. (1996). *Constitutional law of India* (4th ed.). Universal Law Publishing.

The Guardian. (2025). India's electoral roll revision threatens democracy, critics say. The Guardian.

The Telegraph. (2024). *NRC concerns and migrant anxieties in West Bengal*. The Telegraph.

Times of India. (2025). Assam rights groups urge resolution of NRC-related exclusions. The Times of India.

Torpey, J. (2000). *The invention of the passport: Surveillance, citizenship, and the state*. Cambridge University Press.

Xaxa, V. (2008). *State, society, and tribes: Issues in post-colonial India*. Pearson Education.

Chapter 17

Pluralism in Motion: Migration, Multiculturalism, and the Future of Indian Democracy

Kusum Lata
http://orcid.org/0009-0005-2938-4129
D.G.C. Gurugram, Gurugram University, India

ABSTRACT

This chapter investigates how migration and multiculturalism reshape the foundations of India's pluralist democracy. It examines the interaction between internal and international mobility, social diversity, and political inclusion, drawing upon secondary data from the Census of India, National Sample Survey, United Nations reports, and academic studies. The chapter argues that migration places Indian pluralism "in motion," compelling institutions to reconcile constitutional ideals with demographic realities. It develops a theoretical framework combining democratic pluralism, citizenship theory, and the sociology of migration to interpret mobility as both a challenge and an opportunity for democratic renewal. The chapter concludes by proposing a shift toward a mobile and inclusive democracy that embeds portability of rights, participatory governance, and intercultural education. Migration emerges not as a threat to pluralism but as its contemporary expression, redefining belonging within a dynamic democratic framework.

1. INTRODUCTION

India's democratic experiment has unfolded within an environment of deep and persistent diversity. From its inception, the Indian Republic embedded pluralism within its constitutional order, codifying equality, secularism, and protection of cultural and religious freedoms under Articles 14 to 30 of the Constitution of In-

DOI: 10.4018/979-8-3373-8500-6.ch017

dia. This framework positioned diversity not as an obstacle but as the normative foundation of citizenship. Over the decades, India's pluralism has been sustained through a delicate balance of linguistic accommodation, regional federalism, and minority rights, yet this equilibrium is undergoing transformation as migration, both internal and international, reconfigures the social and political map of the nation.

According to the Census of India (2011), nearly 450 million individuals approximately 37% of the total population were classified as migrants, based on change in place of residence. Among these, about 139 million were interstate migrants, while 315 million migrated within the same state. India's internal mobility constitutes one of the largest in the world, encompassing seasonal labour flows, rural-to-urban transitions, marriage-based migration, and circular mobility. In parallel, India is the largest country of origin for international migrants, with 17.9 million Indians residing abroad as of 2020. Remittance inflows reached nearly USD 87 billion in 2021, representing 3% of India's GDP and ranking the country as the top global recipient (World Bank, 2021). This magnitude of movement, both within and across borders, renders migration not merely a demographic process but a profound social and political transformation.

Migration reshapes the texture of Indian democracy in ways that extend beyond economics. It modifies local compositions of caste, language, and religion, influencing electoral behavior and public policy priorities. The consequences are visible in India's major cities, where migrants sustain urban economies yet remain marginalized in civic participation. Such conditions challenge the inclusivity promised by the constitutional framework and expose the tension between mobility and belonging. The implications extend to the realm of political representation. Estimates by the Election Commission of India (2019) indicate that over 45 million internal migrants were unable to vote in their home constituencies during the 2019 general elections due to residency-linked voter registration rules. The spatial immobility of electoral rights within a highly mobile society effectively disenfranchises a significant share of the population. This disjunction invites reflection on the nature of citizenship in a democracy where the boundaries of community and territory are increasingly fluid. Migration compels reconsideration of democratic inclusion as a process that must accommodate movement, multiplicity, and hybridity.

In a broader sense, the relationship between migration and pluralism illuminates the evolving character of Indian modernity. Historically, pluralism in India was managed through spatial compartmentalization linguistic states, community-specific personal laws, and affirmative action regimes that localized diversity within stable categories. Migration disrupts these arrangements by bringing heterogeneity into direct and continuous interaction, particularly in urban spaces. Cities such as Mumbai, Bengaluru, and Delhi function as microcosms of multicultural negotiation, where new solidarities and conflicts emerge across regional, religious, and class lines

(Chatterjee, 2004; Deshingkar & Akter, 2009). The lived experience of pluralism in these spaces demonstrates that diversity is not static but dynamically produced through mobility.

This dynamic demands a theoretical reframing of pluralism itself. Rather than viewing pluralism as coexistence among fixed identities, it must be seen as a democratic process that evolves through the circulation of people, ideas, and cultures. Bhikhu Parekh (2000) conceptualized multiculturalism as an ongoing dialogue between shared civic values and the recognition of particular identities. In the Indian case, this dialogue is intensified by migration, which continuously reconstitutes the cultural composition of the polity. The pluralist ethos of Indian democracy thus becomes a moving equilibrium, shaped by negotiation rather than consensus.

The study of migration as a political phenomenon remains underdeveloped in Indian scholarship, which has traditionally emphasized economic and developmental dimensions. Yet, as scholars such as Holston (2008) and Rajan & Zachariah (2019) argue, mobility has direct implications for citizenship and democratic participation. Migrants' experiences of exclusion and adaptation serve as indicators of how well democratic institutions translate constitutional ideals into lived equality. By foregrounding migration as a force that both tests and transforms pluralism, this chapter seeks to contribute to a deeper understanding of how Indian democracy can sustain its inclusivity amid unprecedented mobility. In essence, India's pluralism is in motion. The constitutional promise of equality encounters new pressures from patterns of movement that unsettle established social hierarchies and territorial identities. Whether democracy can evolve to absorb this motion without fracturing its pluralist foundations will determine not only the future of India's democratic project but also its capacity to offer lessons for other diverse societies in an age of global mobility.

2. THEORETICAL FRAMEWORK

The analytical foundation of this chapter rests on three intersecting theoretical traditions: democratic pluralism, citizenship theory, and the political sociology of migration. Together they frame migration as both a structural and normative phenomenon that reconfigures the relationship between diversity and democracy in India.

Democratic pluralism, as articulated by political theorists such as Bhikhu Parekh (2000) and Will Kymlicka (1995), posits that the stability of diverse societies depends on institutionalized recognition of group identities within a shared civic framework. Pluralism thus requires that equality not be achieved through assimilation but through negotiated coexistence. In the Indian context, this principle is embedded in constitutional guarantees that uphold cultural autonomy and minority rights (Austin, 1999). The idea aligns with what Parekh describes as the dialogical nature of multiculturalism societies must continuously renegotiate the moral and institutional balance between common citizenship and cultural diversity.

The second pillar of this framework is citizenship theory. T. H. Marshall's (1950) tripartite schema civil, political, and social rights remains a key reference for evaluating how rights are distributed and enacted. While formal citizenship in India is universal, the lived experience of migrants reveals the uneven realization of these rights. Holston's (2008) concept of "insurgent citizenship" extends Marshall's framework by highlighting how marginalized groups assert claims to recognition and participation through everyday struggles. In the Indian case, internal migrants exercise insurgent citizenship when they contest exclusion from welfare programs, electoral registration, or urban services. Citizenship thus becomes performative and mobile, expanding through the political practices of those who move.

A third theoretical strand derives from the sociology of migration, which situates movement as a driver of social transformation. Stephen Castles' (2010) concept of "migration-as-development nexus" reveal how labour mobility both reflects and produces shifts in governance and identity. Applying this lens to India positions migration not as an anomaly but as a constitutive feature of modernization. Migration functions as a mechanism through which pluralism becomes dynamic people bring their languages, customs, and political orientations into new spatial contexts, transforming the social bases of democracy itself.

Integrating these traditions allows the chapter to interpret migration as a test of democratic adaptability. The pluralist ideal of equal respect encounters its practical limits in the conditions of mobility. Citizenship, once territorially anchored, becomes translocal and fluid. The theoretical framework thus conceptualizes pluralism as "in motion" a continuous process of institutional adjustment and civic negotiation prompted by migration's reordering of demographic, cultural, and political boundaries. Through this lens, India's democratic trajectory can be read as an evolving dialogue between movement and belonging.

3. MAPPING MIGRATION IN INDIA

Migration in India operates on a scale that reshapes its social structure and political geography. Both internal and international movements have accelerated since the 1990s, coinciding with economic liberalization, urban expansion, and demographic transitions. Examining the magnitude, composition, and spatial patterns of migration reveals how mobility has become integral to India's pluralist democracy.

Internal Migration

The 2011 Census of India remains the most comprehensive official dataset on mobility. It recorded 450 million migrants, constituting 37% of the total population. Of these, 315 million moved within the same state, while 139 million crossed state boundaries (Census of India, 2011). Women accounted for nearly 70% of all migrants, largely due to marriage-related mobility, whereas employment and business motives predominated among male migrants. The National Sample Survey Office (NSSO) 64th Round (2007–08) provided complementary insights, showing that 28.3% of rural and 35.4% of urban households reported at least one migrant member (Government of India, 2010).

The acceleration of rural-to-urban migration is most visible in states with expanding service and manufacturing sectors. Maharashtra, Delhi, Gujarat, Karnataka, and Tamil Nadu together attracted over 40% of interstate migrants (Kundu, 2011). States such as Uttar Pradesh, Bihar, Rajasthan, and Odisha serve as major sources of out-migration. The movement is predominantly circular; millions of workers oscillate seasonally between rural origins and urban workplaces in construction, manufacturing, and informal services (Deshingkar & Akter, 2009).

This flow has altered the demographic and cultural profiles of Indian cities. Mumbai and Delhi host migrant populations exceeding 40% of their total residents (Registrar General of India, 2016). Bengaluru, Pune, and Hyderabad have emerged as multilingual metropolises where linguistic boundaries are blurred by occupational diversity. These transformations generate new urban pluralisms spaces where regional, linguistic, and religious affiliations intersect and coexist, sometimes uneasily. Migrants sustain economic growth but remain socially peripheral, often excluded from welfare schemes tied to domicile requirements.

Statistical Summary: Internal Migration Patterns in India

Table 1. Internal migration indicators in India, compiled from official secondary sources.

Indicator	Data Value	Primary Source
Total migrants in India (2011)	450 million (37% of population)	Census of India, 2011
Intra-state migrants	315 million	Census of India, 2011
Inter-state migrants	139 million	Census of India, 2011
Women among total migrants	70%	Census of India, 2011

continued on following page

Table 1. Continued

Indicator	Data Value	Primary Source
Rural households with migrant members	28.3%	NSSO 64th Round (2007–08)
Major destination states	Maharashtra, Delhi, Gujarat, Karnataka, Tamil Nadu	Kundu, 2011
Major source states	Uttar Pradesh, Bihar, Rajasthan, Odisha	Kundu, 2011
Urban share of migrants in Mumbai and Delhi	Over 40% of city population	Registrar General of India, 2016

The scale of movement revealed in Table 1 underlines that internal migration is not a marginal phenomenon but a defining social condition. It drives urbanization, sustains industry, and mediates rural distress. Yet the persistence of informality keeps many migrants invisible to policy systems. The 2017–18 Periodic Labour Force Survey (PLFS) reported that migrant workers are disproportionately represented in informal employment, with limited job security or social protection (Ministry of Statistics and Programme Implementation, 2019). The COVID-19 lockdown of 2020 exposed this vulnerability, as millions of migrant workers undertook reverse migrations to rural areas, highlighting the fragility of India's mobility-based economy (Aajeevika Bureau, 2020).

Regional Variations and Social Composition

Migration in India also exhibits marked regional asymmetries. The southern and western states dominate in attracting skilled and semi-skilled labour, while northern and eastern regions remain sending zones. This pattern reinforces existing economic inequalities. According to the Economic Survey of India (2017), inter-state labour mobility increased from 4.1 million annually during 2001–2011 to 5–6 million per year in the subsequent decade, reflecting deepening spatial integration. The same report estimated that nine million people migrate interstate each year for work, implying a significant redistribution of labour across the federal landscape.

Caste and community remain important determinants of migration outcomes. Studies have found that Scheduled Castes and Scheduled Tribes experience higher precarity in urban labour markets compared to upper-caste migrants, who often leverage social networks for mobility. Gender adds another dimension; women migrants, though numerically dominant, are concentrated in low-paid informal work or confined to domestic spheres following marriage migration (Deshingkar & Akter, 2009). These patterns complicate the relationship between migration and equality, revealing that mobility does not automatically translate into social advancement.

International Migration

Beyond internal movement, India's global diaspora represents another axis of pluralism. According to UN DESA (2020), 17.9 million Indians lived abroad, accounting for 6.5% of the world's total migrant stock. The distribution is geographically diverse: Gulf Cooperation Council (GCC) countries host about 9 million Indian workers, North America houses 4.5 million, and the United Kingdom about 1.4 million. The World Bank (2022) reported that India received USD 89 billion in remittances in 2021, surpassing China and Mexico, making remittances a critical source of household income and foreign exchange. Kerala, Tamil Nadu, and Punjab are leading sender states, with remittances constituting over 30% of Kerala's Net State Domestic Product (Rajan & Zachariah (2019).

Migration to the Gulf, largely driven by temporary labour contracts, has transformed social structures in sending regions. Villages in Kerala and coastal Andhra Pradesh display patterns of transnational household economies, where remittances finance education, housing, and political participation. At the same time, dependence on short-term migration exposes workers to precarious conditions and limited rights abroad (Rajan & Zachariah (2019)). Recent diversification toward high-skilled migration particularly to the United States and Canada has added a new dimension of cultural influence, visible in India's expanding global professional diaspora.

Comparative Scale and Global Position

India's migratory patterns situate it among the world's most mobile societies. Table 2 summarizes comparative data on international migration.

Table 2. Comparative international migration and remittance indicators.

Indicator	India	China	Mexico	Philippines	Source
International migrants abroad (2020)	17.9 million	10.5 million	11.8 million	6.1 million	UN DESA, 2020
Remittance inflows (2021, USD billion)	89.0	53.0	54.1	36.7	World Bank, 2022
Remittances as % of GDP	3.1	0.4	4.0	9.4	World Bank, 2022

India's scale of mobility exceeds other major developing economies both in absolute numbers and in the economic significance of remittances. Yet, unlike Mexico or the Philippines, Indian migration is characterized by duality: a large pool of low-skilled Gulf labour coexists with a substantial high-skilled diaspora in OECD countries. This dual structure reflects domestic inequalities in education and opportunity, projecting internal hierarchies into the global labour market.

Migration as a Demographic and Political Force

Demographically, migration moderates regional population pressures while accelerating urbanization. Between 2001 and 2011, India's urban population grew by 31.8%, with migration contributing roughly one-third of this increase (Census of India, 2011). The ongoing 2021–2031 decade is expected to witness urban residents surpassing 40% of the total population (NITI Aayog, 2021). Politically, such demographic redistribution reshapes constituency boundaries, labour relations, and demands for welfare. Migrants' presence in cities diversifies electorates and compels parties to respond to new identities, even as institutional barriers limit their participation. Migration also influences regionalism and federal relations. Destination states bear the burden of service provision, while source states experience remittance-led consumption booms without commensurate industrial development. The resulting asymmetries produce political friction over resource allocation and representation. Despite these challenges, migration fosters inter-regional integration and the diffusion of pluralistic practices across linguistic and cultural boundaries.

The 450 million migrants identified in the 2011 Census make India's internal mobility larger than the total population of the European Union. This magnitude underscores that migration is not peripheral but central to India's democratic evolution. Its effects permeate electoral politics, labour markets, and urban governance, compelling continuous redefinition of pluralism as a lived democratic process.

Mapping India's migration landscape reveals that movement operates simultaneously as an economic necessity, social strategy, and political phenomenon. Internal migration links agrarian distress with urban growth, while international migration integrates India into global labour circuits. Both dimensions reshape pluralism by relocating diversity into new contexts. The data underscore that India's democracy functions within constant demographic flux. Understanding this motion is essential to analyzing how pluralism adapts under the pressures of mobility a theme explored in subsequent sections on social spaces, participation, and policy inclusion.

4. MIGRATION AND THE RECONFIGURATION OF SOCIAL SPACES

4.1 Urban Transformation and Everyday Multiculturalism

Migration reshapes India's urban landscape more profoundly than any other social process of the twenty-first century. Cities such as Mumbai, Delhi, Bengaluru, Hyderabad, and Pune have become labouratories of multicultural coexistence, where linguistic, regional, and religious diversities interact daily. The 2011 Census reported that migrants comprise 42 percent of Mumbai's population and 39 percent of Delhi's (Registrar General of India, 2016). These proportions signify that nearly every urban encounter in workplaces, markets, or neighborhoods occurs across lines of origin and identity.

Urban sociologists note that the city functions as both a site of economic opportunity and a terrain of cultural negotiation. Partha Chatterjee (2004) described Indian cities as arenas where "the politics of the governed" unfolds through informal practices rather than formal rights. Migrants, often excluded from planning frameworks, carve out spaces of survival through informal settlements, street vending, and self-organized welfare networks. Such practices create hybrid social orders that defy rigid administrative boundaries.

In Mumbai's Dharavi or Delhi's Seelampur, migrants from Uttar Pradesh, Bihar, and West Bengal coexist with long-term residents under precarious tenure arrangements. Jan Breman (2016) characterizes these zones as "neither urban nor rural," embodying a mobile citizenship that is simultaneously excluded and indispensable. Linguistic pluralism manifests in the proliferation of vernacular media and cultural associations: Bhojpuri film screenings in Mumbai, Odia community festivals in Surat, or Tamil cultural centers in Bengaluru. These activities sustain collective identity while facilitating adaptation to host environments.

Everyday multiculturalism operates through mundane interactions food sharing, festival observance, or labour cooperation rather than through state policies alone. However, this coexistence is unevenly distributed. Migrants in high-skill sectors experience cosmopolitan inclusion, while low-income labourers face segregation in informal housing and limited social mobility. The urban form thus mirrors India's hierarchical pluralism, where proximity does not automatically translate into equality.

4.2 Housing, Labour, and the Spatial Politics of Inclusion

Housing constitutes a primary axis through which migration reconfigures social space. Rapid urbanization has produced acute shortages: the Technical Group on Urban Housing Shortage (Ministry of Housing and Urban Affairs, 2012) estimated a deficit of 18.8 million dwelling units, 96 percent of which affect economically weaker sections. Migrant workers, lacking proof of residence or credit access, inhabit informal settlements that operate outside municipal recognition. This spatial marginality translates into political invisibility; residents often remain unregistered voters despite decades of urban residence (Aajeevika Bureau, 2020).

Labour segmentation reinforces these spatial hierarchies. The Periodic Labour Force Survey (2017–18) found that 81 percent of India's workforce remains in informal employment (Ministry of Statistics and Programme Implementation [MoSPI], 2019). Migrants constitute a disproportionate share of construction, domestic work, and street vending sectors, where regulatory protections are minimal. The Code on Social Security (2020) aims to extend benefits to unorganized workers, yet its implementation depends on digital registration platforms that exclude those lacking documentation or literacy (ILO, 2021).

Empirical studies show that migrant neighborhoods often become nodes of inter-regional cultural exchange. In Surat's textile districts, Odia and Bihari workers share dormitory housing, generating hybrid dialects and culinary practices (Deshingkar & Akter, 2009). Similar fusions occur in Bengaluru's service sector, where Hindi and Kannada intermingle in workplace communication. Such interactions gradually transform host cultures while softening regional boundaries. However, competition for housing and jobs can also trigger exclusionary politics. The "sons of the soil" campaigns in Maharashtra during the 2000s, directed against North Indian migrants, exemplify how economic anxiety can be reframed as cultural.

4.3 Gendered Dimensions of Migrant Social Worlds

Gender fundamentally structures the reconfiguration of social spaces. Women constitute nearly 70 percent of India's migrants (Census of India, 2011), though most move for marriage rather than employment. Nevertheless, female labour migration has expanded in domestic work, garment manufacturing, and care economies. Studies in Delhi and Chennai show that women migrants frequently create dense informal networks for childcare, credit, and housing, compensating for the absence of state support. These solidarities illustrate what Nandini Gooptu (2016) terms the "micro-politics of survival," where collective agency emerges from everyday cooperation.

Marriage migration, while often reinforcing patriarchal control, also contributes to cultural diffusion. Inter-regional marriages link linguistic and caste groups, particularly among economically mobile households in peri-urban areas. Research in Haryana and Uttar Pradesh finds rising instances of cross-regional unions involving women from eastern India, reshaping local kinship structures (Rajan & Zachariah (2019). Migration thus unsettles social norms even as it reproduces gendered vulnerabilities.

Women migrants encounter compounded exclusion in housing and employment markets due to lack of documentation and safety concerns. Yet their presence in informal sectors especially domestic work sustains urban middle-class lifestyles, revealing an invisible foundation of India's urban pluralism. The persistence of gendered precarity underscores the need to view migration as a social transformation that is simultaneously empowering and exploitative.

4.4 Migrant Associations, Religion, and Civic Belonging

Community associations serve as vehicles for negotiating belonging within multicultural cities. Ethnic welfare societies, trade unions, and religious institutions offer migrants emotional security and collective voice. In Kerala's Gulf diaspora, expatriate associations such as the Kerala Muslim Cultural Centre (KMCC) provide welfare assistance and maintain transnational ties (Rajan & Zachariah (2019). Within India, city-based organizations like the *Bihar Foundation* in Mumbai or Odia Samaj in Delhi facilitate social integration while preserving cultural distinctiveness.

Religious networks often provide material support independent of state intervention. Sikh *gurdwaras* in Delhi's industrial areas, for example, offer free meals and shelter to unemployed workers regardless of origin. Hindu and Muslim charitable trusts similarly function as parallel welfare institutions, compensating for gaps in municipal provisioning. The politicization of migrant identities can also deepen fragmentation. Electoral mobilization around regional or linguistic blocs such as the *Telangana Praja Samithi* in the 1970s or contemporary Marathi regionalism demonstrates how migration feeds into territorial politics. The balance between solidarity and competition determines whether civic life evolves toward inclusion or polarization. Migration, by multiplying associational forms, expands democratic participation but also generates new cleavages requiring institutional mediation.

4.5 Cultural Production, Language, and Media

The proliferation of regional media in metropolitan centers illustrates how migrants reshape cultural industries. Satellite television, digital platforms, and vernacular newspapers cater to dispersed linguistic publics. For instance Malayalam-language media houses in the Middle East maintain continuous communication with Kerala, creating a transnational public sphere (Rajan & Zachariah, 2019).

Language adaptation within workplaces and education reinforces multilingual competence. The rise of "Hinglish" and other mixed registers exemplifies linguistic hybridization driven by migration (Annamalai, 2001). Urban schools accommodate this fluidity by adopting bilingual instruction, while private academies teach Hindi and English to southern migrants seeking service employment. Such trends demonstrate that cultural production is no longer bounded by regional identity; it circulates through networks of labour and mobility. Cultural hybridity is also visible in food and festival cultures. Cities host cross-regional festivals such as *Chhath Puja* in Delhi's Yamuna Ghat or *Onam* celebrations in Mumbai, attracting participants beyond the originating communities. These practices normalize diversity as routine urban experience. At the same time, commodification of culture through tourism and branding risks reducing pluralism to spectacle, detaching it from the social realities of migrant labour.

4.6 Conflict, Negotiation, and Emerging Cosmopolitanism

While migration generates integration, it also introduces friction. Tensions arise over employment competition, language policy, and urban resources. The 2008 Maharashtra riots targeting North Indian workers and periodic clashes between Assamese and Bengali migrants exemplify how local politics can reframe economic disputes as cultural conflicts (Jaffrelot, 2021). Such events underscore that multicultural coexistence requires active governance rather than spontaneous harmony.

Municipal and state governments have adopted varying strategies. Bengaluru's *Samagra Nagar* initiative incorporates migrant communities into local consultative bodies, while Kerala's *Aawaz Insurance Scheme* provides accident coverage and registration for interstate labourers. Surveys by the Centre for the Study of Developing Societies (2019) show increasing public acceptance of linguistic and regional diversity in cities with sustained migration histories. Exposure and interdependence produce pragmatic cosmopolitanism: an urban ethos valuing cooperation over homogeneity. This emergent cosmopolitanism, though uneven, demonstrates pluralism's adaptive capacity in motion.

4.7 Comparative Glimpses and Global Resonances

India's urban pluralism resonates with experiences in other multicultural democracies. Toronto's neighborhood-based integration policies, London's community cohesion framework, and Singapore's ethnic-integration housing model all institutionalize diversity within spatial planning. While these examples differ in governance capacity, they highlight the potential of spatial design to promote inclusion. Indian cities, constrained by informality and fragmented jurisdiction, rely more on social negotiation than state planning. The comparison underscores that pluralism in India is largely self-organized, emerging from below rather than engineered from above.

4.8 Synthesis: Pluralism Re-imagined through Mobility

The cumulative effect of migration on India's social spaces is a redefinition of pluralism from static coexistence to fluid interaction. Cities have become frontiers where identities are negotiated through labour, language, and everyday practice. Housing precarity, informal employment, and gendered labour patterns reveal the constraints of inclusion, yet they also generate solidarities that expand democratic participation. Migrant associations and cultural production reproduce community while enabling dialogue across difference. Migration transforms the spatial grammar of democracy. Political representation, once anchored to locality, must adapt to transient populations. Welfare systems designed for sedentary citizens require portability. Cultural recognition shifts from protection of fixed minorities to facilitation of inter-group engagement. These adjustments exemplify what Holston (2008) calls the "insurgent horizon" of citizenship: new rights and institutions emerging from mobility itself.

In this evolving milieu, pluralism is no longer confined to constitutional text; it becomes lived through the improvisations of millions who navigate movement and belonging. Urban India, despite inequality and conflict, demonstrates that diversity can function as a connective tissue rather than a fault line. Migration's reconfiguration of social space thus stands at the heart of India's democratic resilience, setting the stage for subsequent analysis of political participation and policy responses.

5. MIGRATION AND THE DEMOCRATIC DEFICIT

5.1 Introduction: Mobility and the Paradox of Representation

Migration transforms not only economies and social structures but also the texture of political participation. India's democracy, premised on universal suffrage and equality of citizenship, presupposes a stable relationship between citizens and place. Yet mobility complicates this relationship. The democratic framework assumes fixed constituencies and residence-based registration, while the lived reality of migration is fluid, circular, and transregional. This disjuncture produces what scholars term a democratic deficit a gap between constitutional inclusion and practical participation.

Migrants in India are legally citizens but often politically peripheral. The inability to vote, limited access to political institutions, and exclusion from welfare-based entitlements erode substantive citizenship. Internal migrants who constitute more than one-third of India's population carry their political identities across spaces but seldom find representation where they work and live. Their mobility exposes structural weaknesses in electoral design, governance capacity, and social rights frameworks.

5.2 Electoral Exclusion and Mobility Barriers

The most visible manifestation of the democratic deficit is electoral disenfranchisement. The Election Commission of India (ECI) requires voters to register in constituencies of permanent residence. For internal migrants, this condition effectively ties the right to vote to geographic immobility. The ECI's 2019 report estimated that 45 million internal migrants were unable to exercise their franchise during the general elections due to lack of voter registration portability. Urban surveys conducted by Aajeevika Bureau (2020) in Rajasthan and Gujarat found that over 70 percent of migrant workers were not enrolled in electoral rolls of their destination cities despite long-term residence.

Such exclusion is not a matter of apathy but structural design. Circular migrants often travel during election periods, lack proof-of-residence documents required for registration, or reside in informal settlements unrecognized by municipal authorities. The system's dependence on fixed addresses renders millions politically invisible. The problem persists despite repeated proposals for portable voting mechanisms. Pilot projects for *remote voting machines (RVMs)* were initiated in 2022 but have yet to be operationalized nationwide.

Table 3. Indicators of Electoral Exclusion among Internal Migrants

Indicator	Data Value	Source
Estimated internal migrants unable to vote in 2019 elections	45 million	Election Commission of India (2019)
Migrant workers not registered in destination cities	70%	Aajeevika Bureau (2020)
Circular migrants who missed elections due to travel	23%	CSDS-Lokniti Survey (2019)
States piloting Remote Voting Machine (RVM) projects	8	Election Commission of India (2022)

Table 3 demonstrates the systemic gap between formal citizenship and actual participation, highlighting structural impediments that disproportionately affect mobile populations.

Migrants' political invisibility carries broader implications. Electoral incentives for addressing their concerns remain weak; political parties prioritize resident voters who can influence local outcomes. As a result, issues central to migrant welfare portable social protection, affordable housing, or workplace safety receive limited policy attention. This dynamic perpetuates a cycle of neglect: exclusion breeds apathy, which in turn reinforces exclusion.

Call-Out: India's 45 million "missing voters" among migrants constitute a population larger than that of Spain or Kenya.

Their absence from electoral rolls represents not disinterest but a structural design flaw in the world's largest democracy.

5.3 Representation and Local Governance

Beyond voting, representation in governance institutions remains skewed against migrants. Panchayats, municipalities, and state legislatures are territorially anchored, privileging long-term residents. Migrants who contribute to urban economies rarely appear in consultative forums or local decision-making bodies. Studies by the Indian Institute for Human Settlements (2021) show that less than 2 percent of elected representatives in major cities identify migration-related concerns in their manifestos or constituency work.

Municipal governance compounds exclusion through documentation requirements. Access to urban welfare programs such as the *Pradhan Mantri Awas Yojana (PMAY)* or public distribution system (PDS) depends on residence certificates and ration cards. For mobile workers, obtaining these documents involves navigating multiple jurisdictions. The *One Nation One Ration Card* scheme, operational in all states by 2021, addresses part of this problem but remains limited to food security entitlements. Political representation, however, still lacks portability.

At the national level, diaspora engagement presents a contrasting story. Non-Resident Indians (NRIs) enjoy online voter registration and can cast ballots via postal proxy. The differential treatment between international migrants and internal migrants underscores a paradox: cross-border mobility receives institutional accommodation, while domestic mobility remains administratively invisible.

5.4 The Informal Economy and Political Marginalization

The democratic deficit also stems from migrants' concentration in the informal economy. Informality limits unionization, collective bargaining, and political voice. The Periodic Labour Force Survey (2019–20) reported that approximately 81 percent of India's workforce remains informal, with migrants disproportionately represented in construction, transport, and domestic work. Informal workers often depend on intermediaries rather than formal employers, blurring accountability for rights violations or political engagement.

Labour migration networks thus function as both enablers of mobility and mechanisms of control. Contractors and middlemen frequently mediate migrants' access to jobs, housing, and welfare benefits, creating dependencies that discourage open political participation. In cities like Surat and Ahmedabad, studies reveal that workers are compelled to avoid political visibility to maintain job security (Breman, 2016). The absence of stable organizational structures weakens migrants' bargaining capacity, further entrenching their marginality. The introduction of digital labour platforms adds complexity. Gig workers, many of whom are internal migrants, operate outside traditional union frameworks. Despite efforts by emerging collectives such as the Indian Federation of App-based Transport Workers, representation remains fragmented. Without institutional mechanisms linking economic contribution to political representation, democracy risks reproducing inequalities embedded in the labour market.

5.5 Migrant Citizenship and Access to Welfare

Citizenship in practice is mediated through welfare access. Migrants' exclusion from housing, healthcare, and education services limits their effective membership in the polity. A 2021 study by NITI Aayog and the International Labour Organization found that only 27 percent of interstate migrant workers were covered by any form of social protection scheme. The portability gap persists despite initiatives such as the *e-Shram* portal, which had registered over 290 million informal workers by 2023 but faced challenges linking databases across states.

Education access for migrant children remains uneven. The Ministry of Education (2021) reported that approximately 10 million children of migrant workers face disruptions each year due to school transfers. Lack of language support and documentation forces many into informal labour, perpetuating intergenerational exclusion. Similarly, health insurance schemes like *Ayushman Bharat* operate primarily through state-specific empanelments, making them difficult to access for mobile populations. These welfare exclusions amount to a democratic deficit of capability. While the Constitution guarantees equality and mobility, the administrative architecture of welfare remains territorially bounded. Migrants' inability to claim entitlements at the point of residence transforms legal rights into theoretical abstractions.

5.6 Institutional Innovation: Emerging Correctives

Recognizing these deficits, several Indian states have initiated corrective measures. Kerala's *Aawaz* health and accident insurance program has registered over 5 million interstate workers, providing identification cards and grievance redressal mechanisms. Odisha's *Shramika* portal facilitates interstate coordination of welfare benefits, while Rajasthan's *Labour Welfare Fund* extends portable insurance to construction workers. These initiatives represent localized efforts to bridge the citizenship gap by linking welfare registration to mobility rather than domicile.At the federal level, the ECI's proposal for remote electronic voting seeks to enfranchise migrants without requiring physical relocation. The success of such innovations depends on inter-state cooperation and political will. Without systemic alignment between electoral law, welfare administration, and labour governance, fragmented solutions risk reproducing inequalities.

Comparatively, other democracies have demonstrated models of mobile citizenship. In the Philippines, absentee voting for overseas workers was institutionalized in 2003, achieving a 25 percent turnout among registered overseas voters in 2016. Canada allows internal migrants to vote via postal ballots at temporary addresses. These examples show that technological and legal barriers to mobility-inclusive democracy are surmountable. India's challenge lies less in capacity than in political prioritization.

5.7 Migrant Politics and Collective Agency

Despite institutional inertia, migrants exhibit growing political consciousness. In major cities, labour collectives and rights organizations act as intermediaries between migrants and the state. Groups such as the Aajeevika Bureau and the Migrant Workers Solidarity Network facilitate documentation, legal aid, and advocacy. Their efforts gained prominence during the COVID-19 pandemic, when mass reverse migration exposed administrative neglect. Public outcry led to renewed attention to migrant rights, including parliamentary debates and judicial interventions.

The emergence of "migrant politics" marks a subtle shift from invisibility to assertion. In Delhi and Mumbai, resident welfare associations now coexist with migrant welfare committees that engage local authorities on sanitation, housing, and safety. Electoral candidates increasingly address migrant issues, albeit selectively. Field data from the Naik (2022) show that migrant-related policy mentions in urban manifestos rose from 3 percent in 2014 to 11 percent in 2020. While modest, this trend signals that mobility is entering political discourse.

Social media further amplifies migrants' voices. WhatsApp networks, regional YouTube channels, and digital advocacy campaigns enable cross-regional mobilization. During the pandemic, online solidarity initiatives connected return migrants across states, demanding wage payments and transport assistance. This digital activism functions as an informal participatory mechanism, expanding the democratic sphere beyond institutional confines.

5.8 The Role of Judiciary and Civil Society

The Indian judiciary has intermittently acted as an arbiter of inclusion. The Supreme Court's rulings in cases concerning bonded labour, pavement dwellers, and migrant workers underscore the constitutional linkage between dignity and participation. In *People's Union for Democratic Rights v. Union of India* (1982), the Court affirmed labourers' right to humane conditions as integral to constitutional equality. More recently, during the COVID-19 crisis, the Court directed states to ensure free transportation and food for stranded migrants, implicitly recognizing mobility as a constitutional dimension of citizenship.

Civil society organizations supplement these judicial interventions. Trade unions, rights NGOs, and faith-based charities provide services that the state fails to deliver. Their role, while compensatory, also demonstrates the decentralized nature of democratic inclusion. Yet reliance on non-state actors risks uneven coverage and reinforces the perception that migrant welfare is an act of charity rather than a right. For democracy to function substantively, inclusion must be institutionalized, not improvised.

Table 4. Quantitative Snapshot of India's Democratic Deficit

Domain	Key Indicator	Data Value	Year
Internal migrants unable to vote	45 million	2019	Election Commission of India
Urban voter registration deficit (migrant workers)	70% unregistered	2019	Aajeevika Bureau
Workforce in informal sector	81%	2019–20	MoSPI (PLFS)
Migrant workers covered by social protection	27%	2021	NITI Aayog & ILO
Children of migrant workers facing educational disruption	10 million	2021	Ministry of Education
Migrant manifestos in urban elections	11%	2022	Naik, M.
Registered workers under e-Shram portal	290 million	2023	Ministry of Labour & Employment

Table 4 consolidates critical indicators across electoral, social, and labour dimensions to illustrate the multifaceted nature of India's democratic deficit as it pertains to migration.

When over one-third of a nation's population remains only partially enfranchised, the question is not whether democracy exists but for whom it effectively functions.

Migration reveals that participation cannot be confined to residence; it must travel with citizens wherever they contribute.

5.10 Towards a Mobility-Inclusive Democracy

Bridging the democratic deficit requires reimagining citizenship as portable and inclusive. Electoral reform must decouple voting rights from fixed residence through mechanisms such as remote ballots, digital voter verification, and inter-state roll synchronization. Administrative reforms should integrate welfare and labour databases to enable portability of benefits across state lines. The success of the *One Nation One Ration Card* initiative demonstrates feasibility; similar models can extend to healthcare and housing.

Democracy must also cultivate representational sensitivity to mobility. Political parties and civil society actors should recognize migrants as constituencies, not transient labour pools. Inclusion in local governance through reserved consultative seats or participatory councils can institutionalize migrant voice. Technology can bridge informational gaps; voter awareness drives, mobile registration kiosks, and multilingual electoral materials can expand access.

Comparative experience suggests that inclusion enhances rather than threatens stability. In South Africa, municipal migrant councils facilitate policy input from non-native residents. Brazil's participatory budgeting allows internal migrants equal voice in local expenditure decisions. India's pluralist tradition provides a normative foundation for similar experimentation.

6. INSTITUTIONAL AND POLICY RESPONSES

The governance of migration in India has historically been reactive rather than anticipatory. For decades, internal mobility was treated primarily as a private livelihood decision, not a subject of state policy. The absence of a national migration framework reflected the assumption that mobility was temporary and peripheral to development. Only recently especially after the 2020 pandemic crisis has migration become visible within policy discourse as a structural component of India's economy and democracy. Institutional responses are now emerging at multiple levels, from national legislation to state welfare innovations and local governance initiatives.

6.1 National-Level Frameworks and Legislative Measures

The principal legal instruments relevant to migration remain fragmented across labour, welfare, and urban governance domains. The Code on Social Security (2020) represents a major consolidation effort, merging nine earlier labour laws into a single framework to extend coverage to unorganized workers, including migrants. It mandates a national database of informal workers linked to the e-Shram portal, which by 2023 had registered over 290 million individuals. Registration enables access to insurance and welfare benefits independent of domicile, signaling a modest step toward portability.

Complementary initiatives include the One Nation One Ration Card (ONORC) scheme, introduced in 2019 and fully operational by 2021 across all states. The scheme allows beneficiaries to access subsidized food grains from any fair-price shop nationwide, effectively decoupling entitlement from residence. Early evaluations by NITI Aayog (2022) indicate that more than 85 million inter-state transactions occurred within the first two years, demonstrating high adaptability once administrative interoperability was achieved.

Urban development programs also incorporate migrant considerations. The Smart Cities Mission and the Pradhan Mantri Awas Yojana (PMAY-Urban) aim to expand affordable housing stock and improve service delivery. Yet implementation remains skewed toward formal sectors. A 2021 audit by the Comptroller and Auditor General found that only 8 percent of PMAY-Urban beneficiaries were renters or mobile workers. Policies continue to privilege property ownership over rental security, leaving most migrants outside formal shelter systems.

6.2 State-Level Innovations

States have developed more context-sensitive responses. Kerala's *Aawaz Insurance Scheme* (2016) provides health and accidental coverage for interstate workers, with registration numbers exceeding 5 million by 2022. The program also issues biometric identity cards recognized by police and health departments, enhancing both protection and visibility. Odisha's *Shramika* initiative coordinates interstate welfare transfer for Odia migrants working in Gujarat and Tamil Nadu, including skill certification and emergency support. Rajasthan's *Labour Welfare Fund* and *Shubh Shakti Yojana* link cash incentives to education for daughters of construction workers, indirectly targeting migrant households.

These state programs reflect federal diversity in approach but share a common orientation toward welfare rather than political inclusion. They enhance security and recognition without necessarily altering migrants' participation in decision-making. The focus remains on mitigating vulnerability, not expanding democratic agency.

6.3 Institutional Coordination and Data Gaps

A central obstacle to coherent policy lies in fragmented jurisdiction. Migration intersects multiple ministries Labour, Housing, Rural Development, and Home Affairs without a unified coordinating body. The Working Group on Migration (2017) recommended an inter-ministerial council to harmonize data and policy, but implementation has been limited. The absence of consistent migration statistics beyond the decennial Census impedes evidence-based planning. The Periodic Labour Force Survey (PLFS) collects limited information on mobility and cannot track circular migration or gender dynamics accurately.

Digital initiatives like e-Shram partially address this gap, yet integration with state databases remains incomplete. Without interoperable systems, portability of welfare and electoral rights cannot be achieved. Policy coherence requires a migration information system that links demographic, employment, and welfare data while protecting privacy.

6.4 Civil Society and Private Sector Engagement

Non-governmental organizations fill critical gaps in service delivery. The Aajeevika Bureau, Jan Sahas, and Migrant Workers Solidarity Network provide documentation support, legal aid, and shelter facilities across industrial corridors. Partnerships between these organizations and local governments such as the *Migrant Resource Centres* in Rajasthan and Gujarat illustrate emerging hybrid governance models. The private sector is also engaging through corporate social responsibility (CSR) initiatives. Construction firms and garment exporters increasingly collabourate with NGOs to provide health check-ups, safety gear, and education for workers' children. While such initiatives remain voluntary, they signal recognition that migrant welfare underpins productivity. A rights-based legal mandate for employer contributions could institutionalize these practices more equitably.

6.5 Global Engagement and Bilateral Mechanisms

For international migrants, India has developed a more coherent institutional apparatus. The Ministry of External Affairs (MEA) oversees 17 Indian Community Welfare Funds operating across major destination countries, offering legal and repatriation assistance. The *eMigrate* platform (2015) regulates recruitment agencies and tracks overseas employment contracts. Bilateral labour agreements with Gulf Cooperation Council states address wage protection and grievance redressal. These mechanisms reflect stronger institutionalization of transnational migration governance than of internal migration, underscoring policy asymmetry.Diaspora engagement policies, including the *Pravasi Bharatiya Divas* and *Overseas Citizenship of India (OCI)* schemes, cultivate transnational political and economic ties. While external mobility is valorized as a symbol of national success, internal migration continues to evoke ambivalence a divide that mirrors India's class and skill hierarchies.

6.6 Emerging Post-Pandemic Shifts

The COVID-19 crisis marked a turning point in policy consciousness. The mass return of migrant workers in 2020 exposed administrative unpreparedness and galvanized reform. The Atmanirbhar Bharat package included provisions for portable ration cards, rental housing complexes for workers, and the creation of *Migrant Support Cells* in all districts. By 2023, more than 80 such complexes were under construction, though occupancy remained limited. The experience highlighted the importance of proactive institutional design rather than emergency response.

The post-pandemic policy discourse now frames migration as integral to development and urban resilience. NITI Aayog's *National Policy Draft on Internal Migration and Human Development* (2022) proposes portable social security, gender-responsive planning, and participatory governance structures involving migrant representatives. Its eventual adoption could mark India's first comprehensive migration policy.

Institutional responses have evolved from silence to selective recognition. Yet most initiatives remain welfare-centric, addressing symptoms rather than structural causes of democratic exclusion. The challenge ahead lies in transforming migrants from beneficiaries into participants. A rights-based approach linking welfare entitlements with electoral and civic inclusion would align institutional design with constitutional pluralism. Migration policy, when fully articulated, has the potential to renew India's democratic contract by translating mobility into belonging.

7. CHALLENGES TO PLURALISM

Pluralism is the normative foundation of Indian democracy, yet it remains perpetually contested. Migration intensifies this paradox by bringing heterogeneous groups into immediate contact within limited urban spaces and competitive labour markets. While mobility broadens cultural exchange, it also provokes anxiety among host communities confronting economic insecurity and rapid change. These frictions provide fertile ground for populist mobilization and identity politics that threaten the inclusive ethos of democracy.

7.1 Regionalism and the "Sons of the Soil" Politics

One major challenge to pluralism arises from regional nativism. In several states, political movements have constructed "insider–outsider" binaries, framing migrants as economic or cultural interlopers. The *Maharashtra Navnirman Sena (MNS)* campaigns of 2008 and subsequent linguistic agitations in Karnataka and Assam exemplify this pattern.

Populism derives potency from local economic discontent. Migrants' visibility in low-wage sectors makes them convenient scapegoats for unemployment or resource scarcity. Nativist movements often conflate economic competition with cultural defense, asserting that migrants dilute linguistic identity or strain infrastructure. The persistence of these narratives indicates that pluralism's institutional safeguards federalism and linguistic autonomy can also reinforce fragmentation when weaponized politically.

7.2 Communalization and Cultural Polarization

Migration intersects with religion in complex ways. Cities experiencing rapid demographic change sometimes witness politicized interpretations of settlement patterns. Rumors of "vote bank migration" or "demographic imbalance" circulate in electoral discourse, feeding communal polarization. The 2021 National Crime Records Bureau data recorded sporadic communal incidents in urban centers where migrant inflows were highest, suggesting correlation though not causation.

Religious polarization also manifests through the targeting of specific migrant groups, such as Bengali Muslims in Assam or Rohingya refugees in Delhi and Jammu. These populations face dual exclusion as migrants and as minorities blurring the line between security policy and identity politics. Political entrepreneurs exploit such anxieties to consolidate majoritarian solidarity, eroding pluralism's civic foundation. The media environment amplifies fragmentation. Regional news channels and social media networks often reproduce echo chambers that reinforce prejudice. Disinformation linking migrants to crime or disease circulates rapidly, shaping public opinion and electoral strategies. Counter-narratives of solidarity rarely receive comparable visibility.

7.3 Populism and the Erosion of Democratic Deliberation

Populism thrives in environments of inequality and mobility. It personalizes politics, framing complex structural issues like joblessness or urban congestion as moral struggles between virtuous locals and corrupt elites or outsiders. The rhetorical simplicity of populism undermines deliberative pluralism, replacing negotiation with antagonism.

Empirical studies by the Centre for the Study of Developing Societies (2022) reveal that regions with high interstate migration display both greater ethnic diversity and stronger support for populist rhetoric invoking local identity. The correlation suggests that where institutions fail to manage diversity inclusively, populism fills the vacuum with emotional appeals. Social media platforms further accelerate this dynamic by privileging polarizing content that fosters in-group cohesion and out-group hostility. Populism also distorts representation. Migrants, lacking organized voice, are rarely the subjects of populist mobilization except as symbols of threat. Their invisibility allows populist actors to define them unilaterally, deepening exclusion while claiming democratic legitimacy through electoral mandate.

7.4 Economic Inequality and the Fracturing of Solidarity

Economic disparity exacerbates pluralism's fragility. Migrants sustain urban economies yet remain concentrated in precarious work. The absence of social protection creates resentment among both migrants and host populations one perceiving neglect, the other competition. Without redistributive policies, diversity translates into stratification.

Urban inequality manifests spatially through segregation of informal settlements and gated enclaves. This spatial polarization weakens civic solidarity, replacing interaction with isolation. Where daily contact diminishes, stereotypes flourish. The weakening of trade unions and collective bargaining further erodes cross-class alliances that once bridged regional or linguistic divides. Pluralism, deprived of economic foundations, risks devolving into coexistence without cohesion.

7.5 Digital Nationalism and the Reinvention of Identity

The digital sphere has become a new terrain for identity construction. Online platforms enable the rapid circulation of cultural symbols and political claims that transcend geography. While this connectivity can foster cross-regional empathy, it often amplifies majoritarian nationalism. Narratives of cultural purity or authenticity circulate widely, marginalizing hybrid or migrant identities.

Digital nationalism reframes pluralism as cultural hierarchy, privileging a homogenized idea of nationhood. Migrants who embody multiplicity speaking different languages, practicing syncretic customs are portrayed as ambiguous or suspect. The resulting polarization erodes the dialogical space essential to democracy. Countervailing efforts by fact-checking groups and intercultural digital initiatives remain limited in reach.

7.6 Institutional Weakness and Governance Gaps

Pluralism's endurance depends on robust institutions capable of mediating conflict. Weaknesses in policing, urban governance, and judicial processes allow identity-based violence to persist with impunity. Delays in prosecuting hate crimes or enforcing anti-discrimination laws send signals of tolerance for exclusion. Local governments, constrained by resources and jurisdiction, often lack capacity to implement inclusive urban planning.

Federal structures, while designed to manage diversity, sometimes incentivize competitive regionalism. Fiscal and political autonomy enable states to cultivate distinctive identities, but without national coordination this autonomy can foster inter-state tension over migration flows and resource allocation. Institutional fragmentation thus mirrors the social fragmentation it is meant to regulate.

The interplay of migration, identity, and populism reveals both the vulnerabilities and the adaptive strengths of Indian pluralism. Mobility destabilizes established hierarchies but also creates new solidarities. Populism exploits anxiety yet inadvertently reaffirms the salience of diversity as a central political issue. The task for democratic institutions is not to eliminate conflict but to channel it through deliberation and equity.

For pluralism to remain viable, policy must address material inequality alongside cultural recognition. Urban governance should institutionalize intercultural contact through inclusive planning, participatory forums, and equitable service distribution. Education and media literacy programs can counter polarization by fostering critical empathy. Above all, political leadership must reassert pluralism as a shared value rather than a partisan slogan. India's pluralism, though under strain, continues to function as the moral compass of its democracy. Its survival depends on translating mobility into opportunity and diversity into dialogue an endeavor that demands not only institutional reform but a renewal of democratic imagination.

8. TOWARD A MOBILE AND INCLUSIVE DEMOCRACY

Migration has redefined the meaning of belonging within India's democratic framework. The patterns of movement that have reshaped cities, labour markets, and social relations also challenge the institutional logic of citizenship. The twentieth-century model of democracy was built upon fixed territorial constituencies, stable residence, and localized political participation. The twenty-first-century reality, however, is characterized by mobility and multiplicity. A democratic order that remains territorially rigid risks excluding those whose livelihoods depend on movement. The transition toward a mobile and inclusive democracy therefore requires structural as well as normative adaptation.

A mobile democracy begins by recognizing movement as a legitimate mode of citizenship rather than an administrative anomaly. Electoral reforms must align with the demographic realities of internal migration by enabling portable voter registration and remote voting mechanisms. The Election Commission's pilot projects with remote voting machines represent an initial step, yet technological innovation must be accompanied by procedural flexibility and outreach. Migrants' participation depends as much on awareness and trust as on access. Urban local bodies could introduce temporary voter registration facilities linked to verified employment or rental records, thereby bridging the gap between presence and representation.

Inclusive democracy extends beyond the ballot box. Welfare and social protection systems must follow citizens across regions. The One Nation One Ration Card initiative has demonstrated that portability is administratively feasible when backed by digital interoperability. Similar frameworks can be extended to health insurance, education, and housing through linked databases integrating e-Shram registration and state welfare platforms. Such systems should safeguard privacy while ensuring universal accessibility. Institutional coordination across ministries and state governments is vital to prevent fragmentation.

Education and cultural policy also hold transformative potential. Schools, community centers, and digital platforms can serve as spaces for intercultural exchange where migrant and host populations engage as equals. The pedagogy of citizenship must emphasize adaptability, empathy, and civic dialogue rather than static identity. Public communication campaigns celebrating linguistic diversity and migrant contributions can counteract nativist narratives. The role of civil society and local media in constructing inclusive imaginaries is indispensable.

A mobile democracy requires participatory institutions that reflect translocal realities. Municipal councils, welfare boards, and consultative bodies should include migrant representatives. Kerala's Aawaz model offers a prototype of institutionalized participation through registration and grievance redressal. Expanding such models across states could operationalize pluralism in governance practice. Simultaneously, labour policy must recognize migrants not as temporary workers but as full economic citizens entitled to fair wages, safety, and voice.

CONCLUSION

The analysis across eight sections demonstrates that migration has become a central force reshaping India's democratic order. The scale of internal and international mobility nearly half a billion individuals within national borders and almost eighteen million abroad renders mobility an enduring structural condition rather than an episodic phenomenon. Migration challenges the traditional alignment of citizenship, territory, and participation that underpinned the post-independence democratic model. It exposes the distance between formal equality guaranteed by the Constitution and the uneven realization of substantive rights. Pluralism, long celebrated as India's distinctive strength, now operates within new spatial and social configurations. Migrants transform cities into multicultural arenas where difference is negotiated daily through work, housing, and civic life. These encounters produce hybrid forms of identity but also generate tension when institutions fail to mediate inclusion. The democratic deficit identified in this chapter manifested in electoral exclusion, welfare inaccessibility, and political invisibility illustrates the mismatch between mobility and governance. Yet migration simultaneously revitalizes democracy by compelling adaptation. The expanding discourse on portable rights, participatory urban policy, and labour protection suggests that reform is underway.

Institutional responses reveal a gradual shift from neglect to recognition. Initiatives such as the Code on Social Security, One Nation One Ration Card, e-Shram registration, and state programs like Kerala's Aawaz and Odisha's Shramika indicate an emerging framework for mobile citizenship. However, welfare-centric measures must evolve into mechanisms of political inclusion. Migrants must be recognized as full participants in governance rather than transient beneficiaries.

The broader challenge to pluralism arises from the politicization of identity and populism's exploitation of mobility-related anxieties. Nativism and communal polarization threaten to erode the moral fabric of democracy. Sustaining pluralism requires strengthening institutions, promoting equitable development, and fostering civic education that valorizes diversity. Migration reveals that difference is not a weakness but a constitutive element of democratic vitality. The chapter concludes that the future of Indian democracy depends on transforming mobility from a source of exclusion into an axis of inclusion. A mobile and inclusive democracy anchored in portability of rights, participatory governance, and intercultural dialogue offers the pathway to reconciling diversity with equality. In institutionalizing pluralism as a dynamic, lived process, India reaffirms the constitutional promise of freedom and fraternity for a society perpetually in motion.

REFERENCES

Aajeevika Bureau. (2020). Unlocking the urban: Reimagining migrant lives in cities post-COVID-19. https://ruralindiaonline.org/en/library/resource/unlocking-the-urban-reimagining-migrant-lives-in-cities-post-covid-19/

NITI Aayog. (2021–2022). Annual report 2021–22. Government of India.

Annamalai, E. (2001). *Managing multilingualism in India.* Sage Publications.

Austin, G. (1999). *Working a democratic constitution: The Indian experience.* Oxford University Press.

Breman, J. (2016). *At work in the informal economy of India.* Oxford University Press.

Castles, S. (2010). Understanding global migration: A social transformation perspective. *Journal of Ethnic and Migration Studies, 36*(10), 1565–1586. DOI: 10.1080/1369183X.2010.489381

Census of India. (2011). Migration tables. Government of India. https://censusindia.gov.in/census.website/data/census-tables

Centre for the Study of Developing Societies. (2019, 2022). State of democracy in South Asia surveys. CSDS. https://www.lokniti.org/otherstudies/state-of-democracy-in-south-asia-i-198

Chatterjee, P. (2004). *The politics of the governed: Reflections on popular politics in most of the world.* Columbia University Press.

Deshingkar, P., & Akter, S. (2009). Migration and human development in India (Human Development Research Paper 2009/13). United Nations Development Programme. https://hdr.undp.org/system/files/documents/hdrp200913.pdf

Election Commission of India. (2019, 2022). General election reports & remote voting machine pilot notes. Government of India. https://www.pib.gov.in/PressReleasePage.aspx?PRID=1887248

Gooptu, N. (2016). *Enterprise culture in neoliberal India.* Routledge.

Holston, J. (2008). *Insurgent citizenship: Disjunctions of democracy and modernity in Brazil.* Princeton University Press.

Indian Institute for Human Settlements. (2021). *Urban governance and migration inclusion in India.* IIHS.

International Labour Organization. (2021). Extending social security to workers in the informal economy: Lessons from international experience. https://www.ilo.org/publications/extending-social-security-workers-informal-economy-lessons-international

Jaffrelot, C. (2021). *Modi's India: Hindu nationalism and the rise of ethnic democracy*. Princeton University Press.

Kundu, A. (2011). Trends and processes of urbanisation in India. International Institute for Environment and Development. https://www.iied.org/10597iied

Kymlicka, W. (1995). *Multicultural citizenship: A liberal theory of minority rights*. Oxford University Press.

Marshall, T. H. (1950). *Citizenship and social class*. Cambridge University Press.

Ministry of Education. (2021). Report on education of migrant children. Government of India. https://www.education.gov.in/en/annual-report-2021-2022-moe-english

Ministry of Housing and Urban Affairs. (2012). Report of the Technical Group on Urban Housing Shortage (2012–2017). Government of India. https://www.pib.gov.in/newsite/erelcontent.aspx

Ministry of Statistics and Programme Implementation. (2019–2020). Periodic Labour Force Survey reports. Government of India. https://microdata.gov.in/NADA/index.php/catalog/217

Naik, M. (2022). *A "mainstreaming" approach to uplifting migrant households*. Centre for Policy Research.

Parekh, B. (2000). *Rethinking multiculturalism: Cultural diversity and political theory*. Harvard University Press.

Rajan, S. I., & Zachariah, K. C. (2019, January). Emigration and remittances: New evidences from the Kerala Migration Survey, 2018 (Working Paper No. 483). Centre for Development Studies.

Registrar General of India. (2016). *Population projections for India and states 2011–2036*. Government of India.

World Bank. (2021, November). Migration and development brief 35: Recovery from the COVID-19 crisis through a migration lens. https://documents1.worldbank.org/curated/en/099738408132414027/pdf/IDU110e1541c1704b14821196441e301ab86ff0b.pdf

World Bank. (2022, November). Migration and development brief 36: Remittances grow 5% in 2022, despite global headwinds. https://www.worldbank.org/en/news/press-release/2022/11/30/remittances-grow-5-percent-2022

Chapter 18

Transnational Remittances and Socio-Economic Transformation:
A Study of Nepalese Migrant Labor Networks

Sushil Dhakal
http://orcid.org/0000-0002-7638-9636
Brainware University, India

Suvasmita Dey
http://orcid.org/0009-0000-5642-5866
Jharkhand Rai University, India

ABSTRACT

Traditionally, Nepal has undergone chronic labor out-migration due to the lack of domestic labor markets, poverty, and inequalities in the regions. This paper discusses the functioning of Nepal's migrant labor networks across borders and the way in which remittances produced by such networks, results into socio-economic change on both the household and community level. It examines past and present trends of migration, recruitment procedures, labor channels, and presence of informal brokers and social networks. The paper also examines formal and informal remittance channels, online platforms and regulatory bodies that oversee remittance. At the household level, it evaluates the effects on consumption, education, health, savings,

DOI: 10.4018/979-8-3373-8500-6.ch018

repayment of debt and social mobility. Lastly, the work also presents issues of labor exploitation, high migration costs, financial dependency and policy gap and sheds light on vulnerabilities of the remittance-based economy in Nepal.

1. INTRODUCTION

Nepal is the traditionally country which is characterized by the enormous number of people relocating abroad to work. This has been increasing dramatically in the last several decades. Initially, a significant number of the Nepali workers used to attend neighboring India or armies in foreign countries. As global demand on labor grew beyond 1980s, increased numbers of people started moving to the Gulf and other countries in search of jobs (Sijapati et al., 2017). As the number of individuals who came out of Nepal to seek jobs in foreign countries increased, this started altering the social and economic environment of the Nepali family. Migration not only became a short-term approach but also a structural aspect of life to many Nepali families (Mishra & Kunwar, 2020).

Along with this increasing stream of labor migration, there were increasing inflows of money from migrants sent back home. These sums, also called remittances, rapidly became one of the most significant foreign exchange earners of Nepal. With time remittances increased to constitute a huge portion of the national income of Nepal. Within a few years they contributed almost one-quarter to one-third of the gross domestic product of the country (Ministry of Labor, Employment and Social Security, 2022). Remittance money became a staple resource to many Nepal households; it allowed access to improved food, education, health services and housing (Sharma, 2024). Simultaneously with the entry of this foreign income, Nepal changed its economy, needing less foreign aid or foreign investment, and, in the process, reforming how communities, families, and individuals perceive work, migration, and opportunity (Kharel & Kharel, 2020).

On this basis, the phenomenon of migrant labor networks and remittance economy in Nepal seems worth studying critically. This study seeks to comprehend the effects of migrant labor flows and remittance flows on the socio-economic reality of households and communities. The range of studies involves the analysis of remittance effect on incomes, consumption, poverty alleviation, social organization and long-term development outcomes. It is also about the way networks between migrants, their families and communities can be practiced across the borders to maintain migration and remittance flows.

In order to provide some direction to such research some questions arise. Why is it that so many Nepalis prefer to migrate to work other than find a job at home? What are the key destination countries, nature of work, duration, and remittance behavior patterns of migration? What are the effects of remittances on the household income, livelihoods, poverty rates, social status and ambitions in home countries? Are the remittances utilized to accumulate long run economic assets (as an investment in business, education or property) or are they primarily used to fund consumption and basic needs? What is the sustainability of a remittance-based model of development in Nepal, particularly in the context of changing global labor demand and potential weaknesses? In addition, there is the question of how returnees re-integrate, and what is the social or economic implication of their experiences in foreign countries with regard to their local communities?

The research relies on a combination of data sources to answer these questions. The secondary data is based on national surveys and government reports, central bank documents, and published research papers. A quantitative picture is formed by using statistics on remittance inflows, migration, destination countries and labor market trends, based on national and international studies. The qualitative information on the academic literature and the reports of the organizations, who perform research on migration and development, allow exploring the social and cultural impacts that occur at the social, cultural, and household levels of remittances and migration.

Simultaneously the study also recognizes some of these limitations and challenges. The official data does not always reflect the real migration, and remittance flows since most migrants move through less formal, or informal streams. The variety of different migrant experiences in various regions, caste or social categories may not be fully reflected in qualitative data that relies on case study or survey research. The impact of the remittance can be very diverse and different based on the background of the household, education, available assets and social-network, and thus, can hardly be generalized.

Despite these complications, the analysis of the remittance economy and migrant labor networks in Nepal can be of great significance to policy and development of the country. Since the level of remittance inflows is quite high and the percentage of households reliant on migration income is also quite high, the findings of such studies can be used to inform government policies related to labor migration, social protection, financial inclusion, and the development planning. They could assist in formulating plans to stimulate positive application of remittances, offer more assistance to migrant employees and their families, and decrease the reliance on foreign labor and stimulate domestic jobs. The shifting migration patterns and the rapidly changing global economic scenery have made it very important to take cognizance of these dynamic, so that remittances not only stand to guarantee the well-being of the household, but also to provide sustainable socio-economic change to Nepal and the citizens.

2. PATTERNS OF NEPALESE LABOR MIGRATION

2.1 Historical Trajectories of Out Migration from Nepal

The migration of Nepalese labor has strong historical foundations dating back to more than two hundred years. The historical studies indicate that the phenomenon had origins in the early nineteenth century when Nepalese soldiers began to work in foreign armies (Thieme & Wyss, 2005). The flow had initially been instigated by recruiting Nepalese as soldiers in foreign powers. Recruitment of Nepali "Gurkhas" into the British army started with the Anglo-Nepal war (1814-1816), the treaty of 1816 that allowed the recruitment of Nepali soldiers into British regiments (National Statistics Office, 2021). This gave rise to the tradition of serving in the military abroad creating an alternative source of livelihood among the Nepalese youth in the economically disadvantaged rural areas (Thieme & Wyss, 2005).

Gradually, this "Lahure" or "Gurkha" tradition spread outside of the military service. Based on an extensive assessment, historically Nepali migrant workers migrated as a survival tactic, particularly among people with poor rural origins and limited opportunities back home (Khatiwada & Basyal, 2022). When the internal economic mechanisms in Nepal failed to generate enough jobs, overseas jobs offered a convincing and often only effective way of many households to uphold their livelihood and social progress (International Organization for Migration (IOM), 2023).

In this way, Nepalese out-migration was historically evolving, as the recruitment of soldiers in the colonial era, into wider trends of labor migration, which were based on structural economic limitations and the pursuit of incomes that were stable. This tradition runs deep in the modern migration processes.

2.2 Contemporary Destination Countries and Labor Corridors

In recent decades, especially post-1990, the destination landscape for Nepalese labor migrants has broadened significantly beyond traditional military corridors and neighboring India. The broad liberalization of Nepal's economy and increased global demand for labor in rapidly industrializing and construction-oriented economies transformed migration patterns (Sijapati et al., 2015).

According to a recent study, since 1990 there has been a rapid shift as large flows of Nepalese labor have moved to Gulf Cooperation Council (GCC) countries (for example Qatar, Saudi Arabia, United Arab Emirates) and to Malaysia (Aryal, 2023). These countries constitute major corridors for foreign employment. Indeed, one policy brief confirms that the six GCC countries and Malaysia remain the central destinations for Nepali migrant workers (International Organization for Migration (IOM), 2023).

Statistical data corroborates this pattern. In the most recent decades, authors note that migration to India, once the dominant destination, has drastically declined, while the share migrating to "other countries" (outside India) has risen steeply (Aryal, 2023). The diversification of destination nations has also increased: beyond GCC and Malaysia, there is growing migration to "new" countries beyond traditional corridors, reflecting changing global labor demands and Nepalese ambition for broader opportunities (Ministry of Labour, Employment and Social Security, 2022).

Thus, contemporary Nepalese migration exhibits a pattern of concentrated labor corridors (GCC, Malaysia) combined with increasing diversification outward, a shift from historic soldier- or India-oriented migration.

2.3 Recruitment Processes and Labor Mobility Chains

The present-day recruitment and labor mobility of the Nepal migrants is largely mediated with formal mechanisms as well as the structured supply-chain of labor. Dedicated institutions create this official record; the Department of Foreign Employment (DoFE), Ministry of Labor, Employment and Social Security (MoLESS), Nepal Rastra Bank (NRB) and other agencies list labor approvals, labor returns, labor renewals, labor remittances and so on (Ministry of Labor, Employment and Social Security, 2020).

The government of Nepal reports that the system of labor permits is a major cause of migration of foreign jobs (excluding the migration to India and through irregular channels, however) (Ministry of Labor, Employment and Social Security, 2020).). In this case in fiscal years 2017/18 and 2018/19, migrant workers, who renewed labor approvals, were numerous, which cannot be attributed to a single movement to another place, but to repeated migration cycles of departure-return-and migration (Ministry of Labor, Employment and Social Security, 2020).

The labor mobility chains thus are carried out as a combination of formal approvals, contract-based hiring as well as repetitive migration trend. Such an arrangement may affect the career paths of migrants and the livelihoods of households: remittances, mastery of new skills in new countries and eventual re-entry or recurring cycles of migration. An official record-keeping and permit system is aimed at making the process more regulated and organized, particularly since 2008/09 when a great number of labor permissions began to be issued on a regular basis (Ministry of Labor, Employment and Social Security, 2020).

Nonetheless, despite formal procedures, there is still a large number of migrants who resort to informal or irregular channels, particularly those who move to India or pass through India to other countries, which remains important, but gets increasingly overshadowed by the formal foreign-employment system (Ministry of Labor, Employment and Social Security, 2020).

2.4 Role of Informal Brokers and Community Networks

Although formal institutional structures exist, informal participants such as brokers, agencies in Nepal, as well as local networks continue to play a pivotal role in meditating the Nepalese labor migration. The migration of Nepal, as reported by a number of scholarly authors, is impossible to comprehend without valuing the enduring role of such informal networks (Khatiwada & Basyal, 2022).

These brokers usually operate at the point of origin, in rural villages or poor agrarian communities, local intermediaries find migrant worthy youths, help them connect with recruitment agencies, handle labor-permit requests or informal contracts, and even arrange group migration. These brokers provide easy yet unsafe avenues in situations where formal access is both expensive and scarce (Khatiwada & Basyal, 2022).

Community networks and most importantly past migrants or the families of the returns is an important factor in determining migration flow. Migration can be a household or community livelihood policy: When one member of the family leaves and gets a job in another country or region, the money sent home and news of the life there enhances other people in the same social circle to emulate. This creates what is termed by some researchers as a chain of migration (Thieme & Wyss, 2005).

In addition, the networks may also affect destination preference, contracting, and even predictive frequency of repeat migration. As an example, the families that already had migrants in other countries might possess more information and social capital to accommodate any bureaucratic or informal obstacles and facilitate the further migration of other family members. With this dynamic, migration has not been a singular activity as it is a constant approach towards economic betterment and diversification of risks (Thieme & Wyss, 2005).

Dependence on informal brokers has, in most instances, been linked with vulnerabilities: exploitation, high recruitment expenses, contract substitution, and poor protection particularly to the unskilled migrants. Researchers have cautioned that in the event that there is no enhanced governance and control systems, such informal networks might end up perpetuating inequality and instability (Khatiwada & Basyal, 2022).

3. TRANSNATIONAL REMITTANCES: FLOWS AND MECHANISMS

3.1 Formal and Informal Remittance Channels

The flow of remittances in Nepal by its migrant workforce is based on a combination of both formal and informal channels. Extensive research released recently "Status of Remittances in Nepal (2025) states that there exists a combination of formal (banks, licensed money-transfer operators) and informal and semi-formal systems (Kharel et al., 2025). The informal sector can include personal couriers, unlicensed money-transfer agents or community-based networks, particularly where the banking services are not readily available in the earlier decades. Part of these informal flows can also be based on the systems, which are similar to the traditional trust-based value transfer networks (e.g., informal "hawala/hewala" networks) instead of regular banking or licensed remittance operators.

Formal remittance has gained prominence with time. The Nepal government collaborated with international organizations to support formal remittance system in order to make transfers more transparent, more affordable, and more secure (Governance of Labour Migration in South and South-east Asia (GOALS), 2024). Central to the country assessment conducted by the International Organization for Migration (IOM) and other organizations shows that informal flows are suggested to make up approximately 20 to 30 per cent of the total remittance inflows (United Nations Capital Development Fund, 2022).

Under a macro economic background, formal remittance inflows are listed on the balance of payments by central bank (Nepal Rastra Bank, NRB) and are also important sources of convertible foreign exchange (Kharel et al., 2025). Informal remittances, on the contrary, are often not recorded or under-recorded, which complicates the process of track them correctly. The duality of the remittance transfer channels indicates the institutional constraint of the Nepal financial architecture, as well as the practicality of migrant communities who prefer inexpensive, high-quality techniques, especially in the countries or situations where the availability of formal banking lags behind.

3.2 Digital Payment Platforms and Financial Inclusion

Over the past years, electronic finances and mobile-wallet applications have been on the rise in Nepal as a solution to streamlining the flow of remittances and supporting financial inclusion. One interesting case is IME Pay, a partnership project developed by remittances service providers and development organizations (including UNCDF) to develop a digital mobile-wallet system enabling remittance recipients to access the funds directly, even in rural regions (United Nations Capital Development Fund, 2022).

The IOM (2024) argues that digital and formal remittance services contributed to a reduction in transaction costs and the cost of sending remittances through formal channels went as low as 3.7 per cent in 2022 (IOM Nepal, 2024). This cost saving promotes a low cost and a motivation towards migrants and their families to adopt formal/digital channels instead of more informal, and frequently more hazardous options.

Financial inclusion is also assisted by the development of digital remittance platforms. In a study conducted at a micro-level by Sadichchha Shrestha and Nayan Krishna Joshi (2018), households in Nepal receiving remittance were more likely to utilize formal financial services (deposit accounts or loans) when they received remittance flows on a regular basis (Shrestha & Joshi, 2018). But, rather counterintuitive, the paper found that the true demand of formal deposit or credit is declining sometimes, possibly due to remittance-driven income lowering a short-term demand of loans or savings (Shrestha & Joshi, 2018).

In most general terms, the empirical studies conducted globally highlight that remittances play a positive role in realizing development objectives, especially when they are accompanied by financial inclusion (Barkat et al., 2024). In the case of Nepal, this implies that the digital remittance solution, such as IME Pay, as well as the bank-based system, could be used not only to transfer the funds but also include migrant-household families into the formal financial system, which would offer them additional benefits such as savings, credit access, and monetary planning.

3.3 Determinants of Remittance Sending Behavior

The decision of Nepalese migrants to send remittances, and the frequency and amount thereof, depend on multiple factors: origin household economic condition, destination earnings, cost and accessibility of transfer channels, household composition, and intended use of remittances. The 2025 "Status of Remittances" report provides detailed empirical data indicating that households receiving remittances tend to belong to certain socio-demographic profiles: many come from households with no stable domestic income, limited productive assets, and often rural origins (Kharel et al., 2025).

Remittance receipt tends to be more significant in certain provinces of Nepal (e.g. Bagmati, Gandaki, Koshi), compared to relatively poorer provinces (e.g. Karnali, Sudurpaschim, Madhesh) (Kharel et al., 2025). The reason appears to be that migrants from wealthier provinces more frequently access higher-wage foreign jobs (outside India), thereby remitting larger amounts; migrants from poorer provinces often migrate to lower-paying jobs, or to India where wages (and remittances) are comparatively lower (Kharel et al., 2025).

Academic analysis also suggests that remittances are directed largely towards consumption, household expenditure, education, healthcare, and sometimes savings or investment (Kharel et al., 2025). A time-series study using ARDL bounds testing identified a positive long-term relationship between remittance inflows and financial savings in Nepal (Lamsal & Soneja, 2025).

Beyond household-level determinants, macroeconomic factors also influence remittance sending behavior. For instance, demand for migrant labor abroad (especially in high-wage destinations), wage levels in host countries, exchange rates, and cost and convenience of transfer channels play a role. Also, policies and institutional frameworks that facilitate easy formal remittance, such as lower transfer costs, availability of digital transfer platforms, and regulatory facilitation, encourage migrants to remit more and regularly through formal channels. This institutional effect is captured in policy analyses by international agencies working with the Nepal government (Governance of Labour Migration in South and South-east Asia (GOALS), 2024).

3.4 Volatility, Exchange Rate Sensitivity and Global Economic Shocks

The inflows of remittance into Nepal are not exempt to the global economic conditions and exchange rate variations and macro-economic shocks. Empirical and institutional research has shown that in fact remittances have acted as a buffer in crises, including natural disasters or global recessions, to the Nepalese economy, but they are vulnerable to adverse global shocks (Kharel et al., 2025).

Indicatively, the 2025 Nepal economic update notes that the past years of increasing remittances were partly due to the increasing numbers of Nepali migrants working in emerging destinations with higher wage rates (e.g., Japan, South Korea) and partly because of a weaker Nepali Rupee to foreign currencies (Mijiyawa et al., 2025). This implies that the devaluation of the exchange rate can see the value of remittances in the local currency go up and therefore encourage more remittances to be sent by the migrant. Nonetheless, excessive use of favorable exchange rates also causes instability to households and the macro-economy; any appreciation of Nepal currency or negative effects caused by any economic recession in the hosts countries can severely diminish remittance value.

Remittance flows may also be affected by global economic shocks such as international recessions, pandemics, or changes in demand of migrant labor. It is important to mark that during the COVID-19 pandemic, remittance inflows were expected to go down because of lockdowns and loss of jobs in foreign countries.

However, according to the IOM-UNCDF partnership, digital remittance platforms and formal avenues also served to keep the flows going, and Nepal continued to receive significant remittances even amidst the crisis time period (Rashid et al., 2023).

However, such reliance on remittance in the long-term suggests a possible form of vulnerability: global economic factors may slow down, or lower labor demand in the host country, or the mobility of migrants may be restricted and, as a result, remittance inflows, and, accordingly, the income of the household will decrease, which will place the livelihoods and the stability of the macroeconomic environment at risk. Others have expressed concern of overdependence on remittances as sources of foreign exchange, savings and consumption which would lead to failure in domestic productive investments and diversification of the economy (Sharma, 2024)

3.5 Regulatory Institutions Governing Remittance Transfers

In Nepal, remittance environment is becoming more defined by the institutional structures and regulations. The Nepal Rastra Bank (NRB) is the main institution that regulates the flow of remittances and foreign exchange, and records the flow of workers remittances as part of a balance-of-payments information (Kharel et al., 2025). The reports by NRB have changed with time, with older ones featuring remittances by foreign-service soldiers (including Gurkhas) as part of Gorkha remittance, whereas in the 80s the language was broadened to wage-earners (and civilians abroad), and other remittances made by foreign servicemen (Kharel et al., 2025).

There is the regulation of the remittance service providers which is a part of licensing and supervision. According to the IOM Migration Governance Profile of Nepal, 2024, since 2018 the government has implemented new remittance plans under the watch of the Ministry of Finance and its other regulatory bodies (International Organization for Migration (IOM), 2024). The intention of these schemes is to make remittance faster, safer and less expensive processes to the migrant workers and their relatives. (Governance of Labour Migration in South and South-east Asia (GOALS), 2024)

Moreover, this can be supported by policy briefs and academic research, which encourages migrants to send remittances through formal banking strategies, ensuring the quality of data as well as directing the funds to beneficial investment and savings (Lamsal & Soneja, 2025). A study based on ARDL was able to conclude that there is a positive impact of formal remittance flows on long-term financial savings in Nepal thus leading to capital formation, investment and subsequently job creation (Lamsal & Soneja, 2025).

Simultaneously, regulatory initiatives deal with the risk of informal transfer, including money laundering, deficiency of consumer protection, and disruptive underground capital networks. Status of Remittances in Nepal report explains registration processes of remittance service providers, compliance with Anti-money laundering (AML) frameworks as well as regular monitoring of remittance operators (Kharel et al., 2025).

However, there are still issues. The informal channels persist, particularly among the migrants in the isolated areas or those individuals employed in countries where formal bank system and access to remittance services are unavailable or unaffordable (Bisheshta Shrestha, 2023). In addition, inequality in the financial inclusions among regions and households, founded on income, literacy and access to banking infrastructures can constrain accessibility of formal and online remittance systems. Researchers and policy-makers observe that, unless such gaps are filled, remittance flows might continue to be somewhat informal in nature; this demeans the full potential of remittances in terms of economic growth and the deepening of the financial sector (Pant, 2011).

The existence of regulatory institutions and policies is vital towards governance and transparency besides contributing to the productive utilization of remittances. A classic study by Bhubanesh Pant explains that there is a big potential in remittances to finance entrepreneurship, investment in education, better human capital but policy frameworks need to be in place so that remittances can be channeled towards productive purposes and not just consumption (Pant, 2011).

The efforts of the past few years by the international organizations operating in Nepal, including IOM, International Fund for Agricultural Development (IFAD), UNCDF and others were aimed at helping to modernize remittance infrastructure: a switch to digital wallets, licensing remittance companies, a lower cost of transactions, and awareness amongst migrant households of the benefits of the formal channels (Yamini Lohia, 2024). These activities are associated with global best practices as prescribed by organizations like World Bank and Global Knowledge Partnership on Migration and Development (KNOMAD) that examine the flow of migration and remittances between countries (World Bank, 2025).

4. SOCIO ECONOMIC IMPACTS OF REMITTANCES IN NEPAL

4.1 Household Income, Consumption and Poverty Reduction

Remittances represent a vital and, in some cases, major source of income to a significant number of Nepali households especially in the rural and marginal areas. In empirical studies, there is a consistent indication that the foreign remittances increase the per capita income, and total consumption expenditure in recipient households in a considerable manner. To give an example, a more recent study by the title of Impact of Remittance on Household Income, Consumption and Poverty Reduction of Nepal reveals a significant positive impact of becoming a recipient of remittance income on the welfare of households, with significant increases in income levels and consumption abilities of households (Bam et al., 2018).

On the same note, another recent cross-sectional study involving 5,645 rural households in 50 districts indicated that households that received remittances were less likely to be poor (Byanjanakar & Shakha, 2021). Research has also made distinctions between food and non-food aspects of poverty. In the analysis of Nepal Living Standards Survey problem (NLSS II), remittances were found to decrease food poverty, and non-food poverty across Nepal, but the impact was stronger on the non-food poverty (i.e., spending beyond subsistence) such as clothing, utilities, and other living expenses (Tiwari, 2022).

Households tend to use remittance inflows to enhance their living standards. Housing conditions have been improved such as better building materials, increased or more secure dwelling unit, reportedly, particularly in rural peripheries where earlier housing may have been primitive. The remittances therefore not only result in short-term consumption but also lead to medium-term growth in material standards of living. In the long run, this system of inflow of foreign earnings assists in protecting households in the event of income shocks (such as crop failure or local job losses), which is their individual social insurance and allows them to be more economically sound. This pattern reaffirms such theoretical models as the "Household Strategy Model" in the paradigm of New Economics of Labor Migration, where migration and the remittance sending is not always a personal choice, but a risk-coping and income-diversification approach at the household level (Rai, 2025).

Considered on a macro level, remittances stand out to Nepal with significant aggregate economic impacts. Analyses conducted by the central banking and the economic research institutions indicate that, the inflows of remittance has relieved the foreign exchange pressure, improved the balance of payment of the country, and added on to the national savings and home investments abilities (Pant, 2006). In certain years, they surpass other external inflows like foreign direct investment or development aid, thus they form a significant and consistently stable source of external revenue to the nation (The World Bank, 2024).

But there is a certain amount of caution to be prudently observed. As receiving remittance families experience increased consumption and better standards of living, the net social impact might be increased inequality in the society. Such growth in per-capita expenditure is frequently also followed by a growth in measures of inequality (such as a rising Gini coefficient), because wealthier households or those already advantaged are more likely to have a number of their members migrate to other countries, thereby receiving foreign income. This implies that remittance is capable of decreasing the absolute poverty, but at the same time, they can increase relative inequality among households, which are or are not reliant on migration. This trend had been experienced in the past where there is an increase in the inflows of remittances (Lokshin et al., 2010).

4.2 Education, Health and Human Capital Enhancement

The remittance inflow has one of the greatest social effects on human capital in Nepal, affecting levels of education and health outcomes among remittance-receiving households. There are studies that show remittances are positively related with an increase in the expenditure on education. Considering the examples, families to whom the remittance is sent tend to enroll their children to school, purchase school supplies, and invest in higher education (Sharma, 2024). Such a rise is particularly remarkable in the rural environments, where the remittances compensate the local constraints of low household income, the unpredictability of seasons in agricultural activities, and insufficient liquidity to afford initial educational expenditure. The economic stagnation in some parts of Nepal makes this remittance-based investment in education a sometimes the only available route to potentially enhanced future opportunities on next generations.

There is also an improvement in health outcomes with flows of remittance. It is found in studies that, medical services are more highly utilized among remittance-receiving households, with increased probability of visiting a clinic or hospital, improved postnatal and prenatal care services, increased birth weight and reduced child mortality rates (Sharma, 2024). The higher purchasing power enables households to obtain nutritious diets, proper household hygiene and access to preventive and therapeutic healthcare services, investments that would be forgotten in the restrictive budgets.

These transformations are not only of greater material good but are also an indicator of improvements in the long-term formation of human capital. Healthier and educated children will have better opportunities to serve the economy well either through a skilled job within the country or remitting themselves later. This is a possible generational payoff supporting the debate that remittances should be seen as consumption income and as developmental capital. This viewpoint is highlighted in some scholarly approaches (e.g., Human Capital Theory and Sustainable Livelihoods Framework) that are implemented in research on Nepal (Rai, 2025).

However, researchers have warned that there is an uneven use of remittance in human capital improvement. However, not every recipient is focused on education or health, some might switch funds to consumption or non-consumption spending. Remittances in certain households are spent to address daily needs, debt repayment (which is usually incurred in the recruitment or migration process), or conspicuous consumption instead of making long-term investments (Pasa & Kharel, 2024). So, despite the high possibility of human capital enhancement, its achievement should be reliant on domestic decisions, service access, and macroeconomic circumstances (school accessibility, good healthcare availability, etc.).

4.3 Gender Roles and Changing Family Dynamics

Remittance flows and migration of relatives especially male relatives have a great impact on gender roles and family dynamics in Nepal. In most Nepali rural families, remittance receiving migrants are male workers in foreign countries who leave behind wives, children, or other family members. This often leads to more decision-making power in the hands of women on household issues such as the handling of remittance funds, decision-making on expenditures as well as house repairs. There is a set of descriptive reports and policy accounts that indicate that women become de facto heads of the household in absence of men, making financial choices, educational needs of their children, health care and everyday subsistence spending.

This transformation can result in a socio-economic empowerment of women who are in charge of remittance money, women can have more freedom, they become active in making decisions regarding schooling, health, housing, and investments. Increased financial accountability among women and remittance inflow helped reduce fertility, child health expectations, and educational attainment all of which are indications of a shift in gender-family relationships in the migrant sending societies.

Simultaneously, these changes are not entirely good or harmless. Prolonged absence of male household members may bring emotional and social expenses that can mean additional workload of females, performing multiple roles, social isolation, or becoming overdependent on remittance income. Traditional gender roles come in conflict with emerging economic realities in certain communities causing tension or social stress. Critics claim that family reorganization due to remittances can even destroy ancient social organizations, making society weak, or burdening women in the long term (Nicander, 2015).

In addition, the remittance-dependent households can find themselves feeling socially dislocated or with shifting identity. Women, the elderly and children can stay behind in villages where there is high outmigration of men, shifting the demographic balances and social positions in whole communities. Social norms and generational aspirations and expectations evolve; examples include a focus on educational opportunities of children, migration desires of younger generation, altered attitude to traditional jobs (agriculture), and a restructuring of occupational roles by gender (Nicander, 2015).

4.4 Community Development and Local Infrastructure

At a broader level, remittances do have consequences on community development and the infrastructure of the locality, but with mixed results depending on local factors, institutions, and decisions. Remittance inflows have helped to provide better housing, better utilities (water, electricity, sanitation), local small-scale building, and renovation of community facilities (educational, medical, and retail) in certain areas. In rural municipalities like those analyzed in Harion Municipality and other localities, overseas employment and remittances have given rise to better standards of living, housing and certain levels of investment on local infrastructure and community services.

Local economies are also prone to be affected by remittances. The growth of the household consumption increases the demand of goods and services supplied by local businesses and, as a result, the number of retail shops, services, transport, small construction businesses, and informal enterprises grows. The remittance-based consumption has a multiplier effect on creating employment even to families who do not migrate. According to some research, collective investments may be formed by pooled remittances (where more than one household invests within the community), i.e. investment in communal structures, roads, small businesses, thus improving the welfare of the community. (Pant, 2006)

Additionally, at the macroeconomic-nation level, remittances have been playing a role in national savings and aggregate demand, and when appropriately channeled, may be able to support capital formation, business investments and rural development projects. Previous studies have highlighted that inflows of remittances ease foreign exchange limitations and impact positively national balance of payments, that further may allow the government to invest in infrastructure and state services. (Pant, 2006)

However, there are also limitations that can be observed in empirical studies. Remittance inflows have not been converted into community investments or better infrastructure in certain localities. Rather, benefits are still only limited to individual households, which implies the existence of disparities between remittance-receiving and non-receiving households. Remittances through increases in consumption or construction (in sensitive or ecologically sensitive zones such as surrounding national parks) could have the effect of causing environmental stress, resource over exploitation, and unsustainable local development, particularly without proper regulation. Research in the buffer zone of a national park found both positive impacts (better household consumption, access to health and education) and negative impacts of the ecological integrity forced by more resource use and development pressures (Dhakal, 2024).

Moreover, the dependency on remittances might deter investment in productive activities including agriculture or local businesses, therefore the long-term structuring development can be minimal unless the remittance income is invested in the productive activities. In fact, other studies observe that although household welfare gains, in most cases, remittance inflows are not converted into local entrepreneurship, modernization of agriculture, or permanent development of the community (Pasa & Kharel, 2024).

4.5 Regional Disparities in Remittance Utilization

Effects of the remittances are not uniform in Nepal which has varied geographical and socio-economic areas. Research indicates that the food and non-food poverty decreases attributable to remittances vary across geography, e.g., mountain-region, hilly-region and the Terai plains have varied patterns of remittance flows and effects. In a study based on NLSS II, the authors discovered that remittances diminished poverty in all regions, but the extent of the decrease was smaller in remote mountain compared to the Terai or urban-proximate regions (Tiwari, 2022).

The issue of rural-urban differences is also relevant. Rural and remote households may be sending money primarily to satisfy consumption demands (food, basic utilities, debt payment), but in many cases may not be able to invest the money in education, health or business. Conversely, families located in more convenient places, close to towns or with more accessible markets can be able to utilize remittances to fund education, health, projects or renovate housing or invest in small-scale ventures more easily. The accessibility of services, quality of local institutions (schools, health centers, transport, markets) is an important factor in determining remittance use.

In addition, social and environmental settings are significant. Remittance-based consumption and construction can cause non-sustainable resource exploitation, environmental harm, or land and resource contention in densely populated or ecologically sensitive regions (e.g. buffer zones around national parks), going against the potential benefits in long-term sustainability (Dhakal, 2024).

Moreover, migrated households (such as families of former soldiers, e.g., Gurkhas / lahures) tend to be better informed about the remittance mechanisms, have more stable remittance inflows, and possibly well-connected social networks, thus using the remittance income more strategically than first-generation civilian labor migrants. These households are better informed on financial planning, knowledgeable on cross border financial flows and are more effective in utilizing remittances. Nonetheless, there is no specific empirical evidence that can draw the line between these legacy migrant households and new migrant households; the majority of research does not distinguish between origin of remittance (military pension or civilian labor).

Therefore, the regional differences in utilization indicate not only geography, but also the differences in social network, institutional access, previous migration history, and the local infrastructure. Remittances have limited potential of transformative changes in the long run without facilitating and supporting services and a favorable local environment.

5. MIGRANT LABOR NETWORKS AND TRANSNATIONAL LINKAGES

5.1 Social Capital, Kinship and Diaspora Support Systems

The social capital and kinship networks play a central role in determining the migration of labor in Nepal. The literature on migrant networks illustrates the maintaining of migration flows by previously established social relations and how relations offer resources, material and informational, contributing to the process of migration and its accommodation in another country (Sha, 2021).

In the Nepali context, empirical studies show that decisions to migrate for foreign employment often rely heavily on family connections or acquaintances who have already migrated. As observed in the ethnographic study from Sindhupalchowk district, many households view migration not solely as an economic strategy but as a long-term livelihood option shaped by transnational social spaces linking origin and destination (Shakya, 2024). This corresponds with the theoretical framework of transnational social fields, where migrants and non-migrants remain connected across borders through kinship, shared community identity, and mutual obligations. (Hâncean et al., 2021)

Such networks provide several forms of support. First, there is emotional and social support, for example, guidance regarding life in the destination country, cultural adaptation, and coping with separation from home. Second, there is practical support, help in finding jobs, accommodation, navigating bureaucratic procedures, or even initial settle-in assistance. Third, many migrants channel remittances not just to immediate family, but to extended family or community networks, including investments in housing, education, or community-based ventures. In studies from other migrant communities, researchers have identified categories of remittance beyond purely personal/household, including network remittances, welfare remittances, and investment remittances. (Tharmalingam, 2011)

In Nepal too, such dynamics seem to operate as diaspora communities abroad, by virtue of their social capital, contribute to strengthening transnational linkages that go beyond remittance in cash, encompassing social, cultural, and informational exchanges. As documented in a review of Nepali diaspora involvement, emigrants contribute through financial remittances, transfer of knowledge and skills, and in some cases community mobilization or development initiatives oriented toward their places of origin (Adhikari, 2022).

5.2 Circulatory Migration and Returnee Experiences

Circulatory migration where individuals move to other countries and come back periodically (or forever) constitutes an important aspect of Nepalese labor migration. The recent Nepal Labor Migration Report 2022 states that return migration is a significant phenomenon, to which a significant number of Nepali workers has returned after a time of foreign work (Ministry of Labour, Employment and Social Security, 2022).

Returnees have complicated experience. On one hand, due to remittances that are frequently brought by the returnee, it may help to enhance the living standards, pay debts, or invest in property or small business. Conversely, the reintegration process of the returned is not easy; they are unable to adjust to the new developments back home, obtain constructive jobs, or transform their skills and savings into long-term livelihood systems. According to the report, the governance structure of labor migration, particularly in the period after the disruptions such as the COVID-19 pandemic, includes reintegration activities, such as certifying skills and providing welfare (Ministry of Labour, Employment and Social Security, 2022).

Academically, returnees bring about what some scholars refer to as social remittances, exchange of ideas, cultural practices and social norms learnt in the foreign land to communities in home countries. Returnees in Nepal have been suggested to deliver some form of transnational identity that exceeds any economic calculation, and the act of migrating, returning, and maintaining connections between the two countries influences the social life, ambitions, and strategies of migrant families (Shakya, 2024).

Additionally, the circulatory character of migration occasionally implies that migrants maintain close links to the home and destination. Such continuous connections also may have impact on future migration patterns, social responsibility, and community life. Returnees who have foreign jobs also contribute to the generation of role models to other immigrant who may be considering migration hence sustaining the migration and remittance flow cycle. These dynamics are similar to a wider theory of migration-network, which emphasizes how current migrants lower the expenses and risks incurred by new migrants (Sha, 2021).

5.3 Cross Border Information Exchange and Employment Facilitation

The cross-border exchange of information through the networks of migration is a key intermediate and determinant in the patterns of labor migration. It is social relationships, kinship, friendships, community associations, that tend to contribute to the transmission of information regarding potential employment, recruitment procedures, living conditions in foreign countries and realities of immigration. In migration literature, these information flows tend to have a greater impact on decision-making than recruitment agents (Williams et al., 2020).

When it comes to Nepal, research indicates that these unofficial channels of information are important to the migrants. As an illustration, a cross-border migration study between the Nepal-India migration points out that social network, low communicability (similarities among languages), low price of traveling and open border are one of the key components of cross-border migration (Bhatt, 2023). This highlights the role of exchange of information via informal networks in decreasing transaction costs, decreasing uncertainty about employment in foreign countries, and speeding up the migration process.

International bodies and labor governance reports also acknowledge the role of exchange of information through migrant networks. According to the ILO-backed report on migration and remittance in Nepal, the face-to-face network, peer recommendation, diaspora relations, and community-based knowledge-sharing are the ones that contribute to safe and informed migration choice (Khadka et al., 2016).

This flow of cross-border information usually incorporates information on employment prospects, workplace situations, labor contracts, housing and even the credibility of recruitment firms. Moreover, migrants in foreign countries can offer direct support to applicants to enable them have contacts with employers, provide temporary housing or support them to have access to informal employment sectors.

5.4 Role of Migrant Associations and Community Groups

The migrant associations, local organizations, and diaspora groups contribute to the institutionalization of the migrant support system to their relatives and close ones. Generally similar to what sociological literature calls as hometown associations (HTA), mutual-aid societies of immigrants of the same city or region, these groups facilitate remittance organization, provision of social support and development or welfare activities back at home.

Similarly, in Nepal, there is evidence that the diaspora and migrant organizations lead to development, knowledge exchange, and community mobilization in the native regions. As per one study on Nepali diaspora, the emigrants abroad tend to participate in investments, transfer of technology or skills, and other types of contribution beyond the remittance (Adhikari, 2022). These associations can also offer informal but necessary assistance to the new migrants, exchange experience regarding the processes of labor migration, recruitment, and working conditions in foreign countries.

In addition to this, the international non-governmental organizations (INGOs) and intergovernmental agencies present in Nepal have acknowledged the role of such community groups. As one of the migration governance indicators, the report by International Organization for Migration (IOM) Nepal (2024) describes the ways migrant associations and community groups can connect migrant workers to welfare schemes, insurance benefits (accident, disability, repatriation), and services to dependents. (International Organization for Migration (IOM), 2024).

On the policy and governance level discussed in the Nepal Labor Migration Report 2022, the Government of Nepal, in collaboration with I/NGOs and global partners, envisions the need to involve migrant associations as a stakeholder in labor migration management, such as reintegrating returned migrants, certifying migrants skills, and supporting families who remain behind (Ministry of Labour, Employment and Social Security, 2022). This is because it indicates a realization that groups in the community can be used to supplement state-based mechanisms particularly where formal institutions have restrictions due to inadequacy or failure to reach.

6. CHALLENGES AND VULNERABILITIES IN THE REMITTANCE ECONOMY

This dependency on the income of migrant workers is one of the cornerstones of the Nepalese economy, and it maintains the livelihoods of a large number of households (The World Bank, 2024). However, this remittance-led economy has a number of structural weaknesses. These are the result of exploitative labor practices, expensive migration, domestic financial mismanagement, and large policy, regulation, and institutional loopholes. It is these challenges that weaken the progressive long-term development and several potential socio-economic changes attributed to remittances.

6.1 Labor Exploitation, Contractual Abuse and Safety Issues

Frequent cases of labor exploitations, contractual exploitations and severe safety issues experienced by migrant workers in foreign countries form one of the most severe vulnerabilities to Nepal remittance economy. A recent academic study named as *Beyond Remittances: The Real Cost of Nepal Labor Migration* reported on how failure in the basic foundations of the Nepalese governance framework around labor migration leads to abuses on a massive scale, particularly in the Gulf States and Malaysia (Ghimire, 2025). The author claims that exploitation is structural, not casual, that fraudulent hiring procedures, misleading contracts, inadequate pre-departure protections, and ineffective supervision altogether lead to the creation of a dangerous situation within Nepali workers (Ghimire, 2025).

This is supported by empirical facts gathered by human rights organizations. A report by Amnesty International found that in numerous instances, Nepali migrant workers in foreign countries faced low wages, fraudulent agreements in languages that they could not understand, seizure of passports, limited freedom of movement and denial of fundamental rights (Amnesty International, 2011). In practice, such conditions are frequently equivalent to forced labor or some kind of quasi-bondage, which harms the dignity and security of migrant workers.

Risks associated with safety are also common. Studies have reported common threats to the occupational safety of Nepali employees overseas, particularly in the construction industry, the manufacturing business and other dangerous industries (Hajariya, 2016). It has been reported to have high cases of workplace injuries, fatal accidents, heat related illnesses, and in some cases death. An example is a study that projected staggering mortality rates among the workers in the Gulf especially those in the construction and other risk sectors (Hajariya, 2016).

Moreover, psychological pressures, loneliness, and mental health issues are also becoming more common among migrant workers, particularly when employers modify working conditions negatively, salaries are postponed or refused, or when employees face any mistreatment or hazardous working/living conditions (Ghimire, 2025).

These tendencies of exploitation and safety risks indicate that the remittance economy is sustained by the institutional system of labor migration in which institutional protections fail and in which the rights and dignity of migrants are frequently violated.

6.2 High Cost of Migration and Remittance Transfer Charges

The other major weakness is that Nepali workers have high migration costs and some burdens related to remittance transfer. The Nepal Labor Migration Report 2022 states that migration expenses such as recruitment fee, visa fees, medical tests, and traveling fee, as well as, commissions to brokers can have a substantial financial burden particularly to weaker families (Ministry of Labour, Employment and Social Security, 2022).

According to academic and policy discussions, most Nepali migrants turn to informal lenders or borrow in order to take in initial expenses of traveling overseas. These debt related burdens may cycle migrants into dependency forcing them to take poor workplace jobs and pressuring them to send money fast, even at the expense of their rights or wellbeing. The article "Beyond Remittances" notes that this high entry cost contributes to vulnerability, and especially to low-income and marginalized populations (Ghimire, 2025).

Migrants are exposed to financial leakage due to charges on transfer of remittances even after securing jobs overseas. Despite the growth of formal remittance channels over the past years, informal or intermediaries remain an option to many migrants because of convenience, time or unavailability of formal banking facilities. A country evaluation by the United Nations Capital Development Fund (UNCDF) of Nepal has detailed that reliance on informal transfer systems remains, partially due to the fact that formal mechanisms can be too costly, out of reach, or cumbersome particularly to the low-income migrants (United Nations Capital Development Fund, 2022).

Such financial expenses decrease the net gain of remittances in beneficiary households. The high cost of transfer and debt repayment makes a sort of poor or marginalized family feel that the real disposable income is still low.

6.3 Financial Mismanagement and Dependency Risks

Remittance is also known to increase household spending and can enhance access to education, health and basic living conditions in most Nepali households. In a recent empirical investigation based on the data collected in rural Nepal, it was observed that the inflows of remittances are a significant factor in raising household spending on food, healthcare, and education (Thapa-Parajuli et al., 2025). This very evidence however also indicates structural weaknesses, particularly with remittances being the major or sole source of income to the households with little investment in productive or long-term economic activity.

According to the 2022 migration report, most households spend remittances on day-to-day spending or debt repayment as opposed to investing it in business or farmlands or other income-intensive activities (Ministry of Labour, Employment and Social Security, 2022). Researchers have warned that this will give rise to a dependency syndrome in the long term as families will lose interest in local labor markets making them less productive at home and lose incentive to invest in skills training or in local businesses. This risk is reflected in the UNCDF country assessment which notes that excessive reliance on the remittances can undermine the dynamism of the local economy and restrict the growth of sustainable development (United Nations Capital Development Fund, 2022).

This dependency leaves households highly exposed to external shocks like job losses in foreign countries, wage reductions, sudden returns as a result of economic crunch or medical/emergency crises in receiving countries. As an example, global recessions or alterations in labor demand may cause an abrupt loss of revenue to households thus leading the households into debt or into poverty. The nature of volatile remittance inflows therefore highlights the reality of the risks of over-relying on overseas jobs to improve the welfare of the household.

6.4 Policy Gaps, Weak Enforcement and Institutional Failures

The major policy gaps with poor enforcement systems and institutional failures are some of the critical vulnerabilities because they curb the ability to protect migrant workers and adequately govern foreign employment. According to the Nepal Labor Migration Report 2022, though foreign employment is still at the center of the economy of Nepal, there is still a challenge in managing migration in an informed, safe and rights-based manner (Ministry of Labour, Employment and Social Security, 2022).

According to recent studies, the major threat to the safety of Nepali migrant workers is systemic failures, lack of regulation of recruitment agencies, predeparture training, bilateral agreements to protect labor rights in foreign countries, fragmented institutional accountabilities (Ghimire, 2025). Although there is legal policy in presence, real implementation in Nepal and destination countries is still weak since a large number of recruitment agencies push the limits of regulations, contract replacement, excessive fees and inadequate disclosure.

Moreover, there is a lack of institutional coordination. The governance of migration falls on various ministries, governmental agencies and local jurisdictions with overlapping mandates, which result in gaps due to weak implementation frameworks. According to the UNCDF country assessment, financial inclusion and remittance programs that have been implemented since 2018 have had some achievements, but even now, many migrant workers do not have access to any formal financial services, secure mechanisms of transferring funds, or redressing grievances (International Organization for Migration (IOM), 2024).

The orientation before the departure and the dissemination of information are poor, particularly among workers who belong to the rural or marginalized group with low literacy. Consequently, migrants can go abroad without being aware of their rights, terms of contracts or the help of institutions, which makes them more susceptible to exploitation (Ghimire, 2025).

There is also poor reintegration support to the returnees. Despite having a policy framework that envisages support to the returning people, skill certification, reintegration programs, and welfare services, there is imbalance in implementation. Finding decent jobs, transferring overseas acquired skills to the home country, and receiving social security and assistance are among the challenges faced by many returnees (Ministry of Labour, Employment and Social Security, 2022).

In addition, the excessive reliance on remittance inflows within the country seems to shadow investments in the creation of domestic jobs and structural economic growth. This kind of orientation in policy, as suggested by the migration governance literature, leaves foreign employment as a must, not a choice, leading to a cycle of labor export instead of diversified and self-sufficient domestic economy (Ghimire, 2025).

Lastly, accountability mechanisms are poor, both at the domestic and international levels. Often, the victims of exploitation have massive barriers to redress because the legal procedures are complicated, issues of cross-border jurisdictions appear, and the institutional support can be insufficient or even unavailable. Such failure in protection and enforcement is a major factor that compromises the rights of migrants, which strengthens structural vulnerability in the remittance economy. (Amnesty International, 2011)

7. CONCLUSION

On the basis of the reflections about the phenomena of migrant labor and Nepalese remittance flows, several salient insights are uncovered. To begin with, remittances continue to form central determinants to the livelihoods of a very large proportion of Nepali households and play an important role in economic stability of the country. According to one of the studies, remittance inflows have played a critical role when it comes to sustaining consumption, education, and household welfare in the face of no domestic employment avenues, hence protecting a large portion of Nepali households against poverty and increasing access to services that would otherwise be out of reach (Dinesh, 2020). Secondly, the migrant workforce can offer an avenue to excess labor in Nepal when the country has limited domestic non-farm jobs; skilled and unskilled laborers alike are willing to be recruited in foreign markets and thus households are able to access foreign incomes where domestic labor markets falter in providing stable employment opportunities (Pudasaini, 2025). Thirdly, even with beneficial impact on economies systemically there are drawbacks to dependence on remittances: remittance-oriented income tends to interfere with long-term solutions to domestic job creation, skills investment, or local entrepreneurship. According to recent reports, excessive reliance on foreign labor exports and remittance inflows can only plunge Nepal into a hole of emigration and under-development instead of developing a self-sufficient economy (Giri, 2025).

Policy-wise, there is some indication that current laws and institutional structures aimed at safeguarding migrant labor and utilizing the remittances to develop the nation are promising but still insufficient. Legal and regulatory frameworks governing foreign employment, such as the Foreign Employment Act, 2007 and its associated regulations and policies endorses the aim of having control of foreign employment, workers protection, and promotion of safe migration; in theory the policies include pre-departure orientation, registration of recruitment agencies, insurance coverage and welfare funds of migrants (Pudasaini, 2025). Meanwhile, institutional breakdowns, sporadic implementation and disjointed supervision have stunted their performance. Systemic failures in governance of recruitment procedures, the lack of pre-departure protections and a poor enforcement, continue to be some of the leading factors behind exploitation and abuse of Nepali workers in foreign countries (Ghimire, 2025).

Based on these insights a set of policy recommendations towards the inclusive development emerges. First, migration governance needs to become more proactive towards protecting migration rights and offering wholesome working environments abroad, instead of merely facilitating labor export. This will require better controls, fair and transparent hiring procedures, implementation of the contract conformity to the norms and availability of grievance redress systems. Agreements should be sought at bilateral levels and through coordinated labor diplomacy to ensure minimum labor standards are achieved as well as to allow destination country recourse mechanisms to workers. Second, the use of remittance inflows should be more productive instead of being consumed. The government and the financial institutions are supposed to advance financial literacy among the migrant households, encourage savings and investment in small businesses, agriculture or skills training, and offering access to credit and business services to the returnees. Current measures to promote more formal remittance transfer and returnee entrepreneurship through subsidized lending programs and banking outreach has to be reinforced (Ministry of Labor, Employment and Social Security, 2020). Third, Nepal needs to simultaneously promote the creation of domestic jobs and diversification of the economy. To minimize reliance on foreign employment as the main livelihood strategy, it is necessary to increase the non-farm employment opportunities, foster vocational training, and establish links between skills training and the labor market. Research indicates that non-farm employment and earnings may increase greatly, especially among women, through vocational training programs that are designed in a proper way (Chakravarty et al., 2019). Fourth, the mechanisms of pre-departure orientation and migrant protection should be strengthened and made available. That means workers know their terms of the contract, rights, insurance cover and remittance opportunities; and government agencies, destination countries embassies or labor attaches have ability to handle upset workers or families. Report implies institutional reinforcing in this direction (Ministry of Labor, Employment and Social Security; European Union Delegation, et al., 2024).

In future studies of Nepalese migrant workers, some directions seem particularly significant. Further longitudinal, empirical studies are required to discuss the dynamics of remittance-based households, whether the remittances are a pathway to sustainable socio-economic mobility, asset accumulations or dependency. Comparisons of the impacts of migration between districts, caste and gender and education backgrounds can help shed light on the disparities and inequalities in benefiting in migration.

The study should also examine the efficacy of financial literacy programs, formal remittance plans and returnee entrepreneurship plans in changing remittance into long term economic resources. Research on the experiences of migrants in foreign countries, particularly in destinations that are less researched, in women, and climate-displaced and informal workers can reveal the structural vulnerability and direct rights-based policy. Most importantly, research that measures the macro-economic effects of high dependence on remittances, domestic supply of labor, agriculture, retention of human capital, and sector growth will assist policymakers to understand trade-offs in migration strategy as economic and map the diversification paths.

Although migrant labor and remittances provide temporary refuge to most Nepali families and bring a lot of development to the national economy, unless policies are carefully considered, institutional changes and vision, the potential of socio-economic transformation may still be limited. Coexistence between securing of the rights of migrants and productive entry of the remittances domestically coupled with job creation and intensive research is a condition which may contribute to forming a more inclusive and sustainable development in Nepal.

REFERENCES

Adhikari, A. P. (2022). A review of Nepali diaspora and their role in Nepal's development and lessons for developing countries. *UNM Digital Repository. Himalayan Research Papers Archive*, (90), 27.

Amnesty International. (2011). *False Promises Exploitation and Forced Labour of Nepalese Migrant Workers* (p. 109). Amnesty International, International Secretariat, United Kingdom. https://www.amnesty.org/es/wp-content/uploads/2021/06/asa310072011en.pdf

Aryal, G. R. (2023). Overseas Labour Migration of Nepal: Trends and Patterns. *Journal of Population and Development*, *4*(1), 21–29. DOI: 10.3126/jpd.v4i1.64235

Bam, N., Thagurathi, R. K., & Neupane, D. (2018). Impact of Remittance on Household Income, Consumption and Poverty Reduction of Nepal. *Economic Literature*, *13*, 32. DOI: 10.3126/el.v13i0.19148

Barkat, K., Mimouni, K., Alsamara, M., & Mrabet, Z. (2024). Achieving the sustainable development goals in developing countries: The role of remittances and the mediating effect of financial inclusion. *International Review of Economics & Finance*, *95*, 103460. DOI: 10.1016/j.iref.2024.103460

Bhatt, D. C. (2023). Why do Labour Migrants Cross their Border? : A Comparative Analysis between Nepal and India. *Journal of Tikapur Multiple Campus*, 143–159. DOI: 10.3126/jotmc.v6i01.56373

Bisheshta Shrestha. (2023). *Incentivizing Migrant Workers to Send Remittance Through Formal Channels*. Daayitwa Nepal Public Policy Nepal. https://www.daayitwa.org/storage/archives/1704262558.pdf

Byanjanakar, R., & Shakha, M. (2021). Role of Remittances on Rural Poverty in Nepal-Evidence from Cross-Section Data. *NRB Economic Review*, *33*(1–2), 45–72. DOI: 10.3126/nrber.v33i1-2.47989

Chakravarty, S., Lundberg, M., Nikolov, P., & Zenker, J. (2019). Vocational training programs and youth labor market outcomes: Evidence from Nepal. *Journal of Development Economics*, *136*, 71–110. DOI: 10.1016/j.jdeveco.2018.09.002

Dhakal, K. R. (2024). Socio-Economic Influence of Remittances on Households In The Patihani Buffer Zone, Chitwan National Park, Nepal. *The Third Pole: Journal of Geography Education*, *24*, 77–87. DOI: 10.3126/ttp.v24i1.73369

Dinesh, K. C. (2020). The Impact of Migrant Remittance on the future of Nepal's Economy. *Migration and Diasporas: An Interdisciplinary Journal, 1*(1), 122–148.

Ghimire, A. (2025). Beyond Remittances: The True Cost of Nepali Labor Migration. *Journal of Human Rights and Social Work, 10*(4), 756–767. Advance online publication. DOI: 10.1007/s41134-025-00409-4

Giri, M. (2025). *Emigration from Nepal and its impact on the economy*. Friedrich Naumann Foundation for Freedom, South Asia., https://www.freiheit.org/sites/default/files/2025-09/emigration-from-nepal-and-its-impact-on-economy_0.pdf

Governance of Labour Migration in South and South-east Asia (GOALS). (2024). *Promoting Faster, Cheaper and Safer Remittance Processes for Migrant Workers and Their Families: A Snapshot of Colombo Process Member States Achievements* (International Organization for Migration (IOM), p. 20).

Hajariya, A. (2016). Nepalese migrant workers and their hardship in the desert. *Sustainability and Social Justice*, 154.

Hâncean, M.-G., Lubbers, M. J., & Molina, J. L. (2021). Measuring transnational social fields through binational link-tracing sampling. *PLoS One, 16*(6), e0253042. DOI: 10.1371/journal.pone.0253042 PMID: 34125853

International Organization for Migration (IOM). (2023). *Migration and Skills Development*. POLICY BRIEF.

International Organization for Migration (IOM). (2024). *Migration Governance Indicators Second Profile 2024 – Nepal* (p. 42). IOM, Geneva. https://nepal.iom.int/sites/g/files/tmzbdl1116/files/documents/2025-05/pub2024-088-el-mgi-nepal-second-profile.pdf

Khadka, R., Rimal, S., & Dev Pant, B. (2016). *Promoting informed policy dialogue on migration, remittances and development in Nepal*. ILO.

Kharel, A., Shrestha, S., & Limbu, C. (2025). *Status of Remittances in Nepal*. Centre for the Study of Labour and Mobility., https://www.ceslam.org/wp-content/uploads/2025/06/Status-of-Remittances-in-Nepal-230625.pdf

Kharel, K. R., & Kharel, S. (2020). Analyzing the economic impact of foreign employment on development prospective of Nepal. *Management Dynamics, 23*(2), 119–130. DOI: 10.3126/md.v23i2.35814

Khatiwada, P. P., & Basyal, K. (2022). Labour Migration in Nepal: Policy, Institutions, and Governance. *Molung Educational Frontier, 12*(01), 144–172. DOI: 10.3126/mef.v12i01.45922

Lamsal, M. R., & Soneja, S. (2025). Effects of Remittance on Financial Savings in Nepal: An Exploration through Auto-Regressive Distributed Lag Approach. *A Bi-Annual South Asian Journal of Research & Innovation (JORI), 12*(1), 94–108. DOI: 10.3126/jori.v12i1.84833

Lokshin, M., Bontch-Osmolovski, M., & Glinskaya, E. (2010). Work-Related Migration and Poverty Reduction in Nepal. *Review of Development Economics, 14*(2), 323–332. DOI: 10.1111/j.1467-9361.2010.00555.x

Mijiyawa, A. G., Joshi, N. K., & Dongol, P. (2025). *Nepal Development Update: Reforms to Accelerate Public Investment* (No. 206571; Nepal Development Update). The World Bank. https://documents1.worldbank.org/curated/en/099548411112541261/pdf/IDU-ba05d530-4963-4bbf-88e3-c094e89fbf3d.pdf

Ministry of Labour. Employment and Social Security. (2020). *Nepal Labour Migration Report 2020*. Government of Nepal. https://www.developmentaid.org/api/frontend/cms/file/2020/12/Migration-Report-2020-English.pdf

Ministry of Labour. Employment and Social Security. (2022). *Nepal Labour Migration Report 2022* (p. 250). Government of Nepal. https://giwmscdnone.gov.np/media/app/public/298/posts/1715249334_10.pdf

Ministry of Labour. Employment and Social Security; European Union Delegation, Embassy of Japan; Embassy of Sweden; Swiss Agency for Development and Cooperation (SDC); International Labour Organization; International Organization for Migration; & United Nations Development Program. (2024). *Nepal's Labour Migration Governance Through Business and Human Rights Perspective* (p. 4). POLICY BRIEF. https://mbhr.iom.int/system/files/crest/resources/document/joint-un-final-policy-brief.pdf

Mishra, M., & Kunwar, L. S. (2020). Overview of foreign labour migration in Nepal. *Patan Pragya, 7*(1), 123–134. DOI: 10.3126/pragya.v7i1.35114

National Statistics Office. (2021). *National Population and Housing Census 2021: International Migration in Nepal* (p. 191). National Statistics Office, Government of Nepal. http://censusnepal.cbs.gov.np/results/files/result-folder/International%20Migration%20in%20Nepal%20Report.pdf

Nepal, I. O. M. (2024, June 16). Nepal on the Right Track to Achieve Cost-effective Remittance Transfers. *International Organization for Migration*. https://nepal.iom.int/news/nepal-right-track-achieve-cost-effective-remittance-transfers

Nicander, J. (2015). *Impacts from Migration and Remittances in the Nepali Society—Analysing the Migration Process in Nepal* [Bachelor Thesis, Lund University]. https://lup.lub.lu.se/student-papers/record/5463257

Pant, B. (2006). Remittance Inflows to Nepal: Economic Impact and Policy Options. *NRB Economic Review*, 20–36. DOI: 10.3126/nrber.v18i1.53046

Pant, B. (2011). Harnessing Remittances for Productive Use in Nepal. *NRB Economic Review, 23*(1), 1–20. DOI: 10.3126/nrber.v23i1.52747

Pasa, R. B., & Kharel, S. (2024). Effect of Remittance on Household Welfare in Nepal. *Panauti Journal, 2*, 57–75. DOI: 10.3126/panauti.v2i1.66581

Pudasaini, S. (2025). Labour Migration, Policies and Skills Development. *Political Science Journal, 3*(1), 87–94. DOI: 10.3126/psj.v3i1.77457

Rai, J. C. (2025). *Impact Of Remittances On The Socio-Economic Development Of Nepal: A Study On Remittance Contributions, Challenges, And Policy Implications In Nepal (2014–2024)* [Bachelor's Thesis, Oulu University of Applied Sciences]. https://www.theseus.fi/bitstream/handle/10024/893920/Chamling%20Rai_Jiten.pdf

Rashid, A. A., Cao, H., & Gravesteijn, R. (2023). Integrating Remittance and Mobile Wallet Services: A Case Study of IME Pay in Nepal. *Migrant Money, UN Capital Development Fund*. https://migrantmoney.uncdf.org/resources/insights/integrating-remittance-and-mobile-wallet-services-a-case-study-of-ime-pay-in-nepal/

Sha, H. (2021). Migrant networks as social capital: The social infrastructure of migration. *MIDEQ*, 30.

Shakya, S. (2024). Implications of International Labor Migration from the Perspective of Migrants and Returnees: Symbolic Interactionism Approach. *The Harvest, 3*(1), 91–106. DOI: 10.3126/harvest.v3i1.64186

Sharma, L. (2024). Impact of Remittances on the Nepalese Economy: Opportunities and Challenges. *Rural Development Journal, 4*(1), 37–57. DOI: 10.3126/rdj.v4i1.64026

Shrestha, S., & Joshi, N. K. (2018). *Remittances and Financial Inclusion: Evidence from Nepal*. New York University.

Sijapati, B., Bhattarai, A., & Pathak, D. (2015). *Analysis of labour market and migration trends in Nepal* (p. 112). Deutsche Gesellschaft für Internationale Zusammenarbeit (GIZ) GmbH & International Labour Organization. https://www.voced.edu.au/content/ngv:70423

Sijapati, B., Lama, A. S., Baniya, J., Rinck, J., Jha, K., & Gurung, A. (with Centre for the Study of Labour and Mobility). (2017). *Labour migration and the remittance economy: The socio-political impact.* Centre for the Study of Labour and Mobility.

Thapa-Parajuli, R., Kshetri, T., & Thapa, S. S. (2025). The Role of Remittances in Household Spending in Rural Nepal. *Economies, 13*(6), 163. DOI: 10.3390/economies13060163

Tharmalingam, S. (2011). Remittance practices and transnational social spaces of tamils and somalis in Norway. *Nordic Journal of Migration Research, 1*(3), 166–175. DOI: 10.2478/v10202-011-0017-x

The World Bank. (2024). *Nepal Development Update: International Migration and Well-being in Nepal.* The World Bank.

Thieme, S., & Wyss, S. (2005). Migration Patterns and Remittance Transfer in Nepal: A Case Study of Sainik Basti in Western Nepal. *International Migration (Geneva, Switzerland), 43*(5), 59–98. DOI: 10.1111/j.1468-2435.2005.00342.x

Tiwari, S. (2022). Impact of Remittance on Food and Non-Food Poverty in Nepal. *Nepal Journal of Multidisciplinary Research, 5*(3), 70–81. DOI: 10.3126/njmr.v5i3.48016

United Nations Capital Development Fund. (2022). *Report On Inclusive Innovation Strategies in Migrant Remittances and Financial Services* (Migrant Money, p. 54). UNCDF. https://migrantmoney.uncdf.org/wp-content/uploads/2023/02/Nepal-Country-Assessments.pdf

Williams, N. E., Hughes, C., Bhandari, P., Thornton, A., Young-DeMarco, L., Sun, C., & Swindle, J. (2020). When Does Social Capital Matter for Migration? A Study of Networks, Brokers, and Migrants in Nepal. *The International Migration Review, 54*(4), 964–991. DOI: 10.1177/0197918319882634 PMID: 33814660

World Bank. (2025). *Migration: Overview.* World Bank. https://www.worldbank.org/en/topic/migration/overview

Yamini Lohia. (2024, June 11). *IFAD, IOM Celebrate Vital Role of Remittances in Nepal's Development.* International Fund for Agricultural Development (IFAD). https://www.ifad.org/en/w/news/ifad-iom-celebrate-vital-role-of-remittances-in-nepal-development

Chapter 19
Workplace Discrimination, Job Satisfaction, and Length of Stay Among Lusophone Immigrants in Portugal:
Beyond Language Proficiency

Eva Gonçalves
http://orcid.org/0009-0002-6976-9451
Polytechnic University of Cávado and Ave, Portugal

Márcia Duarte
http://orcid.org/0000-0002-8863-2402
School of Management, Polytechnic University of Cávado and Ave, Portugal

Oscarina Conceição
http://orcid.org/0000-0001-8072-8250
School of Management, Polytechnic University of Cávado and Ave, Portugal

ABSTRACT

This study examines the impact of language proficiency in Portuguese on workplace discrimination and job satisfaction among immigrants in Braga, Portugal (n=161), using a questionnaire. The sample is predominantly composed of Brazilian immigrants (60.2%) and PALOP immigrants (5.6%) (Lusophone immigrants) — populations for whom Portuguese is already the official language. The study employs Mann-

DOI: 10.4018/979-8-3373-8500-6.ch019

Whitney U tests and Spearman's rank correlation. Results indicate that language proficiency does not significantly differentiate either workplace discrimination or job satisfaction. A significant negative correlation is found between workplace discrimination and job satisfaction, and between length of stay in Portugal and perceived discrimination. One possible explanation is that discrimination among Lusophone immigrants in Braga, Portugal, is rooted in accentism, rather than linguistic barriers. Going beyond language proficiency involves examining the impact of accentism—which stems from structural, racial, and cultural stereotypes and prejudices—on job satisfaction.

1. INTRODUCTION

According to the International Organisation for Migration (IOM), in 2024, there were more than 281 million people in immigration-related situations worldwide (IOM, 2024). Portugal and Spain are among the main European destinations for immigrants, with significant growth in the number of foreign residents relative to the native population (Ennes et al., 2018). Among the migrant populations that have settled in Portugal, Brazilians and immigrants from the Portuguese-speaking African countries — collectively known as PALOP (Países Africanos de Língua Oficial Portuguesa) — constitute a historically significant group, bound to Portugal by a shared language, a colonial past, and deep cultural ties.

According to the 2024 Migration and Asylum Report, the municipality of Braga had 28,538 immigrants, and most of them are Brazilian immigrants (AIMA, 2024).

This shared linguistic heritage has often been invoked — both in public discourse and in migration policy — as a key issue for the integration of Lusophone immigrants into Portuguese society and the labour market. The logic is compelling at first glance: if language is one of the primary barriers to workplace integration, then immigrants who already speak the host country's language should be at a structural advantage. However, this assumption has received surprisingly little empirical scrutiny in the Portuguese context. The study by Śliwa et al. (2024), published in the prestigious journal *Human Relations*, is an exception; it is a pioneering study that analyses the role of accentism in workplace discrimination.

The choice of this topic was based on the importance that immigrant employees currently assume in the labour market of host countries. This community plays a fundamental role in strengthening local economies, contributing to filling labour shortages in certain sectors and regions. By filling existing gaps, immigrant workers boost and revitalise the communities where they operate. Thus, it is essential to value this workforce and recognise its contribution to economic and social growth (Peri, 2016). It is also important to promote equality and respect among all people, regardless of their origin or culture, ensuring fair conditions of treatment and opportunities.

For immigrant employees to feel satisfied with their jobs and not experience exclusion or discrimination based on their culture or nationality, organisations must implement effective integration practices. In this regard, the role of Human Resources is crucial, as it ensures the inclusion of workers through effective management of cultural diversity within the organisational context, thereby respecting and valuing the different cultures that may be present in this environment.

Within an organization, diversity management can foster behaviors and practices aimed at responding effectively and constructively to situations of discrimination through the integration of culturally diverse work teams. These practices can consequently lead to greater job satisfaction among the workforce (Kamal & Ferdousi, 2009; Koç et al., 2025).

The present study addresses this gap by examining whether proficiency in European Portuguese — the specific variety spoken in Portugal, which differs phonologically and lexically from Brazilian Portuguese and African varieties — has a meaningful impact on two key workplace outcomes: job satisfaction and workplace discrimination.

To achieve the study's overall objective, research questions were defined to guide the analysis and formulate specific hypotheses. The questions outlined were as follows: *Do immigrant employees with* language proficiency *feel less discriminated against and more satisfied at work? Could workplace discrimination be linked to lower levels of job satisfaction? Could the variable 'length of stay' have any influence on job satisfaction and workplace discrimination?*

2. LITERATURE REVIEW

2.1 Workplace Discrimination: Theoretical Framework

The integration of immigrants into the labour market is a key issue. Problems and obstacles, such as discrimination, are observed for immigrants in the workplace. Discrimination is when people are treated differently because of their group membership. Discrimination is usually considered negative, disadvantaging individuals and causing exclusion, restriction, or mistreatment (Lopes, 2024).

Although the terms are often confused, prejudice and discrimination are not synonymous: prejudice refers to an attitude that encompasses various dimensions: cognitive (stereotypes), affective (feelings) and behavioural (discrimination), whereas discrimination manifests itself in concrete actions that result in exclusion, restrictions, lack of integration or unfair treatment (Lopes, 2024). In the labour market, for example, discrimination manifests itself in the assignment of less valued roles to a particular group or in the pay gap between two individuals even when they perform the same duties, leading to a lack of workplace integration and low job satisfaction (Lopes, 2024).

According to Human Capital Theory (Becker, 1993), knowledge, skills, and abilities constitute valuable capital when they increase productivity and have a positive impact on an individual's career. Proficiency in a foreign language is a form of human capital that can facilitate immigrant integration. A low language proficiency not only affects a person's professional performance but also their equality with other workers, placing these immigrants at a disadvantage compared to native employees and immigrant employees who already speak the language of the host country (Dostie & Javdani, 2020; Park, 2011). The integration and inclusion of immigrant workers can be problematic, especially when they face difficulties understanding and using the language of the host country (Cheng et al., 2021; Ghio et al., 2022; Lang, 2022). The language barrier is considered one of the main factors excluding these workers, since the poor language proficiency negatively affects how they are perceived in the performance of their work duties (Ghio et al., 2022). Language proficiency and length of stay in the host country are important variables in the acculturation and integration process of immigrants (Tsang & Nguyen, 2023).

In the labor market, for example, discrimination manifests itself in the assignment of less valued functions to a particular group or in the salary difference between two individuals even when they perform the same functions, causing a lack of labor integration and low job satisfaction (Lopes, 2024). These situations of injustice create inequalities between immigrant workers and native workers, hindering integration and the development of a more equitable working environment (Dietz et al., 2015). It has been possible to verify, through some studies, that proficiency in the host country's language plays a central role in an individual's integration, particularly in the workplace.

Additionally, Social Exchange Theory (Blau, 1964) argues that when immigrants communicate easily, good language proficiency can lead to the exchange of information between colleagues, which leads to better relationships with their colleagues and supervisors. A sense of belonging is fostered, which contributes to less discrimination at work. Difficulty of communication in the host country's language can lead to the perception of discrimination in relation to other work colleagues, which in turn can lead to lower levels of job satisfaction and less engagement with their duties (Salleh et al., 2021).

Furthermore, a lack of familiarity with the specific language used in the organizational context leads to situations of insecurity or feelings of a lack of belonging. This insecurity compromises the integration and adaptation of immigrant workers in the work context (Cheng et al., 2021). These situations of unfamiliarity and linguistic difficulties can generate a perception of discrimination against these workers (Ghio et al., 2022).

However, it is important to note that language discrimination is a form of discrimination. Wei et al. (2012) emphasise that language discrimination involves being discriminated against for not using the country's language as a second language or for speaking the country's language with an accent.

Based on these assumptions, the following hypothesis was formulated:

H1: Language proficiency in European Portuguese is negatively associated with the perception of workplace discrimination; the higher the proficiency, the lower the perception of discrimination.

2.2 Job Satisfaction: Theoretical Framework

Communication can be a significant obstacle to the integration of immigrants, particularly newcomers. Difficulties with phonology, such as accent and speech rate, compromise understanding and interaction in the professional environment, negatively affecting the work experience of these employees (Hua et al., 2024).

Despite the challenges, it is essential that immigrant employees feel satisfied in their work. Job satisfaction is defined as a pleasurable or positive emotional state resulting from an individual's appraisal of their job or job experiences (Locke, 1976). It is among the most studied constructs in Organisational Behaviour and Human Resource Management, given its well-established associations with employee performance, turnover intention, organisational commitment, and wellbeing (Judge & Klinger, 2008).

Job satisfaction is understood as an employee's overall evaluation of their job, work environment, compensation, colleagues, and other factors (Warr et al., 1979; Wang & Jing, 2017)

The role of language in migrant labour market integration has been extensively studied in the economics of migration literature. Therefore, Human Capital Theory (Becker, 1993) posits that language proficiency in the host country's dominant language is a form of human capital that enhances worker productivity, facilitates communication, and signals employability to employers (Chiswick & Miller, 2014). Consistent with this, studies in the Netherlands found that male migrants with higher proficiency levels were more satisfied with their work and employed at higher professional levels, suggesting that language proficiency improves job match quality. Lack of language skills can push immigrants into lower-level roles, leading, in turn, to lower job satisfaction (Bloemen, 2023).

In this sense, the language barrier and the lack of support for language training in the host country's language can compromise job satisfaction for these workers, since the difficulty in communicating effectively also increases the perception of discrimination in the workplace (Salleh et al., 2021).

However, the provision of adequate language training contributes significantly to the integration of immigrants into the work environment. When they are able to develop stronger language skills, workers tend to feel more satisfied with their work, the organisation, and their colleagues, thus reducing the perception of discrimination and leading to better integration into the organisational context (Cheng et al., 2021; Hua et al., 2024).

The level of self-confidence and comfort in using a particular foreign language may be negatively related to workplace discrimination and positively related to job satisfaction. (Hua et al., 2024).

Once again, the theoretical framework of Social Exchange Theory (Blau, 1964) makes sense. High proficiency in a language can lead to easier communication with coworkers and supervisors, which, in turn, strengthens relationships with peers and managers. Good relationships with colleagues and supervisors have been identified as factors that prevent job dissatisfaction (Herzberg et al., 1959).

The seminal work of Herzberg et al. (1959) distinguishes between *motivators* — intrinsic factors such as achievement, recognition, and responsibility that produce genuine satisfaction when present — and *hygiene factors* — extrinsic factors such as working conditions, interpersonal relations, and company policy that, when inadequate, produce dissatisfaction. Herzberg's framework suggests that dissatisfaction is produced not by the absence of positive experiences but by the active presence of negative ones. Workplace discrimination, as an interpersonal and organisational phenomenon, can be theorised as a hygiene factor: its presence actively produces dissatisfaction, while its absence merely removes a source of negative experience (Herzberg et al., 1959). Therefore, workplace discrimination can lead to greater job dissatisfaction (Roberts et al., 2004; Wadsworth et al., 2007). This theoretical framing aligns with the empirical literature on discrimination and workplace well-being, which consistently finds that perceived discrimination has a direct, negative effect on job satisfaction, organisational commitment, and psychological wellbeing (Roberts et al., 2004). For immigrant workers, this effect may be compounded by additional stressors, including precarious employment, under-qualification in host-country terms, and social isolation (Intungane et al., 2024).

Based on these statements, the following hypothesis was formulated:

H2: Language proficiency in European Portuguese is associated with job satisfaction; the higher the proficiency, the greater the job satisfaction.

H3: Workplace discrimination is negatively associated with job satisfaction among migrants in Portugal.

2.3 Length of Stay and Workplace Integration

Length of stay in the host country is a well-established variable in migration research, typically associated with gradual improvement in labour market outcomes over time. Longer-established immigrants tend to develop stronger social networks, greater cultural competence, and a more sophisticated understanding of their rights and opportunities in the host country (Radu & Virga, 2020). Research on workplace inclusion has confirmed that length of stay significantly contributes to migrants' sense of belonging and professional integration (Adam et al., 2023; Adam et al., 2025.

H4: Length of stay in Portugal is negatively associated with perceived workplace discrimination.

3. METHOD

3.1 Sample and Data Collection

The study is based on a convenience sample of 161 immigrants residing and working in Portugal. Data were collected through a structured self-administered questionnaire.

The main advantage of collecting data via questionnaires is their speed and efficiency, enabling information to be gathered from many individuals quickly and very efficiently (Gideon, 2016). In addition to this benefit, the anonymity guaranteed in the responses allows respondents to feel more at ease and motivated to answer honestly, particularly when addressing more sensitive topics. The questionnaires are tailored to the study's objectives, allowing for the collection of different types of information. Regarding data processing, the data can be easily quantified and analysed, enabling statistical analyses such as descriptions, correlations, tests and regression models, amongst others (Ahmad et al., 2019).

The questionnaire survey used in this study was developed and presented in two languages, Portuguese and English. The English version was provided to ensure that all workers felt comfortable responding, given that Portuguese is not the mother tongue of some of them. Thus, by making the questionnaire available in two languages, the range of choice was broadened, and greater accessibility to participation was ensured.

The questionnaires were distributed via digital networks, such as Facebook and LinkedIn, and sent directly to communities of immigrant workers in Portugal, specifically to immigrant communities in the district of Braga. This survey was also administered to immigrant workers within the researcher's immediate circle, including people at her workplace, in her community, Braga. The survey was anonymous, and for this reason, there are no questions in the survey that identify the participants.

Finally, the survey was available online for approximately one month, between 11 June and 19 July 2025, during which time all the responses analysed in this research were collected.

The most represented age group in the sample is between 30 and 39 years old (46.58%), followed by the 18–29 age group (32.92%). Regarding gender, 56.52% are male and 43.48% are female.

The sample is predominantly composed of Brazilian immigrants (n=97, 60.2%), with a smaller representation of PALOP migrants (n=9, 5.6%) and other nationalities (n=55, 34.2%), including Venezuelan, Ukrainian, Bangladeshi, German-Indian, Swedish, Ecuadorian, and Bolivian respondents. The demographic characteristics of the sample are presented in Table 1.

Table 1. Sample Characteristics (N=161)

Variable	**Category**	**N (%)**
Origin		
	Brazilian	**97 (60.2%)**
	PALOP	**9 (5.6%)**
	Other	**55 (34.2%)**
Proficiency in Portuguese		
	Fluent	**111 (68.9%)**
	Advanced	**16 (9.9%)**
	Intermediate	**25 (15.5%)**
	Basic	**9 (5.6%)**
Length of Stay in Portugal		
	Less than 1 year	**15 (9.3%)**
	1–3 years	**65 (40.4%)**
	4–6 years	**45 (28.0%)**
	6 or more years	**36 (22.4%)**

Note. PALOP = Países Africanos de Língua Oficial Portuguesa.

A key characteristic of this sample is that the majority of respondents — specifically Brazilian and PALOP migrants — are native or near-native speakers of Portuguese for whom the language was already the official language of their country of origin. Their proficiency in European Portuguese, therefore, reflects adaptation to a specific linguistic variety rather than the acquisition of a foreign language. Notably, 127 respondents (78.9%) reported advanced or fluent proficiency in Portuguese. The question did not specify whether it was European Portuguese, Brazilian Portuguese, or the African variants of Portuguese (Angola, Mozambique, Cape Verde, etc.)

3.2 Measures

Language proficiency in Portuguese was measured using a single self-report item with four response categories: Basic, Intermediate, Advanced, and Fluent. For the Mann-Whitney U tests, respondents were grouped into two categories: low proficiency (Basic + Intermediate, n=34) and high proficiency (Advanced + Fluent, n=127).

Workplace discrimination was measured using a multi-item Likert scale capturing respondents' perceived frequency of discriminatory treatment in their current workplace. To understand perceptions of discrimination in an organisational context, the Everyday Discrimination Scale, developed by Williams et al. (1997), was used. This scale allows for the identification of everyday experiences of discrimination. In the present study, the scale was applied to measure perceptions of workplace discrimination experienced by immigrant workers.

The original version of the scale consists of 9 items. In this study, 7 of these items were used, selected for their relevance and suitability to the organisational context. The scale was thus adapted to the workplace, including only those items that best fit the reality under analysis. Examples of items: You are treated with less courtesy than your other work colleagues; People act as if they think you are not intelligent; People act as if they think you are dishonest.

It is important to note that the original discrimination scale is measured using a 6-point Likert scale, where 1 corresponds to 'almost every day' and 6 to 'never'. Given the items on the scale, the categories must be recoded inversely, such that 6 (never) equals 0 and 1 (almost every day) equals 5. This inversion ensures that a higher overall score reflects a greater perception of everyday discrimination (Williams et al., 1997). Thus, the data obtained on the dimension of workplace discrimination will be treated in the same way. The internal reliability coefficient was calculated to assess the scale's consistency. The reliability of the scale is excellent, as demonstrated by the value obtained for Cronbach's alpha ($\alpha = 0.912$), which indicates high internal consistency of the scale items.

Job satisfaction was measured using a validated multi-item Likert scale assessing overall satisfaction with the respondent's current employment. The job satisfaction measurement tool was developed by Warr et al. (1979) and comprises 15 items, which assess individuals' level of satisfaction with various aspects of their working environment, including the role they perform, their relationships with colleagues and superiors, and working conditions, amongst other factors. In addition to these 15 items, the scale also includes an independent item, also used in this study, which allows respondents to assess their overall job satisfaction.

The chosen scale, the Job Satisfaction Scale, was developed in the 1970s within the context of Organisational and Industrial Psychology research in the United Kingdom. The aim in creating this scale was to assess job satisfaction in a more comprehensive and holistic manner, considering both intrinsic and extrinsic aspects of the work environment.

For the development of the questionnaire survey in this study, 11 of the 15 items from the original scale were used, as shown in the table below. The decision not to include all the items provided for in the scale stemmed from the need to ensure the instrument's relevance and suitability to the context under analysis. Consequently, it was decided to exclude items relating to the organisation's management style, as well as others that were not deemed appropriate for the specific objectives of the study. Furthermore, including all items could have made the questionnaire excessively long, compromising the clarity of the responses and reducing participants' motivation to complete it (Rolstad et al., 2011).

In this study, the dimension of job satisfaction will be analysed holistically, considering the combination of all items used. It is important to note that the standalone question on workers' general satisfaction was also included and will be assessed alongside the other items. Cronbach's alpha was also calculated to assess the internal reliability of the items comprising the scale. The reliability of the scale is excellent, as demonstrated by the value obtained for Cronbach's alpha ($\alpha = 0.954$), which indicates high internal consistency of the items.

Length of stay was measured using a four-category ordinal variable: less than 1 year, 1–3 years, 4–6 years, and 6 or more years.

3.3 Analytical Strategy

Given the ordinal nature of the key variables, non-parametric tests were employed throughout. Mann-Whitney U tests were used to compare workplace discrimination and job satisfaction between high and low proficiency groups. Spearman rank-order correlations were used to examine bivariate associations between proficiency, length of stay, workplace discrimination, and job satisfaction using the full sample (n=161). To assess the robustness of the findings, the Spearman analysis was replicated among the fluent migrant subsample (n=111). All analyses were conducted using IBM SPSS Statistics.

4. RESULTS

4.1 Mann-Whitney U Tests: Proficiency and Workplace Outcomes

A *dummy* variable was created for the level of proficiency in Portuguese, classified as follows: High Proficiency (including advanced levels and fluency); Low Proficiency (including basic and intermediate levels). Two Mann-Whitney U tests were conducted to compare workplace discrimination and job satisfaction between low-proficiency (n=34) and high-proficiency (n=127) groups. The results are presented in Table 2.

Table 2. Mann-Whitney U Test Results: Proficiency Groups vs. Workplace Outcomes

Dependent Variable	Groups (n)	U	Z	p-value
Workplace Discrimination	Low (n=34) vs High (n=127)	1694.500	-1.940	.052
Job Satisfaction	Low (n=34) vs High (n=127)	2368.000	.866	.386

Note. Low proficiency = Basic + Intermediate (n=34); High proficiency = Advanced + Fluent (n=127).

Neither workplace discrimination (U = 1694.500, Z = -1.940, p = .052) nor job satisfaction (U = 2368.000, Z = .866, p = .386) differed significantly between the two proficiency groups, leading to the rejection of both H1 and H2. Although the p-value for workplace discrimination approaches conventional significance, it does not meet the threshold of $p<.05$. These results suggest that, within this sample, proficiency in European Portuguese does not significantly differentiate migrants' experiences of discrimination or satisfaction in the workplace.

4.2 Spearman Correlations: Full Sample (n=161)

The main objective of correlation analyses is to investigate the presence and nature of the relationship between two variables. This procedure is essential in research, as it provides important information on how variables relate to one another. Through correlations, it is possible to determine whether the variables tend to increase or decrease simultaneously, or whether they show no significant association (Schober et al., 2018). Spearman's rank-order correlation analysis was conducted to examine the bivariate associations between all key variables. The results are presented in Table 3.

Table 3. Spearman Correlation Matrix (N=161)

Relationship	P	p-value	Significant?
Proficiency → Workplace Discrimination	−.112	.157	No
Proficiency → Job Satisfaction	.073	.359	No
Workplace Discrimination → Job Satisfaction	−.373**	< .001	Yes
Length of Stay → Workplace Discrimination	−.189*	.017	Yes
Length of Stay → Job Satisfaction	.119	.133	No

Note. * p < .05; ** p < .001.

Consistent with the Mann-Whitney results, proficiency showed no significant correlation with either workplace discrimination (ρ=−.112, p=.157) or job satisfaction (ρ=.073, p=.359), confirming the rejection of H1 and H2. However, two significant relationships were identified. First, a statistically significant moderate negative correlation was found between workplace discrimination and job satisfaction (ρ=−.373, p<.001), supporting H3. Second, a significant negative correlation was found between length of stay and perceived workplace discrimination (ρ=−.189, p=.017), supporting H4. Length of stay was not significantly associated with job satisfaction (ρ=.119, p=.133).

4.3 Complementary Analysis: Fluent Migrant Subsample (n=111)

To examine the robustness of the observed relationships within a linguistically homogeneous subgroup, the Spearman analysis was replicated among fluent migrants only (n=111). A comparison of results across the two samples is presented in Table 4.

Table 4. Spearman Correlations: Full Sample vs. Fluent Migrants Only

Relationship	Full Sample (n=161)	Fluent Only (n=111)
Discrimination → Job Satisfaction	ρ=−.373, p<.001 *	ρ=−.362, p<.001 *
Length of Stay → Discrimination	ρ=−.189, p=.017 *	ρ=−.149, p=.120
Length of Stay → Job Satisfaction	ρ=.119, p=.133	ρ=.140, p=.143

Note. * = statistically significant (p < .05)

The negative correlation between workplace discrimination and job satisfaction remained significant and of similar magnitude among fluent migrants (ρ=−.362, p<.001), confirming the robustness of this relationship. However, the association between length of stay and perceived discrimination, significant in the full sample, did not reach significance among fluent migrants alone (ρ=−.149, p=.120), suggesting an attenuation of this effect within the most proficient subgroup.

5. DISCUSSION

5.1 The Absence of Statistical Significance Between Language Proficiency and Workplace Discrimination, Language Proficiency and Job Satisfaction

The fact that the relationships between language proficiency and workplace discrimination, and between language proficiency and job satisfaction, are not statistically significant warrants further, careful consideration. It is important to note that the correlation between language proficiency and workplace discrimination is negative (albeit weak), and that the correlation between language proficiency and job satisfaction is positive (albeit very weak); however, these correlations are not statistically significant.

Proficiency in Portuguese doesn't seem to protect immigrants from workplace discrimination, nor does it enhance their job satisfaction. In fact, there does not seem to be a statistically significant relationship between language proficiency and workplace discrimination, nor between language proficiency and job satisfaction.

This finding seems to challenge the migration policy discourse, which holds that language proficiency is a key factor in integration into society and the workplace.

It also appears to be at odds with Human Capital Theory (Becker, 1993), which argues that skills and abilities are valuable assets for an individual's career, in the sense that proficiency in a language serves as a resource for the integration of immigrants into the workplace, fostering job satisfaction and reducing workplace discrimination. It also appears to be inconsistent with Social Exchange Theory (Blau, 1964), which supports the view that language proficiency can lead to better communication with colleagues and supervisors, thereby improving workplace relationships, reducing workplace discrimination, and increasing perceived well-being at work.

However, there is a large body of research suggesting a negative statistical relationship between language proficiency and workplace discrimination, and a statistically significant positive relationship between language proficiency and job satisfaction (Bloemen, 2023; Cheng et al., 2021; Dosti & Javdani, 2020; Ghio et al., 2022; Hua et al., 2024; Lang, 2022; Tsang & Nguyen, 2023).

At first glance, the data we obtained was somewhat disappointing, but a more in-depth analysis led to a clearer understanding that was consistent with the characteristics of the sample.

The absence of statistical significance doesn't imply that there is no relationship between the variables; it may reflect limitations in the sample or insufficient variability in the observed data (Visentin et al., 2020).

In fact, the sample is highly homogeneous due to the predominance of Brazilian employees. This lack of diversity in the sample may be attributable to the data collection method, as the survey was administered in the Braga district, and to the researcher's personal contacts. Braga has a high number of Brazilian immigrants, which explains why so many of the participants are Brazilian. According to the Report on Immigration, Borders and Asylum (AIMA, 2024), Brazilian nationals remained the largest foreign community residing in Portugal, accounting for 31.4% of the national total, and were also the most numerous foreign group in the district of Braga in 2023 (INE). Although Brazilian immigrants face poor working conditions and difficulties in having their professional qualifications recognised, they choose to live in Portugal because they believe it offers a better quality of life (Azevedo et al., 2022).

The research predominantly focuses on contexts in which migrants must acquire a new language — a condition that does not apply to the same extent for migrants who already speak the host country's official language. For Brazilian and PALOP immigrants in Portugal, the relevant linguistic challenge is not the acquisition of Portuguese per se but the adaptation to the specific phonological, lexical, and pragmatic features of European Portuguese.

These immigrants aren't learning a foreign language — they are adapting to a specific variety of a language – the European Portuguese, with a typical accent, different from the Portuguese Brazilian accent or from the Portuguese accent of PALOP immigrants (Angolans, Mozambicans, Cape Verdeans). It is tempting to think that linguistic similarity can facilitate integration. That was the basis of our analysis. In fact, it is the same language—Portuguese—but different speakers have distinct accents. Native Portuguese speakers speak European Portuguese, while Brazilian and African immigrants (non native speakers) speak Portuguese with accents.

Accent discrimination refers to the effects of nonstandard accents, a variation of language that deviates from the standard accent of a particular language. We must distinguish between non-native accents, when speakers who learn a different language later in life continue to apply certain aspects of their first language (e.g., intonation, pronunciation) and regional accents or dialects (Hideg et al., 2024). Another way to look at the phenomenon is the term 'accentism' which refers to 'accent-based discrimination often connected to one's non-standard accent along with one's linguistic and social class background, nationality, and country of origin' (Orelus, 2016).

There are two main forms of accentism in the workplace: (1) overt accentism, which involves an explicit, direct reference to a person's accent, and (2) accent-activated stigmatisation, which occurs when the listener realises that the speaker is a member of a particular group, specifically a particular nation (Śliwa et al., 2024).

Colonial power relations can also underpin workplace discrimination. Portugal is the country of the former coloniser, and Brazilians are members of a former colonised nation. The same is true for African immigrants from PALOP: Portugal is the country of the former coloniser, and PALOP immigrants are members of a former colonised nation. In this sense, the historical and cultural context can legitimise accentism. The colonial past may also influence the experiences of accentism faced by Brazilians in Portugal (Śliwa et al., 2024).

This study didn´t examine the educational qualifications of immigrants, nor did it check the professions they had in Portugal. Research has documented persistent conditions of underemployment, symbolic devaluation, and workplace discrimination among Brazilian immigrants in Portugal, rooted in racialised labour hierarchies that position Lusophone immigrants in subaltern roles irrespective of their qualifications or linguistic competence (Intungane et al., 2024). Brazilian immigrants carry an immediately recognisable accent that signals national origin and triggers discrimination based on stereotypes associated with Brazilian identity rather than with communicative competence.

In addition to the power dynamics underlying the coloniser-colonised relationship, there remain prejudices based on a devaluation of the education received by professionals in their country of origin, as well as prejudices and stereotypes regarding involvement in illegal activities, such as prostitution, theft, and drug trafficking (Sardinha, 2011).

PALOP immigrants, many of whom are of African descent, face an additional and distinct layer of racial discrimination that language cannot mitigate.

It seems that the analysis cannot be so simplistic. To assume that fluency in a language is important for improving job satisfaction and reducing discrimination is a reductionist view, because it fails to recognise that even within the same language, there are different accents, and that these accents can reactivate power dynamics rooted deep in the past and, as such, may underlie discriminatory behaviour. The Lusophonia – the cultural and linguistic community that links Portugal to its former colonies and to Brazil – is often discussed, but this narrative may, paradoxically, minimise the importance of inequalities of power, status, and race.

5.2 Relationship Between Workplace Discrimination and Job Satisfaction

The most robust finding of this study is the significant negative correlation between workplace discrimination and job satisfaction ($\rho=-.373$, $p<.001$), a relationship that holds across both the full sample and the fluent migrant subsample ($\rho=-.362$,

$p<.001$). Studies have shown that discrimination results in reduced psychological well-being and lower job satisfaction (Roberts et al., 2004; Wadsworth et al., 2007).

This seems to be in line with Herzberg's Two-Factor framework: discrimination constitutes a hygiene factor — an interpersonal and environmental condition that, when present, actively produces dissatisfaction and cannot be compensated for by the presence of motivating factors such as achievement or recognition (Herzberg et al., 1959). Workplace discrimination is negatively associated with job satisfaction; the greater the discrimination, the lower the sense of well-being at work, and thus the lower the job satisfaction. This finding is consistent across the full sample and the fluent subsample. Consequently, workplace discrimination may be an antecedent of job satisfaction, acting as a hygiene factor within company policies and relationships between colleagues. Hygiene factors, when present, prevent job dissatisfaction (Herzberg et al., 1959).

Another perspective is that, based on Social Exchange Theory (Blau, 1964): when individuals experience positive friendships in the workplace, they perceive a higher level of social support in their environment and develop a greater sense of trust and belonging. These feelings, in turn, contribute to the individual's sense of well-being (Chen et al., 2024). If employees perceive discriminatory behaviour from their colleagues, their sense of belonging and trust is undermined, which in turn affects their job satisfaction.

On the other hand, workplace discrimination tends to place immigrant employees in lower-level roles, failing to recognise their skills, educational qualifications and previous professional experience. As a result, job satisfaction declines. If the organisation fails to recognise the immigrant employee, the immigrant employee does not develop a positive view of their work, according to Social Exchange Theory (Blau, 1964).

In the study by Teixeira et al. (2025), which was based on interviews, women revealed that they were victims of racial discrimination and reported instances of explicit racism and stigmatisation, combined with gender stereotypes, which exacerbated their vulnerability in the workplace.

5.3 Relationship Between Length of Stay and Workplace Discrimination and Length of Stay and Job Satisfaction

The significant negative association between length of stay and perceived workplace discrimination ($\rho=-.189$, $p=.017$) introduces an important temporal dimension to the analysis. Migrants who have resided in Portugal for longer periods report lower levels of workplace discrimination, suggesting that social and professional integration accumulates over time in ways that may reduce exposure to or perception of discriminatory treatment.

Several mechanisms may account for this finding. Longer-established migrants may develop stronger professional networks and greater organisational knowledge, enabling them to navigate or avoid discriminatory contexts more effectively (Radu & Virga, 2020). They may also develop greater awareness of their legal rights, making them more likely to resist or report discriminatory practices rather than passively absorb them. Additionally, research has consistently shown that newcomers are the most sensitive to inclusion struggles in the workplace (Adam et al., 2025), suggesting that early-stage migrants face a period of heightened vulnerability that diminishes as they become established.

This effect is replicated within the fluent subsample ($\rho = -.149$, $p = .120$). Among immigrants with lower proficiency, time in Portugal may be especially important in compensating for the additional vulnerabilities associated with linguistic distance. Among fluent migrants, the baseline of linguistic integration may already reduce vulnerability sufficiently that the additional effect of time is no longer statistically detectable.

However, an alternative explanation deserves consideration: the observed negative relationship may reflect a selection effect, whereby immigrants who experience severe or persistent discrimination are more likely to return to their country of origin or move to a third country, leaving behind a self-selected group of longer-term residents with more positive workplace experiences. Future longitudinal research should attempt to disentangle these competing mechanisms.

Regarding the relationship between length of stay and job satisfaction, although the relationship is positive, it is not statistically significant. Factors such as good relationships with co-workers and supervisors, recognition of high performance by managers, and anti-discrimination policies in the workplace may be more significant predictors of job satisfaction and may moderate the relationship between length of stay and job satisfaction.

5.4 Implications for HRM Practice

The findings of this study challenge a premise in the HRM literature on migrant workforce integration: that language proficiency is an important variable in determining workplace outcomes, namely workplace discrimination and job satisfaction. In the Lusophone context, this assumption may not be true. The structural and racial determinants of workplace discrimination appear to operate independently of language, requiring HRM interventions that target these deeper mechanisms directly.

For organisations operating in Portugal with diverse workforces, the findings suggest several practical priorities. First, diversity and inclusion strategies must go beyond language support programmes to address the racial and ethnic dimensions of workplace discrimination. Second, the onboarding and integration of newly arrived immigrants deserves particular attention, given that newcomers face the highest risk of discriminatory treatment. Third, organisations should evaluate and monitor organisational climate and discrimination behaviours among immigrant employees, given that workplace discrimination contributes to lower job satisfaction, which, in turn, may affect performance, organisational commitment, and turnover intentions.

From an HRM perspective, this finding carries direct practical implications. This means that HRM interventions focused solely on linguistic integration or onboarding support are insufficient. Organisations that employ immigrant employees must actively address the interpersonal and structural conditions that enable discriminatory treatent, including unconscious bias training, robust anti-discrimination policies, and inclusive HR practices.

Considering these findings, it is worth reflecting on the role of HRM in reducing discrimination and increasing job satisfaction among migrant workers. Managing cultural differences at an organisational level is a significant responsibility, as these differences are becoming increasingly apparent. Managing cultural diversity is essential to prevent discriminatory situations (Shore et al., 2009) and to promote greater job satisfaction (Xia et al., 2022).

Every organisation has its own culture and integration methods (Abrantes et al., 2021), and it is crucial that HRM understands how to optimise these processes. It is therefore important to develop practices that prevent discrimination and promote job satisfaction. Solutions thus emerge, such as the implementation of training programmes that promote knowledge of other cultures, as well as awareness-raising initiatives on the importance of cultural diversity (Edewor & Aluko, 2007; Patrick & Kumar, 2012).

In contexts where such support is lacking, the likelihood of feelings of exclusion and discrimination increases. Furthermore, strategies such as mentoring by colleagues or line managers, particularly for employees who are new to the organisation or the country, contribute to their inclusion in a more positive way (Patrick & Kumar, 2012).

At the policy level, the findings underscore the need for stronger enforcement of anti-discrimination legislation in the Portuguese labour market. Strengthening institutional support for discrimination complaints, particularly for immigrant workers in precarious employment situations, would represent an important step towards the inclusive labour market that Portugal's integration policy nominally aspires to achieve.

6. CONCLUSIONS

This study set out to examine whether proficiency in Portuguese influences workplace discrimination and job satisfaction among immigrants in Portugal. Among a sample predominantly composed of Lusophone immigrants — Brazilians and PALOP nationals who already speak Portuguese — proficiency in the European variety of the language neither seems to protect against workplace discrimination nor enhances job satisfaction. Indeed, the correlations are not statistically significant.

The data suggests that shared linguistic heritage fails to protect Lusophone immigrants from workplace discrimination in Portugal — and argues that the barriers faced by Lusophone immigrants are not communicative but structural, racial, and cultural in nature. Our study highlights the importance of further research in accentism, a form of discrimination based on accent. The narrative of linguistic and cultural proximity present in the concept of Lusophonia may obscure these dynamics and mask inequalities that lead to workplace discrimination.

Despite these findings, the association between workplace discrimination and job satisfaction appears to be robust, suggesting that it is important to remove discriminatory barriers in order to increase job satisfaction.

Length of stay emerges as a predictor of lower perceived discrimination. Length of stay leads to a temporal integration, through the gradual accumulation of social capital, network ties, and institutional knowledge. The length of stay may be a better predictor of workplace discrimination than language proficiency.

Looking beyond language proficiency requires a more in-depth examination of how accentism – that is, discrimination based on accent – influences job satisfaction. In the case of Lusophone immigrants, accentism may be rooted in racial and cultural stereotypes stemming from the colonial past.

It is suggested that future studies should examine African Lusophone immigrants separately from Brazilian Lusophone immigrants, since in the former case, accentism may be compounded by racial discrimination.

Future studies should include cultural intelligence as an individual variable that may act as a mediator between workplace discrimination and job satisfaction. It is also suggested that the relationship between cultural intelligence and discrimination be analysed in conjunction with other factors, including socio-demographic variables, to gain a deeper understanding of the factors that influence perceptions of discrimination. Such approaches could contribute to more effective and inclusive organisational strategies in the workplace for migrant workers. Studies involving larger samples are also needed.

ETHICS DECLARATION

This study did not require ethical clearance for the research referred to in this paper.

AI DECLARATION

The authors utilized Grammarly, an AI-based writing assistant, solely to enhance language clarity, grammar, and style. All conceptual contributions, analyses, and conclusions presented in this manuscript are entirely the responsibility of the authors.

ACKNOWLEDGEMENT

This work was supported by national funds through FCT/MCTES (PIDDAC): UID/04752 – Applied Management Research Unit (UNIAG).

REFERENCES

Adam, I., Agyeiwaah, E., & Boateng, F. O. (2023). Migrant worker inclusion and psychological well-being: Insights from the hospitality and tourism workplace. *Tourism Management Perspectives*, *47*, 101112.

Adam, I., Agyeiwaah, E., & Boateng, F. O. (2025). Workplace inclusion struggles and consequences on migrant workers — A multi-group invariance analysis. *Journal of Sustainable Tourism*. Advance online publication.

Ahmad, S., Wasim, S., Irfan, S., Gogoi, S., Srivastava, A., & Farheen, Z. (2019). Qualitative versus. quantitative research: A summarized review. *Journal of Evidence Based Medicine and Healthcare*, *6*(43), 2828–2832. DOI: 10.18410/jebmh/2019/587

AIMA - Agência para a Integração, Migrações e Asilo (2024). *Relatório de migrações e asilo 2024*. AIMA. https://aima.gov.pt/pt/noticias/relatorio-de-migracoes-e-asilo

Azevedo, L. F. D., França, T., & Cairns, D. (2022). You're better being poor here: Migration decision-making and political and lifestyle considerations among qualified Brazilians in Portugal. *Migraciones*, *56*(56), 1–16. DOI: 10.14422/mig.2022.020

Becker, G. S. (1993). *Human capital: A theoretical and empirical analysis, with special reference to education* (3rd ed.). University of Chicago Press. DOI: 10.7208/chicago/9780226041223.001.0001

Blau, P. M. (1964). *Exchange and power in social life*. John Wiley & Sons.

Bloemen, H. G. (2023). Language proficiency of migrants: The relation with job satisfaction and skill matching. *Empirical Economics*, *65*(6), 2899–2952. DOI: 10.1007/s00181-023-02445-3

Cheng, L., Im, G., Doe, C., & Douglas, S. R. (2021). Identifying English Language Use and Communication Challenges Facing "Entry-Level" Workplace Immigrants in Canada. *Journal of International Migration and Integration*, *22*(3), 865–886. DOI: 10.1007/s12134-020-00779-w

Chiswick, B. R., & Miller, P. W. (2014). International migration and the economics of language. IZA Discussion Paper No. 7880.

Dietz, J., Joshi, C., Esses, V., Hamilton, L., & Gabarrot, F. (2015). The skill paradox: Explaining and reducing employment discrimination against skilled immigrants. *International Journal of Human Resource Management, 26*(10), 1318–1334. DOI: 10.1080/09585192.2014.990398

Dostie, B., & Javdani, M. (2020). Immigrants and Workplace Training: Evidence from Canadian Linked Employer–Employee Data. *Industrial Relations, 59*(2), 275–315. DOI: 10.1111/irel.12255

Edewor, P., & Aluko, Y. (2007). Diversity Management, Challenges and Oportunities in Multicultural Organizations. *The International Journal of Diversity in Organisations, Communities and Nations, 6*(6), 189–196. DOI: 10.18848/1447-9532/CGP/v06i06/39285

Ennes, M., Ramos, N., & Suaréz, B. (2018). O Lugar do Interculturalismo nas Políticas Imigratórias em Portugal e Espanha. *Revista TOMO, 32*, 243-268. http://hdl.handle.net/10400.2/7337

Ghio, D., Bratti, M., & Bignami, S. (2022). Linguistic Barriers to Immigrants' Labor Market Integration in Italy. *The International Migration Review, 57*(1), 357–394. DOI: 10.1177/01979183221107923

Gideon, L. (2016). *Handbook of Survey Methodology for the Social Sciences*. Springer.

Herzberg, F., Mausner, B., & Snyderman, B. B. (1959). *The motivation to work*. John Wiley & Sons.

Hideg, I., Shen, W., & Koval, C. Z. (2024). Hear, hear! A review of accent discrimination at work. *Current Opinion in Psychology, 60*, 1–6. DOI: 10.1016/j.copsyc.2024.101906 PMID: 39321607

Hua, J., Kondo, A., Wang, C., & Ganchulun, S. (2024). Language confidence and job satisfaction among foreign-born nurses in Japan: Mediating efect of workplace discrimination and moderating efect of immigration duration. *BMC Nursing, 23*(1), 450. DOI: 10.1186/s12912-024-02116-3 PMID: 38956549

INE - Instituto Nacional de Estatística. (2023.). *População estrangeira com estatuto legal de residente (N.º) por Local de residência (NUTS) e Nacionalidade:* https://www.ine.pt/xportal/xmain?xpid=INE&xpgid=ine_indicadores&indOcorrCod=0013219&contexto=bd&selTab=tab2

International Organisation for Migration. (2024). [International Organization for Migration] [IOM]. *World Migration Report*, •••, 2024.

Intungane, D., Long, J., Gateri, H., & Dhungel, R. (2024). Employment barriers for racialized immigrants: A review of economic and social integration support and gaps in Edmonton, Alberta. *Genealogy*, *8*(2), 40. DOI: 10.3390/genealogy8020040

Judge, T. A., & Klinger, R. (2008). Job satisfaction: Subjective well-being at work. In Eid, M., & Larsen, R. J. (Eds.), *The science of subjective well-being* (pp. 393–413). Guilford Press.

Kamal, Y., & Ferdousi, M. (2009). Managing Diversity at Workplace: A Case Study of Hp. *ASA University Review, 3* (2), 157-170. https://ssrn.com/abstract=1944511

Koç, D. E., Solanas, J., Dağıstan, S. I., & Hasan, E. A. (2025). Diversity, equity, and inclusion in the hospitality and tourism workplace: A quantitative systematic literature review. *International Journal of Hospitality Management*, *128*, 1–13. DOI: 10.1016/j.ijhm.2025.104171

Lang, J. (2022). Employment effects of language training for unemployed immigrants. *Journal of Population Economics*, *35*(2), 719–754. DOI: 10.1007/s00148-021-00832-7

Locke, E. A. (1976). The nature and causes of job satisfaction. In Dunnette, M. D. (Ed.), *Handbook of industrial and organizational psychology* (pp. 1297–1343). Rand McNally.

Lopes, R. C. (2024). *Preconceito e Discriminação em Portugal.* Fundação Francisco Manuel dos Santos.

Orelus, P. W. (2016) An anticolonial analysis of accent discrimination with some implications for minority languages. In: Orelus PW (ed.) *Language, Race, and Power in Schools* (127–137): Routledge.

Park, J. (2011). Job-related training of immigrants. *Perspectives on Labour and Income*, *12*(8), 3–15.

Patrick, H., & Kumar, V. (2012). Managing Workplace Diversity: Issues and Challenges. *SAGE Open*, *2*(2), 2158244012444615. Advance online publication. DOI: 10.1177/2158244012444615

Peri, G. (2016). Immigrants, Productivity, and Labor Markets. *The Journal of Economic Perspectives*, *30*(4), 3–30. DOI: 10.1257/jep.30.4.3

Radu, D., & Virga, D. (2020). Work and stay: Explaining perceived discrimination among Romanian labor migrants. *Journal of International Migration and Integration*, *22*, 1051–1070.

Roberts, R. K., Swanson, N. G., & Murphy, L. R. (2004). Discrimination and occupational mental health. *Journal of Mental Health (Abingdon, England), 13*(2), 129–142. DOI: 10.1080/09638230410001669264

Rolstad, S., Adler, J., & Rydén, A. (2011). Response burden and questionnaire length: Is shorter better? A review and meta-analysis. *Value in Health, 14*(8), 1001–1008. DOI: 10.1016/j.jval.2011.06.003 PMID: 22152180

Salleh, M. M., Mohi, Z., Nordin, N., Mohamad, N. A., & Razali, N. (2021). The Impact of Language Barriers and Discrimination Issues on Work Productivity of Foreign Workers. *International Journal of Academic Research in Business & Social Sciences, 11*(16), 42–52. DOI: 10.6007/IJARBSS/v11-i16/11215

Sardinha, J. (2011). Highlighting the contrasts, downplaying the divergences: Insertion and visibility tactics of Brazilians in Portugal. *Ethnic and Racial Studies, 34*(6), 986–1005. DOI: 10.1080/01419870.2010.526237

Shore, L., Chung-Herrera, B., Dean, M., Ehrhart, K., Jung, D., Randel, A., & Singh, R. (2009). Diversity in organizations: Where are we now and where are we going? *Human Resource Management Review, 19*(2), 117–133. DOI: 10.1016/j.hrmr.2008.10.004

Śliwa, M., Aguzzoli, R., Brewster, C., & Lengler, J. (2024). Workplace accentism as a postcolonial and intersectional phenomenon: The experiences of Brazilians in Portugal. *Human Relations, 77*(10), 1468–1501. DOI: 10.1177/00187267231198965

Teixeira, I., Silva, P., Alckmin-Carvalho, F., Wendt, G. W., & Pereira, H. (2025). We Help Each Other Through It: Community Support and Labor Experiences Among Brazilian Immigrants in Portugal. *Behavioral Sciences (Basel, Switzerland), 15*(9), 1283. DOI: 10.3390/bs15091283 PMID: 41009313

Tsang, S. S., & Nguyen, T. V. T. (2023). Sociocultural adaptation and job satisfaction as mediators between cultural competence and intention to stay among Vietnamese workers in Taiwan. *Humanities & Social Sciences Communications, 10*(1), 292. Advance online publication. DOI: 10.1057/s41599-023-01798-5

Visentin, D. C., Cleary, M., & Hunt, G. E. (2020). The earnestness of being important: Reporting non-significant statistical results. *Journal of Advanced Nursing, 76*(4), 917–1089. DOI: 10.1111/jan.14283 PMID: 31793043

Wadsworth, E., Dhillon, K., Shaw, C., Bhui, K., Stansfeld, S., & Smith, A. (2007). Racial discrimination, ethnicity and work stress. *Occupational Medicine, 57*(1), 18–24. DOI: 10.1093/occmed/kql088 PMID: 16928781

Wang, Z., & Jing, X. (2017). Job Satisfaction Among Immigrant Workers: A Review of Determinants. *Social Indicators Research*, *139*(1), 381–401. DOI: 10.1007/s11205-017-1708-z

Warr, P., Cook, J., & Wall, T. (1979). Scales for the measurement of some work attitudes and aspects of psychological well-being. *Journal of Occupational Psychology*, *52*(2), 129–148. DOI: 10.1111/j.2044-8325.1979.tb00448.x

Wei, M., Wang, K., & Ku, T. (2012). A Development and Validation of the Perceived Language Discrimination Scale. *Cultural Diversity & Ethnic Minority Psychology*, *18*(4), 340–351. DOI: 10.1037/a0029453 PMID: 22866690

Williams, D. R., Yu, Y., Jackson, J. S., & Anderson, N. B. (1997). Racial Differences in Physical and Mental Health. *Journal of Health Psychology*, *2*(3), 335–351. DOI: 10.1177/135910539700200305 PMID: 22013026

Xia, L. C., Lopes, B. F., Pinto, G., Sequeiros, A. M., & Oliveira, M. (2022). A gestão da diversidade cultural e o seu impacto no bem-estar dos colaboradores). *Proceedings of the 6th International Conference on Innovation and Entrepreneurship in Marketing & Consumer Behaviour* (pp. 350-361). DOI: 10.34624/iciemc.v0i3.29812

About the Contributors

Emre Cengiz completed his PhD at Istanbul University in 2017. His research focuses on displacement, migration, urbanisation policy, climate change and global warming. He is currently an Associate Professor in the Department of Political Science and Public Administration at the Faculty of Economics and Administrative Sciences, Gümüşhane University.

Metin Aksoy completed his PhD at the University of Münster in 2007. His research focuses on foreign policy, migration, security and integration. He is a professor in the Department of Political Science and International Relations at the Faculty of Economics and Administrative Sciences, Gümüşhane University.

***

Handan Akkaş is an Associate Professor of Management and Organization whose work focuses on organizational behavior, cross-cultural studies, human resource management, and research methodology. She earned her PhD from Hacettepe University, where she also worked as a Research Assistant in the Department of Business Administration. She conducted her postdoctoral research in social psychology and acculturation as a TÜBİTAK 2219 fellow at Tilburg University. Dr. Akkaş has an extensive publication record, including studies on work behavior, qualitative research methods in multicultural contexts, and organizational dynamics. She has contributed to internationally co-authored research addressing contemporary organizational phenomena, including emerging workplace trends and employee attitudes. She is currently a faculty member in the Department of Business Administration at Ankara Medipol University. In addition, she teaches part-time at Hacettepe University. Her academic work spans cross-cultural organizational psychology, employee well-being, and the interplay between technology, work dynamics, and cultural values

José Almeida is an Assistant Professor and Director of the Master's Programme in Social Work at the University of Trás-os-Montes e Alto Douro (UTAD), Portugal. He holds a doctoral degree in Social Work and is a senior researcher at CETRAD (Centre for Transdisciplinary Development Studies). He is the national coordinator of RiiSSE (Network for Research and Intervention in School Social Work) and is regarded as a leading authority on social work within educational systems. His research explores the epistemology of Social Work, focusing on how theoretical frameworks are mobilised in professional practice and on the development of competencies required to address contemporary social challenges. He has contributed extensively to the scientific advancement of Social Work in Portugal through academic publications, curriculum development, and the supervision of doctoral and master's research.

Muhlise Canlı completed her B.A. (2014) and M.A. (2017) degrees in Sociology at Cumhuriyet University. She is currently a Ph.D. candidate in the Department of Social Work at Hacettepe University. Since 2018, she has been serving as a Lecturer in the Department of Social Work at Gümüşhane University. Her primary research interests encompass social work with migrants and refugees, field studies involving vulnerable populations, human rights, social policy, gender, and disability.

Fernando Casado Gutierrez is an international analyst born in Córdoba, Spain. Graduated in Law and PhD in Social Communication, he is a tenured professor at the Institute of High National Studies of Ecuador and a teacher in the Master of Public International Law at the Bolivarian University of Venezuela. He has written the books Introduction to Human Rights from a Bolivarian and Revolutionary perspective and in 2015 with the Akal publishing house another book entitled Anti-journalists: confessions of media attacks against Venezuela.

Oscarina Conceição is Professor at Polytechnic University of Cávado and Ave and researcher at Applied Management Research Unit (UNIAG) and Dinâmia'CET - Iscte (Instituto Universitário de Lisboa). She has a PhD in Economics from University of Minho. Her research interests include the following topics: innovation process and their socio-economic effects; knowledge transfer; knowledge and innovation networks; entrepreneurship; Academic entrepreneurship; Blue Economy.

Suvasmita Dey is a legal professional specialising in criminal law, with a focused interest in cross border movements and transborder crime in South Asia. She brings over a decade of professional experience in criminal practice, which provides her with strong practical insight into criminal justice processes and enforcement challenges. Alongside her practice background, she has developed a solid academic profile, engaging with issues at the intersection of criminal law, border regulation, and regional security.

Sushil Dhakal serves as an Assistant Professor of Law at the School of Law, Brainware University. His academic work is primarily situated within the field of comparative constitutional law, with a focused research interest in the constitutional frameworks and democratic institutions of India and Nepal. He has published scholarly work examining various dimensions of India Nepal relations, particularly in the context of constitutional governance and cross border interactions. His research also emphasises the need for integrating emerging technologies as regulatory tools for managing and strengthening legal and administrative mechanisms along the Indo Nepal border, with a view to enhancing cooperation, security, and institutional efficiency.

Marcia Duarte holds a PhD in Management, specialising in Organisation and Business Policy. Her research focuses on topics related to Human Resource Management and Organisational Behaviour. She has been an assistant professor at the School of Management of the Polytechnic University of Cávado and Ave for around 23 years. She teaches courses at both undergraduate and postgraduate levels, including Organisational Behaviour and Leadership and Team Development.

Anwesha Ghosh is an Assistant Professor at the Kirit P. Mehta School of Law; Shri Vile Parle Kelvani Mandal's Narsee Monjee Institute of Management Studies (Deemed to be University), Mumbai, India. Previously, she served as an Assistant Professor at Amity Law School, Mumbai, Amity Law School, Kolkata, and Rajiv Gandhi National University of Law (RGNUL), Patiala. She was also a UGC-sponsored Senior Research Fellow at the Central University of Punjab, where she earned her Ph.D. on gender diversity in Indian corporate boards. A University Gold Medalist in both LL.B. and LL.M., Dr. Ghosh's research focuses on Corporate Law, Corporate Governance, Gender Diversity, ESG, Competition Law, Sustainability, and Business and Human Rights. Her work has been published in Scopus-indexed, Web of Science-indexed, UGC-CARE-listed, and other peer-reviewed journals. She is the author of An Introspection of Corporate Criminal Liability in India and has presented her research at international conferences in Thailand, Türkiye, and Indonesia, receiving Best Paper Awards for her work on women's leadership and LGBTQ+ inclusion.

Sunay Güngör is an Assistant Professor in the Department of Psychology at Gümüşhane University, Türkiye, where he also serves as the Head of the Department of Applied Psychology. His academic interests include migration, social acceptance of foreign nationals, social identity, and cross-cultural adaptation. Drawing on both his academic work and his personal experience as a migrant, he integrates psychological and sociological perspectives to examine identity formation and belonging in migration contexts. His recent work introduces the concept of Borrowed Identity as a theoretical framework for understanding the psychological and social consequences of identity transformation among migrants.

Sovanna Huot is a PhD candidate in Political Science at the University of Delhi, India. He serves as Vice Principal at a Cambodian Government High School, overseeing academic leadership and school administration. He earned a Master of Education in High School Principalship from the National Institute of Education (NIE) in Phnom Penh in 2022. His research focuses on education governance, digital transformation in education, policy implementation, school leadership, and comparative public policy in developing countries. With teaching and publication experience in political science and education—his work appears in Scopus-indexed publications (Author ID: 59316244400)—his interdisciplinary background makes him well-equipped to edit a volume exploring governance, policy, and education across global, national, and local (glonalcal) contexts.

Tamari Kajaia is an Associate Professor at the Faculty of Business Technologies at the Georgian Technical University. She holds a PhD in Economics. Her research interests primarily focus on economics and business administration, with a specific expertise in migration and emigration trends and their impact on market dynamics. She is actively involved in international academic projects, including Erasmus+ initiatives, and has a robust track record of participating in international scientific conferences. Dr. Kajaia has authored numerous research papers published in both local and prestigious international peer-reviewed journals, contributing significantly to the fields of economic development and labor migration studies.

Khatuna Kharkhelauri has held various academic positions at authorised higher education institutions in Georgia since 2011. She is currently an Associate Professor and Scientific Secretary of the Faculty of Business Technology at Georgian Technical University, where she supervises doctoral and master's thesis research. She participates as a principal investigator in an internal university research project and is an active contributor to international scientific conferences. She has published articles in both local and international peer-reviewed scientific journals. She regularly participates in professional development trainings and seminars within the framework of Erasmus+ and Iowa State University's Centre for Excellence in Learning and Teaching projects. She also holds 10 years of experience as a financial manager.

Neslihan Koç completed her B.A. in Public Administration at Anadolu University in 2015. She is currently an M.A. candidate in the Department of Political Science and Public Administration at Gümüşhane University. Her research focuses on the sociology of migration, specifically exploring the socio-cultural dynamics of integration between immigrants and local communities.

Pardeep Kumar holds a Ph.D. in Mathematics from Lovely Professional University (2021). His research expertise lies in Stochastic Processes, with a specialized focus on Markov Models, Engineering System Reliability, and Reliability Theory. He actively contributes to the modeling and reliability analysis of IoT-enabled and sensor-integrated systems for next-generation engineering applications. Dr. Kumar has a profound command of Stochastic Modelling, Reliability Testing, and advanced analytical methods for complex system behavior under uncertainty. His work emphasises practical implementations in smart technologies and cyber-physical systems. He has an exceptional academic track record, having qualified the prestigious CSIR-UGC NET twice, securing All India Ranks (AIR) of 15 and 32, respectively. To date, Dr. Kumar has published 26 high-quality research papers in reputed national and international journals, reflecting his continued contribution to the advancement of mathematical reliability and its engineering applications.

Sanjeev Kumar is a Professor in Lovely Professional University Punjab India. He received Undergraduate in Hotel Management from Osmania University, Postgraduate in Tourism Management from Madurai Kamaraj University. He completed Doctor of Philosophy in Hospitality Management in 2019 from Amity University Jaipur India. His research areas lies in food Service Industry, his research focuses on Alcoholic beverages, Event management and Sustainable Management Practices, Metaverse, AI Machine Learning and Artificial Intelligence. He published more than 80 research papers, articles and chapters in Scopus Indexed, UGC Approved and peer reviewed Journals and books. Dr. Sanjeev Kumar participated and acted as resource person in various National and International conferences, seminars, session chair, research workshops and industry talks and his work has been widely cited. Dr. Sanjeev also edited more than 20 books with various International Publishers such as IGI Global, Cambridge Scholars, Emerald, CABI, Bentham Science, Taylor & Francis. Dr Sanjeev is an active researcher and has published numerous research articles in prestigious National and International journals and books.

Lovleen Marwaha is a Professor at the Department of Zoology, School of Bioengineering and Biosciences, Lovely Professional University, Phagwara, India. She has completed her M.S. and Ph.D. in Cytogenetics from the Department of

Zoology, Punjab University, Chandigarh. She has worked on the evaluation of pesticide genotoxicity using insect genomes, specifically on different mosquito species and Drosophila melanogaster. She has carried out an intensive study on the correlation between pesticide exposure limit and inductive genotoxic consequences on Dipteran larval salivary polytene chromosomes. Furthermore, she has studied chromosomal and gene mutations in mosquito and fruit fly genomes due to pesticide exposure. Currently, she is working on Apiculture and Sericulture-related topics. She has many research papers published in National and International Journals of repute. Presently, she is working on insecticide resistance in mosquitoes, pesticide genotoxicity evaluation, honey bee development, honey processing, silk fiber, and pearl quality improvement. She has published three authored books on Apiculture and on Mobile Genetic Elements. Forthcoming books include Worker Honey Bees, Apiculture Products, Basic Concepts of Genetics, and Introduction to Sericulture.

Daniela Monteiro holds a Doctorate, a Master's degree, and a Bachelor's degree in Social Work from the Catholic University of Portugal (UCP). She is an Assistant Professor in the Department of Economics, Sociology and Management (DESG) at the University of Trás-os-Montes e Alto Douro (UTAD) and a researcher at CLISSIS (Lusíada Centre for Research in Social Work and Social Intervention) . Her research specialises in Social Gerontology and the study of the life cycle, with particular attention to the challenges of demographic ageing, family dynamics, and the effectiveness of social support networks. She bridges specific social intervention methods with broader regional development goals, contributing to an integrated understanding of ageing and welfare in contemporary Portuguese society.

Kimyut Phin is an educator and PhD research scholar in English at the University of Delhi, India. He serves as the director of the Institute of Foreign Languages of the University of Heng Samrin Thbongkhmum, Cambodia. Kimyut has also had teaching experiences in linguistics, applied linguistics, teaching methodology, second language acquisition, academic writing skills, global studies, and literature studies for years. Further, he has experience in lesson planning, classroom management, assessment and evaluation, and technology for teaching and learning. His research centers on ELT and linguistics, education, digital pedagogy, literary and theoretical studies, cultural and gender studies, and translation studies, and his work also gains Scopus-indexed publications (Scopus Author ID: 60516584900).

Naresh Prajapati is an Assistant Professor of Law at Bennett University, India, and a recipient of the Chancellor's Award for Best Ph.D. Scholar. His research focuses on climate change law, human rights, and international environmental governance, with a comparative emphasis on South Asia. He holds a Ph.D. from the Central University of Punjab and has published extensively in Scopus-indexed journals and edited volumes. Dr. Prajapati actively contributes to global academic discourse through international conferences and editorial roles. His work engages interdisciplinary perspectives, advancing legal scholarship on sustainability, climate justice, and governance.

Rebeca Sánchez is employed at the Universidad Técnica “Luis Vargas Torres” de Ecuador. Sociologist graduated at the Central University of Venezuela in 2004. Master on Research on Latin American Studies & International Relations in the Simon Bolívar University (2014-2016). Member of the Research Team in Critical Studies for Social Justice at the Technical University of Manabí. PhD Student at the Universidad Rey Juan Carlos in Spain.

Paula Sousa is an Assistant Professor in the Department of Economics, Sociology and Management (DESG) at the University of Trás-os-Montes e Alto Douro (UTAD), Portugal. She holds degrees in Social Work, Educational Sciences, and Cultural Studies, and is a researcher at CETRAD (Centre for Transdisciplinary Development Studies). Her research focuses on cultural competence in social work practice, the management of diversity, and the construction of professional identity among social workers. She is particularly interested in how practitioners navigate complex social differences in contemporary multicultural societies. Paula Sousa is an active member of the European Social Work Research Association (ESWRA), through which she contributes to international dialogue on social work education and research standards. Her work applies a transdisciplinary lens to issues of equality, social inclusion, and the professional development of social work as a discipline.

Zahid Thoker is a serious research Scholar at Lovely Professional University who is working on Insects (Entomology), specifically on Honey Bees. He graduated with his Master's degree in Zoology from Chandigarh University, Gharuan, Mohali, where he developed a very solid academic grounding in life sciences. Zahid has already contributed greatly to academia; he has published one research paper, one review paper, and over 25 book chapters in reputable national and international volumes. His academic publication is an indication of the desire to promote science, especially in the biological sciences. As a visionary who desires to make a difference in the research world and in society, Zahid hopes to broaden his academic and professional experiences with integrity and excellence. He is also strongly driven by the goal of benefiting society with his research work and making his parents proud by leaving his mark on the field of science and scholarship.

Index

A

B

C

D

E

F

G

H

I

L

M

T

U

V

W

www.ingramcontent.com/pod-product-compliance
Lightning Source LLC
LaVergne TN
LVHW062028101126
852251LV00005B/51
* 9 7 9 8 3 3 7 3 8 5 0 0 6 *